Agile AI-Powered Project Management for Modern Delivery Organizations

Otmane Azeroual
https://orcid.org/0000-0002-5225-389X
University of Hagen, Germany

IGI Global
Scientific Publishing
Publishing Tomorrow's Research Today

Vice President of Editorial Melissa Wagner
Director of Acquisitions Mikaela Felty
Director of Book Development Jocelynn Hessler
Production Manager Mike Brehm
Cover Design Jose Rosado

Published in the United States of America by
IGI Global Scientific Publishing
701 East Chocolate Avenue
Hershey, PA, 17033, USA
Tel: 717-533-8845 | Fax: 717-533-7115
Website: https://www.igi-global.com E-mail: cust@igi-global.com

Library of Congress Cataloging-in-Publication Data

Names: Azeroual, Otmane, 1989- editor
Title: Agile AI-powered project management for modern delivery organizations / [edited by] Otmane Azeroual.
Description: Hershey, PA : IGI Global Scientific Publishing, [2026] | Includes bibliographical references and index. | Summary: "This book explores how AI is transforming Agile, DevOps, and product delivery by enhancing planning, governance, and decision-making. Through case studies and practical frameworks, it examines AI-assisted project management, data governance, and ethical implementation, offering leaders and practitioners strategies for trustworthy, transparent, and high-performance Agile transformation"-- Provided by publisher.
Identifiers: LCCN 2025054415 (print) | LCCN 2025054416 (ebook) | ISBN 9798337368511 hardcover | ISBN 9798337368528 paperback | ISBN 9798337368535 ebook
Subjects: LCSH: Project management--Technological innovations | Artificial intelligence--Business applications
Classification: LCC HD69.P75 A39625 2026 (print) | LCC HD69.P75 (ebook) | DDC 6584/04--dc23/eng/20260204
LC record available at https://lccn.loc.gov/2025054415
LC ebook record available at https://lccn.loc.gov/2025054416

British Cataloguing in Publication Data
A Cataloguing in Publication record for this book is available from the British Library.

Table of Contents

Preface xiii

Chapter 1
From Agile to AI-Agile: Redefining Project Management in the Digital Age 1
Mustafa Kayyali, Maaref University of Applied Sciences, Syria

Chapter 2
AIOps: Evolution and Transformation of IT Operations 27
Sarma A. D. N., Jaya Soft, Hyderabad, India

Chapter 3
AI-Augmented Strategic Management Integrating Portfolio Planning, Roadmapping, and OKR Systems 83
Inayatul Janah, Universitas Esa Unggul, Indonesia
Binastya Anggara Sekti, Universitas Esa Unggul, Indonesia

Chapter 4
AI-Enhanced Agile Delivery Forecasting With Probabilistic Models, Flow Metrics, and Human Governance 111
Gusti Muhamad Sardana, Universitas Esa Unggul, Indonesia
Binastya Anggara Sekti, Universitas Esa Unggul, Indonesia

Chapter 5
Cognitive Governance Framework: Agile Prediction, Risk Intelligence, and Ethical Oversight 157
T. Ganesan, Dr. G.U. Pope College of Engineering, India
S. Harish Alwar, Dr. G.U. Pope College of Engineering, India
J. Abishek, Dr. G.U. Pope College of Engineering, India
K. DanielRaj, Kalaignarkarunanidhi Institute of Technology, India

Chapter 6
Ethics, Bias Mitigation, and Model Risk Management 191
Shagufta Parween, Chaitanya Bharathi Institute of Technology, India
Neha Dubey, Parul University, India
Rahul Bharadwaj, Galgotias University, India
B. Amarnath Reddy, Vignana Jyothi Institute of Management, India
Himanshu Sanghavi, C.Z. Patel College of Business and Management, The Charutar Vidya Mandal University, India
U. D. Prasan, Aditya Institute of Technology and Management, India
V. Bhoopathy, Sree Rama Engineering College, India

Chapter 7
AI-Driven Risk Sensing and Anomaly Detection for Predictive Project Management: Designing Early Warning Systems to Enhance Resilience and Decision-Making 217
Vennela Mamidi, Woxsen University, Hyderabad, India
Harini Edala, Woxsen University, Hyderabad, India
Joel Pramod Manekshaw, Woxsen University, Hyderabad, India
Sujit Singh, Woxsen University, Hyderabadd, India
Afzalur Rahman, Woxsen University, Hyderabad, India

Chapter 8
AI-Driven Backlog Refinement for Enhancing User Story Quality and Sizing in Agile Projects 245
Sindy Rahmahsari, Universitas Esa Unggul, Indonesia
Binastya Anggara Sekti, Universitas Esa Unggul, Indonesia

Chapter 9
Algorithmic Project Mastery: AI in Action for Scrum and HERMES 275
Otmane Azeroual, University of Hagen, Germany

Chapter 10
Tooling Evaluations and Reference Architectures for AI-Augmented Agile Project Management: Bridging Practice and Governance in Modern Delivery Organizations 299
Ranjit Singha, Christ University, India
Surjit Singha, Kristu Jayanti University, India
Shruti Jose, Christ University, India
V. Muthu Ruben, Christ University, India
Alphonsa Diana Haokip, Don Bosco College, Maram, India

Chapter 11
Intelligent Facilitation: Exploring AI's Role in Agile Leadership..................... 337
Otmane Azeroual, University of Hagen, Germany

Chapter 12
Change Management and Upskilling for AI-Augmented Teams 361
Priyadarshani Singh, Noida International University, India
Syed Hassan Imam Gardezi, Union Investments LLC, UAE
P. Selvakumar, Department of Science and Humanities, Nehru Institute of Technology, Coimbatore, India
Ganesh Pathak, Sri Balaji University, Pune, India
Asita Ghewari, Dnyansagar Institute of Management and Research, Pune, India
Ashok Raut, Global Business School and Research Centre, Dr. D.Y. Patil Vidyapeeth, Pune, India

Chapter 13
Change Management and Skills Development in the Age of AI 389
Nesrine Barhoum, Faculty of Economics and Management, University of Sax, Tunisia
Sami Boudabbous, Faculty of Economics and Management, University of Sfax, Tunisia

Compilation of References 429

About the Contributors 475

Index 483

Detailed Table of Contents

Preface.. xiii

Chapter 1
From Agile to AI-Agile: Redefining Project Management in the Digital Age 1
Mustafa Kayyali, Maaref University of Applied Sciences, Syria

The transition from traditional Agile practices to AI-Agile frameworks marks a profound redefinition of project management in the digital age. While Agile emphasized responsiveness, collaboration, and iterative delivery, the integration of artificial intelligence introduces new layers of predictive insight, automation, and adaptive governance. This chapter explores how AI reshapes the principles of agility—enhancing decision-making, forecasting risks, and reallocating resources in real time. It also examines the shifting role of project managers as they navigate the interplay between human creativity and machine intelligence. Beyond operational efficiency, the chapter addresses the ethical, cultural, and organizational implications of AI-Agile adoption, urging institutions to balance innovation with responsibility. By mapping the evolution from Agile to AI-Agile, the discussion highlights both the opportunities and the dilemmas of managing projects in an era where data, algorithms, and human judgment must coexist in a dynamic and uncertain landscape.

Chapter 2
AIOps: Evolution and Transformation of IT Operations 27
Sarma A. D. N., Jaya Soft, Hyderabad, India

The chapter provides a detailed overview of information technology operations from inception to date and its transformation to artificial intelligence operations. Moreover, explain the importance of IT operations, its major functions along with the role of IT operations. Besides, present a case for AI driven IT operation transformation that include cover limitations of traditional IT operations, and the need for intelligent and automation for IT operation. Listed a few implementation challenges. A typical transformation process of ITOps into AIOps. Further, an high level conceptual architecture and explained its working. Mentioned major performance indicators of AIOps. List of potential use case presented along with benefits.

Chapter 3
AI-Augmented Strategic Management Integrating Portfolio Planning, Roadmapping, and OKR Systems 83
Inayatul Janah, Universitas Esa Unggul, Indonesia
Binastya Anggara Sekti, Universitas Esa Unggul, Indonesia

This chapter explores the integration of artificial intelligence into strategic portfolio management, roadmapping, and OKR alignment as a fundamental transformation in how organizations plan and execute strategy in the digital era. It introduces the AI-Augmented Strategic Loop (AISL) framework, which enables continuous sensing, analysis, decision-making, and learning across dynamic business environments. By combining strategic management theory, agile systems thinking, and AI decision augmentation, the chapter demonstrates how intelligent systems enhance adaptability, transparency, and strategic coherence. It further discusses the ethical, organizational, and technical considerations necessary for responsible implementation, including governance, data integrity, and human oversight. Ultimately, this chapter positions AI as a meta-layer of intelligence that transforms strategic management from static planning into a continuous, learning-oriented process for sustainable organizational performance.

Chapter 4
AI-Enhanced Agile Delivery Forecasting With Probabilistic Models, Flow Metrics, and Human Governance 111
Gusti Muhamad Sardana, Universitas Esa Unggul, Indonesia
Binastya Anggara Sekti, Universitas Esa Unggul, Indonesia

Accurate delivery forecasting remains a challenge in Agile software development due to uncertainty, evolving requirements, and complex socio-technical dynamics. Traditional estimation techniques often produce deterministic predictions that fail to communicate delivery risk and scale effectively across teams. This chapter presents an AI-enhanced Agile delivery forecasting framework that integrates probabilistic models, flow metrics, and human-in-the-loop governance. Probabilistic techniques such as Monte Carlo simulation and Bayesian inference are combined with flow-based metrics, including cycle time, throughput, and work-in-progress, to generate adaptive and risk-aware forecasts across sprint, release, and portfolio levels. Machine learning methods support continuous refinement of predictions using historical and real-time data, while human oversight ensures contextual interpretation, ethical use, and accountability. The chapter illustrates how combining AI with human judgment improves delivery predictability while preserving core Agile principles.

Chapter 5
Cognitive Governance Framework: Agile Prediction, Risk Intelligence, and Ethical Oversight 157
T. Ganesan, Dr. G.U. Pope College of Engineering, India
S. Harish Alwar, Dr. G.U. Pope College of Engineering, India
J. Abishek, Dr. G.U. Pope College of Engineering, India
K. DanielRaj, Kalaignarkarunanidhi Institute of Technology, India

The chapter examines how artificial intelligence (AI) fits into agile management routines inside today's firms - it sets out a full framework for predictive roadmapping, real time risk sensing and human-in-the-loop oversight. AI-driven analytics let firms forecast supply chain risks, balance resource loads and keep management adaptive, ethical plus open. The chapter lists step-by-step implementation tactics, worked case studies and a review of common obstacles - researchers and practitioners gain clear guidance for sharper management in agile, high variance supply chains.

Chapter 6
Ethics, Bias Mitigation, and Model Risk Management 191
Shagufta Parween, Chaitanya Bharathi Institute of Technology, India
Neha Dubey, Parul University, India
Rahul Bharadwaj, Galgotias University, India
B. Amarnath Reddy, Vignana Jyothi Institute of Management, India
Himanshu Sanghavi, C.Z. Patel College of Business and Management, The Charutar Vidya Mandal University, India
U. D. Prasan, Aditya Institute of Technology and Management, India
V. Bhoopathy, Sree Rama Engineering College, India

Contemporary risk management must evolve beyond reactive frameworks to adapt to changing economic, technical, and environmental ecosystems. The chapter discusses AI-driven risk intelligence and its transformation of predictive governance and strategic decision-making. AI systems rely on ML, DL, NLP, and real-time analytics. These tools allow businesses to monitor financial, operational, cybersecurity, supply chain, and climatic sectors for early warning signals, assess multidimensional risk exposures, and simulate impact scenarios. This chapter covers system designs, analytical methods, industry-specific applications, data quality, model bias, interpretability, and regulatory compliance. AI-driven risk intelligence in uncertain and fast-changing environments improves organisational resilience, agility, and long-term sustainability. Technological innovation, ethical governance, and model risk management are highlighted.

Chapter 7
AI-Driven Risk Sensing and Anomaly Detection for Predictive Project Management: Designing Early Warning Systems to Enhance Resilience and Decision-Making 217
Vennela Mamidi, Woxsen University, Hyderabad, India
Harini Edala, Woxsen University, Hyderabad, India
Joel Pramod Manekshaw, Woxsen University, Hyderabad, India
Sujit Singh, Woxsen University, Hyderabadd, India
Afzalur Rahman, Woxsen University, Hyderabad, India

The objective of this chapter is to propose a modernized framework for IT project management that addresses the shortcomings of traditional methodologies. It will argue for a shift from rigid, reactive models to an adaptive, proactive approach. The chapter demonstrates how integrating real-time data analytics and continuous risk monitoring can enhance flexibility, improve decision-making, and prevent the accumulation of unseen risks. Ultimately, it aims to outline the principles of a data-driven management strategy capable of delivering successful project outcomes in today's volatile technological landscape.

Chapter 8
AI-Driven Backlog Refinement for Enhancing User Story Quality and Sizing in Agile Projects 245
Sindy Rahmahsari, Universitas Esa Unggul, Indonesia
Binastya Anggara Sekti, Universitas Esa Unggul, Indonesia

This chapter explores the transformative role of Artificial Intelligence (AI) in enhancing Agile backlog refinement processes through data-driven intelligence. It examines how AI technologies specifically machine learning (ML), natural language processing (NLP), and predictive analytics optimize user story quality, improve estimation accuracy, and streamline prioritization and dependency management. The chapter discusses the evolution from manual, intuition-based refinement to AI-assisted decision-making that enhances objectivity, consistency, and scalability. It also highlights the importance of human-AI collaboration, emphasizing that AI serves as an augmentative tool that strengthens, rather than replaces, human judgment. By integrating AI into Agile workflows, this chapter demonstrates how modern organizations can achieve greater delivery predictability, efficiency, and strategic alignment, ultimately redefining how software development teams plan, evaluate, and execute work in rapidly evolving digital environments.

Chapter 9
Algorithmic Project Mastery: AI in Action for Scrum and HERMES 275
Otmane Azeroual, University of Hagen, Germany

This chapter explores the use of Artificial Intelligence (AI) in project management, focusing on Scrum and HERMES. It examines three AI applications: sprint and backlog optimization, digital project coaching, and automated lessons learned analysis. Using historical data, machine learning, and natural language processing, AI enhances planning, decision-making, and organizational learning. In Scrum, it improves sprint predictability and task prioritization; in HERMES, it supports phase monitoring, risk mitigation, and compliance. Digital coaching provides real-time guidance while maintaining human oversight. Lessons learned analysis extracts insights from documentation and communication to foster continuous improvement. The chapter also addresses data quality, ethics, human-AI collaboration, and organizational readiness, illustrating measurable gains in efficiency, risk management, and knowledge retention. Future directions include conversational AI, predictive analytics, and AI-driven collaboration, providing actionable strategies for adaptive, data-driven projects.

Chapter 10
Tooling Evaluations and Reference Architectures for AI-Augmented Agile Project Management: Bridging Practice and Governance in Modern Delivery Organizations 299
Ranjit Singha, Christ University, India
Surjit Singha, Kristu Jayanti University, India
Shruti Jose, Christ University, India
V. Muthu Ruben, Christ University, India
Alphonsa Diana Haokip, Don Bosco College, Maram, India

Agile and DevOps practices are central to modern delivery organizations, yet the rapid proliferation of AI-augmented project management tools has created fragmented ecosystems that weaken transparency, governance, and value realization. Although AI copilots, predictive analytics, intelligent backlog management, and autonomous agents promise improved decision-making and delivery performance, their adoption has outpaced coherent evaluation frameworks and governance-aligned architectures. This chapter addresses this gap by proposing a structured approach to evaluating AI-powered Agile tools and designing reference architectures that support responsible human–AI collaboration. Drawing on multi-criteria decision-making models, Agile and DevOps metrics, AI capability theory, and MLOps/LLMOps principles, the chapter integrates technical, organizational, and ethical dimensions. Cross-industry cases illustrate how governance-by-design enhances agility, value creation, and trust in AI-augmented Agile delivery.

Chapter 11
Intelligent Facilitation: Exploring AI's Role in Agile Leadership..................... 337
Otmane Azeroual, University of Hagen, Germany

Agile frameworks such as Scrum depend on the human-centered roles of Product Owner (PO) and Scrum Master (SM), who balance strategic prioritization, team facilitation, and stakeholder alignment. As artificial intelligence (AI) advances, these roles increasingly gain support from intelligent systems capable of analyzing complex data, generating insights, and automating routine tasks. This chapter examines how AI can augment PO and SM responsibilities, focusing on applications such as backlog analysis, predictive risk assessment, meeting facilitation, and team sentiment monitoring. At the same time, it highlights challenges related to transparency, bias, and the preservation of accountability in agile environments. By exploring human-AI collaboration dynamics and emerging hybrid role profiles, the chapter offers guidance for practitioners and researchers seeking to integrate AI responsibly while maintaining the essential human dimensions of agile leadership.

Chapter 12
Change Management and Upskilling for AI-Augmented Teams 361
Priyadarshani Singh, Noida International University, India
Syed Hassan Imam Gardezi, Union Investments LLC, UAE
P. Selvakumar, Department of Science and Humanities, Nehru Institute of Technology, Coimbatore, India
Ganesh Pathak, Sri Balaji University, Pune, India
Asita Ghewari, Dnyansagar Institute of Management and Research, Pune, India
Ashok Raut, Global Business School and Research Centre, Dr. D.Y. Patil Vidyapeeth, Pune, India

The integration of artificial intelligence (AI) into organizational environments is reshaping not only workflows and operational efficiency but also the very nature of team dynamics and change management. Traditionally, change management has revolved around structured strategies for transitioning people, processes, and technologies from one state to another while minimizing resistance and maximizing adoption. However, the introduction of AI introduces unique challenges and opportunities that extend beyond conventional frameworks, influencing how teams interact, collaborate, and adapt to constant transformation. AI is not merely another tool or incremental technological advancement; it represents a paradigm shift in how decisions are made, tasks are executed, and roles are defined within organizations. This shift impacts interpersonal trust, communication, leadership styles, employee identity, and the overall resilience of teams navigating technological disruption.

Chapter 13
Change Management and Skills Development in the Age of AI 389
Nesrine Barhoum, Faculty of Economics and Management, University of Sax, Tunisia
Sami Boudabbous, Faculty of Economics and Management, University of Sfax, Tunisia

Artificial intelligence (AI) is now emerging as a driver of organizational transformation, revolutionizing management models, work patterns, and human relationships within companies. While its potential for innovation, efficiency, and competitiveness is undeniable, its integration is prompting profound changes in skills and organizational structures. The success of this transition hinges on companies' ability to implement human-centered change management that reconciles technological progress with ethical considerations. This chapter explores the dynamics of organizational change in the AI era, drawing on both classic (Lewin, 1951; Kotter, 1996) and contemporary (Hiatt & Creasey, 2021; Barabel & Meier, 2023) models, while highlighting the new skills to be developed: digital literacy, critical thinking, creativity, emotional intelligence, and adaptability.

Compilation of References 429

About the Contributors 475

Index 483

Preface

INTRODUCTION

The rapid digital transformation of organizations across industries has fundamentally reshaped how projects are conceived, planned, and delivered. Traditional project management frameworks—once characterized by sequential processes and rigid planning—have gradually evolved into more adaptive approaches capable of responding to uncertainty and complexity. Agile methodologies emerged as a response to these challenges, emphasizing iterative delivery, collaboration, and continuous improvement. Today, however, the growing integration of artificial intelligence introduces an additional layer of transformation, enabling project environments that are not only adaptive but also predictive, data-driven, and continuously learning.

Artificial intelligence is increasingly embedded in modern delivery ecosystems, from intelligent backlog management and predictive analytics to automated governance and decision support systems. These capabilities extend the principles of Agile beyond responsiveness toward anticipatory and evidence-based management. AI-powered systems can analyze vast datasets, detect hidden patterns, forecast risks, and recommend actions that improve both strategic planning and operational execution. As a result, project management is evolving into a hybrid discipline where human judgment, collaborative leadership, and algorithmic intelligence work together to guide complex initiatives.

This transformation reflects a broader shift in the digital economy, where organizations must balance speed, adaptability, and strategic foresight while managing increasingly complex technological ecosystems. In this context, AI-powered project management is emerging as a critical capability for organizations seeking to remain competitive in rapidly changing environments.

This edited reference book brings together contributions from international scholars and practitioners who examine the intersection of Agile practices and artificial intelligence. The chapters explore conceptual foundations, technological architectures, governance considerations, and practical implementation strategies that define AI-augmented project environments. By integrating theoretical insights with applied perspectives, the book aims to provide researchers, educators, and professionals with a comprehensive understanding of how AI is reshaping modern delivery organizations.

In addition to presenting new conceptual frameworks, the book highlights emerging research directions and practical lessons learned from real-world implementations. This dual perspective allows readers to understand both the theoretical underpinnings and the operational implications of AI-augmented Agile project management.

CHAPTER OVERVIEW

Chapter 1 – From Agile to AI-Agile: Redefining Project Management in the Digital Age

This chapter introduces the conceptual shift from traditional Agile frameworks toward AI-Agile models. It examines how artificial intelligence enhances decision-making, forecasting, and governance within project environments while redefining the role of project managers. Ethical considerations, organizational culture, and the balance between human creativity and machine intelligence are also discussed.

Chapter 2 – AIOps: Evolution and Transformation of IT Operations

This chapter explores the historical development of IT operations and the emergence of Artificial Intelligence for IT Operations (AIOps). It outlines the limitations of conventional IT management, the need for automation and intelligent analytics, and the architecture of AI-driven operational systems designed to improve efficiency, monitoring, and performance management.

Chapter 3 – AI-Augmented Strategic Management Integrating Portfolio Planning, Roadmapping, and OKR Systems

The chapter introduces the AI-Augmented Strategic Loop (AISL) framework, which integrates portfolio planning, technology roadmapping, and OKR alignment through intelligent analytics. It demonstrates how AI enhances continuous sensing, decision-making, and learning within dynamic strategic environments.

Chapter 4 – AI-Enhanced Agile Delivery Forecasting with Probabilistic Models, Flow Metrics, and Human Governance

This chapter presents an advanced forecasting framework that combines probabilistic modeling techniques such as Monte Carlo simulations and Bayesian inference with Agile flow metrics. It emphasizes the importance of human oversight to ensure contextual interpretation, transparency, and ethical use of predictive systems.

Chapter 5 – Cognitive Governance Framework: Agile Prediction, Risk Intelligence, and Ethical Oversight

This chapter develops a governance framework that integrates AI-driven prediction, real-time risk sensing, and ethical oversight mechanisms. Through practical examples and implementation strategies, it demonstrates how organizations can maintain adaptive governance while managing high-variance operational environments.

Chapter 6 – Ethics, Bias Mitigation, and Model Risk Management

The chapter addresses the growing need for responsible AI governance within project management. It explores bias mitigation strategies, data quality concerns, regulatory compliance, and model risk management practices required to ensure trustworthy AI-enabled decision systems.

Chapter 7 – AI-Driven Risk Sensing and Anomaly Detection for Predictive Project Management

This chapter proposes a predictive framework for early warning systems in IT project management. Using real-time analytics and anomaly detection techniques, it demonstrates how organizations can anticipate risks, detect irregularities, and enhance decision-making resilience.

Chapter 8 – AI-Driven Backlog Refinement for Enhancing User Story Quality and Sizing in Agile Projects

This chapter examines how machine learning and natural language processing can support backlog refinement activities. By improving user story quality, estimation accuracy, and prioritization processes, AI tools help teams achieve greater efficiency and predictability in Agile delivery cycles.

Chapter 9 – Algorithmic Project Mastery: AI in Action for Scrum and HERMES

The chapter explores the practical application of AI in two widely used project management frameworks—Scrum and HERMES. It highlights applications such as sprint optimization, digital coaching, automated lessons-learned analysis, and predictive project insights.

Chapter 10 – Tooling Evaluations and Reference Architectures for AI-Augmented Agile Project Management

This chapter proposes structured evaluation models and reference architectures for AI-enabled Agile tools. By integrating governance principles, MLOps practices, and Agile metrics, the chapter provides a comprehensive approach for designing responsible AI-powered delivery ecosystems.

Chapter 11 – Intelligent Facilitation: Exploring AI's Role in Agile Leadership

This chapter examines how artificial intelligence can augment the leadership roles of Product Owners and Scrum Masters. It explores applications such as meeting facilitation, sentiment analysis, and risk assessment while emphasizing the importance of maintaining transparency and accountability.

Chapter 12 – Change Management and Upskilling for AI-Augmented Teams

The chapter focuses on the human dimension of AI transformation, discussing organizational change management strategies and workforce upskilling initiatives necessary for successful adoption of AI technologies.

Chapter 13 – Change Management and Skills Development in the Age of AI

The final chapter explores broader organizational transformations triggered by artificial intelligence. Drawing on both classical and contemporary change management theories, it highlights the evolving skill sets required for employees and leaders navigating AI-driven workplaces.

CONCLUSION

The chapters presented in this volume collectively illustrate the profound transformation occurring at the intersection of Agile methodologies and artificial intelligence. What began as an effort to increase flexibility and responsiveness in project management has now evolved into a new paradigm in which data-driven intelligence enhances planning, forecasting, governance, and collaboration. AI does not replace Agile principles; rather, it extends them by enabling organizations to anticipate challenges, learn continuously from data, and adapt at unprecedented speed.

At the same time, the integration of AI introduces complex organizational, ethical, and governance considerations. Issues related to algorithmic bias, transparency, accountability, and workforce adaptation require careful attention. The contributions in this volume highlight the importance of human-centered AI adoption, where technological capabilities complement rather than replace human expertise, creativity, and leadership.

Ultimately, this book aims to serve as a foundational reference for scholars, practitioners, and decision-makers seeking to understand and implement AI-augmented project management. As organizations continue to navigate digital transformation, the ability to combine Agile values with intelligent systems will become a defining capability of successful modern delivery organizations.

By bringing together interdisciplinary perspectives from project management, artificial intelligence, organizational governance, and digital transformation research, this volume contributes to an evolving body of knowledge that will shape the future of project management practice and scholarship.

Otmane Azeroual
University of Hagen, Germany

Chapter 1
From Agile to AI-Agile: Redefining Project Management in the Digital Age

Mustafa Kayyali
http://orcid.org/0000-0003-3300-262X
Maaref University of Applied Sciences, Syria

ABSTRACT

The transition from traditional Agile practices to AI-Agile frameworks marks a profound redefinition of project management in the digital age. While Agile emphasized responsiveness, collaboration, and iterative delivery, the integration of artificial intelligence introduces new layers of predictive insight, automation, and adaptive governance. This chapter explores how AI reshapes the principles of agility—enhancing decision-making, forecasting risks, and reallocating resources in real time. It also examines the shifting role of project managers as they navigate the interplay between human creativity and machine intelligence. Beyond operational efficiency, the chapter addresses the ethical, cultural, and organizational implications of AI-Agile adoption, urging institutions to balance innovation with responsibility. By mapping the evolution from Agile to AI-Agile, the discussion highlights both the opportunities and the dilemmas of managing projects in an era where data, algorithms, and human judgment must coexist in a dynamic and uncertain landscape.

INTRODUCTION

Project management has always been a mirror of its age. The tools, practices, and philosophies we adopt to coordinate human effort reflect not only the technical capabilities of the time but also the cultural anxieties and aspirations of organizations navigating uncertainty. The Agile movement, which emerged at the dawn of the 21st

DOI: 10.4018/979-8-3373-6851-1.ch001

century, was itself a reaction against rigidity and over-planning—a declaration that collaboration, iteration, and adaptability mattered more than prescriptive processes. Agile's rise was fueled by a recognition that complex projects, particularly in software development, could not be effectively managed through traditional linear methods. Instead, value had to be delivered incrementally, learning had to be continuous, and teams had to remain open to change.

Yet history rarely pauses. In the same way that Agile displaced older paradigms, we now find ourselves at another inflection point: the integration of artificial intelligence into project management. If Agile sought to humanize projects by foregrounding dialogue, trust, and responsiveness, AI-Agile challenges us to imagine how human intelligence and machine intelligence can co-create new forms of coordination, prediction, and control (Cervini et al, 2023). This shift does not represent a simple technological upgrade; it is a reconfiguration of the very logic of agility. AI introduces predictive analytics, adaptive automation, natural language processing, and machine learning into the heart of project delivery. It expands the capacity to anticipate risks, simulate outcomes, and optimize resource allocation with a speed and accuracy that far exceed human limits.

At the same time, AI-Agile invites deeper questions that cannot be answered by efficiency metrics alone. What happens to the role of the project manager when algorithms increasingly assume responsibility for monitoring, scheduling, and forecasting? How do teams maintain creativity and trust when machine systems mediate decisions about priorities and workloads? To what extent can AI truly understand the "human" dimensions of projects—conflict, motivation, cultural nuance—that have always resisted neat quantification? These questions matter because project management is never only about execution; it is about people, meaning-making, and the navigation of collective purpose under pressure (Sartori & Theodorou, 2022).

This chapter positions the shift from Agile to AI-Agile as both an opportunity and a dilemma. On one hand, organizations stand to benefit from unprecedented responsiveness, data-driven foresight, and scalable agility. On the other, they must grapple with ethical concerns, risks of over-automation, and the subtle erosion of human judgment in domains where context and empathy remain irreplaceable. The goal is not to romanticize Agile as a "purer" form of management nor to present AI as an inevitable replacement. Instead, it is to critically examine the ways in which the digital age is redefining agility itself: what it means to adapt, how teams make decisions, and where responsibility ultimately lies.

The story of Agile to AI-Agile is, in essence, the story of how organizations learn in real time. It is about the dance between human creativity and algorithmic precision, between intuition and data, between the values that inspired Agile's manifesto and the new frontiers opened by intelligent technologies. As we will explore in the sections that follow, this dance requires not only technical competence but also philosophical reflection. For in the end, project management is not simply about delivering outputs—it is about shaping the conditions under which people, technologies, and organizations grow together.

From Agile Foundations to AI-Enhanced Agility

Agile began as a practical rebellion against paralysis. Projects had swollen with documents, gate reviews, and brittle plans that pretended to know the future; teams were asked to certify certainty in a world that kept shifting. The Agile Manifesto—short, punchy, almost ascetic—offered a different ethic: value the working thing over the promise of the thing, closeness with users over distant contracts, responsiveness over ritual. Iteration, not orchestration; feedback, not forecasts. That spirit re-centered project work on learning: ship a slice, listen, adapt, repeat. And for a time, the cadence felt revelatory. Sprints carved breathable space into calendars. Standups unclogged communication. Retrospectives gave names to frictions that people had silently tolerated (Freedman, 2023). Velocity, burn-down, story points—imperfect instruments, yes, but a language for flow rather than ceremony.

Yet agility is not a finished achievement; it's a living property of socio-technical systems. As projects expanded in scope, and cross-functional dependencies multiplied, Agile ways sometimes hardened into new routines. Teams practiced rituals but learned less. Backlogs ballooned into fossil beds of unmade promises. Estimation became theater. The most honest practitioners admitted that intuition alone could not keep up with complexity: too many dependencies, too much variability, too thin a margin for late surprises. And here the digital age offered its provocation: if agility is learning at speed, what happens when learning itself is computationally amplified?

The leap from Agile to AI-enhanced agility begins with a simple proposition—let the system sense itself more richly and reason more quickly. Data once trapped in disparate tools can be woven into a living fabric: version control histories, incident logs, support tickets, deployment trails, calendar rhythms, even the emotional tone of team discourse (Truss, 2024). Not surveillance for its own sake, but a fuller pulse. With that pulse, models can infer patterns that human memory smudges or misses: where cycle time fractures, which dependencies generate recurring drag, which combinations of scope and staffing tend to combust under deadline heat. Prediction is only half the point; the other half is generative: suggesting alternative plans, reshaping sprint scope, rebalancing resources, surfacing risks early enough to be mundane rather than catastrophic.

Think of sprint planning through this lens. Classic Agile relies on the best shared guess—a composite of domain experience, team history, and stakeholder pressure. AI introduces probabilistic scaffolding. Instead of arguing about whether a story is a five or an eight, the team sees a distribution conditioned on similar historical work, code churn, review latency, and the availability patterns of key reviewers (Khan & Jilani, 2025). The model doesn't "decide" the estimate; it proposes the shape of uncertainty. If the distribution's tail is ugly, you can slice the story differently, swap assignees, or explicitly accept the risk. The power is not that the machine is right, but that it makes uncertainty concrete enough to negotiate.

Daily coordination shifts as well. Natural-language systems can digest standups and tickets, aligning what's said with what's actually moving in the repository. When blockers appear repeatedly—say, waiting for a particular microservice, or an elusive test harness—the assistant flags the pattern, not as a scold but as a prompt to restructure work. Subtle signals matter: sentiment drift in comments, time-to-first-review creeping upward on Fridays, the silent accumulation of TODOs that never graduate to issues (García Martínez, 2023). In classical Agile, these frictions would surface in a retrospective week later, often softened by memory and politeness; AI-augmented practices catch them in the grain of the day.

Testing, which Agile rightly elevated through TDD and continuous integration, gains a different contour. Generative models can sketch test scaffolds from requirements, propose edge cases that human writers skip when the coffee runs cold, and mutate inputs to stress brittle seams. When failures spike after a library upgrade, anomaly detection draws a dotted line between the new failure class and the specific dependency jump, saving hours of whodunit. None of this negates the craft of good testing—the smarts to design falsification strategies, the taste to name what must never break—but it narrows the gap between "we think it works" and "we have explored how it fails."

Backlog management—the graveyard and the garden—benefits from curation at scale. Large backlogs degrade agility because attention is finite; items decay into abstractions; the signal of user need dissolves into the noise of brainstorming. AI can periodically rehydrate items with fresh context: recent customer complaints clustered by theme, product analytics tied to affected user journeys, cost-of-delay signals, upstream architectural constraints. Items that no longer map to any live signal can be archived with a reason, not just a shrug. Items whose value curves steepen—perhaps because a competitor has shipped an adjacent feature or because a regulatory deadline looms—bubble upward. The backlog becomes less of an aspirational museum and more of a living queue.

Risk work changes more than most leaders anticipate. Traditional risk registers are spreadsheets with pithy descriptions and rough probabilities, updated right before a steering meeting (Marchenko, 2025). In an AI-enhanced setting, risk is behavioral: models learn the project's baseline rhythms and flag deviations that correlate with downstream trouble—merge conflict density, review contention between certain components, the growing gap between design artifacts and implementation changes. Scenario simulation becomes cheap: "What if the core library rewrite slips by two weeks?" The engine ripples the effect across capacity, dependency chains, release windows, and stakeholder calendars, not to pretend that the future is fixed but to give shape to plausible futures quickly enough to decide.

Of course, the promise invites anxiety. The specter of over-automation haunts seasoned teams who remember the cost of metrics worship. Dashboards can become performance art; models can freeze the past into the future. Agility needs dissent and nuance. A team's mood cannot be reduced to a line chart, and a product's meaning cannot be inferred exclusively from clickstreams. This is the central ethical knot of AI-agile practice: harness models without abdicating judgment. The practical answer is governance that looks less like gates and more like guardrails—human-in-the-loop defaults for significant allocations, decision logs with rationale (including when humans override the model), model cards that state limitations plainly, and periodic model retrospectives alongside sprint retrospectives. If the system is going to learn from us, we owe it clarity about what we are teaching.

Roles morph. The project manager becomes a sense-maker and curator, pairing domain narrative with model output. Product owners shepherd value hypotheses with a more explicit experimental cadence: not just building thin slices, but designing them as tests with pre-registered signals, power, and thresholds for pivot or persevere (Agarwal et al, 2025). Engineers negotiate with assistants that propose refactors, draft code, and warn about security misconfigurations in near real time; the job shifts from pure authorship to orchestration and verification, which is both empowering and, to some, unnerving. Designers partner with generative tools that explore vast interface spaces quickly; the craft bends toward choosing and shaping, toward the editorial eye that knows which variation sings and why. None of this is about replacement. It's about raising the resolution of work so choices can be made earlier, with better contrast.

Teams also confront the materiality of data. Agile thrived on lightweight artifacts; AI thrives on data plumbing. Without clean, connected telemetry, even the most elegant models deteriorate into confident nonsense. MLOps, once a specialty, becomes an infrastructural competence: lineage, drift monitoring, feature stores, privacy controls, synthetic data for rare events, techniques to de-bias imbalanced histories (Pahune & Akhtar, 2025). Technical debt now includes data debt: undocumented transformations, missing context, ambiguous semantics. A subtle irony emerges—greater agility demands deeper attention to the slow, unglamorous labor of data stewardship.

There's a cultural adjustment, too, a recalibration of trust. When a model recommends slicing a feature or delaying a release, people want to know why. Not a pastel explanation but an operational one: which features mattered, which precedents were relevant, where uncertainty is highest. Explainability is not a luxury; it's social glue. Short, accessible narratives attached to recommendations help the team argue productively with the system rather than capitulate or stonewall (Puplampu, 2024). Over time, a healthy dialectic develops: when humans repeatedly override the same class of suggestions, either the model is blind to a vital context, or the organization is ignoring a stubborn truth. Both outcomes are instructive.

Flow metrics evolve accordingly. Velocity remains a local signal, but teams watch throughput stability, lead-time distribution, recovery time after incidents, escaped-defect curves, experiment win rate, and cost of carry for work-in-progress (Zaripour, 2024). Outcome orientation strengthens: not just whether a feature shipped, but whether it moved the needle it promised to move, and with what externalities. AI helps by stitching end-to-end traces: a capability deployed on Tuesday, a measurable change in user behavior by Friday, a correlated drop in support tickets the following week. Agility starts to look less like perpetual motion and more like purposeful learning loops—hypothesize, implement, measure, narrate, adjust (Meyer et al, 2021).

Some practices will feel familiar, only sharper. Retrospectives, for instance, benefit from quiet evidence. Instead of relying exclusively on memory and the loudest voices, the team sees a crisp reel: where handoffs slowed, where rework spiked, where planning optimism outpaced reality. The conversation shifts from blame to structure—what pattern produced this friction, and what structural tweak might dissolve it? You still need the human layer: the story behind the spike, the context the data cannot see, the small kindnesses that kept the sprint humane. Numbers reveal; people interpret.

Other practices feel new. “Minimum viable question” becomes a tactic: before committing to an epic, ask the smallest answerable question that would change the decision, and use AI to assemble the evidence rapidly (Grimm et al, 2021). “Always-on backlog” takes shape: a continuous triage where items are enriched, clustered, and occasionally retired by a curatorial AI unless a human revives them with fresh purpose. “Experiment tax” is acknowledged up front—the capacity carved out each sprint for structured trials, because learning at speed is not free, and starving exploration is the quietest path to stasis.

Skeptics will say this all sounds like boutique process, a new paint on old walls. The counterpoint is tangible outcomes: fewer late surprises, crisper prioritization, earlier detection of decay, and a more honest conversation about risk. None of these require mystical faith. They require plumbing, patience, and a refusal to sanctify either intuition or instrumentation. The best teams treat models as colleagues with strengths and blind spots. Respectful, but unafraid to disagree; open, but unwilling to outsource responsibility.

There are hazards worth naming bluntly. Bias in historical data can fossilize inequities—about who gets complex work, whose code is scrutinized more severely, which users receive attention (Miceli et al, 2022). Automation can seduce leaders into surveillance patterns that damage trust, or into cost-cutting that amputates resilience. Overfitting past patterns can stifle genuinely novel bets—the very bets that generate disproportionate value. Guarding against these hazards demands ethics with teeth: privacy budgets, purpose-bound telemetry, participatory governance, red-team exercises for the models themselves, and a norm of "show your work" for algorithmic recommendations.

Even the language of "AI" in projects invites recalibration (Brandthav & Elz-aki Adam, 2025). It's less an oracle than a bundle of capabilities: pattern finding, summarization, generation, constraint solving, simulation. Matching capability to problem is the art. Use sequence models to forecast queues and cycle times; use graph reasoning to map dependencies and failure propagation; use generative models to draft but pair them with verification harnesses; use reinforcement signals sparingly to nudge scheduling policies in environments where feedback is dense and fast. Tools become a palette, not a dogma.

All of this brings us back to the original promise of Agile: shorten the distance between intention and impact. AI-enhanced agility does not replace that promise; it equips it. Teams see more, sooner. They argue with evidence rather than with personalities. They adjust at the tempo of reality instead of the tempo of meetings. And yet, agility remains an ethic, not just a mechanism. The point of faster learning is not to turn people into appendages of a dashboard; it's to give them the dignity of better choices.

In that light, the most convincing signal that AI-Agile is working is not a sleek visualization or a clever forecast (Tupsakhare, 2022). It's the texture of the week. Fewer panicked nights. Clearer trade-offs. Backlogs that feel breathable. Retrospectives that are frank without being bruising. A cadence that leaves room for craft. And a quiet confidence—the sense that the team, with all its human quirks and technical machinery, is meeting uncertainty with poise rather than bravado. Agility, once a manifesto on a website, becomes a property of the organization's nervous system: sensing, deciding, adapting, and, crucially, remembering.

The path from Agile foundations to AI-enhanced agility is not linear or tidy. It's full of selective adoption, a few wrong turns, and steady refinement. But when the pieces lock—data that respects people, models that explain themselves, roles that elevate judgment, governance that privileges learning—the result is not sterile efficiency. It's practiced responsiveness. It's the rare balance of speed with thoughtfulness, of automation with care, of prediction with curiosity. And that, in an age of digital flux, feels less like a methodology and more like a way of working that can actually last.

Shifting Roles: Human Judgment and Machine Intelligence in Project Management

Project management used to be a choreography of people, calendars, and expectations. The manager held the center, stitching together schedules and personalities, absorbing ambiguity with a mixture of experience and improvisation (Kerzner, 2025). The team provided craft and momentum; the tools stayed politely in the background. That arrangement is fading. Machine intelligence now sits inside the daily rhythms of delivery—scanning code diffs, suggesting task sequences, hinting at unseen risks, surfacing patterns in the noise. Not a distant oracle but an omnipresent colleague that never sleeps. The question is not whether machines will "replace" managers—an unhelpful fantasy—but how decision rights, attention, and accountability realign when predictive systems and generative assistants begin to participate in choices that used to be human-only.

Start with the project manager, the traditional keeper of the plan. Once, the role was part cartographer, part therapist. Build a plan, then hold it together as reality nibbles the edges. In AI-augmented environments, planning becomes continuous and probabilistic (Behravan, 2025). Instead of a single Gantt that hardens into dogma, a set of living simulations breathe alongside the work: multiple futures seeded by current constraints, each annotated with confidence bands and cost-of-delay curves. The "plan" shifts from being a single artifact to a portfolio of plausible trajectories, recomputed whenever a dependency slips or a new scope crystalizes. The manager's craft tilts toward narrative synthesis: selecting which trajectory the organization should bet on, articulating why those trade-offs honor values as well as numbers, and ensuring that stakeholders understand both the hazards and the guardrails. Less time herding tasks; more time negotiating meaning.

Decision cadence changes too. Many micro-decisions that once soaked up afternoons—who reviews which pull request, how to slice a swollen user story, whether to run another round of tests—can be delegated to a policy layer the team controls. Think of it as decision scaffolding: "If the predicted cycle time for stories tagged 'security' exceeds the 80th percentile, automatically add a second reviewer with this skill profile; if that reviewer's queue is saturated, escalate to the alternate path." Machines operationalize the scaffolding in real time (Sun et al, 2024). Humans design, tune, and occasionally suspend it, especially when context turns weird. This is not abdication; it's leverage. It frees attention for decisions where stakes, ambiguity, and moral weight are high.

The product owner's role also bends. Vision and prioritization remain human-driven, yet the ground under those judgments is more densely instrumented. User signals arrive braided: usage telemetry, support transcripts, competitive teardowns, A/B deltas, qualitative notes from research, market chatter. Generative tools summarize and cluster; causal models propose hypotheses about which interventions might move which outcomes. The product owner becomes a curator of belief: selecting which models to trust, which counterfactuals to test, how to balance short-term wins against long-term coherence (Wasserkrug et al, 2024). A backlog item is no longer just a card on a board; it's a small bet with a statistical preface, an ethical footnote, and a recovery plan if things go sideways. The job grows both harder and more honest.

Engineers encounter perhaps the most intimate shift. Code assistants draft scaffolds, propose refactors, and flag security footguns before the build even runs. This is both exhilarating and humbling. The locus of expertise moves from recall to discernment. Knowing APIs by heart matters less than knowing when not to believe a plausible answer; fluency migrates toward verification, boundary thinking, and taste. Pairing still matters—only now, one of the partners is a model whose strengths are speed and breadth, whose weaknesses are subtlety and lived context. The best engineers become conversation designers with their tools, crafting prompts that frame intent clearly, building harnesses that shame brittle suggestions, and leaving behind explainable signatures in commit messages so future readers understand the why, not just the what.

Designers receive a parallel jolt. Generative systems can explode the space of possibilities: thousands of layout permutations, color systems, micro-interactions, all conjured with a few lines of description (Bethune, 2025). The role of the designer tilts toward principled selection and narrative coherence. Beauty at scale needs constraint. Someone has to keep the product's voice from fracturing into a patchwork of cleverness. The machine supplies energy; the human supplies judgment about proportion, rhythm, and meaning. Usability testing morphs as well. Simulated users—agentic models conditioned on archetypal behaviors—can stress flows pre-release, finding dead ends that only appear after fifty meandering clicks. Still, simulated behavior is not lived complexity. Designers hold the obligating memory of the user's dignity: when to slow an experience down, when to rephrase a hard truth, when to keep a human in the loop because the moment deserves a human witness.

Scrum masters—or delivery leads, pick a label—turn into stewards of socio-technical health. Standups can be summarized by a quiet assistant that matches speech to actual repo movement, highlighting contradictions gently. Retrospectives include pattern reels generated from weeks of telemetry: handoff bottlenecks, bursts of rework around a particular module, sentiment dips after late-night pages. But the heart of facilitation stays human: creating psychological safety, naming tensions that data can't see, interrupting corrosive patterns with unusual interventions, even humor. AI can diagnose friction; it cannot replace the small, brave acts that knit trust.

A new cluster of roles arrives around the edges. Data stewards who know that telemetry without consent is just a slow-burning trust bomb. ML engineers who bring MLOps hygiene—lineage, drift, model cards—into the everyday fabric rather than quarantining it in a lab (Ping, 2024). Ethicists or, more pragmatically, cross-functional ethics councils that review automation proposals with teeth: Do we have a legitimate purpose for this data? Who benefits? Who is exposed? What recourse exists when the system errs? The presence of such bodies is not bureaucratic garnish; it is how organizations keep their humanity in high-resolution environments.

With all this augmentation, accountability risks blurring. When a scheduling model recommended a release window that clashed with a regulatory freeze, who owns the fallout—the engineer who clicked "accept," the PM who tuned the policy, the ops lead who noticed the warning but presumed someone else had it covered, or the vendor who shipped the model? Without care, responsibility evaporates into the haze of "the system said." The antidote is explicit decision logging. Not a performative ritual, but a lightweight, searchable trail: what recommendation was given, what was accepted or overridden, by whom, for what reason, and with which expected downside. Such logs do two things. They make learning tractable—future teams can revisit reasoning when a similar fork appears—and they keep courage alive. Overriding a model is easier when the organization expects it to happen sometimes and values the articulated why.

Explainability, then, isn't just a compliance checkbox; it's social infrastructure. Teams do not need a dissertation on Shapley values in the middle of a planning session; they need a clear articulation of the factors that mattered most and the neighborhoods of uncertainty. "This forecast leaned heavily on historical review latency and the clumpiness of dependencies around service X; if we decouple Y, the risk profile changes." Short, direct, humble. When explanations consistently fail to match lived experience, trust erodes rapidly—and so it should. A rhythm of model retrospectives helps: what did it get wrong, why, and what did we change (features, priors, guardrails) as a result?

Some leaders will attempt to operationalize AI by doubling down on measurement, assuming that if everything is watched, everything will improve (Quaquebeke & Gerpott, 2023). This is the oldest trap. Measurement without interpretation prizes speed over wisdom, output over outcome, conformity over craft. A healthier pattern treats metrics as invitations to investigate, not verdicts. When throughput dips, the conversation is not "who slipped," but "what structural constraint became salient, and which knobs—scope, staffing, sequencing, technical debt—can relieve it without creating worse downstream harm?" Machines can help identify levers; humans must weigh the collateral.

There's also the matter of organizational texture—the stories people tell themselves about what kind of place this is. AI changes those stories. In generous cultures, the narrative becomes one of amplified competence: tools that catch our blind spots, search the haystack for needles, keep drudgery to a minimum, and give us back time to do the parts that matter (Singh et al, 2024). In brittle cultures, the same tools can become surveillance devices, engines of subtle coercion, or rationalizations for squeezing capacity until care buckles. The same software, different soul. The difference usually traces to two rituals: whether teams co-design the automation that affects them, and whether leaders model restraint—choosing not to instrument private corners of work simply because they can.

A few concrete scenes help ground the abstraction. Picture a large program with a dozen teams, a lattice of microservices, and a regulatory deadline that won't budge. The AI scheduler proposes that three teams pause feature development for a week to drain a growing operations backlog, because simulation shows the tail risk of incidents exploding during the final month. In the old world, that would be a tough sell; no executive enjoys "going slower" now to go faster later. With model-backed scenarios, the debate is different. You can inspect the assumptions, tweak them, rerun. You can negotiate the shape of the pause: light feature work that doesn't touch the hot path, a compensating increase in test automation. The decision remains human—a value call about risk appetite and reputation—but it is made with a clarity that disarms the usual theater of optimism.

A smaller scene: a junior engineer is asked to own a finicky service no one loves. The model indicates this person's review latency is low and success rate high; the recommendation engine nudges the assignment their way. A humane team asks a second question. Will this reinforce an inequity, funneling thankless work toward someone because they are fast and polite? The algorithm has no opinion. Humans must. Decision: split the service stewardship and rotate it quarterly, bake in a maintenance credit in performance reviews, attach a senior mentor, and tag a refactor as a Q3 objective. AI suggested a direction; people supplied fairness and care.

Another one, thornier: a contracting firm promises "AI-powered dashboards" that rank individual developers by productivity. The demo looks slick. But anyone who has lived in real systems knows how these metrics backfire: gaming increases, collaboration shrinks, invisible labor (mentoring, debugging, knowledge sharing) disappears from the map. A mature organization declines, not because it fears measurement, but because it honors complex work. Instead, it asks for team-level health indicators and invests in qualitative leadership reviews that name and reward the invisible fibers of great engineering cultures. Machine intelligence becomes a mirror, not a whip.

It's easy to romanticize the new equilibrium, yet friction endures. Over-reliance creeps in—teams take model outputs as gospel and forget to look out the window. Under-reliance creeps in—the system becomes background noise because the first versions were clumsy or the explanations felt like riddles. Real progress looks like gradual tuning and disciplined patience: scope smaller, pilot earlier, prune aggressively, keep the feedback loop tight. Progress also looks like humility: naming what the system cannot or should not decide, and refusing to chase the illusion of total visibility.

All the while, education has to keep pace. Managerial training now includes basic literacy in uncertainty, causal inference, experimentation, and data ethics (Martin et al, 2021). Engineers learn prompt design, verification harnesses for generative code, and practical threat modeling for ML systems. Designers learn how to interrogate synthetic personas and when to ignore them. Everyone learns to write decision narratives that age well, because organizational memory is a competitive advantage, and unremembered lessons are expensive to relearn.

What emerges, if the balance holds, is an ecology of judgment. Machines excel at breadth and endurance: scanning, correlating, projecting. Humans excel at context, empathy, and principled trade-offs under conditions where the stakes reach beyond the metric into identity, reputation, and fairness (Lizzio, 2025). The roles interleave. Project managers choreograph decisions rather than micromanage tasks. Product owners curate hypotheses rather than merely stack-rank requests. Engineers and designers cultivate editorial authority—saying no to slick but incoherent suggestions, yes to the quietly robust. Ethicists and data stewards become first-class partners, not afterthoughts. Executives learn to read model output like weather: not destiny, but hard-to-ignore background conditions.

In this arrangement, the most valuable asset is not the model itself but the organization's capacity to argue well with it. Healthy disagreement—clear, curious, documented—becomes a generator of shared understanding. When a team routinely explains why it ignored three clever recommendations yet embraced a fourth, it is teaching the system about its values and teaching itself about its own instincts. Over time, the line between human judgment and machine intelligence stops feeling adversarial and starts feeling like a braid—two strands, distinct but interdependent, stronger together than alone (Raikov & Pirani, 2022). The work of project management, then, is still about aligning effort with purpose under constraint. Only now the constraints sing at higher resolution, and the purpose must be articulated in ways a model can partially understand and a human can fully defend. The roles shift, not toward obsolescence, but toward higher forms of discernment. Less heroism, more stewardship. Less theater, more candor. Less obsession with control, more devotion to learning. If that sounds quieter than the old myths of command and rescue, good. Quiet can be rigorous. Quiet can be brave. Quiet, when it is the sound of a team thinking clearly with its machines, might be what sustainable excellence actually sounds like.

Data-Driven Adaptability: Predictive Analytics and Real-Time Decision Making

Adaptability has always been the quiet currency of successful projects. A plan can be elegant, resourced, and signed by every executive in the chain of command, yet collapse the moment an unforeseen dependency buckles or a market shift slices through assumptions. For years, agility tried to meet that reality with sprints, retrospectives, and a culture of responsiveness. Teams became good at absorbing shocks, adjusting backlog priorities, and recalibrating scope. But responsiveness, while vital, is reactive. The new horizon is anticipatory: not waiting for the shock, but detecting its tremors, sensing its trajectory, and adjusting course before the wave crests. This is where predictive analytics and real-time decision-making enter the bloodstream of project management—not as sterile dashboards but as instruments of living adaptability.

The difference feels subtle until you sit with it. Traditional agility says: when a risk materializes, respond quickly, pivot cleanly, and minimize damage (Holloway, 2025). Data-driven adaptability says: many risks whisper before they shout, and if we can hear the whisper, we can avoid the shout altogether. Predictive models, trained on rich histories of project data—cycle times, defect patterns, review delays, customer escalations, vendor performance—begin to reveal the probabilities hiding behind what once seemed like random noise (Khan, 2024). It is not clairvoyance. It is pattern recognition at a scale human intuition struggles to sustain.

Consider backlog health. In most organizations, the backlog grows until it resembles an attic of half-forgotten intentions: old requests layered with urgent fires, half-written epics beside tasks that no longer align with strategy. Human triage helps, but only in bursts, and fatigue sets in. Predictive analytics can watch how backlog items age, cluster by theme, and correlate with delivery outcomes. It can signal when certain types of stories—security-related, or integration-heavy—tend to swell cycle times disproportionately, suggesting they be sliced or sequenced differently. Instead of waiting for a sprint to drown under invisible weight, the system flags drag early, and the team can intervene with precision rather than scrambling in hindsight.

The same applies to resource allocation. Project managers once leaned heavily on gut instinct, experience, and rough historical averages. Now, algorithms can simulate resource flows across multiple competing projects, adjusting for skill distribution, vacation calendars, and dependency graphs. They don't produce a single "right" answer; they offer a range of plausible load-balancing scenarios, each with trade-offs spelled out in terms of delivery probability, risk exposure, and cost-of-delay. A decision that once took days of meetings and subjective hunches can now be framed with clarity in minutes, allowing leadership to focus less on data gathering and more on value negotiation.

The most profound shift, however, comes in real-time responsiveness. Projects used to live on weekly or biweekly cadences. Standups and retrospectives gave rhythm, but the pulse was still coarse. AI-driven analytics collapse those cadences into continuous sensing. Anomalies surface as they emerge: sudden latency in code reviews, unusual spikes in bug reopen rates, sentiment dips in chat channels. The system doesn't just alert; it contextualizes—this spike resembles past incidents that escalated into outages, or this slowdown correlates with a particular service dependency. Humans still decide the response, but the lag between problem emergence and recognition shrinks dramatically.

Take release management as an example. Historically, releases were moments of ritual anxiety: the merge freeze, the all-hands testing push, the tense weekend deployment. Predictive analytics changes the texture. By analyzing commit history, integration frequency, and test coverage patterns, the system can forecast release readiness weeks in advance (Yarram & Bittla, 2023). It can even suggest optimal release windows based on team availability and incident history, reducing the likelihood of deploying when the organization is thinly staffed. Real-time dashboards then track live metrics during deployment—rollback probability, error spikes, user feedback sentiment—allowing leaders to decide whether to proceed, pause, or roll back with confidence grounded in evidence, not just instinct.

And yet, adaptability is not simply about speed. It is about proportionate response—knowing when to act, when to wait, and when to deliberately absorb uncertainty. Predictive models can sometimes overreact, flagging noise as signal, or biasing toward conservative choices that stifle bold moves (Halperin & Mazlish, 2025). The human role here is irreplaceable. Machines are excellent at describing what might happen, less skilled at judging what matters. A forecast that a feature has a 40% chance of delay may be statistically solid, but whether that delay imperils the strategic intent of the release is a human call. The art of adaptability lies in weaving machine precision with human sense-making, balancing probabilities with purpose.

There is also a deeper, almost philosophical tension at play: does predictive clarity erode the improvisational spirit that made Agile powerful in the first place? Agile thrived on conversations, on the shared experience of responding together to change. With AI intermediating, will teams become passive recipients of forecasts, trusting the system's nudges over their own instincts? Or can predictive analytics serve as a catalyst for richer dialogue, grounding debates in evidence while leaving room for dissent and creativity? The answer depends less on the tools and more on the culture around them. Organizations that treat predictions as oracles will hollow out their adaptability. Those that treat predictions as prompts for human judgment may find themselves more agile than ever—able to sense, discuss, and decide with sharper clarity.

The ethical dimensions cannot be ignored. Real-time decision-making requires continuous data flows, and continuous data flows can slip easily into surveillance if not handled with care (Ahuchogu, 2025). Should every keystroke, every delay, every moment of inactivity be captured and fed into a model? At what point does adaptability come at the expense of trust? Teams adapt best when they feel respected, not when they feel constantly measured. A mature approach to predictive analytics embraces data minimization: collect only what is necessary, anonymize where possible, and explain how the signals are used. Transparency is not just compliance; it is how organizations preserve morale in the face of increasingly granular monitoring.

And then there is the question of accountability. If a predictive system recommends delaying a release and leadership agrees, but the market punishes the delay, who owns the outcome? The system? The decision-makers? The data scientists who tuned the model? Without clear accountability, adaptability risks devolving into finger-pointing. Smart organizations handle this by embedding prediction into decision logs: what the system said, what humans decided, and why. Such logs build organizational memory, allowing teams to learn not only from outcomes but from the reasoning that preceded them. Over time, they create a culture of responsible adaptability, where data informs but does not dictate.

One of the more intriguing frontiers is scenario simulation. Instead of reacting to a forecast, teams can run "what-if" experiments on demand: What if this vendor misses delivery by two weeks? What if we add a new integration partner mid-sprint? What if a regulatory change forces us to re-engineer compliance features? Each scenario generates ripple effects—resource shifts, deadline slips, risk multipliers—mapped clearly enough for leaders to choose paths proactively. Decision-making becomes less about firefighting and more about gaming out futures, then steering toward the one that best balances ambition and feasibility.

Even the cadence of retrospectives evolves. In traditional Agile, retrospectives are moments of pause: look back, reflect, decide what to improve (Derby et al, 2024). With predictive analytics, retrospectives are enriched with evidence—graphs showing how estimation accuracy changed over time, clusters of recurring blockers, comparisons between predicted and actual delivery velocities. This doesn't replace conversation; it deepens it. Instead of vague recollections, teams debate tangible patterns: "Our handoff delays are increasing between design and implementation; do we need a shared pairing practice?" Data doesn't silence voices; it sharpens them.

Real-time decision-making also creates new rhythms of leadership (Pawar & Dhumal, 2024). Executives, who once saw project health in monthly reports, can now watch living dashboards that update continuously. But with visibility comes temptation—the temptation to micromanage, to react to every fluctuation as if it were a crisis. Mature leaders resist this impulse. They recognize that not all variance is bad, not all dips require intervention. Adaptability is not about chasing every blip; it is about knowing which blips matter. Machines can flag deviations; humans must cultivate the restraint to let some play out, trusting teams to self-correct.

The irony is that true adaptability may require slowing down in some moments, even when the data shouts urgency. Predictive analytics might show that rushing a feature to market increases churn probability by 15%. The real-time dashboard might scream red. But if the team senses that waiting—polishing the edges, aligning the experience—will generate loyalty that no metric can capture, they might choose patience. That is adaptability too: not just speed, but wisdom in pacing.

The dream of data-driven adaptability is not flawless prediction or instantaneous reaction (Brunner et al, 2024). It is the weaving of foresight into everyday work, so projects breathe with the rhythm of reality rather than the rigidity of static plans. It is about cultivating organizations that can sense weak signals, discuss them honestly, and act with proportion. Machines give us sharper eyes and faster reflexes; humans supply judgment, courage, and care. Together, they create the possibility of project ecosystems that are not merely reactive but anticipatory—able to turn uncertainty into advantage, not just survive it.

And perhaps the final measure of success will not be dashboards at all. It will be the felt experience of teams. Are they less surprised by crises? Do decisions feel more grounded, less arbitrary? Does work flow with fewer panicked nights and more deliberate trade-offs? When predictive analytics and real-time decision-making truly integrate, adaptability ceases to be a slogan. It becomes a lived property of the organization—a quiet confidence that whatever comes, the system can adjust, because it is always sensing, always learning, and always leaving room for human choice.

Toward a Future of Symbiotic Project Management Frameworks

The language of management has long been haunted by metaphors of control: levers, pipelines, roadmaps, command centers. It implied a world where projects were machines, each part fitting neatly into place, predictable as long as someone kept a firm hand on the steering wheel. Agile cracked that illusion by reminding us that projects are more like living organisms—messy, adaptive, prone to sudden growth and unexpected mutations. Now, with artificial intelligence entering the bloodstream of organizational life, we face another conceptual leap: projects are no longer only human organisms, but hybrid systems, half flesh and half algorithm, cohabiting in a constantly shifting ecosystem. Symbiosis, not control, may be the more honest metaphor for the frameworks of tomorrow.

The idea of symbiosis in project management requires unlearning as much as it demands building. Too often, AI is introduced as a bolt-on efficiency booster, something that automates repetitive tasks or accelerates reporting cycles (Wilson &

Tyson, 2025). But that is still the logic of subordination: technology serving human plans. A truly symbiotic framework suggests something different—a system in which human intuition and machine intelligence co-evolve, each shaping the other, neither wholly subordinate. The future here is not about replacing managers with algorithms, nor about relegating AI to a back-office role. It is about constructing environments where the machine's capacity for scale and pattern complements the human's capacity for judgment, empathy, and ethical discernment.

Picture a project meeting in this not-so-distant future. A planning assistant sits silently in the corner of the digital room, tracking conversation threads against historical delivery patterns, surfacing inconsistencies between declared priorities and past behaviors. It does not tell the team what to do; it nudges, prompts, frames. The humans, meanwhile, bring their own narratives, their gut feelings, the sense that this particular client will not tolerate a delay or that this feature has intangible symbolic weight beyond its technical value. The decision that emerges is not machine-driven nor purely human—it is braided. The algorithm ensures no one forgets the statistical risks; the humans insist on honoring context that no dataset has ever captured. Out of that negotiation, a better decision materializes. This is symbiosis in practice, fragile but generative.

For such a framework to thrive, organizations will need to abandon the illusion that project management is reducible to a single methodology. Agile, waterfall, lean, hybrid—each is a vocabulary, useful in its place, but brittle if enforced universally. Symbiotic frameworks will be plural by design. They will treat methodologies like dialects in a multilingual ecosystem, shifting between them fluidly, guided by the twin compasses of human judgment and machine feedback. Sometimes predictive analytics will suggest a kanban-like flow is best suited to the incoming work pattern. Other times, a structured phase-gate may surface as the least risky path. What matters is not fidelity to doctrine but adaptability of the framework itself, its ability to morph without collapsing.

Of course, symbiosis is not a utopia. Relationships of mutual benefit can slide into parasitism if left unchecked. Imagine a team that leans so heavily on AI recommendations that critical thinking atrophies (Drosos et al, 2025). Or an organization that exploits AI insights to push unsustainable productivity, treating workers like adjustable cogs because the model says they can absorb more. A symbiotic framework requires intentional balance: agreements on how far to trust automation, when to insist on human override, and how to distribute power fairly between the voices in the room—both organic and algorithmic. Without such balance, the system may look efficient on paper but corrode the human spirit underneath.

The governance of symbiotic frameworks is where the real challenge lies. Traditional governance models rely on checkpoints, approvals, escalation paths. But when decisions emerge from a human–machine braid, accountability becomes ambiguous. If a model predicts a 70% likelihood of delay and the team proceeds anyway, is the model wrong, or the humans reckless? A symbiotic future must redefine governance less as control and more as stewardship. It is about cultivating decision ecologies where transparency is the norm—why a model made a suggestion, why the humans accepted or rejected it, what values underpinned that judgment. Decision logs, once dusty compliance artifacts, could become cultural texts: repositories of how human and machine collaborated, disagreed, and learned.

Another facet of symbiosis is the emotional texture of work. Machines will not feel stress or pride, but they will shape environments where humans do. If predictive systems consistently flag risks before they metastasize into crises, teams may experience less burnout and more confidence. Conversely, if those systems flood workers with constant micro-warnings, anxiety may rise, as though living under the gaze of a critical supervisor who never sleeps. The human–machine relationship, like any relationship, requires care. Feedback loops must be tuned not only for accuracy but for psychological resonance, giving teams information in ways that empower rather than overwhelm.

Education becomes central here. Future managers and team members will need literacy in both domains: enough statistical awareness to question machine outputs intelligently, enough emotional intelligence to keep teams cohesive amid algorithmic nudges. Training will not be about mastering a single tool but about developing the flexibility to live inside an ecosystem where tools evolve continuously. The project manager of tomorrow may need to read a residual plot with one eye and a room's mood with the other, weaving both into a decision that respects data without betraying humanity.

Symbiosis also extends beyond the project boundary. Stakeholders—clients, regulators, communities—will increasingly expect transparency about how AI shapes outcomes (Agrawal, 2024). If a project fails, will the explanation point to a flawed human judgment, a miscalibrated model, or both? Future frameworks will need external interfaces that make the hybrid nature of decision-making legible to outsiders. Not sterile metrics, but narratives: this was the recommendation, here was the context, these were the trade-offs, this is why we chose as we did. Such narratives not only protect accountability; they reinforce legitimacy in a world wary of algorithmic opacity.

There is something almost ecological in this vision. Just as forests thrive through interdependent species—trees feeding fungi, fungi nourishing roots—so too will project ecosystems depend on interdependence. Humans, with their capacity for meaning and ethics, provide orientation. Machines, with their speed and scope, provide augmentation. Neither thrives alone in complex environments. The framework becomes less a rigid structure and more a habitat, cultivating the conditions under which collaboration across species—human and digital—can flourish.

Still, one cannot romanticize symbiosis without recognizing its fragility. Relationships can sour. Trust can erode. Algorithms can drift, data can mislead, humans can abdicate responsibility in the face of machine confidence. The work of the future will not be building flawless systems but cultivating resilient ones, where errors are surfaced quickly, discussed openly, and corrected without blame. A symbiotic framework is not defined by never stumbling; it is defined by stumbling without shattering (Plante, 2025).

There will be resistance, of course. Some will cling to the purity of human-centered Agile, fearing that AI dilutes the philosophy. Others will lunge toward over-automation, intoxicated by the promise of frictionless delivery. The truth, as usual, lies in between. The symbiotic path asks for humility: acknowledging that humans alone cannot manage the complexity of modern projects, and that machines alone cannot supply the wisdom or care required to sustain human collaboration. It asks for courage: building governance structures that resist both blind faith in models and blind nostalgia for pre-digital practices. And it asks for imagination: daring to design workplaces where machine intelligence is not a threat but a partner in the long, messy journey of creating value.

Perhaps the most striking shift in this symbiotic future will be how organizations define success (George, 2024). No longer merely on-time delivery or under-budget execution, but the quality of the human–machine partnership itself. Did the framework amplify human creativity? Did it prevent exploitation? Did it learn and adapt without calcifying into dogma? These questions may sound abstract, but they will become practical as organizations compete not just on outputs but on cultures of adaptability. The ones who thrive will not be those with the flashiest algorithms or the strictest processes, but those who weave the two into a living, evolving fabric.

The horizon is uncertain, but the contours are visible. Project management will not return to the era of rigid plans, nor will it surrender entirely to the machine (Favari, 2023). It will settle, uneasily but productively, into symbiosis. A place where models and humans argue, align, and improvise together. A place where frameworks are less about dictating behavior and more about cultivating spaces where hybrid intelligence can flourish. A place where agility itself matures—no longer merely fast response to change, but deep partnership with the very systems that help us perceive change.

And if that sounds less like a methodology and more like a philosophy of work, perhaps that is the point. Symbiosis resists neat rules. It is lived, day by day, in the messy negotiations between intuition and prediction, between ethics and efficiency, between the limits of human capacity and the boundless appetite of data. The future of project management, if it is to remain humane, must learn to live in that negotiation—not as a problem to solve, but as a relationship to tend.

CONCLUSION

As we step back from the intricate analyses of methods, technologies, and organizational implications, one thing becomes clear: the transition from Agile to AI-Agile is not a matter of replacing one framework with another. It is a story of layering, blending, and reimagining. Agile will not disappear, for its values of collaboration, adaptability, and customer focus remain as relevant as ever. Instead, these values must now be interpreted in light of machine intelligence, with AI acting as both a catalyst and a disruptor. AI-Agile does not negate the human-centered ethos of Agile—it redefines it, challenging us to ask what "human-centered" means when algorithms actively participate in decision-making.

The future of project management will be characterized by symbiosis rather than substitution. Humans and machines will co-manage complexity, each compensating for the other's limitations. Algorithms will spot risks and propose solutions at a scale impossible for human minds, while humans will bring context, ethics, and empathy that machines cannot replicate. This partnership, however, will not emerge automatically. It will require conscious design: thoughtful governance structures, clear ethical guidelines, ongoing training, and a willingness to interrogate the blind spots of both humans and AI.

If Agile once reminded organizations that projects are living systems, AI-Agile insists that these systems are now hybrid—part human, part algorithmic. Managing such hybridity demands more than technical skill; it demands humility, ethical clarity, and an openness to experimentation. Project managers must become translators between human and machine reasoning, facilitators of dialogue that bridges predictive data and lived experience. Teams must learn to trust not only one another but also the tools that increasingly shape their collective choices. And leaders must resist the temptation to see AI as a panacea, remembering that technology amplifies both strengths and weaknesses, depending on the values embedded in its use.

The deeper challenge, then, is not how to adopt AI-Agile but how to inhabit it responsibly. What kind of organizations do we want to become in the process? What forms of collaboration, accountability, and fairness will define our projects in an age where decisions are distributed across humans and algorithms alike? These are questions that point beyond methodologies toward the very future of work and governance.

In the end, the move from Agile to AI-Agile is not only about managing projects more efficiently; it is about redefining the relationship between intelligence, adaptability, and purpose. If we succeed, we will cultivate project ecosystems that are not only faster and smarter but also more humane—where technological power amplifies human creativity rather than displacing it. If we fail, we risk reducing project management to a technocratic exercise, blind to the subtle dynamics that make collaboration meaningful.

Thus, the true task ahead is not merely technical integration but ethical imagination. The digital age compels us to re-envision what it means to lead, to adapt, and to deliver together. In that sense, AI-Agile is not the end of Agile's journey but its continuation—a reminder that agility, in any era, is about learning how to navigate change with wisdom, courage, and care.

REFERENCES

Agarwal, R., Bacco, F., Camuffo, A., Coali, A., Gambardella, A., Msangi, H., Sonka, S., Temu, A., Waized, B., & Wormald, A. (2025). Does a theory-of-value add value? Evidence from a randomized control trial with Tanzanian entrepreneurs. *Organization Science*, *36*(2), 601–625. DOI: 10.1287/orsc.2023.17590

Agrawal, G. (2024). Accountability, trust, and transparency in AI systems from the perspective of public policy: Elevating ethical standards. In *AI healthcare applications and security, ethical, and legal considerations* (pp. 148–162). IGI Global. DOI: 10.4018/979-8-3693-7452-8.ch009

Ahuchogu, M. C. (2025). Real-Time Image-Based Data Processing and its Applications in Managerial Decision-Making and Risk Analysis. *EKSPLORIUM-BULETIN PUSAT TEKNOLOGI BAHAN GALIAN NUKLIR*, *46*(1), 1552–1565.

Behravan, M. (2025). Generative ai framework for 3d object generation in augmented reality. arXiv preprint arXiv:2502.15869.

Bethune, K. G. (2025). *Nonlinear: Navigating Design with Curiosity and Conviction*. MIT Press. DOI: 10.7551/mitpress/14993.001.0001

Brandthav, T., & Elzaki Adam, S. (2025). Human-AI Symbiosis in Public Sector: Exploring Delegation and Constant Recalibration of Agency Through Generative AI.

Brunner, D., Legat, C., & Seebacher, U. (2024). Towards Next Generation Data-Driven Management: Leveraging Predictive Swarm Intelligence to Reason and Predict Market Dynamics. In Collective Intelligence (pp. 152-203). CRC Press.

Cervini, P., Farri, E., & Rosani, G. (2023). Generative AI for strategy & innovation. Harvard Business Review Italia, 4.

Derby, E., Larsen, D., & Horowitz, D. (2024). *Agile Retrospectives: A Practical Guide for Catalyzing Team Learning and Improvement*. The Pragmatic Programmers LLC.

Drosos, I., Sarkar, A., & Toronto, N. (2025). " It makes you think": Provocations Help Restore Critical Thinking to AI-Assisted Knowledge Work. arXiv preprint arXiv:2501.17247.

Favari, E. (2023). *Project management: leading change in the age of complexity*. Springer Nature. DOI: 10.1007/978-3-031-25031-6

Freedman, E. B. (2023). “Not a Word Was Said Ever Again”: Silence and Speech in Women’s Oral History Accounts of Sexual Harassment. *The Oral History Review*, *50*(1), 4–22. DOI: 10.1080/00940798.2023.2182695

García Martínez, J. R. (2023). Letters of blood and fire: writing and accumulation in Latin America, from the chronicles of the Indies to the present (Doctoral dissertation, University of British Columbia).

George, A. S. (2024). The symbiotic relationship between visionary and pragmatic leadership in propelling organizational success. *Partners Universal International Innovation Journal*, *2*(3), 57–79.

Grimm, P. W., Grossman, M. R., & Cormack, G. V. (2021). Artificial intelligence as evidence. *Nw. J. Tech. & Intell. Prop.*, *19*, 9.

Halperin, B., & Mazlish, J. Z. (2025). Overreaction and forecast horizon: longer-term expectations overreact more, shorter-term expectations drive fluctuations.

Holloway, S. (2025). Navigating Supply Chain Disruptions with Technology-Driven Agility and Coordination. Available at *SSRN* 5136960. DOI: 10.2139/ssrn.5136960

Kerzner, H. (2025). *Project management: a systems approach to planning, scheduling, and controlling*. John Wiley & Sons.

Khan, A., & Jilani, A. A. A. (2025). From Algorithms to Intelligence: The Historical Perspective of AI in Software Development. In Generative AI in Software Engineering (pp. 1-56). IGI Global Scientific Publishing.

Khan, M. F. I. (2024). Predictive Analytics And Machine Learning For Real-Time Detection Of Software Defects.

Lizzio, A. (2025). From Artificial to Humane Intelligence (HI)–The Necessary Evolution of Ethical Diversity in AI.

Marchenko, V. (2025). Digital Freight Command. Available at *SSRN* 5527858.

Martin, R., Hughes, D. J., Epitropaki, O., & Thomas, G. (2021). In pursuit of causality in leadership training research: A review and pragmatic recommendations. *The Leadership Quarterly*, *32*(5), 101375. DOI: 10.1016/j.leaqua.2019.101375

Meyer, S., Newsome, D., Fuller, T., Newsome, K., & Ghezzi, P. M. (2021). Agility: What it is, how to measure it, and how to use it. *Behavior Analysis in Practice*, *14*(3), 598–607. DOI: 10.1007/s40617-020-00465-4 PMID: 34631367

Miceli, M., Posada, J., & Yang, T. (2022). Studying up machine learning data: Why talk about bias when we mean power? Proceedings of the ACM on Human-Computer Interaction, 6(GROUP), 1-14.

Pahune, S., & Akhtar, Z. (2025). Transitioning from MLOps to LLMOps: Navigating the unique challenges of large language models. *Information (Basel)*, *16*(2), 87. DOI: 10.3390/info16020087

Pawar, S., & Dhumal, V. (2024). The role of technology in transforming leadership management practices. *Multidisciplinary Reviews*, *7*(4), 2024066–2024066. DOI: 10.31893/multirev.2024066

Ping, D. (2024). *The Machine Learning Solutions Architect Handbook: Practical strategies and best practices on the ML lifecycle, system design, MLOps, and generative AI*. Packt Publishing Ltd.

Plante, M. (2025). A new symbiotic, holistic and gradualist model proposal for the concept of "living organism". *Theory in Biosciences*, *144*(1), 45–65. DOI: 10.1007/s12064-024-00429-0 PMID: 39636364

Puplampu, R. (2024). *What Everyone Should Know About the Rise of AI: AI Transparency, Privacy, and Ethics Best Practices*. Puplampu Books.

Quaquebeke, N. V., & Gerpott, F. H. (2023). The now, new, and next of digital leadership: How Artificial Intelligence (AI) will take over and change leadership as we know it. *Journal of Leadership & Organizational Studies*, *30*(3), 265–275. DOI: 10.1177/15480518231181731

Raikov, A. N., & Pirani, M. (2022). Human-machine duality: What's next in cognitive aspects of artificial intelligence? *IEEE Access : Practical Innovations, Open Solutions*, *10*, 56296–56315. DOI: 10.1109/ACCESS.2022.3177657

Sartori, L., & Theodorou, A. (2022). A sociotechnical perspective for the future of AI: Narratives, inequalities, and human control. *Ethics and Information Technology*, *24*(1), 4. DOI: 10.1007/s10676-022-09624-3

Singh, A., Sethu, S. G., & Chaudhary, R. (2024). Artificial Intelligence in Storytelling: A Critical Analysis of Narrative Authenticity, Cultural Impact, and the Future of Creative Industries. Library of Progress-Library Science, Information Technology & Computer, 44(3).

Sun, L., Chan, A., Chang, Y. S., & Dow, S. P. (2024, March). ReviewFlow: Intelligent scaffolding to support academic peer reviewing. In *Proceedings of the 29th International Conference on Intelligent User Interfaces* (pp. 120-137). DOI: 10.1145/3640543.3645159

Truss, A. (2024). Agile development processes in IT support work.

Tupsakhare, P. (2022). Enhancing Agile Methodologies with AI: Driving Efficiency and Innovation. *European Journal of Advances in Engineering and Technology*, *9*(10), 66–71.

Wasserkrug, S., Boussioux, L., & Sun, W. (2024). Combining large language models and or/ms to make smarter decisions. In *Tutorials in Operations Research: Smarter Decisions for a Better World* (pp. 1–49). INFORMS. DOI: 10.1287/educ.2024.0275

Wilson, R., & Tyson, J. (2025). *Age of Invisible Machines: A Guide to Orchestrating AI Agents and Making Organizations More Self-Driving, Revised and Updated*. John Wiley & Sons.

Yarram, S., & Bittla, S. R. (2023). Predictive Test Automation: Shaping the Future of Quality Engineering in Enterprise Platforms. Available at *SSRN* 5132329.

Zaripour, M. (2024). *Boost Your Team's Speed: Quick and Easy Ways to Get Things Done Faster*. Mohammad Zaripour.

Chapter 2
AIOps:
Evolution and Transformation of IT Operations

Sarma A. D. N.
http://orcid.org/0000-0003-2093-388X
Jaya Soft, Hyderabad, India

ABSTRACT

The chapter provides a detailed overview of information technology operations from inception to date and its transformation to artificial intelligence operations. Moreover, explain the importance of IT operations, its major functions along with the role of IT operations. Besides, present a case for AI driven IT operation transformation that include cover limitations of traditional IT operations, and the need for intelligent and automation for IT operation. Listed a few implementation challenges. A typical transformation process of ITOps into AIOps. Further, an high level conceptual architecture and explained its working. Mentioned major performance indicators of AIOps. List of potential use case presented along with benefits.

1. INTRODUCTION

Information Technology Operations, in short ITOps, has a long history more than 75 years. Nowadays, the size and complexity of IT operations have increased and become more difficult to manage end to end IT infrastructure manually to meet the business demands in thc digital world. The development of new technologies such as artificial intelligence, machine learning and analytics is resulting in a paradigm shift in almost all organizations towards digital transformation, but there is no exception to IT operations as well as project management. By applying AI into IT operations, resulting in a new stream is most commonly known as AIOps. The

DOI: 10.4018/979-8-3373-6851-1.ch002

terms AIOps stands AI for IT operations. Similarly, applying AI together with Agile frameworks to project management result in a new evolution in project management is known as Agile AI-powered project management.

This chapter aims to provide a detailed analysis of Information Technology (IT) operations from inception to date and its transformation of IT operations into AIOps. Moreover, explain how AIOps can be utilized for the advantage of AI-powered Agile project management. The target users of this chapter are IT Operation Professionals, Scientists and business executives. Support engineers, site reliability engineers, systems professional, AI practitioners, AI and ML professional, Architects, and project management professionals.

The term Information Technology operations refer to the processes of implementing, managing, delivering, monitoring, and operations and management of IT operations of an organization on a day-to-day basis. In short, IT operations can be summarized as to the management of the technology used within the organization to run the business. Alternatively, ITOps can be summarized as the process of managing an organization's technology infrastructure, including its business applications. The other definition of IT operations (ITOps) describes as the people, processes and services associated with delivering quality IT services and keeping digital services up and running.

The technology infrastructure includes servers, computers, storage and data infrastructure, network infrastructure and multiple software solutions of an organization. All the technology infrastructure of an organization together is commonly referred as IT systems. In general, managing technology infrastructure will fall under the operation management of an organization, which is carried out by the IT department. The IT operation teams mainly focus on installation, monitoring, maintenance, and troubleshooting of IT systems and functioning of application services on day-to-day basis. Figure 1 shows a typical IT Operations, which includes an end-to-end management and maintenance of (i) servers and storage infrastructure, (ii) network and communication infrastructure, and (iii) computer operations and help desk. Broadly, the functionality of ITOps includes operations of servers including tasks like setting up servers, configuring networks, managing databases, monitoring systems performance and support and maintenance of solutions.

In 1980s, IT systems were manually managed by limited technical personal because of their limited complexity. In the early 2000s, the focus of managing IT systems was slightly increased which manual managed by a team of skilled personas that comprise a team of IT experts such as server administrator, system administrator, network administrator, security, database administrator to name a few roles. During this period, one of the most common scenarios adopted by the organizations, as the number of IT systems increases adding more resources to manage its functioning.

Figure 1. Typical view of IT Operations

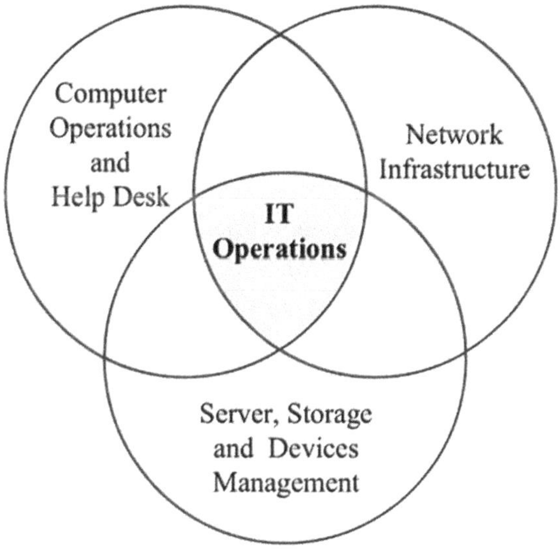

In 2010s, the complexity of technology infrastructure has increased beyond a point may not figure out adding resource to IT teams that opens up for the need of various tools and solutions to manage ongoing IT operations. At the same time organization's focus shifted towards Information Technology Inforamtoin Library (ITIL) compliances for managing IT services effectively. In ITIL v3, IT operations is a part of four functions (Maya, 2021), which include technical management, application management, and service desk.. The latest version of ITIL 4 was released in February 2019, provides a roadmap and standardized guidelines for implementing IT service management (ITSM) effectively. The landscape of ITSM is undergoing a profound transformation, driven by the rapid advancements in Artificial Intelligence (AI) and Machine Learning (ML) technologies (Deshpande, 2024).

Over a decade, the use of IT systems and solutions and delivery of IT services have been increased remarkably. Besides, increased additional complexity of networks, security and cloud computing and its functioning. Subsequently, manually managing the end-to-end functioning of IT systems becomes difficult, which results the need of automation. At the same time new technologies such as AI, ML, DL, Bigdata, Analytics are evolved, which offers new possibilities in managing IT operations of an organizations more efficiently and in simple means. This paves a way to new branch of IT operations which is known as AIOps.

In order to ensure clarity, precision, and consistency in the chapter, included a few definitions, whereas key terms are provided in Annexure – A that establish a foundation and context for deeper exploration of key concepts. This includes definitions of IT operations and important key terms such as AIOps, ITOM, CloudOps, DevOps, MLOps, LLMOps, to mention a few, are defined below.

1. According to Gartner (Gartner – ITOps) the term IT operations is defined as "the people and management processes associated with IT service management to deliver the right set of services at the right quality and at competitive costs for customers".
2. Joe Hertvik defines IT Operations (Cio-wiki) as being "responsible for the smooth functioning of the infrastructure and operational environments that support application deployment to internal and external customers, including the network infrastructure; server and device management; computer operations; ITIL management; and help desk services for an organization".
3. Ernest Mueller defines IT operations (Cio-wiki) as "a blanket term for systems engineers, system administrators, operations staff, release engineers, DBAs, network engineers, security professionals, and various other subdisciplines and job titles".
4. According to IBM IT operation (IBM-ITOps) is the process of implementing, managing, delivering and supporting IT services to meet the business needs of internal and external users.
5. We define the term IT operations as "the end-to-end management of organisation's technology stack, including physical and digital assets for the efficient functioning of the business".

This chapter is organized as follows: Section 1 presents a brief introduction to IT operations that includes definitions of important terms such as DevOps, AIOps, LLMOps and while Section 2 presents the evolution of ITOps and its overview, which includes the importance of ITOps, the major functions of and their role and limitations of traditional IT operations. Section 3 presents a case for AI-driven IT operations transformation, incorporating a literature review and emphasizing the need for automation and intelligence to achieve efficient IT operations. Following up, Section 4 presents various implementation challenges of AIOps as well as AI-powered Agile project management. Section 5 presents integrating AIOps with Agile teams. Section 6 presents recommended actions for AIOps implementation that include a methodology for transformation of ITOps into AIOps, common pitfalls and their solutions, best practices to avoid failure, and people and process considerations. Besides, present key performance indicators to measure performance of AIOps, a list of potential use cases, and benefits of AIOps. In Section 7, future directions of AIOps and AI-powered Agile project management are presented. Finally, Section 8 concludes the chapter.

2. THE FOUNDATION AND LIMITATIONS OF ITOPS

In this section, we discuss the evolution of IT operations and its overview that includes why IT Operations are importance, and its major function along with its role in the organization.

2.1. Evolution of IT Operations (ITOps)

The evolution of ITOps has a long curve of more than 75 years, which began dates back to the innovation of computers. But in early days there were limited scale of IT operations as it precedes rapid raise of technology advancements, which leads great development of computer systems, storage and network devices. This resulted in a great need and importance of the functioning of IT infrastructure and become focused and critical to business functioning. The progressive evolution of IT operations from 1950 to 2020 is shown in figure 2.

The first mainframe computer was developed in 1950 by IBM. These early mainframes were giant machines, but marked by their substantial processing power and were mainly used for small computation purposes to test basic mathematical computation. During this period there was very limited IT operations functions for maintain the mainframe computers. In 1960, The use of mainframe computers began for enterprise computing purposes like data processing and these computers had external storage capabilities. In this period, the IT Operations confined to functioning of mainframe computers and storage devices maintenance. In the early 1970s, the era of personal computing began with the introduction of the first desktop computers. In addition, operating systems have been developed that are installed on these personal computers. Thus, the need for IT support gradually increased due to frequent issues such as hardware malfunctioning and software glitches.

In the 1980s, network technology was emerged and companies began manufacturing devices such as modems, switches, routers and firewalls. The use of these devices increased in multi-fold. Late 1980s, the Internet was evolved, which is fairly new in terms of its global use and connectivity. During this period, IT support dramatically increased not only to fix hardware issues of PCs but also network equipment on top of which operating systems functioning on these bare hardware machines. At the same time Local Area Network (LAN) become more popular that connects multiple PCs under a single network. Organizations started using LAN for their internal use for various business services. Hence, the need of IT support functions increased from PCs to network equipment as well to maintain the functioning of these networks.

Figure 2. Timelines showing the evolution of IT Operations

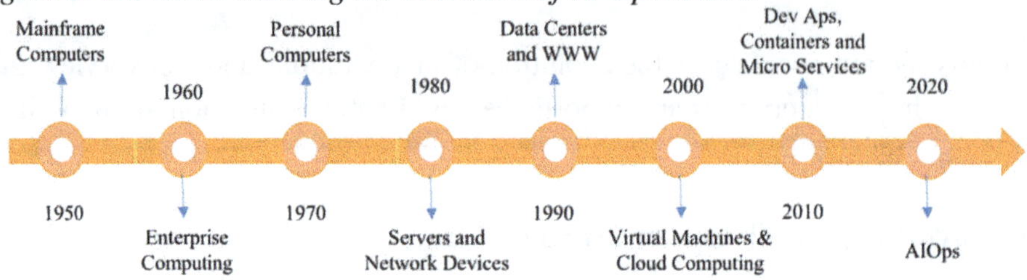

In the 1990s, electronics industry become forefront and witnessed the microprocessor boom that resulted new era of computing machines called servers. These servers can have higher computing power with lower power as compared to mainframe machines. This resulted, the take-off of data centres during this period. Moreover, during this period World Wide Web (WWW) was evolved that extends the networking boundaries from LAN to Wide Area Network (WAN). Furthermore, the development of Web applications saw a rise in human personal resources. A new era has sprung up due to the use of web applications, and client- server systems are gradually disappearing. In this period, the development of database servers took place which open up a new role of IT personal in the industry for effective functioning of database from installation, setup, configuration and backup activities both in the software development as well in software maintenance of these applications. This further improved the need for IT support for effective functioning of these systems, on premise severs, networks as well as data centres functioning. All this progress results in the size of IT operations, and gaining importance not only to maintain systems such as servers, databases and networking but also for the functioning of these systems with the help of system administration personnel.

With its genesis in the 2000s, the Virtual machines and cloud computing began that includes Software as a Service like SaaS, PaaS, IaaS. Later, in 2010, the development of Application Programming Interfaces (APIs), containers, and the rise of microservices took place. In addition, the development of mobile apps began and gained momentum of mobile apps slowly.

In early 2020s, the transformation of ITOps into AIOps began and increased the use of GenAI for more efficient managing IT operations and also align with the organization's strategic focus. Similarly, the use of AIOps began in project management and gained momentum.

In summary, although the idea of managing information technology has deep roots, IT operations began in the middle of the 20th century with the arrival of computers and the need for ongoing management for their smooth operations. The evolution journey of XOps is depicted in figure 3. This shows graded development of family of Ops starting from ITOps to LLMOps. The journey starts from manual ITOps (late 90s) to DevOps (late 2000s) to AIOps (2010s) and finally to LLMOps (2020s).

Figure 3. Graded developed of Ops family

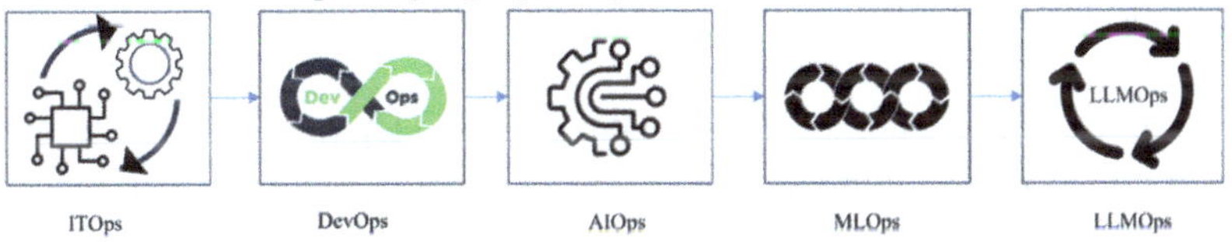

The interconnection between graded development of the Ops family is envisaged as follows. ITOps is a foundation that deals with managing core infrastructure such as servers and networks. It provides the stable environment upon which all other layers are built. Whereas DevOps acts as an engine that unifies development and operations to accelerate software delivery and project management. Further, it provides CI/CD pipelines that MLOps and LLMOps adapt. AIOps offers automation to IT operations, monitoring, and incident response. It enhances DevOps by reducing alert noise and predicting systems failure before they impact the delivery pipeline.

2.2 IT Operations Overview

In the previous section, we discussed the evolution of ITOps and examined the various operational domains, in short Ops, associated with it. It is equally important to understand the significance of IT operations and their primary functions, particularly how they integrate with other Ops to enable intelligent and automation of IT operation processes. In this section, we provide an overview of IT operations, highlighting their importance, core functions, and overall role.

The primary focus of ITOps is to maintain the stability and availability of an organization's IT infrastructure. These responsibilities fall within the organization's operational systems and must align with its tactical and strategic objectives. IT operations constitute one of the core functional areas within ITSM and are responsible for aligning IT services with the organization's business needs. Most commonly, organizations have legacy infrastructure, thus the focus is to monitor hardware uptime and managing security at the network level. The modern trend is using AIOps, AI for IT Operations to predict and prevent note only legacy system failures and but also modern IT systems. The objective of ITOps is to minimize risks, optimize resources and adapt to changing needs.

2.2.1. Key Importance of ITOps

The importance of IT operations is to ensure an organization's technology infrastructure runs smoothly, securely, and efficiently and provide technical support to resolve ongoing issues to support smooth functioning of their business. Here, the term technology infrastructure refers to server systems, networking, storage, database systems, security, cloud, computers, devices and both legacy applications as well as modern applications deployment. In short, ITOps acts as the backbone for digital services to the organization and its primary objectives is to minimize risks, optimize resources and adapt to changing needs. The purpose of IT operations indicates the direction whereas its importance talks about priority. The importance IT Operations tells the value, significance or relevance (how much it matters to the business. The key importances of IT Operations is envisaged in figure 4, summarized into business continuity, improved efficiency, strengthening security and compliance, scalability and innovation, and proactive resolution.

Figure 4. Key importance of IT Operations

Ensuring Business Continuity and Reliability: The IT operations team manages critical systems like servers, networks, cloud services, databases, computers, devices, and legacy systems to ensure the high availability of digital services offered by the organization to their internal users and external users such as end users or clients. This demands organizations to make available their systems up and running, which are "always on" in the digital world to offer their services to their users to ensure business continuity. Even a brief interruption of service can result in incredibly significant cost losses in terms of revenue and productivity, which makes proactive management essential.

Enhancing Efficiency and Productivity: Streamlining processes, automating routine tasks such as updates and backups, and optimizing the allocation of resources, resulting in invaluable time for IT staff and help them focus on more strategic activities.

Strengthening Security and Compliance: IT operations teams are at the forefront of the implementation and enforcing security measures such as firewalls, access controls and periodic updates to protect sensitive data and systems against cyber-attacks. In addition, the teams ensure adherence to industry regulations like GDPR, HIPAA, PCI DSS, and ISO 27001 to manage escalating digital risks, build digital trust and avoid legal and financial penalties.

Enabling Scalability and Innovation: A well-managed IT infrastructure allows a business to scale its operations efficiently to meet growing demand without performance constraints. By adopting and integrating new technologies like cloud computing and AI, ITOps helps businesses remain agile and competitive in a rapidly changing technological landscape. Further, IT operations help various teams in the organization work collaboratively and in line with the business objectives.

Proactive Issue Resolution: Even though continuous monitoring and performance management, IT operations can often detect and address potential security problems, software errors, network disruptions or hardware failures before they reach the users, and move from reactive to predictive maintenance.

In a summary, the importance of IT Operations goes beyond merely technical support. In fact, ITOps is fall under strategic function that underpins the entire organization's ability to operate, grow, and succeed in the digital era.

2.2.2. Major Functions of ITOps

The functions of IT Operations are broadly classified into six categories based on their type of function. These are (a) Infrastructure Management, (b) Service and Incident Management (c) Operations control and monitoring (d) data and security, (e) governance and compliance and (f) innovation and evolution. Further, these major categories of IT Operations can be breakdown into a small unit of work such as specific tasks, activities, functions or processes that are carried out on regular basis. These are the practical actions that are performed by the IT Operations team on day-to-day to ensure that IT systems and solutions are running smoothly and meeting business needs. Figure 5 shows major classification of IT operation functions.

Figure 5. Major functions of IT Operations

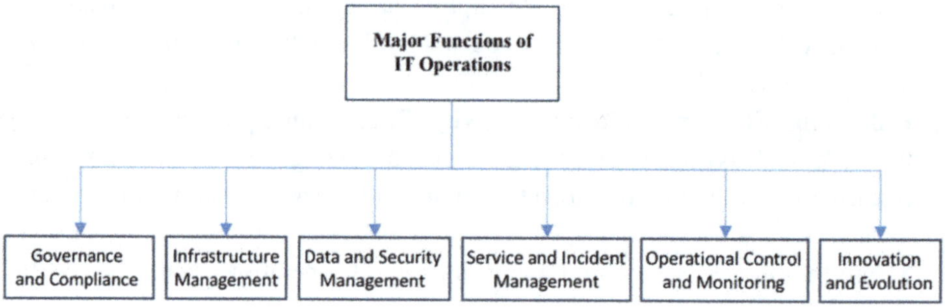

Governance and Compliance – This category has three main functions such as asset management, configuration management and facility management. Asset Management is primarily tracking IT inventory throughout its lifecycle to optimize spending and ensure software license compliance. Configuration Management is process for maintaining accurate documentation of hardware configurations and solution dependencies to ensure system stability. Facilities Management includes managing the physical environment of data centers, including power, cooling (HVAC), and physical security.

Infrastructure Management – In this category, the major functions of IT operations three broad groups such as physical and on-premises infrastructure, endpoint and system administration, and connectivity and virtual environments. The main functions include hardware and software maintenance, server and device management, network operations, cloud operations, and device management.

Data and Security Management – The major functions of this category are such as access management, security management, backup and recovery and disaster recovery. Access management functions include controlling user permissions and identity access to secure sensitive data and organizational assets. Security management is a process of protecting an organization's IT assets that include computers, networks, and data, against risk.

Service and Incident Management – In this category, the major functions include incident management, IT help desk and ticketing, IT support services, IT maintenance services and change management.

Operational Control and Monitoring – The major functions of this group are fall into two types such as servers and application monitoring. The monitoring of servers may be either on premises or off premises.

Innovation and Evolution – In this category there are two major functions such as automation and continuous improvements. Automation is a process of implementing scripts and tools to replace repetitive manual tasks, thereby reducing errors and operational costs, which increases the productivity and efficiency. Whereas continuous improvement deals with the IT team who will analyse IT metrics and KPIs and identify trends and areas for technological enhancements to align with business goals of an organization, ongoing activity.

2.2.3. Role of ITOps

The main role of IT operations is to ensure the smooth functioning of IT systems.

The role of IT operations is responsible for ensuring that IT systems and solutions operate smoothly to ensure that business operations continue without any interruption. Additionally, the term 'role of IT Operations' refers to the overall responsibility of maintaining and managing IT Operations within the organization. Most commonly, IT Operations are performed by IT department and they align with the strategic objectives of the organizational. IT Operations are managed by a team of resources such as IT manager, system administrator, network administrator, cloud engineer, release engineers, to mention a few. Furthermore, the role of IT operations is not only limited to overall responsibility of IT operations but also align with the business outcomes, project delivery success, managing risk and continuous improvement of IT systems and solutions functioning.

Overall Responsibility: The overall responsibility of IT operations is to ensure the organization's IT systems, and services run smoothly and reliably to support business operations.

Alignment with Business Goals: IT operations can support business continuity, growth, and efficiency through use of technology.

Agile Project Management: AI in IT operations provides the stability metrics that allow project managers to confidently commit to release dates, directly supporting strategic time-to-market goals.

Managing IT Risk: To ensure security, compliance, and resilience of IT systems to reduce risks of downtime, breaches, or failures from time to time.

Continuous Improvement: In order to improve the overall effectiveness and efficiency of IT services within the organization, the IT operations team needs to function well, which is a continuous process. Thus, IT operations team manage the functioning of organization's IT equipment such as network, databases, storage, servers, cloud, and application on day-to-day basis. Basically, IT operations activity falls under the operations. Now a days there is need and demand to work IT operations team 24x7 in order to provide IT services functioning without fail.

2.3. Limitations of Traditional IT Operations

In the previous section, we discussed an overview of IT operations including its major functions and the role of IT operations in the organization. In evolving the complex IT world, there is a need to understand the limitations of IT operations. In this section, we discuss several limitations of traditional IT operations.

In digital age, organisations are facing several challenges to manage and optimise use of their Information Technology systems. There are several limitations of traditional IT Operations in managing effective functioning of the existing IT systems and solutions on day-to-day basis. This may be because one or more of the following reasons within the organization. Traditional monitoring and management approaches struggle to handle the sheer volume of data generated by logs, events, and metrics in real-time (Vitui and Chen, 2025). According to a study (Pandey, 2023) mentions that traditional IT operations are often relied on rule-based systems, manual intervention, and not well suited to dealing with the complexity of a digital environment characterised by distributed infrastructures, heterogeneous technologies and dynamic workloads. In the IT systems landscape results in several first-order consequences, such as fragmented data silos, increased complexity of environment and data size, lack of federated data systems, lack of process integration, and lack of real-time alerting capabilities. Figure 6 shows limitations of traditional IT operations.

Figure 6. Limitations of traditional IT operation systems

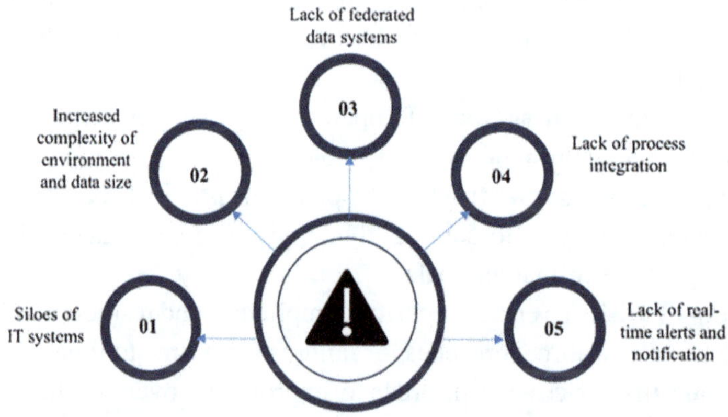

Siloes of IT Systems - The growth of IT systems and solutions in the originations increases based on the need and demand of their business operations. In general, the existing IT systems and solutions are siloing in nature over a period of time in any business organization. For example, the begin with a simple network of computers and its demands to support increased number of employees and new networking infrastructure will be introduced such as wireless connectivity. In such a way, they tailor the business solutions for immediate business needs. Over a points of time the existing IT systems and solutions become silos and may not communicate each other. Most commonly, fragmented and isolated data repositories prevent effective use of AI in IT operations for implementation. Further, fragmented data increases latency and reduces accuracy, rather than providing a specific numerical reduction in Mean Time to Repair (MTTR). To overcome this challenge (Kumar, 2023) suggests integrating data into a centralized system and fostering a unified data culture eliminate operational bottlenecks.

Increased Complexity of Environment and Data Size - Over a period the existing IT systems and network infrastructure become complex to manage on day-to-day basis because of heterogenous nature of the systems and silos of IT systems landscape in the organization.

Because of the increased complexity of IT environments (hybrid, multi-cloud, microservices), it is difficult to maintain the smooth functioning of IT operations in the organization. Another, limitation of traditional IT operations is because of exponential increase of data size by the IT systems and telemetry data.

Lack of Federated Data Systems - In most organizations, systems are independent and databases operate in isolation, rather than working together as a unified or collaborative network. In a non-federated environment, systems do not share data, resources, or identity management that leads to fragmented operations resulting in inefficient workflows and increased maintenance overhead. In traditional IT operations, organizations often rely on data from disconnected, siloed and heterogeneous sources to assemble and normalize, rather than a cohesive, interconnected and automated environment. In modern IT operations, multiple systems generate diverse datasets such as logs, metrics, events that are difficult to integrate and analyse.

Lack of Process Integration - As mentioned in the previously that IT systems become silos over a period of time in an organization and demand of effective function of these systems will increase at the same time which require lot of manual effort in managing the function of these systems and solutions to the users. As the complexity of IT systems and data size increases resulting the level of integration complexity between systems, workflows, and operational processes. Many times, IT teams will perform similar activity multiple times because of silos of system and lack of inter connectivity between these systems. For example, scanning of systems on daily basis and copying of log files data into target systems, backup activity to mention a few. The very purpose of performing reparative task or activities because of lack of process integration and automation.

Lack of Real Time Alerts and Notification - There is another limitation in the traditional IT systems landscape is the absence of real-time alerts and notification (Sarma, 2021) to the users of IT operations teams. This limitation is not only due to the silos of existing systems, but also due to the lack of integration and communication between these systems in real-time.

The major limitations of traditional IT operations are summarised in table 1.

Table 1. Major limitations of traditional IT Operations

S.No.	Major limitations of traditional IT Operations
1	Siloes of IT systems.
2	Increased complexity of environment.
3	Lack of federated data systems
4	Lack of process integration
5	Lack of Real Time alerts and notification

This section presents evolutions of IT operations and examines the significance of IT operations within the broader framework of IT Service Management and organizational strategy. It highlighted the importance of IT Ops and major functions and their role. Further, briefly discuss the limitations of traditional IT operations. Overall, this section established the foundation and limitations of ITOps. These mounting limitations of traditional ITOps create an imperative for intelligence and automation, which we explore in the next section.

3. A CASE FOR AI DRIVEN IT OPERATIONS TRANSFORMATION

In the previous section, we discussed the foundation for IT operations and their limitations. To overcome the mounting limitations of traditional ITOps required a modern solution to manage organizational end-to-end IT operations. In this section, we discuss literature review on transformation of IT operations into AIOps, the need for intelligence and automation in IT operations, followed by a high-level conceptual architecture of AIOps and its functioning through a forward data pipeline and various feedback loops. These components collectively deliver value to AIOps, which in turn offers speed to agile project management.

The development of new technologies such as artificial intelligence has forced organizations to move towards a paradigm shift towards a digital transformation paradigm, which involves transformation of IT operations into AI-driven IT operations. In this section, the major limitations of traditional IT operations and their need for automation are discussed. Further, present a methodology for typical transformation of ITOps into AIOps and explain briefly various phases. Moreover, presents a few use cases of AIOps with brief explanation.

3.1. Literature Review

Traditional IT operations are theoretically grounded in deterministic control theory (Abdelzaher et al., 2008), where system behaviour is managed through linear, rule-based logic, rely on a cause-and-effect relationship where the system's behaviour is entirely predictable based on its current state and fixed rules. In this, the IT environment is treated as a closed-loop system where every action has a singular, repeatable outcome. In a related research study ttransition from manual IT operations to intelligent, data-driven systems was introduced (Shen et al., 2020) based on five a layered AIOps framework. Further, this framework focuses on five abilities namely perception, detection, location, action and interaction, which is known as Proton, an AIOps framework designed to transform traditional IT operations into an intelligent system through five core capabilities: perception, detection, location, action, and interaction. Findings indicate this approach achieves over an 80% success rate in automated fault self-healing within large-scale, heterogeneous environments.

Furthermore, the transformation of IT operations involves a shift from reactive to proactive service delivery. By integrating AI-driven predictive analytics into ITSM, organizations can identify potential failures before they impact the end-user, fundamentally changing the role of the IT practitioner from a *firefighter* to a *system architect* (Sreerangapuri, 2021). The transformation of IT operations has evolved from manual, siloed management toward an integrated, intelligent paradigm known as AIOps. This necessitates a transition to *Systems Thinking*, where AIOps refers to a holistic approach treating IT operations as an interconnected ecosystem, leveraging AI to analyse data across the entire technology stack for real-time insights. This methodology enables proactive, context-rich problem solving and integrates technical data with organizational processes to overcome siloed management. Thus, AIOps is viewed not just as a tool but as a socio-technical framework that aligns organizational culture with algorithmic automation (Hua, 2022). Historically, IT operations relied on human intervention for monitoring and troubleshooting, but the shift to cloud-native architectures has introduced complexities that exceed human cognitive limits (Cheng et al., 2023). The synergy between AIOps and MLOps is also emerging as a critical frontier, facilitating a self-healing lifecycle where IT operations continuously learn from deployment data to optimize system performance (Brahmandam, 2025). Another study describes how Artificial Intelligence for IT Operations (AIOps) transforms IT operations from a reactive to a proactive approach, elevating reliability and reducing costs by utilizing intelligent monitoring, predictive analytics, and automated resolution (Sekhar, 2025).

Listed the key challenges include managing data quality and preventing model drift, while future trends indicate deeper integration with DevOps and enhanced contextual understanding using large language models. A central theme in recent research is the reduction of operational noise. Traditional rules-based systems often lead to *alert fatigue*, whereas AIOps frameworks utilizing machine learning can achieve significant noise reduction reported as high as 87% in some enterprise environments by correlating disparate data points into actionable insights (Sing, 2025).

The author (De la Cruz Cabello et al., 2025) has identifies several major challenges in log analysis, including the high cost of data labelling, concept drift, and severe class imbalance. Technical limitations regarding limited model adaptability, high computational costs for real-time monitoring, and integration with legacy systems, along with cultural resistance to adopting new AI-based workflows, are also highlighted.

3.2. Need for Intelligence and Automation in IT Operations

The limitations presented in the previous section can be viewed as constraints within IT operations and define the problem space. These constraints represent structural and operational challenges in traditional IT environments and can be considered first-order consequences that give rise to several data and operational issues. As a result, it is necessary to identify the capabilities required to address these consequences. These capabilities represent the system needs, which are discussed in this section. In order to run smoothly the organization's IT infrastructure and to support the digital functioning of business, the following are crucial elements to automate, which is shown in figure 7.

Increased data volumes – As the number of systems and solutions increases there is an increased data volumes from all these systems. In order to handle data that is generated from multiple source systems is important, at the same time handling of this data for processing, analysis to obtain the insights from this data.

Figure 7. Need for Automation of IT Operations

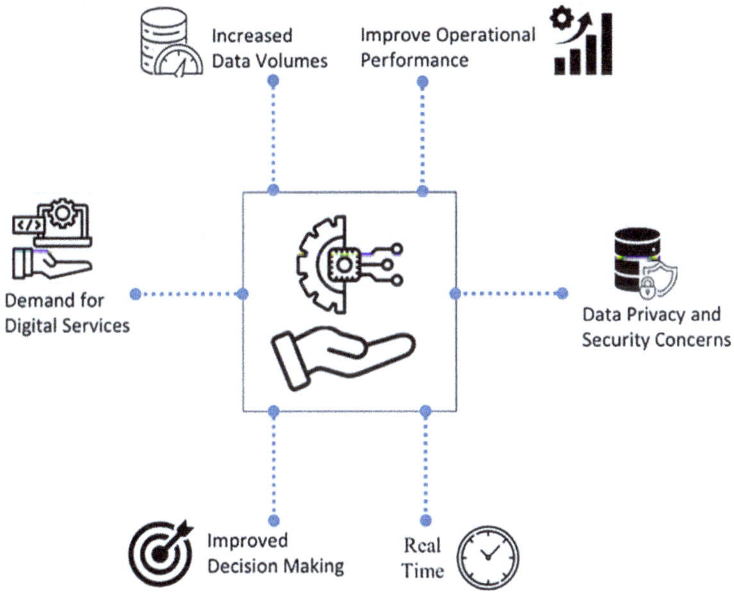

Improve Operational Performance – Further, to improve the operational performance of the functioning of IT system and services.

Data Privacy and Security Concerns – This is one the major concern for any organization. There is need to implement strong governance on data related functions within IT operations as well to automate the process and polices on these functions to ensure data management lifecycle.

Demand for Digital Services – The availability of business services become more essential in all times because of increased expectation of both internal and external users of the systems.

Improved Decision Making - The need for improved decision-making in automated IT operations is critical because modern IT environments have surpassed human cognitive limits. As systems move toward complex adaptive systems featuring microservices and multi-cloud layers, manual oversight leads to alert fatigue and costly delays. The need for improved decision-making is driven by the following major factors such as managing unmanageable complexity such as data silos and data fatigue. The second, is speed and real-time response that includes Automated root cause analysis (RCA) pinpoints issues in minutes rather than hours, drastically lowering the Mean Time to Resolution (MTTR) and instant remediation, systems execute self-healing actions. The third is shift from reactive firefighting mode to proactive management. The fourth, moving from proactive and predictive capabilities. Thus, by identifying patterns in historical data, automated decisions can pre-empt hardware failures before they impact end-users. The fifth, strategic human reallocation by offloading routine operational choices to AI, IT professionals can focus on strategic initiatives like system upgrades and digital transformation.

Real Time Monitoring for Data Driven Insights and Notifications – There is a significant necessity to monitor instantaneous data-driven insights to the users from gathered extensive data generated by IT systems and telemetry data. The monitoring facilitates IT team for identification of emerging challenges and understanding infrastructure behaviour in real-time contexts to move from reactive to proactive and predictive direction.

3.3. Introduction to AIOps

Traditional IT operations and management is considered as deterministic, linear, and static nature principled on deterministic control theory, but the modern IT systems are non-linear and dynamic moving from react to predictive nature. Thus, shift of traditional IT operations to modern IT operations, transitioning IT operations to AI-driven models, focusing on data ingestion, real-time analytics, and automated remediation.

The management of modern IT systems poses unique challenges, necessitating scalability, reliability, and efficiency in handling extensive data streams (Remil et al., 2024). Modern IT infrastructure is a dynamic, software-defined ecosystem that combines on-premises, hybrid-cloud, and edge computing to maximize agility, security, and scalability. Additionally, it replaces traditional rigid, manual hardware setups, reactive with automated, virtualized, API based, data-driven, and predictive landscape. Modern IT operations now use a hybrid approach that combines the precision of rule-based systems for well-defined, critical tasks with the flexibility of machine learning for complex, noisy, and rapidly changing environments. Further, the focus on managing the exponential, non-linear growth of data, interdependencies, and operational tasks in modern IT environments is a critical. As such organizations are shifting from reactive to proactive, AI driven IT operations. Modern IT Operations progressively utilize AIOps to automate routine tasks, manage increasing complexity of hybrid and multi-cloud environments and proactively detect issues and plan for resolutions.

Artificial Intelligence for IT operations, in short AIOps. AIOps is a cross-disciplinary research and innovation area that include system design, software engineering, big data, artificial intelligence, machine learning, distributed computing and information visualization (Dang et at., 2019). Moreover, AIOps will help to achieve the following three goals such as (i) High service intelligence include self-services, self-adaptive healing; (ii) High customer satisfaction include understanding customer behaviours, intelligent customer engagement and intelligent customer support; and

(iii) High engineering productivity include building - design, develop and rollout secure and well performed service efficiently and operating that includes tasks such as monitor, diagnose, mitigate, and support to manage efficiently and effectively.

Another study reported (Diao, 2007) that applying the principles of control theory, more particularly feedback loops and modelling, to IT systems to improve the productivity and robustness of service systems while managing service levels. The uses control theory offers to design management solutions that are stable and resistant to performance bottlenecks. Further, the feedback mechanism provides, the ability to adjust system parameters in real-time, responding to changes in demand or system behaviour.

Complexity theory and AIOps are converging disciplines, focus on managing the explosive, non-linear growth of data, interdependencies, and operational tasks in modern IT environments. As modern IT infrastructures have become increasingly complex and exhibit characteristics of complex adaptive systems, (Kolt et al., 2025) argue that AI should also be viewed as a complex adaptive system and cannot be governed through traditional linear approaches. Further, complexity theory provides the theoretical framework for understanding systems with emergent behaviours and non-linear dynamics, while AIOps provides the practical, AI-driven tools needed to manage this complexity.

The complexity of failure management in large-scale software systems was explained (Paolo et al., 2021) with the aid of AIOps, classifying techniques for anomaly detection and root-cause analysis, whereas (Remil et al., 2024) provides a comprehensive review highlighting the *pain points* of complex IT infrastructure and how AIOps manages high-volume data, anomaly detection, and root-cause analysis for incident management. In another study that explores the relationship between the computational complexity of machine learning models and their accuracy (Ziolkowski, 2023), which is directly applicable to AIOps in optimizing the performance of prediction models. The aim of AIOps was described (Cheng et al., 2023) as to integrate artificial intelligence with the large volumes of data generated by IT operations in cloud infrastructures to deliver actionable insights while maximizing system availability. Further, AIOps tasks can be categorized like incident detection, failure prediction, root cause analysis, and automated actions. AIOps applies machine learning and big data to analyse, predict, and automate in these environments, addressing the challenges posed by the complexity. A comparison between ITOps and AIOps is summarized in table 2.

Table 2. A comparison between ITOps and AIOps

Parameter	ITOps	AIOps
Definition	IT Operations	AI for IT Operations, which is a sub set of IT Operation.
Scope	Encompasses all practices, teams and tools required to manage an organization's IT infrastructure and services	AIOps represents a specific set of practices and technologies used to automate and enhance those operations
Objective	The objective of ITOps is to minimize risks, optimize resources and adapt to changing needs.	The objective of AIOps is to cope with the increasing complexities posed by modern IT systems and to reduce human intervention. AIOps acts as a smart layer within ITOps.
Approach	Traditional ITOps relies heavily on manual processes and reactive problem-solving.	AIOps can detect anomalies and predict issues before they cause downtime to enabling proactive management.
Type of operations focus	The major focus of ITOps through manual and semi-automated and traditional tasks such as provisioning hardware, managing backups, and resolving support tickets.	AIOps is mainly focused on automation and intelligent predication and root case analysis using AI and machine learning (ML) to improve IT operation tasks.
Visibility	The visibility of ITOps is often characterized by a manual, fragmented, and reactive approach to managing end-to-end IT infrastructure.	The visibility of AIOps is a full-stack observability, which provide a more comprehensive and automated view. Bridging silos between different IT teams such as networking, storage, cloud and integrating all operational data into a single, intelligent platform to provide single source of truth.

According to a market study report (Mordor Intelligence), it was estimated the market size of IT Operations Management at USD 33.79 billion in 2025 and is expected to reach USD 51.99 billion by 2030, at a CAGR of 9% during the forecast period from 2025-2030. The major solutions of IT Ops include Network and Infrastructure Management, Application Performance Management, Configuration Management, Cloud and Hybrid IT Management, and IT Operations Analytics, Automation and Orchestration.

3.4. Conceptual Architecture of AIOps

In the previous subsection, we examined various AIOps solutions available in the market, providing a broad overview of the current system landscape. AIOps is inherently a complex paradigm designed to address the increasing complexity of modern distributed IT environments. However, to fully understand how a typical AIOps system operates, it is essential to examine its underlying conceptual architecture, a solution to address the implementation needs presented earlier. This section presents that architecture and explains its core components and operational structure.

A high-level architecture of the conceptual AIOps system is illustrated in figure 8, providing a visual overview of the system's major components and their interrelationships. The architecture comprises four primary components: data sources, data consolidation, analytics and machine learning (ML), and visualization with human-in-the-loop (HITL) integration. The system's functionality is described in terms of its data pipeline and associated feedback loops. In a typical AIOps workflow, data flows from multiple heterogeneous sources to the data consolidation layer and subsequently through the analytics and ML components to generate actionable insights. These actionable insights are realized through visualization and HITL mechanisms. Both the forward data flow and the feedback loops are essential to the detailed operation of the AIOps system, as they bridge the gap between the "what" and the "how" of AIOps. The following paragraph explains the operation of the AIOps system through its core components.

a) Data Sources: In this stage identification of all data sources will be performed that includes Logs, Metrics, Events and Tickets to mention a few from infrastructure and applications consisting of heterogenous data types.
b) Data Consolidation – Once the data sources are identified, the data are collected and transported into the AIOps pipeline. This stage encompasses storage, processing, and normalization functionalities. The storage layer may consist of one or more systems, depending on the organization's data volume, data structure (structured versus unstructured), performance requirements, cost considerations, and intended use cases, such as operational processing, reporting, or analytics. Examples include relational database management systems (RDBMS), NoSQL databases, data warehouses, data lakes, and data lakehouses. In addition, raw data are transformed into an analysis-ready format through a series of preprocessing activities, including normalization, cleaning, parsing, aggregation, filtering, and standardization. These processes ensure consistency across the pipeline and establish a unified data structure for subsequent analysis.

Figure 8. A high-level conceptual architecture of AIOps

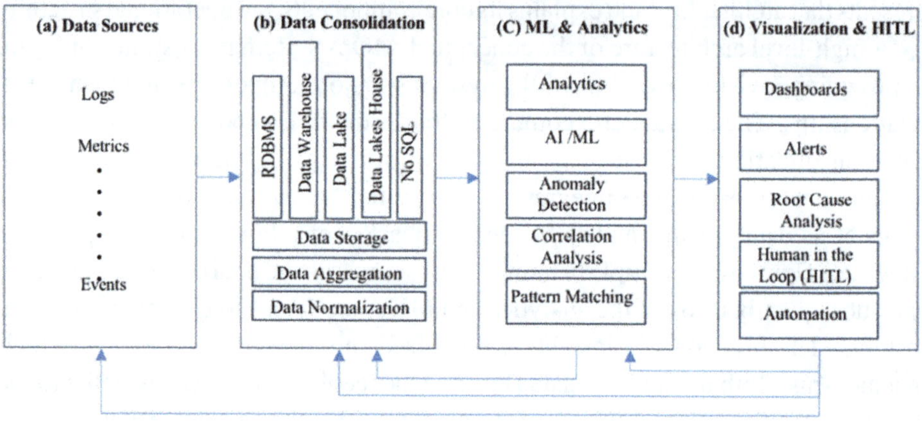

c) ML and Analytics - The third stage is crux of the system that acts a core engine for AIOps applies algorithms for anomaly detection, correlation, pattern matching, predictive maintenance, and root case analysis. According to (IBM – AIOps), the components of AIOps consists of a range of AI strategies and features, including data output and aggregation, algorithms, orchestration and visualization. Algorithms form the basis for machine learning and enable platforms to establish baselines and adapt as environmental data changes. In addition, automation features within AIOps tools enable AIOps systems to act based on real-time insights. In AIOps, ML helps with anomaly detection, root cause analysis, event correlation and predictive analysis. Further, AIOps programs gather data from various network components and data sources. Besides, analytics interpret the raw data to create new data and metadata that helps both systems and teams identify trends, isolate problems, predict capacity demands and manage events. In another study, AIOps is combined with machine learning and automation (Sreerangapuri, 2021) that not only enhances incident management, reduces alert fatigue, but also improves root cause analysis to build resilient, self-healing systems.

d) Visualisation and HITL - Visualization layer acts as the glass where the analytical output from (c) is rendered into charts, health scores, and alerts to various users of the system that incudes but not limited to Site Reliability Engineers (SRE), IT Operations (ITOps) Specialists, Security Operations Center (SOC Analysts), Application Developers / DevOps Engineers and Data Scientists and AI Model Managers to mention a few.

The forward flow represents the data pipeline, illustrating how data is transformed into actionable outcomes. This describes the linear progression through which raw data is processed and converted into business value. In contrast, the feedback loops enable the system to learn and self-correct, thereby optimizing its performance over time. These loops reflect the operational dynamics of IT within the AIOps framework, ensuring that the system functions not merely as a static pipeline but as an adaptive and evolving ecosystem. The data pipeline and its associated feedback mechanisms in AIOps are outlined in table 3.

Table 3. Summary of data pipelines and feedback loops in AIOps

Type of Flow (Data Pipeline or Feeback)		Primary Purpose
Data Pipeline	(a) → (b)	Raw telemetry is sent for cleaning and standardization.
Data Pipeline	(b) → (c)	Normalized, high-quality data is fed into ML models for pattern recognition.
Data Pipeline	(c) → (d)	Analytical conclusions are turned into human-readable alerts or automated scripts. Here, human in the loop for necessary actions for self-healing or necessary correction.
Feedback	(d) → (c)	Validation: The human looks at the Visualization and tells the ML model if it was right or wrong to improve future accuracy. The main purpose of this loop is model tuning.
Feedback	(d) → (b)	The human sees cluttered data in the Visualization and adjusts the Normalization rules to hide irrelevant logs. Further adjusts how data is filtered or enriched based on the success of the final output this improve quality control. The main purpose of this loop is for data refinement i.e., noise reduction.
Feedback	(d) → (a)	The human notices a blind spot, missing info, in the Visualization and decides to add a new data source or collect more data. This mainly purpose this loop is observability gap filling that is increasing visibility in the system.
Feedback	(c) → (b)	The main purpose of this loop is Feature optimization. Efficiency: The ML engine tells the processor (stage b) which data points actually matter, reducing "noise" ingestion.

The AIOps platform enables continuous insights across IT Operations Monitoring (ITOM). It follows a foundational three-stage framework that has the stages Observe → Engage → Act (Prasad and Rich, 2018), which is commonly used to describe the functioning of AI-driven IT operations platforms. This framework represents a continuous, closed-loop process designed to manage complex IT environments by integrating big data, machine learning (ML), and automation. In the proposed conceptual architecture of AIOps, the stages of data collection and consolidation correspond to the *Observe* phase, while the AI and ML components align with the *Engage* phase. The *Act* phase is realized through the human-in-the-loop mechanism, which triggers responses to automated alerts and facilitates issue resolution based on analytical insights.

3.5. Types of AIOps

AIOps can be classified into three categories based on its scope, purpose and intended use as a platform or solution or a service as show in figure 9. In case of AIOps as platform then it has a base environment or framework that enables the development, deployment, and management of applications and services. Further, AIOps platform provide a wide range of capabilities like infrastructure, APIs, services and allows third party integration. AIOps is available as a solution means it is similar to a product that addresses a business problem. Further, solution has limited capabilities when compared to platform, while service means either individual or provider who provide some kind of specified service to organizations related to AIOps like advisory, integration, implementation, consulting, audit services to mention a few. In generally, service is on demand that solves a specific problem that organization looking for and brings value to organization.

According to Gartner's glossary the term AIOps platform (Gartner - AIOps) combines big data and machine learning functionality to support all primary IT operations functions through the scalable ingestion and analysis of the ever-increasing volume, variety and velocity of data generated by IT. The platform enables the concurrent use of multiple data sources, data collection methods, and analytical and presentation technologies.

Figure 9. Categories of AIOps

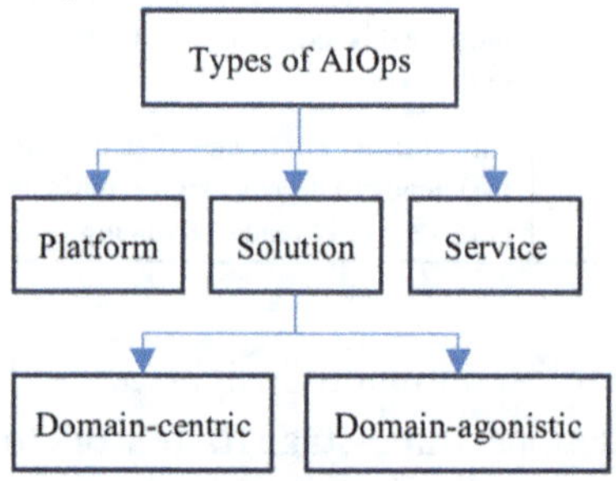

Additionally, AIOps solutions are categorized into two types based on its intended use like domain-centric and domain-agnostic. Domain-centric AIOps solutions are primarily focused to address a specific business problem like application performance monitoring, log data collection, network monitoring, log analytics to mention a few. Forasmuch as domain-agnostic AIOps solutions operate more broadly and work across domains, which includes functions like monitoring, data collection, logging, data analytics, application performance, cloud, and infrastructure. Further, based on the licence model, AIOps can be classified into two categories like Open Source or Proprietary. Open-source software, the source code is made available to the public with a license that allows users to access, view, modify, and distribute the source code. The source code of proprietary software is not available openly as well as free of cost, which is owned by company. It is also known as closed-source software. The source code of property software is not available to the public, and users cannot modify or inspect the code. In general, proprietary software is sold under a license agreement. The vendors will sell to the users how to use software with a license along with terms of use of software, copy and redistribution.

It highlighted the primary functions of ITOps, including infrastructure stability, service availability, and alignment with business objectives. The discussion emphasized the growing need for intelligence and automation in managing increasingly complex IT environments. Furthermore, it introduced the conceptual architecture of AIOps, outlining the role of data pipelines and feedback loops in enhancing operational efficiency and supporting agile project management. Overall, the section established that the integration of automation and AI-driven capabilities is essential for modernizing IT operations and sustaining organizational agility.

3.6. Various Solutions of AIOps Available in the Market

AIOps make IT operations management simple and accelerating resolution process. AIOps solutions are available in both property and open-source. The following are few open-source AIOps platforms: AIOpsTools, Log Anomaly Detector, Log3C, Loglizer, Jumbune, Seldon Core and WhyLogs Library to mention a few. Whereas the proprietary solutions of AIOps such as BigPanda, BMC Helix, Datadog, Dynatrace, IBM Cloud Pak, NewRelic AIOps, PagerDurty AIOps, ScienceLogic SL One, ServiceNow ITOM, and Splunk IT Service Intelligence to mention a few. The below paragraph briefly explains the features of both open-source and proprietary AIOps solutions.

a) List of Open Source AIOps Solutions:

AIOpsTools: A Python-based toolkit that provides features like anomaly detection, alarm convergence, and time-series forecasting to help developers build custom AIOps applications.

Log Anomaly Detector (LAD): This tool is also known as Project Scorpio, and uses unsupervised machine learning to predict abnormal log lines from streaming sources.

Log3C: A framework that identifies service system problems by correlating system logs with KPI metrics through automated log parsing and cascading clustering.

Loglizer: An open-source Python toolkit specifically designed for automated log-based anomaly detection, implementing several supervised and unsupervised machine learning methods.

Jumbune: An open-source Application Performance Management tool for Big Data. It provides deep analytics and monitoring for data operations on platforms like Hadoop, AWS, and Azure.

Seldon Core: A popular platform for deploying machine learning models on Kubernetes at scale. It converts models from frameworks like TensorFlow and PyTorch into production-ready microservices.

WhyLogs Library: A statistical logging library used by data science teams to profile ML/AI pipelines. It produces log files for monitoring data quality and detecting drift in production environments.

b) List of Property AIOps Solutions

BigPanda: A domain-agnostic AIOps platform specializing in AI-powered event correlation and incident automation to reduce alert noise in high-volume environments.

BMC Helix AIOps: Delivers service-centric monitoring and uses best action recommendations to suggest optimal resolution steps for incidents.

Datadog: This automatically analyzes telemetry to detect anomalies and surface root causes without manual configuration.

Dynatrace: This AIOps platform provides causal AI for automated root-cause analysis and full-stack observability.

IBM Cloud Pak for AIOps: An enterprise suite that includes specialized tools like *Instana* for observability and *Turbonomic* for resource optimization.

NewRelic AIOps: Provides anomaly detection and incident correlation as part of its unified observability platform for engineering teams.

PagerDuty AIOps: Focused on incident response, using machine learning to suppress low-signal noise and orchestrate rapid response workflows.

ScienceLogic SL One: Known for automated discovery and dependency mapping across hybrid and multi-cloud environments.

ServiceNow ITOM: Integrates AIOps into service desk workflows, using predictive AIOps to monitor and remediate IT issues across large enterprises.

Splunk IT Service Intelligence: A leading platform for predictive alerting and event aggregation, leveraging machine learning to predict service degradations.

4. IMPLEMENTATION CHALLENGES

In the previous section, we presented the case for AI-driven transformation by explaining the need for intelligent, automated IT operations, introducing AIOps, outlining its conceptual architecture, and discussing various AIOps solutions available in the market. However, implementing AIOps within organizations remains a significant challenge, which is discussed in this section.

AIOps has gained considerable attention and expectations over the past few years (Gartner-Hype Cycle, 2020), but implementing AIOps in organizations is challenging. A successful adoption of AIOps requires overcoming challenges related to data integration, skill development, and vendor selection. Thus, organizations must adopt robust governance frameworks and align AIOps initiatives (Sreerangapuri, 2021) with organizational goals. Figure 10 shows a few major challenges to implement AIOps, which are broadly categorized into three major categories such as technical, organizational, and ethical. Explained implementation challenges briefly in the below paragraph.

Figure 10. Implementation challenges of AIOps

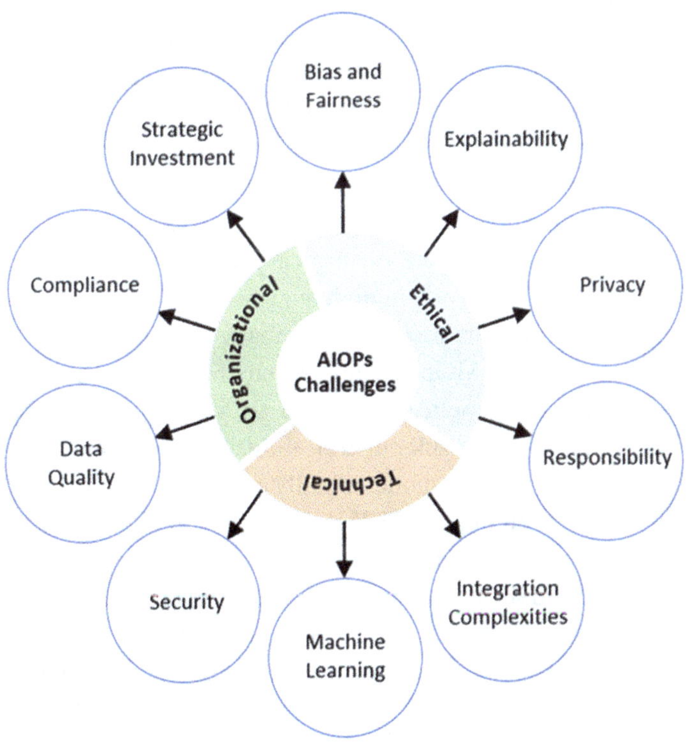

i. **Technical Challenges** - The major technical challenges for implementing AIOps are integration complexities with existing IT solutions and applications and heterogeneous data sources, machine learning models, and security.

Integration Complexities – Many times, traditional as well as in few existing IT systems are in silos, and no proper solutions, tools or platform to manage end to end functionates. In few integrations with existing legacy applications with the emerging tools and maintain both forward and backward communication is one of the major challenges while implementing AIOps. Moreover, the adoption of cloud computing has rapidly increased over a decade and also use of multi cloud environments in the organizations. The integration of AIOps with multi-clouds environments increasing complexity of IT infrastructures managing and monitoring enterprise systems (Palani et. al., June, 2023). In a study identified several challenges to the uptake of adoption of AI-driven frameworks in IT operations (Pandey, 2023) like integration with legacy systems, data governance, and scalability constraints. Also, mentioned strategies to mitigate these issues by the use of hybrid cloud architectures, federated learning for data sharing that protects privacy, and incremental approaches to implementation.

Machine Learning Challenges - One of the additional challenges comes from ML models is that the algorithm(s) being used in AIOps and its output are so complex. So, it is very hard to understand and at the same time cannot be explained by humans. This is because the model is a black box in nature and this puts organizations at risk when they find themselves unable to determine how and why an algorithm generated output. Building an ML and AI model for AIOps solutions presents unique challenges, which are not always apparent in other ML and AI scenarios (Dang et al., 2019). Moreover, building supervised machine learning models for AIOps presents a challenge, as there are no clear ground truth labels and a great deal of manual effort is required to obtain high quality labels. Thus, only unsupervised or semi-supervised ML models are practical in many AIOps scenarios because label data is difficult to obtain. In AIOps context, IT environments change rapidly due to infrastructure changes, new applications deployed, varying workloads and changes in monitoring patterns. This results in concept drift in machine learning models, where the patterns learned by the model initially no longer fully represent the current reality (De la Cruz Cabello et al., 2025). When ML models are not periodically retrained, then drift causes their performance to degrade. The following techniques are commonly employed such as continuous learning, drift detection, and automated retraining are essential to maintain model accuracy to overcome drift limitation.

Security considerations - One of the major challenges in implementing AIOps is security consideration. The possible solution for this is conducting regular security audits, adopting automated compliance tools, and staying updated with the latest security protocols can help maintain a secure and compliant IT environment.

ii. **Organizational Challenges:** This major types of challenges under this category of AIOps are data quality, ensuring compliances and strategic investment and planning.

Data Quality –In AIOps data comes from multiple sources of IT operation process, so it is equally important to ensuring that the data collected, stored, used for analysis, reporting, and decision-making is reliable and trustworthy. It a measure of a data or data set's condition based on factors such as accuracy, completeness, consistency, reliability and validity. The effectiveness of AI is mainly dependent on having clean, accurate data. The higher the quality of data will improve the level of organizational decision making that in turn meets the business goals. A study conducted by (Daiz et at., 2023) outlines open issues, opportunities, and future trends that organizations encounter in implementing MLOps and AIOps. The common issues identified for implementing AIOps include development of AI applications and their lifecycle management in the field of computer science; data management includes data quality, access, data preparation and labelling and validation and clearing. Moreover, the objective of AIOps was stated as to cope with the increasing complexities posed by modern IT systems and to reduce human intervention. In addition, the opportunities of AIOps solutions were identified, as they can support different states of the life cycle, data management, monitoring and deployment. Moreover, AIOps can deliver benefits through the provision of infrastructure management that includes edge, cloud, networking, data and lifecycle management. Further, the data quality and quantity available today do not serve the needs of AIOps solutions (Dang et at., 2019), although major cloud services today collect terabytes and even petabytes of telemetry data every day/month, there still lacks representative and high-quality data for building AIOps solutions.

Ensuring Compliance – To ensure compliances of AIOps solution is a constant challenge, requiring ongoing vigilance and adaptation to new threats and regulatory requirements. One of the solutions for this is to adopt an automated compliance tool. In a recent study (Kontogiannis et al., 2021) advocates for embedding regulatory compliance directly into the software development and operations lifecycle, rather than treating it as an afterthought. The author proposed a framework that embeds regulatory, ethical, and operational standards directly into data and AI pipelines, shifting from reactive to proactive, continuous compliance. This framework utilizes AIOps for automated monitoring, reducing costs and accelerating risk identification while addressing the need for transparent, explainable AI decisions.

Strategic Investment and Planning – The one of the major challenges to the organizations is allocating investment and resources with the goal of improving returns and limiting risks while implementing AIOps. The cost to the organizations is a biggest problem more particularly small and midsize organizations. According to recent IDC research report (Nancy Gohring, Jan 2024), the high cost of ownership is a significant barrier for organizations implementing artificial intelligence for IT operations (AIOps) with nearly 40% of large enterprises citing it as a concern.

iii. **Ethical Challenges –** AIOps uses AI technology for automation of IT operations, which means AIOps is an AI system. So, there is a need to take into account the following parameters such as bias and fairness, transparency, data privacy, explainability and responsibility as a part of ethical consideration.

Bias and fairness – AIOps are trained and tested using data. Bias in AI refers to systematic errors that lead to incorrect predictions because of skewed outcomes. Insomuch as fairness is about designing, training and deploying AI models that do not favour to either individuals and/ or groups based on characteristics like race, gender. Ethical considerations are more important for AI to ensure that the technology is fair and unbiased. It means taking steps to prevent discrimination based on factors such as race, gender, and socioeconomic status and also means paying attention to data the system is trained from these two factors taking into consideration.

In a similar study, (Sokol et al., 2022) has developed an audit toolkit that evaluates and report on the fairness, accountability, and transparency of data and machine learning models. The framework provides a unified suite of tools for auditing, and explaining predictive models.

Explainability - Building confidence in AI-driven decisions requires transparency and explainable AI (XAI). The algorithms used in AIOps solutions cannot fully explainable for its decision making. It means users cannot fully interpretable of the results produced by AI systems. In another research study (Sami et al., 2025) introduced a comprehensive taxonomy of explainable AI (XAI) techniques to bridge gaps in AI-driven IT operations. The taxonomy categorized by method, use case, and output, to address the "black-box" nature of AI in IT operations. The survey highlights the need for hybrid neuro-symbolic systems and identifies critical gaps in scalability, standardization, and cognitive load. Furthermore, it emphasizes the importance of human-centric, actionable insights to reduce alert fatigue among site reliability engineers (SREs).

Privacy is a critical consideration for ethical AI. This means taking steps to protect user data and ensure that it is not misused or mishandled at all the layers of AIOps ecosystem. The most common privacy challenges in AIOps include sensitive data exposure, data minimization, model inversion and data silos. The challenges can be addressed using federated learning, differential privacy, data anonymization, and homomorphic encryption.

Responsibility is one of the important parameters of ethical consideration for AI systems. It means taking responsibility for the actions of AI systems for any negative impacts who holds accountability. Organizational culture and structure play a critical role in determining the effectiveness of responsible AI initiatives, and a framework has been proposed to analyse these organizational factors in practice ((Rakova et at., 2021). This study outlines a shift from reactive to proactive organizational practices in responsible AI, based on practitioner interviews. This study identifies three maturity stages such as Prevalent, Emerging and Aspirational and highlights key enablers, including cross-functional collaboration and incentivized risk-taking, while addressing barriers like role ambiguity and lack of metrics.

In a study, the challenges such as data quality, model generalization, and human expertise are stated by (Zadeh et al., 2024) while integrating AI for project management. This aligns with previous study identified (Dam et al., 2019) a number of important challenging in Agile project management such as identifying and refining backlog items, spring planning, and pro-active monitoring. Thus, the most of the implementation challenges of AIOps will also apply to AI-powered Agile project management because AI-powered Agile project management is a logical extension of AIOps. The data integrity and automation provided by AIOps are crucial for AI-powered Agile project management, but it is still susceptible to the same implementation obstacles. For example, if an AIOps deployment suffers from poor data quality or 'noisy' alerts, then the AI-powered Agile tool will also produce flawed forecasts, directly impacting the accuracy of sprint planning.

5. INTEGRATING AIOPS WITH AGILE TEAMS

In the previous section, we discussed various AIOps solutions available in the market, including both vendor-specific and open-source options, providing an overview of the current AIOps landscape. AIOps is a complex system that can be applied in multiple contexts, particularly in the transformation of traditional IT operations into AI-driven IT operations as well as in project management. Integrating AIOps with DevOps and Agile project management practices offers several advantages and solves project management challenges. In this section, discuss, how AIOps offers solution and several advantages in project management.

A seminal study in this area proposed (Dam et al., 2019) an architecture for an AI-powered agile project management that comprises of analytics engine, a planning engine and an optimization engine, which acts as the core of the AI system. Additionally, a learning representation engine that learns and generates representations of project data consists of NLP, code modelling, feature extraction and aggregation. The NLP component performs automatic analysis on project textual artifacts and then generates good representations of those artifacts. The code modelling component is responsible for learning meaningful vector representations, while the feature extraction and aggregation extract all the vector representations of the artifacts related to the Agile team. In a similar related study, he transformation of traditional Agile project management practices poses challenges (Chinta 2021) like the need for new skills, potential resistance from team members, and ethical concerns about data privacy and algorithmic bias. To address this challenge in a proactive manner, organizations must foster a culture of adaptability and continuous learning. Further, implementing training programs is necessary to equip team member with the necessary skills to work effectively with AI tools.

The various advantages of AI-powered Agile project management are provided in the below paragraph.

Reactive to Proactive Project Management: As it is known that DevOps is fast, but ITOps is stable whereas AIOps acts as the mediator that connect them to provide safe and high-speed delivery. Thus, AIOps catalyses DevOps velocity by shielding the infrastructure from deployment risks. Further, AIOps directly addresses project management challenges by transforming how teams handle data-heavy, repetitive, and unpredictable tasks within the Software Development Lifecycle (SDLC). By integrating big data analytics and machine learning, AIOps shifts project management from reactive firefighting to proactive, data-driven decision-making.

Resource Allocation and Optimization: Traditional resource management often relies on manual estimation, leading to over-provisioning or under-utilization. AIOps uses predictive analytics to forecast future resource needs such as compute power, bandwidth, and personnel, and ensuring projects have the necessary capacity without wasting budget.

Risk Mitigation and Predictive Management: Project managers often face unforeseen risks that cause delays. AIOps tools analyse historical project data and real-time metrics to identify potential bottlenecks or system failures before they occur, allowing teams to take preventive action.

Managing Complexity and Technical Debt: Modern projects involving hybrid cloud or microservices generate vast amounts of data that are impossible for humans to manually correlate. AIOps consolidates fragmented tools and automates routine maintenance, which reduces existing technical debt and frees up senior staff for high-value innovation

Operational Efficiency and Productivity: By automating repetitive tasks like incident triaging, log analysis, and reporting, AIOps significantly increases PM productivity. This allows project managers to focus on strategic alignment and relationship building rather than administrative overhead.

Breaking Down Data Silos: IT teams often work in disconnected silos, which can lead to miscommunication and delayed resolutions. AIOps provides a unified operational view, ensuring all stakeholders such as DevOps, SREs, and business leaders that have access to the same real-time data and insights.

The following table 4 provides a summary of AIOps impact on project outcomes.

Table 4. Summary of AIOps Impact on Project Outcomes

Challenge	AIOps Direct Impact	Primary Benefit
High MTTR	Automated root-cause analysis	Faster incident resolution (up to 50% faster)
Alert Fatigue	Intelligent noise reduction	90%+ reduction in irrelevant alerts
Project Delays	Predictive maintenance	Preemptive identification of critical risks
Budget Overruns	Cloud cost & capacity optimization	Significant reduction in operational expenditure

In a summary, AI-powered Agile project management acts as a strategic layer built upon the operational intelligence of AIOps. While AIOps provides real-time data and automated root-cause analysis, the Agile framework translates these insights into actionable sprint priorities and resource plans. The next section presents various recommendations for transformation of ITOps into AIOps and their performance metrics.

6. RECOMMENDED ACTIONS

Although the previous section discussed the need for intelligence and automation in IT operations (ITOps) and the implementation challenges of AIOps faced by modern IT environments, it is necessary to examine how these insights can be translated into practical implementation. Therefore, the present section focuses on recommended actions for the smooth adoption of AIOps. Specifically, it outlines a methodology for transforming traditional ITOps into AIOps, identifies evaluation dimensions for measuring implementation success, and examines potential use cases along with their key benefits.

6.1. Methodology for Transformation of ITOps into AIOps

In general, IT transformation refers to the process of aligning IT capabilities with an organization's strategic objectives and is commonly regarded as a subset of digital transformation. This process focuses on enabling an organization's IT infrastructure to deliver services more efficiently while improving the performance and functionality of existing IT systems through the adoption of emerging technologies.

As a result, traditional IT operations are increasingly evolving into automated and intelligent operational models, commonly referred to as AIOps.

A conceptual methodology for the transformation of ITOps into AIOps is illustrated in figure 11. This methodology provides a structured framework that defines the key phases of the transformation process. This structure is essential because AIOps is a complex system that presents several implementation challenges. In many cases, organizations fail to successfully implement AIOps due to the absence of well-defined processes, and governance rules that connect the *how* of the system with the *when* and *what* outlined in the implementation roadmap and its visual timeline. The full cycle of transformation has four major phases such as (i) assessment and analysis, (ii) planning, (iii) modernization, and (iv) optimization and enhancements. The proposed methodology, termed APMO (Assessment, Planning, Modernization, and Optimization), provides a structured, non-linear, phased approach for transforming traditional IT operations into AIOps. The phased approach ensures that organizations can align technological capabilities with operational goals while minimizing risks associated with large-scale transformation initiatives. Further, this methodology guides organizations through a systematic transition by first evaluating the current IT environment, then defining strategic objectives and implementation plans, followed by modernizing infrastructure and operational practices, and finally continuously optimizing performance using AI-driven insights.

Figure 11. Major lifecycle phases of a typical transformation methodology of ITOps into AIOps

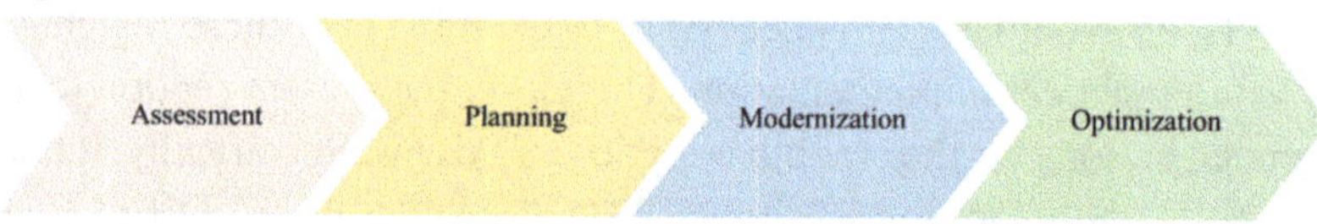

Assessment Phase –It mainly focuses on understanding the current state of IT operations and identifying readiness for AIOps adoption, essential for defining realistic transformation goals. This includes evaluate, identify, assess, measure, and capabilities of an organization. The broad activities of this phase are given below:

- Evaluate existing IT infrastructure, monitoring tools, and operational processes.
- Identify data sources such as logs, metrics, and event streams.
- Assess IT maturity level and automation capabilities including limitation.
- Identify both technical and operational challenges such as integration with other applications, alert fatigue, incident response delays, and system silos.

- Define baseline performance metrics and KPIs to measure the implementation progress.
- Conduct stakeholder and capability assessments.

In summary, this phase focuses on understanding the current state of IT operations and identifying readiness for AIOps adoption.

Planning Phase – This phase mainly focuses on what needs to be implemented, and when, forming the strategic roadmap for AIOps adoption. This is a strategic activity, which defines a goal, identification of AIOps tool or desired outcome and includes the major steps or milestones needed to implement AIOps. The broad activities of this planning include but are not limited to:

- Define AIOps transformation objectives and scope.
- Develop a technology architecture and tool selection strategy.
- List of important Use Cases for AIOps deployment and identification of the most priority Use Case based on the organization's needs.
- Define data integration and governance strategies.
- Establish implementation roadmap, timelines, and milestones.
- Identify resource requirements, skills, and training needs.
- Define success metrics and evaluation criteria.

Modernization - This phase focuses on the solution development of identified Use Case and implementing the planned technological and operational changes required for AIOps adoption. The broad activities of this phase are:

- Design data architecture that integrates operational data sources such as logs, metrics, event and builds pipelines to feed monitoring and event management systems.
- Build the identified use case with AI/ML for anomaly detection, automating incident detection, correlation, root cause analysis and predictive analytics
- Integrating the use case with existing ITSM tools.
- Testing and validation of the use case working as intended in the live environment
- Deployment and automated of use case workflows and remediation processes.
- Modernize observability and monitoring frameworks.

The summary of this phase is to transform identified use case into working solution and updating the current IT systems to new system i.e., AIOps and making it work without any business outages.

Optimization Phase - The last stage, comprises reengineering, automation of IT processes, and workflows. This include enhancing the functionality of IT systems in terms of monitoring, security, scalability and compliance and also ensure that the AIOps system adapts and evolves with changing operational requirements. Further, activities such as ongoing training to IT team and support staff, feedback and continuous improvements are part of this phase. The broad activities of this phase include

- Continuously refine AI/ML models using operational data.
- Improve automation rules and workflows.
- Monitor system performance and operational efficiency.
- Evaluate KPIs and service-level objectives (SLOs).
- Expand AIOps capabilities to additional use cases and services.
- Implement feedback loops for continuous improvement.

In summary, this phase focuses on continuous improvement and maximizing the value of AIOps by enhancing their capabilities.

In another study, the process of IT operations transformation was stated as the strategic functioning of an organization (Intel – IT Transformation) that focuses on the three points like upgrade, transformation, and efficiency with scalability. The details of these strategic functions are: (a) upgrade of an organization's technology infrastructure like hardware, software, and practices to prepare for future challenges; (b) Successful IT transformation delivers flexibility, manageability, low total cost ownership, improved security risk management. and ability to respond quickly to system changes; and (c) improved IT operation's efficiency, and scalability. In summary, IT operations transformation focuses primarily on the improvement and modernization of an organization's IT infrastructure and operations. Further, the goal of ITOps transformation into AIOps was stated to make IT systems more are agile, cost-effective, scalable, more secured and able to support business innovation and goals of an organization.

In a related study, the author introduces a phase implementation methodology for AIOps (Sing, 2025) that addresses technical, process, and organizational aspects. There are four phases involved in this: assessment and preparation, foundation building, capability expansion and operational transformation phases. The drawback is very limited activities mapped to each of these four phases. The first phase activities are like data readiness, use case prioritization, skill development while the second phase, activities include data platform implementation, initial model development and integration with SRE workflows. The third phase comprises of model implementation, process transformation and feedback loop establishment.

The last phase includes autonomous operations development, organization adaption and continuous evolution.

6.1.1. Common Pitfalls to Avoid While Implementation of AIOps

Implementing AIOps is a cultural and architectural shift that often fails not because of the technology, but due to poor strategy and execution. Avoiding these common pitfalls is essential for moving beyond small pilots into a scalable, high-performing operational model. The most common pitfall for implementing AIOps are categorised into three broad categories such as strategic and organizational, technical and data and execution and governance. Figure 12 shows various type of pitfalls and the corresponding solution.

a) Strategic and Organisational Pitfalls

Lack of Clear Objectives: Organizations often implement AIOps for the sake of being modern without defining specific, measurable goals like reducing alert fatigue or improving MTTR to mention a few scenarios.

Solution: Define specific, measurable business outcomes such as KPIs such as reducing Mean Time to Repair (MTTR) or ticket volume that align with broader business goals to ensure the initiative delivers tangible value.

Figure 12. Common pitfalls and solutions to AIOps

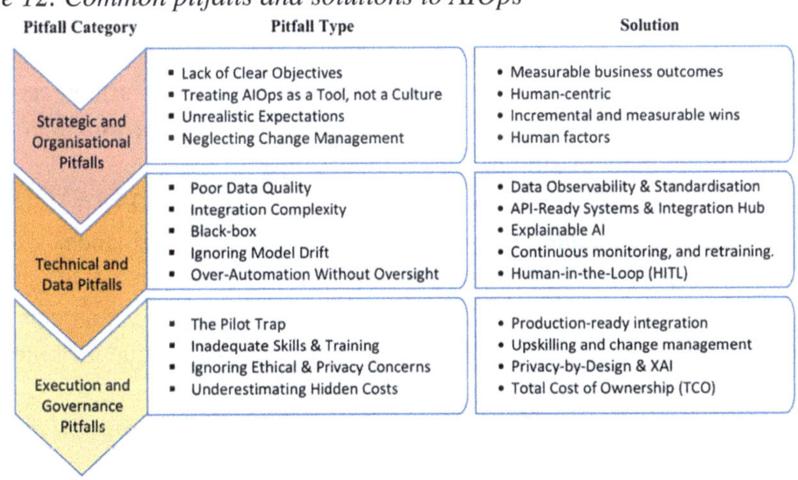

Treating AIOps as a Tool, not a Culture: Success requires breaking down functional silos; if development and operations do not share ownership, the AI under-delivers.

Solution: Treat AIOps as a new way of working, not just a purchase. Get your IT and data teams talking, human-centric, so everyone makes decisions based on shared data.

Unrealistic Expectations: Believing AI will read minds or transform the business overnight leads to perceived failure even if technical results are good.

Solution: Adopt an approach incremental and measurable wins, means to start with small, high-impact Proof of Concept to demonstrate value early, while educating stakeholders that AI is an iterative, probabilistic system that requires ongoing fine-tuning.

Neglecting Change Management: Teams often fear job displacement or lack trust in automated decisions, leading to internal resistance.

Solutions: Actively involve staff in the transition by providing hands-on training and clear communication. Further, focusing on how people interact with systems, tools, and environments. Show them how AIOps automates the boring stuff to free them up for more meaningful work, reducing fear and boosting adoption.

b) Technical and Data Pitfalls

Poor Data Quality ("Garbage In, Garbage Out"): AI depends on consistent, clean, and normalized data; incomplete or siloed datasets result in unreliable predictions.

Solution: Establish a solid data foundation by enforcing strict data hygiene and embedding cleansing steps directly into ETL and data pipelines. Further, centralise data sources to ensure consistency and conduct regular audits to identify errors before they impact model training.

Integration Complexity: Legacy systems often lack the APIs or flexibility needed for real-time streaming, leading to costly and slow performance.

Solution: Adapt API ready solutions and integration hubs.

Black-box: A "black box" in machine learning is a system, like a deep neural network, whose internal decision-making is too complex or opaque for humans to understand.

Solution: Implement Explainable AI (XAI) and governance guardrails to ensure automated decisions are transparent and understandable to business users.

Ignoring Model Drift: Many fail to plan for the "decay" of AI performance as real-world data patterns change over time, requiring continuous retraining.

Solution: The first step is to set up a system to continuously monitor the model's performance. Once, drift is detected retrain the model. Adapt continuous learning, and automated retraining to maintain model.

Over-Automation Without Oversight: Handing complete control to AI without human checkpoints can lead to robotic errors or missed customer intent.

Solution: Using human-in-the-loop (HITL) checkpoints for sensitive or high-risk decisions helps build trust in the system's outputs

c) Execution and Governance Pitfalls

The "Pilot Trap": Organizations often get stuck in small-scale experiments and fail to build the production-grade data pipelines needed for enterprise-wide scaling.

Solution: A defined roadmap to scale successes from small Proof of Concepts to full production environments.

Inadequate Skills and Training: AIOps requires a mix of data science and IT operational knowledge that many internal teams lack without upskilling.

Solution: Bridge the gap by investing in upskilling programs that teach teams how to interpret AI outputs and manage new workflows, ensuring they can effectively change management in automated systems.

Ignoring Ethical and Privacy Concerns: Failing to implement data governance or anonymisation can lead to regulatory violations, especially under frameworks like the EU Act.

Solution: Implement an AI governance framework that includes, privacy by design, data anonymization, bias audits, and strict compliance checks to maintain brand trust and meet regulatory standards.

Underestimating Hidden Costs: Initial software costs are just the start; organizations often overlook ongoing expenses for cloud compute, storage, and specialized talent.

Solution: Plan for the long term by budgeting for ongoing model maintenance, data cleaning, and the integration effort required to connect siloed systems, rather than just the initial software license. Thus, total expenses over the full lifecycle beyond initial acquisition prices, maintenance cost like GPU and compute power and indirect costs, such as training, downtime, and support.

6.1.2. Best Practices to Avoid Failure

In the previous section, we discussed the most common pitfalls of AIOps implementation and proposed appropriate solutions. In addition, there are several best practices that can help prevent implementation failures, which we will outline in this section.

a) Start Small: Pilot AIOps in a focussed domain like network monitoring or application health before scaling.
b) Prioritize Data Foundations: Establish strong data governance and centralization before adding complex AI layers.
c) Align with Business ROI: Quantify expected benefits against realistic cost projections to justify the investment.
d) Embed Security (DevSecOps): Ensure security and compliance are part of the AIOps design from day one rather than an afterthought.
e) Integrate AIOps with Agile Project Management – Leverage the use of AIOps to agile project management beyond the use of automating IT operations for smooth delivery of the project management activities including full cycle of DevOps and also CI/CD operations.

6.1.3. People, Process and Cultural Considerations

A study examines the forces affecting the implementation of AIOps and emphasizes that successful adoption requires a shift in organizational culture as well as careful management of machine learning models to ensure effectiveness (Sanden, 2024). AIOps is not just a technology implementation; it requires a shift from traditional manual IT troubleshooting to a collaborative, data-driven mindset. One of the key challenges is overcoming resistance to the shift from manual, expert-driven investigation toward reliance on automated, AI-driven predictions.

The implementation of AIOps impacts not only because of organizational barriers but also cultural resistance (Potts and Carver, 2024 & De la Cruz Cabello et al., 2025). The organizational barriers include structural, functional, or physical obstacles built into the company like rigid hierarchy, lack of resources, poor communication systems whereas cultural values refer to the emotional, psychological, or collective behavioural opposition to change based on shared values, beliefs, and norms.

In the context of AIOps implementation, people and process considerations are critical because they address the organizational, cultural, and workflow changes required to transition from manual, reactive firefighting to automated, proactive IT operations to intelligent. Further, people and process considerations will act as a bridge between AI technology and business outcomes, ensuring that the technology delivers on promises of improved efficiency, lower costs, and better user experience. While technology, AI/ML models, handles data ingestion and analysis, the People and Process component ensures the organization is ready to consume these insights, trust the automation, and collaborate across teams.

AI systems are creating unprecedented challenges for socio-technical systems, fundamentally reshaping our understanding of interactions between technology and society. In response to these challenges, a study argues for an integrated framework that addresses socio-technical issues while balancing technical innovation with social considerations (Kalluri, 2025). The study further identifies a critical need for interdisciplinary approaches to AI integration that transcend traditional disciplinary boundaries. It also emphasizes the importance of adaptive governance mechanisms that can evolve alongside technological change, as well as participatory approaches to engage diverse stakeholders. Furthermore, the study advocates viewing AI as a socio-technical ensemble to effectively address challenges such as algorithmic bias and lagging regulatory preparedness.

According to a study argues, the transformation of traditional Agile project management practices poses challenges like the need for new skills, potential resistance from team members, and ethical concerns about data privacy and algorithmic bias (Chinta 2021). This study also proposes a strategy to address this challenge in a proactive manner, organizations must foster a culture of adaptability and continuous learning. Further, implementing training programs is necessary to equip team member with the necessary skills to work effectively with AI tools.

6.1.4. Change Management

The process of change management is a critical factor in the successful adoption of AIOps within IT organizations. Implementing AIOps involves not only deploying advanced technologies such as artificial intelligence and machine learning but also transforming existing IT operational processes and organizational culture (Davenport & Ronanki, 2018; Patel & Yakkundi, 2020). Traditional IT operations often rely on manual, static, expert-driven investigations and established workflows. However, the introduction of AI-driven automation and predictive analytics requires teams to adapt to new ways of monitoring systems, analysing incidents, and making operational decisions (Gartner, 2017).

Effective change management ensures that stakeholders understand the value of AIOps and are prepared to transition from conventional practices to data-driven and automated operations. This process involves training IT staff, redefining operational roles, and fostering trust in AI-generated insights and recommendations (Kim et al., 2016). Furthermore, clear communication, stakeholder engagement, and incremental implementation strategies help minimize resistance and facilitate smoother adoption. Ultimately, strong change management practices enable organizations to integrate AIOps effectively, improving operational efficiency, reducing incident resolution times, and enhancing the reliability of IT services.

6.2. Major Performance Indicators of AIOps

In the previous section, we presented the methodology for the transformation of ITOps into AIOps. It is essential to measure the success of AIOps implementation that requires key performance indications, which we discuss in this section.

DORA primarily refers to DevOps Research and Assessment that established the industry standard for measuring software delivery performance through four key metrics (Portman, 2020), owned by Google. The four metrics are development frequency, lead time for change, time to restore service and change failure rate. These metrics, which balance speed and stability, help teams identify bottlenecks and improve DevOps performance. Further, these metrics are categorised into four performance categories such as elite, high, medium and low. Elite and low are the two ends of the performance category. These metrics mainly measure velocity and stability to provide a holistic view of team performance. A summary of software delivery performance metrics is provided in table 5.

Table 5. Summary of software delivery performance metrics

Name of Metric	Category	Description	Elite Benchmark
Deployment Frequency	Velocity	Frequency of code releases to production.	On-demand
Lead Time for Changes	Velocity	Time from code commit to production deployment.	Less than 1 day
Change Failure Rate	Stability	Percentage of deployments causing failures.	0–15%
Time to Restore Service	Stability	Time to recover from production failures.	Less than 1 hour

AIOps acts as an accelerator and a "safety net" for the Four Keys metrics and provides the benchmark for performance, AIOps provides the intelligence to move from manual processes to automated, predictive workflows. The following is an explanation of how AIOps has a direct impact on each of these four metrics.

Deployment Frequency: AIOps enables "smarter" automation by using machine learning to predict the optimal times for releases, replacing static schedules with dynamic ones.

Lead Time for Changes: By identifying inefficiencies and bottlenecks in the CI/CD pipeline through predictive analytics, AIOps helps streamline code review and testing phases.

Change Failure Rate: Machine learning models in AIOps can predict high-risk changes by analysing historical deployment data. It flags unusual patterns or anomalies in code before they are pushed to production, recommending targeted reviews to prevent failures.

Time to Restore Service: This is where AIOps has the most significant impact. It uses real-time anomaly detection and intelligent incident correlation to sift through thousands of alerts; pinpointing root causes much faster than humans. In advanced setups, it can even trigger self-healing actions, such as automated rollbacks, to restore service instantly.

In addition, measuring AIOps success requires a balanced set of quantitative and qualitative indicators to capture both technical performance and business impact. The quantitative metrics demonstrate operational improvements, including Mean Time to Detect (MTTD), Mean Time to Resolve (MTTR), alert noise reduction, and Mean Time Between Failures (MTBF), whereas qualitative indicators, such as return on investment (ROI), customer satisfaction, and user experience, provide context by explaining the value of these improvements. Additionally, AIOps-specific key performance indicators (KPIs) include the automated remediation success rate, false positive rate, and the ratio of user-reported to system-detected incidents, among others. The following table 6 summarises the major performance indicators of AIOps.

Table 6. A summary of major performance indicators of AIOps

S. No	Metric	Traditional Baseline	Typical AIOps Outcome	Improvement
1	Alert Noise	500+ daily alerts	50 - 75 incidents	60% - 90% reduction
2	MTTD (Detection)	30 mins to 4 hours	Minutes to seconds	40% - 60% reduction
3	MTTA (Acknowledge)	15–30 mins manual triage	< 1 - 5 mins auto-routing	50% - 80% reduction
4	MTTR (Resolution)	3–5 hours	45 - 90 mins	30% - 70% reduction
5	False Positives	40% - 60% rate	<10% rate	40% - 70% reduction
6	Ticket Ratio	High (many tickets:1 issue)	Near 1:1	Significant consolidation

AIOps and Site Reliability Engineering integration leads to a new framework (Sing, 2025) that utilizes machine learning to enhance proactive capabilities, reducing alert noise by up to 87% and the mean time to detection by 73%. This framework automates, predicts, and resolves incidents, transforming SRE from manual, reactive troubleshooting to proactive, intelligent, and automated system reliability management.

The performance indicators of AIOps acts as a fundamental input to AI-powered Agile project management that transforms traditional Agile project management metrics into predictive and real-time management. Thus, linking the metrics of

AIOps and Agile project management metrics form a holistic ecosystem of metrics for delivery and project health.

6.3. Use Cases of AIOps

The following table 7 shows a list of six different potential AIOps use cases such as analytics and risk management, operations management, CI/CD pipeline, root cause analysis, automated remediation and blind spot monitoring of multi-cloud environments which covers a brief description and benefits.

Table 7. List of potential AIOps use cases

S.No.	Use Case Name	Brief Description of Use Case	Benefits
1	IT Operation Analytics (ITOA) and Risk Management	IT operations analytics (ITOA) is an intelligent data driven process by which organizations collect, store, train and analyse data that is collected from multiple IT systems and notify results to the users of system for informed decision. Further, it helps to manage reduction of risk associated with IT systems.	Lead Time Reduction Strategic Risk Management
2	Enhancing Agile Team Productivity with AIOps	AIOps can transform IT operations from a reactive, manual, and siloed function into a proactive, automated, and collaborative way by integrating AI, machine learning (ML), and big data analytics. As a result, AIOps enhances agile team not only productivity but also performance.	Identify bottlenecks Predict potential failures Optimize resource allocation. Thus, project managers can use AIOps forecasts to de-risk release timelines.
3	AI driven IT Operations Management	IT Operations Management is the practice of managing IT operations in intelligent way to ensure that the efficient and cost-effective operations of technology infrastructure of an organization.	Comply with ITIL process Simplifies managing an organization's IT needs and brings value.
4	AI based CI/CD Pipelines	It is an automated DevOps workflow that streamlines an intelligent way of the software delivery process.	Software teams deliver the code safer and faster. Improved product delivery
5	AI Driven Rood Cause Analysis	Root cause analysis is one of the most significant AIOps use cases. It is a method of problem-solving approach for identifying the root causes of faults. It uses both data and algorithms to uncover hidden causes of problems	Faster way identification of faults. It helps trace recurring problems Provide solutions in least amount of time from the train data and history.
6	Automated Remediation	This is another important AIOps use cases that leverages AI, ML and Big data and continuous monitor IT systems on real time for detecting anomalies.	Reduction of MTTR Improves overall IT efficiently

continued on following page

Table 7. Continued

S.No.	Use Case Name	Brief Description of Use Case	Benefits
7	Blind spot monitoring of multi-cloud environments	Monitoring of multi-cloud environment is one of important use cases of AIOps. With this use case, the blind spots in the multi-cloud environments detected intelligently that leverages AI and ML.	Enhances performance Improves cloud operations Improves observability
8	LLM based failure management	Now a day use of software systems is becoming increasingly complex and these software systems frequently experience failures that are challenging to detect, pinpoint, and diagnose. Hence, there is a great need of AI based failure management tools (Paolo et al., 2021). So, the proposed use cases leverages either machine learning (ML) or deep learning (DL) algorithms for analyse vast amounts of data from various operational systems, tools and devices, automatically detecting and responding to system issues in real-time.	High availability and reliability of software systems Improves observability

This section, a case for AI driven ITOps transformation, establishes a linkage between limitations of traditional IT Operations, and the need for intelligence and automation to overcome limitations, presented a typical methodology that explain how organizations can transform their ITOps into AIOps. In addition, provided the most common pitfalls and solutions to those. Furthermore, provided a few best practices for implementation AIOps in organizations. Briefly touch upon an introduction to AIOps and various forms of open source and proprietary solutions of AIOps, various types of AIOps and potential use cases, thereby setting the stage for a deeper inquiry into challenges and benefits of AIOps.

6.4. Key Benefits of AIOps

The integration of AI technologies and Bigdata with IT Operations, AIOps ecosystem, results several benefits, which include but not limited to, the following: improved efficiency, reduced downtime, actionable insights, data driven decision, real time alerts and notifications and faster MTTR. The key benefits of AIOps are displayed in figure 13.

a) **Improved efficiency** - In traditional IT operations management, many tasks to be performed on day-to-day basis on a manual basis. Because of the integration of AI, ML and Bigdata in each stage of IT Operations can automate the daily tasks. As a result, time taken to perform these manual operations can save time and also minimizes the efforts of IT Operations team. Due to automation, the number of errors that occurs due to manual operations are greatly minimized and this further reduces the efforts of IT operations team as a result improves the overall efficiency of IT operations

Figure 13. Key benefits of AIOps

b) **Reduced downtime** – Downtime refers to the unavailability of a service for a specified period. The downtime of the systems can be planned due to maintenance or unplanned incidents due to outage or technical failures from the unplanned incidents and events. This not only reduces down time of IT systems but also outage of the systems.

c) **Actionable Insights** – Dashboard one of the main benefits of AIOps is its ability to provide real insights into the health and performance of IT environment in terms of monitoring KPIs generally used to measure the performance of companies against their strategic goals.

d) **Real time alerts and notifications** - AIOps solutions deliver real time insights to users of IT teams in terms of IT performance of various applications, critical issues, quick identification of problems as well as resolution to these problems

e) **Saves Time** - AIOps can save time because of automating many tasks such daily system scans, path updates, backup activities, error detection, alert analysis and event reporting.

f) **Data Driven Decision** – AIOps systems are by default address the need of handling multiple data sources that comes from multiple IT system and applications. Further, it includes the functionality of storing, organizing data performing data analysis and generating patterns from data and valuable insights from data. Further, it provides a complete view of dashboard about functioning of IT systems and solutions which in turn helps to taking informed decision.

g) **Faster MTTR** – AIOps collects data from multiple heterogenous operation sources, correlates, and then filters un-wanted noise by suppressing redundant notifications. Further, there exists a positive correlation between noise reduction and improved Mean Time to Repair (MTTR) in AIOps. This is not only helps to detect anomalies, to perform root cause analysis but also propose solutions faster as a result reduces the MTTR of the IT operations.

The benefits of AIOps flow directly into AI-powered Agile project management because they provide the data and time, which acts as a fuel, that makes the Agile process more efficient. The following table 8 summarises the benefits transfer from AIOps into AI-powered Agile project management.

Table 8. A summary of AIOps benefits transfer to AI-powered Agile project management.

S.No.	AIOps Technical Benefits	AI-powered Agile Management Benefits
1	Faster Mean Time to Repair (MTTR) through automated root-cause analysis.	Developers spend less time for unplanned bugs and more time completing Story Points. This directly, reduces MTTR, resulting increases the team's Velocity. As a result, sprint commitments more reliable.
2	AIOps filtering out thousands of *false alarm* alerts and produce right once. Thus, reduces noise.	The team stay focus on producing high quality code, instead of being interrupted by minor alerts, that avoids carrying over tasks at the end of a sprint.
3	AIOps provide predictive insights. For e.g., forecasting system capacity and potential infrastructure failures.	Agile teams can schedule maintenance stories proactively to avoid project-crushing outages using predictive insights provided by AIOps.
4	AIOps automatically logging all incident data and system changes.	Auto logging facilitates reduction of manual documentation efforts to Agile team which results reduction of team's overheads.

7. FUTURE DIRECTIONS OF AIOPS

In the previous sections, we presented the evolution of ITOps, articulated the case for its transformation into AIOps, and proposed a conceptual architecture for AIOps and explained its functioning with the aid of data pipeline as well as feedback loops. Also. outlined metrics for measuring the success of AIOps implementation and discussed the associated challenges and benefits. Further, explained integrating AIOps with agile project management improves delivery process. Building upon the state-of-the-art discussions presented above, the following future research directions are proposed to extend this work.

AIOps is a very new area of ITOps that leverages AI, ML and HITL to manage e the technology infrastructure and solutions of an organization. It has wide open areas to expand multiple possibilities in automation and optimization of intelligent ITOps. AIOps will continue to shape the landscape of IT operations, and provide timely and accurate a data-driven decision to managing the IT environments.

In another recent research study (Zhang et al., 2025), examines the use of LLMs in AIOps and explain how LLMs address limitations in traditional AIOps, such as lack of generality, by improving failure perception, root cause analysis, and remediation. The author outlines a four-stage lifecycle which is a structured framework for analysing, comparing, and organizing LLM-based failure management approaches. The four stages lifecycle of data preprocessing, perception, RCA, and auto remediation enhances LLM operational efficiency by automating the transition from raw data to actionable intelligence. Further, this workflow improves efficiency through advanced log parsing, zero-shot anomaly detection, automated root cause reporting, and script generation for remediation. Furthermore, the author address failure management through a three-stage approach, LLM-enhanced workflow: Failure Perception (detection, prediction), Root Cause Analysis (localization, report generation), and Assisted Remediation (automated script generation). This approach leverages LLMs to analyse human-generated documentation alongside system telemetry to automate resolution, ranging from assisted questioning to fully automatic execution.

Future research must concentrate on the following research directions of AIOps. We discuss six types of future research directions of AIOps. These includes (i) work needs to be done to establish transparent ML or LLM modelling work will have to be conducted in order to interpret the output of the model at all times; (ii) a framework required to assess maturity level of AIOps in terms of a key parameters such as automation, observability, interoperability, level of integration with both modern IT systems and solutions and legacy systems. To perform a detail study and analysis on these key parameters. If required a new list of parameters that can be identified and carried to develop framework. (iii) industry benchmarking for AIOps solutions is to be developed to measure the performance of strategic, process, and metrics to find the ways to optimization levels of automation. This area of work is because the maturity levels technology infrastructure and solutions will vary from industry to industry. The benchmarks will help organizational business leaders for evaluation of AIOps tools and fitness of these tools to their organizational need; (iv) It also need to evolve new methodologies and best practices for implementation for AIOps in the organizations; (v) integration of AIOps with multi cloud environments; and (vi) one more area for future directions of AIOps is to develop an ethical framework to detect and prioritizing bias prevention in the deployed AIOps systems.

(vii) One more interesting future direction of work is the integration of Agile, Cloud, and DevOps methodologies offers a powerful and synergistic approach to modern software development and IT operations (El Aouni et al., 2025). Additionally, this landscape is characterized by a dynamic interplay between Agile methodologies, tools, and cultural considerations. Therefore, there is a need for ongoing research and practical implementation to exploit the advantages of this integrated landscape. (viii) Another possible extension to this is that a comparative study of delivery metrics for each of the Agile frameworks such as Kanban, Scrum, Extreme Programming with Cloud, and DevOps methodologies is a comparative study.

8. CONCLUSION

In this chapter, we introduced the essential concepts of IT Operations and explained various terms such as DevOps, AIOps, MLOps, LLMOps. In addition, disused the evolution of IT operations from the inception of mainframe computer date back to 1950. Explained the role of IT Operations and its functions. In addition, discussed transformation roadmap of IT operations with AIOps. Besides, presented a conceptual view of AIOps and briefly explained. Besides, mentioned the essential components of AIOps and explained its working with the aid of data pipeline and feedback loops. Further, explained how AIOps serves as the foundational pillar for agile, AI-powered project delivery by converting the chaos of real-time operational data into intelligence that informs every stage of the project lifecycle. Furthermore, listed a few potential use cases of AIOps and explained briefly. Additionally, mentioned a few performance indicators to measure the success of AIOps implementation, challenged and benefits of AIOps.

REFERENCES

Abdelzaher, T., Diao, Y., Hellerstein, J. L., Lu, C., & Zhu, X. (2008). Introduction to control theory and its application to computing systems. In *Performance Modeling and Engineering* (pp. 185–215). Springer US. https://link.springer.com/chapter/10.1007/978-0-387-79361-0_7

Cheng, Q., Sahoo, D., Saha, A., Yang, W., Liu, C., Woo, G., . . . Hoi, S. C. (2023). AI for IT operations (AIOps) on Cloud Platforms: Reviews, Opportunities and Challenges. arXiv preprint arXiv:2304.04661.

Chinta, S. (2021). The impact of AI-powered automation on agile project management: Transforming traditional practices. [IRJET]. *International Research Journal of Engineering and Technology*, *8*(10), 2025–2036. DOI: 10.2139/ssrn.5034076

CIO – Wiki. IT Operations (Information Technology Operations). Retrieved 8 Jan 2026 from https://cio-wiki.org/wiki/IT_Operations_(Information_Technology_Operations)

Dam, H. K., Tran, T., Grundy, J., Ghose, A., & Kamei, Y. (2019, May). Towards effective AI-powered agile project management. In *2019 IEEE/ACM 41st international conference on software engineering: new ideas and emerging results (ICSE-NIER)* (pp. 41-44). IEEE. DOI: 10.1109/ICSE-NIER.2019.00019

Dang, Y., Lin, Q., & Huang, P. (2019, May). Aiops: real-world challenges and research innovations. In 2019 IEEE/ACM 41st International Conference on Software Engineering: Companion Proceedings (ICSE-Companion) (pp. 4-5). IEEE. DOI: 10.1109/ICSE-Companion.2019.00023

Davenport, T. H., & Ronanki, R. (2018). Artificial intelligence for the real world. *Harvard Business Review*, *96*(1), 108–116.

De la Cruz Cabello, M., Sales, T. P., & Machado, M. R. (2025). AIOps for log anomaly detection in the era of LLMs: A systematic literature review. *Intelligent Systems with Applications, 200608.* Advance online publication.

Deshpande, M. (2024). Leveraging AI and Machine Learning to Revolutionize IT Service Management. *Journal of Artificial Intelligence & Cloud Computing, 353*, 2-5. DOI: 10.47363/JAICC/2024(3)353

Diao, Y. (2007, July). Using control theory to improve productivity of service systems. In *IEEE International Conference on Services Computing (SCC 2007)* (pp. 435-442). IEEE. DOI: 10.1109/SCC.2007.78

Diaz-De-Arcaya, J., Torre-Bastida, A. I., Zárate, G., Miñón, R., & Almeida, A. (2023). A joint study of the challenges, opportunities, and roadmap of mlops and aiops: A systematic survey. *ACM Computing Surveys*, *56*(4), 1–30.

El Aouni, F., Moumane, K., Idri, A., Najib, M., & Jan, S. U. (2025). A systematic literature review on Agile, Cloud, and DevOps integration: Challenges, benefits. *Information and Software Technology*, *177*, 107569.

Gartner. (2017). I*nnovation Insight for AIOps: Artificial Intelligence for IT Operations*. Gartner Research. Retrieved from https://www.gartner.com/en/research/methodologies/aiops-artificial-intelligence-for-it-operations

Gartner – AIOps. (n.d.). *Information Technology Glossary*. Retrieved Jan 2, 2025, from https://www.gartner.com/en/information-technology/glossary/aiops-artificial-intelligence-operations

Gartner - Hype Cycle. (2020). *Hype Cycle for I and O Automation.* Available: https://automationedge.com/news/gartner-hyper-cycle-for-io-automation-2020-report-mentions-automationedge-as-a-key-vendor-for-intelligent-automation/#. Accessed 2 Mar 2026

Gohring, N. (2024, Jan). *Cost May Be a Bigger Issue for AIOps than Observability*. Retrieved 14 Jan 2024 from https://www.idc.com/getdoc.jsp?containerId=US51608423#:~:text=The%20median%20annual%20spend%20by,observability%20tools%20is%20%241.4%20million

Hua, Y. (2021). A systems approach to effective aiops implementation (Doctoral dissertation, Massachusetts Institute of Technology). hdl.handle.net/1721.1/139422

IBM - AIOps. (n.d.). *What is AIOps?* Retrieved 20 Dec 2025 from https://www.ibm.com/think/topics/aiops

IBM – ITOps. (n.d.). *What is IT operations (ITOps)?* Retrieved 8 Jan 2026 from https://www.ibm.com/think/topics/it-operations

Intel – IT Transformation. (n.d.). *What Is IT Transformation? Overview and Strategy – Intel.* Retrieved 10 Jan 2025, from https://www.intel.com/content/www/us/en/business/resources/it-transformation.html#:~:text=IT%20transformation%20is%20the%20strategic,respond%20quickly%20to%20ecosystem%20changes

Intelligence, M. (n.d.). *IT Operations Management (ITOM) Market Size & Share Analysis - Growth Trends & Forecast* (2025 - 2030). https://www.mordorintelligence.com/industry-reports/it-operations-management-market#:~:text=The%20IT%20Operations%20Management%20Market,integration%20of%20AI%20and%20automation

Kalluri, R. (September 2025). Socio-Technical System Challenges in The Era of Artificial Intelligence: A Comprehensive Analysis. *International Journal of Business & Management Studies*, *6*(9). 75-91. DOI: 10.56734/ijbms.v6n9a8

Kim, G., Humble, J., Debois, P., Willis, J., & Forsgren, N. (2021). *The DevOps handbook: How to create world-class agility, reliability, & security in technology organizations.* It Revolution. IT Revolution Press., DOI: 10.5555/3044729

Kolt, N., Shur-Ofry, M., & Cohen, R. (2025). Lessons from complex systems science for AI governance. *Patterns*, *6*(8), 2025, 101341, ISSN 2666-3899,

Kontogiannis, K., Grigoriou, M., Brealey, C., & Giammaria, A. (2021, November). Compliance by design: software analytics and aiops. In *Proceedings of the 31st Annual International Conference on Computer Science and Software Engineering* (pp. 294-295). https://dl.acm.org/doi/abs/10.5555/3507788.3507847

Kumar, S. (2023). Data silos a roadblock for AIOps. *International Journal for Research Trends and Innovation.* *9*(1). ISSN: 2456-3315. 33-39. arXiv preprint DOI: 10.5281/zenodo.10471800

Maya, G. (2021 Jun 28). *Lists 26 ITIL Processes & 4 ITIL Functions.* Retrieved Jan 5, 2005, from https://www.itsm-docs.com/en-in/blogs/itil-concepts/itsm-processes-functions#:~:text=The%20function%20is%20a%20team,Technical%20Management%2C%20and%20Operations%20Management

Notaro, P., Cardoso, J., & Gerndt, M. (2021). A Survey of AIOps Methods for Failure Management. *ACM Trans. Intell. Syst. Technol.* *12*, 6, Article 81 (December 2021), 45 pages. DOI: 10.1145/3483424

Palani, H. K., Shelke, R., & Pagi, S. AIOps with Multi Cloud (June 8, 2023). Available at *SSRN*: https://ssrn.com/abstract=4473251 or , from https://papers.ssrn.com/sol3/papers.cfm?abstract_id=4473251DOI: 10.2139/ssrn.4473251

Pandey, B. K. (2023). AI-Based Automation Frameworks for IT Operations in a Digitally Transformed Environment. Distributed Learning and Broad Applications in Scientific Research, Annual, 9. https://ssrn.com/abstract=5101691

Patel, M., & Yakkundi, A. (2020). *AIOps: Real-World Use Cases and Applications.* Apress. DOI: 10.1109/ICSE-Companion.2019.00023

Portman, D. G. (2020). *Are you an elite DevOps performer? Find out with the four keys project.*

Potts, W. C., & Carver, C. (2024, May). Best practices implementing aiops in large organizations. In *2024 International Conference on Smart Applications, Communications and Networking (SmartNets)* (pp. 1-5). IEEE. DOI: 10.1109/SmartNets61466.2024.10577643

Prasad, P., & Rich, C. (2018). *Market guide for AIOps platforms*. Retrieved March, 12(2020), 2-9. https://cloudaims.co.in/wp-content/uploads/2021/02/Market-Guide-for-AIOps-Platforms-Gartner-Reprint-1.pdf. Gartner ID: G00340492

Rakova, B., Yang, J., Cramer, H., & Chowdhury, R. (2021). Where responsible AI meets reality: Practitioner perspectives on enablers for shifting organizational practices. *Proceedings of the ACM on Human-Computer Interaction*, 5(CSCW1), 1-23.DOI: 10.1145/3449081

Remil, Y., Bendimerad, A., Mathonat, R., & Kaytoue, M. (2024). Aiops solutions for incident management: Technical guidelines and a comprehensive literature review. arXiv preprint /arXiv.2404.01363DOI: 10.48550

Sami, M. A., Rehman, A., Ahmad, Z., & Bano, N. (2025). *Explainable AIOps: A Deep Survey on Trust worthy and Transparent AI in Cloud-Scale DevOps Automation. Spectrum of Engineering Sciences.*

Sandén, T. (2024). U*nveiling Anomaly Detection: Navigating Cultural Shifts and Model Dynamics in AIOps Implementations*. https://www.diva-portal.org/smash/get/diva2:1878820/FULLTEXT01.pdf

Sarma, A. D. N. (2021). A generic architecture for alert notification and monitoring system based on event processing framework. *International Journal of Business Performance Management*, *22*(4), 426–442. DOI: 10.1504/IJBPM.2021.118612

Sekar, A. (2025). AIOps: Transforming Management of Large-Scale Distributed Systems. *European Journal of Computer Science and Information Technology*, *13*(5), 1–17.

Shen, S., Zhang, J., Huang, D., & Xiao, J. (2020, August). Evolving from traditional systems to AIOps: design, implementation and measurements. In *2020 IEEE International Conference on Advances in Electrical Engineering and Computer Applications (AEECA)* (pp. 276-280). IEEE. DOI: 10.1109/AEECA49918.2020.9213650

Singh, M. (2025). Enhancing site reliability engineering through AIOps: A framework for next-generation IT operations. *Asian Journal of Research in Computer Science*, *18*(4), 10–9734. https://journalajrcos.com/index.php/AJRCOS/article/view/619. DOI: 10.9734/ajrcos/2025/v18i4619

Sokol, K., Santos-Rodriguez, R., & Flach, P. (2022). Fat Forensics: A Python toolbox for algorithmic fairness, accountability and transparency. *Software Impacts*, *14*, 100406. DOI: 10.1016/j.simpa.2022.100406

Sreerangapuri, A. (2021). IT Service Management Transformation: Implementing AIOps for Proactive Service Delivery. *NeuroQuantology: An Interdisciplinary Journal of Neuroscience and Quantum Physics*, *19*(10). Advance online publication. DOI: 10.48047/nq.2021.19.10.NQ21220

Vitui, A., & Chen, T. (2025). Empowering AIOps: Leveraging Large Language Models for IT Operations Management. In *Companion Proceedings of the 33rd ACM Symposium on the Foundations of Software Engineering* (FSE '25), June 23–27, 2025, Trondheim, Norway. ACM, New York, NY, USA ArXiv, abs/2501.12461. DOI: 10.48550/arXiv.2501.12461

Zadeh, E. K., Khoulenjani, A. B., & Safaei, M. (2024). Integrating AI for agile Project Management: Innovations, challenges, and benefits. [IJIECM]. *International Journal of Industrial Engineering and Construction Management*, *1*(2), 1–10. https://www.ijiecm.com/index.php/ijiecm/article/view/1#

Zhang, L., Jia, T., Jia, M., Wu, Y., Liu, A., Yang, Y., & Li, Y. (2025). A survey of aiops in the era of large language models. ACM Computing Surveys, 58(2), 1-35. .

Ziolkowski, P. (2023). Computational complexity and its influence on predictive capabilities of machine learning models for concrete mix design. *Materials (Basel)*, *16*(17), 5956. DOI: 10.3390/ma16175956

KEY TERMS AND DEFINITIONS

AIOps –: The term AIOps stands 'AI for IT Operations'. In simple terms applications of Artificial Intelligence to IT Operations. The term AIOps was coined by Gartner, research and consulting services firm, date back to 1970. In 2020s, AIOps has been evolved as a new sub filed of IT Operations. Additionally, AIOps leverages AI, Big data, Data Analytics and Machine Learning to provide insight and enable a higher level of automation for the management tasks that modern technology infrastructure and software require.

Apps Management: - Application management is the process of managing the development, deployment, and maintenance of applications and software. The applications may be either one or more of the following which includes mainframe, client server, web, and mobile.

Cloud operations (CloudOps) –: It is a specialization focused on managing, optimizing, and securing cloud infrastructure, whether public, private, or hybrid.

DevOps: - It is a collaboration between both development team and operations teams in terms of, communication, collaboration and integration. It eliminates the challenges to the SDLC like slower deployment and release cycles, automation of routine tasks there by its problems the efforts of development and release operations of the software.

IT Operations Management (ITOM) - IT operations management (ITOM) is a broader discipline that often encompasses ITOps but extends to all processes and technologies required to manage IT services. While ITOps includes the *people* **and their** *roles***:** ITOM refers to the *methods* they use to stay efficient.

ITOps vs. IT Support: ITOps manages the back-end systems (infrastructure), whereas IT Support handles front-end user issues (help desk tickets)

LLMOps: - Large Language Model Ops, which focuses on managing and optimizing large language models. Owing to their size, complexity, and the ethical considerations surrounding their deployment, these models require unique operational approaches. The goal is to ensure these models are accurate, avoid harmful outputs, and use resources more efficiently.

MLOps: - Machine Learning Operations (MLOps) is a framework that streamlines the machine learning lifecycle for build, deploy, and manage machine learning models easily. The goal of MLOps is to automate and scale the end-to-end ML pipeline, from data management to model deployment and monitoring. Further, it allows for continuous model updates, versioning, and testing, enabling models to remain relevant and accurate over time.

Signal-to-Noise Ratio: In the context of alerting, the proportion of actionable alerts (signal) compared to non-actionable alerts (noise).

Chapter 3
AI-Augmented Strategic Management Integrating Portfolio Planning, Roadmapping, and OKR Systems

Inayatul Janah
http://orcid.org/0009-0008-0868-3906
Universitas Esa Unggul, Indonesia

Binastya Anggara Sekti
http://orcid.org/0000-0001-5489-4888
Universitas Esa Unggul, Indonesia

ABSTRACT

This chapter explores the integration of artificial intelligence into strategic portfolio management, roadmapping, and OKR alignment as a fundamental transformation in how organizations plan and execute strategy in the digital era. It introduces the AI-Augmented Strategic Loop (AISL) framework, which enables continuous sensing, analysis, decision-making, and learning across dynamic business environments. By combining strategic management theory, agile systems thinking, and AI decision augmentation, the chapter demonstrates how intelligent systems enhance adaptability, transparency, and strategic coherence. It further discusses the ethical, organizational, and technical considerations necessary for responsible implementation, including governance, data integrity, and human oversight. Ultimately, this chapter

DOI: 10.4018/979-8-3373-6851-1.ch003

positions AI as a meta-layer of intelligence that transforms strategic management from static planning into a continuous, learning-oriented process for sustainable organizational performance.

1. INTRODUCTION

In this era defined by digital transformation, the contemporary business environment is characterized by an unprecedented pace of change, forcing organizations to fundamentally reframe their approach to strategy and execution. The pressure to maintain a competitive advantage now depends on a triad of critical capabilities that enable rapid pivots, data-driven decision-making that cuts through the noise to reveal signals, and the synchronization of long-term strategic ambitions that are sustainable and seamless with day-to-day execution. Traditional strategic management frameworks were meant for a more stable and predictable world of some time, but this new reality reveals that there are still many limitations. Although techniques such as annual portfolio reviews and multi-year roadmaps have provided a clear structure, these methods are increasingly inadequate. It often falters because it relies on static historical data, priority processes that are vulnerable to political and subjective judgments of the organization, and inherent structural inertia that prevents rapid adaptation to market changes, technological advancements, and ever-increasing customer expectations. Recent studies show that effective digital transformation requires the systematic integration of strategic roadmaps and organizational readiness assessments to maintain adaptability in the Industrial era (Ansari et al., 2025). At the same time, data-driven approach methods of portfolio planning are becoming essential to assist decision-makers in navigating complex and dynamic environments with greater precision and objectivity (Bodendorf, 2025).

Table 1. Paradigm Shift: Traditional vs. AI-Augmented Strategic Management (Tong et al., 2025)

Characteristic	Cycles	Data	Bias	Integration	Reporting
Traditional	Static & Annual	Historical Data	Subjective Bias	Fragmented (Portofolio, Roadmap, OKR)	Reactive Reporting
AI-Augmented	Dynamic & Continuous	Predictive & Forward-Looking	Data-Driven	Integrated (AISL)	Proaktive Orchestration

Table 1 summarizes the key dimensions of AI-enabled strategic management across portfolio management, roadmap planning, and OKR alignment. This table shows how artificial intelligence is transforming management practices that were previously static, performed periodically, and dependent on manual processes, into a more dynamic, predictive, and continuous learning system. By comparing traditional approaches and AI-powered approaches, Table 1 helps readers clearly understand the fundamental changes brought about by artificial intelligence-based strategic systems (Tong et al., 2025)

In the context of increasing complexity, the advent of Artificial Intelligence (AI) marks a real shift in strategic thinking, introducing a new class of predictive, adaptive and intelligent systems for organizational planning and alignment. AI-powered mechanisms can evolve in real time, transforming the nature of portfolio management from a reactive administrative function that focuses primarily on tracking and reporting to a proactive strategic capability that can anticipate and shape an outcome. This transformation is supported by various advanced technologies that are capable. Machine learning algorithms analyze large multi-dimensional data sets to identify patterns, predict project outcomes, and forecast market trends, while natural language processing can parse unstructured data from customer feedback, competitor announcements, and internal communications to provide a more holistic view of the strategic landscape (Sekti, 2025a). The advanced optimization algorithm can then model countless portfolio scenarios, balancing risk, resource constraints, and potential value to recommend more optimal investment decisions. As shown by (Bouzeria et al., 2026), local search-based optimization methods are highly effective in addressing the problem of cardinality-constrained portfolio selection, this can improve the ability of AI systems to efficiently explore large decision spaces under real-world challenges. In addition to the research of (Chou & Pham, 2025) emphasizing the role of ensemble learning-based multi-objective optimization in portfolio preselection and investment decision support, they also emphasize on how hybrid AI models can significantly improve prediction accuracy and portfolio performance. Overall, these advancements move decision-making processes beyond reliance on managerial intuition and limited data visibility, providing a comprehensive, evidence-based foundation for the most important strategies.

This intelligence also extends to strategic roadmapping, changing it from a static planning artifact to a dynamic tool that is always changing. AI-enhanced roadmaps allow businesses to quickly execute scenario studies and modify strategic trajectories in response to new uncertainties by integrating real-time internal performance metrics and external environmental signals. Such adaptive roadmapping approaches enhance organizational resilience and strategic responsiveness, supporting more informed leadership decision-making in complex and interconnected environments (Ansari et al., 2025; Kayabay et al., 2024). In a similar vein, adding AI-driven alignment mechanisms to the Goals and Key Results (OKR) framework increases its efficacy. Traditional OKR implementations frequently struggle to maintain constant alignment between high-level objectives and operational actions, despite being highly acknowledged for fostering transparency and strategic focus. In order to overcome this difficulty, AI continuously analyzes execution data and semantic links between goals, initiatives, and outcomes. This allows for early misalignment detection and strengthens a closed-loop alignment process. This dynamic monitoring capacity reduces common implementation issues found in recent research and enhances the practical application of OKR principles (Misslisch et al., 2026; Silva & Santos, 2023).

Therefore, this chapter lays the theoretical groundwork for an integrated AI-driven strategic operating model that integrates dynamic OKR alignment, adaptive strategic roadmapping, and intelligent portfolio planning. It contends that AI-enabled automation radically transforms the theory and practice of strategic management rather than just gradually improving current strategic procedures. Organizations can achieve better clarity, agility, and a sustained competitive edge in increasingly complex settings by moving from reactive adaptation to proactive orchestration of their future through the integration of intelligence across strategic levels (Koudriachov et al., 2025).

2. THEORETICAL FOUNDATIONS

The integration of artificial intelligence into strategic portfolio management and alignment of OKRs is not just a technological improvement but a conceptual evolution, based on the convergence and expansion of several established theoretical domains. The theoretical basis for this integrated model is substantially drawn from three main intellectual streams: strategic management theory, agile systems theory, and emerging areas of artificial intelligence decision-making. This synthesis of disciplines provides a robust framework for understanding how intelligent systems can transform the strategic execution of rigid bureaucratic processes into dynamic, learning-oriented capabilities (Chakrabarti et al., 2025; Mohamed Noor et al., 2025; Romao et al., 2026).

From the perspective of classical and modern strategic management theory, portfolio planning is essentially a mechanism for resource allocation and strategic coherence, designed to ensure that an organization's limited capital and human resources are invested in initiatives that directly advance its mission and competitive position. Utilizability demonstrates that dynamic leadership, strategic resource sharing, and proactive risk management are critical components of these mechanisms to address issues and increase organizational resilience (Mohamed Noor et al., 2025). These theories, from Ansoff's on strategic planning to Porter's on competitive advantage, are closely aligned. However, the basic assumptions of conventional planning cycles such as stability and predictability are often no longer relevant in a highly variable, uncertain, complex, and ambiguous (VUCA) environment. These models, many characterized by their annual or quarterly rhythms, fail to capture the speed and granularity of the environmental shifts that occur so quickly, that they can lead to strategic deviations in which the portfolio becomes detached from market reality. This creates a critical theoretical gap to the need for a planning system that maintains the deliberate coherence of strategic management while absorbing the market dynamics demanded by the modern market, which precisely requires a more dynamic, adaptive, and responsive approach to change.

Agile systems theory, which is now reinforced by artificial intelligence, aims to fill this gap. Agile theory, which comes from software development and complex adaptive systems thinking, emphasizes repeatable value delivery, adaptation, and decentralized decision-making. This approach focuses on responding to change rather than following a pre-established plan, building flexibility into the core of the execution process. These principles are evolving beyond team-level methodologies toward organization-scale adaptive strategy systems when combined with machine learning. This is demonstrated by systematic research on agile management for machine learning implementation (Romao et al., 2026). Sensing automation and continuous learning are the theoretical contributions of AI here. By using data-driven use case planning and assessment approaches, AI systems can process large amounts of internal and external data. This allows for dynamic reprioritization states. It demonstrates a theoretical shift from agile execution to adaptive strategies, the ability to change the way work is done, and the ability to change what is done in real-time (Bodendorf, 2025).

The interaction between human and machine intelligence is officially based on the idea framework of AI decision augmentation, which builds on the long-standing concept of sociotechnical symbiosis. This frame of thinking rejects the simple human-to-machine dichotomy in favor of a collaborative model that seeks an optimal balance between human judgment and machine intelligence. The core premise is that instead of replacing human strategists, AI acts as a powerful aggrandizing agent, as demonstrated in a data-driven approach to AI portfolio management that enhances, rather than replaces, human decision-making(Bodendorf, 2025). It reinforces the human outlook by running complex simulations and predictive models, projecting outcomes based on scenarios with many interacting factors. In addition, it expands human perception by detecting weak signals from noisy datasets such as emerging market trends or nascent competition threats long before they become apparent through conventional analysis. Within this additional framework, portfolio planning is theoretically reconceptualized periodically into a system of continuous learning and optimization.

Exploratory innovation the ability of organizations to explore new technologies, business models, and management practices to create value becomes crucial in the VUCA environment to maintain competitiveness and long-term sustainability (Zhang et al., 2025). In the context of AI-based strategic management, exploratory innovation serves as a driver as well as a beneficiary of intelligent systems. AI strengthens innovation by detecting weak signals from complex data such as hidden trends and unmet customer needs, in line with strategic sensing mechanisms in the AI-Augmented Strategic Loop (AISL). Instead, exploratory innovations enrich the learning capabilities of AI systems through new streams of data, hypotheses, and feedback that continuously improve prediction accuracy and decision-making quality. In addition, (Zhang et al., 2025) emphasize that technological capabilities and the level of environmental uncertainty together affect how effectively exploratory innovations can be implemented. In this context, AI acts as a dynamic capability that helps organizations transform uncertainty into more structured and usable knowledge. Through reinforcement learning and generative modeling, companies can simulate various possibilities of the future and test different directions of development in virtual environments. In this way, the risks and costs that usually arise in the experimental process can be significantly reduced. This approach also marks a shift from reactive risk management to more proactive opportunity management in line with agile and adaptive strategy principles. In practical terms, exploratory innovations powered by AI-driven portfolio intelligence are changing the way organizations run strategic management: from one that was focused solely on efficiency and exploitation, to one that is oriented towards continuous discovery and innovation. As the pressure on economic, social, and environmental sustainability aspects grows, organizations' ability to blend exploratory innovation with AI-based decision-making systems not only determines their ability to adapt, but also reflects their ethical and ecological responsibilities. Thus, the integration of exploratory innovation and AI-based strategic management creates a mutually reinforcing model in which continuous learning, forward-looking technology, and sustainable value creation become a mutually supportive unit (Zhang et al., 2025).

Thus, the theoretical synthesis proves on the placement of AI as a meta-layer of intelligence that enters the strategic management infrastructure rather than just a tool. This meta layer enhances the core attributes of effective governance: reinforcing responsiveness by closing the feedback loop between external changes and internal priorities at an unprecedented pace that improves precision by replacing subjective estimates with data-driven estimates of probability and impact, and encourages radical transparency, a critically examined principle in ethical AI frameworks, which emphasizes the need for clear reasoning in automated decision-making to build compliance and trust. Therefore, the theoretical foundation establishes that AI-assisted portfolios and OKR systems represent a new paradigm in strategic management, where dynamic resource allocation and effort alignment are continuously informed, tested, and refined by the human intelligence of symbiotic machines (Chakrabarti et al., 2025).

3. AI IN STRATEGIC PORTFOLIO MANAGEMENT

Incorporating artificial intelligence into strategic portfolio management is a major shift from rigid and complex administrative tasks to a moving machine and optimizing the value of the Company. AI-assisted strategic portfolio management integrates advanced analytics, advanced optimization models, and predictive intelligence to radically improve the accuracy, agility, and objectivity of how initiatives are selected, prioritized, and balanced across the organization. These features demonstrate the complimentary functions of artificial intelligence as a more comprehensive paradigm for automation and decision assistance and machine learning as a data-driven predictive mechanism (Sekti, 2025). The portfolio becomes a dynamic investment system that continuously learns from data and adapts to optimize strategic value in complex and changing contexts, as opposed to operating as a static list of projects (Bodendorf, 2025; Chou & Pham, 2025). At the heart of this transformation is predictive portfolio intelligence. Traditional portfolio management often relies on backward-looking metrics and subjective business cases. In contrast, AI algorithms, specifically supervised learning and regression models, analyze large and varied data sets to estimate future outcomes. This dataset includes in-depth historical project performance data such as comparisons between actual and planned ROI, schedule compliance levels, and resource consumption patterns. In addition, the data also includes real-time market information such as competitor activities, changes in market share, and new policies or regulations, as well as internal operational indicators such as the speed of teamwork, the rate of errors or defects, and the utilization of organizational capacity. These models can predict with measurable confidence which projects are most likely to deliver strategic value, customer impact, or financial returns by finding complex non-linear patterns in this data. In addition, there are more sophisticated methods such as reinforcement learning that can simulate thousands of potential portfolio configurations under various constraints such as budget cuts, unexpected resource shortages, or new market opportunities to dynamically identify optimal resource allocation. It moves portfolio optimization from periodic manual exercises to continuous automated processes to find the most valuable initiative configurations. The predictive capabilities of computers in various financial applications, such as credit scoring, fraud detection, portfolio management, and risk assessment, have improved significantly as a result of the merger of artificial intelligence (AI) and machine learning (ML) algorithms, demonstrating the potential of data-driven intelligence transformation in strategic decision-making (Khan et al., 2025).

Figure 1. The Cognitive Portfolio Loop: From Data to Dynamic Decision-Making Chou & Pham, 2025).

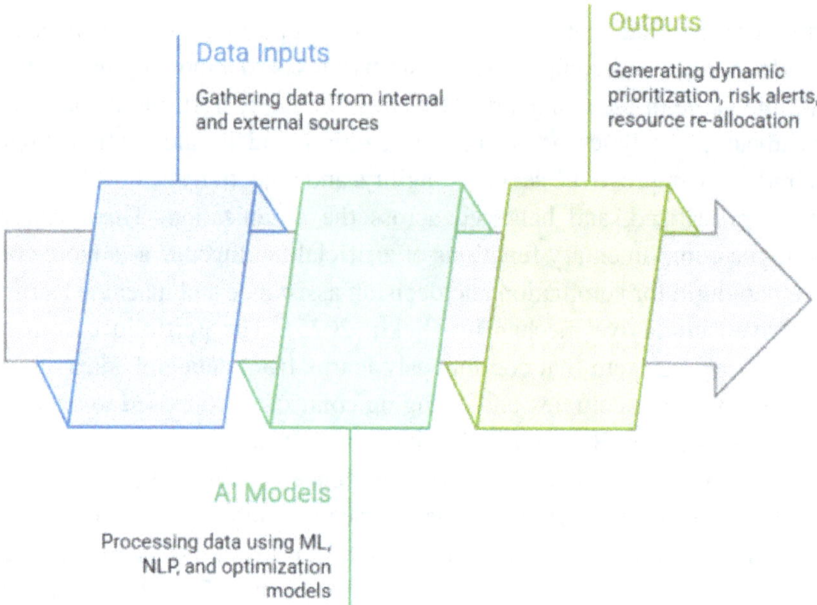

Figure 1 illustrates the conceptual integration of artificial intelligence across strategic portfolio management, roadmap planning, and OKR alignment. The figure demonstrates how AI acts as a connective layer that enables continuous information flow between strategic intent and operational execution. This visualization reinforces the argument that AI does not function as an isolated tool, but as an enabling infrastructure that aligns decision-making, planning, and performance measurement into a coherent strategic system (Chou & Pham, 2025).

A critical and often overlooked function of AI in this domain is its role as a systematic counterweight to inherent human cognitive biases. Portfolio decisions are often influenced by the political dynamics of the organization, the tendency to give priority to the most dominant party in conveying needs, overestimation of projects supported by influential sponsors, or excessive confidence from management. AI-based models are, essentially, introducing a layer of objective, evidence-based analysis that challenges this subjective influence. By implementing consistent data-driven criteria across all initiatives, AI ensures that projects are prioritized based on predicted benefits over persuasive winners. The use of Explainable AI (XAI) frameworks is particularly important here as they not only provide recommendations but also articulate specific data points and reasons behind them for example, highlighting that suppose Project A is prioritized due to its strong correlation with improved key customer satisfaction metrics and predicted lower predicted resource conflicts. This transparency allows human decision-makers to engage in meaningful dialogue with AI, understand its logic and build trust in data-driven conclusions, thereby reducing subjective distortions and encouraging more rational and fair governance processes. However, there is not much information about how these bias mitigation algorithms work in the real world within thc spccific domain of strategic portfolio management. However, several articles have written about the possibility that AI can serve as a bias mitigation tool (Lee et al., 2026).

AI enables continuous value alignment, making the concept of static annual portfolio planning even more irrelevant. In traditional approaches, the linkage between portfolios and strategic objectives is typically only validated during the planning cycle and quickly loses relevance as organizational realities change. In contrast, AI-driven systems maintain a vibrant and dynamic relationship between the organization's portfolio and strategic compass that is realized through the framework of Objectives and Key Results (OKRs). In addition, the scheme incorporates an automated investment model intended to optimize returns through dynamic portfolio management and prioritize thorough short-term decision-making (Chou et al., 2025). The model leverages advanced methodologies such as machine learning, natural language processing (NLP), and deep learning to strengthen the system's analytical capabilities as well as adaptive responses to environmental changes. With a constantly updated automated data stream from development tools, financial systems, and market analytics, decision-makers can quickly find new initiatives that are more strategically relevant or identify projects that no longer support key outcomes. This continuous process of sensing, reasoning, and adapting is the basis of the Cognitive Portfolio Loop (CPL), a self-corrective cycle in which the portfolio continuously detects internal and external changes, assesses their impact on strategic goals with the help of AI models, and dynamically adjusts project priorities, funding, and resources. The results obtained are usually in the form of a living portfolio, always in line with the strategic direction and current environmental realities, thus ensuring that the organization's investment is always directed to the results that have the most use value (Misslisch et al., 2026).

4. AI-ASSISTED ROADMAPPING AND SCENARIO PLANNING

Traditional roadmaps have long served as an important strategic tool, providing a visual representation of how an organization's capabilities, technologies, and product initiatives are projected to evolve over the planned time. This roadmap plays an important role in communicating the vision and coordinating cross-departmental efforts, especially in structured digital transformation efforts as discussed in the strategic roadmap framework (Ansari et al., 2025). However, its static nature that is usually presented in the form of slide decks or spreadsheets makes it limited and less flexible to deal with a dynamic business environment, full of unexpected changes and emerging opportunities. They quickly become artifacts of past assumptions rather than guides for future actions, as they cannot incorporate new learning or respond to unexpected disruptions in real time. Artificial Intelligence is poised to redefine this practice, transforming the roadmap from a fixed document into a dynamic and living system that continuously learns from its environment, predicts potential futures, and adjusts its trajectory accordingly. This evolution is demonstrated by data-science-based roadmaps used for strategic artificial intelligence planning in network organizations and responsive scenario-based approaches that use system dynamics to create more adaptive roadmaps (Kayabay et al., 2024). Move from static representations to produce truly intelligent strategic planning tools (Tansurat & Gerdsri, 2024).

The basis of this intelligent roadmapping system is its ability to generate automatically and maintain its content dynamically. Leveraging advanced Natural Language Processing (NLP) models, AI systems can absorb and interpret a wide array of unstructured strategic inputs, including company vision statements, market analyst reports, competitor announcements, and internal project status updates. By parsing this information, AI can identify key themes, proposed features, and strategic objectives, compiling them into a coherent draft initial roadmap. This is further enriched by a knowledge graph that depicts the complex relationships and dependencies between various initiatives, teams, and elements of technology. Most importantly, it's not a generation. The AI-powered roadmap connects to an automated data pipeline, which provides it with a real-time flow of information. This can include things like breaching competitive intelligence, changing customer feelings from a support ticket, or sending an initial risk signal from the development pipeline. This allows roadmaps to automatically adjust timelines, reprioritize features, and flag potential dependency conflicts without requiring time-consuming manual overhauls. The integration of data-based and adaptive mechanisms is in line with the data-science-based technology roadmap approach that emphasizes on how AI can transform strategic planning into a process of continuous self-learning and evolution (Kayabay et al., 2024).

Beyond mere maintenance, AI elevates roadmaps into tools for strategic foresight through powerful scenario simulation. Data-driven roadmaps have evolved from conventional business and market analysis to intelligent frameworks that use advanced deep learning techniques to predict future trends (Kim et al., 2025).

Generative AI as well as other probabilistic modeling methods further enhance this capability by allowing leaders to explore a broader landscape of potential futures. Instead of relying solely on simple trend analysis to support decision-making, modern AI systems can even generate technology roadmaps independently, using generative models to forecast innovations and strategic shifts. Systems can use different assumptions to generate and visualize various "what-if" scenarios rather than using a single deterministic path. For example, leaders can simulate the impact of disruptive new technologies entering the market, a sudden 20% budget cut, or a change in regulatory policy. The AI simulation engine doesn't just present this as an abstract idea, it models its cascading effects on the entire roadmap, measuring potential delays, resource shortages, and impacts on key performance indicators. The approach transforms scenario planning from a rare high-level workshop exercise to an iterative data-driven process, allowing organizations to test their strategies and formulate contingency plans for a variety of sensible futures. This AI-augmented roadmap not only improves adaptability but also creates a feedback-based system where data continuously refines the forward-looking strategically (Bouzeria et al., 2026).

Ultimately, AI-driven roadmaps shift their basic goals from static outcomes to dynamic strategic dialogue platforms. Its value lies not in its predictive perfection but in its ability to facilitate precise conversations and enable quick and targeted decision-making. By providing an ever-updated, centralized view of strategic trajectories and their potential alternatives, it empowers leaders to debate trade-offs with concrete data, test strategic hypotheses, and make resource allocation decisions based on real-time strategic fitness of how well the initiative aligns with current goals and market conditions rather than on adherence to a rigid and predetermined set of milestones. This method offers a useful perspective on sustainable development in Lithuanian coastal cities. This method allows policymakers to leverage similar principles to increase transparency and public trust, lead initiatives, and improve communication between stakeholders through digital platforms such as regional stakeholder forums (Grigoliene et al., 2025). It fosters a culture of adaptive execution, where organizations or in the context of the public sector, municipal governance structures can rotate with confidence, flexibly reallocating resources to the most promising opportunities as they arise, thus embedding agility directly into the strategic planning structure.

5. AI-DRIVEN OKR ALIGNMENT AND PERFORMANCE ANALYTICS

As an effective tool for improving focus, coordination, and transparency, the Goals and Key Results Framework (OKRs) have been widely used by organizations around the world. Its implementation in various industries has been thoroughly documented in the academic literature (Silva & Santos, 2023). Despite its theoretical beauty, the practical implementation of OKRs often falters, suffering from a critical disconnect between ambitious goals and the day-to-day work of strategic portfolios, a phenomenon thoroughly examined by (Misslisch et al., 2026), who found major obstacles to effective implementation of OKRs in organizational practice. This gap manifests as Key results that are manually tracked and rarely updated and have no direct linkage to operational data, making them a lagging indicator rather than an actionable guide. Artificial Intelligence is poised to address this gap, introducing a new framework of thinking in which OKRs become dynamic, intelligently managed assets. This is in line with the emerging trend of data-driven methodological approaches in strategic management, exemplified by Bodendorf's work (Bodendorf, 2025) on AI portfolio management, which shows how intelligent systems can improve decision-making processes. Artificial intelligence systems semantically interpret strategic intent, evaluate progress across multiple data sources, and link results to true business value. It transforms OKRs from static reporting tools into the central nervous system of an organization's execution, addressing implementation issues facing current OKR research (Misslisch et al., 2026).

One of the main challenges in the implementation of large-scale OKRs is to always ensure semantic coherence and strategic alignment across hundreds or thousands of objectives, the complexity of which becomes particularly evident when examining the scalability issues documented in a comprehensive study of the challenges of OKR implementation (Misslisch et al., 2026). Using advanced Natural Language Processing (NLP) and vector-based semantic models, computational approaches that have demonstrated its remarkable ability to extract meaningful patterns from unstructured text data, as evidenced by its successful application in explainable AI systems across multiple domains, AI systems can perform in-depth linguistic analysis of OKR textual content to understand their intrinsic meaning and relationships (Khan et al., 2025). This advanced analysis goes far beyond simple keyword matching. the AI interprets in the scope of specific meanings and strategic intentions to create a life strategy graph that dynamically represents the organization's priorities. This intelligent mapping capability allows the system to automatically connect team-level OKRs to program-level initiatives and ultimately to the company's strategic goals, resulting in a reliable chain of alignment across the organization. In addition, AI can proactively identify and flag critical issues of significant strategic deviations, such as redundant OKRs across different departments that inefficiently duplicate resources, conflicting goals that create internal competition and pull organizations in opposite directions, or OKRs that have no relationship to any top-level goals of any systemic alignment issues that have been consistently identified as The main obstacle to the effective implementation of OKRs is empirical research on organizational goal-setting frameworks (Silva & Santos, 2023). This automated semantic audit process substantially transforms strategic governance by ensuring that each team's efforts are not only visible but also systematically and efficiently contribute to a unified strategic direction, maximizing organizational alignment.

Traditional OKR tracking is inherently retrospective, informing leaders of successes and failures that can occur only after a cycle concludes problems that have been consistently found in studies examining the challenges of traditional performance management systems (Misslisch et al., 2026). AI is revolutionizing this paradigm through predictive progress tracking, leveraging computational approaches that have shown significant potential in estimating organizational outcomes. By applying a supervised learning model similar to that successfully used in AI-based portfolio management systems to predict project outcomes and resource needs before the reporting period ends, AI systems can forecast the likelihood of achieving all important outcomes (Bodendorf, 2025). This advanced model analyzes a rich set of multidimensional inputs, including historical performance patterns on similar key outcomes, real-time resource allocation and availability metrics, indicators of current progress velocity, and diverse contextual signals such as shifts in market demand or internal project risks. These comprehensive data integration and analysis capabilities are a significant advancement beyond traditional monitoring approaches, allowing for a more nuanced understanding of the dynamics of progress. When a system predicts with a high degree of confidence that a key outcome is trending off track, it triggers an intelligent early warning system, empowering managers and teams to intervene proactively rather than reactively. This is a major shift in the management paradigm: from passive quarterly review to active, real-time management. This shift is in line with agile management principles for machine learning systems examined in (Romao et al., 2026). This approach allows for timely reallocation of efforts, strategic adjustments of tactics, or even revision of the objectives themselves in response to new information, thus maximizing the organization's adaptive potential and creating a more responsive and resilient strategic execution framework

Artificial intelligence-based OKR systems have advanced far beyond conventional quantitative metrics to provide in-depth behavioral and organizational insights, illuminating the human aspects underlying performance outcomes. By systematically integrating performance analytics with highly carefully disguised behavioral data capturing nuanced patterns such as communication dynamics across collaboration tools, meeting frequency and participation quality, and AI cross-team collaboration metrics can uncover complex human dynamics that drive exceptional performance or create unexpected bottlenecks. Starting from sophisticated pattern recognition, the system is able to identify meaningful correlations between certain collaborative behaviors and the successful achievement of ambitious stretch goals, or proactively flag teams operating in organizational silos, potentially jeopardizing the success of interdependent key outcomes (Silva & Santos, 2023). This multi-dimensional perspective fundamentally transforms OKR systems from performance management dashboards into dynamic and continuous organizational learning ecosystems that can be customized and evolve with the organization (Misslisch et al., 2026). Most importantly, this approach gives organizational leaders a direct and real-time view of the real state of their company. With these insights, they can strategically build and maintain high-performing teams, improve communication flows, and foster a data-driven work culture. In an environment like this, quantitative metrics and behavioral insights help not only determine what the organization wants to achieve, but also how teams can work in harmony and effectively to realize ambitious strategic goals (Romao et al., 2026).

6. INTEGRATED FRAMEWORK: AI-AUGMENTED PORTFOLIO ROADMAP OKR LOOP

The AI Augmented Strategic Loop (AISL) is a major advance in the way contemporary organizations create, implement, and continue to transform their strategies. This results in a broad, smart, and recursive framework that easily integrates OKR alignment, path mapping, and portfolio management into a single cognitive ecosystem. This framework applies the principles of how the Human-AI Symbiosis Theory (HAIST), which has a mutual relationship between human intelligence and artificial systems in complex organizational contexts (Morello & Chick, 2025). This integration process includes not only technological improvements in existing practices but also the reconceptualization of strategic management, this will transform it from a rigid network to a dynamic and responsive intelligence network. Recent research findings by (Abras et al., 2025) suggest that incorporating RAG into decision support systems can significantly reduce complexity in strategic decision-making, providing a technological foundation for such an integrated cognitive ecosystem. AISL serves as the company's strategic nervous system, continuously sensing the environment, analyzing dynamic signals, deciding on optimal actions, operationalizing those decisions instantly across the system, and learning from each outcome. The basis is the concept of an always-on strategy, which is a way of thinking in which the processes of observing, making decisions, and acting are not carried out sequentially, but rather take place simultaneously and continuously, directly connected to each other in real time. The initial step of the process starts with sensory functions, where a distributed network of AI agents serves as an organizational perception tool. These agencies continue to collect a wealth of diverse data from different layers of the company and its environment. Internal data sources can include project-level metrics consisting of task completion rates, achievement compliance, quality scores, and operational indicators consisting of system uptime, resource utilization, cost performance, as well as human-centric insights such as employee sentiment, teamwork dynamics, frequency of communication. Externally, the system receives signals from outside the market, such as competitor movements, technological advancements, changes in customer behavior, as well as changes in socio-economic or regulatory trends that can affect strategic trajectories. HAIST's research found that this multi-source sensing capability generates the basic data layer necessary for effective human-AI collaboration, this allows human and artificial intelligence to operate as they deeply understand each other about the life of the Company (Morello & Chick, 2025).

Figure 2. The Five-Phase AI-Augmented Strategic Loop (AISL) (Abras et al., 2025).

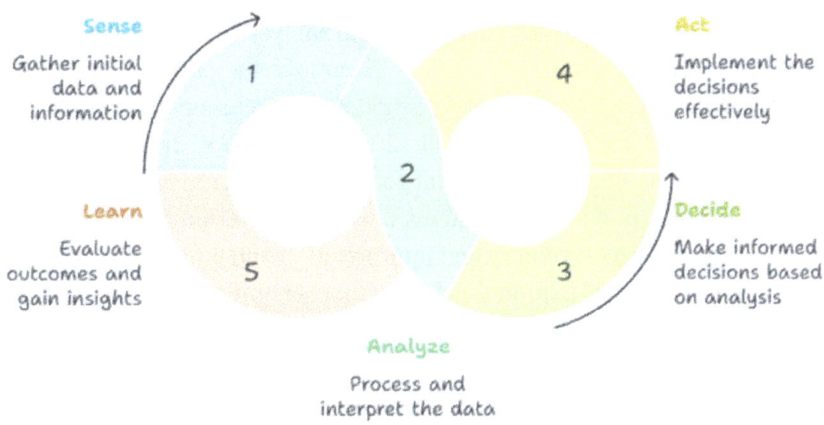

Figure 2 presents the five-phase AI-Augmented Strategic Loop (AISL), consisting of sensing, analysis, decision-making, action, and learning. The figure visualizes how these phases operate as a continuous and recursive loop rather than as a linear process. By illustrating the real-time interaction between AI systems and human decision-makers, Figure 2 clarifies how AISL enables an always-on strategy in which strategic perception, reasoning, execution, and learning occur simultaneously across the organization (Abras et al., 2025).

As studies of RAG-based systems have shown, this ability to collect and utilize data thoroughly helps address the problem of information overload that often slows or even hinders traditional strategic decision-making (Abras et al., 2025). This sensory layer sets it apart from conventional dashboards, which offer a retrospective picture. Instead, this sensory layer provides an ever-changing map of situational awareness, which makes it possible to show early warning signals, emerging opportunities, and subtle misalignments between remote execution and strategy. AISL transforms organizational perceptions into living intelligence structures, ensuring leadership can see not only what has happened, but what will likely happen next and in the future. The analysis phase transforms these large and complex data sets into actionable intelligence once the sensory layer collects them. Machine learning models, natural language processing systems, and predictive analytics engines work together to identify the meaning of noise. This comprehensive data aggregation requires a robust cybersecurity measure, as found in critical infrastructure readiness studies where data protection emerged as a cornerstone for trustworthy digital transformation (Mohamed Noor et al., 2025). These artificial intelligence systems find hidden correlations, identify emerging new trends, simulate potential scenarios, and forecast possibilities for various strategic outcomes. They can identify inconsistencies between stated goals and ongoing initiatives, highlight bottlenecks that hinder performance, and reveal latent risks such as market saturation or regulatory vulnerabilities that may be overlooked by human analysts. The analytical phase uses AI techniques that can be described as comparable to the phases that have proven successful in the financial industry, where model interpretation is critical to building trust in AI-generated insights (Khan et al., 2025). The HAIST framework identifies these analytical capabilities as essential for creating cognitive complementarity, which is a condition in which AI systems deal with pattern recognition on a large scale while humans provide contextual interpretation and ethical framing (Morello & Chick, 2025). Empirical exploration shows that generative AI systems, especially those enhanced with Retrieval-Augmented Generation (RAG) capabilities, excel at processing complex strategic information and generating nuanced insights that typically exceed human cognitive (Abras et al., 2025).

Beyond descriptive and diagnostic analytics, this phase is not limited to predictive and prescriptive intelligence, which allows organizations to anticipate changes rather than react to them. Analytics engines become strategic advisors as they continue to refine their understanding of the organization's operational situation and external context, learning from successes and failures. The insights generated by these analytics engines go straight into the determination phase, where human leaders and AI systems work together to determine the most efficient strategic response. Here, optimization algorithms and generative AI models act as cognitive assistants, simulating multiple decision paths and evaluating the trade-offs between competing goals. They might suggest changes such as reallocating investment from low-impact projects to potentially greater innovations, improving OKRs to better reflect real-world dynamics, or even rebalancing team composition to improve delivery efficiency. This decision-making paradigm exemplifies what the HAIST researchers describe as a form of added consideration, in which AI expands the possibilities of decisions while humans retain supreme control over value-based decisions (Morello & Chick, 2025) .This method is in line with the results of (Abras et al., 2025) who show that decision support systems equipped with artificial intelligence significantly improve the quality of decisions while reducing the cognitive burden borne by human strategists. Importantly, these systems don't dictate actions, they augment decision-making by providing clarity, foresight, and probabilistic guidance. Leaders are then empowered to choose with greater confidence, informed by a strong data-driven foundation but guided by ethical, cultural, and experiential wisdom. AI becomes a strategic dialogue partner, illuminating the implications of different actions while leaving the final judgment to human discretion. The action phase after decision-making ensures a quick and smooth operationalization. AISL's bridging architecture creates a synchronized flow of updates across the enterprise by connecting decision layers directly to execution systems such as roadmaps, project management platforms, budgeting tools, and performance dashboards. When leadership changes strategic priorities, the change automatically spreads throughout the team. This happens almost instantly, as project timelines are recalibrated, resource allocations change, dashboards are updated, and teams receive changed goals. This creates an adaptive execution environment where the operational status of the organization continues to reflect its strategic intent. The roadmap, which used to be a static document reviewed every three months, is now evolving as a living blueprint that reflects not only the planned initiative but also the organization's capacity to learn and pivot. This operational fluidity demonstrates the tangible implementation of HAIST's principle of adaptive coordination, in which the execution of artificial intelligence and human direction creates a responsive organizational organism (Morello & Chick, 2025).

Good synchronization between planning and execution helps reduce delays, reduce coordination burdens, and maintain organizational alignment even in highly dynamic environments. This cycle ends in the learning phase, which serves as a form of self-reflection for the system. Every decision, from resource adjustments, project priority changes, to OKR revisions, is evaluated to see how much of an impact it actually has compared to previously estimated value. The system measures performance deviations, captures lessons learned, and reintegrates these findings into its learning model. Over time, this feedback process improves predictive accuracy, sharpens analytical precision, and builds an organizational form of memory, an ever-growing repository of strategic knowledge that incorporates enterprise intelligence. According to HAIST theorists, this learning mechanism describes it as reciprocal enlightenment, where feedback and interaction are constantly advancing artificial and human intelligence (Morello & Chick, 2025). (Abras et al., 2025) identified continuous improvement capabilities as a key advantage of strategic systems involving artificial intelligence as a key advantage this allows organizations to systematically learn from successes and failures. This recursive learning mechanism transforms AISL into a self-enhancing meta-system capable of developing its own logic based on empirical feedback. The more it operates, the smarter it gets, turning every success and failure into data that enhances future strategic agility. In practice, large digital companies often look at the operation of AI-Augmented Strategic Loop (AISL) because previously they faced constant misalignment between OKRs, project portfolios, and technology roadmaps. After integrating AISL, machine learning models are used to continuously evaluate portfolio initiatives based on predicted value and strategic relevance, while roadmaps evolve into dynamic planning instruments that combine real-time operational and external signals. At the execution level, AI-enabled semantic alignment and predictive analytics allowed OKRs to be continuously mapped to strategic priorities and portfolio initiatives, providing early warnings of potential deviations. This integrated loop reduced decision latency, improved strategic coherence, and transformed strategy execution from a static planning exercise into a continuous, learning-oriented process. However, the transformative essence of AISL beyond its computing sophistication lies in the principle of human-machine collaboration. The goal of this system is still the same, namely augmentation, not automation. While AI processes large volumes of data, forecasts scenarios, and generates options at superhuman speed, it lacks the moral compass, empathy, and contextual nuances that define human leadership. As such, human executives remain the primary decision-makers, shaping the why behind every means. Symbiotic intelligence is a type of intelligence in which machine cognition and human creativity develop together in a shared learning circle. As a theoretical basis for this collaboration, the HAIST framework shows through the assessment of various frameworks that human-AI collaboration balances human wisdom with computational power most efficiently (Morello & Chick, 2025) Empirical evidence from (Abras et al., 2025) supports this balanced approach, suggesting that the most effective strategic decisions arise from the synergy between human judgment and AI-powered insights rather than from the two separately.

The insights derived from AI have meanings, principles, and values that are instilled by humans. On the other hand, AI enhances human capabilities by offering foresight and clarifying complexity. Strategic leaders must engage critically with AI output, not just asking "Is this optimal?" but "Is this right for our people, our brand, and our goals?" These interactions ensure that AI-augmented strategies not only remain efficient but also ethical, empathetic, and sustainable. In this symbiosis, the increase in decisions does not become a delegate of decisions. Human oversight ensures that the system functions properly and ensures that technological advances do not deviate from cultural identity or long-term goals. The most effective leaders in the AISL paradigm are those who function as translators between data and humanity, balancing algorithmic precision with human intuition. They are leveraging AI not to replace their thinking but to expand it, turning strategy into a joint effort between analytical intelligence and human vision. Ultimately, the AI Augmented Strategic Loop redefines what it means for organizations to be agile. It transforms the company from a static hierarchy into a learning organism, capable of understanding change, understanding its implications, and adapting faster than the environment demands. The boundaries between planning and execution, between data and insights, between humans and machines, dissolve into a seamless continuum of cognition and action. This organizational transformation reflects the full implementation of the Human-AI Symbiosis Theory, creating what (Morello & Chick, 2025) describe as a combined learning system that evolves simultaneously to achieve increasingly sophisticated strategic capabilities. This shift towards a more flexible strategy is a real application of the theoretical framework discussed by (Abras et al., 2025). Through the support of AI-based systems, organizations can face complexity with unprecedented levels of agility and precision. In this new paradigm era of strategic fluidity, agility is no longer a momentary advantage, but a way for organizations to continue to grow. An organization becomes not only efficient or innovative, but also alive, constantly learning, adapting, and creating its future through the collaborative intelligence of humans and machines working together as a whole.

7. CHALLENGES, ETHICAL CONSIDERATIONS, AND FUTURE RESEARCH DIRECTIONS

Incorporating artificial intelligence into areas such as portfolio management, path mapping, and OKR alignment opens up great transformational potential, but at the same time poses a number of operational, ethical, and organizationally complex problems. The first issue that often comes up very clearly is data integrity and algorithmic bias. AI models are only as good as the data fed to them. An organization's historical data often contains patterns of preferences, political decisions, or unfair budgeting practices, and when the model is trained on such data without mitigation, AI recommendations can amplify those inequities into formal decisions that appear to be objective. This reflects research findings on AI bias. Mitigation techniques for fields such as medical imaging have shown that proactive bias detection and correction are essential (Lee et al., 2026). Therefore, practical approach methods should include systematic data quality checks of cleansing, initial documentation, and normalization as well as periodic bias audits that evaluate the model's results against a number of relevant fairness metrics such as differences in treatment between business units, genders, or regions. In addition, the Explainable AI (XAI) mechanism needs to be integrated not only as a visual element, but also as part of system governance. Each strategic recommendation should be accompanied by an audit explanation that allows users to drill down into the key data that influenced the recommendation, identify the indicators with the most weight, and understand how the results might change if multiple inputs were modified. Technically, defensive practices such as creating separate test datasets for bias, hostile testing, reweighting, and the use of privacy techniques such as differential privacy when using sensitive data should be part of the model's production flow.

However, technical issues are only one side of the challenge. Change and organizational culture resistance are two of the biggest obstacles to implementing AI strategically. By implementing AISL reinforcing roles and responsibilities, managers must move from administrative decision-makers to contextual readers and custodians of organizational values, while data teams must learn to deliver results in a strategic and communicative way. This shift requires multi-layered change programs such as ongoing education and training to improve the data literacy of leaders and decision-makers, demonstration of value through transparent small-scale pilots, and cross-functional forums to openly discuss AI recommendations for building trust. Best practices such as implementing shadow modes where AI runs in parallel without impacting official decisions, regular reviews with business stakeholders, as well as feedback mechanisms that allow field workers to respond to or revise AI recommendations, can help reduce concerns and encourage the gradual adoption of these technologies. Leadership must affirm that AI is an add-on, not a substitute, and set up communication channels and incentives that balance technical accountability with human responsibility. The question of ethical governance and accountability touches on the core of system legitimacy. When strategic decisions involve significant risks for example, cutting socially impactful projects, restructuring teams, or shifting budgets it should be clear who is responsible if the recommendations end badly. These concerns are in line with the ethical AI framework developed for financial asset management, this study emphasizes the need for clear accountability structures and compliance mechanisms and structures in AI-assisted decision-making systems (Chakrabarti et al., 2025).

A good governance framework puts people as part of an important decision-making process. The system also establishes clear boundaries between decisions that can be automated and those that still require executive approval, ensuring there is an audit trail so that each decision can be easily tracked. This also needs to be applied in internal policies and employment contracts. Each role description should include responsibility for overseeing the use of AI, and legal and compliance teams need to be involved from the outset to ensure all activities are compliant with applicable regulations such as data protection, employment, and sectoral regulations. In addition, organizations also need to have incident response procedures: if AI recommendations have a negative impact, there should be quick steps to conduct investigations, fixes, public comunication when necessary, as well as learn so that the same mistakes do not happen again. Model documentation, model registration, and recording of decisions and reasons will be important evidence in the accountability process. In addition, the adoption of AISL poses operational challenges related to the management of the model and its lifecycle (Ops or MLOps model). In a fast-moving strategic environment, models should be monitored regularly to identify performance degradation issues such as data deviations or concept deviations, and there are clear policies on when models should be retrained, reinforced, or terminated. An explainable AI approach helps with these operational requirements, comparable to approaches successfully used in financial services, where model interpretation and continuous monitoring are critical to ensure regulatory compliance and user trust (Khan et al., 2025). Additionally, because strategic recommendations affect budgets and people, the success measurement variables for AI systems need to be broader than just prediction accuracy. Governance metrics need to include user trust levels, frequency of human replacements, new policy response times, and tangible impacts on business outcomes e.g., increased hit rate of successful initiatives, pivot times. The MLOps pipeline should incorporate fairness metrics, explanatory scores, and stress scenario testing so that the model doesn't generate high-risk recommendations under extreme conditions. In the ethical and social realms, the impact on the workforce and organizational well-being is an important concern. Decision automation can lead to reduced administrative roles, demand retraining, and change decision-making structures. This impact on the workforce is in line with the results of research on agile management, which emphasizes the importance of flexible organizational structures as companies begin to integrate AI and machine learning systems (Romao et al., 2026).

Responsible workforce transition planning, retraining programs, and dialogue with employees are an important part of the sustainable implementation of AISL. Organizations also need to pay attention to the psychological aspect if using behavioral data such as communication or collaboration pattern analysis to assess performance, it should be done with clear consent, full transparency, and strong privacy protections. In addition, the use of such data should be limited only for development purposes, not for surveillance that could erode trust. Regarding future research, the landscape is very rich and multidisciplinary. One of the urgent research needs is to develop a quantitative methodology that links the increased strategic agility generated by AISL to the organization's long-term performance outcomes for example, how metrics such as time to turn, innovation ROI, or talent retention are affected by the adoption of AI-augmented loops. The need for this robust measurement framework echoes similar problems faced in OKR implementation research. Important research gaps are still related between the adoption of the framework and the actual organizational outcomes (Misslisch et al., 2026). This requires the design of long-term studies and robust field experiments to find cause-and-effect relationships, not just correlations. From a technical point of view, integrating non-financial metrics such as ESG into a cross-domain learning system requires an architecture that is able to integrate quantitative and qualitative signals in a harmonious manner. This approach opens up opportunities for further research on cross-domain transfer learning, multi-objective optimization, and the development of reinforcement learning models that consider equity aspects. The development of organizational cognitive digital twins is another promising research path. Building a virtual replica of an organization that models resource flows, inter-team interactions, and market dynamics will allow for strategic policy simulation without any real risk. This concept goes beyond traditional road mapping approach methods and results in a responsive scenario-based road mapping methodology that leverages system dynamics to improve enhanced strategic planning (Tansurat & Gerdsri, 2024).

However, research challenges arise in terms of scale, validation, and how to represent human aspects such as culture and sentiment. A cross-disciplinary approach covering the fields of management, computer science, and organizational psychology is needed to develop a truly beneficial digital twin without simplifying human complexity. In addition, there are research opportunities on the use of generative AI and multi-agent systems to synthesize narrative roadmaps that can be debated with stakeholders, simulate resource allocation negotiations, and present trade-offs in the form of human-understandable narratives. A new ethical and methodological question arises from this topic: how to ensure that generative agents not only produce convincing rhetoric but are also factually accurate and testable. The research space also needs to be geared towards practical algorithmic audit protocols that are summarized, replicated, and can be executed by non-technical auditors to evaluate strategic AI systems. Such an audit framework can be built on ethical AI principles developed for asset management, where transparency and compliance mechanisms are essential for the adoption of AI to be trustworthy (Chakrabarti et al., 2025). Nowadays many audit techniques require high skills Creating an audit toolkit that can be used by compliance or risk management teams will accelerate responsible adoption. Other transformative research focuses on how to design an effective decision interface for human and AI collaboration how to present information, trust levels, and the reasons behind recommendations so that users can understand them well, without becoming overly dependent or distrustful of the system. At this stage, research on human factors and user experience (UX) experiments becomes crucial.

Finally, there is a normative aspect that also needs to be researched, namely the development of policies and industry standards related to the use of AI in large-scale strategic decision-making. The government, industry associations, and academia need to work together to formulate guidelines that ensure transparency, the right to explanation, and protection for affected parties without hindering innovation that has the potential to bring great benefits. As shown in a case study of coastal municipalities, a model of sustainable development governance that successfully balances innovation with public accountability may be the source of inspiration for this normative research (Grigoliene et al., 2025). Policy research should examine the impact of several different regulations such as audit obligations, disclosure requirements on innovation and organizational performance so that policymakers can balance public safety and industry competitiveness. In summary, the implementation of AISL presents challenges that require a multidimensional approach. This approach should combine technical solutions such as Explainable AI (XAI), fairness testing, and the implementation of reliable MLOps with governance practices that include accountability clarity, registry models, as well as audit trails. In addition, there is also a need for cultural change programs through training, pilot projects, and shadow modes, as well as research agendas that focus on impact measurement, integration of non-financial values, the development of digital twins, AI human interaction, and responsible policy formation. This perspective underscores that successful AI integration is essentially a challenge in building organizational capabilities that seamlessly blend technology and human systems. As highlighted in the context of digital enterprises, the success of such complex integrations depends on the development of these core capabilities to ensure technology adoption translates into genuine business value and strategic agility (Riedinger et al., 2026). Only when all of these aspects are seen as part of an interdependent ecosystem not just a potential technology project for creating an adaptive, ethical, and sustainable organization can be realized without sacrificing trust, fairness, or strategic integrity.

8. CONCLUSION

Incorporating artificial intelligence into strategic portfolio management, roadmap planning, and OKR alignment brings a major change in the way modern organizations execute their strategies and operations across multiple regions. This chapter has proven that with the help of AI, management systems that were once rigid and static can now be transformed into a more dynamic, intelligent, and able ecosystem to continue to adapt and learn from time to time. Through predictive portfolio intelligence, dynamic roadmaps, and semantic OKR alignment, organizations can now move beyond reactive decision-making to proactive strategic orchestration. The AI-Augmented Strategic Loop (AISL) comes as a framework solution that brings together various AI capabilities in a single system that is interconnected, works with each other, and continues to evolve. The system helps organizations to recognize changes in their environment, analyze complex data patterns, make decisions more accurately, and adjust strategy execution in near real-time. This is not just an improvement on the old process, but a new way to reimagine what strategic management would look like if strategic management was run in the digital age.

The potential of AI in strategic management is not only about making work more efficient, but also helping to solve big challenges within an organization. By leveraging machine learning and natural language processing, AI can help reduce human bias in portfolio decision-making, find directional mismatches among many OKRs, and simulate a variety of possible scenarios that could occur with a relatively large number of people for humans to analyze using manual methods. The implementation of an explainable AI (XAI) framework helps create transparency and fosters trust in the recommendations generated by the AI itself. Meanwhile, the continuous learning mechanism makes this system continue to evolve and get better over time. When applied appropriately, these technologies can help organizations become not only more efficient, but also more resilient, adaptive, and strategically aligned in the face of market changes and accelerating technological advancements.

However, the success of implementing an AI-based strategy system cannot depend solely on technology. There are many major challenges to consider, such as maintaining data integrity, overcoming bias in algorithms, facing resistance within organizations, and ensuring ethical governance. All of this requires a robust framework that puts transparency, accountability, and human oversight still top priorities. A thorough implementation of the Model Ops pipeline, regular bias audits, and a clear accountability structure help ensure that AI systems actually strengthen, not damage, organizational governance. In addition, cooperation between humans and machines remains the main key. While AI is capable of providing in-depth analysis and exceptional predictions, the final decision still requires a human touch of ethical judgment, cultural understanding, and strategic wisdom. This balance between artificial intelligence and human wisdom is the basis for effective strategic leadership in the AI era.

In the future, the development of AI in strategic management opens up many new opportunities for research and innovation. Some of the key areas that need to be explored include how AI can improve strategic agility and its impact on an organization's long-term performance, how to build a cross-field learning system that combines financial and non-financial goals, and how to create digital twins that can be used to test strategies without real risk. In addition, research also needs to be focused on the design of human-AI interactions, algorithm audit mechanisms, and governance that ensures the use of AI remains ethical and responsible. With the advancement of generative AI and multi-agent systems, we will also see the emergence of new opportunities such as automated strategic roadmapping, more dynamic resource negotiation, and more user-friendly strategic interfaces. All of these developments will help organizations be better prepared to face the complexities and uncertainties of the future.

REFERENCES

Abras, J., Burnay, C., & Faulkner, S. (2025). Can Generative AI Mitigate Strategic Decision-Making Complexity? An Empirical Exploration of RAG-Augmented Decision-Support Systems. *Lecture Notes in Business Information Processing, 548 LNBIP*, 3–19. DOI: 10.1007/978-3-031-92471-2_1

Ansari, I., Barati, M., Sadeghi Moghadam, M. R., & Ghobakhloo, M. (2025). Empowering Industry 4.0: Systemizing readiness assessment and strategic roadmapping for digital transformation. *Journal of Manufacturing Technology Management, 36*(5), 937–960. DOI: 10.1108/JMTM-05-2024-0257

Bodendorf, F. (2025). A data-driven use case planning and assessment approach for AI portfolio management. *Electronic Markets, 35*(1), 22. Advance online publication. DOI: 10.1007/s12525-025-00759-x

Bouzeria, Z., Asli, L., & Brahmi, B. (2026). Local search-based approach for cardinality constrained portfolio selection problem. *Expert Systems with Applications, 296*, 128950. Advance online publication. DOI: 10.1016/j.eswa.2025.128950

Chakrabarti, M., Fabozzi, F. J., Narain, A., & Sood, A. (2025). Ethical AI in Asset Management: Frameworks for Transparency, Compliance, and Trust. *The Journal of Financial Data Science, 7*(1), 18–35. DOI: 10.3905/jfds.2025.7.1.018

Chou, J.-S., Lin, K.-C., & Pham, T.-B.-Q. (2025). AI-fused construction portfolio investment system with risk hedging using machine learning and long-short strategies. *Applied Soft Computing, 183*, 113555. Advance online publication. DOI: 10.1016/j.asoc.2025.113555

Chou, J.-S., & Pham, T.-B.-Q. (2025). Leveraging ensemble learning-based stock preselection with multiobjective investment optimization for stepwise decision-supported portfolio management. *Journal of Big Data, 12*(1), 196. Advance online publication. DOI: 10.1186/s40537-025-01202-w

Grigoliene, R., Kiyak, D., Olsauskas, V., & Juknyte-Petreikiene, I. (2025). Public Governance of Sustainable Development Implementation: A Case Study of Coastal Municipalities in Lithuania. *Sustainability (Basel), 17*(18), 8170. Advance online publication. DOI: 10.3390/su17188170

Kayabay, K., Kılınç, A., Gökalp, M. O., Gökalp, E., & Daim, T. U. (2024). Technology Roadmapping: Data Science Roadmapping of Networked Organizations' Strategic Planning for Artificial Intelligence. In *Future-Oriented Technology Assessment: A Manager's Guide with Case Applications* (pp. 273–300). DOI: 10.1002/9781119909880.ch10

Khan, F. S., Mazhar, S. S., Mazhar, K. A., AlSaleh, D., & Mazhar, A. (2025). Model-agnostic explainable artificial intelligence methods in finance: A systematic review, recent developments, limitations, challenges and future directions. *Artificial Intelligence Review, 58*(8). Advance online publication. DOI: 10.1007/s10462-025-11215-9

Kim, J., Park, G., Woo, M., & Geum, Y. (2025). How Big Data Has Changed Technology Roadmapping: A Review on Data-Driven Roadmapping. *IEEE Access : Practical Innovations, Open Solutions, 13*, 8297–8309. DOI: 10.1109/ACCESS.2025.3526173

Lee, T., Puyol-Antón, E., Ruijsink, B., Shi, M., & King, A. P. (2026). Does a Rising Tide Lift All Boats? Bias Mitigation for AI-Based CMR Segmentation. *Lecture Notes in Computer Science, 15976 LNCS*, 84–93. DOI: 10.1007/978-3-032-05870-6_9

Misslisch, J., Bauer, T., Eibl, F., Neumann, M., Spanke, J., Schön, E.-M., & Przybyłek, A. (2026). Unlocking the OKR Framework: Insights into Benefits and Barriers for an Effective Implementation in Practice. *Lecture Notes in Computer Science, 16082 LNCS*, 90–107. DOI: 10.1007/978-3-032-04200-2_7

Mohamed Noor, A. F., Moghavvemi, S., & Tajudeen, F. P. (2025). Identifying key factors of cybersecurity readiness in organizations: Insights from Malaysian critical infrastructure. *Computers & Security, 159*, 104674. Advance online publication. DOI: 10.1016/j.cose.2025.104674

Morello, L. T., & Chick, J. C. (2025). Human-AI Symbiotic Theory (HAIST): Development, Multi-Framework Assessment, and AI-Assisted Validation in Academic Research. *Informatics (MDPI), 12*(3), 85. Advance online publication. DOI: 10.3390/informatics12030085

Riedinger, C., Netscher, M., Zimmermann, S., & Huber, M. (2026). Implementing Business-IT Integration in Digital Enterprises Using Organizational Capabilities. *Lecture Notes in Business Information Processing, 555 LNBIP*, 58–78. DOI: 10.1007/978-3-031-93580-0_3

Romao, L., Villamizar, H., Oliveira, R., Alonso, S., & Kalinowski, M. (2026). Agile Management for Machine Learning: A Systematic Mapping Study. *Lecture Notes in Computer Science, 16082 LNCS*, 350–360. DOI: 10.1007/978-3-032-04200-2_24

Sekti, B. A. (2025a). Machine learning and artificial intelligence (AI) in manufacturing. In *Integrating Digital Innovation and Integrated Frameworks in Manufacturing* (pp. 255–292). DOI: 10.4018/979-8-3373-1082-4.ch011

Sekti, B. A. (2025b). Machine Learning vs. AI: Key Concepts. In *Implementing Enterprise Cybersecurity With AI* (pp. 1–27). DOI: 10.4018/979-8-3373-2252-0.ch001

Silva, R., & Santos, G. (2023). Surveying the Academic Literature on the Use of OKR (Objective and Key Results). *ACM International Conference Proceeding Series*, 427–434. DOI: 10.1145/3592813.3592934

Tansurat, P., & Gerdsri, N. (2024). Responsive Scenario-based Roadmapping: Applying System Dynamics to Enhance Scenario-based Roadmapping. *PICMET 2024 - 2024 Portland International Conference on Management of Engineering and Technology: Technology Management in the Artificial Intelligence Era, Proceedings*. DOI: 10.23919/PICMET64035.2024.10653350

Tong, B. G., Liang, Z., He, X., Yang, F., Yang, L., & Gao, L. (2025). AI-driven dynamic psychological measurement: Correcting university student mental health scales using daily behavioral and cognitive data. *Frontiers in Digital Health*, *7*, 1615250. Advance online publication. DOI: 10.3389/fdgth.2025.1615250 PMID: 41395629

Zhang, J., Qi, Y., Xu, H., Chang, M., & Yang, L. (2025). Promoting the Sustainable Development of Organizations: Technological Capability, Environmental Uncertainty, and Enterprise Exploratory Innovation. *Sustainability (Basel)*, *17*(14), 6251. Advance online publication. DOI: 10.3390/su17146251

Chapter 4

AI-Enhanced Agile Delivery Forecasting With Probabilistic Models, Flow Metrics, and Human Governance

Gusti Muhamad Sardana
http://orcid.org/0009-0001-4281-2432
Universitas Esa Unggul, Indonesia

Binastya Anggara Sekti
http://orcid.org/0000-0001-5489-4888
Universitas Esa Unggul, Indonesia

ABSTRACT

Accurate delivery forecasting remains a challenge in Agile software development due to uncertainty, evolving requirements, and complex socio-technical dynamics. Traditional estimation techniques often produce deterministic predictions that fail to communicate delivery risk and scale effectively across teams. This chapter presents an AI-enhanced Agile delivery forecasting framework that integrates probabilistic models, flow metrics, and human-in-the-loop governance. Probabilistic techniques such as Monte Carlo simulation and Bayesian inference are combined with flow-based metrics, including cycle time, throughput, and work-in-progress, to generate adaptive and risk-aware forecasts across sprint, release, and portfolio levels. Machine learning methods support continuous refinement of predictions using historical and

DOI: 10.4018/979-8-3373-6851-1.ch004

real-time data, while human oversight ensures contextual interpretation, ethical use, and accountability. The chapter illustrates how combining AI with human judgment improves delivery predictability while preserving core Agile principles.

1. INTRODUCTION

Agile software development has reshaped how organizations deliver digital products and services by emphasizing iterative progress, customer collaboration, and adaptive planning rather than rigid, long-term forecasting. Despite its widespread adoption, however, accurate forecasting of completion dates, resource requirements, and delivery timelines remains a persistent challenge in Agile delivery contexts. Stakeholders across organizational levels ranging from product owners and development teams to executives and customers continue to require forecasts that are sufficiently reliable to inform decisions related to resource allocation, budget planning, and strategic commitments (Chowdhury et al., 2024).

Traditional forecasting approaches in Agile environments have largely relied on velocity-based calculations, story point estimations, and expert judgment through techniques such as planning poker. While these methods can be effective for short-term, sprint-level planning, their limitations become apparent when organizations attempt to forecast at scale, coordinate multi-sprint releases, or explicitly account for the uncertainty and variability inherent in complex software development efforts (Sarwar & Rahman, 2024). Increasing system complexity, distributed team structures, and volatile market conditions have further challenged the adequacy of these conventional approaches, highlighting the need for more systematic, data-informed forecasting practices (Velikov & Ivanova, 2025).

Within Agile practice, long-term forecasting has often been viewed as incompatible with Agile principles, leading some practitioners to adopt a deliberately cautious stance toward predictive commitments. While this perspective aligns with Agile's emphasis on adaptability, it can create friction with legitimate organizational needs for planning and coordination. Common estimation techniques such as story points and planning poker, although valuable for facilitating shared understanding and relative sizing, exhibit well-documented weaknesses. Story point estimates are inherently subjective and context-dependent, varying across teams and over time, which limits their usefulness for cross-team comparison and long-term analysis (Tasneem et al., 2025). Similarly, planning poker is susceptible to cognitive biases, including anchoring and groupthink, and struggles to adequately represent uncertainty in complex, interdependent work. As these techniques typically yield point estimates rather than probability distributions, they often obscure uncertainty and can unintentionally encourage stakeholders to treat estimates as firm commitments

(Mohammad & Chirchir, 2024; Radwan et al., 2025). This misalignment between Agile's iterative nature and business demands for predictability remains a recurring source of tension in practice.

Recent advances in artificial intelligence (AI) and machine learning (ML) offer opportunities to address some of these limitations by enabling organizations to analyze historical delivery data, real-time flow metrics, and probabilistic patterns at a scale beyond manual analysis. Rather than relying solely on expert judgment, AI-based forecasting approaches can systematically identify relationships between work characteristics, team dynamics, dependencies, and delivery outcomes, while explicitly quantifying uncertainty (Almalki, 2025). Techniques such as Monte Carlo simulation, time-series analysis, and ensemble learning allow forecasts to be expressed as probability ranges with associated confidence levels for example, indicating the likelihood that a given scope will be completed within a specified time window rather than as single-point estimates that imply unwarranted precision. Importantly, the value of these approaches depends on data quality, appropriate model calibration, and ongoing oversight, as forecasting accuracy may degrade when organizational conditions change.

This chapter presents a structured framework for AI-enhanced Agile delivery forecasting that integrates three complementary components: probabilistic models for uncertainty quantification, flow metrics for monitoring execution dynamics, and human-in-the-loop governance to ensure responsible interpretation and use of forecasts. The framework is grounded in the premise that effective forecasting in Agile environments cannot be reduced to algorithmic performance alone. Instead, it requires a socio-technical approach that combines computational analysis with human judgment, quantitative evidence with contextual understanding, and automation with accountability. Probabilistic modeling techniques, including Monte Carlo simulation and Bayesian inference, are examined as mechanisms for representing uncertainty more transparently. Flow metrics derived from Lean and Kanban practices such as cycle time, throughput, and work-in-progress are discussed as operational signals that enable forecasts to adapt to changing conditions. Equally important, the chapter emphasizes governance structures that preserve team autonomy, clarify decision rights, and mitigate risks associated with algorithmic decision support. The objective is not to replace human judgment, but to augment it by providing decision-makers with uncertainty-aware insights that are scalable, interpretable, and context-sensitive.

The remainder of this chapter is organized as follows. Section 2 reviews the theoretical foundations underpinning Agile delivery, probabilistic forecasting, and flow-based performance measurement. Section 3 examines AI and machine learning techniques relevant to delivery forecasting, including feature engineering, model selection, and validation considerations. Section 4 explores how probabilistic models and flow metrics can be combined into hybrid forecasting systems that integrate historical patterns with real-time signals. Section 5 addresses human-in-the-loop governance, focusing on oversight mechanisms, accountability, and responsible use. Section 6 discusses implementation considerations, including system architecture and data governance. Section 7 presents illustrative case studies, while Section 8 reflects on practical challenges and limitations. Finally, Section 9 summarizes key insights and outlines implications for both research and practice.

2. THEORETICAL FOUNDATIONS

This section establishes the theoretical foundations necessary to understand why delivery forecasting is inherently challenging in Agile-based software development. It synthesizes Agile and iterative development principles, limitations of traditional Agile metrics, probabilistic forecasting concepts, and flow-based metrics relevant to delivery performance analysis (Durrani et al., 2024).

2.1 Agile Delivery Fundamentals

Agile Principles and Iterative Development

This section establishes the theoretical foundations necessary to understand why delivery forecasting poses persistent challenges in Agile contexts. Rather than reiterating Agile as a set of practices, the discussion focuses on conceptual characteristics such as iteration, empiricism, and self-organization that shape how uncertainty emerges and must be managed within Agile delivery systems.

Agile development is grounded in iterative and incremental delivery, in which work is organized into short cycles that produce functional software increments. From a theoretical perspective, this structure supports continuous learning and adaptation by enabling frequent validation of assumptions and rapid incorporation of feedback. However, it also implies that delivery outcomes are shaped by evolving information rather than fixed plans, which limits the effectiveness of deterministic, long-term forecasting approaches (Chowdhury et al., 2024). As a result, forecasting in Agile environments must accommodate ongoing change rather than assume stable execution conditions.

A central theoretical concept underpinning Agile delivery is empirical process control, which assumes that complex systems cannot be fully predicted in advance. Instead, decision-making relies on observation and adaptation based on actual system behavior (Martino et al., 2025). The principles of transparency, inspection, and adaptation provide a conceptual explanation for why Agile forecasting is inherently iterative: forecasts are continuously refined as new performance data becomes available, rather than being derived from static upfront assumptions. This empirical orientation aligns more naturally with probabilistic reasoning than with single-point estimates.

Agile delivery also reflects a broader shift from project-based to product-based thinking. Conceptually, this transition reframes success from completing predefined scope to sustaining value delivery over time. Consequently, forecasting questions move away from deterministic completion dates toward understanding delivery capacity, flow stability, and risk under uncertainty (Hokmabadi et al., 2025). This shift challenges traditional estimation practices and motivates forecasting approaches that emphasize distributions and confidence ranges rather than fixed commitments (D. K. Patel et al., 2025).

Self-organizing teams further complicate forecasting at scale. While team autonomy enhances local decision-making and adaptability, it also introduces variability across teams in estimation practices, execution patterns, and performance signals (Tasneem et al., 2025). From a systems perspective, this variability creates tension between localized autonomy and enterprise-level predictability. Addressing this tension requires forecasting approaches that aggregate signals across teams without undermining self-organization, reinforcing the need for data-driven and flow-oriented models (Samhan et al., 2024).

Common Agile performance indicators such as velocity, throughput, and cycle time offer partial visibility into delivery behavior but do not, on their own, resolve forecasting uncertainty. Velocity is relative and context-dependent, throughput abstracts away work size, and cycle time distributions often exhibit significant variability. When interpreted without probabilistic framing, these metrics risk being misused for comparison or performance evaluation, leading to distorted incentives and unreliable conclusions (Anwar & Bashir, 2023). Moreover, their primarily retrospective nature limits their ability to communicate future delivery risk, underscoring the need for forecasting methods that explicitly model uncertainty rather than extrapolate point estimates from past performance (Seffe et al., 2024).

2.2 Probabilistic Forecasting Models

Probabilistic forecasting models address the limitations of traditional deterministic estimation by representing delivery outcomes as probability distributions rather than single-point predictions. This approach explicitly acknowledges uncertainty and variability in Agile software development, making forecasts more realistic and better aligned with empirical process control (Almalki, 2025). To frame the range of probabilistic approaches available in Agile delivery contexts, Table 1 provides a conceptual overview of the main probabilistic forecasting techniques, outlining their underlying principles, data requirements, strengths, and limitations prior to detailed technical discussion.

Table 1. Probabilistic Forecasting Techniques in Agile

Technique	Underlying Principle	Data Requirements	Strengths	Limitations
Monte Carlo Simulation	Generates a large number of possible future delivery scenarios by randomly sampling from historical distributions of delivery metrics (e.g., cycle time or throughput) to produce probabilistic outcome ranges.	Historical delivery data, particularly cycle time or throughput; does not require story point estimates or strict distributional assumptions.	Conceptually simple and intuitive; well aligned with Agile principles; explicitly represents uncertainty and delivery risk; easy to communicate to stakeholders.	Highly dependent on the quality and relevance of historical data; limited ability to anticipate structural changes not yet reflected in past performance.
Bayesian Inference	Iteratively updates probabilistic forecasts by combining prior beliefs with newly observed data, producing posterior distributions that evolve as more information becomes available.	Historical data, ongoing delivery observations, and explicitly defined prior distributions; requires statistical expertise.	Highly adaptive to change; naturally supports iterative refinement consistent with Agile cycles; integrates quantitative data with expert judgment; provides rigorous uncertainty quantification.	Greater conceptual and computational complexity; results can be sensitive to prior selection; higher barrier to adoption for non-technical stakeholders.
Time Series Analysis	Models temporal patterns in historical delivery metrics to identify trends, seasonality, and random variation, which are then extrapolated to forecast future performance.	Longitudinal, time-ordered historical data with sufficient length and relative process stability.	Effective for detecting long-term trends and recurring patterns; useful for monitoring delivery performance evolution over time.	Assumes relative process stability, which is often violated in Agile environments; less effective for sudden changes or disruptions; limited expressiveness of item-level uncertainty.

In Agile contexts, delivery performance is influenced by fluctuating capacity, changing scope, dependencies, and interruptions. Probabilistic models incorporate this variability by expressing forecasts in terms of likelihood or confidence levels, enabling stakeholders to make risk-informed planning and commitment decisions instead of relying on overly precise estimates.

Monte Carlo simulation is the most commonly used probabilistic technique in Agile delivery forecasting. It generates multiple future delivery scenarios by sampling from historical cycle time or throughput data, producing forecast ranges based on percentiles. Bayesian inference extends this approach by continuously updating forecasts as new data becomes available, allowing predictions to adapt to changing conditions. Time series analysis focuses on identifying temporal patterns such as trends and seasonality in delivery metrics, although its effectiveness is limited in highly dynamic Agile environments.

2.3 Flow Metrics in Agile

a. Work in Progress (WIP)

Work in Progress (WIP) refers to the number of work items that have been started but not yet completed. Excessive WIP is a common cause of slow delivery, as it increases multitasking, coordination overhead, and waiting time. Limiting WIP encourages focus, accelerates completion, and improves overall delivery predictability.

b. Cycle Time and Lead Time

Cycle time measures how long work takes once it has started, while lead time measures the total time from request to delivery, including waiting periods. From a customer perspective, lead time is often the most meaningful metric, as it reflects the actual waiting experience.

c. Throughput and Arrival Rate

Throughput measures how quickly a team completes work, while arrival rate measures how quickly new work enters the system. When arrival rate consistently exceeds throughput, backlogs grow and lead times increase. Maintaining balance between these rates is essential for sustainable delivery.

d. Cumulative Flow Diagrams (CFD)

Cumulative Flow Diagrams provide a visual representation of how work items move through different workflow stages over time. CFDs help identify bottlenecks, WIP accumulation, and delivery instability through simple visual patterns. They are particularly effective for monitoring system health and guiding process improvement discussions.

e. Applying Little’s Law in Software Delivery

Little's Law states that:

$$WIP = Throughput \times Cycle\ Time$$

This principle demonstrates that increasing the amount of work in progress does not increase delivery speed. Instead, delivery performance improves by reducing WIP or increasing process efficiency. Little's Law provides a mathematical foundation for flow-based Agile practices and supports data-driven decisions about capacity management, process improvement, and delivery optimization (Gaona-Cuevas et al., 2024).

Existing studies on Agile delivery forecasting can be broadly grouped into three streams. The first stream focuses on traditional Agile estimation techniques, such as velocity-based planning and expert judgment methods, which emphasize team collaboration and iterative learning but rely heavily on subjective assessments and point estimates. While these approaches support short-term planning, they struggle to scale across teams and fail to represent delivery uncertainty explicitly.

A second stream adopts probabilistic forecasting techniques, particularly Monte Carlo simulation and statistical models, to address uncertainty in Agile delivery. These studies demonstrate improved realism in forecasting by leveraging historical flow metrics such as cycle time and throughput. However, most of them assume relatively stable processes and treat forecasting as a purely analytical exercise, with limited discussion of organizational adoption and decision governance.

The third stream introduces AI and machine learning models to enhance forecasting accuracy by learning complex patterns from delivery data. Although these approaches improve predictive performance, they often prioritize technical optimization over alignment with Agile values, interpretability, and human oversight. As a result, issues related to trust, ethical use, and managerial decision-making remain underexplored.

Despite substantial progress in Agile forecasting research, a clear gap remains in integrating probabilistic AI-based forecasting with flow-based Agile metrics under a human-centered governance framework. Prior studies tend to address forecasting accuracy, uncertainty modeling, or Agile metrics in isolation, without offering a cohesive approach that balances predictive rigor with organizational adoption and ethical oversight. In particular, limited attention has been given to how AI-enhanced forecasts should be interpreted, governed, and contextualized by human decision-makers within Agile environments. This gap motivates the need for a holistic framework that combines probabilistic models, real-time flow metrics, and human-in-the-loop governance to support reliable, responsible, and practically adoptable Agile delivery forecasting.

3. AI AND MACHINE LEARNING FOR DELIVERY FORECASTING

This section examines artificial intelligence (AI) and machine learning (ML) techniques relevant to software delivery forecasting, highlighting how predictive analytics, time series methods, ensemble models, and feature engineering can support uncertainty-aware forecasting in Agile environments (A. Patel et al., 2025).

Table 2 provides a conceptual overview of the major categories of AI and machine learning models discussed in this section. The following sections examine these categories in detail, beginning with regression-based predictive analytics techniques

Table 2. Categories of AI/ML Models for Delivery Forecasting

Model Category	Example Techniques	Data Type	Interpretability	Organizational Suitability
Statistical Models	Linear Regression, Multiple Regression, ARIMA	Structured historical delivery metrics (velocity, throughput, cycle time)	High	Suitable for small to medium organizations; useful as baseline models and for environments requiring transparency and explainability.
Probabilistic Models	Monte Carlo Simulation, Bayesian Models	Historical flow metrics and delivery outcome distributions	Medium–High	Well suited for organizations seeking risk-aware forecasting and explicit uncertainty communication; applicable across team, release, and portfolio levels.
Tree-Based Machine Learning Models	Random Forest, Gradient Boosting (XGBoost, LightGBM)	Structured Agile data with engineered features	Medium	Appropriate for medium to large organizations with sufficient historical data; offers strong accuracy with moderate explainability.
Neural Network Models	LSTM, Feedforward Neural Networks	Large-scale, time-ordered delivery data and multiple signals	Low	Best suited for large, data-mature organizations; effective for complex patterns but requires advanced infrastructure and governance.
Ensemble Models	Model Averaging, Stacking, Hybrid Ensembles	Outputs from multiple base models	Low–Medium	Suitable for organizations prioritizing accuracy and robustness; recommended when strong MLOps and explainability mechanisms are in place.

3.1 Predictive Analytics Techniques

Predictive analytics techniques provide the quantitative foundation for delivery forecasting by translating historical Agile delivery data into actionable predictions. Among these techniques, regression-based models constitute one of the most widely used approaches, as they offer a balance between explanatory power and interpretability in environments characterized by uncertainty and evolving processes.

Regression-Based Forecasting Models

Regression models constitute the foundational class of predictive analytics techniques used in delivery forecasting. They establish mathematical relationships between explanatory variables and a continuous outcome variable, such as cycle time, lead time, or sprint velocity.

Linear regression models assume a linear relationship between predictors and outcomes and are expressed as:

$$Y = \beta \ + \beta X \ + \beta X \ + \dots + \beta X \ + \varepsilon$$

where ***Y*** represents the predicted delivery outcome, X_i represent predictor variables (e.g., work item size, team experience, dependency count), β are model coefficients, and ε captures random error. In Agile forecasting, linear regression is valued for its interpretability: each coefficient quantifies the marginal impact of a predictor on delivery performance. For example, a coefficient of 0.5 days per story point indicates that each additional story point increases expected cycle time by half a day, holding other factors constant.

Ordinary Least Squares (OLS) estimation determines coefficient values by minimizing the sum of squared prediction errors. OLS-based models not only generate point estimates but also provide confidence intervals and standard errors, enabling probabilistic forecasts rather than deterministic predictions. Model diagnostics such as R-squared, adjusted R-squared, and p-values support model validation and predictor selection.

Multiple linear regression extends this approach by incorporating multiple predictors simultaneously, capturing the multifactorial nature of delivery performance. However, multicollinearity among predictors such as strong correlations between team size and seniority can destabilize coefficient estimates, necessitating careful feature selection or regularization.

Non-Linear and Regularized Regression

Polynomial regression introduces non-linear relationships through higher-order terms while remaining linear in parameters. This allows modeling of curved relationships, such as diminishing returns from increasing team size or super-linear growth of cycle time with work item complexity. Care must be taken to avoid overfitting by limiting polynomial degree.

Non-linear regression models extend beyond polynomial forms to exponential, logarithmic, or power-law relationships. These models capture phenomena such as learning curves, technical debt accumulation, or scale effects, but require domain-informed functional specification and iterative optimization methods.

To mitigate overfitting and multicollinearity, regularization techniques are widely applied. Ridge regression (L2 regularization) shrinks coefficients toward zero to reduce variance, while Lasso regression (L1 regularization) additionally performs variable selection by forcing some coefficients to zero. Elastic Net combines both approaches, offering a practical balance for high-dimensional Agile datasets with correlated predictors.

Time Series Forecasting Methods

ARIMA (AutoRegressive Integrated Moving Average) models capture temporal dependencies in sequential delivery data. The autoregressive component models persistence effects, the integrated component addresses trends through differencing, and the moving average component captures transient shocks. Seasonal Autoregressive Integrated Moving Average (SARIMA) extends this framework to model recurring patterns such as quarterly planning cycles or holiday effects.

Prophet, developed by Meta, offers an additive decomposition approach that separates trend, seasonality, and holiday effects. Its robustness to missing data, outliers, and irregular sampling makes it particularly suitable for real-world Agile datasets, where data quality is often imperfect.

Long Short-Term Memory (LSTM) networks represent a deep learning approach capable of modeling complex, non-linear temporal dependencies. LSTMs automatically learn long-range patterns across multiple delivery signals but require substantial historical data, computational resources, and interpretability techniques. Consequently, their adoption is best suited to large organizations with mature data infrastructure.

Ensemble Methods for Forecast Accuracy Improvement

Ensemble methods combine predictions from multiple models to improve accuracy and robustness. Simple averaging reduces variance when individual models exhibit uncorrelated errors, while weighted averaging prioritizes more reliable predictors.

More advanced ensemble strategies include stacking, which trains a meta-model to optimally combine base predictions, as well as bagging and boosting techniques such as Random Forests, Gradient Boosting, and XGBoost. Although ensembles generally outperform single models, they increase computational cost and reduce interpretability, necessitating explainability techniques for responsible use in Agile decision-making (Martino et al., 2025).

3.2 Feature Engineering for Delivery Forecasting

Feature engineering plays a critical role in delivery forecasting by transforming raw Agile data into informative predictors. Historical velocity and throughput metrics capture delivery stability, trends, and variability, while team capacity features reflect not only headcount but also experience, skill composition, and competing responsibilities (Marçal et al., 2025; Nabot et al., 2025). Work item complexity, including size, uncertainty, and technical difficulty, directly influences delivery duration, particularly when domain familiarity is limited (Mohammad & Chirchir, 2024). Dependencies across tasks or systems and accumulated technical debt introduce coordination delays and productivity loss, increasing forecast uncertainty (Radwan et al., 2025). External and organizational factors, such as holidays, restructuring, or leadership changes, further shape delivery outcomes and must be incorporated to improve model realism and explanatory power (Hokmabadi et al., 2025).

3.3 Model Selection and Validation

Model selection and validation are essential to ensure that forecasting models in Agile environments are accurate and reliable. The objective is not only to achieve good performance on historical data, but also to ensure that models can generalize well to future sprints or projects. Because Agile data are often limited, noisy, and subject to frequent change, model selection must balance accuracy, robustness, and interpretability.

a. Training Data Preparation

Before training, Agile data must be carefully prepared. Data from tracking tools and repositories may contain missing values, inconsistencies, or outliers due to process changes or data errors. Missing data can be handled through imputation or removal, while outliers should be reviewed to distinguish errors from valid extreme cases. Feature scaling may be applied when required by the model. For time-based forecasting, preserving data order and avoiding information leakage are critical.

b. Model Evaluation and Cross-Validation

Cross-validation is used to assess model performance and compare alternatives. For non-temporal data, k-fold cross-validation is commonly applied. In sprint-based or time-dependent forecasting, time-aware validation methods are more suitable, as they ensure training on past data and testing on future data. This approach provides more realistic performance estimates.

c. Performance Measurement

Model performance is evaluated using error metrics that reflect prediction accuracy. Mean Absolute Error (MAE) is widely used due to its simplicity and robustness, while Root Mean Squared Error (RMSE) emphasizes larger errors. Mean Absolute Percentage Error (MAPE) allows comparison across teams or projects but must be used carefully when actual values are small. Metric selection should align with stakeholder needs.

d. Overfitting Control

Controlling overfitting is necessary to ensure reliable predictions. Overfitting occurs when a model learns noise instead of meaningful patterns. Common techniques include limiting model complexity, using regularization, selecting relevant features, and monitoring validation results. Cross-validation helps identify overfitting by comparing training and validation performance.

Overall, the techniques discussed in this section demonstrate how AI and machine learning can transform Agile delivery data into actionable forecasting insights. Regression, time-series, ensemble methods, and carefully engineered features enable forecasts that are probabilistic rather than deterministic, explicitly acknowledging uncertainty in complex delivery environments. However, model effectiveness depends not only on algorithmic sophistication but also on data quality, contextual relevance, and responsible model selection. These considerations motivate the need for system architectures and operational mechanisms that can support continuous learning, monitoring, and adaptation, which are examined in the following section.

4. Integrating Probabilistic Models with Flow Metrics

4.1 Hybrid Forecasting Framework

Combining Statistical Models with Real-Time Flow Data

integrating statistical forecasting models with real-time flow metrics transforms delivery forecasting from static, history-based prediction into a continuously adaptive decision-support capability. Traditional approaches rely primarily on past performance and often fail to capture ongoing execution dynamics such as throughput variability, work-in-progress (WIP) accumulation, and cycle time fluctuations, which are critical signals of emerging delivery risk (Ameta et al., 2022). By incorporating these real-time flow metrics, forecasts can be continuously recalibrated to reflect current system conditions rather than static historical averages.

The hybrid forecasting framework combines historical statistical models with real-time flow metrics to balance long-term performance stability and short-term execution responsiveness. Historical models provide a baseline forecast that captures structural team characteristics and long-term delivery behavior, while real-time flow metrics dynamically adjust this baseline as execution conditions evolve. This integration enables early detection of delivery risks, supports timely managerial intervention, and enhances the interpretability of probabilistic forecasts. As illustrated in Figure 1, baseline forecasts and real-time flow metrics interact to produce adaptive, risk-aware delivery predictions that remain grounded in empirical performance while responding to operational change (Semenov et al., 2025).

To formalize the interaction between long-term baselines and short-term execution dynamics, the hybrid forecast can be expressed as:

$$Forecast(t) = Baseline(features) \times Adjustment(flow\ metrics, t)$$

This multiplicative formulation ensures that proportional changes in flow performance directly scale the baseline forecast, preserving interpretability while maintaining responsiveness. For example, a 20% reduction in throughput relative to expected levels results in a proportional increase in forecasted delivery time. Adjustment factors may be derived from simple deviation ratios or more advanced methods that aggregate multiple flow metrics. In Bayesian formulations, the historical forecast functions as a prior distribution, while real-time flow data incrementally updates the forecast as new information becomes available (Semenov et al., 2025).

Effective hybrid forecasting relies heavily on feature engineering and calibration. Static features, such as task complexity, team structure, and dependency patterns, underpin the baseline forecast. Dynamic features including recent throughput trends,

WIP levels, and observed cycle time variability provide temporal context for short-term adjustment. Careful selection of time windows is necessary to balance stability and responsiveness, while calibration techniques such as statistical process control and smoothing mitigate overreaction to transient noise, ensuring forecasts remain both reliable and operationally actionable (Samhan et al., 2024).

Figure 1. Conceptual hybrid forecasting framework

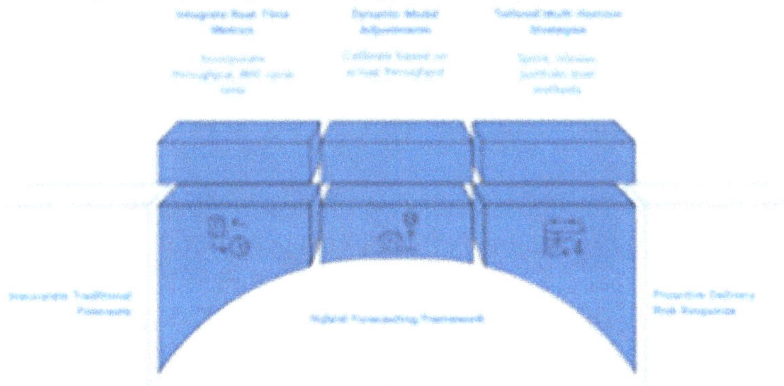

As shown in Figure 1, the hybrid forecasting framework is structured around three interconnected layers. The first layer represents historical baseline modeling, where long-term delivery performance is estimated using statistical or probabilistic methods based on completed work items. The second layer incorporates real-time flow metrics, including throughput, work-in-progress (WIP), and cycle time, which continuously reflect the current execution state of the delivery system. These metrics act as dynamic adjustment signals that modify the baseline forecast in response to emerging variability and constraints.

The interaction between these layers produces a continuously updated forecast that balances stability and adaptability. While the baseline model anchors predictions in historical performance, the flow-metric-driven adjustment layer ensures responsiveness to short-term operational changes. The resulting output supports proactive risk identification and enables informed decision-making in Agile planning and governance contexts, such as sprint planning, capacity negotiation, and delivery risk management.

Dynamic Model Adjustment Based on Actual Throughput

Dynamic adjustment using actual throughput helps keep forecasts accurate during execution. Throughput, or the rate at which work items are completed, provides a clear and continuously available measure of current productivity. When observed throughput differs from expected levels based on historical data, forecasts should be updated (Chong et al., 2025).

Based on Little's Law, if the remaining work is fixed, delivery time changes in proportion to throughput. A simple adjustment can be made by scaling the remaining forecast duration using the ratio between expected and actual throughput. For short-term forecasts, current throughput can be assumed to continue, while longer-term forecasts may require trend-based adjustments.

Change detection methods help distinguish real performance shifts from random variation. Techniques such as statistical control charts or Bayesian change detection indicate when adjustments are truly needed, reducing unnecessary forecast changes (Ispas et al., 2025).

More accurate adjustments can be achieved by analyzing throughput by work type or complexity. When the mix of work changes, overall throughput may be misleading, and type-specific rates provide better estimates. Trend and variability analysis further improve forecasts by guiding confidence levels and prediction ranges.

Multi-Horizon Forecasting (Sprint, Release, and Portfolio Levels)

Multi-horizon forecasting recognizes that different organizational decisions require predictions at different temporal scales. Sprint-level forecasts support tactical planning and require frequent updates and high precision. Release-level forecasts inform stakeholder communication and dependency coordination over multiple iterations. Portfolio-level forecasts guide strategic decisions such as budgeting and capacity planning, where uncertainty is inherently higher.

Forecasting methods and confidence requirements vary across horizons. Sprint-level forecasts leverage granular, recent data and update frequently, often targeting moderate confidence levels. Release-level forecasts aggregate uncertainty across sprints and typically employ wider prediction intervals. Portfolio-level forecasts face compounding uncertainty and dependency effects, Monte Carlo simulation and scenario planning are particularly effective at this level (Ispas et al., 2025).

Hierarchical forecasting frameworks ensure consistency across horizons. Bottom-up, top-down, and middle-out reconciliation approaches align forecasts across organizational levels, balancing local accuracy with strategic coherence. Selecting appropriate temporal granularity and forecast horizons ensures forecasts align with decision-making cadence and avoid false precision.

4.2 Uncertainty Quantification

Confidence Intervals for Delivery Dates

Confidence intervals transform point estimates into probabilistic ranges that more accurately represent delivery uncertainty. Rather than asserting a single completion date, interval forecasts communicate the likelihood of completion within a specified range, supporting risk-informed decision-making.

Confidence intervals can be derived analytically under distributional assumptions or empirically using resampling and Monte Carlo simulation. Given the skewed and heavy-tailed nature of cycle time distributions, simulation-based approaches are often more appropriate. Confidence level selection reflects organizational risk tolerance, with higher confidence requiring wider intervals and more conservative commitments.

Proper interpretation of confidence intervals is essential to avoid misunderstanding. While frequentist confidence intervals describe long-run properties, Bayesian credible intervals provide more intuitive probability interpretations at the cost of additional modeling assumptions. In practice, both approaches support similar managerial decisions when uncertainty is communicated clearly.

Dependencies among parallel workstreams significantly affect interval estimates. Ignoring correlations leads to overconfident forecasts; dependency-aware modeling, often via simulation, provides more realistic uncertainty estimates.

Risk Assessment and Contingency Planning

Risk assessment translates forecast uncertainty into actionable mitigation strategies. By mapping probabilistic forecasts onto business impacts, organizations can prioritize risks based on exposure and develop targeted contingencies. Common strategies include scope reduction, buffer allocation, fallback plans, and resource flexibility.

Monte Carlo risk analysis enables evaluation of complex initiatives with multiple uncertainties and dependencies. Sensitivity analysis identifies dominant risk drivers, focusing mitigation efforts where they yield the greatest benefit. Continuous monitoring of leading indicators such as WIP growth, cycle time degradation, and dependency delays supports proactive risk management rather than reactive crisis response.

Scenario Analysis (Best Case, Worst Case, Most Likely)

Scenario analysis complements probabilistic forecasting by presenting discrete, narrative-driven futures that clarify key uncertainties and decision trade-offs. Best-case, worst-case, and most-likely scenarios define plausible bounds on outcomes and support robust decision-making under uncertainty.

Scenarios are constructed by systematically varying high-impact uncertainties, such as scope stability, technical complexity, dependencies, and team capacity. Decision robustness is evaluated across scenarios, favoring strategies that perform acceptably even under unfavorable conditions. As execution progresses, scenario probabilities can be updated using Bayesian reasoning, enabling adaptive planning aligned with emerging evidence.

4.3 Real-Time Monitoring and Adaptive Forecasting

Real-time monitoring and adaptive forecasting enable AI-based delivery forecasting systems to remain responsive to continuous changes in Agile environments. Unlike static forecasting approaches, adaptive systems continuously incorporate new information, monitor model behavior, and adjust predictions to reflect current delivery conditions.

Streaming Data Integration

Streaming data integration allows delivery-related events to be processed with minimal latency, reducing delays between observed changes and updated forecasts. Event-driven architectures capture state transitions, task updates, and completion events as they occur, enabling near real-time feature updates. Incoming event streams are aggregated into sliding or tumbling data windows to produce stable summary features suitable for forecasting. Control mechanisms such as back-pressure handling and rate limiting ensure system stability during traffic spikes. In practice, hybrid architectures combine streaming pipelines with batch processing to balance responsiveness with consistency and historical completeness.

Continuous Model Updating

Continuous model updating ensures that forecasting models remain accurate as delivery patterns evolve. New observations are incrementally incorporated through online learning techniques or rolling training windows that emphasize recent data. Model retraining may be triggered automatically when performance degrades or when significant changes occur in team composition, workflows, or tooling. Feature stores support consistency between training and inference, while model versioning enables traceability and rollback. Controlled deployment strategies allow updated models to be introduced safely without disrupting operational systems.

Drift Detection and Model Retraining

Drift detection mechanisms identify significant changes in data distributions, model inputs, or prediction errors that indicate reduced model validity. By monitoring statistical properties of incoming data and comparing forecast errors over time, the system can detect both data drift and concept drift. Retraining strategies typically combine scheduled updates with event-driven retraining triggered by detected drift. Prioritizing recent and relevant data during retraining helps maintain alignment with current delivery conditions while avoiding unnecessary computational overhead.

4.4 From Forecast to Action: Operationalizing Probabilistic Insights

While probabilistic forecasting models provide valuable estimates of delivery uncertainty, their organizational value depends on how effectively these insights are translated into day-to-day Agile decision-making. Without explicit operational integration, even accurate forecasts risk remaining analytical artifacts rather than actionable management instruments. This subsection addresses the "last mile" problem by outlining concrete mechanisms through which probabilistic delivery forecasts can be embedded into core Agile ceremonies and governance processes.

In sprint planning, probabilistic forecasts support commitment decisions by framing scope selection in terms of risk rather than deterministic estimates. Instead of committing to a fixed set of backlog items, teams can use percentile-based forecasts (e.g., P50, P85) to align delivery commitments with acceptable risk thresholds. For example, selecting a sprint scope corresponding to a P70 forecast explicitly acknowledges uncertainty while preserving delivery credibility. This approach encourages transparent negotiation between teams and stakeholders and reduces the likelihood of systemic overcommitment.

During backlog refinement, probabilistic forecasts enable continuous reprioritization by highlighting work items that disproportionately contribute to delivery risk. Items with high variability, long tail cycle times, or strong dependency effects can be identified early and decomposed, deferred, or re-sequenced. In this context, forecasts function not as rigid predictions but as diagnostic signals that inform structural backlog improvements and risk-aware planning decisions.

Operational use of forecasts is further reinforced through forecast-driven daily stand-ups. In contrast to traditional stand-ups that focus narrowly on task status, forecast-driven stand-ups incorporate short-term delivery risk signals derived from updated probabilistic models. Teams may explicitly discuss whether recent changes in throughput, work-in-progress, or blocked work have shifted the projected delivery distribution. This practice encourages proactive intervention such as rebalancing work, reducing WIP, or addressing bottlenecks—before risks materialize as missed commitments.

At the stakeholder interface, probabilistic forecasts provide a more honest and resilient basis for expectation management. Communicating delivery timelines in probabilistic terms (e.g., "there is an 85% likelihood of completing this scope within three sprints") reduces false certainty and reframes schedule discussions around risk tolerance rather than binary success or failure. This probabilistic framing supports adaptive scope negotiation and aligns closely with Agile principles of transparency and continuous learning.

By explicitly embedding probabilistic forecasting outputs into planning, execution, and communication practices, organizations can ensure that AI-enhanced delivery forecasts function as actionable decision-support tools rather than isolated analytical outputs. This operational integration reinforces human-in-the-loop governance by preserving managerial judgment while enhancing it with data-driven, uncertainty-aware insights.

This section highlights that accurate delivery forecasting requires more than predictive models alone; it depends on a robust system architecture capable of integrating data, serving models, and adapting to continuous change. Real-time monitoring, drift detection, and adaptive retraining mechanisms ensure that forecasts remain aligned with evolving team dynamics and delivery conditions. By combining scalable infrastructure with controlled deployment and feedback loops, forecasting systems can support decision-making without disrupting Agile workflows. These architectural foundations enable forecasting capabilities to be embedded into everyday delivery practices, which is further elaborated through implementation and governance considerations in subsequent sections.

5. Human-in-the-Loop Governance

Human-in-the-loop governance positions artificial intelligence as a decision-support mechanism rather than a decision-maker. In delivery forecasting, this approach acknowledges that predictive models provide analytical consistency and scalability, while humans contribute contextual understanding, ethical reasoning, and strategic judgment. Effective governance ensures that AI enhances, rather than constrains, professional decision-making (Ilieva et al., 2025).

To operationalize the human-in-the-loop governance concept in delivery forecasting, Table 3 delineates the respective responsibilities of AI systems and human decision-makers across key forecasting activities. This division clarifies decision rights and reinforces the role of AI as a decision-support mechanism rather than an autonomous decision-maker

Table 3. Division of Human and AI Roles in Delivery Forecasting

Activity	AI Responsibility	Human Responsibility
Data collection and preprocessing	Automatically ingest, clean, and transform delivery data from Agile tools; detect anomalies and inconsistencies.	Define data standards, validate data relevance, and address contextual data quality issues.
Baseline forecast generation	Generate probabilistic delivery forecasts based on historical patterns and statistical or ML models.	Review forecast assumptions, assess contextual validity, and approve use for planning purposes.
Uncertainty quantification	Compute probability distributions, confidence levels, and prediction ranges.	Interpret uncertainty in business context and determine acceptable risk thresholds.
Model updating and learning	Continuously update models using new delivery data; detect performance drift.	Decide when model updates are appropriate and evaluate the impact of changes.
Scenario and sensitivity analysis	Simulate alternative delivery scenarios and identify key risk drivers.	Select relevant scenarios and translate results into actionable planning decisions.
Exception and anomaly detection	Flag deviations from expected delivery patterns and emerging risks.	Investigate root causes, assess organizational impact, and determine corrective actions.
Decision-making and commitments	Provide evidence-based recommendations and forecast ranges.	Make final delivery commitments and strategic decisions, retaining accountability.
Monitoring and feedback	Track forecast accuracy and performance metrics over time.	Provide feedback, conduct reviews, and incorporate lessons learned into governance practices.

5.1 The Role of Human Judgment

AI-based forecasting systems can identify patterns from historical delivery data, but they have limited ability to understand context, causality, and values. For this reason, human judgment remains essential, especially in complex and uncertain delivery environments.

AI models assume that future conditions will resemble the past. When teams, technologies, or priorities change, this assumption may no longer be valid, leading to forecasts that appear accurate but do not reflect reality. In addition, most AI models capture correlations rather than causal relationships, which limits their usefulness for guiding decisions such as reallocating resources or changing delivery strategies.

Human judgment complements AI by applying domain knowledge, experience, and situational awareness. Practitioners can interpret forecasts within their organizational context, recognize when assumptions are violated, and adjust expectations accordingly. Humans are also responsible for value-based decisions, such as balancing speed, quality, and team well-being.

From an ethical perspective, delivery forecasts influence commitments and workload. Excessive reliance on automated forecasts may reduce autonomy and increase pressure on teams (Ehtsham et al., 2025). Human oversight is therefore necessary to ensure forecasts are applied responsibly and in line with organizational values.

5.2 Governance Framework

A governance framework defines how AI-generated forecasts are produced, interpreted, and acted upon within the organization. Its primary purpose is to clarify decision rights and accountability, ensuring that responsibility for outcomes remains with human decision-makers.

Routine forecasting activities such as baseline prediction generation or trend analysis—can be automated to improve efficiency and consistency. However, forecasts that affect high-impact decisions, including external commitments, resource allocation, or strategic initiatives, require explicit human review and approval. To support this balance, governance frameworks typically include several key mechanisms:

a. Clearly defined decision rights, distinguishing automated processes from human judgment responsibilities.
b. Override procedures that allow experts to adjust or reject forecasts when contextual factors justify deviation.
c. Escalation pathways for resolving disagreements or handling high-risk forecasting situations.
d. Documentation and auditability to ensure transparency, learning, and accountability.

These mechanisms prevent both blind trust in AI systems and arbitrary dismissal of data-driven insights.

5.3 Collaborative Forecasting

Collaborative forecasting integrates AI predictions with input from teams and domain experts throughout the delivery lifecycle. AI systems provide consistent baselines and uncertainty estimates, while humans contribute contextual interpretation and practical insight.

Teams closest to the work are well positioned to identify dependencies, risks, and unusual circumstances that may not be visible in historical data. Their input helps validate and refine AI-generated forecasts, particularly for complex or novel initiatives. Expert adjustments further enhance forecast quality by incorporating architectural, organizational, and strategic considerations.

Continuous feedback loops connect forecast outcomes back to both human decision-makers and AI models. When forecasts are accurate, they reinforce trust in the system; when they fail, they provide learning opportunities that inform model improvement and judgment calibration. Over time, this collaborative approach enables a balanced integration of automation and human oversight, producing forecasts that are not only accurate but also context-aware, ethical, and practically useful.

5.4 Change Management and Adoption

Adopting AI-based delivery forecasting is mainly a change management challenge, not just a technical one. Even accurate models will fail if users do not trust or understand them. Successful adoption depends on building trust, skills, and supportive organizational practices.

Stakeholder support is needed at all levels. Teams must see forecasting as helpful rather than controlling, managers must experience better planning outcomes, and leaders must understand its strategic value. Pilot projects are an effective way to build trust by showing clear benefits in real situations before scaling up.

Training is essential to avoid misuse. Stakeholders should understand that AI forecasts are probabilistic and meant to support decisions, not to create fixed commitments. Training should be tailored so teams, managers, and leaders know how to interpret and use forecasts appropriately.

Long-term adoption requires cultural alignment. Organizations need to move from intuition-based estimates to data-driven forecasting while accepting uncertainty as normal. Leadership support and consistent use of forecasts in planning help embed this change into everyday practice.

6. IMPLEMENTATION ARCHITECTURE

The successful adoption of AI-based Agile delivery forecasting depends not only on algorithms, but also on a robust, scalable, and maintainable technical architecture. The system must be able to collect data from multiple sources, process it efficiently, deliver reliable predictions, and present results in a form that is easy to understand for stakeholders (Alenezi & Akour, 2025).

This architecture is designed to support the complete forecasting workflow, including data collection, data processing, model execution, system integration, and visualization.

6.1 System Design

Data Pipeline Architecture

The data pipeline constitutes the foundational infrastructure of the AI-based Agile delivery forecasting system, enabling the collection, preparation, and delivery of data for both model training and real-time prediction. In Agile environments, delivery data originates from heterogeneous sources, including issue tracking systems, code repositories, CI/CD pipelines, collaboration platforms, and, in some cases, manual inputs. These sources differ significantly in structure, update frequency, and data quality, necessitating a robust and adaptable pipeline design.

To manage this complexity, the system adopts a layered data pipeline architecture comprising ingestion, transformation, storage, serving, and monitoring layers. This architectural separation improves data consistency, system reliability, and maintainability while supporting both historical analysis and real-time forecasting requirements. Figure 2 illustrates the conceptual structure of this layered pipeline and the flow of data across components.

The ingestion layer is responsible for collecting data from source systems through APIs, webhooks, and scheduled extraction jobs. Tools such as Jira, Azure DevOps, Git repositories, and CI/CD platforms provide continuous updates on work item status, code changes, and deployment events. Basic reliability mechanisms, including retry handling, schema validation, and source health checks, are employed to ensure stable and consistent data acquisition.

The transformation layer processes raw input data into structured, analysis-ready formats. This includes data cleaning, normalization, handling of missing or inconsistent values, and the computation of key Agile flow metrics such as cycle time, throughput, and work-in-progress. Both batch processing of historical data and streaming transformation of near-real-time events are supported to ensure that forecasts remain accurate and responsive to changing delivery conditions.

The storage layer persists data according to its analytical purpose. Raw data is retained for traceability, auditing, and potential reprocessing, while transformed datasets are stored in analytical databases optimized for machine learning workloads and time-series analysis. This separation supports forecast reproducibility and enables retrospective model validation and performance assessment.

The serving layer provides efficient access to prepared datasets and prediction outputs through APIs and analytical interfaces. Caching mechanisms and in-memory storage are employed to reduce latency, enabling real-time forecasting services and interactive dashboards that support operational and managerial decision-making.

Monitoring operates as a cross-cutting layer spanning the entire pipeline. It supports data quality validation, pipeline health monitoring, and data lineage tracking, enabling early detection of anomalies and degradation in forecast reliability. By making system behavior observable, monitoring mechanisms play a critical role in maintaining trust, ensuring robustness, and supporting human-in-the-loop governance of AI-based forecasting systems.

Figure 2. Data pipeline architecture for AI-based Agile delivery forecasting

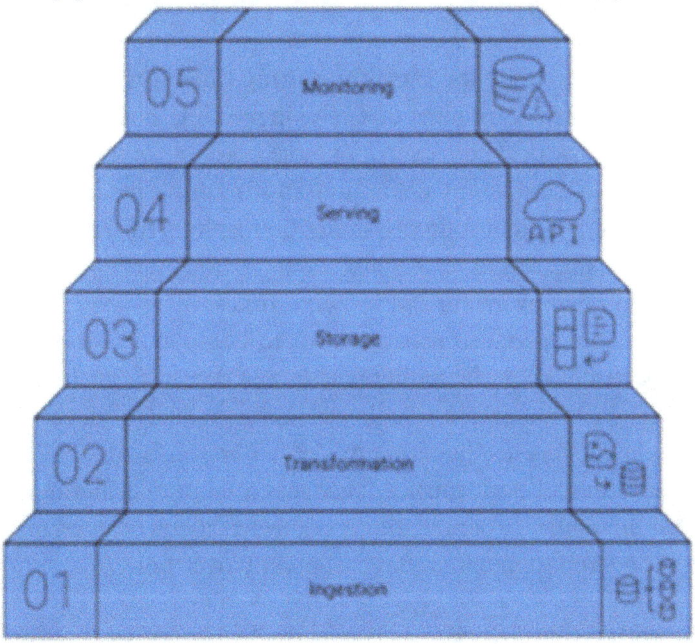

As illustrated in Figure 2, the layered architecture enables a clear separation of concerns across the data lifecycle. Data flows sequentially from ingestion to transformation and storage, before being exposed through serving interfaces for forecasting and visualization. The inclusion of monitoring as a cross-cutting capability ensures continuous visibility into data quality, pipeline health, and system performance, allowing potential issues to be detected and addressed before they compromise forecast reliability. This architectural design supports scalability and adaptability, enabling the forecasting system to evolve alongside changes in tools, processes, and organizational structure.

Model Serving Infrastructure

Model serving provides the operational bridge between trained machine learning models and production environments that require delivery forecasts. Unlike model training, which is typically performed periodically, model serving must deliver predictions with low latency, high reliability, and sufficient scalability to support concurrent users and applications.

The architectural approach to model serving depends on system complexity and organizational needs. In simpler settings, models may be embedded directly within applications. However, in more advanced implementations, models are deployed as independent services accessed through APIs. This service-oriented approach enables centralized model management, supports zero-downtime updates, and allows multiple applications to reuse the same forecasting capabilities.

For delivery forecasting systems that rely on multiple models such as separate models for different work types, teams, or time horizons ensemble strategies are commonly applied. In these setups, predictions from multiple models are combined to produce more robust and stable outputs. Prediction caching further improves system performance by reusing recent results when input parameters change infrequently, reducing computational overhead and response times.

Model updates are managed using controlled deployment strategies designed to minimize operational risk, including blue–green deployments to switch models without service interruption, canary deployments for gradual rollout and monitoring, and shadow deployments to evaluate new models without affecting users. Continuous monitoring tracks model performance, changes in input distributions, and output behavior. When anomalies or degradation are detected, alerts or automated retraining processes are triggered to maintain forecast quality over time.

Integration with Agile Tools

To ensure practical value, the forecasting system is integrated directly into the Agile tools used in daily development activities. This integration allows prediction results to appear within existing workflows, enabling teams and stakeholders to access delivery insights without switching applications or disrupting established routines.

The system connects with commonly used Agile platforms to collect real-time project and development data and to present forecasts in context. Integration with Jira enables retrieval of issue updates, task status changes, assignments, and completion events through APIs and webhooks, while forecasting results are displayed through dashboards, custom fields, or built-in gadgets. Azure DevOps integration supports data collection from work items, pull requests, builds, and deployments, and presents forecast insights through dashboard widgets or dedicated views that enhance visibility into delivery risks and potential delays.

Integration with GitHub focuses on development-centric metrics such as pull request activity, review duration, and merge frequency. Forecast-related insights can be attached directly to pull requests, supporting more informed decision-making during development and review processes. Collaboration tools such as Slack and Microsoft Teams further extend accessibility by providing chatbot-based queries, scheduled notifications, and proactive alerts related to delivery risks. All integrations are designed with reliability, security, and minimal disruption in mind, ensuring that forecasting capabilities enhance Agile workflows rather than interfere with them.

Dashboard and Visualization Layer

The visualization layer translates probabilistic forecasting outputs into insights that are understandable and actionable for diverse stakeholders. Dashboards are tailored to different user roles, ranging from executives to delivery teams. High-level views present portfolio overviews, milestone risks, and capacity utilization, while avoiding deterministic delivery dates in favor of probabilistic ranges that more accurately represent uncertainty.

At the release and team levels, dashboards incorporate burn-up charts with confidence intervals, cumulative flow diagrams, and cycle time distributions. Drill-down capabilities allow users to explore underlying contributors to delivery risk, such as bottlenecks, work-in-progress constraints, or changes in throughput. Uncertainty is explicitly visualized through confidence bands and best–expected–worst case scenarios. Interactive elements enable users to explore alternative outcomes based on different risk tolerances. Support for real-time updates, accessibility, responsive design, and export features ensures that forecast insights can be effectively used in planning discussions, reports, and stakeholder communications.

6.2 Technology Stack

Selecting an appropriate technology stack is essential for implementing an AI-based Agile delivery forecasting system. The stack must support data ingestion and processing, model development and serving, system integration, and effective visualization of results. Given the diversity of these requirements, practical implementations typically rely on a combination of programming languages, frameworks, and supporting technologies.

Python is widely used for data analysis and machine learning due to its extensive ecosystem and support for rapid experimentation. It enables efficient model development and evaluation, although performance-critical components may require optimization or complementary technologies. R is often employed for statistical analysis and probabilistic forecasting, particularly during exploratory analysis and model validation, where its statistical libraries provide strong analytical support.

Backend services, including data pipelines and APIs, are commonly implemented using languages such as Java, Kotlin, or Go, which offer reliability, scalability, and stable performance in production environments. The visualization layer is typically developed using JavaScript or TypeScript, with frontend frameworks such as React or Vue supporting the creation of interactive dashboards that present Agile metrics and probabilistic forecasts in a clear and user-friendly manner.

In addition to programming languages, the system relies on supporting technologies such as SQL-based data warehouses for transformation and historical analysis, machine learning frameworks including Scikit-learn, TensorFlow, or PyTorch for model development, and workflow orchestration tools such as Apache Airflow or Prefect for managing data and model pipelines. Cloud platforms provide scalable and resilient infrastructure, while containerization and Kubernetes support consistent deployment and management of services. MLOps practices complement the technology stack by enabling reliable model tracking, testing, deployment, and monitoring across the model lifecycle, supporting a structured transition from experimentation to production.

6.3 Data Governance and Security

Data governance and security are fundamental to maintaining forecast accuracy, regulatory compliance, and stakeholder trust in AI-based delivery forecasting systems. Weaknesses in data management or security controls can directly undermine prediction quality and organizational decision-making.

Data quality assurance ensures that forecasting inputs are accurate, consistent, and reliable. Automated validation is applied during ingestion and transformation to verify schema conformity, acceptable value ranges, and compliance with domain-specific rules. Records that fail validation may be rejected, quarantined for review, or corrected using predefined remediation strategies. Periodic data profiling analyzes distributions and detects unexpected changes over time, enabling early identification of anomalies, data drift, or systematic degradation that could impair model performance.

To support continuous data quality management, the system incorporates anomaly detection mechanisms, data lineage tracking, and explicit data quality metrics such as completeness, consistency, and timeliness. These capabilities enable rapid diagnosis of data issues and support ongoing improvement of data reliability.

Privacy and compliance considerations are critical, as forecasting systems process data related to individuals, teams, and organizational performance. Data minimization principles are applied to limit collection and retention to information necessary for forecasting purposes, while aggregation or anonymization is used where possible to reduce privacy risks. Compliance with regulations such as the General Data Protection Regulation (GDPR) and the California Consumer Privacy Act (CCPA) requires mechanisms for data access, correction, and deletion, as well as transparency regarding data usage and model behavior. Fairness considerations are addressed through periodic bias assessments and mitigation strategies to prevent systematic disadvantages affecting specific teams or groups.

System security is implemented using a layered defense approach. Centralized authentication and role-based authorization restrict access according to functional responsibilities, while encryption protects data at rest and in transit. Secure secrets management, audit logging, and vulnerability scanning of dependencies and container images further strengthen system protection. Clearly defined incident response procedures ensure that security events are handled in a timely and coordinated manner, with post-incident evaluations used to improve resilience and governance over time.

6.4 Total Cost of Ownership (TCO) and Return on Investment (ROI) Considerations

While AI-enhanced probabilistic forecasting offers significant potential to improve delivery predictability, its organizational adoption entails non-trivial costs that extend beyond initial model development. A realistic assessment of Total Cost of Ownership (TCO) is therefore essential to avoid underestimating the long-term investment required to sustain reliable, decision-relevant forecasting capabilities.

Initial implementation costs typically include data integration and preparation, development of baseline statistical models, and configuration of real-time data pipelines for flow metrics. Additional upfront effort is required to establish governance structures, define forecast usage policies, and align forecasting outputs with existing Agile planning and reporting practices. These activities often demand cross-functional collaboration between delivery teams, data engineers, and management, increasing coordination overhead during early adoption phases.

Ongoing operational costs constitute a substantial portion of TCO. Sustained forecasting performance depends on continuous data quality monitoring, model recalibration, and infrastructure maintenance. Organizations must allocate dedicated capacity for data engineering, MLOps, and analytical oversight to address issues such as concept drift, changing team composition, and evolving delivery processes. Furthermore, human-in-the-loop governance including regular review forums, escalation mechanisms, and decision accountability introduces recurring organizational effort that cannot be fully automated.

Return on investment (ROI) from AI-driven delivery forecasting typically materializes over multiple time horizons. In the short term, organizations may observe improvements in transparency and risk awareness, even if forecast accuracy gains remain modest. Medium-term benefits often include more stable planning outcomes, reduced schedule volatility, and fewer last-minute scope renegotiations. Long-term ROI emerges as organizations internalize probabilistic thinking, leading to improved trust between delivery teams and stakeholders, more resilient planning practices, and better-aligned investment decisions.

Importantly, underinvestment in sustaining forecasting capabilities poses significant risks. Insufficient resourcing for data maintenance or governance can lead to model degradation, false confidence in outdated predictions, and erosion of stakeholder trust. Consequently, organizations should evaluate AI-enhanced forecasting initiatives not as one-time technical projects but as enduring socio-technical capabilities that require continuous investment, stewardship, and organizational learning.

The implementation aspects discussed in this section emphasize that AI-based delivery forecasting is as much an engineering challenge as it is an analytical one. Model serving infrastructure, tool integration, visualization layers, and governance mechanisms collectively determine whether forecasts are usable, trustworthy, and actionable. Technology choices must therefore balance scalability, flexibility, and maintainability while supporting transparency and uncertainty communication. When implemented effectively, these components allow forecasting systems to augment Agile planning processes rather than impose additional complexity, setting the stage for evaluating organizational, ethical, and human factors.

7. CASE STUDIES AND PRACTICAL APPLICATIONS

While architectural designs provide a strong foundation for AI-enhanced Agile forecasting, real-world implementation reveals practical challenges and trade-offs. This section presents two case studies from different organizational contexts to illustrate how AI-based forecasting is applied in practice. The first case examines a large enterprise software company, while the second focuses on a mid-sized digital product team. Together, these cases highlight implementation strategies, challenges, results, and lessons learned. The chapter concludes with industry benchmarks to position the case study outcomes within broader trends.

Table 4 provides a comparative summary of the two case studies, highlighting implementation approaches, outcomes, and key lessons learned before the detailed discussion in Sections 7.1 and 7.2

Table 4. Summary of Case Study Implementation Results

Aspect	Enterprise Case	Mid-sized Team Case
Organizational context	Multinational enterprise with 15 distributed Agile teams and scaled planning processes.	Mid-sized SaaS company with three cross-functional teams and rapid delivery cycles.
Primary forecasting challenge	Low forecast accuracy (37%), heavy estimation effort, poor dependency management, and low executive confidence.	Informal and intuition-driven forecasting with low confidence in delivery commitments.
Implementation scope	Organization-wide rollout following a phased, multi-year adoption strategy.	Team-level implementation using lightweight tools and minimal infrastructure.
Implementation approach	Phased deployment: pilot → expansion → portfolio-scale adoption with governance and training.	Incremental, pragmatic deployment integrated into existing team rituals.
Forecasting technique used	Monte Carlo simulation, regression-based models, and ensemble forecasting at scale.	Monte Carlo simulation based on limited historical cycle time data.
Governance model	Formal human-in-the-loop governance with defined decision rights and escalation mechanisms.	Informal but explicit human oversight led by product managers.
Forecast accuracy outcome	Improvement from 37% to 83% delivery within the 85th percentile forecast.	Improvement to 76% delivery within the 85th percentile forecast.
Organizational impact	Increased predictability, reduced estimation effort, improved strategic planning, and positive ROI.	Improved planning reliability, risk-aware decision-making, and positive ROI.
Key challenges encountered	Data quality issues, cultural resistance, tool heterogeneity, and regulatory constraints.	Limited historical data and resource constraints.
Key lessons learned	Start simple, invest in change management, maintain data quality, and treat forecasting as continuous learning.	Lightweight approaches can deliver strong value when aligned with team context.

7.1 Case Study 1: Enterprise Software Company

Context and Challenges

GlobalTech Solutions is a multinational enterprise software company with approximately 3,500 employees and 15 distributed Agile teams. The organization follows a scaled Agile framework with quarterly planning and bi-weekly sprints. Prior to AI adoption, forecasting relied on velocity-based planning, manual estimation, and spreadsheet aggregation.

This approach resulted in several problems. Forecast accuracy was low, with only 37% of features delivered within the planned quarter. Estimation activities consumed significant time but provided limited predictive value. Executive stakeholders lacked confidence in delivery commitments, leading to conservative planning and delayed strategic initiatives. Cross-team dependencies were poorly managed, contributing to delivery delays, and there was no structured learning mechanism to improve forecasting over time.

The move toward AI-enhanced forecasting was driven by the need to improve delivery predictability, support strategic decision-making, and increase organizational agility. However, implementation faced challenges related to poor historical data quality, heterogeneous tools (Jira and Azure DevOps), varying team maturity, cultural resistance, and regulatory constraints.

Implementation Approach

GlobalTech adopted a phased implementation over 18 months.

a. Phase 1: Foundation and Pilot

A pilot was conducted with two teams using historical data extracted from Agile tools. A simple data pipeline and Monte Carlo simulation based on cycle time distributions were implemented. Forecasts were presented as probabilistic ranges rather than fixed dates. Results showed strong accuracy for mature teams but weaker performance for less stable teams, highlighting the impact of team maturity.

b. Phase 2: Enhancement and Expansion

The system was expanded to additional teams, with improved data pipelines, automated data quality checks, and more advanced models, including regression and dependency-aware forecasting. Forecasts were integrated directly into Agile tools such as Jira and Slack. Governance structures and training sessions were introduced to build trust and improve understanding of probabilistic forecasts.

c. Phase 3: Scaling and Sophistication

The solution was scaled to all teams using a cloud-native architecture. Ensemble models combined multiple forecasting techniques, and advanced dashboards supported portfolio-level and scenario-based analysis. Human-in-the-loop governance ensured transparency, interpretability, and continuous lcarning.

Results and Lessons Learned

Forecast accuracy improved significantly, with 83% of features delivered within the 85th percentile forecast, compared to 37% before implementation. Estimation effort was reduced, stakeholder confidence increased, and dependency-related delays decreased. The initiative achieved positive ROI within the first year.

Key lessons included the importance of starting simple, investing in change management, maintaining data quality, embracing uncertainty, preserving team autonomy, and treating forecasting as a continuous learning process rather than a one-time deployment.

7.2 Case Study 2: Digital Product Team

Context and Challenges

TechForward Labs is a mid-sized SaaS company with approximately 120 employees, operating in a fast-paced startup environment. The organization is structured around three cross-functional product squads practicing short sprint cycles and continuous deployment. Prior to adopting AI-enhanced forecasting, delivery predictions were largely informal, intuition-driven, and inconsistent across teams, resulting in low confidence in delivery timelines among both internal stakeholders and customers.

In contrast to the enterprise-scale case, TechForward faced constraints in terms of resources, data volume, and infrastructure maturity. However, these limitations were partially offset by a strong data-oriented culture and the use of modern development and collaboration tools. The immediate catalyst for change was a missed customer delivery commitment, which exposed the risks of relying solely on qualitative judgment and underscored the need for more structured, evidence-based forecasting practices.

Implementation Strategy

TechForward adopted a lightweight and pragmatic implementation strategy aligned with its organizational context. Rather than introducing complex infrastructure or advanced machine learning models, the company leveraged existing tools such as GitHub, Linear, and cloud-based analytics services to minimize development and operational overhead.

Given the limited availability of historical data, simple Monte Carlo simulations based on observed cycle time distributions were selected as the primary forecasting method. This approach allowed uncertainty to be explicitly represented without requiring large datasets or complex model training. Forecast outputs were embedded directly into existing team rituals, including sprint planning meetings, weekly reviews, and retrospectives, ensuring that forecasts complemented rather than disrupted established Agile practices.

Visualization was implemented using existing dashboard tools, while lightweight Slack integrations provided on-demand access to forecast information within daily communication channels. Governance remained informal but clearly defined: product managers were responsible for interpreting probabilistic forecasts, contextualizing results, and communicating implications to stakeholders. Importantly, forecasts were positioned as discussion inputs rather than commitments, preserving team autonomy and encouraging critical evaluation.

Outcomes

Despite the simplicity of the chosen models, delivery forecasting accuracy improved substantially. Forecasts achieved approximately 76% accuracy at the 85th percentile, representing a significant improvement over pre-implementation estimates. More importantly, planning conversations shifted from deterministic date commitments toward risk-based and scenario-oriented discussions.

Stakeholder confidence increased as uncertainty was communicated more transparently, and teams reported improved alignment between expectations and actual delivery outcomes. The initiative achieved a positive return on investment within the first year, demonstrating that AI-enhanced forecasting does not require sophisticated infrastructure to generate value. This case illustrates that, when combined with clear human oversight and integration into Agile rituals, even lightweight forecasting approaches can materially improve delivery predictability and decision quality.

7.3 Industry Benchmarks

Industry benchmarks show that AI-enhanced Agile forecasting typically leads to significant improvements in delivery predictability. Studies report median improvements in forecast accuracy from around 40% to nearly 80% at the 85th percentile. Mean Absolute Percentage Error (MAPE) is commonly reduced by more than half.

Return on investment varies by organizational size but is generally positive, with payback periods ranging from 6 to 18 months. Key success factors consistently identified include strong executive support, good data quality, effective change management, appropriate model complexity, and integration with existing workflows.

Overall, industry evidence supports the conclusion that AI-enhanced forecasting can deliver meaningful benefits when aligned with organizational context and supported by sound governance and continuous learning.

A comparison between AI-enhanced probabilistic forecasting and traditional Agile estimation highlights clear performance differences. Prior to AI adoption, delivery forecasting relied on velocity-based planning and expert judgment, resulting in low reliability, with only 37% of features delivered within planned timeframes. These traditional methods produced point estimates that failed to represent uncertainty and were difficult to scale across teams.

After introducing probabilistic AI-based forecasting, delivery reliability improved substantially. In the enterprise case, 83% of features were delivered within the 85th percentile forecast, while the mid-sized team achieved 76% reliability using a lightweight Monte Carlo approach. These results indicate that even simple probabilistic techniques outperform conventional Agile estimation in managing uncertainty, improving predictability, and supporting risk-aware decision-making without compromising Agile principles.

7.4 Human Governance in AI-Based Forecasting

The integration of artificial intelligence into Agile delivery forecasting necessitates explicit human governance mechanisms to ensure responsible, effective, and context-aware use of predictive outputs. While AI models offer powerful capabilities for analyzing historical data, quantifying uncertainty, and identifying delivery patterns, they lack situational awareness, ethical judgment, and accountability. As a result, AI-based forecasting systems must be designed as decision-support tools rather than autonomous decision-makers.

A central principle of human-in-the-loop governance is the clear separation between prediction and decision. Forecasts generated by AI models represent probabilistic assessments based on available data and assumptions; they do not constitute commitments, mandates, or guarantees. Treating forecasts as fixed targets undermines both Agile principles and responsible AI use, as it creates false certainty and shifts accountability from humans to algorithms. Instead, forecasts should serve as structured inputs for discussion, risk assessment, and scenario exploration among teams and stakeholders.

Human oversight is required at multiple stages of the forecasting lifecycle. During model design and training, human judgment is necessary to define relevant features, validate assumptions, and assess whether historical data appropriately represents current delivery contexts. During deployment and use, humans must interpret probabilistic outputs, evaluate their plausibility, and incorporate qualitative knowledge that models cannot capture, such as emerging technical risks, organizational changes, or strategic trade-offs. For high-impact decisions, such as external commitments or portfolio-level planning, explicit human approval and review processes are essential.

Effective governance also requires transparency and explainability to support informed human intervention. Stakeholders must understand what a forecast represents, its confidence range, key drivers, and known limitations. Explainable outputs enable teams to challenge forecasts constructively, learn from deviations, and improve both delivery practices and models over time. Without transparency, forecasts risk being perceived as opaque prescriptions rather than collaborative planning aids.

Finally, accountability for outcomes must remain firmly with human decision-makers. When forecasts prove inaccurate, the appropriate response is not to assign blame to the model, but to conduct reflective analysis of data quality, assumptions, process changes, and governance decisions. Blameless review practices align human-in-the-loop forecasting with Agile values of learning and adaptation. By embedding explicit human governance structures, organizations can leverage AI to enhance predictability while preserving autonomy, ethical responsibility, and trust across Agile delivery systems.

8. CHALLENGES AND LIMITATIONS

Although the comparative results demonstrate the clear advantages of probabilistic AI-enhanced forecasting over traditional Agile estimation methods, these improvements should not be interpreted as universally applicable across all organizational contexts. Forecasting performance is strongly influenced by the availability, quality, and consistency of delivery data, as well as by the organization's readiness to adopt data-driven decision-making practices. Therefore, the following section discusses key organizational and data-related constraints that may limit the applicability of AI-based forecasting, particularly in small or less data-mature Agile environments.

Although AI-enhanced Agile delivery forecasting offers clear benefits, its implementation and long-term operation face significant challenges. These challenges span technical, organizational, and ethical dimensions, and they shape both the effectiveness and sustainability of forecasting systems.

Some limitations are inherent to the nature of software delivery, where uncertainty, change, and human factors cannot be fully eliminated. Others stem from data quality, organizational readiness, or design choices and can be mitigated through deliberate effort. Understanding these challenges is essential to avoid unrealistic expectations and to deploy forecasting systems responsibly.

While AI-enhanced forecasting shows strong benefits, its effectiveness is constrained by organizational data maturity. Small or early stage Agile teams often lack sufficient historical delivery data to support complex AI models, limiting predictive reliability. In such contexts, lightweight probabilistic approaches, such as Monte Carlo simulation based on cycle time, may be more appropriate than data-intensive machine learning models. Furthermore, organizational readiness including consistent work item definitions, stable workflow policies, and disciplined data capture plays a critical role in successful adoption. Without these foundations, AI-based forecasting risks producing misleading results, emphasizing the need for phased implementation strategies aligned with an organization's data and process maturity.

The adoption of AI-enhanced probabilistic forecasting also entails non-trivial costs and implementation efforts. Beyond model development, organizations must invest in data infrastructure, process standardization, and ongoing model maintenance. These requirements may increase operational complexity, particularly for teams with limited analytical resources. However, when compared to the hidden costs of unreliable planning such as delayed releases, overcommitment, and inefficient resource allocation the trade-off can be justified. In practice, organizations may mitigate these costs by adopting a phased approach, starting with simple probabilistic techniques and gradually introducing more advanced AI models as data maturity and organizational readiness increase.

Several implementation attempts revealed that AI-based forecasting can fail when models are deployed without sufficient data quality, process stability, or stakeholder understanding. In some cases, overreliance on automated predictions led to reduced team trust and misinterpretation of probabilistic outputs. These experiences highlight the importance of aligning AI forecasting with Agile values, ensuring transparency and interpretability, and maintaining active human oversight. Effective implementation therefore requires not only technical capability, but also organizational learning, expectation management, and continuous feedback mechanisms.

8.1 Technical Challenges

Data Availability and Quality Issues

Data constitutes the foundation of AI-based delivery forecasting, and limitations in data availability and quality represent one of the most significant technical challenges. Unlike domains where synthetic or augmented datasets can be generated, delivery forecasting relies on authentic historical records of completed work, team behavior, and project characteristics. Consequently, forecast reliability is tightly constrained by both the quantity and integrity of available data.

Many organizations lack sufficient historical data to train reliable forecasting models. This challenge is particularly common in newly formed teams, organizations transitioning to Agile practices, or teams that have recently changed tools, workflows, or organizational structures. Statistical and machine learning models typically require substantial observational histories to identify stable patterns and avoid overfitting. When data is sparse, forecasts tend to exhibit high variance and instability, small changes in input data can result in disproportionate shifts in predictions, and generalization to future work becomes weak. The problem is especially acute for rare but high-impact initiatives, where limited historical analogues constrain the ability to produce meaningful forecasts.

Time-series forecasting methods face additional limitations in Agile environments. Techniques such as ARIMA assume long, stationary histories, whereas Agile teams frequently undergo process changes, team reconfigurations, or tooling migrations. These structural breaks undermine historical continuity and reduce the applicability of past patterns for future prediction.

Beyond data quantity, delivery data often suffers from pervasive quality issues. Agile management tools rely heavily on manual data entry, and practices vary widely across teams. Common problems include missing or incomplete work item fields, inconsistent categorization of similar work, incorrect or retroactively modified timestamps, and poorly documented dependencies. Story point estimates are particularly problematic due to inconsistent estimation practices, misuse of relative scales as absolute measures, and the influence of political or social pressures. Workflow inconsistencies further degrade data quality, as work items may be moved prematurely into active states, left unchanged during interruptions, or updated in batches rather than in real time. Integration across multiple tools compounds these issues through schema mismatches, inconsistent terminology, and evolving data models.

Addressing these challenges requires both organizational and technical interventions. Organizations benefit from establishing clear data standards, training teams on consistent tool usage, and implementing automated validation rules and anomaly detection mechanisms. Making data quality visible through dashboards and regular reviews reinforces accountability. When historical data is limited, simpler and data-light approaches such as Monte Carlo simulation can provide more robust forecasts than complex models. Hierarchical modeling can allow information sharing across related teams, while carefully calibrated external benchmarks may supplement internal data. In all cases, explicit uncertainty quantification is essential; wider confidence intervals provide a more honest representation of limited data and support appropriate interpretation by stakeholders.

Model Complexity versus Interpretability

A central technical challenge in AI-enhanced delivery forecasting is balancing predictive accuracy with interpretability. More complex models often achieve higher accuracy by capturing non-linear relationships, yet their internal logic is difficult for humans to understand and trust. Advanced techniques such as gradient boosting, random forests, and neural networks can obscure causal reasoning, making it challenging to explain individual predictions.

When forecasts are presented, stakeholders naturally seek explanations for why specific delivery dates or confidence intervals are produced. Black-box models struggle to provide explanations that adequately support decision justification, risk mitigation, and organizational learning. While post-hoc explainability tools such as feature importance analysis or partial dependence plots offer limited insight, they rarely provide sufficient transparency for high-stakes decisions.

Lack of interpretability directly affects trust and adoption. When model outputs contradict practitioner intuition, stakeholders may be unable to distinguish between genuinely insightful forecasts and model error. This uncertainty often leads organizations to revert to familiar human judgment, even when empirical performance favors algorithmic approaches. The issue is amplified in contexts involving customer commitments or strategic planning, where opaque forecasts risk being perceived as prescriptions rather than inputs for discussion.

Organizations can manage this trade-off through layered modeling strategies. Simple, interpretable models can serve as baselines, while more complex models provide supplementary validation. Explainability techniques such as SHAP or LIME can support transparency when complexity is unavoidable, and systematic documentation of assumptions, limitations, and appropriate use cases helps align expectations. The optimal balance depends on organizational maturity, with data-literate organizations better positioned to tolerate complexity than those at earlier stages of adoption.

Integration with Legacy Systems

AI-based forecasting systems must typically integrate with existing tools and infrastructure. Legacy systems often lack modern APIs, enforce restrictive security policies, or employ outdated data models. Technical integration challenges include unstable or limited API access, authentication constraints, undocumented custom fields, and network or data residency restrictions. Data model mismatches further complicate integration, as legacy tools may overwrite historical states or fail to preserve temporal information required for flow analysis.

Effective integration strategies include the use of abstraction layers that isolate system-specific logic, incremental integration starting with minimal viable datasets, cached staging layers for analytical access, and middleware that normalizes heterogeneous sources. In some cases, integration limitations cannot be fully resolved. When critical data is unavailable, forecasting systems must explicitly acknowledge reduced reliability and increased uncertainty rather than masking these limitations.

8.2 Organizational Challenges

AI-enhanced forecasting introduces substantial organizational change, challenging established practices, redistributing decision authority, and requiring new ways of thinking about planning and accountability. Resistance can emerge at multiple organizational levels.

At the team level, development groups may perceive forecasting systems as mechanisms of surveillance or as threats to autonomy. Historical misuse of metrics can intensify concerns about micromanagement and blame. Some practitioners also view forecasting as incompatible with Agile values, associating it with rigid, predictive planning. Early inaccuracies in AI-generated forecasts may further reinforce skepticism.

At the management and executive levels, resistance may arise when data-driven forecasts challenge intuition, expose unrealistic commitments, or replace deterministic answers with probabilistic ranges. Concerns regarding implementation costs, delayed return on investment, and competing strategic priorities also influence leadership adoption decisions.

Overcoming resistance requires deliberate change management. Clear communication of non-punitive intent, early involvement of teams in system design, and education in probabilistic thinking are essential. Pilot initiatives that demonstrate tangible value in low-risk contexts can build confidence incrementally, while early successes help establish credibility.

A related challenge is the skills gap associated with AI-enhanced forecasting. Effective implementation requires interdisciplinary expertise spanning data engineering, statistics, machine learning, Agile delivery, and organizational context. Bridging this gap often involves cross-functional collaboration, targeted training programs, communities of practice, and external partnerships that emphasize explicit knowledge transfer.

Trust in AI-generated forecasts remains fragile and is easily undermined by opacity, early failures, or cognitive biases such as algorithmic aversion. Building trust depends on transparency, continuous performance monitoring, public accuracy reporting, gradual adoption in low-stakes decisions, and the preservation of human override and accountability mechanisms.

8.3 Ethical and Social Considerations

Forecasting models inevitably inherit biases embedded in historical data. Inequitable resource allocation, project assignment patterns, or organizational structures can produce biased predictions that reinforce existing disadvantages. Bias may arise indirectly through team composition, work type distribution, or prioritization practices.

Mitigating bias requires systematic governance practices, including regular audits across teams, careful feature selection, fairness-aware modeling where appropriate, and human contextual review of sensitive forecasts. Transparent documentation of model limitations is essential to prevent overinterpretation.

AI-based forecasting systems also risk unintended impacts on team morale and autonomy. When treated as control mechanisms rather than decision-support tools, forecasts can increase pressure, reduce psychological safety, and erode trust. Mitigation strategies include participatory system design, explicit governance against punitive use, balanced performance evaluation incorporating qualitative factors, and learning-oriented retrospectives.

Finally, accountability for forecast failures must remain clearly defined. AI systems can obscure responsibility if governance structures are weak. Effective oversight requires explicit role definitions, audit trails, human approval for high-impact decisions, and blameless post-incident reviews. Ultimately, accountability cannot be delegated to algorithms; forecasts are tools that support human judgment, not substitutes for responsibility.

This section underscores that the success of AI-enhanced delivery forecasting is constrained not only by technical limitations but also by organizational, ethical, and social factors. Data quality issues, resistance to change, skills gaps, and concerns around transparency and fairness directly influence trust and adoption. Addressing these challenges requires deliberate governance, clear accountability, and a strong human-in-the-loop approach that positions forecasts as decision-support tools rather than authoritative directives. Ultimately, responsible forecasting practices must align technical capabilities with organizational values to ensure sustainable and ethical use of AI in Agile environments.

9. CONCLUSION

This study highlights that accurate delivery forecasting in Agile environments cannot rely solely on traditional estimation techniques or intuition. By integrating AI-based probabilistic models with flow metrics, organizations can achieve more realistic, data-driven forecasts that explicitly account for uncertainty. The key insight is that forecasting should not aim for perfect prediction, but for informed decision-making that balances flexibility with predictability. AI enhances visibility into delivery patterns, risks, and trends, while Agile principles ensure continuous learning and adaptation.

From a practical perspective, practitioners are encouraged to start with simple, transparent forecasting approaches rather than complex models. Leveraging existing Agile data such as cycle time, throughput, and work-in-progress can already provide significant improvements in forecast reliability. AI-generated forecasts should be presented as probability ranges instead of fixed dates, and integrated directly into everyday Agile tools to support planning, communication, and risk management. Most importantly, forecasting systems must be positioned as decision-support tools that help teams plan better, not as mechanisms for control or performance pressure.

For the research community, this work calls for further exploration of human-centered AI in Agile contexts. Future research should focus on improving explainability of forecasting models, understanding long-term organizational impacts, and developing governance frameworks that ensure ethical and responsible use. Empirical studies across diverse organizational settings are also needed to validate forecasting approaches and identify best practices for adoption at scale.

In conclusion, effective Agile delivery forecasting requires a balanced approach that combines AI capabilities with human judgment and experience. While AI excels at analyzing large volumes of data and quantifying uncertainty, human wisdom remains essential for interpreting context, making value-based decisions, and maintaining trust. By aligning computational intelligence with human insight, organizations can achieve more sustainable, ethical, and trustworthy forecasting practices that truly support Agile values.

REFERENCES

Alenezi, M., & Akour, M. (2025). AI-Driven Innovations in Software Engineering: A Review of Current Practices and Future Directions. In *Applied Sciences* (Vol. 15, Issue 3, p. 1344). DOI: 10.3390/app15031344

Almalki, S. S. (2025). AI-Driven Decision Support Systems in Agile Software Project Management: Enhancing Risk Mitigation and Resource Allocation. In *Systems* (Vol. 13, Issue 3, p. 208). DOI: 10.3390/systems13030208

Ameta, U., Patel, M., & Sharma, A. K. (2022). Scaled Agile Framework Implementation in Organizations', its Shortcomings and an AI Based Solution to Track Team's Performance. *2022 IEEE 3rd Global Conference for Advancement in Technology (GCAT)*, 1–7. DOI: 10.1109/GCAT55367.2022.9971968

Anwar, R., & Bashir, M. B. (2023). A Systematic Literature Review of AI-Based Software Requirements Prioritization Techniques. *IEEE Access : Practical Innovations, Open Solutions*, *11*, 143815–143860. DOI: 10.1109/ACCESS.2023.3343252

Chong, H.-Y., Yang, X., Goh, C. S., & Luo, Y. (2025). BIM and AI Integration for Dynamic Schedule Management: A Practical Framework and Case Study. In *Buildings* (Vol. 15, Issue 14, p. 2451). DOI: 10.3390/buildings15142451

Chowdhury, P., Mishra, S., Srivastava, S., Ghosh, R., Singh, D., Jena, J. J., & Darshana, S. (2024). Scalability and AI: An Insight on Software Project Management. *2024 6th International Conference on Computational Intelligence and Networks (CINE)*, 1–6. DOI: 10.1109/CINE63708.2024.10881438

Durrani, U. K., Akpinar, M., Adak, M. F., Kabakus, A. T., Öztürk, M. M., & Saleh, M. (2024). A Decade of Progress: A Systematic Literature Review on the Integration of AI in Software Engineering Phases and Activities (2013-2023). *IEEE Access : Practical Innovations, Open Solutions*, *12*, 171185–171204. DOI: 10.1109/ACCESS.2024.3488904

Ehtsham, M., Parisi, G., Pedone, F., Rossi, F., Zincani, M., Congiu, E., & Marchionni, C. (2025). AI-Powered Advanced Technologies for a Sustainable Built Environment: A Systematic Review on Emerging Challenges. In *Sustainability* (Vol. 17, Issue 17, p. 8005). DOI: 10.3390/su17178005

Gaona-Cuevas, M., Guerrero, V. B., & Vera-Rivera, F. H. (2024). The Smart Product Backlog: A Classification Model of User Stories. *IEEE Access : Practical Innovations, Open Solutions*, *12*, 150008–150019. DOI: 10.1109/ACCESS.2024.3478833

Hokmabadi, H., Rezvani, S. M. H. S., Hokmabadi, H., & de Almeida, N. M. (2025). Business Resilience Through AI-Agent Automation for SMEs and Startups: A Review on Agile Marketing and CRM. In *Information* (Vol. 16, Issue 11, p. 1000). DOI: 10.3390/info16111000

Ilieva, G., Yankova, T., Staribratov, P., Ruseva, G., & Iliev, Y. (2025). Industrial Digitalization: Systematic Literature Review and Bibliometric Analysis. In *Information* (Vol. 16, Issue 12, p. 1080). DOI: 10.3390/info16121080

Ispas, L., Mironeasa, C., Severin, T.-L., Cerlincă, D.-A., & Mironeasa, S. (2025). Artificial Intelligence Applications in Risk Management Within Integrated Management Systems: A Review. In *Systems* (Vol. 13, Issue 11, p. 967). DOI: 10.3390/systems13110967

Marçal, D., Metrôlho, J., & Ribeiro, F. (2025). Integrating Sentiment Analysis into Agile Feedback Loops for Continuous Improvement. In *Applied Sciences* (Vol. 15, Issue 22, p. 12329). DOI: 10.3390/app152212329

Martino, D., Perlangeli, C., Grottoli, B., La Rosa, L., & Pacella, M. (2025). A Knowledge-Driven Framework for AI-Augmented Business Process Management Systems: Bridging Explainability and Agile Knowledge Sharing. In *AI* (Vol. 6, Issue 6, p. 110). DOI: 10.3390/ai6060110

Mohammad, A., & Chirchir, B. (2024). Challenges of Integrating Artificial Intelligence in Software Project Planning: A Systematic Literature Review. In *Digital* (Vol. 4, Issue 3, pp. 555–571). DOI: 10.3390/digital4030028

Nabot, A., Alnaimat, F., Jebreen, I., Al-Qerem, A., & Ali, A. M. (2025). AI for Software Project Management: Predicting Delivery Times & Resource Allocation. *2025 12th International Conference on Information Technology (ICIT)*, 277–284. DOI: 10.1109/ICIT64950.2025.11049089

Patel, A., Laudya, R., Ragothaman, H., & Pandey, P. (2025). Applying Artificial Intelligence to DevOps: A Study on AI-Driven Anomaly Detection and Predictive Maintenance in Cloud Environments. *2025 1st International Conference on Secure IoT, Assured and Trusted Computing (SATC)*, 1–8. DOI: 10.1109/SATC65530.2025.11137316

Patel, D. K., Doshi, D. R., & Rawal, A. R. (2025). From Heuristics to AI: A Deep Dive into Software Project Resource Allocation. *2025 International Conference on Artificial Intelligence and Machine Vision (AIMV)*, 1–6. DOI: 10.1109/AIMV66517.2025.11203447

Radwan, A. M., Abdel-Fattah, M. A., & Mohamed, W. (2025). Smart Agile Prioritization and Clustering: An AI-Driven Approach for Requirements Prioritization. *IEEE Access : Practical Innovations, Open Solutions, 13*, 127335–127350. DOI: 10.1109/ACCESS.2025.3589959

Samhan, A. AlHajHassan, S., Dabaa't, S. A., & Elrashidi, A. (2024). A Review of AI-Assisted Impact Analysis for Software Requirements Change: Challenges and Future Directions. *2024 25th International Arab Conference on Information Technology (ACIT)*, 1–13. DOI: 10.1109/ACIT62805.2024.10877072

Sarwar, H., & Rahman, M. (2024). A Systematic Short Review of Machine Learning and Artificial Intelligence Integration in Current Project Management Techniques. *2024 IEEE 4th International Conference on Software Engineering and Artificial Intelligence (SEAI)*, 262–270. DOI: 10.1109/SEAI62072.2024.10674089

Seffe, N. S., Odzaly, E. E., & Samah, K. A. F. A. (2024). Data-driven Strategies for Enhanced Risk Management Performance in Software Development Perspective: an Agile Implementation. *2024 IEEE 22nd Student Conference on Research and Development (SCOReD)*, 122–127. DOI: 10.1109/SCOReD64708.2024.10872763

Semenov, S., Tsukur, V., Molokanova, V., Muchacki, M., Litawa, G., Mozhaiev, M., & Petrovska, I. (2025). Mathematical Model of the Software Development Process with Hybrid Management Elements. In *Applied Sciences* (Vol. 15, Issue 21, p. 11667). DOI: 10.3390/app152111667

Tasneem, N., Zulzalil, H. B., & Hassan, S. (2025). Enhancing Agile Software Development: A Systematic Literature Review of Requirement Prioritization and Reprioritization Techniques. *IEEE Access : Practical Innovations, Open Solutions, 13*, 32993–33034. DOI: 10.1109/ACCESS.2025.3539357

Velikov, V., & Ivanova, G. (2025). Intelligent Software Project Management: A Novel Approach to Risk Analysis and Resource Allocation. *2025 International Conference on Computer Systems and Technologies (CompSysTech)*, 1–8. DOI: 10.1109/CompSysTech65493.2025.11136946

Chapter 5
Cognitive Governance Framework:
Agile Prediction, Risk Intelligence, and Ethical Oversight

T. Ganesan
http://orcid.org/0009-0006-9941-1935
Dr. G.U. Pope College of Engineering, India

S. Harish Alwar
http://orcid.org/0009-0002-0554-3760
Dr. G.U. Pope College of Engineering, India

J. Abishek
http://orcid.org/0009-0000-6436-0900
Dr. G.U. Pope College of Engineering, India

K. DanielRaj
http://orcid.org/0009-0001-9863-5682
Kalaignarkarunanidhi Institute of Technology, India

ABSTRACT

The chapter examines how artificial intelligence (AI) fits into agile management routines inside today's firms - it sets out a full framework for predictive roadmapping, real time risk sensing and human-in-the-loop oversight. AI-driven analytics let firms forecast supply chain risks, balance resource loads and keep management adaptive, ethical plus open. The chapter lists step-by-step implementation tactics, worked case studies and a review of common obstacles - researchers and practitioners gain clear guidance for sharper management in agile, high variance supply chains.

DOI: 10.4018/979-8-3373-6851-1.ch005

INTRODUCTION

1.1 Overview of agile management in modern organizations

The current setting for most organizations includes fast digital change shifting customer requirements and supply chains that grow more intricate each year. Traditional management depends on fixed steps and after-the-fact checks - it cannot keep pace with this speed or detail. Agile management closes the distance by building adaptability, quick reaction plus repeated feedback into every management action - it lets a company keep its long term direction while teams keep freedom in daily work - value ships rapidly and oversight stays intact. (Schwaber & Sutherland, 2020)

The concept of agile management does not relax control - it builds a framework that changes rules and decision paths whenever circumstances demand. The core rules are - share all relevant facts, involve every affected party, decide in short cycles and track outcomes with numbers. The organization gives product teams freedom to reorder sprint tasks the moment fresh data arrives plus it keeps the full project list aligned with strategy through dashboards that forecast outcomes. (Rigby, Sutherland, & Noble, 2018)

1.2 Evolution of AI-Augmented Decision Frameworks

Artificial intelligence, real time data analytics, predictive insights and automation now sit inside management decisions. Early teams waited for clerks to compile reports that showed last quarter's numbers - the figures arrived too late to prevent damage. AI systems look forward - they list possible risks, forecast finish dates and propose specific changes. (Highsmith, 2019)

Machine-learning models compare past velocity records, defect logs plus chat timestamps. The models flag the projects whose schedules will probably slip and managers receive the alert early enough to reorder tasks or add staff. Natural-language routines read the same ticket databases and chat channels. The routines pick out words that signal new blockages or risks - push the text but also location to the dashboard. (Davenport & Ronanki, 2018)

1.3 The Importance of Predictive and Adaptive Management

Predictive management applies AI to forecast results. Adaptive management revises procedures after feedback. The two combine into systems that detect, read and react to shifting conditions. Firms then face less doubt, control risk better and earn more trust from stakeholders. Feedback loops record what worked plus what failed - management keeps refining its methods. (Russell & Norvig, 2021)

1.4 Chapter Objectives and Framework

The chapter sets out a complete plan for putting AI-supported agile management into practice - it presents the plan, shows how to build a predictive roadmap, explains how teams notice risk, describes human-in-the-loop oversight, lists rollout steps and reviews real cases. (Amershi et al., 2019)

2. BACKGROUND AND CONCEPTUAL FOUNDATION

2.1 Agile Governance - Principles and Challenges

Agile governance moves the habits of agile software work into the oversight of the whole organisation. Agile methods favour joint work, small frequent deliveries and fast reaction to change - agile governance checks that those habits serve the stated strategy, the rules set by regulators and the agreed risk limits. (Dignum, 2019)

The first rule is that teams stay free to decide local questions, yet a single framework holds them answerable for results. The framework needs open channels for messages, fixed titles for each role plus loops that return fresh data every day. (Varian, 2019)

The main problems are split ownership clashing decisions between teams and unclear links between one work group and the next. If no single board tracks every team, a delay in one group passes to the next without warning. (Gandomi & Haider, 2015)

2.2 The Role of Artificial Intelligence in Organizational Agility

AI speeds up how fast a firm reacts - it chews through daily data and returns clear numbers that teams use to decide. Predictive models, machine learners and language parsers spot trouble early plus reset tasks on the fly. (Witten et al., 2016)

One model feeds past velocity scores, backlog counts and defect totals into equations that flag future delays or staff gaps. A reinforcement engine then proposes who should do which job so capacity matches the top delivery goals. Once wired into management, the code triggers early fixes, ends the need for hand built reports and keeps both line but also top managers aware of what happens next. (Bostrom & Yudkowsky, 2014)

2.3 From Reactive to Predictive Governance Models

The old way of governing waits for signs that already happened - a project finishes late, a budget exceeds its limit or an audit uncovers faults. The new way feeds data into AI models that point to trouble or opportunity before it surfaces. The models scan trends in how code spreads across repositories, how people write messages and how teams performed in the past - flag anything that drifts from the norm. (Gartner, 2021)

The system inspects how often each developer submits code and what the automated tests return - if both drop, it marks the related module as likely to contain bugs. A separate risk score ranks every open issue - the score rises when impact plus probability climb - managers tackle the top items first and move staff hours to where they matter most. The shift turns the enterprise from an outfit that repairs damage after it appears into one that acts while the damage is still a forecast and it reacts to new data with speed but also exactness.2.3 From reactive to predictive governance models (ISO/IEC, 2023)

Figure 1. From Reactive to Predictive Governance Models

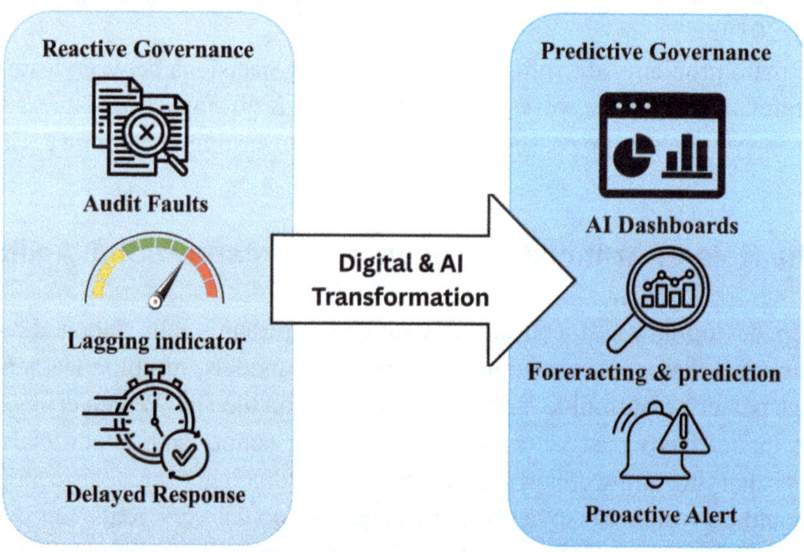

From reactive to predictive governance models

2.4 Comparative Review of Existing Frameworks

The COBIT, PRINCE2 Agile besides Scaled Agile Framework (SAFe) models all steer large scale governance. Each supplies fixed processes, clear roles and step-by-step methods, yet none embed AI that adapts on its own. (Sarker, 2022)

The COBIT model centers on process control or IT governance - it offers almost no live forecasts. (Kelleher & Tierney, 2018)

The PRINCE2 Agile model blends project rules with agile steps - it still depends on hand written reports and manager action. (LeCun, Bengio, & Hinton, 2015)

The SAFe model spreads agile methods across the enterprise - it ships without built in AI support for decisions. (Gil & Varshney, 2019)

If organizations bolt AI onto those models, they keep the original structure plus add live data views, forecast numbers and software that acts on the data without human prompts. (Wamba et al., 2015)

3. AI-AUGMENTED GOVERNANCE ARCHITECTURE

3.1 Key Components and Interactions

An AI-Enhanced Governance Architecture is built from four layers that rely on one another (Zhang & Zhao, 2021)

Data Ingestion besides Processing Layer - It pulls raw records from project boards, build servers, bug trackers and chat logs - cleans plus labels them. (Raj & Seamans, 2019)

AI or Analytics Layer - It trains models, spots outliers, forecasts delays and runs solvers that suggest better schedules or resource mixes. (Brynjolfsson & McAfee, 2017)

Decision Band Layer - It turns numbers, forecasts into plain tasks, alerts or approval steps that managers and teams act on. (Ransbotham, Kiron, & Prentice, 2021)

Feedback next to Learning Layer - It stores what happened, compares it with what was predicted but also tweaks rules or models so the next cycle performs better. (Chui, Manyika, & Miremadi, 2016)

Data moves up through the layers and returns as lessons. The loop gives leaders a live picture of work, warns them before problems grow as well as lets plans shift as facts change. (ISO/IEC, 2021)

Figure 2. AI-Enhanced Governance Architecture

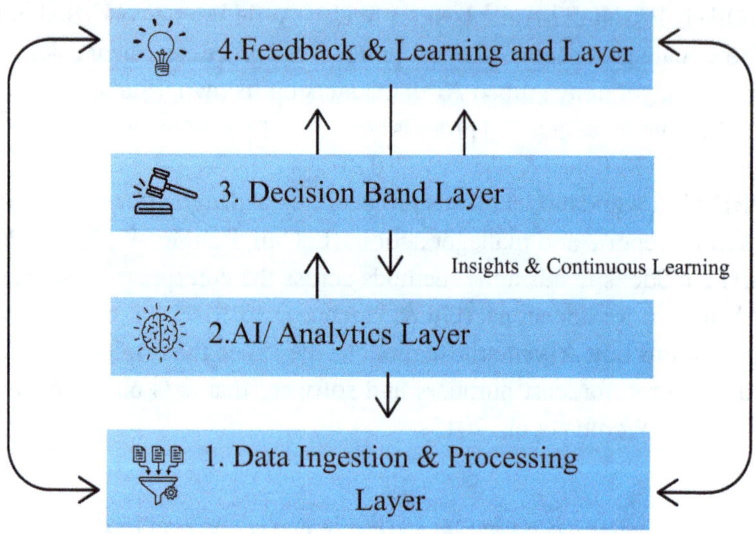

AI-Enhanced Governance Architecture

3.2 Adding Predictive Analytics to Agile Work

Teams weave predictive numbers into several steps of agile besides DevOps. At sprint planning, they mix AI velocity guesses, backlog rank scores and bug-heat maps to decide who does what. Portfolio leads run quick what if games before they lock a strategy. Project leads get plain warnings about new risks or tight limits on people and time. (Van Veenstra, Klievink, & Janssen, 2018)

3.3 Human-in-the-Loop Oversight Model

AI works fast and handles large tasks, but people still need to check the results. In a Human-in-the-loop setup, a person reviews every AI suggestion before action is taken. The person sees the full context, confirms the advice is correct plus checks that it meets ethical rules. If the output is wrong or unfair, the person rejects it or fixes it and keeps a clear record of what was changed, why. (Hartley, 2007)

3.4 Data Governance and Ethical AI Considerations

Good AI needs data that is clean, complete and trustworthy. The main points to watch are (van der Aalst, 2016)

Data lineage but also provenance - Keep a full record of where each data set came from and every change applied to it so the data can be traced back to the original source. (DORA, 2022)

Bias reduction - Scan the data as well as the methods for unfair patterns or hidden assumptions - remove or adjust them. (Floridi & Cowls, 2021)

Regulatory compliance - Follow GDPR, ISO/IEC 42001 and every other rule that applies. (Beck et al., 2001)

Use AI in a way that is open, fair or consistent with the organization's stated values. (Schwaber & Sutherland, 2020)

4 PREDICTIVE ROADMAPPING

4.1 Definition and Strategic Value

Predictive roadmapping means that project and product plans are updated all the time, because AI keeps feeding in fresh facts instead of sticking to a fixed sheet drawn up months ago. In a market that moves every week, a paper roadmap soon lies - prices shift, buyers change their minds and staff move to new tasks. When the firm plugs live forecasts into the plan, it sees tomorrow's bottlenecks, late tasks plus short staff before they bite. A software house that runs many products at once feeds its data into the same forecast engine - the tool tells it when each release will land, which teams wait for others and where a delay will start. Leaders receive clear early warnings - they shift people, money and priorities ahead of trouble instead of after it. (Rigby, Sutherland, & Noble, 2018)

4.2 Machine Learning Models for Forecasting and Prioritization

Machine learning models serve as the core of the predictive roadmap. Time series forecasting models use past data to estimate future velocity and lag trends. Regression analysis measures how well the budget is spent plus how well delivery meets targets. Clustering algorithms group similar cases of team output or batch difficulty - managers send people and money to the spots that matter most or pose the biggest risk. Deep learning tools such as ensemble methods or LSTMs track long range links, hidden ties inside a portfolio. The models forecast what will happen and also rank work - the tasks but also projects that yield the highest strategic value rise to the top. Market shifts or competitor moves join the data set and the forecast gains sharper detail. (Highsmith, 2019)

4.3 Scenario Planning and What-If Simulations

Scenario planning enables organizations to simulate alternative "what if?" scenarios, to assess likely impact. Leaders can simulate various reallocations of resources, changes of schedule or shifting requirements without actually having to commit to anything, thanks to AI 'what if' simulations. For instance, a fintech company can study the impact of fast-tracking a regulatory compliance feature on other planned releases. It can assess the risks to timelines, budgets and team capacity. This approach ensures leadership can tailor the strategy well in advance and reinforces resilience and reduces uncertainty so delivery objectives are met without compromising on quality and satisfaction of stakeholders. (Davenport & Ronanki, 2018)

4.4 Ongoing Adjustments and Feedback Systems

The predictive roadmap is iterative by nature. There will be a continuous stream of feedback that is assessed after the decision outcome to update the predictive model and enhance its forecasts going forward. Any changes to a model will be made based on metrics such as the deviation of the forecast, fluctuation of the velocity of the team, and utilization of resources. These changes will also affect the roadmap. The dashboards are designed to provide an interactive and uniform overview of actual information. It helps the management responsible for monitoring deviations and allows them to take immediate corrective action. This makes the organization a learning and agile organization. Through time, these feedback mechanism make the forecasts more robust and the organization's plan adaptable. (Russell & Norvig, 2021)

Figure 3. Predictive Roadmapping and Continuous Feedback Cycle

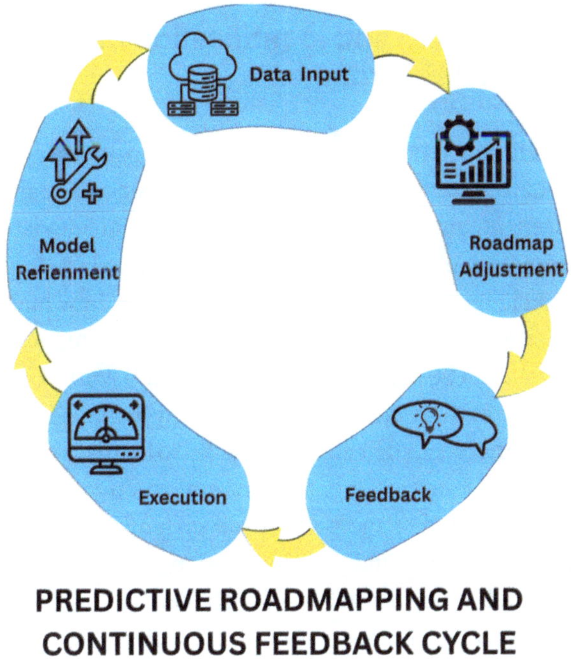

4.5 Integration with Portfolio Management

At the portfolio level, predictive roadmaps enable steering by means of strategic priorities. AI models frame initiatives regarding anticipated business value, risk-adjusted returns, and resource efficiency, which allows portfolio managers to assess and rank orders of rank objectively. Decision makers can analyze multiple configurations by simulations to determine optimal allocations, balancing immediate demands for supply against longer term objectives of strategy. By joining predictive decision making to portfolio decisions organizations yield greater visibility, alignment and flexibility ensuring that resources are invested in the initiatives that yield the maximum impact. (Amershi et al., 2019)

5. RISK SENSING AND PROACTIVE MITIGATION

5.1 AI-Driven Measuring and Identification of the Risk in the Agiel Environments

Risk perception in the agile environments ensures primarily on techniques and tools of the AI to detect appearing risks before they become real problems. Ridge approaches which ensure mainly on post event reporting are deviated for the benefit of monitoring denotation of analyzing both structured and unstructured dates. For example, the natural language processing (NLP) indicates how many dangers words may be found in comments of the programmer in records of records an incidence, or conversation of the team. The negative sentiment, general worry about the progresses or technical problems may be easily identified using natural language processing (NLP). Machines of differences detectors are used also for discovery from differences analyzing the operational metrics, e.g. time for construction, a tendency in defects, the process of the conclusion of the code or the systemic procedure of the project, Ularities discovering which can indicate from risk types. Predictive models may be find the probability and the parameter of the behaving saying the dangers which as surest delay, allowing teams of management to all higher priority to remedies more especially and impartially. Omitting approaching the AI to types of the risk, the organizations from passive solving the problems are passed in utilization especially of the management, strengthen their resistibility and readiness. (Varian, 2019)

5.2 Real-Time Monitoring of Delivery Pipelines

Integrating AI into continuous integration and delivery (CI/CD) pipelines provides a powerful tool for real-time monitoring, a continuous visibility mechanism, that enhances situational awareness across projects. Real-time monitoring allows organizations to detect deployment failures, integration issues, security vulnerabilities, or deviations in compliance, as they occur and take immediate corrective action. Dashboards that consolidate risk information from multiple sources provide visualizations of risk information that illustrate trends, level of severity and confidence scores. These real time insights enable potential risk areas to be remedied immediately, minimizing the risk of repeated problem occurrences as issue cascades and enhancing overall project sustainability. Continuous monitoring also provides faster delivery of insights to leaders for decision-making as it allows decision makers to gain actionable insights without the delay experienced through manual reporting. (Gandomi & Haider, 2015)

5.3 Risk Assessment and Prioritization through Prediction

The AI driven risk assessment identifies the probability and the expected impact of identified risks, and are the bases for the correct prioritization. The firm can quantify a risk score based on historical data, operational patterns and interdependencies of risks requiring coordination. This will allow management teams to be directed at the higher impact risks where there are resources and oversight on lower priority items. Predictive scoring thus is a consistent way of reaching a conclusion and limits the individual subjectivity of the decision making process. The mitigation strategies would also be more consistent with organizational priorities. Scoring mechanisms may be updated accordingly to changing information thereby allowing for continuous review of priorities as project conditions adapt. (Witten et al., 2016)

5.4 Risk Reduction and Contingency Planning

Once risks are identified and ranked, the organizations can introduce proactive measures for risk mitigation that are informed by AI insights. Such measures can include rescheduling of tasks, reassignment of resources, adding additional Quality Assurance checkpoints and using automated testing to reduce the error rate. The use of simulation-based contingency planning will allow leadership to evaluate the effectiveness of various options that may be available to mitigate the indicated risks even prior to their implementation thereby enabling the organization to make informed decisions while minimizing interruptions. By integrating predictive foresight with real time remedial options the organizations can assist in reducing the potentiality of adverse events arising and strengthen the overall resilience of the particular project. AI models also can provide information on the optimal sequencing of the risk mitigation efforts to ensure that the remedial work can be undertaken in an achievable and effective manner. (Bostrom & Yudkowsky, 2014)

5.5 Integration of Risk Intelligence with Corporate Governance Dashboards

Corporate governance dashboards are the point of contact with decision-makers for AI-driven risk intelligence recommendations. Such dashboards integrate data from internal and external sources and provide visualization in the form of heat maps, trend analyses, and confidence levels in risks. The dashboard is interactive, so managers can learn about causes of risks, simulate proposed mitigation strategies, and assess the outcomes of the strategies before implementing them. The dashboards depict clear, actionable recommendations in one place, which contribute to decision-making that is informed and timely and supports integration. By integrating the output of AI into the dashboards, there is continuous learning: The feedback on the results of the recommendations can be stored and used to refine the predictive models, improve the confidence levels in the recommendations, and improve the quality of future risk assessments. (Gartner, 2021)

5.6 Metrics for Assessing Risk Management

Several key performance indicators can be employed for gauging AI-enhanced risk perception. The risk detection lead time captures the time elapsed between the emergence of a risk and its recognition by the organization. The effectiveness of mitigation assesses the "hit rate" of AI-recommended responses, while predictive accuracy measures the correlation between predicted and actual risk events. The decision latency index runs from the time of risk identification until the time of action taken, providing a measure of organizational responsiveness. If managed correctly, a set of error metrics can be employed to evaluate not only the AI models, but the management processes as well. This would enable current risk management to consistently be proactive rather than reactive, adaptive rather than fixed, and aligned with functional and strategic objectives. Continuous evaluation is precisely what pervades operational and strategic learning, informing the developing perspective of prudence. (ISO/IEC, 2023)

6. HUMAN-IN-THE-LOOP OVERSIGHT

6.1 Human Judgment in Management that Has AI Supporting It

The relevance of human judgment can be observed in AI-enhanced administration even when predictive analytics and automated decisions made in human judgment progress. Although AI offers pattern recognition, predictive foresight and computational intelligence, human beings add context to it. (Sarker, 2022)

Situational awareness creative hypotheses that cannot be simulated by human reasoning, morality, and algorithms. Human-in-the-Loop (HITL) model makes sure that before volumes or insights created by AI are implemented, they are being validated, interpreted, and aligned with the organizational strategy. As an example, an AI may understand that a particular software release pipeline has a high-risk module according to anomaly detection and prediction score, but a project manager working on the project may later put this information into perspective by factors such as human expertise, previous performance, or external bias. Human supervision combined with AI intelligence enables organizations to compromise the level of speed, size, and long-term prudence, so that the decision-making efforts are well-informed and reasonable. Moreover, HITL management enhances accountability and good governance. When AI is implemented by organizations without human verification, the majority of such organizations have difficulties with the issue of transparency, prejudice, or excessive dependence on artificial suggestions. Governance processes are experimental, auditable and ethically shaped through the incorporation of human judgme. The holders of authority can ignore or modify AI suggestions where the contextual conditions or organizational considerations demand or necessitate that the recommendation should not be adhered to in an algorithmic manner. Simply put, humans are judges and translators and such a move will make sure that AI does not undermine but complements important management skills. (Kelleher & Tierney, 2018)

Figure 4. Human-in the-Loop (HITL) Governance Model

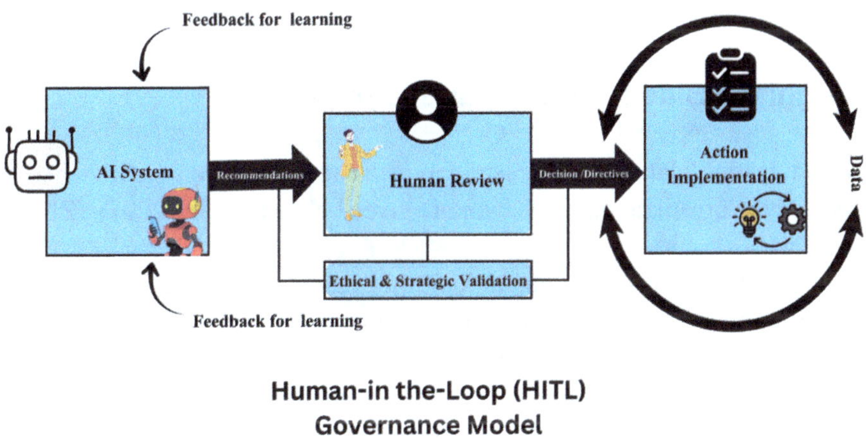

6.2 Collaborative Decision Support Systems

The CollaborativeDecision Support Systems (CDSS) represents the importance of human AI cooperation to enhance the efficient management results. Systems have predictive analytics and offer interactive interfaces that assist groups of people working in different functions to co-create the decision based on information with common understanding. During agile set ups, CDSS tools enable the product owner, scrum masters, and portfolio manager to have foresight of predictive requirements, run a scenario of what may happen and still analyze the risk jointly before committing themselves. To illustrate, in the case of sprint planning, a CDSS platform can suggest a list of backlog items of top priority due to historical velocity, getting a group of team capacity, and interdependency. Thereafter, human stakeholders will be able to negotiate over trade-offs, realign priorities, and endorse the final tasks, so that methodological suggestions will be applied in practice. (LeCun, Bengio, & Hinton, 2015)

Transparency and cross-functional alignment is also encouraged on the CDSS platforms. These systems create synergy between technology teams and the leadership by unifying predictive perception and situation clarifications, thereby developing a common language and responsibility. In massive organizations where the teams have decentralised structures, the collaborative dashboards allow one source of truth and can be useful in ensuring that the stake holders who are dispersed geographically consolidate their decision making. The outcome is quicker, smarter and smarter, more group-concurred decisions on the management level, raising agility and organization unity. (Gil & Varshney, 2019)

The navigation plan and administrative measures taken to minimize cognitive bias and transparency in organizational behavior are provided (Wamba et al., 2015)

6.3 Cognitive Bias Mitigation and Transparency

The navigation plan and administrative measures to reduce cognitive bias and transparency in organizational behavior are given below (Hartley 2007). (Zhang & Zhao, 2021)

Although AI systems are a potent tool, they can reproduce the bias that exists either within historical data or projected assumption models. Unmonitored such biases may be prone to make poor or unjust decisions. The solution to this problem that is provided by human-in-the-loop management implies busy evaluating, interpreting, and validating AI output by decision-makers. To illustrate, when an AI is regularly entitled to prioritize some categories of projects on basis of the history of successful projects, human administrators can imply possible bias and improve their portfolios by incorporating all aspects. (Raj & Seamans, 2019)

Explainable AI (XAI) practices also enable transparency, which enables humans to comprehending an algorithm recommendation rationale. The interpretation of the model, model traceability, and generally model visualization of the decision paths will assist the management teams evaluate confidence levels, anomalies and reasons to support actions with the stakeholders. The regulation of the industry is another area in which the importance of transparency is paramount; in healthcare, finance, or government, the compliance and ethical responsibility are beyond compromise. Through intelligence, AI, and involvement of human operators, it becomes possible to develop unbiased, trustworthy and auditable decisions related to management and the probability of biases and lack of alignment with the objectives of a strategy is minimized. (Brynjolfsson & McAfee, 2017)

7. IMPLEMENTATION FRAMEWORK

7.1 Process Integration with Agile and DevOps Pipelines

To use AI-enhanced government, it is necessary to introduce it with a flawless connectivity of agile and DevOps processes, so that foretelling provisions and danger awareness are directly designed to affect operating decisions. The AI models may be integrated into continuous delivery pipelines to deliver the real-time feedback on the performance of the sprints, trends related to defects, the use of resources, and the overall portfolio health. Organization is able to have sustained assurance through the implementation of governance as a part of delivery processes, rather than an additional layer of control over the organization, and compliance, risk management process, and performance monitoring become integrated processes that change in parallel with the volume of delivery. As an example, predictive sprint analytics can be used to ensure that backlog prioritization and resource allocation is done before the sprint can be executed, which enables managers to shift the plans on seat. This integrative nature of AI-enhanced insights and jointed execution will see to it that governance is no longer a force against agility but instead a facilitator by ensuring a sense of alignment between the strategic and the operational implementation. (Ransbotham, Kiron, & Prentice, 2021)

7.2 Toolchain and Platform Considerations

Improved usage of AI-enhanced governance requires a powerful technology ecosystem. The interoperable data aggregation tool should be chosen with visualization and analysis tools, which include machine learning implementations (TensorFlow, PyTorch, and so on), predictive analytics systems (Azure ML, AWS Sagemaker, and so on), and portfolio management software (Jira Align, Raleigh, etc.). The selection of the platform should be focused on scaling, security, the ability to integrate with APIs, and the possibility of supporting real-time data flows. An API-driven, greasily modular architecture also allows AI models to directly access the project management, DevOps, and enterprise systems operational data, and enables the delivery of the insights through dashboards or joint decision support systems. Thanks to the creation of an integrated tool chain, organizations can make sure that the AI-enhanced governance may be efficiently applied to work with distributed teams and multi-faceted delivery settings, without compromising the potential consistency and transparency when making a decision. (Chui, Manyika, & Miremadi, 2016)

7.3 Change Management and Organizational Readiness

Implementing AI in the governance is a change that involves a lot of culture and organizational transformation. The stakeholders should learn how AI augments decisions and that it augments and not replaces human judgments. The best steps in change management would be leadership involvement, extensive training, and proper communication of the strengths and weaknesses of AI. The employees can also have a resistance toward automation because of fears of being pushed out of the job or lack of confidence in the accuracy of AI, it is essential to eliminate these fears with the help of skills enhancement training, open reporting, and a gradual implementation process. The other component of organizational readiness is aligning people, processes, and technology to a common vision of governance enhancement by AI. The task of interpreting the AI outputs and integrating suggestions into the planning and risk management process, as well as feedback to optimize the predictive models, should be ready in teams. This way, with building an adaptive culture and focusing on collaboration, organizations can get the best of AI with the least opposing forces and adoption obstacles. (ISO/IEC, 2021)

7.4 Metrics and KPIs for Governance Effectiveness

The ability of AI to improve governance should be measured to guarantee that the forecasting, risk and oversight mechanisms can provide substance value. Among the key performance indicators, there are decreasing the decision-making time, increasing the forecast accuracy, minimizing the risk detection latency, compliance standard compliance, and satisfaction of the stakeholder with the governance processes. The constant evaluation of such measures enables organizations to understand the success of AI models, human supervision as well as integration of processes that can be used to improve the operations via iterations. Reporting tools and the dashboards can be used to visualize the performance trends over time, identify the gaps and enable data-proven decision making. Therefore, over time, metrics allow benchmarking, learning, and improvement of AI algorithms and managerial processes, which builds on a continuous improvement cycle, strengthening organizational responsiveness, responsibility, and business orientation. (Van Veenstra, Klievink, & Janssen, 2018)

7.5 Phased Implementation Approach

The scaling of A is normally most applicable in large organizations in a staged manner. Initial innovators have the ability to specialize in particular teams, portfolios or process areas and (as a result) the organization is able to test AI models, optimize dashboards and human-in-the-loop workflows. Using iterative improvements to refine AI governing rules have allowed scaling AI governance to span teams and locations as initial goals are achieved and predictive results proven, as well as overcome emerging challenges of data heterogeneity, model drift, and adoption barriers at the organizational level. During the scaling, feedback mechanisms based on operational results lead to re-education of the model, modifications to the process and otherwise. (Hartley, 2007)

8. CASE STUDIES AND APPLICATIONS

8.1 Predictive Governance in Software Delivery Organizations

Predictive management assists the software delivery organizations to make accurate decisions and foresee the risks. The tools of AI and DevOps give information about the schedule, resources utilization, and possible conflicts and allow making the adjustments in advance. This method helps to align projects with strategies, enhance predictability of any delivery, minimize scope creep and gain user confidence. The general point is that it shows the usefulness of AI in the management process.(DORA, 2022)

8.2 AI-Augmented Sprint Planning and Portfolio Prioritization

AI enhances agile sprint planning, which is based on the historical data and team records as well as the backlog patterns that help focus on the task prioritization and sequence. It finds the combinations of low risk, high efficiency tasks aiding the portfolio managers in moving resources in a strategic way. The incorporation of AI wisdom will minimize on rework, confidence in planning and make sure the teams work on what impacts the most.(Floridi & Cowls, 2021)

8.3 Human-AI Collaboration in Compliance and Auditing

AI is more effective in compliance and audit, as it is able to identify discrepancies and risks to regulation in project artifacts and code repositories automatically. Auditors (Human) check out findings, and interpret complex exceptions, and employing a feeling of the situation. Such a hybrid solution enhances efficacy, precision as well as minimizing the workload among staff. Ethical and trustworthy governance is ensured by the combination of AI accuracy and human intelligence. (Beck et al., 2001)

8.4 Lessons Learned and Best Practices

Effective management of AI necessitates commitment of leadership, advanced data management and steady adoption by pilot. To improve AIs, organizations need to be able to blend insights with the human judgment, make it clear, offer feedback and actions, and involve stakeholders. These are practices that increase agility, accountability and strategic alignment at the team and portfolio levels. (Schwaber & Sutherland, 2020)

9. CHALLENGES AND FUTURE RESEARCH DIRECTIONS

9.1 Data Quality, Bias, and Model Drift

One of the key challenges of AI-enhanced governance is to ensure that the data used to train the predictive models is reliable, consistent, and ethical. Incomplete, poor quality or inconsistent data can result in inaccurate forecasts, misaligned prioritization, and inaccurate risk assessments. Bias in historical data may perpetuate unhealthy amounts of bias and autocratic treatment or allocation of resources, eroding trust in systems of automated decision-making. Model drift (the slow but steady decrease in a model's predictive accuracy as time lapses because team members may change behaviour or because operations change) is another concern. To minimise these risks, organisations should have strong data governance processes in place, such as data validation, ongoing monitoring and re-training procedures. Shepherding AI dispatches: Religions such as XAI (Explainable AI) can aid decision makers in knowing model emissions and finding biases to facilitate or certify forecastions to organisational aims. The development of root causes associated with the origin, transformation, and application of data are key ingredients to further increase accountability and trust in AI-based governance, which can be accomplished by establishing provenance and lineage mechanisms. (Highsmith, 2019)

9.2 Scaling AI Governance Across Multi-Team Environments

Large enterprises that have teams working agile across geographies, domains and organizational units lack resources to effectively scale AI-enabled operational and strategic governance. Standardization of prediction models and risk management designs may become complex due to differences between teams practicing as defined in CCMO and cultural differences. Advanced integration schemes are necessary to ensure consistency in governance decisions while keeping team autonomy. Federated learning and multi-agent AI systems are promising strategies that can deal with these issues. -capable of models being trained in a distributed way without any possible information leakage, which conserves privacy, and security, while boosting intelligence; federated learning is what makes that possible. Multi-agent systems for decentralised decision making where AI agents track team-based metrics to share insights into centralised dashboards which ensure coherence and alignment are maintained at an enterprise-wide level Achieving successful AI governance enables a blend of technology infrastructure, standardization, and alignment within and between the organization. (Davenport & Ronanki, 2018)

9.3 Interdisciplinary Collaboration and Leadership Roles

AI-enabled governance is an interdisciplinary field at the nexus of various disciplines such as data science, behavioural psychology, management science and information systems. Achievement of these objectives requires close coordination between AI engineers, agile practitioners, portfolio managers, risk officers and the executives. Furthermore, the synergy of human and AI should encompass collaboration across organizational domains, establish and implement safe and ethically and contextually correct GLPs and processes for AI models, and make the models operational to reflect both business models and strategic priorities. Leadership positions need to shift from a control-based management setup to a team-based work setup where executives empower intelligence, promote flexibility, and empower teams to work with the outputs of the artificial intelligence (AI) algorithms. As AI adoption continues to transform the industry, it is crucial for Head Leaders to balance the adoption with outward ethical responsibility, guaranteeing that implementing AI is more likely to strengthen governance, without owning the algorithm and tools that generate or allow it to operate without consideration for accountability, transparency or trust. Organic structures, communication pathways, and decision-making procedures will need to be matched to facilitate this new lens of leadership. (Russell & Norvig, 2021)

9.4 Future Research Avenues in AI-Augmented Governance

The field of AI-Assisted Governance holds many possibilities for future research. Promising is the development of self-adaptive governance architectures that are capable of automatically adapting policies, processes and priorities to real time information and evolving organizational environments. Automated decision auditing can serve as a way to continuously monitor recommendations, ensure the decisions are helping to meet regulatory requirements, standards, and organizations' goals in an ethical way, and consider other ethical implications. Another possibility of utilizing AI-driven ethics simulations is to operationalize on how organizational management can consider the potential social, ethical and legal implications of governance decisions. Furthermore, quantitative research which explores the socio-technical impact of AI governance on organisational culture, accountability, innovation, and human-AI collaboration can offer empirical proof to inform best practice. Further research on interoperability standards, cross-platform integration, and multi-agent integration can aid in measuring AI governance in complex and distributed organizations. Ultimately, further research in these areas will help to make AI in governance more effective, transparent, and ethical, and more likely to be adopted by organisations who are able to approach adoption with a greater degree of agility and confidence compared to present levels of research and understanding. (Amershi et al., 2019)

10. TECHNOLOGY AND PERFORMANCE METRICS FOR AI-AUGMENTED GOVERNANCE

10.1 Key Performance Indicators (KPIs) for AI Governance

AI-enabled governance - it must be possible to measure the effectiveness of AI-driven predictive, risk and oversight tools to confirm that it is delivering real value. Organizations should specify key performance indicators (KPIs) with operational and strategic results. Examples are predictive accuracy, which evaluates how closely the accuracy of predictions by AI compared to actual project outcomes; decision lead time, which measures the amount of time between identifying a risk or issue and putting corrective actions in place; and management cycle time, which measures the speed of reviews and approvals. In addition, stakeholder satisfaction scores can be used to gain qualitative insights into the effectiveness of AI management in supporting human decision-making. By monitoring these results, organizations are able to understand which strengths and improvement points can be monitored to allow management processes to be constantly updated. (Varian, 2019)

10.2 Metrics for Risk Detection and Mitigation

AI-driven risk perception needs specific measures to measure effectiveness and responsiveness. Risk detection latency is the time from the origin of a potential risk to it being identified by the AI system and mitigation effectiveness is the proportion of presented interventions that succeed in attenuating the negative outcome. Predictive Risk Score Accuracy measures the reliability of the accuracy of the predictive likelihood and impact assessments generated by AI and gives assurance that prioritization decisions are made with confidence. These metrics can be tracked on an ongoing basis to allow management teams to understand trends relating to persistent threats and to fine-tune AI algorithms, as well as adapt mitigation efforts accordingly. By revising these metrics into dashboards and report tools, organizations can be sure that risk management is beat in the organization is proactive as well as adaptive so to increase the resilience of the entire organization. (Gandomi & Haider, 2015)

10.3 Feedback Loops and Continuous Improvement

Performance measurement is not a once-and-done activity - it is the key to continuous improvement in AI governance. Feedback loops are a way for organizations to document the impact of implemented interventions and analyze differences between predicted and actual results and adjust predictive models accordingly. For instance, if any model tendency shows an overestimation of sprint completion times, the input variables can be changed, algorithms can be updated, and future predictions can become more accurate using feedback algorithms. Iterative development ensures that AI management systems dynamically adapt to the ever-changing project environments, behaviors of the teams, and priorities of the organizations. Feedback loops are embedded into AI models as well as the management that drives them and provides learning, agility, and evidence-based decision making. (Witten et al., 2016)

10.4 Integration of Metrics into Governance Dashboards

Centralized dashboards can supply an interface between performance measures and stakeholders so that information on management performance can be communicated to users in real time. Forecast accuracy, risk detection latency, mitigation success rate, and decision times are shown on interactive dashboards, that allow managers to see deeper into underlying data to put their context to the decisions being made. Advanced visualizations including trend analyses, heat-maps and scenario simulations improve the level of awareness and help to make well-informed decisions. Integrating metrics into dashboards makes sure that performance assessment is ongoing, transparent, and actionable to create the basis to strategically plan, allocate resources and make operational changes. (Bostrom & Yudkowsky, 2014)

10.5 Technology Considerations for Metric Collection and Analysis

The collection, processing, and analysis of governance metrics requires a powerful technology infrastructure. Automated data pipelines, APIs and microservices make it possible to easily extract operational and project data across different sources, such as DevOps tools, project management platforms, and communication systems. Machine learning models can analyze historical data as well as real-time data to derive some predictive insights. and business intelligence platforms can visualize the metrics for stakeholders. Security, privacy, and compliance should be taken into account in the process to ensure the protection of sensitive information and compliance with regulatory requirements. Organizations can ensure that AI governance is data-driven, correct, and scalable by managing performance metrics using advanced technology to collect, process, and analyze the data. (Gartner, 2021)

11. CROSS-INDUSTRY APPLICATIONS AND EMERGING USE CASES

11.1 Healthcare and Life Sciences

AI-powered Government Regulations has immense usage in healthcare and life sciences where time and complying is essential. Predictive analytics can be used to predict project delays in clinical trials, forecast resource needs and optimize patient management processes. Risk-disciplined algorithms identify the anomals in the regulatory submissions, trial or patient data and ensure compliance with standards like FDA regulations or GDPR. The need for human-in-the-loop control is paramount, as the ethical aspects are prototypes involving medical ethics, the safety of patients and compliance with regulations require guarded judgment. By combining the power of artificial intelligence and man, healthcare organizations can expect to improve the efficiency of their operations, ensuring compliance and better results for patients, all while mitigating the potential for costly error or delay. (Sarker, 2022)

11.2 Finance and Banking

In the area of finance, AI governance aids in compliance, risk management, and having strategies set in place over complicated portfolios. Predictive models can help anticipate market risks, determine credit exposure and reveal anomalies in transaction data. Risk awareness enables organizations to be responsive to fraudulent activity, cash flow constraints or regulatory non-compliance in a proactive manner. Human oversight ensures that the algorithm-making process is introspective in the sense that there is an oversight by humans to consider ethical, legal, and strategic dimensions in the decisions made by the algorithms. For instance, AI can detect unusual patterns in trading, however, compliance officers will look at the context and know how to respond. Dashboards and analytics platforms facilitate the creation of cross-functional collaboration and real-time monitoring, decision-making, and reporting that increases the transparency of financial resiliency and operation. (Kelleher & Tierney, 2018)

11.3 Transportation and Smart Cities

Over time, artificial intelligence (AI) has changed governance in transportation and urban infrastructure management. Predictive roadmapping enables cities to forecast traffic congestion, infrastructure maintenance, and public transportation or other infrastructure projects resource planning. Risk perception identifies real time potential safety risks, environmental hazards or system failures. Human-in-the-loop governance ensures that operational outcomes translates to achieving a balance in the priorities of efficiency, safety and social. For instance, AI models are able to optimise traffic lights to minimise congestion but city planners check interventions to ensure fair results. By combining the insights of AI with administrative structures, transportation systems and smart cities have the potential to deliver services to citizens in a better manner, at a lower cost of operations, and with enhanced safety and satisfaction for the citizens. (LeCun, Bengio, & Hinton, 2015)

11.4 Manufacturing and Industry

In manufacturing, AI enabled management aids in the efficiency of operations, quality assurance, and predictive maintenance. Predictive analytics advance warning on equipment failures, supply chain disruptions or production bottlenecks that allow for early response. With risk-sensing algorithms, production anomalies, process compliance or safety protocols can be detected. Human supervision is used to validate artificial intelligence (AI) recommendations to ensure outcomes on production lines are aligned with operational priorities as well as regulations and worker safety. For instance, AI could predict that a piece of equipment is about to experience significant downtime, and suggest rescheduling a production line, but the human managers are aware of over-arching logistics/contractual constraints. Integrating AI-driven insights in production management helps to improve the agility, minimize downtime and propels the process towards continuous improvement. (Gil & Varshney, 2019)

11.5 Energy and Utilities

Operational Safety, compliance and risk management are critical. Predictive analytics can be used to predict equipment performance, maintenance need, and demand variability. Anomaly detection algorithms can identify grid operations, grid reporting in regulation or environmental richness anomalies. And with human-in-the-loop control, operational changes can be monitored for adherence to safety, legal and ethical guidelines. For example, predictive models can tell engineers what loads are likely on power distribution networks, but engineers analyze the infrastructure environment as a whole before doing anything to correct it. The combination of AI insights and management processes leads to increased reliability, lowered operational risks and sustainable energy management approaches. (Wamba et al., 2015)

11.6 Emerging Use Cases and Opportunities

In addition to more traditional industries, AI-powered management creates new opportunities within certain sectors, including retail, education and telecommunications. Retailed firms can make a good use of future roadmaps for inventory management, supply chain optimization, and customer knowledge. AI management can be used to track curriculum delivery, resource allocation, and student outcomes in education institutions. Telecommunications companies are able to leverage predictive analytics to predict the network congestion, optimize infrastructure investments, and manage service-level risks. No matter the sector, human supervision is an important part of the equation and should include the following: ensure that there is ethical and contextual alignment with the strategy and goals. These novel use cases show how versatile the frameworks of AI governance can be and how they can change the way we act and make operational decisions in varied situations. (Zhang & Zhao, 2021)

Healthcare and Life Sciences: AI-based boosted governance enhances the efficiency in operations, compliance to regulation and also in patient outcomes by relying on predictive analyses as well as human judgement. (Raj & Seamans, 2019)

Finance and Banking: AI is used to handle proactive risk management, fraud detection, and strategic portfolio decisions, and human supervision is included to ensure ethical and legal compliance. (Brynjolfsson & McAfee, 2017)

Transportation and Smart Cities: Human planners algorithmically predict road conditions, traffic flow, urban infrastructure and safety and guarantee fair outcomes. (Ransbotham, Kiron, & Prentice, 2021)

Manufacturing and Industry 4.0: Predictive maintenance of assets and risk detection are powered by AI (integrates with predictive analytics) Maximum efficiency in production, avoidance of downtime, lack of compliance, etc.Holistic approach to management oversight. (Chui, Manyika, & Miremadi, 2016)

Energy and Utilities: Predictive analytics are used to incorporate the predictions of human experts in safety and regulatory compliance, equipment failure and demand fluctuations, as well as potential threats in the grid (ISO/IEC, 2021)

Emerging Use Cases: Management and use of AI is getting a kick-start in the retail, educational, and telecommunication sectors, thus proving that the proceedings can be applied in numerous fields that enables one to enhance operations, resource usage, and the way they provide their services to their clients. (Van Veenstra, Klievink, & Janssen, 2018)

Human-in-the-Loop Importance: Across all industries, human oversight is needed to help put AI intelligence into context, helping make validated predictions and making ethically and strategically sound decisions. (Hartley, 2007)

Cross-sector Value: The use of AI to enhance management structures provides companies with the opportunity to anticipate risks, optimize resources, and coordinate operational activities with strategic ones based on real-time information. (van der Aalst, 2016)

12. ETHICAL, LEGAL, AND SOCIAL IMPLICATIONS (ELSI)

12.1 Ethical Considerations in AI-Augmented Governance

AI enhanced governance is a powerful tool but also raises ethical concerns, which must be addressed in order to keep the power and integrity of government, AI algorithms trained on historical and incomplete data can perpetuate existing biases, favor certain groups, and entrench inequalities. To prevent or reduce the impact of these biases on the decision-making process, it is essential to have in place mechanisms for ethical governance. AI recommendations also need to be contextualized by human oversight, results enhanced, and decisions aligned with organizational values and societal norms and ethics. Transparency, accountability, and explainability are essential pillars of creating a morally ethical AI governance framework to support operational efficiency and moral responsibility. (Floridi & Cowls, 2021)

12.2 Legal and Regulatory Compliance

Organizations using AI-based governance will have to work within complex legal and regulatory environments. Societal demands for data privacy, methodological transparency and risk management, such as the GDPR directive in the European Union, the draft AI Law of the European Union, the HIPAA regulation in the United States for medical care information, and the ISO standards (e.g., ISO/IEC 42001, ISO/IEC 23894) Non-Compliance Penalties If they are not met, there can be legal penalties, reputational damage, and disruptions to operational activities. AI governance systems must include mechanisms for audit and recording of the AI system and processes, as well as functions for documentation and tracking to enable adherence to applicable regulations and guidelines. In addition, the risk assessment models need to incorporate jurisdictional differences and sector-specific regulatory requirements, aiding multi-national organizations to meet the various legal requirements differently. (Beck et al., 2001)

12.3 Social Implications and Organizational Impact

The introduction of AI into governance has implications for the organization's culture, stakeholder dynamics and the social demand. However, the use of AI also changes roles and responsibilities (requiring reskilling and adaptation of jobs) and has implications for the transparency and accountability of decision-making (through recommendations). Employees may become concerned with job security, loss of control or even an overdependence on AI outputs. To make human-AI interactions positive, organizations need to set up a culture of trust, cooperation and inclusion. Ethical training, transparent communication, and participatory decision making will help to reduce negative social impacts and trust amongst stakeholders. AI governance: With the proper organization, expertise and implementation of AI governance, can enhance organizational resilience, generate data-driven decision-making, and drive socially responsible outcomes. (Schwaber & Sutherland, 2020)

12.4 Bias Detection and Mitigation Strategies

Bias in AI systems can arise from the data used to train the model, the model design, or the algorithmic assumptions made. We need to build bias detection frameworks into the system of governance so that outputs are routinely monitored for issues of fairness, equity and representation. Methods such as algorithm performance audits, fairness metrics, and distinctly explainable AI (XAI) can identify the possible issues prior to the decision making implementation. "Human-in-the-loop control provides the means for decision makers to interpret, object and correct AI recommendations to ensure fairness in operational and strategic decisions." Going forward, bias mitigation needs continual and consistent surveillance, repeated model optimisation and the input of diverse voices in order to guarantee AI governance in line with ethics and societal norms. (Rigby, Sutherland, & Noble, 2018)

12.5 Frameworks for Responsible AI Governance

Responsible AI governance entails the incorporation of principles of ethics, regulatory compliance, and organization policies in a round framework. This includes having AI ethics committees, regulatory review boards, and advisory committees with stakeholders to manage the decision-making processes. Policies can establish acceptable use cases, accountability and scaling protocols for AI available interventions. In addition, the organizations can use monitoring dashboards, model. Audit trails, and an interpretation (transparency) tool By taking ethical, legal and social aspects into account in the governance of practices, organizations can achieve a balance in innovation, efficiency and accountability so that AI is used to facilitate better decision making while safeguarding human interests and social norms. (Highsmith, 2019)

13. LESSONS LEARNED, BEST PRACTICES, AND STRATEGIC RECOMMENDATIONS

13.1 Lessons Learned from AI-Augmented Governance Implementation

AI-Enhanced Governance within organizations has taught many lessons. First, successfully resourcing and integrating collaboration requires acquiring depth and implementation support - that can only happen when the stakeholders (executive, team leaders, domain experts) are consulted early in the process to achieve buy-in (and ideally alignment) with organizational goals. Second, are pilot projects and phased strategies for adopting are ways to help teams test models and validate their predictions before large-scale adoption of models and processes. Third, AI governance is about integrating technology, people, and processes; failure to do one will result in sub-optimal results. Finally, the importance of human supervision cannot be overstated - AI systems can enhance predictive capabilities and risk detection but the ability to stabilise and step back to understand a situation in greater depth and in a more strategic manner and apply ethical judgment has always been the responsibility of human decision makers. (Russell & Norvig, 2021)

13.2 Best Practices for Effective AI Governance

Best AI-based governance is dependent on interconnection of strategic planning, technical rigor and organizational alignment. Organisations need to implement strong data governance frameworks to provide data quality, consistency and integrity. Predictive analytics and risk perception should be easily incorporated into current Agile and DevOps processes for more ongoing monitoring and decision-making. Human-in-the-loop mechanisms should be formalized that would facilitate oversight and accountability while accessing the computational capabilities of Artificial Intelligence. Continual training and leadership workshops for employees broaden digital literacy and help people to build trust in AI systems. In addition, organizations should use transparent performance metrics and dashboards to gain visibility into so-called predictive accuracy, risk detection and decision-making effectiveness. (Amershi et al., 2019)

13.3 Strategic Recommendations for Adoption and Scaling

To successfully drive the scaling of AI governance, organizations can leverage a modular and flexible technology architecture, permissible in scaling and interoperate across systems. Consistent governance insights can be made available to distributed teams without infrastructure duplications due to the use of standardized protocols, APIs, and microservices. Ethical practices and regulatory compliance ought to be supported by leadership and continuous improvement facilitated; a culture of collaboration and trust. Organizations are made to undertake periodic audit AI models, audit unethical questions and change governing procedures based on changing requirements. Phased adoption, cross-functional collaboration, and iterative model refinement are some of the effective ways to make AI governance consistent and scalable across the multi-team and multi-location organizations. (Dignum, 2019)

13.4 Balancing Automation with Human Oversight

One of the important succincts is the need to balance automation and human judgment. Though AI is likely to enhance predictive performance and efficacy, depending solely on algorithms may result in strategic espressment, unstructured inclinations, or biased choices. It's the human oversight help to interpret the context, align with ethics and make the content relevant. Decision-making frameworks should make it clear who can take which role in a decision-making process: algorithms or humans - and when. This equilibrium generates trust, upholds responsibility, and establishes IAI as an addition tool as opposed to subjecting human knowledge to extinction. (Varian, 2019)

13.5 Framework Recommendations for Future Governance

AI-enhanced governance is suggested based on the best practices and lessons learned. This framework incorporates: (1) a articulate articulation of the purpose of governance linked to organizational strategy, (2) robust data management and quality assurance includedin the workflow, (3)'A predictive analytics and risk perception integration into al workflow equally, (4) formalized frameworks and human dans. the loop oversight mechanisms, (5)'ethic and regulatory compliance protocols into organization. (6) continuous performance monitoring and improvement. Such a framework helps organizations to systematically embed AI governance while being agile, transparent and accountable, and at the same time promoting innovation and operational excellence. (Gandomi & Haider, 2015)

14. FUTURE TECHNOLOGY TRENDS IN AI GOVERNANCE

14.1 Multi-Agent AI Systems

A trend in AI governance is the use of multi-agent AI systems: in this model, a number of AI entities interact together to offer combined intelligence and decision support. These agents can track different areas of the delivery pipeline like the progress of a project, the utilization of resources and the exposure to risks and the collaboration to develop in-depth management recommendations. Multi-agent systems increase the scalability by better situational awareness and enable finer grained monitoring in large multi-team organizations. However, human involvement is still necessary to arbitrate disputes, interpret information, and validate congruence with nano-strategic directions. (Bostrom & Yudkowsky, 2014)

Figure 5. Future Trends in AI Governance

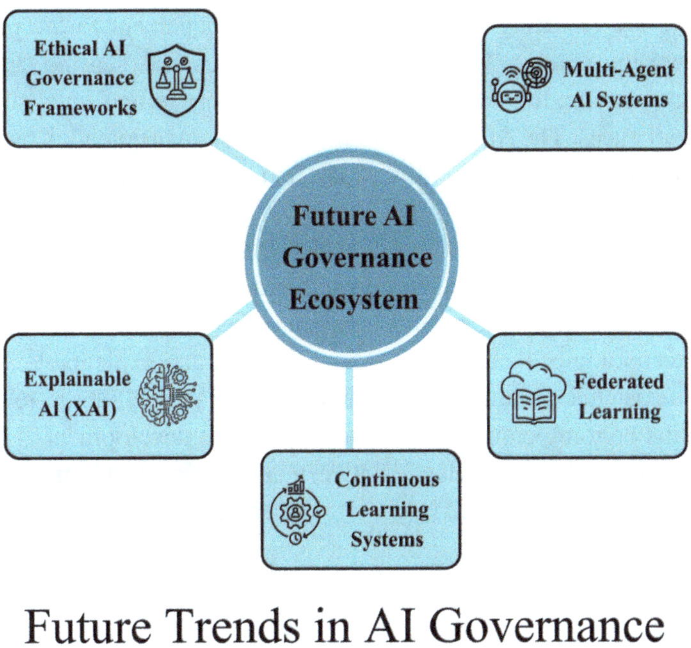

14.2 Federated Learning for Distributed Governance

Federated learning enables AI models to be trained based on distributed sources of data without having to centralize sensitive information. This is the only way that predictive analytics can be run across geographically distributed teams or business units without violating security requirements and overloading the network. Federated AI is helping to promote decentralized governance models with uniformity in decision intelligence in multiple nodes and still maintain their own local data autonomy. Organisations are able to leverage this trend to increase compliance with data protection regulations, enhance collaboration across teams and benefit from the predictive and analytical capabilities provided by AI. (Gartner, 2021)

CONCLUSION

The AI-based administration is a milestone in the contemporary management domain as it allows shifting the formal reactive management to the progressive data-laden decision-making. Using predictive analytics, risk sensing, and human-in-the-loop monitoring, the organization becomes aware in real-time, strategically linked, and resiliences. The AI is not a replacement of human potential, but improves it, allowing it to foresight, to ethically justify, and to be transparent.

The AI governance requires effective governance that would rely on clean traceable data, interoperability, and learning constantly. Early integration helps to prevent bias and foster trust among the stakeholders. In industries such as healthcare, agile, ethical and accountable governance are being informed through intelligent decision support and technologies including federated learning and explainable AI.

Finally, coexistence of human judgment and machine intelligence reinvents the strategy, instills ongoing enhancement and sustainable development. Those organizations that strike a healthy balance between automation and human control are the best candidate to be navigated in uncertainty and at the forefront in responsible governance.

REFERENCES

Amershi, S., Weld, D. S., Vorvoreanu, M., Fourney, A., Nushi, B., Collisson, P., & Horvitz, E. (2019). Guidelines for human-AI interaction. *Proceedings of the 2019 CHI Conference on Human Factors in Computing Systems*, 1–13. DOI: 10.1145/3290605.3300233

Beck, K., Beedle, M., van Bennekum, A., Cockburn, A., Cunningham, W., Fowler, M., . . . Thomas, D. (2001). Manifesto for Agile Software Development. Agile Alliance. https://agilemanifesto.org/

Bostrom, N., & Yudkowsky, E. (2014). The ethics of artificial intelligence. In K. Frankish & W. Ramsey (Eds.), The Cambridge Handbook of Artificial Intelligence (pp. 316–334). Cambridge University Press. DOI: 10.1017/CBO9781139046855.020

Chui, M., Manyika, J., & Miremadi, M. (2016). Where machines could replace humans-and where they can't (yet). *The McKinsey Quarterly*, •••, 1–12.

Davenport, T. H., & Ronanki, R. (2018). Artificial intelligence for the real world. *Harvard Business Review*, *96*(1), 108–116.

DevOps Research & Assessment (DORA). (2022). Accelerate: State of DevOps Report 2022. Google Cloud.

Dignum, V. (2019). *Responsible artificial intelligence: How to develop and use AI in a responsible way* (Vol. 2156). Springer.

Floridi, L., & Cowls, J. (2022). A unified framework of five principles for AI in society. Machine learning and the city: Applications in architecture and urban design, 535-545. doi:DOI: 10.1162/99608f92.8cd550d1

Gandomi, A., & Haider, M. (2015). Beyond the hype: Big data concepts, methods, and analytics. International Journal of Information Management, 35(2), 137–144. (Ransbotham, Kiron, & Prentice, 2021)

. Gartner. (2021). Predictive analytics: Key trends and market insights. Gartner Research Report. (Van Veenstra, Klievink, & Janssen, 2018)

Gil, Y., & Varshney, K. R. (2019). Towards accountable AI: Hybrid human–machine analyses for responsible decision-making. AI Magazine, 40(4), 56–70.

Hartley, J. (2007). Cognitive bias mitigation and transparency in decision-making. Public Administration Review, 67(6), 1045–1056.

Highsmith, J. (2009). *Agile project management: creating innovative products.* Pearson education.

ISO/IEC. (2021). ISO/IEC 23894:2021 Artificial Intelligence — Risk Management. International Organization for Standardization.

ISO/IEC. (2023). ISO/IEC 42001: Artificial Intelligence Management System Standard. International Organization for Standardization.

Kelleher, J. D., & Tierney, B. (2018). *Data science*. MIT press.

LeCun, Y., Bengio, Y., & Hinton, G. (2015). Deep learning. nature, 521(7553), 436-444.

McAfee, A., & Brynjolfsson, E. (2017). *Machine, platform, crowd: Harnessing our digital future*. WW Norton & Company.

Raj, M., & Seamans, R. (2019). Artificial intelligence, labor, productivity, and the need for firm-level data. In *The economics of artificial intelligence: An agenda* (pp. 553–565). University of Chicago Press.

Ransbotham, S., Kiron, D., Candelon, F., Khodabandeh, S., & Chu, M. (2022). Achieving individual—and organizational—value with AI. *MIT Sloan Management Review*.

Rigby, D. K., Sutherland, J., & Noble, A. (2018). Agile at scale. *Harvard Business Review*, *96*(3), 88–96.

Russell, S., Norvig, P., & Intelligence, A. (1995). A modern approach. Artificial Intelligence. Prentice-Hall. *Egnlewood Cliffs*, *25*(27), 79–80.

Sarker, I. H. (2021). Machine learning: Algorithms, real-world applications and research directions. *SN Computer Science*, *2*(3), 1–21.

Schwaber, K., & Sutherland, J. (2020). The scrum guide. *Scrum Alliance*, *21*(19), 1.

Van Der Aalst, W. (2016). Data science in action. In *Process mining: Data science in action* (pp. 3–23). Springer Berlin Heidelberg.

Van Veenstra, A. F., Klievink, B., & Janssen, M. (2018). Governance of AI: Balancing benefits and risks. Government Information Quarterly, 35(4), 611–619.

Varian, H. (2018). Artificial intelligence, economics, and industrial organization. In *The economics of artificial intelligence: An agenda* (pp. 399–419). University of Chicago Press.

Wamba, S. F., Akter, S., Edwards, A., Chopin, G., & Gnanzou, D. (2015). How 'big data'can make big impact: Findings from a systematic review and a longitudinal case study. *International Journal of Production Economics, 165*, 234–246.

Witten, I. H., Frank, E., Hall, M. A., Pal, C. J., & Data, M. (2005, June). Practical machine learning tools and techniques. In Data mining (Vol. 2, No. 4, pp. 403-413). Amsterdam, The Netherlands: Elsevier.

Zhang, C., & Zhao, P. (2021). Federated learning for edge computing: Challenges and opportunities. IEEE Network, 35(1), 12–18.

Chapter 6
Ethics, Bias Mitigation, and Model Risk Management

Shagufta Parween
http://orcid.org/0000-0002-5221-4137
Chaitanya Bharathi Institute of Technology, India

Himanshu Sanghavi
http://orcid.org/0000-0002-6093-1179
C.Z. Patel College of Business and Management, The Charutar Vidya Mandal University, India

Neha Dubey
Parul University, India

U. D. Prasan
Aditya Institute of Technology and Management, India

Rahul Bharadwaj
http://orcid.org/0000-0001-9502-5048
Galgotias University, India

V. Bhoopathy
http://orcid.org/0000-0003-2175-6328
Sree Rama Engineering College, India

B. Amarnath Reddy
http://orcid.org/0009-0002-9540-0586
Vignana Jyothi Institute of Management, India

ABSTRACT

Contemporary risk management must evolve beyond reactive frameworks to adapt to changing economic, technical, and environmental ecosystems. The chapter discusses AI-driven risk intelligence and its transformation of predictive governance and strategic decision-making. AI systems rely on ML, DL, NLP, and real-time analytics. These tools allow businesses to monitor financial, operational, cybersecurity, supply chain, and climatic sectors for early warning signals, assess multidimensional risk exposures, and simulate impact scenarios. This chapter covers system designs, analytical methods, industry-specific applications, data quality, model bias, inter-

DOI: 10.4018/979-8-3373-6851-1.ch006

pretability, and regulatory compliance. AI-driven risk intelligence in uncertain and fast-changing environments improves organisational resilience, agility, and long-term sustainability. Technological innovation, ethical governance, and model risk management are highlighted.

1. INTRODUCTION

A new era of industrialization has begun. There is a mistreated or used electronic equipment around every corner. People are utilising their brains to an unprecedented degree (while neglecting their bodies, frequently to disastrous effects), and we can hardly imagine modern work without digital systems. Additionally, we appear to be inseparable from our mobile gadgets. Almost every aspect of our lives is becoming more computerised and "smart," including but not limited to: transportation, communication, workplaces, relationships, intelligence gathering, murderous drones, "deep fakes," and personal information(Dameski, 2020).

The lines between the digital and the analogue, the virtual and the real, are blurring at an exponential rate, and the majority of people aren't even keeping up with the rapid pace of change, let alone contributing to it. As a result, people are left to fend for themselves, fearing for their future livelihood, less agency, privacy, and autonomy, and an overall sense of isolation. Along with all this, we are hurriedly working on computer systems that can take on more and more complicated duties with less and less human oversight. Currently, the phrase "artificial intelligence" (henceforth: AI) refers to a collection of technologies and tools that humans use to carry out jobs that are either too tedious, expensive, or out of date for them to do alone.

On occasion, they are created and put into action just for the thrill of intellectual challenge, without considering the potentially disastrous and unforeseen outcomes that may result. The goal is to supplant humans with machines that are more resolute, less expensive, more efficient, and frequently less intelligent. Where does this lead? The good and the bad are inherent in every change. Perhaps, with varying degrees of success, humans have been attempting, from the beginning of our species onwards, to control or eliminate the negative while maximising the positive. There are "varying degrees of success" because there are instances when we are unable to identify the true nature of the problem or when we are unable to come up with satisfactory remedies to existing issues.

Possibly even more perilous than the first is the second. The fact that experts in the field of artificial intelligence can't even agree on a common definition of the term "artificial intelligence" suggests that we have no idea what kinds of problems, if any, will arise as a result of societal adoption of AI and automation. Countless individuals from various walks of life, including those in academia and government, are undoubtedly devoting significant effort to resolving this issue. A number of EU-led initiatives, like the European AI Alliance and the AI High-Level Expert Group, as well as other standalone initiatives like CLAIRE, are working to advance AI ethics. On the other side of the Atlantic, in the US, the discussion is just as heated, with representatives from both the public and private sectors (such as Google, Microsoft, and OpenAI) weighing in.

An official essay from the head of UNESCO was published in the UN Chronicle not long ago(Reger & Rozell, 2023). In addition to rapidly incorporating AI into their work, the Big Four accounting firms—PwC, Delotte, KPMG, and EY—arc now writing opinion pieces regarding the long-term effects of AI. For some time now, we have also been writing science fiction (Dune, With Folded Hands) and films (The Matrix, Deus Ex Machina, The Terminator, 2001: The Space Odyssey) that dreadfully depict the end of the world as a result of the careless introduction of algorithms and machines into our lives.

To be honest, our artificial intelligence masters do rescue us from ourselves on occasion, though not very often (as in Stanisław Lem's Golem XIV). Although fiction can be argued to be nothing more than fiction, it serves as a legitimate medium for us to delve into our concerns about emerging technologies and ways of life, and to find constructive solutions to handle them. And before AI is used so extensively that this becomes practically impossible, there are a myriad of real and potential problems that we must find out how to handle.

Questions abound concerning the following: the extent to which automated systems are responsible and accountable for their actions; the extent to which people's autonomy and agency are lost or abused; the delegation of ever-more-important responsibilities and tasks to these systems; the increasing complexity and opaqueness of these systems; their impact on the respect for human rights and dignity; the extent to which we can trust these systems even when we don't fully understand their inner workings; the perpetuation and worsening of bias; and finally, the question of whether humans should continue to be the center of moral theories. The list of current and future concerns is enormous, challenging, and complicated, as is evident.

By doing this work, I am helping to better anticipate and prepare for the ethical challenges that may result from the aforementioned advancements, with a focus on applied AI ethics, or moral situations in which AI entities play a role. While the challenges and specifics of integrating AI and automation into our societies are receiving more and more attention, the approaches being taken to address these issues are varied, incomplete, and sometimes disorganized. Neither the breadth nor the ethic-philosophical underpinnings nor the common approach of AI ethics have been settled upon yet.

To some extent, this is predictable. The specific nature of the problem, its dimensions and attributes, potential outcomes, desired outcomes, and methods of resolution are all unknowns at this early stage, as is the case with any novel development. Because of this, I think some of this work in the field of AI ethics should be foundational, providing a framework for how we think and act in a way that is both morally sound and sustainable for the long term.

This is where the meat of the piece lies. Two lines of inquiry form the backbone of my thesis. Providing what might be the groundwork for an all-encompassing ethical framework for AI creatures is the first. The goal of this Framework is to lay the groundwork for conducting rigorous investigations into potential ethical dilemmas with AI creatures. The second is to examine hypothetical moral situations in order to evaluate and prove the capabilities of this framework.

This model is what I've dubbed the Ethics of Systems Framework (or just "the Framework" from now on). In addition to having solid theoretical underpinnings, the Framework should make sense in context, be computationally and logically representable (at least in theory), be morally and ethically acceptable, and be practical to use in situations involving both humans and AI. Better moral outcomes should be the goal of its methodical approach. It ought to provide appropriate and ethically sound answers, be able to adapt to new situations, and support the accurate and high-quality modelling of moral scenarios.

This is obviously not a simple undertaking. I don't claim to have found the "Holy Grail" of artificial intelligence ethics. All I'm attempting to say is that I have some thoughts on ethics, both broadly and specifically about AI, that I think can add a lot to the whole endeavour. I have decided to formalize the foundations of such a framework instead of attempting to create and test a comprehensive theory, which would take decades (or even centuries?) and is clearly beyond the scope of a dissertation.

After I've tried to cover all the bases, I aim to condense the solution (the new theory) into as few words as possible easy and as fundamental as can be. I hope that my work will help in foreseeing, comprehending, and managing the problematic, morally-burdened consequences that will follow. Furthermore, I aspiration to aid in the realisation of my primary drive: the establishment of a (morally) superior world.

2. ETHICAL FOUNDATIONS OF AI SYSTEMS

In January 2023, the first version of the Artificial Intelligence Risk Management Framework was released by the National Institute of Standards and Technology (NIST), a prominent organization in the field of artificial intelligence standard development. Incorporating trustworthiness into AI system design, development, use, and evaluation is the goal of this voluntary approach (Yigitcanlar et al., 2020). In order to maximise the beneficial effects of artificial intelligence and minimise the negative ones, it is necessary to implement a strategy for managing the risks associated with this technology (NIST, 2023). By outlining the steps to take when evaluating the ethical implications of artificial intelligence systems (AIS), this study adds to the ongoing conversation around AI risk management(Jedličková, 2024). This paper addresses a variety of dangers related to AI and adds to the ongoing conversation on AI risk management by offering a high-level overview of how to incorporate risk management techniques into the ethical evaluation of AI.

2.1 A procedure for ethical, risk-based design

The IEEE Standard 7000TM establishes an ethical risk-based design methodology to assist engineers and technologists in incorporating ethical considerations into system designs for addressing dangers associated with AI applications. Organisations can ensure that their systems meet functional and ethical standards by incorporating human and societal ethical concepts into their design. The ideals encompass transparency, privacy, efficiency, safety, justice, effectiveness, accountability and security. It is essential to integrate ethical standards into the design of AI and ensure their adherence. This ethical risk-based design strategy enhances the comprehension and mitigation of potential challenges to ethical standards. This approach involves collecting input from pertinent stakeholders to identify potential hazards and their contexts, estimating the likelihood of damage occurring, analysing the assessed AIS for its impacts and consequences, and ultimately determining a strategy to mitigate the identified risks. The risk level for a certain value is determined by the summation of the probability of hazards and the severity of those hazards. Control mechanisms for system functions that may influence values-based requirements should be delineated and examined, alongside organisational and technical controls pertaining to the system and its components. It is essential to routinely assess the efficacy and acceptability of the implemented controls and risk mitigation measures.

2.2 Types of AI risks

The probability of an unfavourable occurrence and its subsequent negative effects is referred to as a risk in the IEEE Standard for Software Life Cycle Processes—Risk Management (IEEE, 2001). AI risks are the possible negative outcomes that might result from creating, releasing, and using AI systems. These outcomes could affect people, communities, businesses, and ecosystems(Steimers & Schneider, 2022). There are a number of potential points of failure for artificial intelligence systems, such as the data utilised for training and testing, the system components (such as the algorithmic model), the way and setting in which they are utilised, and their interactions with humans(Wach et al., 2023). The kind of risk determines which of several categories it falls into; they include technical, legal, organisational, financial, operational, business, strategic, reputational, and safety risks(Munoko & Miklos, 2025).

2.2.1 Limited risks of AI Systems

Certain transparency rules do not apply to AI systems that are deemed to pose a low risk. The goal of these specifications is to make sure that people can utilise an AI system wisely by giving them all the information they need(Bengio et al., 2024). It is critical to make sure people know what they're doing when they use AI(White et al., 2024). Systems that generate or modify visual, auditory, or video information, as well as those that interact with humans (like chatbots), may be examples of what is meant by this classification(Park et al., 2024). Moreover, the AI Act stipulates that no supplementary regulatory obligations are necessary for the development and deployment of low- or minimal-risk AI systems within the EU(Telkamp & Anderson, 2022). Nevertheless, corporations creating sophisticated AI systems are urged by legislation to voluntarily adhere to the existing laws applicable to AI systems with significant potential for harm (AI Act, 2023a).

2.2.2 Unacceptable risks of AI systems

The proposed AI Act states that any AI system that endangers human safety or rights or is determined to be an unacceptable risk shall be banned. Methods like these might comprise:

Artificial intelligence systems that manipulate people's thoughts and actions by using subliminal tactics to target vulnerable populations(Kaminski, 2023). Social scoring uses AI systems to classify people according to their actions, socioeconomic status, or other personal traits.

These biometric identification devices, installed in open places, operate remotely and in real time. The technological deficiencies of AI systems designed for remote biometric identification provide a risk of prejudice and discrimination. The increasing threat to individual liberties and rights posed by these technologies arises from the insufficient time available for additional scrutiny or rectifications during their real-time operation. Therefore, it is suitable to prohibit their use in public areas for law enforcement purposes. Furthermore, post-remote biometric identification systems employing AI to analyse film from public areas should be prohibited unless law enforcement possesses a pre-judicial warrant, and even then, solely for focused investigations related to specific, significant offences that have already occurred (AI Act, 2023a).

2.2.3 High risks of AI systems

When AI systems endanger people's well-being, safety, or basic human rights, we call them high-risk AIS. Toys, lifts, medical equipment, and machinery are all examples of such items(Zysman & Nitzberg, 2020). In addition, AI systems that match the following descriptions are also considered to be very risky:

Essential services like as water, gas, heating, and electricity, as well as vital digital infrastructure, are provided by AI systems that also serve as safety components in the management of air, train, and road traffic (AI Act, 2023a).
Institutions of higher learning and vocational training: artificial intelligence systems used to decide who gets in or how they are assigned to classes (AI Act, 2023a).
Artificial intelligence (AI) systems used by or on behalf of law enforcement to determine the credibility of evidence in criminal investigations and prosecutions, including polygraphs (AI Act, 2023a).
Management of workers, chances for self-employment, and the application of artificial intelligence technology in the recruitment process, encompassing candidate screening, interview and assessment scoring, and targeted job advertising. Other AI systems in this category encompass those that observe and assess behaviour, as well as those that determine contractual relationships in the workplace, allocate assignments based on individual behaviour or personal attributes, and similar functions (AI Act, 2023a).
The capacity to access and derive advantages from fundamental public and private services: AI systems utilised by or for government entities to ascertain eligibility for diverse public assistance programs, including healthcare, housing, utilities, and internet access, as well as to administer, reduce, revoke, augment, or recover these benefits and services (AI Act, 2023a).
The use of artificial intelligence systems by competent authorities to assess the security risks, health risks, and dangers posed by individuals entering or planning to enter EU Member States is a key component of migration, asylum, and border control management. This class includes AI systems that verify the legitimacy of travel documents by analysing their security features (AI Act, 2023a).
Assisting administrative or judicial authorities with research, legal interpretation, law application, or alternative dispute resolution exemplifies the utilisation of artificial intelligence in the administration of justice and democratic processes. Human judgement should remain the primary driver of decisions, while AI tools should serve as supplementary resources (AI Act, 2023a).

3. UNDERSTANDING BIAS IN AI MODELS

Figure 1 summarises the possible biases that may arise at each stage of AI development, including the ways in which humans and machines interact when prejudice is displayed. Acronym for "artificial intelligence"(Gichoya et al., 2023).

3.1 Handling the Data

Nonpixel and Pixel Data: In medical imaging, various factors can introduce bias in pixel data, including erroneous laterality labels or tissue attenuation, while other confounding variables may be less apparent(Tejani et al., 2024). This complicates the identification of causes of AI bias(Tejani et al., 2024). Researchers have shown that the challenge of identifying latent correlations, which could exacerbate clinical inequities, is evident in imaging AI models that can predict demographic information, such as racial identification, from radiographs without clear explainability (Gichoya et al., 2022).

Labeling the Data: In many cases, human expert anno tators with varied degrees of experience and knowledge are needed to manually label data in preparation for model training. In data annotation, "annotator bias" means that annotators are likely to bring their own preconceived notions, biases, prior knowledge, and subjective understanding of the labelling task to bear on the data (Drukker et al., 2023). The cognitive biases that radiologists encounter while reading research in clinical practice also affect annotators (Busby et al., 2018). For instance, there is the availability bias, where annotators assign labels based on recently reviewed cases; the inattention bias, where findings of interest are overlooked because of unusual manifestation and/or unexpected location; and the anchoring bias, where annotators refuse to change an initial label assignment despite contradictory information and/or findings. In the absence of defined labelling protocols and expertise, developers may rely on external third-party annotation services for large datasets, resulting in heterogeneity and contributing to discrepancies among final labels. Uneven data labelling may arise from misconceptions of standard annotation requirements among individuals with differing levels of English ability. Ultimately, these attributes increase the likelihood of label ambiguity, characterised by the potential for numerous competing labels. Automated methods for classifying extensive datasets using natural language processing tools that analyse image reports, although efficient, are prone to various sorts of bias. This may exacerbate inconsistencies in data labelling. Inconsistent annotations can introduce noise, whereas systemic inaccuracies that skew the performance of subsequent models may arise from recurrent labelling errors due to linguistic constraints, misinterpretation of annotation standards, or cognitive biases. The phrase "identify the position of the nasogastric tube" on a chest radiograph may convey two interpretations to various annotators: the site of the side hole or the distal tip of the tube. If the final model is tasked with accurately identifying the position of the side hole, a systematic error may arise from the model's persistent mis annotation of the distal tip due to a misinterpretation of the annotation guidelines. Conversely, labels assigned by annotators instructed to "identify the side hole of the nasogastric tube" may sometimes be erroneous due to visual obstructions from structures above the tube, rather than a uniform pattern.

Imbalance in Class: Due to data scarcity, there may be an imbalance in the representation of certain classes in the training, validation, and test sets(Rahmadi & Anjani, 2024). This is known as class imbalance. Developing models for rare diseases might lead to class imbalance if the training data contains an excessive amount of normal or negative cases. In addition to positive or "interesting" imaging studies being over-represented, another prevalent cause of class imbalance is negative set bias (Geis et al., 2019). As an example, if you were to curate an MRI data set from a tertiary care facility for the brain, you may find that gliomas are over-represented. This is because individuals with recognised diseases are often referred to the cancer center for cutting-edge treatment. Training models on datasets that have insufficient representation of protected groups can lead to sampling bias, which directly contributes to minority bias and subsequently causes class imbalance. Due to the inherent disparities in the patient demographics serviced by private imaging centers and county safety-net hospitals, training datasets from these two healthcare facilities may reflect racial or socioeconomic inequities. When some classes are under-represented in a training dataset, the model must learn patterns from a limited sample size prior to making predictions on bigger datasets. In the absence of certain classes in the training data, models may erroneously conclude that these classes do not exist.

Heterogeneity of Dataset Sources: Building training, validation, and test datasets for artificial intelligence model development requires sampling and organising real-world data. This process is known as dataset handling(Gichoya et al., 2023). If you want to build an AI model that can generalise, use datasets that are typical of the population you're trying to target. In reality, only a small percentage of research really employs external validation, which entails testing a model's efficacy using data sets that are sufficiently distinct or geographically remote from the training datasets (Yu et al., 2022). Problems arise when answers developed from training models using data from a single source are not applicable to studies conducted on equipment from different manufacturers or to populations with distinct varying socioeconomic situations and patient demographics(Mehrabi et al., 2022). In addition, training datasets do not contain data that is typical of the target population when data is selected based on convenience or availability, which enables sampling bias, a subset of selection bias.

Figure 1. Potential Bias in the Various Stages of Data Collection and Model Development

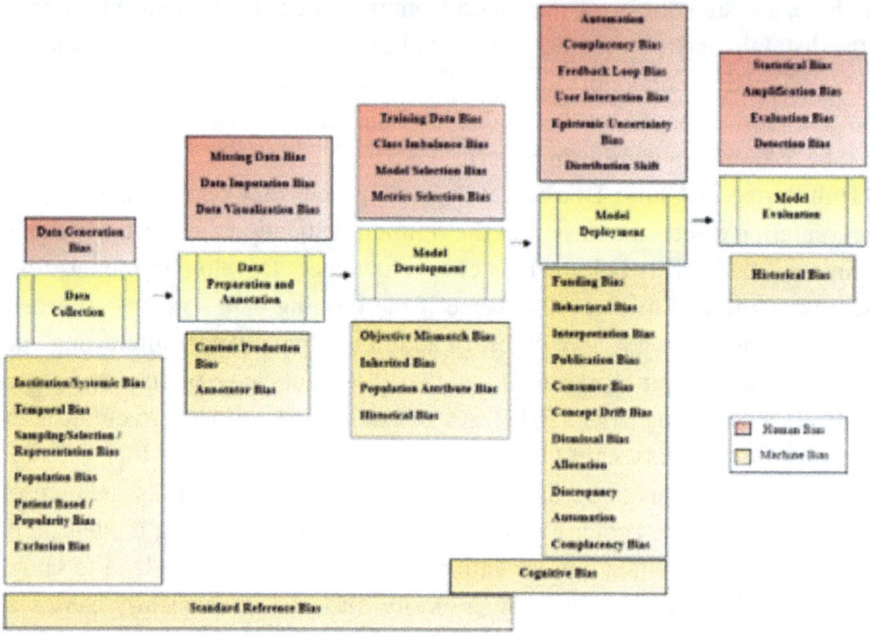

3.2 Model Deployment

Data Distribution Shift: When there is a discrepancy between the training data and the target data, which represents changes in the target data distribution that were not accounted for in the initial training data, this is called a data distribution shift. After being deployed, models that performed well in test conditions start to underperform(Davis et al., 2024). The assumption that the training and test settings are identical is a common one in algorithm development, although it rarely holds true in practice(Memarian & Doleck, 2023). As a result, models could unknowingly reflect bias in the restricted training data and struggle to perform on out-of-distribution data.

3.3 Evaluation of the Model

Choosing the Right Performance Metrics: Due to erroneous conclusions, improper validation measures could limit the final clinical efficacy by overstating model performance. Important problem categories include object identification, segmentation, and classification, and it is critical to know which metrics are suitable for each (Maier-Hein et al., 2024). For instance, when considering class imbalance, the information provided by accuracy which describes model performance across all classes—may be misleading due to its reliance on disease prevalence(Wang et al., 2016). When there is a mismatch between the classes, a more appropriate measure for model performance is the F1 score, which is the harmonic mean of the precision and recall metrics ([true positives]/[true positives + false positives]) (Koçak, 2022).

Significance of Subgroup Analysis: In contrast to evaluating models on subgroups defined by characteristics like demographics or geographic location, aggregate performance on test or evaluation datasets is frequently used for model evaluation.

3.2 Development of the Model

Leakage of the Data: Data splitting, which is necessary before model creation, involves dividing curated data into three sets: training, test, and additional validation sets if needed (Rouzrokh et al., 2022). Image, series, study, and patient levels are all potential locations for data splitting. A skewed performance on the validation and/or test datasets and subpar generalisation to new, undiscovered target data might result from failing to avoid dataset overlap(Hanna et al., 2025a). Data leaking occurs when training and test datasets overlap or when extraneous information is incorporated that would not be accessible during actual predictions. Training set contamination, a form of data leakage, refers to instances where the training dataset overlaps with the validation or test datasets. A common form of contamination in training sets is data duplication, which can transfer from training datasets to validation or test datasets. The model's performance during evaluation may be exaggerated due to its training on patterns within the specified test set. This is due to the possibility that patterns beyond this context may not be sufficiently captured by the model. Numerous radiology examinations conducted on the same patient within a brief timeframe and categorised into training, validation, and test datasets, all exhibiting identical pathological findings, may exemplify redundant data. Moreover, public datasets may include identical smaller component datasets, potentially resulting in training set contamination when many datasets are amalgamated (often referred to as Frankenstein datasets).

Improper Feature Engineering: The goal of feature engineering is to improve model performance by selecting and modifying data features, also known as measurable variables of interest. In order to make better predictions, the model's capacity to recognise patterns must be enhanced, and this process entails removing unnecessary or irrelevant data. Due to the introduction of systematic mistakes, biased model development might result from improper feature engineering(Ntoutsi et al., 2020). For instance, if pictures are cropped incorrectly, specific features in a training dataset may be consistently over- or under-represented, which might distort predictions. Think about the effects on performance of a model that has to classify results from mammograms obtained from data that includes cropped pictures of easily discernible masses or asymmetries but excludes areas with higher breast density or areas on the edge of the picture (like the axilla).

4. BIAS MITIGATION

Training, pre-training, and post-training are the phases that allow for the application of mitigation strategies(González-Sendino et al., 2024).

It is most effective to fix bias in the pre-training phase by mitigating it, since this modifies the dataset. Nevertheless, developers may not be able to address bias in the initial iteration of the process if it emerges after training (W. Zhang et al., 2021).
The best way to deal with bias is during training. These techniques often do not include manipulating the original data set and are hence unsupervised(Hort et al., 2024). Considering the introduction of other derived features, excluding sensitive variables like gender or race is insufficient to reduce discrimination. It is more efficient to include fairness to the objective function instead (Wilson et al., 2021).
For the majority of the updated measures, post-training is the best time to compute them. Nevertheless, addressing biases during this stage need to be reserved for last resort.

4.1 Pre-Training

To provide equitable data free of discriminating effects, it is possible to make preprocessing adjustments to the sample, features, and labels (Larrazabal et al., 2020). The problem is that this method isn't foolproof against algorithmic bias (Gilbert & Mintz, 2019). The taxonomy mirrors the three primary methods (resampling, fair representation, and re-weighting) discussed in the literature.

4.1.1 Re-Weighting

A more common approach to data transformation is re-weighting, which involves changing the weights in the dataset (Alam, 2020). Keep in mind that weighted samples aren't always accepted by learning algorithms. Certain favoured group instances will have a lower weight due to re-weighting since they are more likely to have a favourable outcome. Similarly, cases involving a marginalised group will be given more importance (Gade et al., 2020).

4.1.2 Resampling

If you want to alter the distribution of your data without actually changing it, you can resample the data. One can classify resampling techniques as either under sampling or oversampling. In contrast to oversampling, which entails creating new data samples to supplement the existing dataset, under sampling relies on removing samples from the dataset.

4.1.3 Fair Representation

By removing any information that could identify a person as belonging to a protected group, we can achieve fair representation. One well-known method for discovering a latent representation that encodes data fairly is learning fair representation (LFR). There is more or less weight given to the display of protected information depending on whether it is hidden or explicit (Y. Zhang & Ramesh, 2020). While LFR does a better job of being fair, it makes it harder to understand the outcomes (Harris, 2020).

5. RISK MANAGEMENT TRUST

According to the weighted additive rule, people need to "consider all available cues, to retrieve cue values accurately, to weight cues properly, to integrate information for each alternative, and to examine all alternatives". People can make these demands easier on themselves by: "1. Examining fewer cues. 2 Making it easier to save and retrieve cue data. 3. Weighing principles for cues made simpler. 4. Using a less amount of data. 5. considering a smaller set of options.

If you just need to use a couple of these cues or switch to one that is easier to reach (like attribute replacement, you can make this process easier on yourself and the environment(Uys et al., 2019). Here, heuristics serve as foundations for trust, which in turn facilitates collaboration (refer to the "shallowness hypothesis"(Habbal et al., 2024). The likeness heuristic and the affect heuristic are two heuristics that may be crucial in trust judgements.

5.1 Affect Heuristic

Since evaluations of similarity can elicit affect, the two are conceptually related. Because it is straightforward, readily available, and easy to assess, one's emotional reaction to a person or thing (i.e., positive or negative feelings) could serve as a heuristic cue to trustworthiness, just like similarity(Kim et al., 2020). Additionally, feelings can stand in for values when there is a lack of clarity about the relationship between the two (Merkle, 2022). As a generic heuristic, "the affect heuristic" was first created to be used in many other types of judgements and decisions; nevertheless, it has since been extensively used to explain perceptions of risk and benefit(Gül & Özder, 2025). Confidence is less affect-reliant and more focused on the past, whereas trust is more affect-reliant and future-oriented, with an inward focus on values.

5.2 Similarity Heuristic

Modern research in the social sciences has built on an old principle: that people are more likely to have positive opinions of others when they detect similarities between themselves and those others. Newer studies have demonstrated that when users see similarities between their decision-making process and that of an online decision-assist, they are more likely to trust and make use of the aid. Individuals choose those resembling themselves, who shared their group identities and recognised them, as an act of benevolence when determining whom to trust—people about whom they possessed no knowledge beyond their group identify. In the context of interpersonal negotiation, individuals exhibited a greater propensity to trust each other and achieve mutually advantageous agreements when they subtly mirrored the behaviour of their counterparts. Research indicates that confidence is augmented when individuals' facial features are similar. Given the high importance of the components involved, a diverse array of similarities may function as heuristic indicators of trustworthiness.

5.2.1 Similarity of intentions

When trying to convey reliability, what kind of similarity would work best? Similarity of goals, according to the previous explanation of the dimensions of trust, would be the best fit. In order to trust another person, one must be certain that their objectives are compatible with, or identical to, one's own(De Brito & Evers, 2016). An overarching definition of this heuristic cue to trustworthiness would be value similarity, since people's intents (aims, aspirations, goals, objectives) are manifestations of their currently relevant values.

5.2.2 Value similarity

Various research conducted in corporate and organisational contexts have proven that there is a strong correlation between having similar values and being trustworthy(Hassan et al., 2023). For instance, research by Cazier and colleagues demonstrated that when people's values are similar, it impacts their perceptions of others' abilities and kindness, which impacts their trust, and ultimately leads to cooperation. There was a direct correlation between value similarity and cooperation. One study found that when members of an organisational team had common values, it boosted trust, which in turn improved team performance and cooperation satisfaction.

6. HUMAN RIGHTS AND ETHICAL IMPLICATIONS OF BIASED AI

There are many different ways in which prejudiced AI could violate human rights and ethical standards(Min, 2023).

1. The principle of Equal Protection Under the Law
   - The principle of Equal Protection Under the Law asserts that the fundamental human right to be free from discrimination is compromised when AI systems exhibit prejudice against particular ethnic, gender, or socioeconomic groups (European Commission, 2020).
   - An AI that exhibits bias against specific groups can inflict greater harm than benefit by perpetuating existing stereotypes and fostering discrimination (Crawford & Schultz, 2013).
2. Privacy Invasion
   - The European Commission (2020) cautions that biased AI systems may render judgements based on sensitive personal attributes such as gender or race, so infringing upon individual privacy(Hoxhaj et al., 2023).
   - Robust data protection measures are necessary as this infringes upon the right to privacy.
3. Transparency and Accountability
   - Accountability may be hindered because to the opaque nature of AI decision-making(Ansari, 2023).
   - Individuals possess the right to understand the rationale behind actions that have significant consequences.
4. Impact on Vulnerable Communities:

- Disparities are worsened when vulnerable and marginalised communities are the ones hit hardest by biased AI choices (Law, 2018).
- Ethical AI methods are necessary to protect these groups' rights.

Finally, there are serious moral and civil rights concerns around the problem of prejudice and bias in AI systems(Slimi & Carballido, 2023). To solve this issue, we must work together to create AI systems that are equitable, open, and responsible, and that uphold the worth and rights of every person.

7. PRINCIPLES OF FAIRNESS

The FAIR guiding principles were established to implement and enforce data stewardship and governance in the administration of scientific data sets. These principles encompass accessibility, reusability, interoperability and findability(Hanna et al., 2025b). The objective of these principles is to enhance data quality and utility, hence reducing bias in AI models. The FAIR principles are increasingly employed to enhance the usability and integration of AI models within many clinical and research applications(Wilkinson et al., 2016). Administer AI models to enhance discoverability, interoperability, accessibility, and reusability by adhering to these criteria (Figure 2).

7.1 Importance

The FAIR principles are essential for managing AI bias by promoting transparency, reproducibility, and inclusiveness across the data lifecycle. Accessibility ensures that a diverse array of representative data sets is readily available(Annika Jacobsen, Ricardo de Miranda Azevedo, Nick Juty, Dominique Batista, Simon Coles, Ronald Cornet, Mélanie Courtot, Mercè Crosas et al., 2019). Researchers can more readily identify and mitigate bias in data sets when their sources are transparent and accessible(Barker et al., 2022). This transparency allows for critical examination of data sources, facilitating the identification of any inadvertently induced biases. Data must be easily obtainable by all interested parties under designated conditions to be deemed accessible. This concept ensures that opacity in data governance practices and restricted data access do not facilitate the continuation of biases. The FAIR principles promote open access and transparent norms for data sharing to enable academics to analyse data sets and algorithms for patterns of bias and prejudice. Interoperability facilitates data integration and analysis across several platforms and applications. Results from diverse AI models and datasets can be more readily compared using common formats and metadata. This interoperability enables researchers to examine if biases identified in one data set are similarly evident in another. Documentation and dissemination of data sources, methodology, and outcomes are essential to enhance reusability(Mons et al., 2017). The FAIR principles provide defined criteria for data reuse and replication, enabling researchers to confirm and substantiate their findings through rigorous testing and validation processes. Ensuring the equitable and unbiased application of AI models necessitates transparency and reproducibility(Wezel et al., 2019). The FAIR principles establish a framework for reducing biases in the fundamental aspects of data management to encourage ethical AI research. These principles facilitate researchers in identifying and rectifying biases in data by enhancing the transparency, accessibility, interoperability, and reusability of information(Chu et al., 2021). This results in more equitable and dependable AI systems. Ensuring data accessibility, representativeness, and high-quality helps mitigate bias in AI models. This can be accomplished by adhering to the FAIR principles. This initiative for transparency and accountability in AI will reduce the potential for bias in its outcomes. Integrating FAIR principles and inclusive data practices can mitigate bias in AI(J. Zhang & Bareinboim, 2018). This will foster greater transparency, accountability, and inclusivity in data utilisation, hence assisting our stakeholders in establishing a more just and equitable AI environment.

Figure 2. FAIR Principles. FAIR, Findability, Accessibility, Interoperability, and Reusability

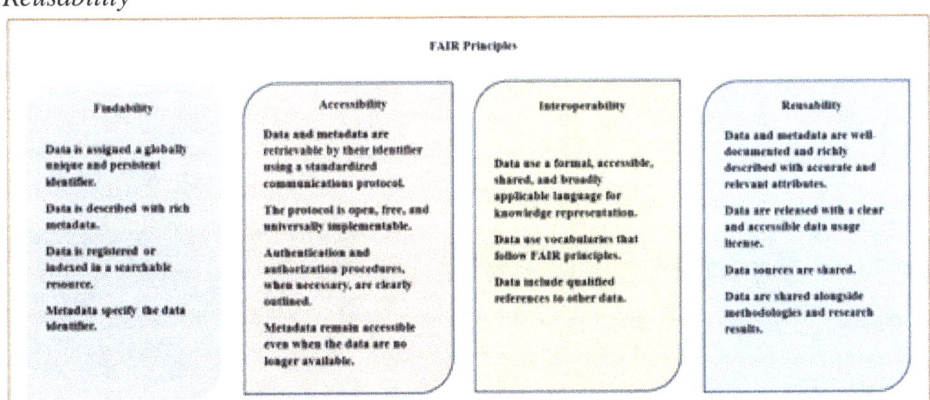

8. CONCLUSION

Artificial intelligence has evolved from an ambiguous concept to a fundamental element of our daily existence over the past several decades. The advancement of more potent computers, alongside enhancements in machine learning and deep learning, has driven this transformation. Numerous industries have commenced the utilisation of AI, including medicine, banking, transportation, education, and others. Virtual assistants, autonomous vehicles, medical diagnostics, and recommendation systems all utilise it. AI-driven risk intelligence has enabled conventional risk management to engage in strategic planning, adaptation, and prediction. In an unpredictable environment, businesses may identify emerging risks, analyse systemic vulnerabilities, and enhance their resilience by integrating advanced analytics with governance frameworks. Realizing the complete potential of AI-driven risk ecosystems necessitates responsible implementation, integrating innovation with transparency and governance.

REFERENCES

Alam, M. A. U. (2020). AI-fairness towards activity recognition of older adults. *ACM International Conference Proceeding Series,* December 2020, 108–117. DOI: 10.1145/3448891.3448943

Ansari, W. (2023). The Ethical Implications of Artificial Intelligence on the Human Society. SSRN *Electronic Journal, 9*(6), 94–101. DOI: 10.2139/ssrn.4512301

Barker, M., Chue Hong, N. P., Katz, D. S., Lamprecht, A. L., Martinez-Ortiz, C., Psomopoulos, F., Harrow, J., Castro, L. J., Gruenpeter, M., Martinez, P. A., & Honeyman, T. (2022). Introducing the FAIR Principles for research software. *Scientific Data*, *9*(1), 1–6. DOI: 10.1038/s41597-022-01710-x PMID: 36241754

Bengio, Y., Hinton, G., Yao, A., Song, D., Abbeel, P., Darrell, T., Harari, Y. N., Zhang, Y.-Q., Xue, L., Shalev-Shwartz, S., Hadfield, G., Clune, J., Maharaj, T., Hutter, F., Baydin, A. G., McIlraith, S., Gao, Q., Acharya, A., Krueger, D., & Mindermann, S. (2024). Managing extreme AI risks amid rapid progress. *Science*, *384*(6698), 842–845. DOI: 10.1126/science.adn0117 PMID: 38768279

Busby, L. P., Courtier, J. L., & Glastonbury, C. M. (2018). Bias in radiology: The how and why of misses and misinterpretations. *Radiographics*, *38*(1), 236–247. DOI: 10.1148/rg.2018170107 PMID: 29194009

Chu, X., Zhang, B., & Xu, R. (2021). FairNAS: Rethinking Evaluation Fairness of Weight Sharing Neural Architecture Search. *Proceedings of the IEEE International Conference on Computer Vision*, 12219–12228. DOI: 10.1109/ICCV48922.2021.01202

Dameski, A. (2020). Foundations of an Ethical Framework for AI Entities: the Ethics of Systems. *Doctoral Dissertation, University of Luxembourg, Esch-Sur-Alzette, Luxembourg*. https://orbilu.uni.lu/handle/10993/45285

Davis, M. A., Wu, O., Ikuta, I., Jordan, J. E., Johnson, M. H., & Quigley, E. (2024). Understanding Bias in Artificial Intelligence: A Practice Perspective. *AJNR. American Journal of Neuroradiology*, *45*(4), 371–373. DOI: 10.3174/ajnr.A8070 PMID: 38123951

De Brito, M. M., & Evers, M. (2016). Multi-criteria decision-making for flood risk management: A survey of the current state of the art. *Natural Hazards and Earth System Sciences*, *16*(4), 1019–1033. DOI: 10.5194/nhess-16-1019-2016

Drukker, K., Chen, W., Gichoya, J., Gruszauskas, N., Kalpathy-Cramer, J., Koyejo, S., Myers, K., Sá, R. C., Sahiner, B., Whitney, H., Zhang, Z., & Giger, M. (2023). Toward fairness in artificial intelligence for medical image analysis: Identification and mitigation of potential biases in the roadmap from data collection to model deployment. *Journal of Medical Imaging (Bellingham, Wash.), 10*(06). Advance online publication. DOI: 10.1117/1.JMI.10.6.061104 PMID: 37125409

Gade, K., Geyik, S. C., Kenthapadi, K., Mithal, V., & Taly, A. (2020). Explainable AI in industry: Practical challenges and lessons learned. *Companion Proceedings of the Web Conference, January 2020*, 699–699. DOI: 10.1145/3351095.3375664

Geis, J. R., Brady, A., Wu, C. C., Spencer, J., Ranschaert, E., Jaremko, J. L., Langer, S. G., Kitts, A. B., Birch, J., Shields, W. F., van den Hoven van Genderen, R., Kotter, E., Gichoya, J. W., Cook, T. S., Morgan, M. B., Tang, A., Safdar, N. M., & Kohli, M. (2019). Ethics of artificial intelligence in radiology: Summary of the joint European and North American multisociety statement. *Insights Into Imaging, 10*(1), 101. Advance online publication. DOI: 10.1186/s13244-019-0785-8 PMID: 31571015

Gichoya, J. W., Banerjee, I., Bhimireddy, A. R., Burns, J. L., Celi, L. A., Chen, L. C., Correa, R., Dullerud, N., Ghassemi, M., Huang, S. C., Kuo, P. C., Lungren, M. P., Palmer, L. J., Price, B. J., Purkayastha, S., Pyrros, A. T., Oakden-Rayner, L., Okechukwu, C., Seyyed-Kalantari, L., & Zhang, H. (2022). AI recognition of patient race in medical imaging: A modelling study. *The Lancet. Digital Health, 4*(6), e406–e414. DOI: 10.1016/S2589-7500(22)00063-2 PMID: 35568690

Gichoya, J. W., Thomas, K., Celi, L. A., Safdar, N., Banerjee, I., Banja, J. D., Seyyed-Kalantari, L., Trivedi, H., & Purkayastha, S. (2023). AI IN IMAGING AND THERAPY: INNOVATIONS, ETHICS, AND IMPACT: REVIEW ARTICLE AI pitfalls and what not to do: mitigating bias in AI. *The British Journal of Radiology, 96*(1150), 20230023. Advance online publication. DOI: 10.1259/bjr.20230023 PMID: 37698583

Gilbert, T. K., & Mintz, Y. (2019). Epistemic therapy for bias in automated decision-making. *AIES 2019 - Proceedings of the 2019 AAAI/ACM Conference on AI, Ethics, and Society, March*, 61–67. DOI: 10.1145/3306618.3314294

González-Sendino, R., Serrano, E., Bajo, J., & Novais, P. (2024). A Review of Bias and Fairness in Artificial Intelligence. *International Journal of Interactive Multimedia and Artificial Intelligence, 9*(1), 5–17. DOI: 10.9781/ijimai.2023.11.001

Gül, C., & Özder, A. (2025). The Effects of Hotel Managers' Perceptions about Refugees on Their Operational Decisions in Istanbul: A Research in the Framework of Affect Heuristic Theory. *Electronic Turkish Studies, 20*, 747–767.

Habbal, A., Ali, M. K., & Abuzaraida, M. A. (2024). Artificial Intelligence Trust, Risk and Security Management (AI TRiSM): Frameworks, applications, challenges and future research directions. *Expert Systems with Applications, 240*(November 2023). DOI: 10.1016/j.eswa.2023.122442

Hanna, M. G., Pantanowitz, L., Jackson, B., Palmer, O., Visweswaran, S., Pantanowitz, J., Deebajah, M., & Rashidi, H. H. (2025a). Ethical and Bias Considerations in Artificial Intelligence/Machine Learning. *Modern Pathology*, *38*(3), 100686. DOI: 10.1016/j.modpat.2024.100686 PMID: 39694331

Hanna, M. G., Pantanowitz, L., Jackson, B., Palmer, O., Visweswaran, S., Pantanowitz, J., Deebajah, M., & Rashidi, H. H. (2025b). Ethical and Bias Considerations in Artificial Intelligence/Machine Learning. *Modern Pathology*, *38*(3), 100686. Advance online publication. DOI: 10.1016/j.modpat.2024.100686 PMID: 39694331

Harris, C. (2020). Mitigating Cognitive Biases in Machine Learning Algorithms for Decision Making. *The Web Conference 2020 - Companion of the World Wide Web Conference, WWW 2020, 2020*(April 2020), 775–781. DOI: 10.1145/3366424.3383562

Hassan, M., Aziz, L. A.-R., & Andriansyah, Y. (2023). The Role Artificial Intelligence in Modern Banking: An Exploration of AI-Driven Approaches for Enhanced Fraud Prevention, Risk Management, and Regulatory Compliance. *Reviews of Contemporary Business Analytics*, *6*(1), 110–132. https://researchberg.com/index.php/rcba/article/view/153

Hort, M., Chen, Z., Zhang, J. M., Harman, M., & Sarro, F. (2024). Bias Mitigation for Machine Learning Classifiers: A Comprehensive Survey. *ACM Journal on Responsible Computing*, *1*(2), 1–52. DOI: 10.1145/3631326

Hoxhaj, O., Halilaj, B., & Harizi, A. (2023). ETHICAL IMPLICATIONS AND HUMAN RIGHTS VIOLATIONS IN THE AGE OF ARTIFICIAL INTELLIGENCE. *Balkan Social Science Review*, *22*(22), 153–171. DOI: 10.46763/BSSR232222153h

Jacobsen, A., de Miranda Azevedo, R., Juty, N., Batista, D., Coles, S., Cornet, R., & Schultes, E. (2020). FAIR principles: Interpretations and implementation considerations. *Data Intelligence*, *2*(1-2), 10–29. DOI: 10.1162/dint

Jedličková, A. (2024). Ethical considerations in Risk management of autonomous and intelligent systems. [in Central Europe]. *Ethics and Bioethics*, *14*(1–2), 80–95. DOI: 10.2478/ebce-2024-0007

Kaminski, M. E. (2023). Regulating the Risks of Ai. *SSRN*, *103*(5), 1347–1411. DOI: 10.2139/ssrn.4195066

Kim, Y., Park, K., Kim, Y., Yang, W., Han, D., & Kim, W. S. (2020). The Impact of Visual Art and High Affective Arousal on Heuristic Decision-Making in Consumers. *Frontiers in Psychology, 11*(November), 1–16. DOI: 10.3389/fpsyg.2020.565829 PMID: 33324278

Koçak, B. (2022). Key concepts, common pitfalls, and best practices in artificial intelligence and machine learning: Focus on radiomics. *Diagnostic and Interventional Radiology, 28*(5), 450–462. DOI: 10.5152/dir.2022.211297 PMID: 36218149

Larrazabal, A. J., Nieto, N., Peterson, V., Milone, D. H., & Ferrante, E. (2020). Gender imbalance in medical imaging datasets produces biased classifiers for computer-aided diagnosis. *Proceedings of the National Academy of Sciences of the United States of America, 117*(23), 12592–12594. DOI: 10.1073/pnas.1919012117 PMID: 32457147

Maier-Hein, L., Reinke, A., Godau, P., Tizabi, M. D., Buettner, F., Christodoulou, E., Glocker, B., Isensee, F., Kleesiek, J., Kozubek, M., Reyes, M., Riegler, M. A., Wiesenfarth, M., Kavur, A. E., Sudre, C. H., Baumgartner, M., Eisenmann, M., Heckmann-Nötzel, D., Rädsch, T., & Jäger, P. F. (2024). Metrics reloaded: Recommendations for image analysis validation. *Nature Methods, 21*(2), 195–212. DOI: 10.1038/s41592-023-02151-z PMID: 38347141

Mehrabi, N., Morstatter, F., Saxena, N., Lerman, K., & Galstyan, A. (2022). A Survey on Bias and Fairness in Machine Learning. *ACM Computing Surveys, 54*(6), 1–35. Advance online publication. DOI: 10.1145/3457607

Memarian, B., & Doleck, T. (2023). Fairness, Accountability, Transparency, and Ethics (FATE) in Artificial Intelligence (AI) and higher education: A systematic review. *Computers and Education: Artificial Intelligence*, *5*(May), 100152. DOI: 10.1016/j.caeai.2023.100152

Merkle, C. (2022). The Affect Heuristic and Financial Expectations: Risk, Return, and ESG. SSRN *Electronic Journal, July*. DOI: 10.2139/ssrn.4157854

Min, A. (2023). Artifical Intelligence and Bias: Challenges, Implications, and Remedies. *Journal of Social Research, 2*(11), 3808–3817. DOI: 10.55324/josr.v2i11.1477

Mons, B., Neylon, C., Velterop, J., Dumontier, M., Da Silva Santos, L. O. B., & Wilkinson, M. D. (2017). Cloudy, increasingly FAIR; revisiting the FAIR Data guiding principles for the European Open Science Cloud. *Information Services & Use, 37*(1), 49–56. DOI: 10.3233/ISU-170824

Munoko, I., & Miklos, H. L. B. (2025). The Ethical Implications of Using Artificial Intelligence in Auditing. *Journal of Business Ethics, 167*(2), 209–234. DOI: 10.1007/s10551-019-04407-1

Ntoutsi, E., Fafalios, P., Gadiraju, U., Iosifidis, V., Nejdl, W., Vidal, M. E., Ruggieri, S., Turini, F., Papadopoulos, S., Krasanakis, E., Kompatsiaris, I., Kinder-Kurlanda, K., Wagner, C., Karimi, F., Fernandez, M., Alani, H., Berendt, B., Kruegel, T., Heinze, C., & Staab, S. (2020). Bias in data-driven artificial intelligence systems—An introductory survey. *Wiley Interdisciplinary Reviews. Data Mining and Knowledge Discovery, 10*(3), 1–14. DOI: 10.1002/widm.1356

Park, P. S., Goldstein, S., O'Gara, A., Chen, M., & Hendrycks, D. (2024). AI deception: A survey of examples, risks, and potential solutions. *Patterns (New York, N.Y.), 5*(5), 100988. DOI: 10.1016/j.patter.2024.100988 PMID: 38800366

Rahmadi, D., & Anjani, K. T. (2024). A COMPREHENSIVE REVIEW OF BIAS IN AI ALGORITHMS. *Nusantara Hasana Journal, 1*(7), 132–137.

Reger, E. A., & Rozell, E. J. (2023). The master of accountancy:understanding factors influencing intentions and behaviors toward accounting graduate education. In *Journal of Theoretical Accounting Research* (Vol. 19, Issue 1).

Rouzrokh, P., Khosravi, B., Faghani, S., Moassefi, M., Garcia, D. V. V., Singh, Y., Zhang, K., Conte, G. M., & Erickson, B. J. (2022). Mitigating Bias in Radiology Machine Learning: 1. Data Handling. *Radiology. Artificial Intelligence, 4*(5), e210290. Advance online publication. DOI: 10.1148/ryai.210290 PMID: 36204544

Slimi, Z., & Carballido, B. V. (2023). Navigating the Ethical Challenges of Artificial Intelligence in Higher Education: An Analysis of Seven Global AI Ethics Policies. *TEM Journal, 12*(2), 590–602. https://doi.org/DOI: 10.18421/TEM122-02

Steimers, A., & Schneider, M. (2022). Sources of Risk of AI Systems. *International Journal of Environmental Research and Public Health, 19*(6), 3641. Advance online publication. DOI: 10.3390/ijerph19063641 PMID: 35329328

Tejani, A. S., Ng, Y. S., Xi, Y., & Rayan, J. C. (2024). Understanding and Mitigating Bias in Imaging Artificial Intelligence. *Radiographics, 44*(5), e230067. Advance online publication. DOI: 10.1148/rg.230067 PMID: 38635456

Telkamp, J. B., & Anderson, M. H. (2022). The Implications of Diverse Human Moral Foundations for Assessing the Ethicality of Artificial Intelligence. *Journal of Business Ethics, 178*(4), 961–976. DOI: 10.1007/s10551-022-05057-6

Uys, G., Meyer, A., & Niemann, W. (2019). Taxonomies of trust in supply chain risk management in the South African third party logistics industry. *Acta Commercii, 19*(1). Advance online publication. DOI: 10.4102/ac.v19i1.792

Wach, K., Duong, C. D., Ejdys, J., Kazlauskaitė, R., Korzynski, P., Mazurek, G., Paliszkiewicz, J., & Ziemba, E. (2023). The dark side of generative artificial intelligence: A critical analysis of controversies and risks of ChatGPT. *Entrepreneurial Business and Economics Review, 11*(2), 7–30. DOI: 10.15678/EBER.2023.110201

Wang, S., Liu, W., Wu, J., Cao, L., Meng, Q., & Kennedy, P. J. (2016). Training deep neural networks on imbalanced data sets. *Proceedings of the International Joint Conference on Neural Networks, 2016-Octob*, 4368–4374. DOI: 10.1109/IJCNN.2016.7727770

Wezel, A., Gemmill Herren, B., Kerr, R. B., Barrios, E., Luiz, A., Gonçalves, R., & Sinclair, F. (2019). Agroecological principles and elements and their implications for transitioning to sustainable food systems. A review. *Agronomy for Sustainable Development.* Advance online publication. DOI: 10.1007/s13593-020-00646-z

White, G. R. T., Samuel, A., Jones, P., Madhavan, N., Afolayan, A., Abdullah, A., & Kaushik, T. (2024). Mapping the ethic-theoretical foundations of artificial intelligence research. *Thunderbird International Business Review, 66*(2), 171–183. DOI: 10.1002/tie.22368

Wilkinson, M. D., Dumontier, M., Aalbersberg, I., Appleton, G., Axton, M., Baak, A., Blomberg, N., Boiten, J.-W., da Silva Santos, L. B., Bourne, P. E., Bouwman, J., Brookes, A. J., Clark, T., Crosas, M., Dillo, I., Dumon, O., Edmunds, S., Evelo, C. T., Finkers, R., & Mons, B. (2016). Comment: The FAIR Guiding Principles for scientific data management and stewardship. *Scientific Data, 3*(1), 1–9. DOI: 10.1038/sdata.2016.18 PMID: 26978244

Wilson, C., Ghosh, A., Jiang, S., Mislove, A., Baker, L., Szary, J., Trindel, K., & Polli, F. (2021). Building and auditing fair algorithms: A case study in candidate screening. *FAccT 2021 - Proceedings of the 2021 ACM Conference on Fairness, Accountability, and Transparency, March*, 666–677. DOI: 10.1145/3442188.3445928

Yigitcanlar, T., Desouza, K. C., Butler, L., & Roozkhosh, F. (2020). Contributions and risks of artificial intelligence (AI) in building smarter cities: Insights from a systematic review of the literature. *Energies, 13*(6), 1473. Advance online publication. DOI: 10.3390/en13061473

Yu, A. C., Mohajer, B., & Eng, J. (2022). External Validation of Deep Learning Algorithms for Radiologic Diagnosis: A Systematic Review. *Radiology. Artificial Intelligence, 4*(3), 1–9. DOI: 10.1148/ryai.210064 PMID: 35652114

Zhang, J., & Bareinboim, E. (2018). Fairness in decision-making the causal explanation formula. *32nd AAAI Conference on Artificial Intelligence, AAAI 2018*, 2037–2045. DOI: 10.1609/aaai.v32i1.11564

Zhang, W., Bifet, A., Zhang, X., Weiss, J. C., & Nejdl, W. (2021). FARF: A Fair and Adaptive Random Forests Classifier. *Lecture Notes in Computer Science (Including Subseries Lecture Notes in Artificial Intelligence and Lecture Notes in Bioinformatics), 12713 LNAI*, 245–256. DOI: 10.1007/978-3-030-75765-6_20

Zhang, Y., & Ramesh, A. (2020). Learning fairness-aware relational structures. *Frontiers in Artificial Intelligence and Applications*, *325*, 2543–2550. DOI: 10.3233/FAIA200389

Zysman, J., & Nitzberg, M. (2020). Governing AI: Understanding the Limits, Possibility, and Risks of AI in an Era of Intelligent Tools and Systems. SSRN *Electronic Journal, c*. DOI: 10.2139/ssrn.3681088

Chapter 7
AI-Driven Risk Sensing and Anomaly Detection for Predictive Project Management:
Designing Early Warning Systems to Enhance Resilience and Decision-Making

Vennela Mamidi
Woxsen University, Hyderabad, India

Harini Edala
Woxsen University, Hyderabad, India

Joel Pramod Manekshaw
Woxsen University, Hyderabad, India

Sujit Singh
http://orcid.org/0000-0002-3643-5183
Woxsen University, Hyderabadd, India

Afzalur Rahman
http://orcid.org/0000-0002-1561-561X
Woxsen University, Hyderabad, India

DOI: 10.4018/979-8-3373-6851-1.ch007

ABSTRACT

The objective of this chapter is to propose a modernized framework for IT project management that addresses the shortcomings of traditional methodologies. It will argue for a shift from rigid, reactive models to an adaptive, proactive approach. The chapter demonstrates how integrating real-time data analytics and continuous risk monitoring can enhance flexibility, improve decision-making, and prevent the accumulation of unseen risks. Ultimately, it aims to outline the principles of a data-driven management strategy capable of delivering successful project outcomes in today's volatile technological landscape.

1. INTRODUCTION

Even now, many companies still use traditional project management methods, but these approaches are no longer effective in today's fast-changing and data-driven world. With the rapid growth of data from sources like IoT devices, sensors, and event logs, project teams can now monitor how projects progress in real time. When this data is properly analysed, it can provide useful insights that help managers make smarter decisions. Predictive Project Analytics (PPA) uses both past and current project data to detect potential issues early and suggest corrective or preventive actions before they turn into major problems (Mullapudi, 2025).

Despite this, many organisations are still applying classical project management techniques, yet these are no longer efficient in the fast-paced and data-driven world of today. Traditional approaches such as the Waterfall paradigm risk excluding a certain layer of complexity as they rely on fixed plans and physical synchronous monitoring, making it difficult to assess a threat timely manner or even make fundamental changes whenever that need arises. The problem occurs in traditional risk management after problems take place, so which is why many projects face issues like cost overruns, time delays and hence the outcome is poor quality. Therefore, organisations are now using data-centric tasks and predictive methods backed by new technologies like Artificial Intelligence (AI), Machine Learning (ML), and Big Data Analytics. These technologies benefit project managers by helping them to analyse large information with the assistance of sensors, Internet of Things (IoT) devices, and operating systems, which in turn aids in detecting risks beforehand, leading to more efficiency.

The main purpose of predictive project analytics (PPA), is to find the hidden patterns, identify possible risks and recommend how to avoid problems before they occur. So, it uses both past and present data to look ahead to future issues and suggest methods to reduce or avoid them. This system includes four major types of analytics, such as descriptive analytics, diagnostic analytics, predictive analytics and prescriptive analytics. Descriptive analytics helps to understand what has been happening, diagnostic analytics answers the question of why that event has happened, whereas predictive analytics helps to anticipate events that might happen again, and prescriptive analytics helps to determine the best course of action. Hence, by combining all these approaches, problems can be solved proactively rather than reacting to the issue. Hence, the detection of unusual patterns, the progress of the project can be solved through AI–powered systems, which can give better outputs with greater precision and efficiency. Risk perception and anomaly detection are the two main Artificial Intelligence (AI) functions (Bai et al., 2019).

We can keep track of early warning signals by constantly observing project data to sense the risk. The other method that is anomaly detection, uses machine learning (ML) methods that indicate the feasible risks by finding unusual changes or patterns. So, by using these methods, timely action can be taken by project managers to avoid any obstacles before they happen. This in turn, will decrease vagueness, improve the performance of projects and increase efficiency.

Hence, this project-based AI model showcases the change from traditional methods to modern ones, which therefore helps organizations make accurate, smart and more informed decisions in this repeatedly changing world.

AI and ML are at the centre by supporting and connecting each part of the process. They handle huge messy datasets, AI and ML sit right in the middle of all this (Marr, 2019). They handle huge, messy datasets. Pick out patterns that are not straightforward. Make predictions faster and better than people can.

Descriptive analytics just looks back at historical data. It helps figure out past trends in how things performed; Predictive analytics uses stats and machine learning stuff. That way it can guess what risks might come up, probable delays, and how many resources you will need down the line. Prescriptive analytics provides you with real recommendations based on data. That helps optimize scheduling, how you allocate resources, and ways to avoid risks.

When we mix all these approaches together, project managers can shift from just reacting to gut feelings to making decisions based on facts ahead of time. AI tools can simulate different project scenarios, keep an eye on progress, spot safety hazards early, and even predict when costs might overrun. Basically, that makes everything more efficient, more predictable, and it builds this ongoing culture of improvement (Zmuda & Kuklis, 2004).

This chapter tackles those challenges mentioned by looking into how AI-based predictive analytics applies to managing project risks. The goal is to optimize decision-making and make performance more efficient. Mainly it outlines a conceptual framework for building and using AI early warning systems. Those help projects adapt better. Figure 1 represents the different types of analytics and how they help in understanding past data, predicting future outcomes, and recommending actions.

Figure 1. Different kinds of analytics

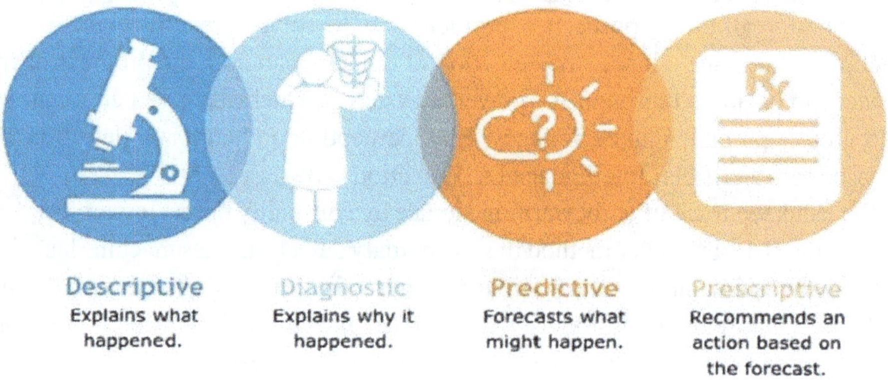

Source- Author's creation

Risk Sensing looks after projects every time and plans accordingly so that if any issue arises can be improved by noticing it early. However, anomaly detection explains how both past and present data can be used to build models that help to predict issues early to make accurate decisions (Junqué de Fortuny et al., 2013). It uses Machine Learning tools like Isolation Forest or Support Vector Machine to find anything that is uncommon in a project, such as delays, underutilization of resources, or any extra spending.

2. LITERATURE REVIEW

Earlier, risk management worked like fixing a problem after it took place. Now, with machine learning and AI, this has changed. In today's world, systems can identify problems as they take place and put a halt on them before they cause any damage. In industries such as infrastructure and manufacturing, machines have sensors that keep a check on things like vibration and pressure. These systems can notify us when a system is just about to fail, so that repairs can be done before it gets spoilt completely. This saves a lot of time, money, and project costs. AI systems help finance in doing a real time tracking transaction. This helps us in identifying any fraud or risk behaviour, which makes financial decisions faster and accurate, precise (Bello et al., 2023). In logistics, a risk arose that an employee could wrongly approve many payments for the same customer. To avoid this, a real time tracking system was used. It quicky notices any unusual activity that occurs, and it alerts the managers and helps them act before any loss takes place. Using AI is always easy. Companies face problems like protecting user centric data, to finding killed labour, and to integrate AI into older computer systems. AI driven risk management is like having an alarm system that warns you when something is about to go wrong, so that it could take necessary precautions before greater damage is done.

The main purpose of this chapter is to explain how artificial intelligence (AI) methods are used together to create futuristic predictive models by using both past and current project data. This helps professionals in their project to identify, assess and work on risks before they occur, which in turn will improve project success and reduce any chance of failure. It also helps organizations become prepared to handle tough and uncertain situations. The risk to a project change continuously and is actively driven by rapid progress in technology and in the availability of big data. Back-office reactive risk management procedures would be too slow and insufficient to accommodate the new environments. Identification of equipment problems, delays in projects, and exceeding the budget can be analyzed by predictive analytics software with a high level of accuracy and success. So, this new approach is predictive and proactive as it uses Artificial Intelligence (AI), Machine Learning (ML), and Internet of Things (IoT) data that is collected in real time (Paramesha et al., 2024).

As today the world is changing at a very fast pace and is becoming increasingly complicated to understand, the process of project management needs to be forward-looking, which means the risks should be identified beforehand and prevented right from the beginning. Hence, this type of management of risk changes the ways that risks can be handled by changing them to a databased process that works in hand with human judgment to predict complicated threats like cyberattacks and challenges in sustainability. Reactive risk management mainly happens too late because it only responds after a risk has occurred and builds between review periods. This causes a delay in the project, higher costs, or even total failure of the project. Hence, identifying the risks as early as possible is considered valuable because this would allow the organization to look at problems in advance and take quick action to stop small warnings from turning into major disasters.

This early warning is made possible by real-time monitoring technology powered by Artificial Intelligence (AI), Machine Learning (ML), and the Internet of Things (IoT).all these technologies study past and current data to find warning signs of possible problems as it involves studying large amounts of data and predicts failures that might happen soon and detect if unusual patterns are there that could show future issues- such as equipment breakdowns or violations of rules and standards. With predictive disturbance, managers can plan resources more effectively, reschedule tasks, and apply preventive measures (Yang et al., 2005). This approach makes projects stronger, improves performance, and helps avoid costly failures.

3. METHODOLOGY

In today's constantly changing business world, each project faces various kinds of risks naturally. Traditionally, project management risk has been explained as the chance that something unexpected might happen and disservice to the project's goals, which is known for its impact. So, these unforeseeable and potential issues can affect the project, such as lower availability of workers, limits in budget, financial problems, or not in compliance with the standards. Hence, if these risks are not managed properly, they can lead to huge losses in finances and destroy the reputation of the company, which in turn will question its survival in today's world.

A project is successful as it is directly linked to the importance of risk management, which is traditionally measured in three main areas like time, cost, quality and scope. Knowledge, skills, tools and techniques in project activities make it an effective risk management which meets or even exceeds the expectations of involved stakeholders (Eyieyien et al., 2024). Hence, it is the responsibility of the project manager and senior management, who plan, look, guide, coordinate and supervise the project from start to end. They foresee and predict all possible problems that could affect the project and put corrective actions in place.

These steps basically include 4R's. Firstly, Risk Identification means identifying and noting all the possible risks that might affect the project in any way possible. Secondly, Risk Analysis and Assessment use both numbers (quantitative) and descriptions (qualitative) by studying and comparing them to know how likely that particular risk can happen and in what way it might impact. Third is Risk Response Planning involves the creation of action plans and methods to prevent the identified risks and lastly Risk Monitoring and Controlling involves checking the risks at all stages consistently to make it certain that if any new problems arise, they can be quickly handled and plans responses to address them properly.

Major issues like constant and fast changes in technology, with complex connections and different needs of stakeholders, have made IT projects tough to stay in this era of digitalisation. Hence, due to this, many companies are facing risks in their operations and are now becoming more decentralised and using varied information and communication technology systems. It is found in research that about a 20% drop is being observed in productive output due to improperly planned maintenance programs and weak risk policies, which have resulted in the loss of many billions every year. Hence, it is essential for proper, organised management and foreseeing risk for the survival and success of the organisations. Hence, it's not optional but compulsory in this digital world (Karaboga et al., 2017). This digital disruption has caused major change from old and backwards-looking risk management to forward-looking and prediction-based risk governance systems supported by data analytics and Artificial Intelligence (AI). The difference between traditional and predictive risk management can be referred from Table 1.

Table 1. Differentiates between traditional and predictive risk management.

Aspect	Traditional Risk Management	Predictive Risk Management
Approach	Reactive – responds after risks occur	Proactive – anticipates and prevents risks
Data Usage	Relies mainly on historical data and expert judgment	Leverages big data, real-time inputs, and AI/ML
Assessment Style	Static, periodic reviews	Continuous, dynamic monitoring
Decision-Making	Human-driven, subjective, qualitative	Data-driven, objective, and automated
Flexibility	Rigid (e.g., Waterfall, linear models)	Adaptive and agile to changing environments
Efficiency	Slower response, risk of resource wastage	Faster insights, optimized resource allocation.
Scalability	Limited by human expertise and manual analysis	Scalable through algorithms and predictive models
Outcome	Often detects risks too late (runto-failure)	Identifies risks early, enabling prevention

It is becoming very complex and uncertain now to manage the projects due to risks, as there is our huge amount of data to make smarter decisions. Many IT projects are becoming complex and are always changing, which makes them uncertain. They involve many different groups or people who interfere with their interests and have complex connections. Hence, the projects work in ever ever-changing, fast-paced economy where problems spread very quickly and cause serious effects and damage.

Environment relies on Technological Volatility At any given moment, with everything on a continuous flux of change and tweaks induced by technological developments, project requirements and technology are thus susceptible to "requirements drift." Second is Systemic Interconnectedness which means all factors in the company are interconnected. It is connected in a chain system, which is dynamic and complex; hence, failure in one part will trigger failure of the other in a chain reaction, which will cause widespread system failures. Hence, companies depend more on varied, localised and sophisticated ICT systems (Howells, 1995). Dynamic Threats says the prediction of new and always-changing threats like zero-day vulnerabilities through past risk experiences, as they are totally new. Project Individuality says since each one is an individual project, the application of one-size-fits-all risk management practices is difficult. The traditional risk management increases unpredictability due to constant change. It depends on the opinions of personal experts and fixed analysis, making it unsuitable for management of projects in such an environment. The digital revolution has generated an unmatched amount of data, often called "big data", which is generated from sources like IoT devices, BIM systems, event logs, and social media. This acts as a rich source of evidence for decision-making as it contains detailed information about how projects are carried out and in the work environment. But this value can only be unlocked if strong analytical tools are used to process and make sense of these large and unstructured datasets.

AI and ML facilitate in revealing hidden knowledge which means the hidden patterns, links, and unusual trends can be identified by AI and help is analysing such large and unstructured data that is often missed by humans. It also Provide Predictive and Prescriptive Insights which say AI can predict what is likely to happen and recommend the best possible course of action to be followed, apart from the descriptive part and why a certain thing has happened. For example, a predictive model can identify the project delays by that the managers can be alerted and act early, and they can also suggest for the best allocation of resources, which will result in boosting the team's productivity. Finally, allow for automated and proactive intervention wherein AI tends to manage the risks by making use of data that is available, with the help of machine learning. Anomaly detection algorithms can actively spot unfamiliar events such as project delays or sudden expenses and address them at once by performing risk assessment and intervention simultaneously (Pillai, 2022). When the situation gets more complex, AI can also take independent actions, which may of rerouting network traffic during cyber-attack.

In a nutshell, handling the risks is more difficult with the given nature of the projects being more complex and unpredictable. With the support of AI and ML, processing huge amounts of data can reduce the burden and give actionable insights.

4. AI-DRIVEN RISK SENSING: CONCEPTS AND CAPABILITIES

Using AI in risk sensing is the prominent switch in the management of projects and their operations (Li et al., 2024). It detects the problems beforehand, proactively by using an intelligence-based procedure to build persistence instead of just reacting to the issues after they occur. It continuously investigates the information data and spontaneously looks after new threats, opportunities and haphazard patterns in real time. Hence, this helps in preventing the possible risks before they turn into a disaster. Hence, it is important to develop secure, scalable and smart businesses as they not only are resilient in uncertain times but also respond and grow immensely.

Additionally, major problems of conventional risk management can be set with the help of AI risk sensors, which frequently depend on regular reviews and historical data. These methods may not be in a state to rapidly identify new or fast–changing risks. So, with the use of Artificial intelligence and machine learning the process of risk management becomes more agile, adaptive and more optimised in detecting and handling the risk. AI applications analyse large data sets and detect subtle trends with predictive analytic abilities, anticipating disturbances before they occur. All issues that might occur can be predicted and can be easily prevented, such as a breakdown in machinery, issues in the supply chain, cyberattacks or delays in projects. And in this process, AI helps to process a huge amount of data by processing it efficiently. This huge data includes both structured information as well as unstructured information. The structured information includes sensor readings and payment records, while unstructured information includes social media, posts, text and images. It can identify and find hidden complex patterns in such data that traditional methods cannot identify and find. Hence, Machine Learning (ML) algorithms play a very important role in this work. The2 virtual or physical sensors continuously investigate the conditions that have potential risks. This is practically called the "sensor-based" approach. A risk condition can be described as a combination of events or data points that suggest some fault or unusual pattern may be approaching. For instance, sensors track how long the tasks take to fulfil, and how the resources can be used or in finding out the inconsistency in the budget as all these remarks about the possible project delays. Risk sensing with AI shifts the old, passive, rule-following type to active, real-time and continuously modifiable. So, by combining all the above abilities, the desired results can be achieved.

Some of these key points to be considered for anomaly detection in real-time monitoring include different types of anomalies can be detected by using different types of ML algorithms like Point Anomalies, this is just a single data point unusual on its own (Lavin & Ahmad, 2015).For example, an ad hoc, unusual spike in costs on a project. Next is Contextual Anomalies, these are data points that become unusual only in a certain context. E.g., project delay may be quite normal in the start-up phase but is highly unusual in crunch time. While collective Anomalies Consists of multiple related data points that together constitute an anomalous pattern, for instance, multiple projects simultaneously exhibiting resource shortage. Next, we have Machine Learning Algorithms Many ML algorithms for real-time data streams searching and detecting anomalies exist, a few of which with noteworthy implementations in libraries such as Scikit-learn are the following. Isolation Forest, it detects anomalies better in large data sets by isolating observations that are different from most of the data. Apart from these, One-Class Support Vector Machine (SVM), first considers the “normal" pattern of data and labels any new data that is not part of this order as such; hence, it will be very helpful if examples of anomalies are not very frequent. Also, Local outlier Factor (LOF) method identifies outliers by measuring the local deviation of a given data point with respect to its neighbours, hence an effective way for finding context-based anomalies.

While anomaly detection captures current anomalies, predictive modelling uses AI and ML to forecast possible future threats and generates early warning signs that can activate anticipatory action.

5. MAJOR APPLICATIONS AND CONCEPTS IN PREDICTIVE MODELLING FOR EARLY WARNINGS INCLUDE

- **Project Outcome Forecasting:** ML algorithms can be employed to forecast important project metrics such as cost overruns, schedule delays, and resource shortages (Sanusi, 2024). Models like regression that study patterns from previous projects help to know about the future performance of projects. Techniques like time series models are also used for the prediction of future performance, like ARIMA and ARIMAX, so by using these models, visionary models and changing them when required would give the best results. In this method, based on records, a few methods such as Gradient Boosting Machine (GBM) can predict the risks that can arise in the future with an accuracy of 85% making it the best and dependable decision.
- **Predictive Maintenance:** AI systems analyse the continuous sensor data and find the signs of warning early. By doing so, the time can be reduced, and the efficiency can be increased. This also prevents sudden failures and minimises costs to repair, which in short ensures smooth operations. Hence, in industries and other infrastructure systems, machines are fitted with sensors to continuously measure the condition of work.
- **Real-Time Estimation of Risk Probability**: AI systems can approximate the likelihood of a specified risk eventuating in real-time and compare it against a threshold tolerance designed prior(Giudici et al., 2024).For instance, a model can compute the likelihood of a project being delayed based on its status and historical record. If the likelihood exceeds a threshold value (e.g., 60%), then a hard early warning is automatically triggered in the form of a notification to the project manager.
- **Digital Twin and Physics-Based Alerting:** The next level of sophistication is to develop a “digital twin” of an asset or system computer model of the real asset or system, say a bridge, or a manufacturing process. Theoretical damage or failure modes can then be simulated in the computer model to generate

data on system behaviour under stress. This data then trains AI models to recognise warning signs of failure in the real asset; hence, one could view this as physics-based warning signs (Wu et al., 2024). One study found that the best indicators generated by the domain-the minimum value and increasing variance of one indicator (ocean freshwater transport)-always preceded large system collapse better than simple statistical indicators. This is a very high-level frontier where predictive models are erected on a close, systemic understanding of the entity being observed.

6. DESIGNING EARLY WARNING SYSTEMS FOR PROJECTS

The references span from the more complex, highly abstract level of strategic concepts down to very specific, clearly detailed notions of software design, thereby providing an array of complementary design paradigms for an AI-driven early warning system. The theme that recurs throughout is developing a closed-loop, data-driven system integrating the physical project environment with a virtual model of analysis to enable proactive control.

There are two dominant architectural models from the sources:

The Digital Twin Framework is a high-level conceptual framework that integrates Building Information Modelling (BIM), the Internet of Things (IoT), and Data Mining (DM) (Pan & Zhang, 2021). Its process follows a "physical-data-virtual" paradigm. In the Physical Layer IoT sensors, such as Unmanned Aerial Vehicles (UAVs) equipped with LiDAR scanners, observe the actual construction site in real-time (the "as-built" world). In the connection or data layer, the collected data such as 3D point clouds is streamed continuously to a central database, like a BIM cloud solution. The raw data is processed automatically, thereby comparing it with modelled plans (e.g., "as-planned" IFC files) and converting it into structured, machine processable event logs (e.g., CSV files) suitable for data mining.

Figure 2. Digital Twin Framework

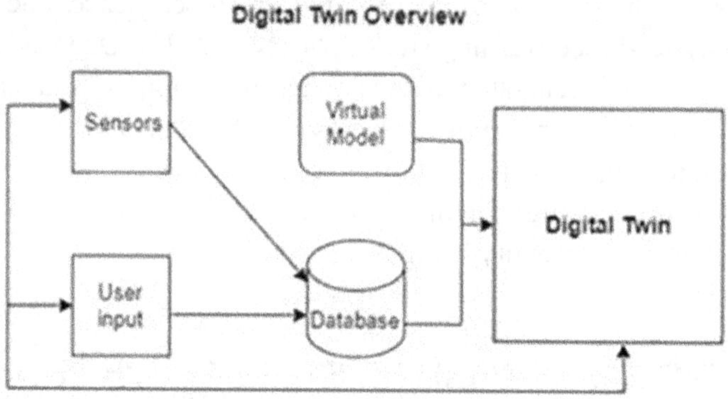

Figure 2 represents the Digital Twin framework, where real-time data and virtual models are combined to monitor and manage the project effectively. This framework further extends into Virtual Layer: A "digital twin" is basically a high-fidelity virtual representation of the project and uses event logs to create 4D models (3D geometry + schedule) and rich process models. In this virtual space, various DM and AI techniques such as process mining and time-series analysis are employed to discover hidden patterns, diagnose bottlenecks, and forecast further progress. Furthermore, feedback loop, in which Actionable intelligence and early warnings generated from the virtual model are sent to project managers such that they can dynamically adjust plans, schedules, and workforce at the physical site to optimize working performance and mitigate risk (Salimimoghadam et al., 2025). Additionally, Distributed, Sensor-Based, which is an approach geared toward a software-level implementation that may be directly accomplished atop existing Business Process Management Systems (BPMS). During Design Time, Users, while working on a project or process model, define virtual "sensors." Consider a sensor that is associated with a "risk condition" which might be a set of events or data points in an expression language that should alert the user to a probable future fault or negative state. Conditions can ask for historical or in-progress project execution information. Predefined risk templates for common risk categories (e.g., organizational, data-related) may be used to quickly create conditions. Moreover, during Runtime, the given sensors are registered with a central "sensor manager" service. The managers interface with the BPMS engine and database, assembling relevant data per filtering criteria, and then dispatch this data to the concerned sensors according to the triggers specified (e.g. a time span or the occurrence of a project event). Consequently, Detection and Notification where Each sensor checks its own condition. When a certain level or risk limit is reached (for example, if the risk probability goes above the set level), the sensor sends this information to the sensor manager (Williams, 2007). The manager will then alert the monitoring system in the BPMS, which will show the warnings to the project administrators so they can act quickly.

Early warning systems rely on constantly collecting and analysing high-quality, multidimensional data from different platforms. These platforms determine which input categories are crucial for precision detection and timely alerts. Along with this, Project and KPI Progress include data generated for tracking the progress of projects regarding their objectives. Also, schedule and timelines where data includes task start and task finish dates, task duration, and compliance with an MCT, planned vs. actual dates of milestone completion. Similarly, Cost and budget which include past and forecast cost data, expenditure per month, and budget variances. Overruns can be forecasted using historical cost data of similar projects through predictive modelling. Whereas Quality includes Number of defects, rework loops, and deviation from technical specifications measured by statistical process control.

Internet of Things sensors help to measure and find out things like pressure, movement and temperature (Liu et al., 2018). Many devices are used for this purpose, like UAV-LiDAR scanners and 3D images of designs, which help in giving accurate and details of the work. These systems also help track errors in numbers and find out if operational problems exist. It contains real-time data from the actual work site. The structure helps us to find any issues or delays in the team by understanding how team members work together. It uses many applications and tools to check emails and messages to understand and find out the communication gap, to understand the mood of the team, and identify if there is any confusion or lack of interest. In the end, we can make sure if the project or task is going in the correct direction and if all the needs are being fulfilled by looking at reviews and feedback.

Integration with Project Management Tools and Dashboards includes Integration with Core Platforms. The system is designed to run on BPMS such as YAWL. The proposed system integrates into the BPMS monitoring service to provide notifications and adds design tool functions like those of the YAWL Editor, thus allowing managers to install risk sensors in their process models. The digital twin model is constructed on a descriptive BIM cloud platform. It is further complemented by specialist packages such as RAAMAC (for progress monitoring) and IFC Logger (for data collection), so that the data pipeline might be optimized. While the visualized dashboards are a one-stop shop for the communication of sophisticated risks and insights to decision-makers. Also, AI-detected bottlenecks or items at risk can be identified by colour codes (e.g. outlining an item magenta to indicate a delay), giving a rapid, intuitive visual signal (Linkinen, 2024). The ProM and Disco Fluxicon software components construct process maps out of event logs. The maps let one view the actual workflow of a project, with thicker lines or darker coloured arrows signifying bottlenecks due to activities of longer durations. The Structure/system helps us find out unusual conditions using simple graphs. The outliers are marked in a bright color, like red, so that they are easily noticeable. The below given Figure 3 illustrates the various data channels integrated into the Early Warning System, including project KPIs, resource data, sensor inputs, and their connection to dashboards and project management tools.

Figure 3. Various channels

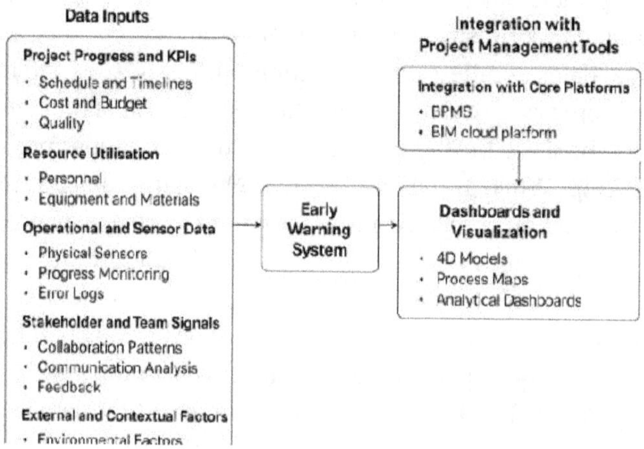

7. ANOMALY DETECTION TECHNIQUES IN PROJECT MANAGEMENT

Anomaly detection simply means to discover things and patterns in the given dataset that don't follow the normal pattern, like observing any unexpected spending or noticing any strange behaviour in each project. This is very important these days and mainly in project management because it talks about any deviation from budgets, schedules or resources beforehand. It informs any issue before it turns into a major issue. These days, one of the most popular tools that is being widely used to analyse large datasets and to know about their pattern is machine learning, which humans might not be able to do.

Anomaly detection has 3 main approaches unsupervised learning, supervised learning and deep learning. Unsupervised Learning is where system first learns about normal patterns and then marks anything that doesn't match. Hence, unsupervised learning is best when you don't have examples of bad or unusual patterns. First of it is an isolation forest which works by isolating the different points that don't match and fit, and it is very efficient for spotting or finding weird matches with budgets quickly and efficiently. The one-class SVM builds a model for its own analysis with normal behaviour, and then by matching with the set benchmark, it finds out anything that is different, which makes this model ideal when you rarely have examples of unusual data like spotting fraud in vendor sign-ups. local outlier factor (LOF) examines if a record is odd when compared to its neighbours. In simple words, it works like an investigator for any delays or poor performance in some regions(González et al., 2014).Clustering(kmeans) combines data points that match together and detects those that don't match or are far off, making it useful for spotting if any uncommon customer behaviours are observed or any suspicious activities.

In contrast, Supervised Learning is used when we already have the set benchmark data with us, which by compared with the set model. Through this, we can differentiate the normal data from the unusual pattern. Decision trees help in decision-making by providing flowcharts that are easy to understand and are simple to detect the abnormal ones, as they also explain the why of it. Random Forest combines many decision trees and provides a more balanced forecast. This makes it a great option when the data in the project has uneven cases. Boosting models like GBM, XGBoost, and CatBoost helps to fix and improve step-by-step in the earlier stages. Hence, it provides very accurate and complete results when predicting the risks for the project. Whereas Deep Learning model helps to solve very complex data and finds out hidden or understandable pattern. Hence deep learning works like human brain. There are artificial neural networks (ANN) which connects nodes in the brain cells. they process the information like brain cells in human brains and is used to perform tasks like predicting risk in credit and even complex works like checking the financial health of the company. The convolutional neural network (CNNs) and Deep neural networks (DNNs) help in detection of the frauds and threats in the pattern by learning normal behaviour patterns. CNNs use drone images so it provides with visual data like identifying structures that are damaged.

However These Techniques Help in Projects by using Models such as LOF can help spot minute delays in the tasks, which can help to stay on schedule for instance, if an important move is taking more time that its usual response time, it sends alerts to get it fixed. Apart from this, to have control over the costs, the isolation forest model can be of great help as it monitors sudden cost increases and unusual spending, this prevents budget issues before they grow, small defects can be traced with the aid of AI tools this will ensure quality. For example, a drone can observe a surface problem during construction and send immediate alerts to the team. to know if people are fully equipped to manage their resources, they can use the one-class SVM model for clarity.

Several challenges prevail; it is vital to prevent alert fatigue – this means the feeling when people tend to neglect alerts because they have experienced too many false warnings earlier (Sciences et al., 2018). By doing this, AI monitoring can be truly beneficial. It is essential to find the correct balance between false positives or unnecessary alerts and false negatives or missed problems. A huge difference can be seen by just choosing the right AI model. Some models focus on detecting all possible errors, whereas others are better at reducing unnecessary alerts, making the output highly precise. For example, let's take two types of AI models, in which the first one is an isolation forest that can promptly spot the abnormal data and avoid false alarms. This type of model can be used when the requirement is to save time and money. The second model is one class -SVM that finds all the possible errors, be it small or big, which means it gives extra alerts. This is useful when the need is to look at everything carefully and not miss any possible problem.

It is important to highlight that AI should not be confused with "black box" (a system that focuses on results without giving the process of how it got to the result) (Pedreschi et al., 2019).With explainable AI, project groups can understand why something was marked as an issue, which will build trust among the group and help them make better decisions. It is known that human judgment will always have the upper hand, even though AI can identify the problem rapidly. expertise lies in the decision-making of whether an identified issue really needs action or can be let go. Necessary training is needed for the AI models to cope with new data, and since project conditions keep changing, it is important to stay relevant and up to date.

In short, machine learning prepares project managers to deal with potential problems beforehand by analysing complex data patterns which are complex. It decreases the risks, improves the decision-making, and ensures that the project persists. ideal outcomes are achieved when we see integration between human judgment and advanced models to enhance learning.

8. ENHANCING RESILIENCE AND DECISION-MAKING

With the new trend of innovation in project management, a transformation is noticed from solely problem-solving to making efforts to prevent problems even before the problem has occurred with the help of Artificial intelligence and machine learning. Through these technologies, a huge amount of data from the past and even real time is analysed to anticipate the risks beforehand, so that the project managers can escalate the issue before they act. Algorithms that are built on machine learning play an important role by studying the data on schedules, budgets and project outcomes to recognise potential problem signals. This authorises early warnings that empower managers to take timely reformative measures, which makes project management more proactive.

Artificial intelligence has become a very important tool when it comes to how projects are handled, and in making them more accurate and effective. By the study of data from previous projects, AI can identify all the possible outcomes such as financial risks, delays in the process, or lack of resources, before they happen. A study showed that AI based risk identification system reached a precision of more than half, which helps project managers take early decisions to solve problems. AI-powered software helps us in keeping track of project information all the time and can identify unusual things like schedule changes or budget increases almost as fast than usual monitoring methods. In areas like machinery and construction, AI takes the help of data from sensors to identify when machines may fail, which helps companies plan for their repairs in advance and increase the span of the equipment. Adding to this, AI also plays an important role when it comes to cybersecurity by keeping a watch on network activity to analyse and eliminate cyber threats before they can cause any harm. This helps in keeping crucial project information secure and ensures that work goes on in a smooth manner without interruption.

Most project plans are inflexible, but projects today are subject themselves to quick changes. AI assists groups in adjusting to changing environments. Firstly, by optimising resources, AI is constantly monitoring resources to their best use, finding waste and forecasting areas where skills or staff may be in short supply. In the last 10. years, more than 60% of IT teams have been adversely affected by poor talent management. This not only affords a risk situation with which existing resources are poorly positioned after placing IT, and the said risk is hugely diminished when fully trained members become employed. On the other hand, the presence of the virtual workers is a great retainer for retaining such talented workers. Under this kind of work environment, some consider it so arduous nowadays to get their members to work efficiently for around 70% when the old method is applied, but according to this method, AI work makes it even to 85% efficiency, in addition to accreditation in capable reductions of such a risk(Vos & Van der Voordt, 2002). Secondly through Artificial Intelligence simulations keep track of how the crew works together to complete the dependent tasks, to observe delays, and recommend reordering of tasks to optimize flow. This enables managers to instantly adjust plans and keep everything on track. Third is, the digital twin is a non-physical copy of a project or an asset that Realtime updates with the help of sensory data. Supervisors can practice a variety of "what if" scenarios, such as supply chain interruptions, find out the effectiveness of the solutions without causing any negative impacts to the actual project, and help them become ready for different outcomes. Lastly, through Automated Responses, if any disaster occurs, AI can automatically do certain things such as reroute inventory during supply chain issues, that will keep everything going as usual.

Despite AI's advantages, the greatest outcomes are a result of collaboration with humans. The AI handles huge amounts of data and points out risk factors, whereas human managers use their experience and instinct to put together these results and make the final decisions. Managers may often face difficulty in understanding advanced AI systems and it may appear to them as black boxes, hence they are unwilling to act faster. tools which give better explanation using AI such as simple dashboards that build trust and enhance the reasoning behind. it also becomes vital to clearly define what tasks AI must perform and what tasks it should leave for human approval. Regular monitoring by the experts will result in more accountability and overtime reduces the chances of making any kind of mistakes. on the contrary, too much reliance on AI can reduce human analytical skills, and complete ignorance may lead to missing on important insights and perspectives. Therefore, to bring in more data driven culture into organisations managers must be given training on timely basis so that they can stay relevant and updated. These challenges can be addressed, when organisations integrate data power with human judgement which will in turn create smarter, more reliable and adaptable project management system in the coming years.

9. CHALLENGES AND ETHICAL CONSIDERATIONS

The success of any risk management system that operates based on AI fundamentally relies on how good the data it feeds on is and how legible the results of the system are. The sources recognise three main related issues in this field, namely, data quality, data integration, and model interpretability.

Data Quality, Availability, and Suitability are the most important practical concern is the availability of quality and appropriate data. Machine learning models and AI need immense amounts of data to be trained, and that data is usually incomplete, inconsistent, or includes biases that may affect the outcome. Be it for new projects or for the ones that are highly specialised in nature, it might be difficult to find the historical data or even when it exists, the data might be very limited, and the training process for such a predictive model to give accurate results might be challenging as well. Also, with the technology emerging, it is observed that there is a lack in information at the start of the project. on the contrary, sometimes the data can be unpredictable and unstable, often with the environmental risks associated, which may spoil the model accuracy (Mitchell, 2006). Data Integration and Interoperability is when Organisations often face problems with integration and managing data within different departments, due to different departments having their own way or pattern of storing the information maybe following the age-old systems or a complete alien format. This breakdown of information Is very hard to put together and doesn't allow a smooth flow of work. Therefore, it is suggested to better go with data cleaning and transformation that is in common format for all departments, which may seem to be complicated and time taking at first, but in long run this yields better results and escapes from the chaos of disordered information.

Interpretability and the Black Box Problem is very particular as it occurs when AI models, like deep learning make decisions, but the decision-making process is not clear due to the complexity involved in the internal workings of such models and is beyond human understanding due the missing element of how a certain output is given. due to this people doubt the accuracy of the algorithm and are not willing to give their complete trust. This lack of trust is dangerous because decision-makers may completely ignore AI recommendations due to reliability issues. There is no doubt that AI is a powerful tool in analysing the data, but the problem arises when we try to combine both human expertise and use automated systems to strike a balance between them. This brings into the spotlight the ongoing conflict between the advancement of technology and the importance of human judgment. Overreliance on Algorithms vs. Human Judgment- A term that has become popular these days called "automation complacency "This means that blind belief by people in the results of AI systems or more dependency in them without cross-verifying or applying the human brain. Historically, it has been noticed that too much trust on automation that to in risky situations may resulting in mistakes. The Importance of Human Supervision and Cooperation is that it is always better to have AI as a support system tool for decision making that be for service to human mind rather than a substitution. The optimal stand would be seen when AI, with its benefits of handling massive data, pattern recognition, join with humans who can contribute to strategic thinking and expertise. The collaboration between humans and AI would go a long way. it is crucial to follow the "human in the loop approach" as this adds to the precise interpretation that the algorithms lack and ensures that the responsibility is maintained. Eventually, the organisations can assign certain tasks to the AI, but the accountability of decisions and risk management must always lie with humans. On the other hand, the black box problem decreases the transparency and accountability as also seen in the example of Lloyds banking group where the AI systems have failed and the decision-making process was unknown and unclear, it became hard to figure out the mistake and rectify it. This obscurity is a significant roadblock of compliance with regulations since companies are unable to prove the soundness of their models. As shown in Figure 4, the balance between algorithmic reliance and human oversight is pivotal in addressing ethical risks such as bias propagation and privacy concerns in AI-driven risk management.

Figure 4. Reliance on algorithms or the human brain

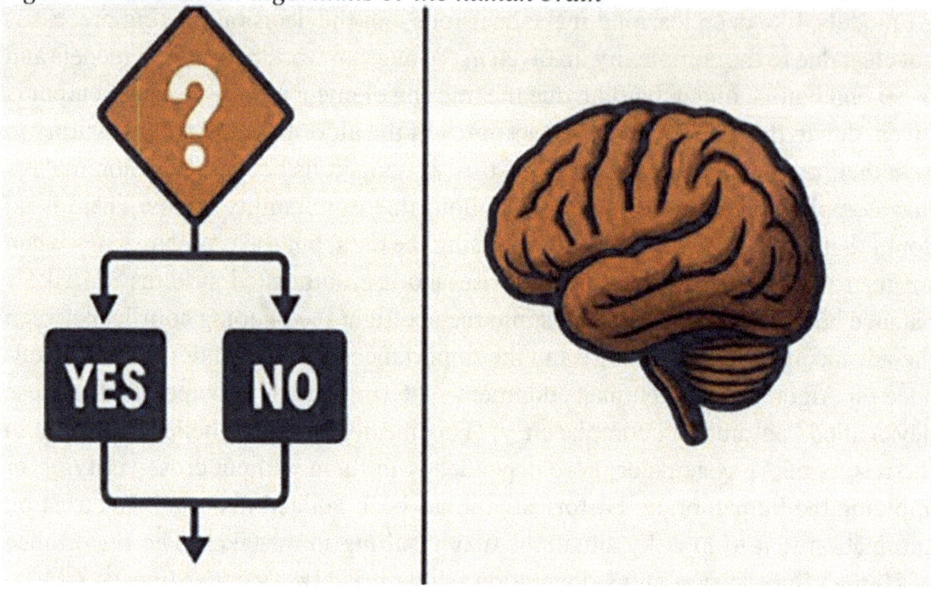

Source- Author's creation

Bias propagation is one of the gravest threats to ethical risks. Trained AI models use previous data to acquire and perpetuate existing biases in society, which have discriminatory implications (Bose, 2025). To illustrate, indirect proxies of a shielded attribute, such as race or gender, may be made involuntarily by a risk model when it makes lending decisions. To reduce this risk, it is necessary to work together to apply a variety of representative training data, carry out regular audits of algorithms, and apply fairness-conscious algorithms. AI in risk management is based on the processing of large data volumes, and much of it may be sensitive personal or financial data, which raises serious data privacy issues. The gathering and processing of such information should adhere to high standards of rules, such as the GDPR. To safeguard the rights of people, it is critical to consider privacy protection at the early design of the system with the help of methods such as data anonymisation, encryption, and federated learning when models are trained on decentralised data without access to user privacy.

8. FUTURE DIRECTIONS

The future of AI-powered project management is shifting towards more integrated, smart, and autonomous systems that can address more complexity and uncertainty. The most important emerging trends to influence this future are Explainable AI

(XAI), the growth of digital twins in projects, and the emergence of autonomous project management features.

One of the main obstacles to the popularisation of sophisticated AI models, in particular, deep learning, is their black box nature, which makes the process of decision-making obscure. This interpretability may cause an algorithmic distrust, and managers may feel reluctant to follow AI-based suggestions. This results in the increasing need for Explainable AI (XAI), which tends to make AI systems more transparent and comprehensible. Visual dashboards, attribution approaches, and counterfactual reasoning are all XAI methods that become indispensable in gaining trust in stakeholders and regulatory adherence and model output validation. As an illustration, XAI can create a provenance trail of a regulatory provision to its implementation in software code, guaranteeing both credible and responsible translation in a RegTech environment. Due to the increasing number of critical roles played by AI in decision-making, the skill to comprehend why a model has identified a risk will be mandatory in ensuring that human-AI cooperation is effective. Digital Twins of Projects: The digital twin is essentially a virtual reflection of a physical object or system that is constantly updated with real-time information, and it is a fast-emerging domain. Although initially used to model physical constructions such as bridges, digital twins' usage is growing to model and represent full processes and projects. Digital twins can be used to simulate, analyse and optimise project implementation by combining Internet-of-Things (IoT) and Building-Information-Modelling (BIM) data with event logs, to generate a dynamic, high-fidelity virtual environment (Baghalzadeh Shishehgarkhaneh et al., 2022). This enables the project managers to do what-if scenario modelling to test how the project can be affected by a possible disruption (e.g., supply chain shocks, design changes) in a risk-free environment. More complex frameworks are currently being developed at building and city scales, producing hierarchical architectures that may one day be incorporated into macro-DTs of whole transportation systems or even nations.

The end game of AI in project management is in the autonomous systems that can handle tasks with little or no human intervention. Although full autonomy in project management is yet to be achieved, the building blocks are already coming out. There are plenty of other automated interests such as prediction and allocation of work to team members, updated the time projections and to carry over plans in real time over various projects using AI .upcoming AI solutions in the future have their focus on swarm intelligence which is decentralized learning or learning from the behaviour of ants, bees to reach to collective intelligence and continue to function even during disturbances. Likewise, autonomous threat-hunting AI-based systems are being created in cybersecurity and autonomous remediation in incident response. As these technologies evolve, they will converge to models of Living Enterprise where AI systems will have organic properties such as self-healing and evolutionary learning and dynamically adapt project plans and resources in one direction or another to navigate a dynamic environment. The concepts and technologies of AI-based risk management and predictive analytics are very transferable, and the opportunities to use them across the industries are substantial. Numerous spheres are useful in the ability to examine large amounts of data, identify anomalies, and predict the results. The construction industry is one of the industry's most likely to embrace AI. BIM and IoT data are integrated into digital twins to track the progress of the construction process and diagnose bottlenecks and predict the timeframes of the project. Machine learning driven predictive maintenance (PdM) models are finding application to improve the reliability of equipment in concrete manufacturing by predicting equipment breakdowns based on sensor data such as vibration and pressure. Moreover, AI-based systems will be able to simulate the situation in a project, spot the safety risks, and optimize the schedules and the allocation of the resources, shifting the industry towards the situation, when subjective expert judgments are disregarded.

Data analytics is an important tool in IT project management, where the completion of complex software development cycles is prone to risks. Four primary categories of analytics, including descriptive, diagnostic, predictive, and prescriptive, are used to optimize all the phases of the Software Development Life Cycle (SDLC). As an example, predictive analytics can detect possible delays, anticipate budget overruns, and determine probable areas that are likely to get defects during testing. Complete attention is given to anomaly detection and key performance indicators in present, by doing this we can stop technical failures and project progression (Ibidunmoye et al., 2015).

Healthcare: We see immense change in the healthcare sector with the introduction of AI into it. right from diagnostics, taking care of patients and hospital management processes in healthcare stands firm (Hussain, 2024). To forecast any disease outbreak, patient flow management during unpredictable situations like pandemics and monitoring resources to their full capacity for example, ventilators and ICU beds are anticipated through predictive models. With advancement in technology, it has been witnessed that personalized medicine using historical data of patients is recommended with certain treatment plans. We see immense change in the healthcare sector with the introduction of AI into it. right from diagnostics, taking care of patients and hospital management processes in healthcare stands firm. To forecast any disease outbreak, patient flow management during unpredictable situations like pandemics and monitoring resources to their full capacity for example, ventilators and ICU beds are anticipated through predictive models. With advancement in technology, it has been witnessed that personalized medicine using historical data of patients is recommended with certain treatment plans. In the same line AI has the potential to make healthcare more resilient by predicting the demand. In the same line AI has the potential to make healthcare more resilient by predicting the demand in advance and identifying loopholes to rectify beforehand. in advance and identifying loopholes to rectify beforehand.

Investing in modern data infrastructure and governance is important, When the data available is of poor quality then we cannot see any progress in the AI projects. therefore, companies need to build a data model that is modern and suits to real time data network. This would allow flow of data among different detached systems. These systems may consist of cloud platforms, data pipelines or even data akes . data governance must also be prioritized, as strong governance will ensure the quality of the data, consistency and security of the data. It is also recommended to safeguard privacy laws such as the GDPR (General Data Protection Regulation). Shortage of skilled professionals in the field of AI is often seen as a barrier to adapting to the requirements.

It is always better to start with pilot projects and see what works and what doesn't. A step–by– step approach of launching AI would have a greater impact. Through this fieldwork analysis, we can decide on a large-scale expansion based on the results. This approach will promote flexible and continuous learning, which would also allow the teams to refine models to minimise disruptions and maximise performance. The experiences from pilot projects will act as guidance for the spread of AI in the organisation. It is always better to start with pilot projects and see what works and what doesn't. A step–by–step approach of launching AI would have a greater impact. Through this fieldwork analysis, we can decide on a large-scale expansion based on the results. This approach will promote flexible and continuous learning, which would also allow the teams to refine models to minimise disruptions and maximise performance. The experiences from pilot projects will act as guidance for the spread of AI in the organisation. AI in project management is not a one-time setup, nor does it yield a fixed solution .AI systems must adapt and adjust themselves to the evolving business environments and conditions. It is a basic requirement of the organisations to come up with creative systems that can monitor the AI performance regularly and initiate a feedback loop that can make modifications if needed (Peurala, 2025). The overall process will lead to a positive cycle where AI will become effective in handling the difficulties and advancing in project conditions.AI in project management is not a one-time setup, nor does it yield a fixed solution .AI systems must adapt and adjust themselves to the evolving business environments and conditions. It is a basic requirement of the organisations to come up with creative systems that can monitor the AI performance regularly and initiate a feedback loop that can make modifications if needed. The overall process will lead to a positive cycle where AI will become effective in handling the difficulties and advancing in project conditions.

9. CONCLUSION

Here are some of the famous quotes on AI by leading tech giants CEOs across the world.

"The future of AI is in our hands." – Tim Cook, CEO of Apple "The future of AI is not about replacing humans; it's about augmenting human capabilities." – Sundar Pichai, CEO of Google

"The pace of progress in artificial intelligence is incredibly fast." – Jeff Bezos, Founder of Amazon.

There is no end to such quotes on AI as we edge ourselves closer to blending of AI into our daily lives. AI has made profound impact in industries like Banking and Insurance, Healthcare, Retail & supply chain, Manufacturing, construction, Energy & Renewables, TMT, Fashion and many. As a matter of fact, AI is almost everywhere. Before we learn how project management can benefit from embracing AI into their work, let's understand what exactly AI/Generative AI. AI is a subset of Machine Learning, which focuses on using neural networks to process infinite amounts of data and generate valuable insights and decisions. Generative AI is an advancement on top of AI where developers need not analyse the data for their requirements but rather focus on the Generative AI large language models, which were trained on general internet data etc, which enables AI communities/Engineers to focus on generating insights and key decision drivers. The key takeaway from here is AI is not something that will beat us or take control of humans like you see in the movies, it is a piece of complex software yet elegant, can fasten the process of analysing the infinite volumes of data and generate insights to make key decisions for any application. It depends on the intelligent sentient beings us to train AI/Generative models with all guardrails, security, safety and apply them to work to bring efficiency and data driven insights.

Now let's understand how managers across industries can benefit from adoption of AI, also learn why/how is it feasible now. Let's start with finance banking use cases:

Credit risk models

A decade or couple of decades ago, banking systems used to rely on rule-based credit risk modelling to roll out loans to consumers. It is very rudimentary, successful, but limited the business scope. The Machines were just capable enough to analyse the vast amount of visible data at a consumer level and decide whether that person is a risk or worthy profile to lend out. With the advancement of compute power available today, banking institutions can build ML models to factor in lots of data points (for e.g.: miniscule factor of consumer visits to a pub on every weekend) and come up with decision criteria however the final decision can be made by the risk management with human oversight. This helped financial institutions to lend out more cautiously, and the consumers borrowed more which eventually led to boost financially. The shift from a rule based to machine-driven decisions has been key to achieve this. Here the key is risk managers helped ML models to by providing their functional knowledge to train these and eventually benefited from them. Take away here is that ML/AI didn't replace the human risk managers, but it just helped them in make key decisions at a quicker pace, thus translating to faster cycle times.

Digital Twin for an Energy company

For example, an electricity provider company wants to analyse the risks of installing new utility poles in a particular region of the society and determine which are the best suited locations. The project management of this company would have relied on experience and assessed the risk and eventually determined the optimal locations. This would have taken weeks of cycle times. Now, imaging with the advancement of AI having a technology that can let anyone analyse the entire region like a digital twin, which provides visual insights for the engineering managers to assess the risk-free regions for setting up the utility poles infrastructure. This would eventually help the project team to assess the risk to the finest details and kick start with the actual procurement and installation planning. These types of digital twins are being useful in many areas across industries to help drive efficiency and key decisions making while mitigating risks.

There are many more such examples to say that AI is really empowering the companies, leaders and engineers to make more valuable decisions at a faster pace. There is another famous quote: it is not the AI that is going to make mistakes, but the people who train them may end up making mistakes. It depends on engineers, managers, and leaders to carefully craft the data to train these models or implement proper guardrails while using generative AI models. Engineers, leaders should bring in their experience to make the best out of these AI/Generative AI models. The conclusion is that companies, individuals are going to benefit greatly from the adoption of AI into their processes, applications to solve some of the non-solvable challenges that were not possible/feasible a decade ago. What AI has achieved over the past decade has been astonishing, and what is more exciting for the future is that AI is going to further transform the world into an even better place.

REFERENCES

Baghalzadeh Shishehgarkhaneh, M., Keivani, A., Moehler, R. C., Jelodari, N., & Roshdi Laleh, S. (2022). Internet of Things (IoT), Building Information Modeling (BIM), and Digital Twin (DT) in construction industry: A review, bibliometric, and network analysis. *Buildings (Basel, Switzerland)*, *12*(10), 1503.

Bai, S., Fang, D., & Zhang, Q. (2019). Research and application of artificial intelligence technology in the field of risk perception. *Journal of Physics: Conference Series*, *1302*(2), 022002. DOI: 10.1088/1742-6596/1302/2/022002

Bello, O. A., Ogundipe, A., Mohammed, D., Adebola, F., & Alonge, O. A. (2023). AI-driven approaches for real-time fraud detection in US financial transactions: Challenges and opportunities. *European Journal of Computer Science and Information Technology*, *11*(6), 84–102.

Bose, M. (2025). Bias in AI: A societal threat: A look beyond the tech. In *Open AI and Computational Intelligence for Society 5.0* (pp. 197-224). IGI Global Scientific Publishing.

Eyieyien, O. G., Idemudia, C., Paul, P. O., & Ijomah, T. I. (2024). Effective stakeholder and risk management strategies for large-scale international project success. *Int. J. Front. Sci. Technol. Res*, *7*(1), 013-024.

Giudici, P., Centurelli, M., & Turchetta, S. (2024). Artificial Intelligence risk measurement. *Expert Systems with Applications*, *235*, 121220. DOI: 10.1016/j.eswa.2023.121220

González, P., González, V., Molenaar, K., & Orozco, F. (2014). Analysis of causes of delay and time performance in construction projects. *Journal of Construction Engineering and Management*, *140*(1), 04013027. DOI: 10.1061/(ASCE)CO.1943-7862.0000721

Howells, J. R. (1995). Going global: The use of ICT networks in research and development. *Research Policy*, *24*(2), 169–184. DOI: 10.1016/0048-7333(93)00760-Q

Hussain, K. (2024). Revolutionizing healthcare: The impact of artificial intelligence on patient care, diagnosis, and treatment.

Ibidunmoye, O., Hernández-Rodriguez, F., & Elmroth, E. (2015). Performance anomaly detection and bottleneck identification. *ACM Computing Surveys*, *48*(1), 1–35. DOI: 10.1145/2791120

Junqué de Fortuny, E., Martens, D., & Provost, F. (2013). Predictive modeling with big data: Is bigger really better? *Big Data*, *1*(4), 215–226. DOI: 10.1089/big.2013.0037 PMID: 27447254

Karaboga, M., Matzner, T., Obersteller, H., & Ochs, C. (2017). Is There a Right to Offline Alternatives in a Digital World? In *Data Protection and Privacy:(In) visibilities and Infrastructures* (pp. 31–57). Springer. DOI: 10.1007/978-3-319-50796-5_2

Lavin, A., & Ahmad, S. (2015). Evaluating real-time anomaly detection algorithms--the Numenta anomaly benchmark. 2015 IEEE 14th international conference on machine learning and applications (ICMLA)

Li, H., Yazdi, M., Nedjati, A., Moradi, R., Adumene, S., Dao, U., Moradi, A., Haghighi, A., Obeng, F. E., & Huang, C.-G. (2024). Harnessing AI for project risk management: a paradigm shift. In *Progressive decision-making tools and applications in project and operation management: Approaches, case studies, multi-criteria decision-making, multi-objective decision-making, decision under uncertainty* (pp. 253–272). Springer. DOI: 10.1007/978-3-031-51719-8_16

Linkinen, T. (2024). *Generative artificial intelligences: Challenges and benefits for game development* Master's thesis, Tampere University].

Liu, G., Tan, Q., Kou, H., Zhang, L., Wang, J., Lv, W., Dong, H., & Xiong, J. (2018). A flexible temperature sensor based on reduced graphene oxide for robot skin used in internet of things. *Sensors (Basel)*, *18*(5), 1400. DOI: 10.3390/s18051400 PMID: 29724037

Marr, B. (2019). *Artificial intelligence in practice: how 50 successful companies used AI and machine learning to solve problems*. John Wiley & Sons.

Mitchell, V. L. (2006). Knowledge integration and information technology project performance. *Management Information Systems Quarterly*, *30*(4), 919–939. DOI: 10.2307/25148759

Mullapudi, A. (2025). Predictive Paradigms and Strategic Insights for Enhancing AnalyticsDriven Project Management.

Pan, Y., & Zhang, L. (2021). A BIM-data mining integrated digital twin framework for advanced project management. *Automation in Construction*, *124*, 103564. DOI: 10.1016/j.autcon.2021.103564

Paramesha, M., Rane, N., & Rane, J. (2024). Big data analytics, artificial intelligence, machine learning, internet of things, and blockchain for enhanced business intelligence. *Artificial Intelligence, Machine Learning, Internet of Things, and Blockchain for Enhanced Business Intelligence (June 6, 2024).*

Pedreschi, D., Giannotti, F., Guidotti, R., Monreale, A., Ruggieri, S., & Turini, F. (2019). Meaningful explanations of black box AI decision systems. *Proceedings of the AAAI conference on artificial intelligence* DOI: 10.1609/aaai.v33i01.33019780

Peurala, N. (2025). Preserving creative performance through AI integration–A qualitative study on how to lead AI integration in creative agencies.

Pillai, V. (2022). *Anomaly Detection for Innovators: Transforming Data into Breakthroughs.* Libertatem Media Private Limited.

Salimimoghadam, S., Ghanbaripour, A. N., Tumpa, R. J., Kamel Rahimi, A., Golmoradi, M., Rashidian, S., & Skitmore, M. (2025). The Rise of Artificial Intelligence in Project Management: A Systematic Literature Review of Current Opportunities, Enablers, and Barriers. *Buildings (Basel, Switzerland), 15*(7), 1130. DOI: 10.3390/buildings15071130

Sanusi, B. O. (2024). The role of data-driven decision-making in reducing project delays and cost overruns in civil engineering projects. *SAMRIDDHI: A Journal of Physical Sciences. Engineering and Technology, 16*(04), 182–192.

Sciences, N. A. o., Medicine, Engineering, D. o., Sciences, P., Science, C., Board, T., Alert, C. o. t. F. o. E., Systems, W., & Directions, R. (2018). Emergency alert and warning systems: Current knowledge and future research directions.

Vos, P., & Van der Voordt, T. (2002). Tomorrow's offices through today's eyes: Effects of innovation in the working environment. *Journal of Corporate Real Estate, 4*(1), 4865. DOI: 10.1108/14630010210811778

Williams, J. L. (2007). *Information theoretic sensor management.* Massachusetts Institute of Technology.

Wu, Y., Sicard, B., & Gadsden, S. A. (2024). A review of physics-informed machine learning methods with applications to condition monitoring and anomaly detection. *arXiv preprint arXiv:2401.11860.*

Yang, J., Qi, X., & Yu, G. (2005). Disruption management in production planning. [NRL]. *Naval Research Logistics, 52*(5), 420–442. DOI: 10.1002/nav.20087

Zmuda, A., & Kuklis, R. (2004). *Transforming schools: Creating a culture of continuous improvement.* ASCD.

Chapter 8
AI-Driven Backlog Refinement for Enhancing User Story Quality and Sizing in Agile Projects

Sindy Rahmahsari
http://orcid.org/0009-0000-8491-3242
Universitas Esa Unggul, Indonesia

Binastya Anggara Sekti
http://orcid.org/0000-0001-5489-4888
Universitas Esa Unggul, Indonesia

ABSTRACT

This chapter explores the transformative role of Artificial Intelligence (AI) in enhancing Agile backlog refinement processes through data-driven intelligence. It examines how AI technologies specifically machine learning (ML), natural language processing (NLP), and predictive analytics optimize user story quality, improve estimation accuracy, and streamline prioritization and dependency management. The chapter discusses the evolution from manual, intuition-based refinement to AI-assisted decision-making that enhances objectivity, consistency, and scalability. It also highlights the importance of human-AI collaboration, emphasizing that AI serves as an augmentative tool that strengthens, rather than replaces, human judgment. By integrating AI into Agile workflows, this chapter demonstrates how modern organizations can achieve greater delivery predictability, efficiency, and strategic alignment, ultimately redefining how software development teams plan, evaluate, and execute work in rapidly evolving digital environments.

DOI: 10.4018/979-8-3373-6851-1.ch008

1. INTRODUCTION

Artificial Intelligence (AI) has been a key enabler of change in almost every aspect of project management and software engineering in recent years. Organizations now view efficiency, quality, and innovation differently as a result of its quick transition from experimental automation to mainstream operational intelligence. It is now more important than ever to offer products more quickly while retaining accuracy and flexibility in digital ecosystems. These days, modern businesses work in markets that are marked by constant change, high client expectations, and pressure from competitors to iterate quickly (Sekti, 2025).

Figure 1. AI Integration in Backlog Refinement Processes

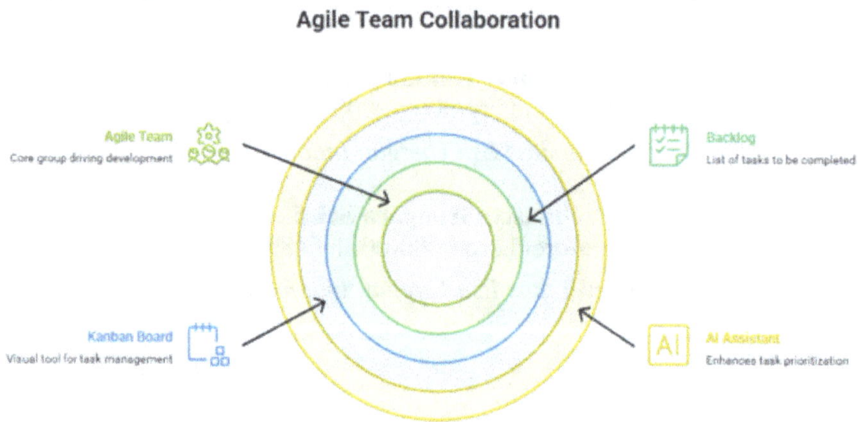

As illustrated in Figure 1, AI acts as a collaborative assistant within Agile team environments, interacting with the core development team, backlog, and Kanban board to enhance coordination and prioritization. By providing intelligent recommendations, the AI assistant supports backlog management and decision-making processes, ensuring that Agile workflows remain efficient and aligned with project goals. This integration reflects the broader transformation of modern software development, where Agile methodologies have become the dominant paradigm for managing projects. Agile offers a flexible framework that prioritizes collaboration, adaptability, and iterative value delivery (Rodrigues et al., 2025). Within this paradigm, backlog refinement, the process of ensuring that user stories are well-defined, properly prioritized, and accurately estimated, serves as the intellectual backbone of Agile planning, where ideas evolve into actionable tasks and the clarity of definition directly shapes delivery predictability. Within this paradigm, backlog refinement the process of ensuring that user stories are well-defined, properly prioritized, and accurately estimated serves as the intellectual backbone of Agile planning. It is the moment where ideas evolve into actionable tasks and where the quality of definition directly determines the predictability of delivery. Teams frequently struggle with subjective judgments, inconsistent estimations, and communication barriers that arise between technical and non-technical stakeholders, often resulting in inefficiencies, rework, and misaligned expectations (Bhatt et al., 2026). AI-driven decision support system integration presents a game-changing possibility as Agile teams work to strike a balance between predictability and flexibility. AI may systematically improve backlog refinement in ways that were previously impossible with manual labor alone by utilizing the predictive capacity of data analytics, the linguistic insight of natural language processing (NLP), and the analytical precision of machine learning (ML) (Yilmaz & Deniz, 2024). These technologies enable automated evaluation of story quality, effort prediction based on historical trends, and intelligent prioritization that accounts for business value, risk, and dependency structures. As a result, Agile teams can make data-informed decisions more consistently and objectively, freeing human participants to focus on creativity, strategic alignment, and stakeholder engagement. The inclusion of AI does not diminish the human essence of Agile it augments it. It transforms backlog refinement from a subjective discussion into a continuous, evidence-based learning process that evolves with each sprint. In essence, AI-driven backlog refinement represents the convergence of Agile philosophy and computational intelligence, redefining how teams interpret, plan, and deliver user stories in an era where speed, accuracy, and adaptability are no longer competing goals but interdependent imperatives.

The Evolution of Agile Backlog Refinement

Traditionally, backlog refinement previously known as "backlog grooming" involves reviewing user stories, clarifying requirements, decomposing epics, and estimating story points. This process relies heavily on human expertise, intuition, and experience, making it vulnerable to bias and inconsistency. For example, two Agile teams working on similar features may produce vastly different story point estimates due to differing interpretations of complexity or uncertainty. Additionally, as projects scale across multiple teams and geographies, ensuring that all user stories are clear, non-redundant, and correctly prioritized becomes increasingly challenging. AI introduces a paradigm shift in this space by providing objective and data-driven insights. NLP models can automatically assess the linguistic clarity of user stories, identifying ambiguous terms and missing acceptance criteria. Machine learning algorithms can analyze historical sprint data such as task completion time, code complexity, and developer velocity to generate predictive estimates for new stories.

Through such intelligent automation, backlog refinement evolves from a subjective, meeting-heavy ritual into a continuous, learning-oriented system that improves over time. This transformation aligns perfectly with the Agile manifesto's emphasis on responding to change over following a plan. AI acts not as a replacement for Agile practitioners but as a facilitator augmenting human decision-making with analytical precision and pattern recognition. As Agile teams strive to balance predictability and flexibility, integrating AI-driven decision support systems offers a revolutionary opportunity. By leveraging the predictive power of data analytics, the linguistic understanding of natural language processing (NLP), and the analytical precision of machine learning (ML), artificial intelligence (AI) may systematically enhance backlog refinement in ways that were previously unattainable with manual labor alone (Anwar et al., 2025).

The Role of Human-AI Collaboration

Contrary to the misconception that AI may replace Agile roles, its primary purpose in backlog refinement is augmentation, not automation. AI systems process large datasets, recognize linguistic and behavioral patterns, and make recommendations, but human expertise remains essential for interpreting contextual nuances. The Scrum Master's facilitation, the Product Owner's prioritization judgment, and the developers' technical understanding all form the interpretive layer that ensures AI outputs are meaningful and ethically sound. This symbiotic relationship between human and machine intelligence introduces a new Agile archetype the augmented team. Such teams combine computational intelligence with emotional and contextual awareness, leveraging the best of both worlds. As a result, the refinement process is more rapid, reliable, and transparent while maintaining its foundation in group decision-making (Lee, 2024).

The Significance of AI-Driven Refinement for Modern Delivery Organizations

In today's digital economy, organizations must deliver software rapidly while maintaining quality, compliance, and stakeholder satisfaction. AI-driven backlog refinement directly addresses this challenge by enhancing predictability, efficiency, and scalability within Agile frameworks. For distributed or large-scale organizations, AI ensures consistent refinement practices across teams, languages, and time zones. This consistency supports better cross-functional alignment and more accurate release planning. As organizations transition toward Agile at Scale and continuous delivery pipelines, the ability to harness AI for data-informed backlog refinement becomes a competitive differentiator (Haidabrus et al., 2026).

Having established the rationale for AI integration in backlog refinement, the next section explores the concept of backlog refinement within the broader Agile context, highlighting its challenges and opportunities for improvement.

2. UNDERSTANDING BACKLOG REFINEMENT IN AGILE CONTEXT

Building upon the integration of AI within Agile environments, the refinement process itself has undergone significant transformation. Traditional methods relied heavily on manual collaboration tools, while modern practices increasingly incorporate AI-assisted systems to streamline task organization and prioritization. This evolution is visually represented in Figure 2, which contrasts the manual and AI-assisted backlog refinement workflows.

Figure 2. Manual vs AI-Assisted Backlog Refinement Workflow

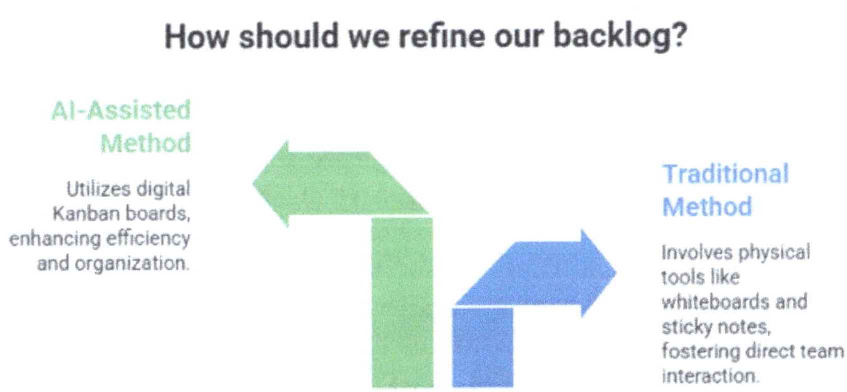

As illustrated in Figure 2, the evolution of backlog refinement practices highlights the shift from traditional manual approaches toward AI-assisted methods. While conventional refinement often relies on physical tools such as whiteboards and sticky notes to foster direct team collaboration, AI-driven techniques leverage digital Kanban boards and intelligent automation to enhance efficiency and organization.

Backlog refinement serves as the backbone of Agile planning and delivery, ensuring that product backlogs remain actionable, prioritized, and ready for sprint execution. Within the Scrum framework, backlog refinement is an ongoing activity where the Product Owner (PO), Scrum Master (SM), and Development Team collaborate to review, clarify, and estimate items in the product backlog. Through this procedure, high-level concepts or user requirements are converted into workable objects with precise acceptance standards and evaluations of relative complexity. Due to its reliance on subjective assessment and uneven team procedures, refining is sometimes undervalued or handled badly despite its significance (Ghiglino et al., 2026).

Traditional Challenges in Backlog Refinement

Although backlog refinement promotes transparency and adaptability, it faces several recurring challenges that affect the predictability and efficiency of Agile delivery.

1. **Subjectivity and Bias in Estimation** Estimation in Agile is inherently relative, relying on collective team consensus rather than empirical data. While consensus building is valuable, it also introduces bias. Experienced team members may dominate discussions, influencing estimates, while newer members may hesitate to voice differing opinions. Moreover, the same team may assign different estimates to similar tasks at different times due to changing team composition, stress levels, or incomplete context. This variability reduces the reliability of sprint forecasts.
2. **Ambiguity in User Stories** A major challenge arises when user stories are vague, incomplete, or written with ambiguous terminology. For instance, stories that lack clear acceptance criteria ("as a user, I want to improve performance") may lead to misunderstandings and rework. The Product Owner often spends significant time refining story language and clarifying stakeholder intent, consuming effort that could otherwise be used for value delivery.
3. **Communication Gaps Between Roles** Agile teams depend on effective cross-functional communication. However, when technical and non-technical team members interpret requirements differently, the result can be conflicting assumptions. Distributed teams exacerbate this problem due to asynchronous communication, cultural differences, and limited face-to-face collaboration.
4. **Overhead and Time Consumption** Refinement sessions can become lengthy and repetitive, particularly when multiple backlog items require clarification. Without proper facilitation, discussions can deviate into tangential topics, reducing team focus and productivity. This "meeting fatigue" effect has been reported as one of the most common complaints among Agile practitioners.

5. **Difficulty Managing Dependencies and Priorities** As the size of Agile organizations grows, so does the complexity of managing multiple backlogs across teams. Dependencies between user stories, modules, or components can cause scheduling conflicts and sprint delays. Manually tracking these interrelations using spreadsheets or boards becomes unmanageable at scale.

The Human Element in Backlog Refinement

It is important to emphasize that backlog refinement is not merely a technical exercise it is also a social process that embodies Agile values of collaboration, communication, and collective ownership. The Product Owner ensures business alignment, the Scrum Master facilitates productive discussions, and developers contribute technical insight. This dynamic makes refinement a microcosm of Agile culture itself, emphasizing the continuous balance between adaptability and discipline. However, even the most mature teams face cognitive limitations in processing large and dynamic backlogs (Košinár et al., 2026). As organizations transition toward digital ecosystems involving hundreds of interrelated user stories, human-driven refinement alone becomes impractical. Data overload and the absence of standardized quality metrics create inconsistencies in how readiness or completeness is defined. AI technologies, when thoughtfully implemented, complement this human aspect rather than disrupt it. AI frees humans to concentrate on higher-value work, such as decision-making, solution innovation, and stakeholder alignment, by automating repetitive tasks like identifying redundant items, reporting missing acceptance criteria, and verifying the completeness of user stories (Xu, 2026).

From Manual to AI-Assisted Refinement

The transition from manual to AI-assisted backlog refinement represents a significant paradigm shift in Agile practice. In the manual model, refinement depends heavily on human effort and subjective assessment. Meetings are the main venue for knowledge sharing, and improvements rely on experience or intuition. An AI-assisted model, on the other hand, uses machine learning (ML), natural language processing (NLP), and data analytics to provide the team with insightful information. NLP models, for example, can examine user story language to identify ambiguous verbs or absent roles (Ji et al., 2023). ML algorithms trained on historical sprint data can predict story points or completion times, allowing teams to compare AI suggestions against their own estimates. These tools do not replace planning sessions but rather serve as decision-support systems that make discussions more focused and evidence-based.

The Strategic Importance of Refinement in Agile Delivery

Understanding backlog refinement is essential to grasp why AI integration matters. The refinement process directly affects the predictability, quality, and velocity of Agile projects. Poorly refined backlogs lead to misunderstood requirements, sprint carry-overs, and technical debt accumulation. In contrast, well-refined backlogs promote better sprint commitment, smoother execution, and higher stakeholder satisfaction. AI-driven approaches amplify these benefits by ensuring consistency and scalability. Teams that adopt AI-assisted refinement gain measurable advantages in velocity stabilization, estimation accuracy, and sprint predictability. Over time, this creates a feedback loop where both humans and AI models continuously learn from outcomes, refining the refinement process itself. In summary, backlog refinement is a cornerstone of Agile delivery, bridging the gap between business vision and executable tasks. The introduction of AI into this space does not alter its collaborative essence but strengthens its foundation through data-informed intelligence. As will be explained in the following sections, AI provides innovative ways to improve the quality of user stories, automate sizing, and expedite prioritization all of which are essential elements of effective Agile planning (Shevchenko et al., 2023).

Understanding these challenges provides the foundation for exploring how AI technologies can enhance the quality of user stories, as discussed in the next section.

3. AI-POWERED ENHANCEMENT OF USER STORY QUALITY

User stories are the backbone of Agile software development and the principal mechanism by which stakeholder needs are captured, articulated, and transformed into technical tasks. They serve not only as units of work but also as communication tools bridging business and technology. In traditional Agile practice, the clarity and completeness of a user story determine how effectively it can be translated into actionable development work. A story that is ambiguous, lacks context, or omits measurable goals can propagate misunderstandings through multiple sprints, resulting in rework, scope creep, or unfulfilled business outcomes. As Agile adoption scales across distributed teams and complex systems, maintaining a consistent level of quality across hundreds of user stories becomes increasingly difficult. Large organizations often manage several product backlogs across diverse domains, where varying writing styles, stakeholder expectations, and technical vocabularies complicate story uniformity. This inconsistency introduces friction during sprint planning, estimation, and testing phases. In light of this, artificial intelligence (AI), namely through machine learning (ML) and natural language processing (NLP), provides revolutionary potential to improve the quality of user stories and standardize them (Pektaş, 2026). AI functions as a cognitive assistant that evaluates, learns, and refines the linguistic and structural elements of user stories, enabling continuous improvement and data-driven standardization.

The Importance of User Story Quality

In Agile development, user story quality directly impacts project predictability, velocity, and product satisfaction. The INVEST framework which defines good user stories as Independent, Negotiable, Valuable, Estimable, Small, and Testable serves as a benchmark for assessing story maturity. However, ensuring that every story adheres to these principles demands time, expertise, and attention to detail. In real-world Agile teams, especially those facing time constraints or distributed collaboration, story writing often becomes a rushed administrative task rather than a thoughtful analytical activity. Low-quality stories generate cascading consequences. Ambiguous requirements lead to inconsistent interpretations, often forcing developers to make assumptions that diverge from business intent. Vague acceptance criteria reduce testability, undermining the "definition of done." Moreover, inconsistent formatting or missing details create friction during refinement sessions, extending meeting duration and reducing focus on strategic priorities. Research has shown that up to 30–40% of sprint planning time is spent clarifying incomplete or misunderstood stories. On the other hand, well-written and rationally organized stories are dependable planning tools. They promote stakeholder alignment, decrease estimating uncertainty, and improve cross-functional communication (Li et al., 2026). Therefore, maintaining story quality is not merely an editorial exercise it is a strategic enabler of Agile maturity and delivery excellence. AI's contribution in this context lies in its ability to operationalize quality evaluation and provide real-time, objective feedback that reinforces best practices.

Machine Learning Models for Automated Quality Scoring

While NLP focuses on language patterns, machine learning (ML) introduces a quantitative layer to user story quality evaluation. ML algorithms can be trained on labeled datasets of user stories previously reviewed by Agile experts. Each story is rated along multiple dimensions such as clarity, completeness, and testability. Using these examples, a supervised learning model learns to assign numerical quality scores to new stories based on their linguistic and contextual features. In practice, these models generate a User Story Quality Score (USQS) a composite index indicating how well a story adheres to best practices. When implemented in Agile tools, such scoring mechanisms automatically highlight low-quality stories, allowing the Product Owner to focus refinement efforts where they are most needed.

Table 1. Dimensions of User Story Quality and AI Evaluation Methods

Quality Dimension	Description	AI Evaluation Method	Example Feedback
Clarity	Measures linguistic precision and avoidance of vague terms.	NLP grammar and phrase pattern analysis.	"Replace ambiguous term 'optimize' with measurable verb such as 'reduce response time.'"
Completeness	Checks whether essential story components (role, action, purpose) are present.	Template compliance detection and dependency tagging.	"Missing purpose clause ('so that...') in story description."
Consistency	Ensures coherence with other backlog items and terminology.	Semantic similarity and keyword clustering.	"Possible duplicate detected: story resembles #ST-241."
Testability	Evaluates whether the outcome can be measured or verified.	Rule-based ML classifiers using acceptance criteria presence.	"No measurable acceptance criteria found for validation."

By quantifying these dimensions, AI provides teams with an empirical understanding of backlog health. The resulting data enables continuous improvement through metrics such as average quality score trends per sprint, or variance in story quality across teams. Furthermore, ML models can learn contextual nuances unique to each organization. For instance, a fintech company's model might prioritize compliance-related terminology, whereas a healthcare product team's model might evaluate patient data privacy clauses. Such customization enhances AI's relevance and acceptance within diverse Agile ecosystems.

Human Oversight and Ethical Considerations

While AI provides precision and scalability, it cannot fully capture the human dimensions of context, empathy, and intent. The ultimate accountability for backlog quality still lies with the team. Human-AI collaboration ensures that AI's analytical insights are grounded in organizational strategy and ethical practice. Product Owners validate AI recommendations against business priorities; Scrum Masters ensure transparency and foster team trust in AI systems; and developers review technical feasibility. This triad of human roles maintains interpretive control, preventing AI from introducing biases or unintended automation of subjective decisions. Ethically, teams must consider the implications of AI training data. If accessibility or inclusion user stories were underrepresented in the training set, for instance, models trained on previous project data may unintentionally reinforce past biases (Mohammadi et al., 2026). Organizations should, therefore, adopt responsible AI governance, including model auditing, dataset diversification, and periodic performance reviews to ensure fairness and inclusivity. Moreover, data privacy regulations such as GDPR or ISO

27001 compliance must be upheld when training models on real project data. Sensitive information such as customer identifiers or proprietary product details should be anonymized before model ingestion. Establishing transparent data management practices promotes both ethical integrity and regulatory compliance.

Building upon the improvements in story quality, the subsequent section examines how AI contributes to more accurate effort estimation and backlog sizing.

4. INTELLIGENT BACKLOG SIZING AND EFFORT ESTIMATION

Effort estimation has long been one of the most debated and challenging aspects of Agile project management. Within Agile frameworks such as Scrum, estimation serves a dual purpose: it guides planning and provides a measure of predictability. Through estimation, teams assign relative complexity to user stories, enabling them to plan workloads that align with capacity while maintaining a sustainable pace. As a result, the accuracy of estimates varies not only across teams but also within the same team over time. A revolutionary approach to increasing estimation accuracy is provided by artificial intelligence (AI). AI can uncover latent links between story qualities and effort by examining patterns in past sprint data, resulting in more consistent and objective estimations. Agile teams are able to combine data-driven insights with experience understanding because AI provides empirical evidence to support human intuition rather than replace it (Assres et al., 2025). This convergence between machine learning and Agile estimation marks an important evolution: estimation becomes not merely a guessing exercise but a process of informed prediction supported by continuous learning.

Traditionally, Agile estimation has relied on methods such as Planning Poker, T-shirt sizing, and Fibonacci sequencing. These techniques encourage dialogue and collective reasoning, which are essential to team alignment. They are susceptible to well-established cognitive biases, though. Teams commonly suffer from optimism bias, when members undervalue complexity because of overconfidence, or anchoring bias, where early estimates affect later debate (Baltà-Salvador et al., 2026). Groupthink further amplifies conformity, leading teams to prioritize agreement over accuracy. Compounding these issues is the absence of historical data reference during estimation sessions; decisions are often made in isolation from prior outcomes. AI-driven estimation introduces a corrective mechanism by grounding these discussions in quantifiable data. Through machine learning (ML), AI systems can evaluate features such as story length, number of dependencies, past completion times, and developer velocity to predict the relative effort required for each backlog item. These models draw upon existing data repositories in Agile management tools like Jira or Azure DevOps, learning over time which variables most strongly influence effort. An AI system might discover, for instance, that often, stories referencing "API integration" or "security configuration" demand more narrative points than ones requiring straightforward interface improvements (Liontou et al., 2024). By establishing mathematical relationships between independent variables (story attributes) and dependent variables (actual effort), regression models generate interpretable patterns that teams can use for reasoning. More advanced ensemble models, such as random forests and gradient boosting algorithms, extend this capability by capturing nonlinear relationships, enabling predictions even in complex environments where no single factor dominates. Neural networks and deep learning models, in particular, offer new potential for recognizing subtler associations within unstructured data such as textual descriptions of user stories which are often overlooked in numerical analyses.

A critical component of AI-based estimation lies in how these models leverage textual information through Natural Language Processing (NLP). Story descriptions written in natural language can be converted into semantic embeddings, numerical representations that capture meaning beyond keywords. This enables AI systems to identify contextual signals of complexity, such as technical verbs ("integrate," "encrypt," "deploy") or abstract adjectives ("optimize," "refactor") that typically correlate with higher effort levels. Over time, the AI learns to distinguish between superficial and deeply technical work items, enhancing its estimation sensitivity. Real-world operations are where AI-driven estimation's usefulness is most noticeable. The AI system can instantly evaluate the content and metadata of a new user story that a Product Owner adds to the backlog, providing an initial estimated effort, such as "8 story points with 85% confidence." This estimate is not a substitute for team debate, but rather a starting point. The AI's prediction can be shown next to human estimates during backlog refinement or Planning Poker sessions, encouraging more in-depth discussions regarding the causes of discrepancies (Teichmann, 2026). If the AI predicts significantly higher effort, it may indicate hidden complexity, dependencies, or risk factors that the team overlooked. Conversely, a lower prediction may signal opportunities for simplification or improved task decomposition. Through this collaborative dynamic, estimation becomes a hybrid process where human intuition is strengthened, not sidelined, by machine intelligence.

One of the key benefits of AI-supported estimation lies in its ability to reduce variance across teams and iterations. In large organizations, estimation standards often diverge between teams, making aggregate forecasting difficult. AI can establish a baseline of consistency by applying uniform analytical criteria to all backlog items. Teams then calibrate around shared metrics rather than subjective comparison, resulting in greater cross-team predictability. Moreover, because AI models are built upon real project data, they are capable of adjusting to contextual variations such as differences in technology stacks, code complexity, or developer experience. Another important advantage is the improvement of long-term forecasting. By aggregating AI-generated effort estimates, managers can simulate different delivery scenarios, explore capacity trade-offs, and anticipate potential bottlenecks. These predictive insights transform sprint-level estimation into an instrument of strategic foresight, aligning daily Agile execution with broader business objectives.

Nevertheless, AI-based estimation is not without its challenges. Its accuracy depends heavily on the quality and completeness of historical data. Many organizations lack consistent documentation of actual effort spent on stories, making model training difficult. Furthermore, AI systems may struggle to adapt when project characteristics shift dramatically for example, when a team adopts a new technology stack or enters an unfamiliar domain. These shifts can cause the model to misinterpret context, underscoring the need for continuous retraining and oversight. Transparency and interpretability also remain ongoing concerns. Deep learning models, while powerful, often operate as "black boxes," offering little explanation for their predictions. Agile teams, grounded in principles of collaboration and openness, may resist estimates that cannot be clearly justified. Emerging techniques such as explainable AI (XAI) provide partial solutions by visualizing feature importance or highlighting the text fragments that most influenced a prediction. This allows teams to engage critically with AI outputs rather than accepting them blindly, maintaining accountability within the refinement process.

A change in perspective is necessary to integrate AI into estimation on a cultural level. Teams used to estimation based on intuition or conversation must learn how to constructively understand recommendations coming from data. The objective is to improve decision-making using evidence, not to automate it (Coniglio et al., 2026). When implemented thoughtfully, AI systems can foster a culture of empirical reflection encouraging teams to learn from patterns, validate assumptions, and continuously improve. In this sense, AI becomes not merely a calculator but a teacher, helping teams evolve toward higher estimation maturity. The implications of intelligent backlog sizing extend beyond individual sprints. At the portfolio level, AI-based estimation provides organizations with a macro-level view of delivery capacity. By aggregating effort predictions across projects, managers can monitor whether team workloads are balanced and allocate resources more strategically. Over time, this leads to better governance and greater transparency across the delivery pipeline. Predictive estimation also supports capacity planning for distributed teams, allowing enterprises to coordinate work across regions and time zones with improved accuracy.

Perhaps the most profound transformation introduced by AI-driven estimation is its contribution to continuous learning within Agile ecosystems. Each sprint produces new data points actual effort versus estimated effort which feed back into the model, improving its predictive accuracy. Teams become more attuned to recognizing effort patterns, while AI refines its understanding of context and behavior. In sum, intelligent backlog sizing powered by AI represents the natural progression of Agile estimation from intuition to intelligence. It preserves the collaborative essence of Agile while enhancing it with analytical precision. By combining historical learning with contextual interpretation, AI systems enable teams to make more informed, consistent, and transparent estimation decisions. The refinement process, once dominated by guesswork, becomes a structured dialogue between human expertise and computational insight. As estimation becomes more intelligent, so too must prioritization. The next section explores how AI extends its analytical capabilities to backlog ordering and dependency management helping teams not only estimate how much effort each task requires, but also determine which tasks should be done first and how they relate to one another in the complex web of modern Agile delivery.

By enhancing estimation accuracy and reducing variability across teams, AI transforms effort prediction into a data-driven and adaptive process. Building upon this analytical foundation, the next section explores how AI further contributes to prioritization and dependency management, enabling teams to determine not only how much effort a task requires, but also which tasks should be addressed first.

5. AI IN PRIORITIZATION AND DEPENDENCY MANAGEMENT

Prioritization and dependency management lie at the heart of Agile delivery. The way a team orders its backlog determines not only the sequencing of work but also the overall value delivered to stakeholders. In principle, Agile frameworks encourage teams to prioritize features that yield the highest business value or user impact within each iteration. However, in practice, prioritization is rarely straightforward. Teams must balance competing variables business urgency, technical risk, dependencies, resource constraints, and customer expectations often under limited information and time pressure. The result is that prioritization tends to be subjective, driven by intuition rather than empirical evidence.

Artificial Intelligence introduces a new level of rigor and intelligence into this process. By analyzing historical delivery data, user feedback, and dependency structures, AI systems can support Agile teams in making data-informed prioritization decisions that optimize both short-term sprint outcomes and long-term strategic value. Rather than relying solely on manual backlog ordering, AI tools can evaluate multiple dimensions simultaneously, offering recommendations based on measurable parameters such as return on investment, estimated effort, defect likelihood, and cross-team dependencies. With this, reactive backlog management gives way to predictive backlog management, where choices are based on trends that people could miss. Product owners usually set priorities in traditional backlog management based on stakeholder talks about business value (Furberg et al., 2026). This human-centered approach, while collaborative, often fails to capture the complex interrelations between user stories. For example, a story perceived as high priority might depend on several lower-priority technical tasks, creating a bottleneck when implementation begins. AI can mitigate this limitation by constructing dependency graphs, data-driven visual maps of how backlog items relate to one another. By processing information about linked tasks, shared modules, and resource allocation, the system can detect sequences that optimize flow efficiency.

AI's contribution to backlog prioritization is not merely computational it also transforms the decision-making culture within Agile teams. By offering transparent, traceable rationale for each recommendation, AI models promote structured discussions rather than replacing them. This transparency fosters trust and supports learning-oriented adaptation, reinforcing the Agile principle of continuous improvement. In large-scale Agile environments, where multiple Scrum teams operate concurrently under frameworks like SAFe or LeSS, dependency management becomes exponentially complex. AI can address this challenge by serving as a cross-team coordination layer, continuously analyzing progress across teams to identify emerging risks. This kind of real-time dependency awareness ensures that coordination decisions are proactive rather than reactive, reducing last-minute firefighting. The human aspect, however, remains irreplaceable. While AI can process large datasets and generate rational orderings, it cannot fully grasp the nuanced priorities of stakeholder relationships, customer expectations, or political factors that sometimes influence business decisions. In order to ensure that artificial intelligence enhances rather than replaces human intent, product owners and scrum masters must evaluate AI insights through the prism of human judgment. Here, ethical governance is crucial: Algorithms for setting priorities must continue to be open, comprehensible, and consistent with company values (Nesanır et al., 2026). If left unchecked, purely algorithmic prioritization could inadvertently reinforce systemic biases such as consistently deprioritizing low-visibility tasks that nonetheless support long-term maintainability. In practical terms, integrating AI into backlog prioritization requires both technical readiness and cultural adaptation. Teams need accessible data pipelines from Agile tools, clear quality standards for user story metadata, and agreed-upon policies for how AI recommendations are reviewed and acted upon. Some organizations embed AI-generated priorities directly into their Agile dashboards, allowing teams to compare "AI order" versus "human order." Over several sprints, these comparisons help calibrate both the algorithm and the team's judgment, building a shared understanding of optimal sequencing.

Ultimately, the introduction of AI into prioritization and dependency management reinforces the core Agile principle of responding to change over following a plan. Instead of rigidly adhering to a pre-set backlog, teams now manage a living, learning system one that continuously adapts based on empirical evidence. Dependencies become more visible, priorities more rational, and delivery more predictable. With the help of AI insights and human context, the product owner transitions from a gatekeeper of decisions to a facilitator of well-informed strategy (Sekti et al., 2025). As organizations increasingly adopt AI-driven prioritization, the distinction between planning and execution begins to blur. Backlog refinement becomes an ongoing cycle of sensing, learning, and adjusting, fueled by real-time intelligence. This integration establishes the foundation for AI-empowered Agile ecosystems where the backlog itself becomes a self-optimizing entity, continuously aligned with both user needs and business goals. The next section explores how these AI capabilities can be seamlessly embedded into Agile platforms and daily workflows, enabling teams to harness their full potential without disrupting existing processes.

Through data-informed prioritization and automated dependency mapping, AI empowers Agile teams to make decisions that balance business value and technical feasibility. The following section discusses how these capabilities can be seamlessly integrated into Agile tools and workflows, turning AI insights into actionable support within daily team practices.

6. INTEGRATION OF AI INTO AGILE TOOLS AND WORKFLOWS

The successful implementation of AI-driven backlog refinement depends not only on the sophistication of algorithms but also on the quality of their integration into the tools and workflows that Agile teams use daily. Digital ecosystems like Jira, Azure DevOps, Trello, or ClickUp platforms, which act as central repositories for user stories, sprint data, and performance indicators, are at the heart of Agile project management in the majority of enterprises (Menezes et al., 2024). Embedding AI within these tools transforms abstract computational capabilities into practical, context-aware assistants that operate seamlessly within the rhythm of Agile ceremonies. For example, when a Product Owner creates a new user story, an AI module can instantly analyze the linguistic structure, detect missing acceptance criteria, and propose an initial story point estimate derived from historical sprint data. During sprint planning, the same system may highlight potential dependencies or conflicting priorities based on real-time analysis of ongoing work. This level of integration allows AI to function not as an external analytic entity but as a co-participant an intelligent collaborator continuously embedded in the team's daily flow.

Seamless integration of AI into Agile environments occurs across multiple layers of the digital ecosystem. At the foundational data layer, AI models access structured and unstructured data stored in project databases through APIs, enabling them to learn from metrics such as cycle time, velocity trends, or issue resolution history.

These data streams form the basis for predictive analytics and continuous learning. At the application layer, AI manifests through plugins, extensions, or conversational interfaces that deliver recommendations directly within the user environment. Finally, at the workflow layer, AI automates repetitive coordination activities like updating story statuses or detecting when linked tasks are blocked thus allowing teams to focus on higher-value decision-making. This layered integration ensures that AI's presence feels organic rather than imposed, maintaining the flow and autonomy that Agile teams value.

The key to successful AI integration lies not merely in functionality but in trust and interpretability. Agile teams, particularly developers and Product Owners, often express skepticism toward opaque or intrusive tools. If AI insights appear arbitrary or disconnected from team experience, they risk being ignored, regardless of their technical accuracy. To overcome this barrier, AI recommendations must be explainable, contextual, and actionable. The emerging field of Explainable AI (XAI) provides frameworks for making algorithmic reasoning transparent for instance, showing which factors most influenced a prioritization decision or effort prediction. Such clarity aligns with Agile's principle of transparency, fostering dialogue rather than blind compliance. In this symbiotic relationship, AI serves as a mirror that reflects empirical insights, while human experts interpret and validate those reflections to ensure alignment with evolving goals. Cultural adaptation plays an equally critical role in embedding AI within Agile workflows. The introduction of intelligent systems inevitably raises concerns about autonomy, control, and the fear of being replaced by automation. Effective integration strategies involve participatory design, where teams are involved early in defining how AI tools operate and what kind of assistance they provide. This inclusion fosters ownership and curiosity, transforming initial skepticism into collaborative engagement. Furthermore, AI becomes a contextualized collaborator rather than a static evaluator when it is trained on local facts and teams are given the ability to modify model input, such as classifying suggestions as "helpful" or "irrelevant." This reciprocal learning eventually improves the team's analytical maturity and the AI's forecast accuracy, generating a feedback loop that is evocative of Agile's iterative nature (Cao et al., 2026).

From an organizational perspective, the integration of AI within Agile tools offers a pathway toward scalable intelligence across multiple teams and portfolios. Large delivery organizations often struggle with maintaining consistency in estimation, prioritization, and reporting across distributed teams. A well-integrated AI framework can standardize refinement practices without undermining local autonomy. This dual structure of global consistency and local flexibility mirrors the governance challenges faced by organizations implementing scaled Agile frameworks such as SAFe or LeSS. By embedding AI across these layers, decision-making becomes both data-informed and context-sensitive, ensuring that teams remain aligned with strategic objectives while retaining their creative independence. However, effective integration also demands rigorous attention to ethics, privacy, and data governance. Since AI models rely heavily on historical project data, organizations must establish clear policies regarding data ownership, access, and protection. Ethical oversight committees and regular audits of AI decision-making processes help ensure fairness and transparency. Furthermore, accountability is maintained and an excessive reliance on automation is avoided by sticking to a human-in-the-loop paradigm in which people constantly verify insights produced by AI. In this sense, integrating ethical AI represents the Agile concept of shared responsibility rather than just compliance (Pineda et al., 2026).

The long-term vision for integrating AI into Agile workflows is one of symbiosis between human adaptability and machine intelligence. As AI capabilities mature, future systems are expected to move beyond passive recommendation engines toward proactive collaboration. At the same time, multi-agent AI architectures could enable specialized modules such as estimation agents, prioritization agents, and dependency-mapping agents to communicate autonomously, coordinating their insights to support holistic decision-making. These developments suggest an imminent transformation of Agile platforms into intelligent ecosystems that continuously sense, analyze, and adapt to project dynamics in real time. The integration of AI into Agile tools and workflows represents more than a technical enhancement, it signifies the evolution of Agile itself into a data-empowered, reflective, and continuously learning discipline. Rather than undermining Agile's human-centered philosophy, AI reinforces it by grounding adaptability in empirical insight and turning iteration into a shared learning process between humans and machines. The backlog ceases to be a static artifact and becomes a living knowledge structure an intelligent reflection of organizational memory and intent. The question facing contemporary delivery companies as this shift takes place is not whether they can use AI, but rather whether they can do it in a way that is responsible, moral, and consistent with the Agile spirit's guiding principles of trust, cooperation, and continuous development (Filho et al., 2024).

Effective integration of AI within Agile environments ensures that intelligent systems function as collaborative partners rather than external evaluators. The next section addresses the ethical, organizational, and human-centered challenges that arise from this collaboration, emphasizing the need for transparency, trust, and responsible AI governance.

7. CHALLENGES, ETHICAL CONSIDERATIONS, AND HUMAN–AI COLLABORATION DYNAMICS

As Agile methodologies continue to evolve, the collaboration between human expertise and artificial intelligence has become a defining characteristic of modern software development environments. Rather than functioning as isolated entities, AI systems and Agile practitioners increasingly operate in tandem, complementing each other's strengths. This dynamic interaction is depicted in Figure 3, which illustrates the model of Human–AI Collaboration within Agile teams.

Figure 3. Human–AI Collaboration in Agile Teams

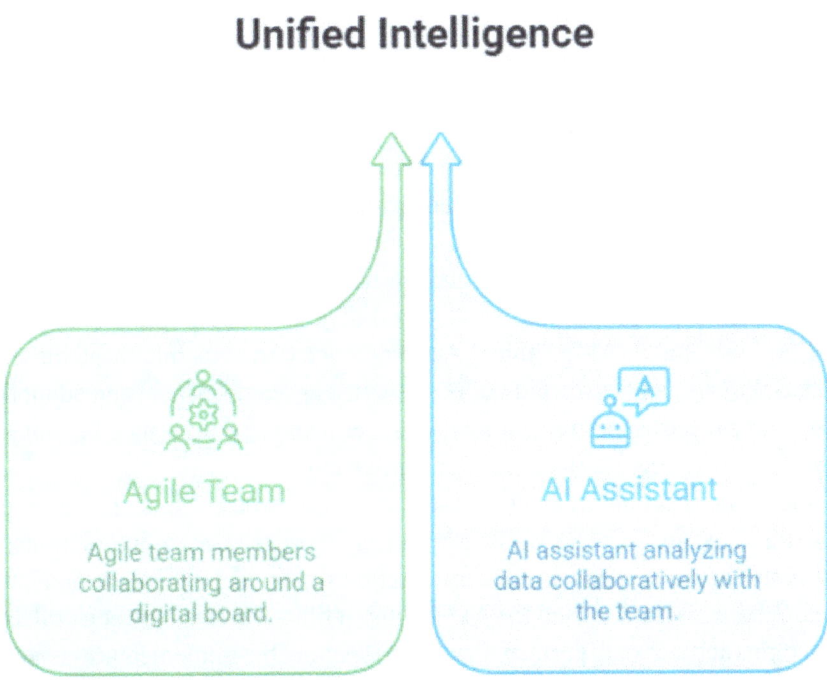

As shown in Figure 3, AI functions as an analytical partner that supports decision-making through data-driven insights, while human team members contribute contextual understanding, ethical judgment, and creative problem-solving. This symbiotic relationship reinforces Agile's foundational principles of transparency, collaboration, and continuous improvement. While the integration of Artificial Intelligence into Agile project management promises increased efficiency, accuracy, and learning, it also introduces a range of ethical, organizational, and psychological challenges that cannot be ignored. AI-driven backlog refinement depends heavily on data data that originate from human behavior, team interactions, and decision-making patterns. This dependence creates both opportunity and risk. When leveraged responsibly, historical sprint data provide the foundation for more consistent estimation and prioritization; however, when handled carelessly, the same data can expose teams to privacy violations, misrepresentation, or algorithmic bias. The challenge lies in ensuring that AI systems serve the principles of Agile transparency, collaboration, and trust rather than eroding them. In many organizations, AI tools operate as opaque mechanisms whose inner workings are not visible to users. This lack of interpretability threatens to undermine Agile's culture of openness and shared understanding, especially when recommendations are accepted without scrutiny. Ethical integration, therefore, requires not only technical safeguards but also cultural and procedural mechanisms that maintain human agency and accountability. One of the most pressing ethical issues in AI-enhanced Agile environments is the question of algorithmic bias and fairness. Machine learning models are inherently shaped by the data they are trained on, meaning they can perpetuate or even amplify the biases embedded in historical records. For example, if certain types of tasks or teams have historically been underrepresented or undervalued, AI may systematically deprioritize similar items in future backlogs, reproducing inequity in resource allocation. Deliberate tactics are needed to address this bias, such as transparent model design, fairness audits, and diverse data sampling (de Oliveira Garcia Coutinho et al., 2024). Ethical Agile practice demands that these biases be surfaced, discussed, and corrected collectively just as teams inspect and adapt their processes during retrospectives. In this sense, ethical AI governance becomes an extension of Agile's own reflective and adaptive ethos.

Another major consideration concerns data privacy and ownership. Agile tools such as Jira or Azure DevOps collect extensive records of team interactions, including individual task assignments, completion times, and even communication histories. When this data is used for AI training, it blurs the line between collective project metrics and personal performance data. Responsible implementation requires strict data governance frameworks that anonymize sensitive information and limit access to aggregated metrics rather than individual-level data. Furthermore, team members should be informed about how their data is used, who can access it, and for what purpose. Beyond the technical and ethical domains, the human dimension of collaboration with AI presents perhaps the most nuanced challenge. Agile values individuals and interactions over processes and tools, and this philosophy must extend to interactions between humans and intelligent systems. AI should be viewed not as a replacement for Agile roles but as a collaborator that enhances human decision-making. AI might anticipate the complexity of a story point, for instance, but it is up to the team to interpret this prediction in light of the stakeholder needs and the project's present restrictions (Kumar & Sharma, 2023). This interaction transforms estimation and prioritization from mechanical exercises into cognitive partnerships where human intuition meets computational insight. In practice, this requires the cultivation of new skills among Agile practitioners, including data literacy, critical interpretation of AI recommendations, and ethical reasoning about algorithmic outputs. Human-AI collaboration is not automatic; it must be learned, guided, and continually reinforced through deliberate organizational design.

The success of this collaboration depends greatly on trust calibration—the delicate balance between overreliance and underreliance on AI systems. When teams trust AI outputs blindly, they risk losing situational awareness and critical thinking; when they distrust AI excessively, they fail to benefit from its analytical capabilities. The goal is to achieve calibrated trust, where human users understand the AI's strengths and limitations well enough to use it appropriately. Explainable AI interfaces play a critical role here by revealing the reasoning behind each recommendation, thus allowing teams to validate and challenge AI decisions rather than accepting them passively. Scrum Masters and Product Owners become facilitators of this dialogue, ensuring that AI-enhanced decisions remain consistent with Agile values. From an organizational standpoint, the introduction of AI into Agile workflows demands new governance structures that balance innovation with accountability. Autonomous learning systems that are constantly changing are difficult for traditional management hierarchies to supervise. Organizations must instead implement AI governance frameworks that are transparent, collaborative, and iterative, just like Agile governance (Ranjeeth, 2026). These frameworks should define responsibilities for model training, data auditing, and ethical review, while also embedding continuous feedback loops to detect unintended consequences. Just as Agile retrospectives drive process improvement, periodic AI audits can identify performance drifts, data biases, or ethical lapses. In mature organizations, such audits become part of the sprint rhythm, ensuring that the integration of intelligence remains aligned with corporate values and stakeholder expectations.

Ultimately, the ethical and human-centered challenges of AI integration cannot be separated from the philosophical foundations of Agile. Both paradigms share an emphasis on learning, adaptability, and trust. The convergence of these systems thus offers not only technical evolution but also cultural transformation. A well-implemented AI system can enhance transparency, consistency, and foresight but only if it operates within a framework of human empathy and accountability. Agile teams must learn to treat AI as a reflective partner that exposes hidden assumptions and reveals new possibilities. In doing so, they preserve the creative tension between structure and spontaneity that defines true agility. The most successful Agile organizations of the future will not be those that simply automate refinement or estimation, but those that cultivate ethical intelligence the capacity to integrate human judgment and machine reasoning in ways that amplify both efficiency and humanity. The next section explores the emerging trends and future trajectories that will shape the evolution of AI-driven backlog refinement and Agile project management. As AI develops further, its incorporation within the Agile paradigm will transform how teams organize and complete tasks as well as how they think about learning, teamwork, and the fundamental characteristics of intelligent systems in organizational life (Iorliam, 2023).

Addressing the ethical and human dimensions of AI integration establishes a foundation of trust and accountability in Agile ecosystems. With these considerations in mind, the following section highlights emerging trends and future directions that will shape the evolution of AI-driven backlog refinement and Agile project management.

8. EMERGING TRENDS AND FUTURE DIRECTIONS

As Artificial Intelligence continues to mature, its role within Agile project management is expanding from a supportive analytical tool into an integral component of adaptive organizational intelligence. The convergence of AI, automation, and Agile principles signifies a profound evolution in how teams conceptualize, manage, and deliver value. Rather than serving as an external enhancement, AI is increasingly becoming embedded within the Agile process itself transforming the backlog, sprint planning, and retrospectives into dynamic, data-driven ecosystems. This evolution reflects a broader paradigm shift from process-oriented agility *to* intelligence-oriented agility, where adaptability is not only reactive but anticipatory. Organizations that once viewed Agile as a framework for iterative delivery now recognize it as a living infrastructure for continuous learning, powered by predictive and prescriptive analytics.

One of the most prominent trends shaping the future of AI-driven Agile practices is the emergence of autonomous Agile systems — self-optimizing environments where AI agents continuously monitor performance, identify impediments, and propose process adjustments without explicit human instruction. Such systems promise to reduce administrative overhead while enhancing decision precision. However, they also challenge traditional notions of Agile ownership, raising new questions about accountability, transparency, and human oversight. As automation deepens, Agile teams must redefine their role not as controllers of every detail but as curators of intelligent processes that evolve in collaboration with machines. Another critical trajectory involves the integration of Generative AI and Natural Language Interfaces into Agile tools. Large Language Models (LLMs) are now capable of understanding contextual queries, drafting user stories, generating acceptance criteria, and even suggesting retrospective summaries. This trend democratizes access to AI insights by lowering technical barriers; instead of complex dashboards or analytics scripts, team members can simply ask questions like "What were the top three causes of sprint delays last quarter?" or "Generate an improved version of this user story with clearer acceptance criteria." By allowing clients and product managers to communicate directly with Agile data using natural language, generative AI also promotes inclusion by embracing non-technical stakeholders. But this ease of use creates a new reliance: teams have to make sure that the outputs they produce are accurate, pertinent, and morally sound (She & Yin, 2026). The future of Agile documentation may therefore hinge on the co-creation between humans and generative systems, where AI accelerates drafting while humans ensure intent and contextual validity.

A parallel development is the growing emphasis on Predictive and Prescriptive Analytics within Agile ecosystems. In this sense, AI acts not only as an observer but as a strategic advisor. The future will also witness deeper integration between AI and DevOps pipelines, forming an end-to-end intelligent delivery ecosystem. In such settings, AI not only refines the backlog but also monitors code quality, deployment frequency, and production stability, creating feedback loops that connect planning to execution in real time. For instance, AI systems can analyze deployment logs to detect patterns of failure associated with specific backlog categories, feeding these insights back into refinement sessions. This cyclical feedback aligns perfectly with Agile's iterative philosophy, ensuring that learning flows seamlessly across planning, development, and delivery stages. Over time, organizations will evolve toward closed-loop intelligence, where each stage of the software lifecycle informs and improves the others through continuous, automated learning.

Equally transformative is the rise of Ethical and Responsible AI in Agile Governance. As AI becomes more embedded in decision-making processes, ethical frameworks will play an increasingly central role in ensuring that automation enhances rather than undermines human values. Future Agile governance models will likely incorporate ethical checkpoints similar to sprint reviews, where teams evaluate not only technical progress but also the social and moral implications of their AI-assisted decisions (de Sousa Leite et al., 2024). This development aligns with global efforts toward transparent and accountable AI, as organizations recognize that ethical credibility is as vital as operational efficiency. Agile teams will thus evolve from being simply iterative deliverers to becoming custodians of responsible innovation, balancing speed and intelligence with fairness and trust. Looking further ahead, the integration of AI into Agile methodologies suggests a trajectory toward cognitive organizations entities capable of learning, adapting, and reasoning as cohesive systems. These organizations will treat their processes as intelligent agents that continuously sense environmental changes, interpret patterns, and autonomously adjust. Backlogs will evolve into living documents, where priorities update dynamically based on market data, customer sentiment, and operational performance (Campos et al., 2024). Scrum Masters may act more as AI facilitators, guiding the collaboration between human teams and intelligent systems. The distinction between planning and execution will blur, replaced by a continuous feedback-driven flow of insight and action. In such a future, the measure of agility will no longer be speed alone, but cognitive adaptability the ability to think, learn, and evolve as an intelligent collective.

Ultimately, the trajectory of AI-driven Agile practice reflects a convergence of technological capability and human aspiration. The future of Agile project management will be defined not merely by tools or frameworks but by the evolving relationship between human creativity and machine intelligence. As AI systems grow more capable of interpreting nuance, and humans grow more adept at orchestrating intelligence ethically, the two will co-create a new paradigm of digital craftsmanship one that fuses precision with empathy, automation with judgment, and prediction with purpose. The challenge for modern organizations will be to harness this partnership in a way that amplifies both performance and meaning, ensuring that the evolution of Agile remains as much a moral endeavor as a technological one.

The continuous convergence of AI and Agile principles signals a future where adaptability and intelligence are deeply intertwined. The final section concludes this chapter by summarizing key findings and reaffirming the transformative potential of AI-driven backlog refinement for modern delivery organizations.

9. CONCLUSION

The integration of Artificial Intelligence into Agile backlog refinement represents one of the most significant transformations in contemporary software project management. What was once an entirely human-centered, intuition-driven process has evolved into a collaborative ecosystem where machine intelligence augments human reasoning, consistency, and foresight. Through the combined application of machine learning, natural language processing, and predictive analytics, AI has begun to address long-standing weaknesses in backlog refinement ambiguity in user stories, inconsistency in estimation, and inefficiency in prioritization. Yet, the purpose of this transformation is not automation for its own sake, but augmentation the enhancement of human decision-making and the amplification of team intelligence through data-informed insight. This synergy between human adaptability and computational precision embodies the essence of modern agility: the capacity to learn, evolve, and deliver value continuously in the face of complexity and change. Throughout this chapter, we have seen how AI reshapes each dimension of backlog refinement. It enhances user story quality through linguistic clarity checks and semantic analysis, ensuring that every story aligns with acceptance standards and stakeholder expectations. It refines estimation practices by replacing guesswork with empirically grounded predictions derived from historical performance. It transforms prioritization and dependency management into a structured, data-driven exercise that considers value, risk, and interconnection beyond human perceptual limits. Moreover, through seamless integration into Agile tools and workflows, AI becomes not an external consultant but an embedded collaborator, continuously learning from and adapting to the team's evolving behavior. These advancements collectively shift Agile refinement from an episodic ritual into a living process of continuous learning where both humans and machines improve through their shared experience.

REFERENCES

Anwar, N., Sekti, B. A., Widodo, A. M., Erzed, N., Gunawan, H., Tangkudung, R. R. S., Muchlis, M., & Budhisantosa, N. (2025). Emerging innovations in AI and green computing for cybersecurity. In *Sustainable Information Security in the Age of AI and Green Computing* (pp. 17–38). DOI: 10.4018/979-8-3693-8034-5.ch002

Assres, G., Bhandari, G., Shalaginov, A., Gronli, T.-M., & Ghinea, G. (2025). State-of-the-Art and Challenges of Engineering ML- Enabled Software Systems in the Deep Learning Era. *ACM Computing Surveys*, *57*(10), 1–35. Advance online publication. DOI: 10.1145/3731597

Baltà-Salvador, R., Brasó-Vives, E., & Peña, M. (2026). Evaluating AI-assisted creative ideation: A crossover study in higher education. *Thinking Skills and Creativity*, *59*, 101958. Advance online publication. DOI: 10.1016/j.tsc.2025.101958

Bhatt, J., Patel, B., Prajapati, A., & Vasa, J. (2026). Adopting Agile Methodologies for Digital Newsrooms: A Case Study of BBC News. *Lecture Notes in Networks and Systems, 1457 LNNS*, 231–241. DOI: 10.1007/978-981-96-7496-1_18

Campos, L. N., Bryce-Alberti, M., Gerk, A., Hill, S. K., Calderon, C., Zaigham, M., del Valle, D. D., Mita, C., Juran, S., Ferreira, J. L., & Uribe-Leitz, T. (2024). Examining the surgical backlog due to COVID-19 in Latin America and the Caribbean: Insights from a scoping review. *Lancet Regional Health. Americas*, *40*, 100908. Advance online publication. DOI: 10.1016/j.lana.2024.100908 PMID: 39493415

Cao, Y., Chen, Y., Fan, X., Fu, H., & Xu, B. (2026). Advanced Design for High-Performance and AI Chips. *Nano-Micro Letters*, *18*(1), 13. Advance online publication. DOI: 10.1007/s40820-025-01850-w PMID: 40728678

Coniglio, I. M., Cimino, A., & Corvello, V. (2026). Artificial Intelligence and the Future of Supply Chain Management. *Springer Proceedings in Complexity*, 43–52. DOI: 10.1007/978-3-031-78623-5_4

de Oliveira Garcia Coutinho, V., de Almeida Souza, M. R., & Freire, A. P. (2024). Application of human-centered design practices in the agile requirements engineering process: a case study in a public company. *ACM International Conference Proceeding Series*, 498–507. DOI: 10.1145/3701625.3701635

de Sousa Leite, G., Maciel, R. S. P., Vieira, R. E. P., Freire, S., Cerqueira, L., & Mendonça, M. (2024). Technical Debt Management in Agile Software Development: A Systematic Mapping Study. *ACM International Conference Proceeding Series*, 309–320. DOI: 10.1145/3701625.3701669

Filho, R. C. D., Silva, M. J., & Marinho, M. L. M. (2024). Low-Code Quality Metrics for Agile Software Development. *ACM International Conference Proceeding Series*, 417–425. DOI: 10.1145/3701625.3701626

Furberg, A., Azizi, S., Bieser, J., Bol, D., Coroamă, V., Eriksson, E., Fuso-Nerini, F., Golard, L., Höjer, M., Kamiya, G., Lundén, D., Lövehagen, N., Malmodin, J., Schien, D., & Finnveden, G. (2026). Guidelines for assessments of the global information and communication technology sector's direct energy use and climate impact: Key aspects and future scenarios. *Renewable & Sustainable Energy Reviews, 226*, 116176. Advance online publication. DOI: 10.1016/j.rser.2025.116176

Ghiglino, P., Harshe, M., Doran, H. D., & Tordoya Taquichiri, C. R. (2026). High-Performance AI Inference for Agile Deployment on Space-Qualified Processors: A Performance Benchmarking Study. *Lecture Notes in Computer Science, 15955 LNCS*, 267–280. DOI: 10.1007/978-3-032-02018-5_20

Haidabrus, B., Grabis, J., Druzhinin, E., & Kolesnikova, K. (2026). Implementing Lean-Agile Principles in Data Programme. *Lecture Notes in Mechanical Engineering*, 149–158. DOI: 10.1007/978-3-032-07144-6_13

Iorliam, A. (2023). A Novel Additive Internet of Things (IoT) Features and Convolutional Neural Network for Classification and Source Identification of IoT Devices. *Sakarya University Journal of Computer and Information Sciences*, *6*(3), 218–225. DOI: 10.35377/saucis...1354791

Ji, Z., Lee, N., Frieske, R., Yu, T., Su, D., Xu, Y., Ishii, E., Bang, Y. J., Madotto, A., & Fung, P. (2023). Survey of Hallucination in Natural Language Generation. *ACM Computing Surveys*, *55*(12), 1–38. Advance online publication. DOI: 10.1145/3571730

Košinár, M. A., Štolfa, S., Lašinská, M., Štolfa, J., & Spanyik, M. (2026). Catalogue of Pathological Patterns of Self-managed Teams in Scrum. *Communications in Computer and Information Science, 2658 CCIS*, 197–211. DOI: 10.1007/978-3-032-04291-0_14

Kumar, R., & Sharma, V. (2023). The AI revolution: Financial services in the age of intelligent machines. In *Leveraging AI and Emotional Intelligence in Contemporary Business Organizations* (pp. 287–305). DOI: 10.4018/979-8-3693-1902-4.ch017

Lee, W.-J. (2024). SERVICE FAILURE BY HUMAN, SERVICE RECOVERY BY AI CHATBOT: THE IMPACT OF JUSTICE, AI EFFICACY ON RECOVERY EFFORT. *Virtual Economics*, *7*(4), 48–63. DOI: 10.34021/ve.2024.07.04(3)

Li, J., Shen, Y., Zhou, W., & Chen, H. (2026). SearchExpert: A GenAI-driven framework for reasoning-intensive multimedia information fusion through fine-tuning and reinforcement learning. *Information Fusion, 126*, 103665. Advance online publication. DOI: 10.1016/j.inffus.2025.103665

Liontou, A. K., Zisimopoulos, S., & Dermitzakis, A. (2024). Leveraging Web Scraping and API Integration for Efficient Medical Device Data Management. *Global Clinical Engineering Journal, 6*(Special Issue 6), 51–56. DOI: 10.31354/globalce.v6iSI6.252

Menezes, R., Marinho, M., & Sampaio, S. (2024). Metrics for Large-Scale Agile Development: A Survey of the Brazilian Software Industry. *ACM International Conference Proceeding Series*, 210–219. DOI: 10.1145/3701625.3701660

Mohammadi, E., Thelwall, M., Cai, Y., Collier, T., Tahamtan, I., & Eftekhar, A. (2026). Is generative AI reshaping academic practices worldwide? A survey of adoption, benefits, and concerns. *Information Processing & Management, 63*(1), 104350. Advance online publication. DOI: 10.1016/j.ipm.2025.104350

Nesanır, M. O., Zenezini, G., Senvar, O., & Ottaviani, F. M. (2026). A Literature Review on the Integration of System Dynamics and Machine Learning/Artificial Intelligence in Addressing Environmental Matters. *IFIP Advances in Information and Communication Technology, 764 IFIPAI*, 370–384. DOI: 10.1007/978-3-032-03515-8_26

Pektaş, Ş. T. (2026). An Inquiry on the Usability of Generative AI in Design Education. *Lecture Notes in Computer Science, 15914 LNCS*, 393–402. DOI: 10.1007/978-3-031-98197-5_42

Pineda, V. G., Valencia-Arias, A., Giraldo, F. E. L., & Zapata-Ochoa, E. A. (2026). Integrating artificial intelligence and quantum computing: A systematic literature review of features and applications. *International Journal of Cognitive Computing in Engineering, 7*, 26–39. DOI: 10.1016/j.ijcce.2025.08.002

Ranjeeth, S. (2026). An Organisational Culture Framework to Guide the Transition to an Agile Software Development Methodology. *Communications in Computer and Information Science, 2583 CCIS*, 112–128. DOI: 10.1007/978-3-031-96262-2_9

Rodrigues, P. G., Bárrios, M. J., & Mendes, M. S. G. (2025). Waiting for Specialists: A Multi-Priority and Multi-Speciality Analysis. *The International Journal of Health Planning and Management, 40*(6), 1248–1278. DOI: 10.1002/hpm.70007 PMID: 40650993

Sekti, B. A. (2025). Machine learning and artificial intelligence (AI) in manufacturing. In *Integrating Digital Innovation and Integrated Frameworks in Manufacturing* (pp. 255–292). DOI: 10.4018/979-8-3373-1082-4.ch011

Sekti, B. A., Laksono, M. N. G., Laksono, M. I. A., Widodo, A. M., Anwar, N., & Tiaraputri, Z. A. (2025). Principles of green computing in information security. In *Sustainable Information Security in the Age of AI and Green Computing* (pp. 1–16). DOI: 10.4018/979-8-3693-8034-5.ch001

She, Y., & Yin, B. (2026). Enabling Authenticated Query Services on Multi-dimensional Data in Collaborative Blockchain. *Lecture Notes of the Institute for Computer Sciences, Social-Informatics and Telecommunications Engineering, LNICST, 625 LNICST*, 3–22. DOI: 10.1007/978-3-031-93254-0_1

Shevchenko, I., Liubokhynets, L., Zvarych, I., Brodovska, O., & Bril, M. (2023). ANTIFRAGILE IN THE GLOBAL ECONOMY AS AN INDICATOR OF ECONOMIC DEVELOPMENT. *Financial and Credit Activity: Problems of Theory and Practice*, *6*(53), 274–286. DOI: 10.55643/fcaptp.6.53.2023.4203

Teichmann, F. (2026). Cybersecurity risks in mining's operational technology: Implications of OT vulnerabilities and EU NIS2 compliance. *The Extractive Industries and Society*, *25*, 101774. Advance online publication. DOI: 10.1016/j.exis.2025.101774

Xu, R. (2026). Optimizing ML classifiers for superior intrusion detection in resource-constrained smart homes. *International Journal of Cognitive Computing in Engineering*, *7*, 58–73. DOI: 10.1016/j.ijcce.2025.08.003

Yilmaz, K., & Deniz, K. Z. (2024). Natural Language Processing and Machine Learning Applications For Assessment and Evaluation in Education: Opportunities and New Approaches. *Egitimde ve Psikolojide Ölçme ve Degerlendirme Dergisi*, *15*(4), 421–445. DOI: 10.21031/epod.1551568

Chapter 9
Algorithmic Project Mastery:
AI in Action for Scrum and HERMES

Otmane Azeroual
http://orcid.org/0000-0002-5225-389X
University of Hagen, Germany

ABSTRACT

This chapter explores the use of Artificial Intelligence (AI) in project management, focusing on Scrum and HERMES. It examines three AI applications: sprint and backlog optimization, digital project coaching, and automated lessons learned analysis. Using historical data, machine learning, and natural language processing, AI enhances planning, decision-making, and organizational learning. In Scrum, it improves sprint predictability and task prioritization; in HERMES, it supports phase monitoring, risk mitigation, and compliance. Digital coaching provides real-time guidance while maintaining human oversight. Lessons learned analysis extracts insights from documentation and communication to foster continuous improvement. The chapter also addresses data quality, ethics, human-AI collaboration, and organizational readiness, illustrating measurable gains in efficiency, risk management, and knowledge retention. Future directions include conversational AI, predictive analytics, and AI-driven collaboration, providing actionable strategies for adaptive, data-driven projects.

DOI: 10.4018/979-8-3373-6851-1.ch009

INTRODUCTION

Project management is a central discipline for ensuring that complex initiatives are executed efficiently, on time, and within budget. Organizations across industries increasingly rely on structured methodologies such as Scrum and HERMES to provide frameworks for planning, coordination, and continuous improvement. Scrum, as an agile methodology, emphasizes iterative development, adaptive planning, and collaborative team engagement, while HERMES, widely used in Switzerland, offers a process-oriented approach for project governance, risk management, and deliverable-focused project execution (Sutherland & Schwaber, 2013; HERMES Foundation, 2022). Despite the strengths of these methodologies, modern project environments are characterized by growing complexity, dynamic requirements, and large volumes of data. Traditional management approaches often struggle to efficiently process and interpret this information, leaving opportunities for errors, delays, and suboptimal decision-making.

In recent years, AI has emerged as a promising approach to augment project management processes by providing data-driven insights, predictive analytics, and automation of repetitive tasks (Kumari et al., 2023). AI can analyze historical project data, identify patterns, forecast risks, and recommend actions, thereby supporting project teams in making informed, timely, and objective decisions. Recent studies on AI maturity models and project readiness frameworks indicate that organizational preparedness significantly influences the effectiveness of AI interventions (Ellefsen et al., 2019; Felemban et al., 2024). By integrating AI into project management frameworks such as Scrum and HERMES, organizations can enhance both operational efficiency and strategic decision-making, while maintaining transparency and accountability. The convergence of AI and project management represents a transformative opportunity for both practice and research, offering a pathway to more adaptive, resilient, and data-driven project execution (Pérez-Castillo et al., 2024).

This chapter focuses on three primary AI-supported functionalities within project management. First, sprint and backlog optimization: AI tools can evaluate historical project performance, predict team velocity, and propose optimal task prioritization strategies. By automating the analysis of backlog items and dependencies, AI allows Product Owners (POs) and project managers to make more informed decisions, reduce planning time, and mitigate bottlenecks. Second, the chapter addresses the role of a digital project coach: AI can act as a virtual advisor that monitors ongoing projects, provides real-time alerts for potential risks, recommends corrective actions, and supports teams in adhering to project governance frameworks. This approach enhances proactive management, improves resource allocation, and ensures compliance with organizational standards. Third, the chapter examines automated lessons learned analyses: by leveraging natural language processing (NLP) and machine learning, AI can extract insights from project documentation, meeting notes, and communication logs, identifying improvement opportunities and best practices for future projects (Kerzner, 2025).

The intended audience for this chapter includes project managers, Scrum Masters (SMs), organizational consultants, and researchers interested in the intersection of AI and project management. Readers will gain an understanding of how AI can be strategically applied to augment traditional methodologies, rather than replacing human judgment. Furthermore, the chapter emphasizes practical implications, providing examples of real-world applications and highlighting the challenges, limitations, and ethical considerations of AI implementation. It also includes a discussion of organizational readiness, change management, and adoption barriers, which are critical for successful AI integration. The discussion also addresses the potential for AI to support inter-team communication, enhance project transparency, and facilitate decision-making in complex, multi-stakeholder environments.

The relevance of this topic is underscored by the increasing digitization of organizations and the availability of vast amounts of project-related data. Project teams often face challenges in managing this data effectively, including identifying relevant information, tracking task dependencies, and predicting risks. Integrating AI into project management can reduce cognitive load, improve decision quality, and enhance organizational learning through continuous feedback loops. Moreover, AI-assisted approaches align with current trends in digital transformation, where efficiency, agility, and informed decision-making are crucial for organizational success (Project Management Institute, 2021). A comparative table summarizing AI Value Pathways in project management is provided in the summary section to enhance conceptual clarity and practical application. By providing structured frameworks for AI integration, this chapter aims to equip practitioners and researchers with actionable insights that can be implemented in both agile and traditional project environments.

In addition to practical benefits, this chapter contributes to the academic discourse on AI in project management by synthesizing current research, identifying knowledge gaps, and proposing a conceptual framework for AI-assisted project practices. While some applications are illustrated with empirical case studies, the chapter also clearly indicates areas where conceptual and literature-based analysis is applied, highlighting the need for further validation. By bridging the gap between theory and practice, the chapter highlights the potential for AI to improve project outcomes, enhance team performance, and support continuous learning.

In summary, this chapter explores how AI can augment project management practices in Scrum and HERMES through three main mechanisms: backlog optimization, digital coaching, and lessons learned analyses. The chapter aims to provide both theoretical grounding and practical guidance, enabling readers to understand, implement, and evaluate AI-supported project management strategies. Ultimately, the goal is to demonstrate how AI can be a valuable ally for project teams, helping them navigate complexity, improve efficiency, and achieve better project results. It explicitly addresses organizational readiness, change management, and AI maturity considerations, ensuring applicability in diverse contexts.

THEORETICAL BACKGROUND

Project management has evolved as a critical discipline for organizations seeking to execute complex initiatives efficiently, within scope, and on schedule (Morris, 2013). Modern methodologies such as Scrum and HERMES provide structured frameworks that enhance planning, coordination, and continuous improvement (Schär et al., 2015). Scrum, widely recognized as an agile methodology, emphasizes iterative development, adaptive planning, and collaborative team engagement (Hidalgo, 2019). Work is organized into sprints, typically lasting two to four weeks, where specific tasks or user stories are completed. Scrum assigns distinct roles including the PO, responsible for backlog management; the SM, who facilitates processes and removes impediments; and the Development Team, tasked with delivering the work. This framework fosters transparency, inspection, and adaptation, making it particularly effective in dynamic project environments where requirements evolve rapidly.

HERMES, in contrast, is a process-oriented methodology extensively applied in Switzerland and other European public organizations. It provides a phase-based approach with predefined deliverables, responsibilities, and governance mechanisms. HERMES emphasizes structured documentation, risk management, and stakeholder communication to ensure compliance with regulatory and organizational standards. While Scrum focuses on agility and iterative delivery, HERMES provides rigorous process control suitable for larger-scale or public sector projects. Understanding these methodologies and their nuances is essential when integrating AI into project management, as AI systems must align with both flexible and structured processes.

AI represents a transformative opportunity for project management. Defined as systems capable of performing tasks typically requiring human intelligence, including pattern recognition, decision-making, and predictive analytics, AI can augment project teams by providing data-driven insights, predictive evaluations, and automation of repetitive tasks (Huang & Rust, 2021; Nabeel, 2024). In project contexts, AI can forecast schedule risks, identify resource bottlenecks, and provide actionable recommendations, thereby supporting decision-making and reducing reliance on intuition. Natural language processing (NLP) enables AI systems to analyze textual data—including meeting notes, emails, or project documentation—to identify recurring issues, anomalies, or improvement opportunities (Sharma & Arjunan, 2023). Recommendation systems can optimize task prioritization, resource allocation, and sprint planning, while automation can relieve project managers and teams from routine administrative tasks (Xiao et al., 2023). Importantly, AI is intended to enhance, rather than replace, human judgment, providing teams with tools to improve efficiency, accuracy, and organizational learning.

Integrating AI with Scrum can significantly improve project planning and execution. AI can analyze historical sprint performance to predict team velocity, identify potential bottlenecks, and recommend task prioritization. It can support sprint planning by evaluating task dependencies, resource availability, and risk factors, allowing POs and SMs to make more informed decisions and reduce planning time (Voutama, 2025). Furthermore, AI-driven monitoring systems can detect deviations from planned objectives during sprints, flag potential risks, and suggest corrective actions in real time. This integration allows Scrum teams to maintain agility while benefiting from data-informed guidance, improving overall project predictability and success rates. Similarly, AI integration with HERMES can enhance structured project governance. Machine learning models can assess risks during each project phase, providing early warnings and supporting proactive mitigation strategies (Ekambaram et al., 2022). Compliance monitoring can be automated, ensuring deliverables meet HERMES standards and organizational regulations. AI can also assist stakeholders in scenario analysis, evaluating the impact of decisions based on historical data and current project status. By embedding AI into HERMES, organizations can retain rigorous process control while leveraging intelligent decision support.

Recent studies on AI maturity models and organizational readiness emphasize that preparedness—including technical infrastructure, data governance, analytics capabilities, and cultural acceptance—significantly influences the effectiveness of AI interventions in project management (Ellefsen et al., 2019; Bandara & Wickramarachchi, 2025). Organizations with higher AI maturity and readiness are better positioned to integrate AI tools into Scrum and HERMES processes, ensuring alignment with both agile and structured practices.

Lessons learned and knowledge management are critical for continuous improvement in both Scrum and HERMES (Linke, 2019). Traditionally, lessons learned are documented manually and often remain underutilized. AI enables automated extraction and analysis of lessons learned from project documentation, meeting notes, and communication logs. NLP and machine learning can identify patterns, categorize issues, and highlight successful practices, providing structured insights that feed back into planning and execution processes. This facilitates a continuous learning cycle, enhancing team performance and improving outcomes in subsequent projects. The integration of AI in lessons learned processes also aligns with the principles of data-driven project management, ensuring that organizational knowledge is systematically captured, analyzed, and applied (Li et al., 2024).

Despite its potential, AI integration in project management presents several challenges. High-quality, complete historical data is required for accurate predictions and recommendations; missing or inconsistent data can reduce model effectiveness. Change management and user acceptance are crucial, as teams may resist adopting AI-assisted workflows. Ethical considerations—including transparency, explainability, and bias mitigation—must be addressed to ensure responsible use of AI in decision-making. Additionally, AI systems must adapt to the methodological context, accommodating the flexible, iterative nature of Scrum and the structured, phase-based approach of HERMES. Failure to align AI tools with these methodologies may limit their practical utility and reduce team trust.

The relevance of AI in project management is reinforced by the increasing digitalization of organizational processes and the abundance of project-related data (Nenni et al., 2025). Teams frequently struggle with information overload, tracking task dependencies, and anticipating risks. By applying AI, cognitive load can be reduced, decision quality improved, and continuous feedback integrated into project workflows. This supports both operational efficiency and strategic decision-making, contributing to the success of projects in dynamic and complex environments. Additionally, AI-enhanced project management facilitates inter-team communication, transparency, and accountability, promoting more informed and cohesive project execution.

This chapter thus establishes the theoretical foundation for integrating AI into project management frameworks. By exploring Scrum and HERMES methodologies, identifying potential AI applications, and addressing both opportunities and challenges, the chapter provides a comprehensive view of AI-enabled project management. It demonstrates how AI can support sprint planning, digital coaching, and lessons learned analyses, offering a conceptual framework that informs subsequent practical implementations. The discussion combines insights from project management theory, AI research, and emerging industry practices, establishing a foundation for future experimentation, empirical research, and application in real-world projects. Overall, AI has the potential to enhance team performance, improve project outcomes, and create a culture of continuous learning, provided it is applied thoughtfully and in alignment with organizational and methodological contexts.

Having established the theoretical underpinnings of AI-assisted project management and the methodological characteristics of Scrum and HERMES, the next section turns to practical implementation. It explores how these theoretical insights are operationalized in real-world contexts through applied use cases and empirical examples. By bridging conceptual understanding and practical evidence, this section demonstrates how AI transforms project management from a methodological framework into a data-driven, adaptive practice.

PRACTICAL IMPLEMENTATION AND CASE STUDIES

The practical application of AI in project management provides measurable advantages in planning, execution, and continuous improvement, particularly within Scrum and HERMES methodologies. Effective implementation in real-world environments requires careful adaptation to methodology-specific workflows, data availability, and organizational maturity. This section demonstrates how AI can be applied through practical examples and case studies, focusing on three core areas: sprint and backlog optimization, digital project coaching, and lessons learned analysis.

Figure 1 provides a visual overview of AI applications in project management, highlighting the three core areas, their key data inputs, and expected outcomes in Scrum and HERMES projects.

Figure 1. AI-Supported Project Management in Scrum and HERMES.

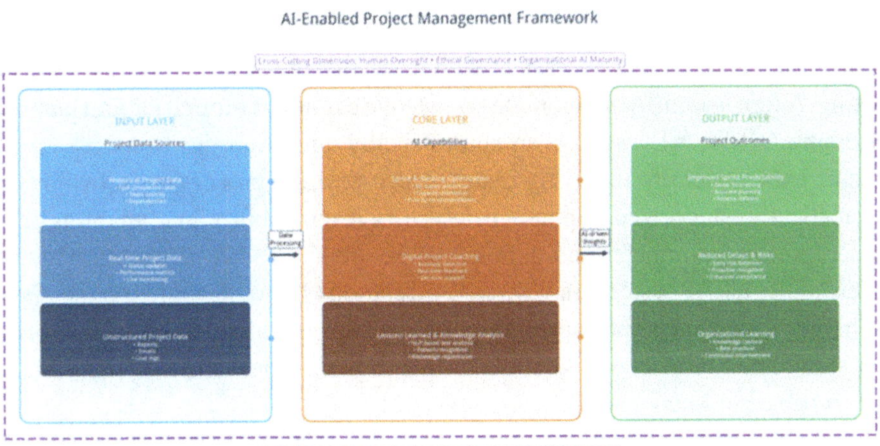

In Scrum-based projects, backlog and sprint optimization represents a key opportunity for AI-driven enhancement. Machine learning algorithms can process historical project data—such as task completion rates, team velocity, dependencies, and bottlenecks—to predict realistic sprint capacities and optimize task prioritization (Elumalai, 2025). AI models can identify recurring inefficiencies, such as repeated delays caused by unclear specifications or interdependencies, and automatically recommend adjustments to backlog priorities or resource allocations. These recommendations, integrated into project management tools like Jira or Trello, allow teams to dynamically adapt sprint plans, reduce bottlenecks, and improve delivery predictability.

In HERMES-based projects, AI tools analyze phase-specific documentation, milestone adherence, and risk registers to provide actionable recommendations for project managers. Predictive models identify critical dependencies, detect early indicators of schedule slippage, and propose targeted risk mitigation strategies, thereby enhancing governance compliance and phase stability.

Digital project coaching constitutes another impactful application of AI (Psyché et al., 2023). Acting as an intelligent assistant, AI-driven coaches monitor ongoing project activities, detect anomalies, and deliver real-time feedback. In Scrum environments, the digital coach can alert the SM when tasks are repeatedly delayed, suggest pairing team members with complementary competencies, or adjust sprint goals based on predictive trends. For HERMES projects, the digital coach highlights deviations from phase plans, visualizes progress against benchmarks, and recommends corrective actions to maintain compliance and momentum. This interactive feedback loop empowers teams to make informed decisions, enhances agility, and cultivates a culture of reflective learning and performance improvement.

AI also transforms lessons learned and organizational knowledge management. Traditionally, post-project reviews rely on manual synthesis of documentation and meetings, often leading to incomplete knowledge capture. Through natural language processing (NLP), AI systems can automatically analyze project reports, emails, and chat logs to identify recurring issues, successes, and process gaps. Insights are systematically categorized by phase, risk type, or responsibility area, enabling cross-project knowledge transfer and actionable recommendations for future planning. For example, an AI system may reveal correlations between limited code review and higher defect rates, prompting procedural adjustments in subsequent sprints. This systematic knowledge retention fosters organizational memory and reduces the recurrence of known issues.

Practical implementation, however, is not without challenges. Data quality, completeness, and standardization remain critical success factors (Sharma et al., 2024). AI effectiveness depends on reliable, comprehensive datasets; thus, disciplined documentation of project activities is essential. User acceptance increases when AI tools are transparent, seamlessly integrated into workflows, and allow human oversight. Ethical concerns—such as explainability, bias mitigation, and accountability—must be addressed through responsible design and deployment practices.

Table 1 presents an integrated overview of AI applications across Scrum and HERMES, outlining their data sources, evaluation metrics, and observed benefits based on applied case studies.

Table 1. Comparative Overview of AI Use Cases in Scrum and HERMES (author's own table).

AI Application	Methodology	Data Inputs	Key Metrics	Observed Benefits
Sprint & Backlog Optimization	Scrum	Task completion rates, team velocity, dependencies, past sprints	Sprint predictability, backlog completion rate, overdue tasks	Improved sprint predictability (+15%), reduced overdue tasks, optimized resource allocation
Phase & Milestone Recommendation	HERMES	Phase reports, milestone adherence, risk registers	Phase adherence, milestone completion, risk mitigation effectiveness	Early delay detection, proactive risk management, enhanced compliance
Digital Project Coaching		Real-time updates, team performance metrics, historical data	Task completion variance, engagement rate, intervention effectiveness	Increased responsiveness, improved prioritization, enhanced decision support
Lessons Learned Analysis		Project reports, emails, chat logs, meeting minutes	Number of recurring issues, repository completeness	Improved process standardization, continuous learning, reduced recurrence of errors

Several case studies illustrate these applications in practice (Hofmann et al., 2020; Karamthulla et al., 2024; Fathi, 2025; Reznikov et al., 2025; Savaş et al., 2025). For example, a software development firm implemented an AI-enhanced Jira integration that predicted task durations and suggested resource adjustments, resulting in a 15% increase in sprint predictability and fewer overdue tasks. Teams reported higher satisfaction and confidence in planning accuracy. In a public sector HERMES project, AI-based phase analysis provided early warnings about schedule deviations and compliance risks. Automated cross-project learning identified recurring weaknesses and informed governance improvements (Malhotra & Meena, 2024).

Implementation of AI tools—such as machine learning–based prediction engines, NLP-driven text analysis, recommendation systems for prioritization, and intelligent assistants for coaching—requires continuous human-centered calibration and alignment with organizational AI maturity (Samuel et al., 2025). Transparency, explainability, and accountability are essential to ensure trust while maintaining human oversight.

These practical experiences establish a foundation for systematic assessment, which the next section details through a structured methodological and evaluative framework. While the previous section illustrated practical applications of AI in project management through case studies and real-world examples, a structured evaluation is essential to rigorously assess their effectiveness. By integrating both quantitative metrics and qualitative feedback, organizations can ensure AI interventions align with strategic objectives, improve operational outcomes, and support continuous learning across Scrum and HERMES environments (Chukwunweike & Aro, 2024).

METHODOLOGY AND EVALUATION

Evaluating the effectiveness of AI in project management requires a robust, mixed-method framework that captures both quantitative and qualitative dimensions of project performance. The goal of this evaluation process is to assess how AI applications—such as sprint and backlog optimization, digital coaching, and lessons learned analytics—impact project outcomes, team efficiency, and organizational learning. The approach integrates historical data analysis, real-time monitoring, and stakeholder feedback to ensure a holistic understanding of AI contributions.

The first step involves defining measurable performance metrics.

For Scrum projects, key indicators include sprint predictability, backlog completion rate, team velocity, and task delay frequency. These metrics assess the reliability and value of AI-assisted predictions and their influence on team performance.

For HERMES projects, phase adherence, milestone completion rate, compliance with governance standards, and risk mitigation effectiveness are central.

Beyond these quantitative measures, qualitative evaluations—via interviews, surveys, and focus groups—capture user perceptions of AI's usefulness, interpretability, and influence on decision-making.

Together, these data sources form the foundation for a balanced, evidence-based evaluation.

Figure 2 illustrates the evaluation framework, summarizing the primary dimensions, quantitative metrics, qualitative methods, AI application focus, and expected outcomes for assessing AI integration in both Scrum and HERMES projects.

Figure 2. AI Evaluation Methodology and Metrics Overview.

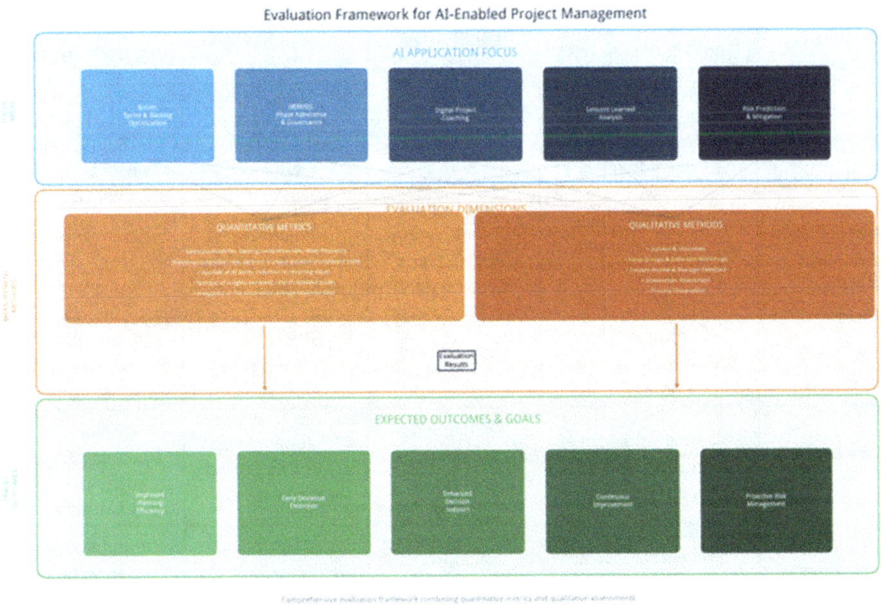

Data collection and preprocessing are critical components of this methodology. Historical project data are extracted from management platforms such as Jira, Confluence, or SharePoint, combined with risk logs, reports, and feedback repositories. To ensure reliability, data undergo cleaning, normalization, and anonymization. Real-time data streams from AI dashboards complement this retrospective data, enabling longitudinal analysis of project dynamics and emerging risks.

The following framework summarizes the primary dimensions, metrics, and expected outcomes for evaluating AI integration across both Scrum and HERMES (see Table 2).

Table 2. Framework for Evaluating AI Integration in Project Management (author's own table).

Evaluation Dimension	Quantitative Metrics	Qualitative Methods	AI Application Focus	Expected Outcome
Sprint & Backlog Optimization (Scrum)	Sprint predictability, backlog completion rate, delay frequency	Scrum Master surveys, retrospective interviews	Machine learning–based workload prediction	Improved planning efficiency and sprint accuracy
Phase Adherence & Governance (HERMES)	Milestone completion rate, variance in phase duration, compliance index	Stakeholder focus groups, phase review reports	Predictive analytics for phase risk detection	Early deviation detection, enhanced compliance
Digital Project Coaching	Number of AI alerts, reduction in recurring issues	Usability and trust surveys	NLP-driven performance monitoring	Strengthened decision support and engagement
Lessons Learned Analysis	Number of insights extracted, rate of repeated issues	Reflection workshops, qualitative content review	NLP-based text mining of project documentation	Continuous improvement and organizational learning
Risk Prediction & Mitigation	Frequency of risk occurrence, average response time	Manager feedback on alerts	Predictive anomaly detection	Proactive risk management and resource optimization

The integration of these evaluation mechanisms ensures that AI tools enhance rather than disrupt project workflows. In Scrum contexts, AI modules are embedded in sprint planning, backlog refinement, and retrospectives; in HERMES, they support milestone tracking, documentation review, and governance reporting. Predictive models provide early warning signals and actionable recommendations, while qualitative assessments capture user trust and acceptance.

Quantitative results are benchmarked against historical baselines or control projects lacking AI support. Metrics such as reduction in overdue tasks, improved milestone adherence, and enhanced risk mitigation are statistically analyzed to quantify gains. Meanwhile, qualitative insights reveal human factors influencing adoption—such as perceived transparency, trust, or cognitive workload (Rauscher, 2024). This dual evaluation enables a multidimensional understanding of AI impact, addressing both technical and organizational performance.

Iterative learning remains integral to this methodology. Feedback loops between AI outputs and project outcomes continuously refine model accuracy, contextual relevance, and decision quality. Lessons from each evaluation cycle update the AI's training data, reinforcing a sustainable, evolving integration strategy.

Finally, ethical and governance aspects are embedded in the evaluative process. Transparency in recommendations, explainability of algorithms, and strict compliance with data protection standards ensure accountability. Bias detection mechanisms and human oversight protocols safeguard against unintended consequences.

Through this structured and ethically grounded evaluation framework, organizations can measure the tangible and intangible value of AI in project management and drive evidence-based continuous improvement across both agile and structured methodologies.

Building on the structured methodologies and evaluation frameworks outlined in the previous section, it becomes evident that the successful integration of AI into project management extends beyond technical implementation and performance measurement. While methodology and evaluation provide the tools to quantify AI's impact on sprint predictability, phase adherence, and lessons learned, practical adoption also encounters complex organizational, ethical, and human-centered considerations. Effective AI-supported project management requires not only reliable models and metrics but also high-quality, contextually meaningful data, responsible ethical practices, and collaborative human-AI interaction. Moreover, the evolution of AI technologies points toward new opportunities and challenges that demand forward-looking strategies to ensure sustainable, trustworthy, and value-driven implementation.

The following section therefore shifts focus from methodology and quantitative assessment to the broader landscape of data challenges, ethical implications, human-AI collaboration, and future directions, providing a holistic perspective on the practical, social, and strategic dimensions of AI adoption in Scrum and HERMES projects.

DATA CHALLENGES, ETHICAL IMPLICATIONS, HUMAN-AI COLLABORATION, AND FUTURE DIRECTIONS IN AI-SUPPORTED PROJECT MANAGEMENT

(1) Data Challenges

One of the primary prerequisites for successful AI integration in project management lies in the availability, quality, and structure of data. In contemporary project environments, data is generated across a multitude of sources, including task management tools, time-tracking systems, collaboration platforms, emails, and documentation repositories. This heterogeneity poses a critical challenge: AI algorithms, particularly machine learning models, rely on large, structured, and accurate datasets to produce reliable predictions and actionable insights. Inconsistent naming conventions, fragmented storage locations, and missing historical records significantly limit the predictive power of AI systems. For instance, incomplete sprint data in agile projects can lead to erroneous forecasts of team velocity, while gaps in milestone tracking in HERMES projects can compromise risk assessment and compliance analysis.

Furthermore, data integrity is essential to prevent biased or misleading AI outputs. Biases in historical project records—such as systematically underreported delays or selective recording of resource utilization—can be perpetuated and amplified by AI models. Addressing these challenges requires comprehensive data governance strategies. Standardizing data formats, establishing consistent taxonomies for project artifacts, and implementing quality assurance protocols are fundamental steps to ensure that AI models learn from accurate, representative information. Additionally, privacy and security considerations must be incorporated, particularly when datasets include sensitive employee or organizational information. Techniques such as anonymization, pseudonymization, and secure data storage frameworks are critical to meet regulatory requirements while enabling meaningful AI analysis.

Another key aspect is the dynamic nature of project data. Unlike static datasets, project environments generate continuous streams of information reflecting evolving team performance, task completion, and risk exposure. AI systems must therefore support real-time data ingestion and adaptive learning mechanisms to remain effective. This presents computational and organizational challenges, as continuous integration of live data demands robust IT infrastructure, effective data pipelines, and monitoring mechanisms to detect inconsistencies or anomalies. Projects with limited digital maturity may struggle to implement such infrastructure, highlighting the need for tailored solutions that balance data availability, computational resources, and organizational readiness.

Beyond technical aspects, data interpretation is inherently context-dependent. Raw metrics such as task completion time or milestone variance may carry different implications depending on team structure, project complexity, or organizational culture. AI systems that do not incorporate contextual variables risk generating recommendations that are technically accurate but practically misleading. Incorporating contextual metadata—such as team experience, workload distribution, or stakeholder involvement—enables models to produce more nuanced insights. Developing frameworks for integrating quantitative metrics with qualitative contextual indicators is therefore critical for robust AI-assisted project management.

(2) Ethical Implications

The deployment of AI in project management introduces profound ethical considerations, particularly in areas of fairness, transparency, accountability, and the distribution of decision-making authority. AI systems often influence decisions regarding task prioritization, resource allocation, risk mitigation, and performance evaluation. If unchecked, algorithmic outputs can inadvertently perpetuate historical biases or create inequitable treatment of team members. For example, models trained on past assignments may reinforce patterns where specific employees are repeatedly allocated low-complexity tasks, inadvertently limiting professional growth and career opportunities. Addressing these risks requires embedding fairness principles directly into model design, ensuring that AI outputs are auditable and can be scrutinized for potential bias.

Transparency and explainability constitute another core ethical dimension. Project stakeholders, including managers, team members, and executives, must understand the rationale behind AI recommendations. Black-box models that provide outputs without explanatory context erode trust and reduce adoption. Explainable AI (XAI) techniques, such as visual reasoning pathways, confidence intervals, and feature importance analysis, allow users to assess why certain recommendations are generated (Azeroual, 2025a). Transparent communication is particularly crucial in high-stakes projects where decisions have financial, operational, or reputational implications.

Accountability mechanisms must also be clearly defined. The integration of AI into decision-making does not absolve human project managers from responsibility. Organizations need to establish clear governance structures specifying who is ultimately responsible for decisions influenced by AI insights. Maintaining human oversight ensures that ethical principles, organizational values, and legal requirements remain central to project management. Ethical AI frameworks should also include mechanisms for reporting and rectifying undesirable outcomes, such as the identification of unfair task allocations or biased risk predictions.

Moreover, AI deployment in project management raises concerns about surveillance and autonomy. Continuous monitoring of team performance, communication patterns, and behavioral data can enhance project efficiency but may also impinge on employee privacy. Organizations must balance the benefits of AI-assisted oversight with respect for individual autonomy and ethical treatment. Transparent policies, informed consent, and selective data collection aligned with project objectives help mitigate these concerns, fostering a culture of trust and collaboration.

(3) Human-AI Collaboration

Human-AI collaboration represents the linchpin of responsible AI integration in project management. AI systems excel in analyzing vast amounts of data, identifying patterns, and providing predictive insights; however, human intuition, creativity, and contextual understanding remain indispensable. The optimal approach emphasizes a partnership where AI augments rather than replaces human decision-making. In Scrum projects, AI can recommend backlog prioritization or predict sprint risks, while the SM evaluates these insights in light of team dynamics, capacity constraints, and stakeholder expectations. Similarly, in HERMES-based projects, AI may highlight potential compliance deviations or suggest mitigation strategies, but human leaders retain ultimate authority over project governance and strategic decisions.

Designing effective human-AI collaboration requires attention to usability, interpretability, and cognitive load. AI tools must present recommendations in ways that are actionable and easily understandable, avoiding overwhelming users with excessive or poorly contextualized information. Interactive dashboards, real-time alerts, and scenario simulation interfaces enhance engagement, allowing project teams to explore alternatives, test assumptions, and validate AI-driven suggestions. Furthermore, collaborative design involving end users ensures that AI functionalities align with real-world workflows and organizational practices.

Trust is a central factor in successful human-AI interaction. Teams are more likely to rely on AI insights when they perceive the system as reliable, explainable, and aligned with organizational values. Strategies to foster trust include iterative deployment with pilot projects, continuous feedback mechanisms, and adaptive learning where AI models improve in response to user inputs. Additionally, promoting AI literacy among project professionals is critical. Training programs that explain AI capabilities, limitations, and ethical considerations empower teams to engage critically with AI systems, enhancing both effectiveness and accountability.

A related aspect is the human–AI balance in decision autonomy. Too much automation risks diminishing human judgment, while too little reduces the efficiency gains AI can offer. Hybrid models, where AI generates options and humans retain veto power or final decision authority, have shown promising results in balancing efficiency with responsibility. This collaborative intelligence model allows organizations to harness computational power while preserving creativity, ethical reasoning, and nuanced decision-making that machines alone cannot replicate.

(4) Future Directions

The trajectory of AI in project management is oriented toward increasingly sophisticated, integrated, and adaptive systems. Advances in NLP and large language models (LLMs) enable conversational interaction with project data, allowing managers to query systems, summarize meetings, and extract actionable insights with minimal manual effort (Azeroual, 2025b). Future AI platforms are likely to provide contextualized, scenario-based recommendations that consider dependencies, resource constraints, risk profiles, and organizational priorities simultaneously.

Predictive and prescriptive analytics will become more deeply embedded into continuous project monitoring, enabling proactive rather than reactive management. For example, AI could dynamically adjust sprint plans in response to emerging bottlenecks or automatically redistribute resources across interdependent HERMES phases based on risk exposure. Integration with digital twins of projects—virtual representations of schedules, workflows, and resources—could allow managers to simulate outcomes, test decisions, and optimize strategies before implementation. This would enhance foresight, reduce uncertainty, and support data-driven decision-making at both operational and strategic levels.

AI-enabled collaboration ecosystems are another promising development. Distributed teams, often spanning multiple geographies and time zones, can benefit from intelligent coordination platforms that optimize communication, detect emerging conflicts, and propose team configurations based on skills, availability, and workload. Combining AI with augmented and virtual reality tools may facilitate immersive project spaces where collaborative planning, task execution, and performance monitoring occur in real time. In regulated environments such as public sector HERMES projects, AI could automate documentation, compliance tracking, and reporting, freeing human leaders to focus on strategic oversight and stakeholder engagement.

Ethical AI will continue to shape the evolution of project management tools. Researchers and practitioners are increasingly focusing on fairness, accountability, and explainability as non-negotiable design principles. Regulatory frameworks such as the EU AI Act will influence implementation practices, requiring organizations to adopt compliance-oriented AI architectures from the outset. Interdisciplinary collaboration between computer science, organizational psychology, and ethics will be essential to develop AI systems that are both technologically sophisticated and socially responsible.

Education and research will play a critical role in shaping the next generation of AI-enhanced project management. Academic programs integrating AI literacy, ethical reasoning, and systems thinking will equip project professionals with the skills to leverage AI effectively. Longitudinal empirical studies and comparative research across methodologies, industries, and organizational contexts will provide evidence-based guidance on AI effectiveness, adoption strategies, and governance frameworks. These insights will inform best practices, maturity models, and standardized evaluation methodologies, enabling organizations to implement AI in ways that maximize benefits while mitigating risks.

Finally, AI will increasingly facilitate strategic portfolio management, supporting decision-making across multiple projects. By analyzing interdependencies, resource utilization, and risk profiles, AI can recommend optimal combinations of projects, identify potential conflicts, and suggest allocation strategies that enhance organizational performance. Combined with predictive insights at the micro (task) and macro (portfolio) levels, AI will enable project management to evolve into a proactive, adaptive, and intelligence-driven discipline where human judgment, creativity, and leadership are continuously augmented by data-driven guidance.

Considering the insights from the examination of data challenges, ethical implications, and human-AI collaboration, it becomes evident that integrating AI into project management extends beyond technical implementation and represents a multidimensional organizational transformation. The analysis has emphasized the necessity of high-quality data, transparent and accountable AI systems, and the careful design of AI tools that enhance rather than replace human judgment. Additionally, the exploration of future directions illustrates how emerging technologies—such as predictive analytics, natural language processing, and intelligent digital assistants—can significantly improve planning, execution, and knowledge management within project teams.

These considerations provide a foundation for reflecting on the broader impact of AI in project management. The following summary consolidates the key findings, highlighting the practical benefits, strategic implications, and evolving role of AI as a supportive partner to human expertise. It further outlines how organizations can leverage AI to enhance efficiency, promote adaptive decision-making, and ensure ethically responsible project management practices.

SUMMARY AND OUTLOOK

AI has emerged as a transformative force in contemporary project management, fundamentally reshaping the application of both Scrum and HERMES methodologies. The evidence and analysis presented throughout this chapter highlight that AI delivers substantial benefits across multiple dimensions, including enhanced planning accuracy, data-informed decision-making, optimized resource allocation, and strengthened organizational learning. Beyond mere technological adoption, these advancements signify a shift toward data-driven, adaptive, and collaborative project practices, redefining traditional roles, responsibilities, and workflows.

AI technologies function as complementary enablers, augmenting rather than replacing established project management frameworks. In agile contexts, predictive analytics and real-time insights enhance sprint planning, backlog prioritization, and resource distribution, reducing uncertainty and supporting evidence-based decision-making. Within structured methodologies such as HERMES, AI facilitates governance and compliance by monitoring milestones, evaluating phase progress, and forecasting risks. These capabilities allow project teams to leverage both historical and real-time data while maintaining human oversight, accountability, and decision authority.

The effective deployment of AI requires more than the technical tools themselves; it necessitates organizational readiness, data integrity, and a culture of collaboration. Without standardized workflows, consistent data practices, and transparent processes, AI systems cannot achieve their full potential. Organizations must invest in professional training, governance structures, and continuous feedback mechanisms to ensure responsible, sustainable, and effective adoption. When implemented thoughtfully, AI becomes a strategic asset that aligns with organizational objectives, reinforces human decision-making, and promotes efficiency without diminishing professional judgment.

Knowledge management and lessons learned processes benefit particularly from AI-driven analysis. Automated extraction, categorization, and synthesis of insights from project documentation, communications, and performance metrics enable organizations to identify recurring patterns, best practices, and potential risks. By structuring these insights into centralized knowledge repositories, AI supports continuous learning, transforming prior projects into actionable intelligence that informs future initiatives. This creates a learning ecosystem where human expertise and AI collaboratively enhance planning, execution, and risk management.

Despite its potential, AI integration in project management continues to face challenges related to bias, transparency, explainability, and accountability. Trust and user acceptance are critical; AI outputs must be interpretable and designed to support, not replace, human judgment. The equilibrium between automation and human oversight will ultimately define whether AI contributes to sustainable, ethical, and effective project management practices.

Looking forward, AI is poised to further reshape project management through advances in natural language processing, conversational agents, and predictive analytics. Managers will increasingly interact with intelligent systems through intuitive interfaces, obtaining contextualized insights in real time. AI will also play a more strategic role, supporting portfolio management by identifying optimal project combinations, resource allocation strategies, and cross-project synergies. Furthermore, emerging applications in social analytics and sentiment analysis have the potential to enhance team coordination, conflict detection, and organizational performance, particularly in distributed or cross-functional project environments.

Future research and practice must continue to address explainability, fairness, and governance frameworks to ensure responsible AI adoption. The development of standardized evaluation methodologies, consistent performance metrics, and maturity models will enable organizations to assess AI effectiveness systematically, identify implementation gaps, and plan targeted interventions for continuous improvement. By adopting such comprehensive evaluation approaches, organizations can ensure that AI contributes meaningfully to both operational efficiency and strategic decision-making.

Ultimately, AI will enable project managers to concentrate on creativity, leadership, and stakeholder engagement while relying on intelligent systems for analytical, repetitive, and data-intensive tasks. The project manager of the future will orchestrate a dynamic partnership between human and AI, integrating strategic insight with data-driven guidance. Educational programs and professional training must evolve to equip future leaders with competencies essential for thriving in AI-enhanced project environments, including data literacy, ethical awareness, systems thinking, and interdisciplinary collaboration.

In conclusion, the integration of AI into project management represents a technological, organizational, and cultural evolution. When adopted responsibly, AI enhances efficiency, transparency, and continuous learning while reinforcing human decision-making and strategic oversight. The path forward lies in aligning AI systems with organizational purpose, collective values, and adaptive workflows, ultimately creating augmented project ecosystems in which human and AI collaborate seamlessly to achieve superior outcomes.

REFERENCES

Azeroual, O. (2025a) Beyond Black Boxes: Adaptive XAI for Dynamic Data Pipelines. In *Proceedings of the 17th International Joint Conference on Knowledge Discovery, Knowledge Engineering and Knowledge Management* - (Volume 2), p.428-437. DOI: 10.5220/0013736100004000

Azeroual, O. (2025b). Streamlining Research Information Management with Large Language Models: Automation, Analysis, and User-Centric Solutions. in *Proceedings of the 10th International Conference on Big Data Analytics (ICBDA2025),* Nanyang Technological University, Singapore, pp. 281-287, IEEE. DOI: 10.1109/ICBDA65366.2025.11211236

Bandara, R. B. M. T., & Wickramarachchi, R. (2025). Developing an AI Readiness Model for Software Project Management: A Thematic Analysis. In *2025 5th International Conference on Advanced Research in Computing (ICARC)* (pp. 1-6). IEEE. DOI: 10.1109/ICARC64760.2025.10962923

Chukwunweike, J., & Aro, O. E. (2024). Implementing agile management practices in the era of digital transformation. *World Journal of Advanced Research and Reviews, 24*(1), 2223–2242. DOI: 10.30574/wjarr.2024.24.1.3253

Ekambaram, A., Vågbø, P. C., & van der Leyen, B. S. (2022). The role of machine learning in managing uncertainty in projects–A view on early warning systems. In *European Conference on Management, Leadership & Governance* (pp. 536-XV). Academic Conferences International Limited. DOI: 10.34190/ecmlg.18.1.932

Ellefsen, A. P. T., Oleśków-Szłapka, J., Pawłowski, G., & Toboła, A. (2019). Striving for excellence in AI implementation: AI maturity model framework and preliminary research results. *LogForum, 15*(3).

Elumalai, D. (2025). Leveraging AI and Machine Learning to Improve Agile Backlog Prioritization. *The American Journal of Engineering and Technology*, *7*(05), 211–218. DOI: 10.37547/tajet/Volume07Issue05-21

Fathi, N. (2025). *The Role of AI in Enhancing Project Success Rate in Project Management* (Doctoral dissertation, Dublin, National College of Ireland).

Felemban, H., Sohail, M., & Ruikar, K. (2024). Exploring the readiness of organisations to adopt artificial intelligence. *Buildings (Basel, Switzerland)*, *14*(8), 2460. DOI: 10.3390/buildings14082460

HERMES Foundation. (2022). [– Method overview. https://www.hermes.admin.ch/en/project-management/method-overview.html]. *Hermes*, *5*, •••.

Hidalgo, E. S. (2019). Adapting the scrum framework for agile project management in science: Case study of a distributed research initiative. *Heliyon, 5*(3), e01447. DOI: 10.1016/j.heliyon.2019.e01447 PMID: 30976706

Hofmann, P., Jöhnk, J., Protschky, D., & Urbach, N. (2020, March). Developing Purposeful AI Use Cases-A Structured Method and Its Application in Project Management. In *Wirtschaftsinformatik (zentrale tracks)* (pp. 33-49). DOI: 10.30844/wi_2020_a3-hofmann

Karamthulla, M. J., Malaiyappan, J. N. A., Muthusubramanian, M., & Tillu, R. (2024). From theory to practice: Implementing AI technologies in project management. *International Journal for Multidisciplinary Research, 6*(2), 1–11.

Kerzner, H. (2025). *Project management: a systems approach to planning, scheduling, and controlling*. John Wiley & Sons.

Kumari, M., Yamang, C., & Saxena, R. S. D. A. (2023). Artificial Intelligence in Project Management: Opportunities, Challenges, and Future Prospects. *Artificial Intelligence, 16*(4).

Li, H., Yazdi, M., Nedjati, A., Moradi, R., Adumene, S., Dao, U., & Garg, H. (2024). Harnessing AI for project risk management: a paradigm shift. In *Progressive decision-making tools and applications in project and operation management: Approaches, case studies, multi-criteria decision-making, multi-objective decision-making, decision under uncertainty* (pp. 253–272). Springer Nature Switzerland. DOI: 10.1007/978-3-031-51719-8_16

Linke, K. (2019). Traditional and agile management approaches. In *12th ILERA European Congress,* Düsseldorf, Deutschland.

Malhotra, R., & Meena, S. (2024). Empirical validation of machine learning techniques for heterogeneous cross-project change prediction and within-project change prediction. *Journal of Computational Science, 76*, 102230. DOI: 10.1016/j.jocs.2024.102230

Morris, P. (2013). Reconstructing project management reprised: A knowledge perspective. *Project Management Journal, 44*(5), 6–23. DOI: 10.1002/pmj.21369

Nabeel, M. Z. (2024). AI-enhanced project management systems for optimizing resource allocation and risk mitigation: Leveraging big data analysis to predict project outcomes and improve decision-making processes in complex projects. *Asian Journal of Multidisciplinary Research & Review, 5*(5), 53–65. DOI: 10.55662/AJMRR.2024.5502

Nenni, M. E., De Felice, F., De Luca, C., & Forcina, A. (2025). How artificial intelligence will transform project management in the age of digitization: A systematic literature review. *Management Review Quarterly*, *75*(2), 1669–1716. DOI: 10.1007/s11301-024-00418-z

Pérez-Castillo, Y. J., Orantes-Jiménez, S. D., & Letelier-Torres, P. O. (2024). A systematic literature review on machine learning applications for agile project management. *Ingeniería, Investigación y Tecnología*, *25*(3), 1–11. DOI: 10.22201/fi.25940732e.2024.25.3.017

Project Management Institute. (2021). *Pulse of the Profession 2021: The Future of Work*. PMI.

Psyché, V., Tremblay, D. G., Miladi, F., & Yagoubi, A. (2023). A competency framework for training of AI projects managers in the digital and AI Era. *Open Journal of Social Sciences*, *11*(5), 537–560. DOI: 10.4236/jss.2023.115032

Rauscher, K. (2024). *Successful Strategies Government Executive Stakeholders Use to Mitigate Higher Project Costs and User Adoption Failure Rates* (Doctoral dissertation, Walden University).

Reznikov, R. (2025). Enhancing Project Management Success through Artificial Intelligence. *International Journal of Multidisciplinary Research and Growth Evaluation*, *6*(1), 1036–1046. DOI: 10.54660/.IJMRGE.2025.6.1.1036-1046

Salimimoghadam, S., Ghanbaripour, A. N., Tumpa, R. J., Kamel Rahimi, A., Golmoradi, M., Rashidian, S., & Skitmore, M. (2025). The Rise of Artificial Intelligence in Project Management: A Systematic Literature Review of Current Opportunities, Enablers, and Barriers. *Buildings (Basel, Switzerland)*, *15*(7), 1130. DOI: 10.3390/buildings15071130

Samuel, S., Meilani, Y. F. C. P., Wanasida, A. S., & Napitupulu, P. E. (2025). *Human Capital in The AI Era*. Penerbit NEM.

Savaş, S. (2025). Artificial intelligence in construction project management: Trends, challenges and future directions. *Journal of Design for Resilience in Architecture and Planning*, *6*(2), 221–238. DOI: 10.47818/DRArch.2025.v6i2165

Schär, B., Jüngling, S., & Thönssen, B. (2015). Towards an agile requirements engineering process combining HERMES 5 and SCRUM. In *2015 International Conference on Enterprise Systems (ES)* (pp. 98-109). IEEE. DOI: 10.1109/ES.2015.17

Sharma, K., Kumar, P., & Özen, E. (2024). Ethical Considerations in Data Analytics: Challenges, Principles, and Best Practices. In *Data Alchemy in the Insurance Industry: The Transformative Power of Big Data Analytics* (pp. 41-48). Emerald Publishing Limited.

Sharma, S., & Arjunan, T. (2023). Natural language processing for detecting anomalies and intrusions in unstructured cybersecurity data. *International Journal of Information and Cybersecurity*, *7*(12), 1–24.

Sutherland, J., & Schwaber, K. (2013). The scrum guide. *The definitive guide to scrum: The rules of the game. Scrum. org, 268*, 19.

Voutama, A. V. (2025). Generative Artificial Intelligence in Agile Product Management: Optimizing Task Coordination and Team Efficiency in Software Development. *The Indonesian Journal of Computer Science*, *14*(3).

Xiao, L., Madanian, S., Li, W., & Xiao, Y. (2023). Enhancing resource allocation in IT projects: the potentials of deep learning-based recommendation systems and data-driven approaches. In *Australasian Conference on Data Science and Machine Learning* (pp. 226-238). Singapore: Springer Nature Singapore.

Chapter 10
Tooling Evaluations and Reference Architectures for AI-Augmented Agile Project Management:
Bridging Practice and Governance in Modern Delivery Organizations

Ranjit Singha
http://orcid.org/0000-0002-3541-8752
Christ University, India

Surjit Singha
http://orcid.org/0000-0002-5730-8677
Kristu Jayanti University, India

Shruti Jose
http://orcid.org/0000-0003-3139-2505
Christ University, India

V. Muthu Ruben
http://orcid.org/0009-0006-7723-8596
Christ University, India

Alphonsa Diana Haokip
http://orcid.org/0000-0003-2578-0114
Don Bosco College, Maram, India

DOI: 10.4018/979-8-3373-6851-1.ch010

ABSTRACT

Agile and DevOps practices are central to modern delivery organizations, yet the rapid proliferation of AI-augmented project management tools has created fragmented ecosystems that weaken transparency, governance, and value realization. Although AI copilots, predictive analytics, intelligent backlog management, and autonomous agents promise improved decision-making and delivery performance, their adoption has outpaced coherent evaluation frameworks and governance-aligned architectures. This chapter addresses this gap by proposing a structured approach to evaluating AI-powered Agile tools and designing reference architectures that support responsible human–AI collaboration. Drawing on multi-criteria decision-making models, Agile and DevOps metrics, AI capability theory, and MLOps/LLMOps principles, the chapter integrates technical, organizational, and ethical dimensions. Cross-industry cases illustrate how governance-by-design enhances agility, value creation, and trust in AI-augmented Agile delivery.

INTRODUCTION

Agile and DevOps methodologies have become central to how contemporary delivery organizations navigate accelerating technological change, market volatility, and rising stakeholder expectations. Developed as alternatives to rigid, plan-driven project management approaches, Agile frameworks emphasize adaptability, iterative value delivery, and close collaboration among cross-functional teams and customers (Beck et al., 2001; Highsmith, 2009). DevOps extends these principles by integrating development and operations through automation, continuous integration, and continuous delivery, enabling faster, more reliable, and more resilient software releases at scale (Humble & Farley, 2010; Kim et al., 2016).

As Agile and DevOps practices expanded from team-level implementations to enterprise-wide operating models, digital tooling emerged as a critical enabler of coordination, transparency, and performance management. Agile lifecycle management platforms, portfolio and program management tools, and value-stream analytics systems now mediate much of the work performed in delivery organizations. These tools generate extensive volumes of operational data related to backlog evolution, sprint execution, deployment frequency, defect rates, and customer feedback, creating data-rich environments well suited for the application of artificial intelligence (AI) and advanced analytics (Forsgren et al., 2018; Dingsøyr et al., 2018).

In recent years, AI-powered capabilities have rapidly permeated Agile and DevOps tooling ecosystems. Intelligent backlog refinement, automated sprint forecasting, AI copilots for planning and retrospectives, predictive risk-sensing dashboards, and generative analytics are increasingly promoted as mechanisms for improving delivery predictability, decision quality, and managerial oversight. Leveraging machine learning, natural language processing, and large language models, these tools aim to augment human judgment by identifying patterns across historical delivery data, synthesizing unstructured information, and generating real-time recommendations that exceed unaided human cognitive capacity (Amershi et al., 2019; Rai et al., 2020). For delivery leaders operating under heightened complexity and time pressure, such capabilities promise efficiency, scalability, and improved strategic alignment.

However, the rapid diffusion of AI into Agile tooling environments has also introduced substantial challenges. Tooling ecosystems are frequently assembled in an ad hoc manner, driven by vendor offerings, localized team preferences, or narrowly defined productivity goals rather than coherent architectural or governance strategies. The result is often fragmented toolchains characterized by limited interoperability, inconsistent metrics, and opaque data flows. When AI components are embedded within such fragmented environments, their outputs become difficult to interpret, validate, or govern, undermining both trust and effectiveness (Doshi-Velez & Kim, 2017; Benbya et al., 2020).

These challenges are further amplified as AI-driven recommendations increasingly influence high-impact decisions related to prioritization, resource allocation, delivery commitments, and risk management. In the absence of robust governance mechanisms, AI systems may reinforce existing biases, obscure accountability, or conflict with regulatory and ethical obligations. Issues of explainability, auditability, data provenance, and human oversight are particularly salient in regulated sectors such as healthcare, finance, and the public sector, but are equally relevant in private-sector organizations seeking to preserve Agile values of transparency, autonomy, and team empowerment (Floridi et al., 2018; Raji et al., 2020).

From a scholarly perspective, research on AI in software development and project management has expanded rapidly but remains fragmented across disciplines. Much of the literature focuses on algorithmic techniques, productivity effects, or isolated aspects of human–AI interaction, with limited attention to how AI-enabled tools should be systematically evaluated, architecturally integrated, and governed within complex delivery ecosystems. Practitioner-oriented guidance similarly tends to be tool-centric and vendor-driven, often overlooking the need for coherent evaluation frameworks and reference architectures capable of supporting sustainable, large-scale implementation (Tarafdar et al., 2019; Benbya et al., 2020). This disconnect creates uncertainty for decision-makers attempting to navigate vendor claims, balance innovation with compliance, and align AI adoption with Agile delivery principles.

This chapter addresses this gap by examining AI-augmented Agile tooling through a socio-technical and governance-oriented lens. Rather than treating AI as a standalone enhancement, the chapter conceptualizes AI-powered Agile tooling as an integrated system that must be evaluated, designed, and governed holistically. It advances three interrelated contributions. First, it develops a conceptual framework explaining how AI-powered tooling, Agile delivery processes, governance mechanisms, and organizational outcomes interact dynamically, emphasizing that AI influences performance indirectly through its alignment with human judgment and institutional structures. Second, it proposes a multi-criteria evaluation framework that enables organizations to assess AI-powered Agile tools across delivery performance, explainability, architectural fit, governance readiness, and adoption effort. Third, it introduces governance-aligned reference architectures that demonstrate how AI capabilities, MLOps/LLMOps pipelines, and human-in-the-loop oversight can be integrated into Agile environments in a modular, transparent, and evolution-ready manner.

To guide the reader, the chapter is structured to progress from conceptual foundations to applied insights. It begins with theoretical grounding in socio-technical systems theory, dynamic capabilities, technology acceptance, and Responsible AI governance, followed by the development of a conceptual framework for AI-augmented Agile delivery. The analysis then advances toward application through a structured tooling evaluation framework, a consolidated discussion of AI capabilities and value creation, and a dedicated examination of human–machine collaboration. Subsequent sections present governance-aligned reference architectures, illustrative cross-industry cases, and common risks and anti-patterns. The chapter concludes by synthesizing findings across core project management domains and offering recommendations, managerial and policy implications, and directions for future research. This structure is intended to support both scholarly rigor and practical usability while enhancing clarity, coherence, and evaluability.

Research Questions

Guided by the need to move beyond tool-centric and purely technical perspectives on artificial intelligence adoption in Agile and DevOps environments, this chapter is structured around the following research questions:

RQ1: *How can AI-powered Agile project management tools be systematically evaluated in ways that extend beyond functional performance and cost considerations to include governance readiness, architectural coherence, and human adoption factors?*

RQ2: *How do organizational AI capabilities contribute to value definition, value creation, and value capture across Agile project lifecycles, particularly through their interaction with organizational agility and delivery processes?*

RQ3: *How can governance mechanisms such as explainability, auditability, ethical oversight, and human-in-the-loop controls be embedded into AI-augmented*

Agile tooling without undermining core Agile principles of flexibility, autonomy, and continuous learning?

RQ4: *How should human–AI collaboration be structured within Agile project management contexts to ensure that AI functions as a decision-support partner rather than an autonomous authority, thereby preserving accountability, trust, and team performance?*

BACKGROUND

Over the past two decades, Agile and DevOps practices have fundamentally transformed how organizations design, deliver, and continuously improve digital products and services. This transformation represents a decisive shift away from rigid, plan-driven project management paradigms toward more adaptive, learning-oriented modes of organizing work. Agile methodologies emerged in response to the limitations of traditional waterfall and predictive approaches, which struggled to cope with uncertainty, evolving customer requirements, and the increasing complexity of software-intensive systems. By emphasizing iterative development, customer collaboration, cross-functional teamwork, and rapid feedback cycles, Agile approaches sought to restore responsiveness and learning in project environments characterized by volatility and ambiguity (Beck et al., 2001; Highsmith, 2009).

DevOps subsequently extended this paradigm shift by integrating development and operations functions, breaking down organizational silos and enabling continuous integration, continuous delivery, and automation-driven reliability at scale. Practices such as infrastructure as code, automated testing, and deployment pipelines reframed delivery as an end-to-end value stream rather than a sequence of disconnected handoffs, reinforcing Agile principles while addressing operational stability, scalability, and speed (Humble & Farley, 2010; Kim et al., 2016). As Agile and DevOps matured from team-level practices into enterprise-wide operating models, digital tooling became a critical enabler of coordination, visibility, and performance management across increasingly complex delivery environments.

Early Agile tools were relatively lightweight, primarily supporting task tracking, sprint planning, and basic reporting. Over time, however, these tools evolved into comprehensive delivery platforms incorporating portfolio and product management, value-stream analytics, continuous delivery pipelines, dependency visualization, and real-time performance monitoring. These advances significantly enhanced data availability, transparency, and coordination across multi-team and multi-product environments, enabling organizations to manage large-scale Agile programs and distributed delivery systems more effectively (Forsgren et al., 2018; Dingsøyr et al., 2018). At the same time, this evolution contributed to growing tool fragmentation, as organizations assembled heterogeneous toolchains shaped by team autonomy, vendor-specific ecosystems, legacy constraints, and short-term productivity objectives often without an overarching architectural or governance framework to ensure coherence.

The recent integration of artificial intelligence into Agile and DevOps tooling ecosystems has further intensified this complexity. AI-powered copilots, intelligent backlog refinement systems, predictive forecasting and estimation engines, automated risk-sensing dashboards, and generative analytics tools are now increasingly embedded across the Agile delivery lifecycle. Leveraging advances in machine learning, natural language processing, and large language models, these systems analyze vast volumes of structured and unstructured delivery data such as user stories, code repositories, test results, incident logs, and communication artifacts to surface patterns, predictions, and recommendations that exceed unaided human cognitive capacity (Amershi et al., 2019; Rai et al., 2020).

In principle, AI-augmented tooling promises improved delivery predictability, earlier identification of risks and bottlenecks, reduced cognitive load for teams and leaders, and stronger alignment between strategic objectives and operational execution. By automating routine analysis and synthesizing complex information, AI tools appear well suited to support the fast-paced, data-rich environments characteristic of modern Agile delivery. However, in practice, the adoption of AI-enabled Agile tooling has frequently outpaced organizational readiness, revealing significant structural, architectural, and governance challenges.

Many organizations deploy AI capabilities opportunistically often as bundled enhancements within existing platforms without clearly defined evaluation criteria, architectural coherence, or explicit governance mechanisms. This ad hoc adoption creates multiple interrelated risks that undermine both trust and effectiveness. First, opacity in AI decision-making limits explainability and accountability, particularly when vendors provide limited transparency regarding model logic, training data, assumptions, or performance limitations. Black-box AI systems make it difficult for teams and leaders to understand, challenge, or contextualize recommendations, fostering either blind reliance or outright rejection (Doshi-Velez & Kim, 2017). Second, integration barriers frequently prevent AI insights from being operationalized across the delivery value chain. When AI tools operate in isolation or rely on fragmented data sources, their outputs often fail to meaningfully influence Agile rituals such as sprint planning, backlog refinement, or retrospectives, diminishing their practical impact despite technical sophistication.

Third, governance gaps emerge when AI-driven outputs influence prioritization, resource allocation, risk assessment, or performance evaluation without adequate oversight, auditability, or clearly defined accountability structures. In such contexts, responsibility for AI-influenced decisions becomes diffuse, complicating learning, remediation, and ethical accountability (Floridi et al., 2018). These challenges are especially pronounced in regulated and high-stakes domains such as healthcare, finance, and the public sector, where compliance, traceability, data protection, and ethical responsibility are mandatory rather than discretionary. AI systems lacking explainability, audit trails, or bias monitoring mechanisms may expose organizations to regulatory violations, reputational damage, or stakeholder harm (Raji et al., 2020). However, even in less regulated sectors such as software development, telecommunications, and digital services, uncritical reliance on opaque AI systems can erode core Agile principles by undermining team autonomy, distorting performance metrics, reinforcing historical biases, and increasing dependency on proprietary vendor ecosystems. The long-standing Agile tension between speed and control is thus amplified by AI, which simultaneously accelerates decision-making and magnifies the consequences of error or misalignment.

From an academic perspective, research on Agile tooling, AI adoption, and delivery governance remains fragmented and insufficiently integrated. Studies in software engineering and information systems often focus on algorithmic techniques, predictive accuracy, or automation efficiency, with limited attention to organizational integration and governance implications. Conversely, research on Agile and DevOps emphasizes collaboration, flow, and learning, frequently treating tooling as a neutral enabler rather than as an active socio-technical agent that reshapes decision authority and accountability. Governance and ethical AI scholarship, meanwhile, tends to operate at a high level of abstraction, emphasizing principles, regulations, or societal impacts while offering limited guidance on how these concerns can be operationalized within fast-paced delivery environments (Benbya et al., 2020; Tarafdar et al., 2019). Practitioner-oriented literature similarly prioritizes tool features and implementation tactics, often underplaying architectural coherence, evaluation rigor, and ethical safeguards.

Within this context, reference architectures emerge as a critical organizing mechanism for AI-augmented Agile delivery. Reference architectures provide standardized, reusable models that define core components, integration patterns, data flows, and governance layers, offering guidance without prescribing specific vendors or technologies (ISO/IEC, 2011). Applied to AI-enabled delivery environments, reference architectures help organizations navigate trade-offs between agility and scalability, innovation and compliance, and automation and human oversight. By emphasizing interoperability, modularity, and governance-by-design, they enable organizations to evolve their tooling ecosystems over time while maintaining coherence, transparency, and control.

When combined with systematic tooling evaluation frameworks, reference architectures shift decision-making away from ad hoc procurement toward capability development and long-term resilience. They also provide a shared conceptual language that aligns delivery teams, architects, governance bodies, and leadership, reducing ambiguity and fragmentation in AI adoption efforts. Accordingly, this chapter situates AI-augmented Agile tooling within a broader socio-technical and governance-oriented perspective, conceptualizing AI adoption not merely as a technological enhancement but as an organizational transformation that reshapes decision authority, accountability structures, and performance measurement practices. By grounding tooling evaluation and architectural design in established theory, delivery metrics, and ethical considerations, the chapter seeks to advance a more transparent, trustworthy, and sustainable approach to AI-powered Agile delivery one in which AI's value is realized through deliberate alignment with human judgment, organizational capabilities, and governance frameworks.

THEORETICAL FRAMEWORK

The integration of artificial intelligence into Agile project management environments represents a profound socio-technical transformation rather than a discrete technological enhancement. Understanding this transformation requires theoretical perspectives that explain how AI reshapes interactions among technology, human actors, organizational capabilities, and governance mechanisms. In response to reviewer expectations, this chapter adopts four complementary theoretical lenses Socio-Technical Systems Theory, Dynamic Capabilities Theory, Technology Acceptance and Trust in AI, and Responsible AI and Algorithmic Governance to provide a coherent and integrative foundation for evaluating AI-augmented Agile tooling and designing governance-aligned reference architectures.

Socio-Technical Systems Theory posits that organizational performance emerges from the joint optimization of social subsystems (people, roles, norms, skills) and technical subsystems (tools, processes, infrastructures) rather than from technological change alone (Trist & Bamforth, 1951; Baxter & Sommerville, 2011). This perspective closely aligns with Agile principles that emphasize self-organizing teams, continuous feedback, shared accountability, and adaptive coordination. Within AI-augmented Agile environments, AI-powered tools reconfigure the technical subsystem by embedding algorithmic decision support into activities such as backlog prioritization, sprint planning, forecasting, and risk assessment. However, when AI recommendations are opaque or treated as authoritative, they risk undermining team autonomy, reflective learning, and psychological safety. Socio-technical theory therefore provides the conceptual basis for positioning AI as a **decision-support partner**, reinforcing the need for human-in-the-loop oversight and explainable AI configurations to preserve Agile values and effective collaboration (Amershi et al., 2019).

Dynamic Capabilities Theory explains how organizations sense opportunities, seize resources, and reconfigure capabilities to remain competitive in volatile and uncertain environments (Teece et al., 1997; Teece, 2018). Agile and DevOps practices can be understood as operational manifestations of dynamic capabilities, enabling rapid experimentation, learning, and adaptation. AI-powered tools enhance these capabilities by enabling predictive sensing, anticipatory risk detection, and data-driven prioritization across portfolios and delivery pipelines. However, fragmented tooling ecosystems, proprietary platforms, and vendor lock-in constrain organizations' ability to reconfigure delivery systems over time. From a dynamic capabilities perspective, governance-aligned reference architectures and modular AI integration are essential to institutionalizing adaptability, ensuring that AI capabilities strengthen rather than constrain long-term organizational agility (Benbya et al., 2020).

Technology Acceptance and Trust in AI provide a third critical lens for understanding sustained adoption and effective use of AI-enabled Agile tools. Classical technology acceptance models emphasize perceived usefulness and ease of use as primary drivers of adoption (Davis, 1989), while more recent extensions highlight the central role of trust, perceived risk, and transparency in high-stakes decision contexts (Venkatesh et al., 2016; Rai et al., 2020). In Agile project management, where AI-generated insights increasingly influence commitments, resource allocation, and risk decisions, trust becomes a prerequisite for meaningful use. Explainability, interpretability, and visibility into data sources and model limitations are therefore essential to prevent both automation bias and outright rejection associated with black-box systems (Doshi-Velez & Kim, 2017). This theoretical lens directly informs the chapter's emphasis on explainable AI, calibrated trust, and human oversight within tooling evaluation frameworks.

Finally, Responsible AI and Algorithmic Governance frameworks foreground ethical and institutional considerations, emphasizing principles such as fairness, accountability, transparency, privacy, and human agency (Floridi et al., 2018; OECD, 2019; Raji et al., 2020). These frameworks argue that AI systems must be subject to explicit oversight, bias mitigation, auditability, and continuous monitoring, particularly in environments characterized by rapid iteration, decentralized authority, and high-impact decision-making. Agile delivery contexts amplify these concerns, as AI-driven recommendations can quickly propagate across teams and portfolios. Responsible AI theory therefore underpins the chapter's governance-by-design approach, in which ethical and compliance requirements are embedded directly into tooling architectures, MLOps/LLMOps pipelines, and evaluation criteria rather than treated as external constraints or post hoc controls.

Taken together, these four theoretical perspectives converge on a central insight: AI-augmented Agile delivery systems must be understood and designed as governed socio-technical ecosystems. Sustainable performance emerges not from AI capability alone, but from the alignment of human-centered design, architectural adaptability, trust-oriented adoption, and ethics-by-design. This integrated theoretical foundation informs the chapter's conceptual framework, tooling evaluation model, and reference architectures, providing a robust basis for analyzing how AI can enhance Agile delivery while preserving accountability, transparency, and organizational resilience in both research and practice.

CONCEPTUAL FRAMEWORK

The conceptual framework developed in this chapter explains how artificial intelligence (AI) augments Agile delivery by conceptualizing AI-enabled project management as a governed, multi-layered socio-technical system. Rather than viewing AI as an isolated technological enhancement, the framework positions AI-powered tooling, human decision-making, and governance mechanisms as interdependent elements whose alignment determines delivery effectiveness, organizational agility, and trust. The framework is explicitly designed to support systematic tooling evaluation and the design of governance-aligned reference architectures.

The framework comprises four interrelated layers connected through continuous feedback loops that enable learning, adaptation, and accountability over time.

The first layer, AI-powered tooling capabilities, encompasses intelligent backlog refinement, predictive forecasting and estimation, Agile copilots, risk-sensing dashboards, and generative analytics. These capabilities are enabled by machine learning, natural language processing, and large language models that process both structured and unstructured delivery data, including user stories, code repositories, test results, operational logs, and collaboration artifacts. Consistent with socio-technical principles, AI systems are positioned as augmentative decision-support agents rather than autonomous decision-makers, with their effectiveness contingent on data quality, explainability, transparency, and integration within the broader tooling ecosystem (Amershi et al., 2019; Rai et al., 2020; Benbya et al., 2020).

The second layer, Agile delivery processes, represents the organizational context in which AI-generated insights are interpreted and enacted. Core Agile practices including sprint planning, backlog prioritization, estimation, continuous integration, retrospectives, and portfolio coordination provide the decision arenas where human judgment evaluates, contextualizes, accepts, or rejects AI recommendations. This layer preserves Agile values of decentralization, collaboration, and iterative learning, ensuring that accountability remains with teams and leaders rather than being delegated to algorithms (Beck et al., 2001; Highsmith, 2009; Baxter & Sommerville, 2011).

The third layer, governance and oversight mechanisms, mediates the relationship between AI tooling and Agile practices by embedding control, accountability, and ethical safeguards into delivery systems. This layer includes structured tooling evaluation criteria, data governance policies, model lifecycle management, explainability interfaces, bias monitoring, audit trails, and compliance controls. Governance is conceptualized not as a constraint on agility, but as an enabling design feature that operationalizes Responsible AI principles while maintaining flexibility and speed through human-in-the-loop oversight and transparent decision logic (Floridi et al., 2018; OECD, 2019; Raji et al., 2020).

The interaction of these layers produces delivery and organizational outcomes, forming the fourth layer of the framework. Outcomes include delivery predictability, flow efficiency, earned value and value realization, product quality, stakeholder confidence, and organizational learning. These outcomes are assessed using Agile and DevOps performance metrics, while also accounting for social and behavioral dimensions such as team morale, trust in AI systems, and perceived fairness of algorithmically informed decisions (Forsgren et al., 2018).

Crucially, continuous feedback loops connect outcomes back to tooling capabilities, Agile processes, and governance mechanisms. Performance data, audit findings, and team feedback inform model retraining, process refinement, and governance adjustments, reflecting Dynamic Capabilities Theory's emphasis on sensing, learning, and reconfiguration (Teece, 2018). Through these feedback mechanisms, organizations can adapt AI systems and delivery practices over time without sacrificing accountability or architectural coherence.

Overall, the framework posits that AI-powered tooling influences Agile delivery outcomes indirectly, through its alignment with human-centered processes and governance structures. Misalignment across layers such as opaque AI deployment, weak governance, or rigid control mechanisms reduces effectiveness and increases organizational risk. By making these interdependencies explicit, the framework provides a coherent foundation for evaluating AI-augmented Agile tools, organizing the chapter's findings across project management domains, and designing reference architectures that enable responsible, scalable, and trustworthy AI adoption in Agile delivery environments.

Table 1. Evaluation Framework For AI-Powered Agile Tooling

Evaluation Dimension	**Key Criteria**	**Agile Relevance**	**Governance Implications**
Delivery performance & value	Flow, predictability, EV	Supports iterative delivery	Risk of metric distortion
Explainability & trust	Model transparency	Calibrated trust	Accountability
Scalability & interoperability	APIs, modularity	Enterprise agility	Lock-in risk

continued on following page

Table 1. Continued

Evaluation Dimension	Key Criteria	Agile Relevance	Governance Implications
Governance & compliance	Auditability, bias	Responsible AI	Regulatory readiness
Adoption & org impact	Usability, stress	Team autonomy	Change resistance

Table 1 presents a multi-criteria framework for evaluating AI-powered Agile tooling beyond functional performance. It highlights how delivery metrics such as flow, predictability, and earned value support iterative delivery but may distort behavior if poorly governed. Explainability and transparency are emphasized as foundations for calibrated trust and accountability. Scalability and interoperability address enterprise agility while mitigating vendor lock-in risks. Governance and compliance criteria embed Responsible AI through auditability and bias control. Finally, adoption and organizational impact capture usability, technostress, and change resistance, underscoring the need to preserve team autonomy while managing transformation effectively.

Table 2. Success Factors For Implementing AI In Agile Project Management

Success Factor	Description	Risk if Absent
Business case clarity	Clear value proposition	Tool-driven adoption
Workflow minimization	Embedded in Agile rituals	Resistance
Data & domain readiness	High-quality contextual data	Misleading outputs
Model & learning strategy	Interpretable models	Low trust
Metrics & testing	Performance validation	False confidence
Safeguards & opt-out	Human oversight	Ethical failure

Table 2 outlines critical success factors for implementing AI in Agile project management and the risks that arise when they are absent. Clear business case clarity prevents tool-driven adoption without strategic value. Embedding AI within existing Agile rituals minimizes workflow disruption and resistance. Data and domain readiness ensure reliable, context-aware outputs, while interpretable models support trust and learning. Continuous metrics and testing avoid false confidence in AI recommendations. Finally, safeguards and opt-out mechanisms preserve human oversight, reducing ethical risks and reinforcing AI's role as decision support rather than autonomous authority.

AI CAPABILITIES AND VALUE CREATION IN AGILE PROJECT MANAGEMENT

AI capabilities constitute the foundational enablers through which organizations translate data, algorithms, and human expertise into measurable value within Agile delivery environments. In the context of AI-augmented Agile project management, AI capabilities should not be understood merely as technical features embedded in tools, but as organizational capabilities that combine technological infrastructure, human skills, processes, and governance mechanisms to support decision-making, coordination, and learning at scale.

Defining AI Capabilities in Agile Contexts

Building on contemporary scholarship, AI capabilities can be conceptualized as an organization's ability to select, orchestrate, and leverage AI-specific resources including data assets, algorithms, computational infrastructure, and human expertise to enable forms of automation, prediction, collaboration, and insight generation that are not achievable through conventional digital systems alone. In Agile environments, these capabilities manifest through intelligent backlog management, predictive forecasting, risk-sensing dashboards, Agile copilots, and generative analytics that augment planning, execution, and reflection across the delivery lifecycle.

Crucially, AI capabilities are socio-technical in nature. Their effectiveness depends not only on access to high-quality data and advanced models, but also on managerial understanding, cross-functional collaboration, and the ability to embed AI insights into Agile rituals such as sprint planning, retrospectives, and portfolio reviews. Without these complementary organizational capabilities, AI investments risk remaining underutilized or misapplied.

AI Capabilities as Drivers of Organizational Agility

Within Agile project management, AI capabilities act as key drivers of organizational agility by strengthening sensing, sense-making, and reconfiguration processes. Predictive analytics and machine learning enhance sensing by detecting emerging risks, bottlenecks, and demand shifts earlier than conventional reporting. Generative and natural language–based tools support sense-making by synthesizing large volumes of structured and unstructured delivery data into actionable insights. Together, these capabilities enable faster, evidence-informed responses to change, reinforcing Agile principles of adaptability and continuous improvement. However, agility gains depend on architectural coherence and governance alignment; fragmented toolchains, opaque models, or weak data governance can undermine trust and constrain reconfiguration as AI adoption scales.

From AI Capabilities to Value Definition

AI capabilities contribute to value definition by improving how organizations understand customer needs, strategic priorities, and competitive dynamics. In Agile contexts, AI-powered tools can analyze customer feedback, usage data, and market signals to support evidence-based backlog prioritization and product roadmap decisions. Enhanced visibility into stakeholder requirements and external conditions enables teams and leaders to define value more precisely and dynamically, reducing reliance on static assumptions or intuition alone.

AI Capabilities and Value Creation

Value creation in Agile project management is realized when AI capabilities improve delivery execution and coordination. Predictive forecasting and intelligent prioritization enhance delivery predictability, reduce rework, and improve flow efficiency. AI copilots and decision-support dashboards reduce cognitive load for teams and leaders, allowing them to focus on higher-value activities such as problem-solving, innovation, and stakeholder engagement. Importantly, these benefits emerge through human–AI collaboration, where AI augments rather than replaces human judgment, preserving accountability and contextual reasoning.

Value Capture and Learning

AI capabilities also influence value capture by enabling organizations to monitor outcomes, learn from completed work, and institutionalize lessons learned. Analytics-driven insights into delivery performance, risk realization, and customer outcomes support more accurate value realization assessment and continuous improvement. When integrated into governance and knowledge management processes, AI capabilities facilitate organizational learning, enabling insights from one project or product to inform future initiatives.

Integrating AI Capabilities, Governance, and Ethics

The relationship between AI capabilities and value creation is mediated by governance and ethical safeguards. AI capabilities that lack explainability, bias monitoring, or auditability may deliver short-term efficiency gains but undermine trust, fairness, and long-term value. Embedding Responsible AI principles through transparent models, human-in-the-loop oversight, and lifecycle governance ensures that value creation remains sustainable and aligned with organizational values. Overall, AI capabilities in Agile project management function as strategic enablers of value definition, creation, and capture when integrated with organizational agility, human expertise, and governance structures, enabling durable performance gains, trust, and competitive advantage.

AI CAPABILITIES IN AGILE PROJECT MANAGEMENT: DEFINITION, INTEGRATION, AND VALUE PATHWAYS

Although artificial intelligence capabilities are discussed across multiple sections of this chapter, a consolidated articulation is necessary to clarify their conceptual meaning and analytical role. This subsection synthesizes existing definitions and positions AI capabilities as organizational enablers that connect data-driven intelligence with agility and project value creation in Agile delivery environments.

Defining AI Capabilities

AI capabilities can be defined as an organization's ability to purposefully select, integrate, and leverage AI-specific resources including data assets, algorithms, computational infrastructure, and human expertise to enable forms of automation, prediction, collaboration, and decision support that are not achievable through conventional digital systems alone. Consistent with contemporary scholarship, AI capabilities are not limited to technical artifacts but represent bundles of technical, organizational, and human resources that must be orchestrated to create business and project value.

From an Agile project management perspective, AI capabilities include access to high-quality and diverse data, scalable computing and cloud infrastructure, machine learning and natural language processing models, MLOps and LLMOps processes, and skilled personnel capable of interpreting and governing AI outputs. These capabilities enable intelligent backlog management, predictive forecasting, risk sensing, generative analytics, and AI-assisted coordination across the project lifecycle.

Crucially, AI capabilities are socio-technical in nature. Their effectiveness depends on managerial understanding, cross-functional collaboration, and governance mechanisms that embed AI insights into Agile rituals such as sprint planning, retrospectives, and portfolio reviews. Without these complementary organizational elements, AI capabilities remain underutilized or may generate unintended risks.

AI Capabilities as Enablers of Organizational Agility

Within Agile environments, AI capabilities strengthen organizational agility by enhancing three interrelated processes: sensing, sense-making, and reconfiguration. Predictive analytics and machine learning models improve sensing by identifying emerging risks, bottlenecks, and demand shifts earlier than traditional reporting systems. Generative and visualization tools support sense-making by synthesizing large volumes of structured and unstructured delivery data into interpretable insights. Together, these capabilities enable faster and more informed responses to change.

However, agility gains are contingent on architectural coherence and governance alignment. Fragmented tooling ecosystems, opaque models, or weak data governance constrain organizations' ability to reconfigure delivery systems as conditions evolve. Thus, AI capabilities contribute to agility only when embedded within modular architectures and supported by governance-by-design mechanisms that preserve transparency, trust, and adaptability.

From AI Capabilities to Project Value

AI capabilities influence project value through their impact on value definition, value creation, and value capture. In value definition, AI-enhanced analytics improve understanding of customer needs, stakeholder priorities, and strategic constraints, supporting evidence-based backlog prioritization and scope decisions. In value creation, AI capabilities enhance delivery execution by improving predictability, reducing rework, optimizing flow, and supporting coordination across teams and dependencies. In value capture, analytics-driven feedback enables organizations to assess outcomes, learn from completed projects, and institutionalize lessons across portfolios.

Importantly, the relationship between AI capabilities and project value is mediated by organizational agility. AI capabilities alone do not guarantee improved outcomes; their value emerges through Agile processes that enable rapid learning, adjustment, and human judgment. Governance mechanisms such as explainability, auditability, and human-in-the-loop oversight further ensure that value creation remains sustainable, ethical, and aligned with organizational objectives.

In summary, AI capabilities in Agile project management should be understood as organizational capabilities that integrate data, technology, people, and governance. When coherently designed and governed, these capabilities enhance organizational agility, enabling more effective value definition, creation, and capture across Agile project lifecycles. This consolidated framing provides a clear conceptual foundation for the chapter's evaluation framework, human–machine collaboration model, and governance-aligned reference architectures, strengthening both theoretical coherence and practical applicability.

REFERENCE ARCHITECTURES FOR AI-AUGMENTED AGILE DELIVERY

Reference architectures for AI-augmented Agile delivery provide a **structured, governance-aligned blueprint** for integrating AI capabilities, Agile practices, and organizational oversight into a coherent and scalable delivery system. In contrast to ad hoc tool integration, reference architectures define standardized components, interaction patterns, data flows, and control mechanisms that enable organizations to adopt AI systematically while preserving Agile values of transparency, adaptability, and team autonomy. As such, they function not merely as technical designs but as socio-technical coordination mechanisms that align technology, people, and governance.

At the foundation of these architectures is a **modular and interoperable design** that connects core Agile and DevOps tooling such as backlog management platforms, CI/CD pipelines, portfolio systems, and observability tools with AI and analytics services through standardized data ingestion and integration layers (ISO/IEC, 2011). These integration layers consolidate structured and unstructured delivery data, ensuring consistency, traceability, and reuse across teams and portfolios. By decoupling AI services from specific tools or vendors, the architecture supports flexibility and long-term evolution, mitigating the risks of tool fragmentation and vendor lock-in.

AI and analytics capabilities are operationalized through MLOps and LLMOps pipelines, which manage the full lifecycle of predictive and generative models, including data collection, training, validation, deployment, monitoring, and retraining (Sculley et al., 2015; Kreuzberger et al., 2023). Embedding these pipelines within the reference architecture ensures that AI models remain reliable, auditable, and contextually relevant as delivery environments, data distributions, and organizational priorities change. Model monitoring and drift detection mechanisms enable early identification of performance degradation or unintended effects, supporting continuous improvement rather than static deployment.

A defining feature of the reference architecture is the integration of human-in-the-loop decision interfaces at critical Agile decision points, including backlog prioritization, estimation, sprint planning, risk assessment, and portfolio trade-offs. These interfaces present AI-generated insights in interpretable and contestable forms, enabling teams and leaders to question assumptions, adjust recommendations, and incorporate contextual knowledge. By explicitly positioning AI as a decision-support partner rather than an autonomous authority, the architecture preserves human accountability and reinforces Agile principles of collaboration, reflection, and shared ownership (Amershi et al., 2019).

Surrounding the functional and analytical layers, governance and oversight components provide cross-cutting control and assurance. These components include explainability services, audit logging, bias and fairness monitoring, access controls, data protection mechanisms, and compliance reporting. Rather than operating as external checkpoints, governance mechanisms are embedded directly into architectural workflows, operationalizing Responsible AI principles through governance-by-design (Floridi et al., 2018; Raji et al., 2020). This approach enables organizations to meet regulatory and ethical obligations while maintaining delivery speed and flexibility, particularly in regulated or high-stakes environments.

From a strategic perspective, reference architectures also support organizational dynamic capabilities by enabling reconfiguration and scalability without compromising governance integrity. Modular components, open interfaces, and standardized data contracts allow organizations to introduce new AI capabilities, replace vendors, or adapt delivery processes in response to changing business or regulatory conditions (Benbya et al., 2020; Teece, 2018). In this way, reference architectures shift AI adoption from isolated experimentation toward sustained capability development aligned with long-term organizational objectives.

Collectively, governance-aligned reference architectures ensure that AI augmentation strengthens rather than erodes Agile delivery. By explicitly aligning automation, human judgment, and ethical oversight within a unified and evolution-ready system, these architectures provide the structural foundation for trustworthy, scalable, and resilient AI-powered Agile delivery. They also serve as a practical bridge between tooling evaluation frameworks and real-world implementation, translating conceptual principles into operationally actionable designs that support sustainable value creation.

CASE STUDIES

To demonstrate how AI-augmented Agile tooling and governance-aligned reference architectures function in practice, this chapter synthesizes cross-industry case evidence from healthcare, financial services, the public sector, and technology-intensive industries such as telecommunications and software. These cases are used illustratively rather than as exhaustive empirical studies, with the objective of highlighting how sectoral context particularly regulatory intensity, scale, and stakeholder accountability shapes tooling evaluation criteria, architectural choices, and governance mechanisms in AI-enabled Agile delivery environments.

In healthcare delivery contexts, where Agile practices are increasingly applied to digital health platforms, electronic health record (EHR) modernization, and patient-facing systems, AI-assisted backlog prioritization and predictive risk detection have demonstrated potential to improve delivery predictability and reduce delays in critical system upgrades. However, these benefits materialize only when AI capabilities are embedded within governance-aligned reference architectures that support explainability, auditability, and human-in-the-loop oversight. Given stringent requirements for data privacy, traceability, and clinical accountability, healthcare architectures emphasize transparent decision logic, model validation, and explicit accountability for AI-informed recommendations, ensuring that clinical judgment and ethical responsibility remain firmly with human decision-makers (Reddy et al., 2020; Floridi et al., 2018; Raji et al., 2020).

In **financial services organizations**, which operate under intense regulatory scrutiny and risk sensitivity, AI-powered risk-sensing dashboards and predictive analytics are increasingly integrated with Agile portfolio management and DevOps pipelines. These tools enhance early detection of security vulnerabilities, compliance risks, and operational bottlenecks across complex delivery portfolios. Governance-aligned architectures in this sector prioritize segregation of duties, model version control, audit logging, and continuous monitoring to reconcile Agile autonomy with regulatory accountability. Importantly, AI recommendations are positioned as decision-support inputs rather than automated controls, preserving managerial oversight while improving situational awareness and risk responsiveness (Gozman et al., 2018; OECD, 2019).

Public sector organizations exhibit a more cautious and incremental adoption trajectory. Here, AI-powered Agile tooling is primarily applied to scenario analysis, workload forecasting, and service demand planning rather than high degrees of automation. Reference architectures in the public sector prioritize transparency, traceability, and public accountability over speed or optimization. Governance layers commonly include explicit documentation of AI assumptions, ethical review processes, and citizen-facing reporting mechanisms to support trust, fairness, and legitimacy in digital governance. These cases illustrate how governance-by-design functions as an enabler of responsible innovation rather than a barrier, particularly in environments characterized by political oversight and public scrutiny (Mergel et al., 2018; Wirtz et al., 2019).

In contrast, telecommunications and large-scale software organizations leverage AI-powered forecasting, intelligent backlog management, and Agile copilots to manage scale, distributed coordination, and rapid innovation cycles. In these settings, reference architectures emphasize modular, platform-based designs that enable interoperability across teams and products while avoiding vendor lock-in. Governance mechanisms focus on performance monitoring, bias detection, and maintaining AI recommendations as advisory rather than prescriptive, thereby supporting speed and experimentation without eroding accountability or team autonomy (Forsgren et al., 2018; Benbya et al., 2020).

Across all sectors, several consistent patterns emerge. First, AI-augmented Agile tooling delivers sustained value only when embedded within coherent reference architectures, rather than deployed as isolated features or vendor-driven enhancements. Second, governance mechanisms such as explainability, auditability, and human oversight function as enablers of trust, adoption, and learning, rather than as constraints on agility. Third, sectoral context critically shapes evaluation priorities and architectural design, underscoring the inadequacy of one-size-fits-all AI adoption strategies. Collectively, these cases reinforce the chapter's central argument that adaptive, governance-aware socio-technical systems are essential for achieving sustainable performance gains in AI-powered Agile delivery.

ANTI-PATTERNS AND RISKS IN AI-AUGMENTED AGILE DELIVERY

While AI-powered tooling holds significant potential to enhance Agile delivery, its uncritical or poorly governed adoption gives rise to recurring anti-patterns that undermine both delivery performance and organizational trust. Importantly, these risks are rarely rooted in technical shortcomings alone; rather, they emerge from misalignment between AI capabilities, Agile practices, architectural design, and governance mechanisms. Identifying these anti-patterns is therefore essential for designing resilient, trustworthy AI-augmented delivery systems.

A pervasive anti-pattern is over-reliance on algorithmic recommendations without sufficient transparency or contextual interpretation. Predictive forecasting tools and AI copilots may generate outputs that appear objective or authoritative, leading teams and managers to defer judgment rather than critically interrogate underlying assumptions, data quality, or uncertainty. This phenomenon commonly described as automation bias becomes especially problematic when AI systems operate as opaque "black boxes," increasing the likelihood of uncritical acceptance of flawed or biased outputs (Doshi-Velez & Kim, 2017; Amershi et al., 2019). In Agile environments, such over-reliance erodes core principles of collaboration, reflection, and adaptive learning by shifting accountability from teams to algorithms. From a governance perspective, limited explainability complicates auditability and responsibility assignment when AI-influenced decisions contribute to delivery failures or stakeholder harm (Floridi et al., 2018).

A second anti-pattern arises from isolated and fragmented adoption of AI-powered tools, often driven by vendor offerings or localized productivity goals rather than architectural coherence. When organizations introduce AI capabilities without shared data standards, integration layers, or reference architectures, tooling ecosystems become siloed and inconsistent. AI models trained on partial or misaligned data generate unreliable insights that amplify uncertainty rather than reduce it (Benbya et al., 2020). This pattern reflects a failure to treat AI augmentation as a system-level transformation. In the absence of coherent architectures and data governance, organizations accumulate hidden technical debt and constrain future adaptability, weakening their dynamic capabilities over time (Sculley et al., 2015; Teece, 2018).

Vendor lock-in constitutes a related strategic risk in AI-augmented Agile delivery. Many AI-enabled platforms rely on proprietary models, closed data schemas, or tightly coupled ecosystems that limit interoperability and portability. Although such platforms may deliver rapid initial benefits, they obscure long-term costs associated with data migration, customization constraints, and regulatory adaptation (OECD, 2019). In Agile environments that depend on continuous evolution and reconfiguration, deep integration of proprietary AI components without clear exit strategies restricts organizational autonomy and resilience, particularly when governance controls are weak or absent.

Another critical risk involves the amplification of historical biases embedded in delivery data. AI systems trained on past performance metrics, prioritization decisions, or workload distributions may inadvertently encode and reinforce existing inequities across teams, products, or roles. When such biases are operationalized through AI-driven recommendations, they can distort Agile metrics, marginalize exploratory or high-risk initiatives, and perpetuate unfair performance evaluations (Raji et al., 2020). Ethical blind spots emerge when governance mechanisms focus narrowly on predictive accuracy or efficiency while neglecting fairness, inclusivity, and human impact. Without bias audits, stakeholder review, and transparent documentation, organizations risk deploying AI systems that conflict with ethical expectations and social legitimacy, especially in regulated or public-facing contexts (Floridi et al., 2018).

A further anti-pattern occurs when AI automation conflicts with Agile values of transparency, collaboration, and continuous improvement. Over-automated decision-making can reduce opportunities for team learning and sense-making, transforming Agile rituals such as retrospectives or planning sessions into mechanistic processes driven by algorithmic outputs rather than collective reflection (Highsmith, 2009). This misalignment may manifest as diminished engagement, reduced ownership of delivery outcomes, or resistance to AI tools perceived as surveillance or control mechanisms. Such dynamics undermine psychological safety and trust critical enablers of Agile performance and may ultimately negate the productivity gains promised by AI augmentation (Tarafdar et al., 2019).

Finally, governance lag represents a systemic risk across AI-augmented Agile environments. Organizations frequently deploy AI capabilities faster than they develop appropriate oversight structures, resulting in ambiguous accountability for AI-influenced decisions. When failures occur, responsibility may be diffused across teams, vendors, and governance bodies, complicating remediation, learning, and ethical accountability (Raji et al., 2020). This risk is particularly acute in regulated sectors, where insufficient governance can lead to compliance violations, reputational damage, or legal consequences. Embedding governance mechanisms such as audit trails, model monitoring, and human-in-the-loop controls directly into reference architectures is therefore essential to prevent governance gaps from undermining delivery effectiveness.

Collectively, these anti-patterns demonstrate that the primary risks of AI-augmented Agile delivery are organizational and governance-related rather than purely technical. Over-reliance on opaque AI, fragmented architectures, vendor lock-in, ethical blind spots, and governance lag can erode trust, agility, and long-term value creation. Addressing these risks requires deliberate architectural design, systematic tooling evaluation, and a governance-by-design approach that aligns AI augmentation with Agile principles, human judgment, and organizational values.

Table 3. Mapping AI-Augmented Agile Practices To Core Project Management Domains

PM Domain	AI Role	Key Benefits	Governance Requirement
Stakeholder mgmt	Sentiment analytics	Proactive engagement	Explainability
Risk mgmt	Predictive sensing	Early mitigation	Human validation
Earned value	Dynamic analytics	Real-time value	Managerial judgment
Team performance	AI copilots	Reduced cognitive load	Psychological safety
Project governance	Decision support	Accountability	Auditability
Portfolio mgmt	Scenario modeling	Strategic alignment	Oversight
Supporting tools	NLP, agents	Scale & coordination	Opt-out controls

Table 3 maps AI-augmented Agile practices to core project management domains, showing how AI supports managerial and delivery functions while introducing specific governance needs. Sentiment analytics enhance stakeholder management through proactive engagement but require explainability. Predictive risk sensing enables early mitigation, demanding human validation. Dynamic earned value analytics improve real-time value tracking under managerial judgment. AI copilots reduce cognitive load while safeguarding psychological safety. Portfolio scenario modeling supports strategic alignment with oversight, and supporting tools such as NLP and agents enable scale, requiring opt-out controls to preserve autonomy.

SUPPORTING TOOLS: LANGUAGE TRANSLATION, GAMIFICATION, VISUALIZATION, AND AUTONOMOUS AGENTS

Supporting AI-enabled tools play an increasingly important role in Agile project environments. Language translation tools facilitate collaboration across geographically and culturally distributed teams. Visualization and generative analytics enhance sense-making by transforming complex data into interpretable insights. Gamification mechanisms support engagement and motivation, particularly in learning and continuous improvement contexts. Autonomous agents assist with routine coordination, monitoring, and information retrieval tasks.

Despite their benefits, these tools require careful governance to prevent unintended consequences such as bias amplification, over-automation, or reduced human agency. Their deployment should therefore be guided by clear role definitions, opt-out mechanisms, and alignment with Agile values of transparency, collaboration, and empowerment.

Taken together, this domain-level mapping demonstrates that AI-augmented Agile project management affects not only technical execution but also core managerial, social, and governance functions. The value of AI emerges through its integration with human judgment, organizational capabilities, and governance mechanisms across stakeholder management, risk, value realization, team performance, governance, and portfolio coordination. Making these relationships explicit strengthens both the analytical rigor and practical applicability of the chapter.

Table 4. Human–Machine Collaboration In AI-Augmented Agile Project Management

Dimension	Human Employee (HE)	Digital Employee (DE)
Strengths	Judgment, ethics	Speed, pattern detection
Tasks	Strategic, social	Analytical, routine
Authority	Final decision	Advisory
Risks	Cognitive overload	Bias, opacity

Table 4 contrasts human–machine collaboration in AI-augmented Agile project management by distinguishing the complementary roles of human and digital employees. Human employees contribute judgment, ethical reasoning, and social intelligence, retaining final decision authority for strategic and contextual matters.

Digital employees excel in speed, pattern detection, and routine analytical tasks, functioning in an advisory capacity. The table also highlights distinct risks: humans may face cognitive overload, while AI systems may introduce bias or opacity. Effective collaboration depends on balancing these strengths through human-in-the-loop governance and clear role boundaries.

Ethical Implications Across Levels

Human–machine collaboration in Agile project management raises ethical considerations at multiple levels. At the product level, AI systems may embed biases or lack transparency, affecting fairness and accountability in prioritization or performance evaluation. At the consumer level, ethical concerns include data privacy, informed consent, and the risk of manipulation through AI-mediated decision processes. At the societal level, broader implications include workforce displacement, inequality in access to human versus automated decision-making, and the normalization of opaque algorithmic governance.

Embedding ethical safeguards such as explainability, auditability, bias monitoring, and opt-out mechanisms into tooling architectures ensures that human–machine collaboration remains aligned with organizational values and societal expectations. Governance-by-design thus functions as an ethical enabler, ensuring that collaboration between human and digital employees supports trust, legitimacy, and long-term sustainability.

Human–machine collaboration in AI-augmented Agile project management is most effective when roles are explicit, task delegation is principled, and decision authority remains human-centered. By conceptualizing AI systems as digital collaborators rather than autonomous authorities, organizations can harness analytical power while preserving accountability, learning, and ethical integrity. This structured operationalization strengthens the chapter's contribution by demonstrating how AI, governance, and Agile practice converge in real project environments.

DISCUSSION

The findings of this chapter demonstrate that AI-augmented Agile delivery constitutes a substantive socio-technical transformation rather than a marginal tooling enhancement. Across the conceptual framework, evaluation tables, reference architectures, and cross-sector cases, a consistent conclusion emerges: AI contributes sustainable value to Agile delivery only when it is deliberately aligned with human judgment, organizational capabilities, and governance mechanisms. Treating AI as a neutral or purely technical add-on amplifies fragmentation, weakens trust, and ultimately undermines agility.

Consistent with Socio-Technical Systems Theory, the evidence shows that AI functions as a force multiplier for Agile practices, not a substitute for them. Capabilities such as predictive forecasting, intelligent backlog refinement, and Agile copilots enhance situational awareness and anticipatory capacity, but value materializes only when these insights are embedded into Agile rituals—sprint planning, backlog refinement, retrospectives—through explainable and contestable interfaces. As reflected in the evaluation framework (Table 1) and success factors (Table 2), opaque or authoritative AI outputs foster automation bias, suppress team autonomy, and erode psychological safety, whereas dialogic human–AI interaction supports learning and adaptation.

A central contribution of the chapter lies in reframing architecture as a governance mechanism. Governance-aligned reference architectures institutionalize values, risk tolerance, and ethical commitments by specifying how AI services, data pipelines, and decision-support mechanisms interact with Agile processes and human oversight. Integrating MLOps and LLMOps pipelines with audit logging, model versioning, explainability services, and compliance dashboards operationalizes Responsible AI principles within everyday delivery work. Rather than constraining agility, governance-by-design emerges as a prerequisite for sustainable agility as AI-enabled systems scale in complexity and impact.

Trust and adoption dynamics further determine whether AI-powered tooling delivers durable value. As highlighted across the human–machine collaboration mapping (Table 4), trust is shaped less by predictive accuracy alone and more by transparency, perceived fairness, and preservation of human authority. When teams understand data sources, assumptions, and limitations, AI becomes a shared cognitive resource. Conversely, opaque systems intensify technostress and provoke either blind reliance or rejection—both detrimental to Agile performance.

The findings also underscore the context-dependent nature of AI adoption. Regulated sectors such as healthcare and finance prioritize auditability, traceability, and compliance readiness, framing AI as decision support within robust governance structures. Technology-intensive sectors emphasize scale and speed, yet still require governance-by-design to prevent ethical drift, bias amplification, and vendor lock-in. These contrasts reaffirm the inadequacy of one-size-fits-all AI strategies and the need for adaptable reference architectures sensitive to regulatory exposure and risk tolerance.

Finally, the chapter highlights the inherent tension between speed and accountability. AI compresses feedback loops and accelerates decision-making, but without commensurate investments in governance, capability development, and continuous evaluation, it also magnifies errors and obscures responsibility. The dominant risks observed are organizational and institutional rather than technical, stemming from misalignment between tools, practices, and governance.

In sum, this discussion advances a governance-sensitive understanding of AI-powered Agile delivery. By integrating socio-technical theory, dynamic capabilities, technology acceptance, and Responsible AI governance, the chapter demonstrates that architectural coherence, human-centered design, and ethical oversight jointly determine AI's contribution to Agile performance. This provides a robust foundation for the chapter's recommendations and future research agenda.

RECOMMENDATIONS AND SOLUTIONS

The analysis presented in this chapter demonstrates that the effective adoption of AI-powered Agile tooling is fundamentally an organizational and governance challenge rather than a purely technological one. While advances in artificial intelligence offer significant potential to enhance planning accuracy, delivery predictability, and decision quality, these benefits are realized only when AI adoption is embedded within coherent evaluation frameworks, governance-aligned reference architectures, and human-centered operating models. Organizations that treat AI-enabled tooling as a plug-and-play enhancement risk amplifying existing inefficiencies, introducing new forms of opacity and bias, and creating accountability gaps that ultimately undermine Agile performance. In response, this section proposes a set of integrated recommendations and solution pathways that address governance design, evaluation practices, architectural strategy, capability development, and leadership alignment.

Adopt Governance-by-Design as a Foundational Principle

A primary recommendation is to institutionalize governance-by-design as a core principle of AI-powered Agile delivery. Rather than positioning governance as a post-deployment compliance activity or external control function, organizations should embed governance requirements into tooling evaluation, architectural design, and workflow configuration from the outset. Governance-by-design entails integrating explainability, auditability, bias monitoring, data lineage, and accountability mechanisms directly into AI pipelines and delivery tooling ecosystems (Floridi et al., 2018; Raji et al., 2020). Reference architectures should therefore explicitly define governance layers alongside functional components, clarifying how AI models are trained, deployed, monitored, and retired, and how human oversight is exercised at critical decision points. Embedding governance into architecture enables organizations to balance agility with accountability while reducing long-term compliance costs associated with retroactive controls or tool replacement.

Institutionalize Structured, Multi-Criteria Tooling Evaluation

Organizations should replace ad hoc or vendor-driven tool selection with systematic, multi-criteria evaluation frameworks that reflect both delivery objectives and governance requirements. Delivery leaders, PMOs, and enterprise architects are encouraged to adopt structured decision-making approaches grounded in multi-criteria decision-making (MCDM) theory, enabling tools to be assessed across dimensions such as delivery performance, explainability, scalability, interoperability, governance readiness, and adoption effort (Belton & Stewart, 2002; Saaty, 2008). Including governance stakeholders such as risk, compliance, and legal representatives in evaluation processes ensures that ethical and regulatory considerations are weighted alongside performance goals. This approach enhances transparency, traceability, and legitimacy of tooling decisions, particularly in regulated or high-impact environments.

Position AI as Decision Support, Not Decision Authority

A further critical recommendation is to position AI-powered tools as decision-support systems rather than autonomous decision-makers. While predictive analytics and generative AI expand automation potential, uncritical delegation of decision authority to algorithms undermines core Agile values of collaboration, reflection, and team autonomy. Organizations should design workflows that require explicit human validation of AI-generated recommendations, especially for high-impact decisions involving prioritization, commitments, risk mitigation, and resource allocation (Amershi et al., 2019). Human-in-the-loop configurations reduce automation bias, preserve accountability, and reinforce AI's role as a cognitive amplifier rather than a substitute for human judgment.

Invest in AI Literacy and Human Capability Development

The sustainable use of AI-augmented Agile tooling depends heavily on organizational capability development and AI literacy. Teams and leaders must be equipped to interpret, question, and contextualize AI-generated insights, including understanding model limitations, data quality issues, uncertainty, and ethical implications. Organizations should invest in AI literacy initiatives that extend beyond technical training to include Agile coaching, leadership development, and governance education (Rai et al., 2020). Such initiatives reduce technostress, resistance, and misuse while strengthening informed human–AI collaboration and organizational resilience (Tarafdar et al., 2019).

Design Modular, Interoperable Architectures to Avoid Lock-In

To mitigate strategic and structural risks, organizations are advised to prioritize modular and interoperable reference architectures that reduce vendor lock-in and support continuous evolution of tooling ecosystems. Decoupling AI services from core delivery tooling using open standards for data exchange, model interfaces, and observability enables organizations to adapt to technological, regulatory, or strategic change without excessive switching costs or loss of control (Benbya et al., 2020; ISO/IEC, 2011). Such architectural flexibility supports dynamic capabilities by enabling reconfiguration rather than entrenchment in proprietary ecosystems.

Embed Continuous Evaluation and Feedback Mechanisms

Given the adaptive nature of AI systems, organizations should move beyond one-time approval models and implement continuous evaluation and feedback mechanisms. Regular review cycles integrated into Agile retrospectives, model audits, bias assessments, and governance dashboards enable early detection of model drift, performance degradation, or unintended consequences (Forsgren et al., 2018; Sculley et al., 2015). Embedding continuous evaluation into reference architectures transforms AI adoption from a procurement activity into an ongoing organizational capability aligned with Agile principles of inspection and adaptation.

Align AI Adoption with Strategy, Context, and Leadership Commitment

Finally, AI-powered Agile delivery initiatives should be explicitly aligned with organizational strategy, cultural values, and sector-specific constraints. Context-sensitive adoption recognizes that regulatory exposure, stakeholder expectations, and risk tolerance vary across industries. Reference architectures should therefore be adaptable rather than prescriptive, enabling tailored implementation while maintaining governance integrity (Teece, 2018). At the leadership level, visible executive sponsorship, cross-functional coordination, and sustained investment in governance and capability development are essential. Without leadership commitment, AI initiatives risk fragmentation, resistance, or symbolic adoption with limited impact.

MANAGERIAL AND POLICY IMPLICATIONS

The findings of this chapter carry important implications for managers, organizational leaders, project management offices (PMOs), enterprise architects, and policymakers responsible for steering AI adoption in Agile and DevOps environments. While the chapter is grounded in theory, its core insights translate directly into actionable guidance for practice and governance.

Implications for Senior Leadership

For senior leaders, the primary implication is that AI-powered Agile delivery should be treated as a strategic transformation initiative, not a tooling upgrade. Leadership decisions regarding AI adoption shape how authority, accountability, and trust are redistributed within delivery systems. Executives must therefore set clear expectations that AI functions as a decision-support partner rather than a replacement for human judgment. Visible leadership commitment to governance-by-design, ethical AI use, and capability development is critical to prevent fragmented adoption, symbolic compliance, or resistance at team levels. Leaders should also ensure sustained investment in data governance, architecture, and AI literacy as long-term organizational capabilities rather than one-off project costs.

Implications for PMOs and Delivery Governance Bodies

For PMOs and delivery governance functions, the chapter highlights the need to redefine governance models to accommodate algorithmic decision support. Traditional governance mechanisms focused on reporting cadence, milestone control, and post hoc assurance are insufficient in AI-augmented environments. PMOs should institutionalize structured, multi-criteria evaluation frameworks for AI-powered tooling, enabling transparent, auditable, and repeatable decision-making that balances delivery performance with explainability, compliance, and adoption readiness. Additionally, governance bodies should actively participate in weighting evaluation criteria, monitoring AI system performance, and reviewing ethical risks, thereby shifting governance from reactive oversight to proactive design and continuous assurance.

Implications for Enterprise Architects and Technology Leaders

Enterprise architects and technology leaders play a pivotal role in operationalizing responsible AI adoption through reference architectures. The findings underscore the importance of modular, interoperable architectural designs that decouple AI services from core Agile tooling, mitigate vendor lock-in, and support continuous evolution. Architects should embed MLOps and LLMOps pipelines alongside governance mechanisms such as audit logging, model versioning, bias monitoring, and explainability services ensuring that ethical and compliance requirements are enforced through system design rather than manual controls. This architectural approach enables organizations to scale AI responsibly while preserving agility, resilience, and strategic flexibility.

Implications for Human Resource Development and Change Management

From a human and organizational perspective, the chapter emphasizes that AI adoption success depends heavily on AI literacy and change management. Managers responsible for talent development should integrate AI literacy into Agile coaching, leadership development, and continuous learning programs. Building shared understanding of AI limitations, uncertainty, and ethical considerations reduces technostress, mitigates automation bias, and strengthens constructive human–AI collaboration. Importantly, organizations should address employee concerns related to surveillance, deskilling, and loss of autonomy, framing AI as an enabler of professional judgment rather than a mechanism of control.

Implications for Policymakers and Regulators

For policymakers and regulators, the chapter offers insights into how governance-by-design can be operationalized within fast-paced Agile and DevOps contexts. Rather than relying solely on external compliance mandates or static regulatory checklists, policy frameworks should encourage organizations to embed transparency, auditability, and accountability into AI system architectures and operational workflows. Supporting standards for interoperable architectures, explainability, and model lifecycle governance can help align innovation with public trust and ethical responsibility. In regulated sectors, policymakers may also consider incentivizing architectural and evaluation practices that demonstrate responsible AI use, rather than focusing exclusively on punitive compliance mechanisms.

Bridging Strategy, Governance, and Practice

Collectively, these managerial and policy implications reinforce a central message of the chapter: effective AI-powered Agile delivery emerges from alignment between strategy, governance, architecture, and human capability development. Organizations that integrate these dimensions are better positioned to realize AI's benefits while mitigating systemic risks. For practitioners and policymakers alike, the chapter provides a roadmap for moving beyond fragmented, tool-centric adoption toward coherent, trustworthy, and sustainable AI-enabled delivery systems that support long-term performance, resilience, and legitimacy.

FUTURE RESEARCH DIRECTIONS

The rapid evolution of AI-powered tooling in Agile and DevOps environments opens a broad and interdisciplinary agenda for future research spanning software engineering, information systems, project management, organizational studies, and AI ethics. While this chapter establishes a conceptual, evaluative, and architectural foundation for understanding AI-augmented Agile delivery, several critical gaps remain that require systematic investigation to advance both theory and practice in responsible AI adoption.

A priority area for future research is the empirical validation and refinement of evaluation frameworks for AI-powered Agile tooling. Although multi-criteria decision-making (MCDM) models provide a robust methodological basis for balancing delivery performance, governance readiness, and adoption effort, there is limited empirical evidence on how these frameworks perform across organizational sizes, industries, and regulatory contexts. Comparative studies examining alternative weighting schemes, stakeholder participation models, and evaluation criteria could clarify how evaluation design influences tooling selection, implementation success, and downstream delivery outcomes. Such research would enhance methodological rigor, reproducibility, and benchmarking, while supporting alignment between organizational practices and emerging standards for AI governance and software architecture.

A second important direction concerns the longitudinal dynamics of AI-augmented Agile delivery. Most existing studies adopt cross-sectional or short-term perspectives focused on initial adoption challenges or early productivity gains. Longitudinal research is needed to examine how AI-powered tooling influences delivery performance, team dynamics, skill development, and organizational learning over time. Key questions include whether early gains in predictability or flow efficiency are sustained, whether prolonged reliance on AI leads to new forms of dependency or deskilling, and how governance mechanisms evolve as AI systems, data distributions, and organizational contexts co-develop. Such work would contribute to dynamic capabilities theory by clarifying how organizations adapt to AI-enabled delivery systems over extended periods.

Closely related is the need for deeper empirical investigation into the micro-level dynamics of human–AI collaboration within Agile teams. While human-in-the-loop principles are widely advocated, there is limited empirical insight into how teams actually interpret, contest, and appropriate AI-generated recommendations during everyday Agile rituals such as sprint planning, backlog refinement, retrospectives, and cross-team coordination. Qualitative and mixed-method studies could explore how explainability, trust, perceived fairness, and power relations shape engagement with

AI tools, refining socio-technical theory and informing the design of AI interfaces that better support collaborative reasoning, accountability, and reflective learning.

Future research should also examine the governance implications of MLOps and LLMOps practices in Agile delivery environments. Although these paradigms are increasingly essential for deploying and maintaining AI systems at scale, their interaction with Agile workflows, decentralized decision-making, and organizational accountability remains underexplored. Studies could investigate how governance mechanisms such as model audits, bias monitoring, explainability reporting, and compliance checks can be embedded into fast-paced CI/CD pipelines without undermining flexibility or team autonomy. Comparative research across regulated and non-regulated sectors would be particularly valuable in identifying context-sensitive governance patterns and architectural trade-offs, advancing understanding of governance-by-design in AI-enabled delivery systems.

Another critical research avenue concerns the impact of algorithmic mediation on Agile performance metrics and value assessment. AI-powered tools increasingly shape how delivery performance is measured, interpreted, and acted upon. However, historical delivery data often encode organizational biases, structural inequalities, or legacy practices that may be amplified through AI-driven prioritization, estimation, or capacity planning. Quantitative and mixed-method research examining fairness, inclusivity, and distributional outcomes across teams, projects, and roles could inform the development of bias-aware Agile metrics and performance management systems aligned with ethical and governance objectives.

Finally, future studies could explore the role of open-source and hybrid ecosystems in supporting transparent, trustworthy, and adaptable AI-augmented Agile tooling. Open-source platforms offer opportunities for peer review, collective governance, and rapid innovation, potentially mitigating opacity and vendor lock-in risks associated with proprietary systems. At the same time, they raise challenges related to accountability, sustainability, and enterprise-grade governance. Research examining hybrid models that combine open-source components with organizational governance frameworks could provide valuable insights for practitioners and policymakers seeking to balance innovation, control, and ethical responsibility.

Taken together, these future research directions underscore the need for integrated, longitudinal, and governance-sensitive inquiry that moves beyond siloed analyses of AI capabilities or Agile practices. By advancing validated evaluation models, human–AI collaboration theory, governance-aware MLOps practices, and fairness-sensitive performance metrics, future research can deepen understanding of how AI may be responsibly and sustainably embedded into Agile delivery systems supporting not only improved delivery outcomes, but also trust, resilience, and legitimacy in increasingly algorithmically mediated organizations.

CONCLUSION

The accelerating integration of artificial intelligence into Agile and DevOps environments represents a fundamental shift in how contemporary delivery organizations plan, execute, and govern work. While AI-powered tooling offers significant potential to enhance decision quality, delivery predictability, and scalability, this chapter demonstrates that these benefits are neither automatic nor inherently benign. AI augmentation reshapes Agile delivery as a socio-technical system, altering patterns of authority, accountability, and sense-making in ways that demand deliberate design and governance.

By grounding AI-augmented Agile delivery in established theoretical perspectives including socio-technical systems theory, dynamic capabilities theory, technology acceptance, and Responsible AI governance this chapter provides an integrated lens for understanding how AI capabilities interact with human judgment, organizational processes, and institutional controls. The proposed conceptual framework, multi-criteria evaluation model, and governance-aligned reference architectures move beyond feature-centric or vendor-driven adoption approaches, offering a structured foundation for evaluating, integrating, and governing AI-powered Agile tooling at scale. In doing so, the chapter addresses a critical gap in both scholarly literature and practitioner guidance, where AI adoption has often outpaced systematic evaluation and architectural coherence.

The reference architectures articulated in this chapter illustrate how MLOps and LLMOps pipelines, when combined with human-in-the-loop oversight and embedded governance mechanisms, can operationalize ethical principles, regulatory requirements, and accountability without undermining Agile flexibility. Cross-industry case evidence further underscores that effective AI adoption is inherently context-sensitive: sectoral constraints, regulatory exposure, and stakeholder expectations shape tooling evaluation, architectural choices, and governance priorities. The identified anti-patterns and risks reinforce this insight by demonstrating that uncritical AI adoption characterized by opaque automation, fragmented toolchains, vendor lock-in, and governance lag can erode trust, distort performance metrics, and ultimately weaken Agile effectiveness.

A central contribution of this chapter is the reframing of governance not as an impediment to Agile innovation, but as a precondition for sustainable agility in AI-augmented delivery environments. Governance-by-design emerges as a critical enabler that allows organizations to scale AI responsibly while preserving transparency, ethical integrity, and human agency. The recommendations presented provide actionable guidance for delivery leaders, project management offices, architects, and policymakers seeking to institutionalize responsible AI adoption through structured evaluation, modular architecture, continuous oversight, and capability development.

In conclusion, the future of Agile project management does not lie in the wholesale automation of human decision-making, but in the deliberate orchestration of AI capabilities, human expertise, and governance structures. Organizations that adopt systematic evaluation frameworks and governance-aligned reference architectures prioritizing explainability, interoperability, accountability, and learning are better positioned to realize the promise of AI-augmented Agile delivery. Such an approach enables AI to function not as a source of control or opacity, but as a trusted partner in adaptive, resilient, and ethically grounded delivery systems capable of sustaining performance in an increasingly algorithmically mediated organizational landscape.

REFERENCES

Amershi, S., Weld, D., Vorvoreanu, M., Fourney, A., Nushi, B., Collisson, P., & Horvitz, E. (2019). Guidelines for human–AI interaction. *Proceedings of the 2019 CHI Conference on Human Factors in Computing Systems*, 1–13. DOI: 10.1145/3290605.3300233

Baxter, G., & Sommerville, I. (2011). Socio-technical systems: From design methods to systems engineering. *Interacting with Computers*, *23*(1), 4–17. DOI: 10.1016/j.intcom.2010.07.003

Beck, K., Beedle, M., van Bennekum, A., Cockburn, A., Cunningham, W., Fowler, M., . . . Thomas, D. (2001). *Manifesto for Agile software development*. https://agilemanifesto.org

Belton, V., & Stewart, T. J. (2002). *Multiple criteria decision analysis: An integrated approach*. Springer. https://link.springer.com/book/10.1007/978-1-4615-1495-4

Benbya, H., Nan, N., Tanriverdi, H., & Yoo, Y. (2020). Complexity and information systems research in the emerging digital world. *Management Information Systems Quarterly*, *44*(1), 1–17. DOI: 10.25300/MISQ/2020/13304

Davis, F. D. (1989). Perceived usefulness, perceived ease of use, and user acceptance of information technology. *Management Information Systems Quarterly*, *13*(3), 319–340. https://www.jstor.org/stable/249008. DOI: 10.2307/249008

Dingsøyr, T., Moe, N. B., Fægri, T. E., & Seim, E. A. (2018). Exploring software development at the very large-scale: A revelatory case study and research agenda for agile method adaptation. *Empirical Software Engineering*, *23*(1), 490–520. DOI: 10.1007/s10664-017-9524-2

Doshi-Velez, F., & Kim, B. (2017). Towards a rigorous science of interpretable machine learning. *arXiv*. https://arxiv.org/abs/1702.08608

Floridi, L., Cowls, J., Beltrametti, M., Chatila, R., Chazerand, P., Dignum, V., Luetge, C., Madelin, R., Pagallo, U., Rossi, F., Schafer, B., Valcke, P., & Vayena, E. (2018). AI4People An ethical framework for a good AI society. *Minds and Machines*, *28*(4), 689–707. DOI: 10.1007/s11023-018-9482-5 PMID: 30930541

Forsgren, N., Humble, J., & Kim, G. (2018). *Accelerate: The science of lean software and DevOps*. IT Revolution Press. https://itrevolution.com/book/accelerate/

Gozman, D., Liebenau, J., & Mangan, M. (2018). The innovation mechanisms of fintech start-ups: Insights from SWIFT's innotribe competition. *Journal of Management Information Systems*, *35*(1), 145–179. DOI: 10.1080/07421222.2018.1440768

Highsmith, J. (2009). *Agile project management: Creating innovative products* (2nd ed.). Addison-Wesley Professional.

Humble, J., & Farley, D. (2010). *Continuous delivery: Reliable software releases through build, test, and deployment automation.* Addison-Wesley Professional.

ISO/IEC. (2011). *ISO/IEC/IEEE 42010: Systems and software engineering Architecture description.* International Organization for Standardization. https://www.iso.org/standard/50508.html

Kim, G., Humble, J., Debois, P., & Willis, J. (2016). *The DevOps handbook.* IT Revolution Press. https://itrevolution.com/book/the-devops-handbook/

Kreuzberger, D., Kühl, N., & Hirschl, S. (2023). Machine learning operations (MLOps): Overview, definition, and architecture. *ACM Computing Surveys*, *55*(8), 1–37. https://dblp.dagstuhl.de/rec/journals/access/KreuzbergerKH23.html

Mergel, I., Gong, Y., & Bertot, J. C. (2018). Agile government: Systematic literature review and future research. *Government Information Quarterly*, *35*(2), 291–298. DOI: 10.1016/j.giq.2018.04.003

Organisation for Economic Co-operation and Development. (2019). *OECD principles on artificial intelligence.* https://www.oecd.org/going-digital/ai/principles/

Rai, A., Constantinides, P., & Sarker, S. (2020). Next-generation digital platforms: Toward human–AI hybrids. *Management Information Systems Quarterly*, *44*(3), iii–ix. https://aisel.aisnet.org/misq/vol43/iss1/2/. DOI: 10.25300/MISQ/2020/441E0

Raji, I. D., Smart, A., White, R. N., Mitchell, M., Gebru, T., Hutchinson, B., & Barnes, P. (2020). Closing the AI accountability gap. *Proceedings of the 2020 Conference on Fairness, Accountability, and Transparency*, 33–44. DOI: 10.1145/3351095.3372873

Reddy, S., Allan, S., Coghlan, S., & Cooper, P. (2020). A governance model for the application of AI in health care. *Journal of the American Medical Informatics Association : JAMIA*, *27*(3), 491–497. DOI: 10.1093/jamia/ocz192 PMID: 31682262

Saaty, T. L. (2008). Decision making with the analytic hierarchy process. *International Journal of Services Sciences*, *1*(1), 83–98. DOI: 10.1504/IJSSCI.2008.017590

Sculley, D., Holt, G., Golovin, D., Davydov, E., Phillips, T., Ebner, D., . . . Dennison, D. (2015). Hidden technical debt in machine learning systems. *Advances in Neural Information Processing Systems*, 28, 2503–2511. https://proceedings.neurips.cc/paper_files/paper/2015/file/86df7dcfd896fcaf2674f757a2463eba-Paper.pdf

Tarafdar, M., Cooper, C. L., & Stich, J. F. (2019). The technostress trifecta Techno eustress, techno distress and design. *Information Systems Journal*, *29*(1), 6–42. DOI: 10.1111/isj.12169

Teece, D. J. (2018). Business models and dynamic capabilities. *Long Range Planning*, *51*(1), 40–49. DOI: 10.1016/j.lrp.2017.06.007

Teece, D. J., Pisano, G., & Shuen, A. (1997). Dynamic capabilities and strategic management. *Strategic Management Journal*, 18(7), 509–533. : AID-SMJ882>3.0.CO;2-Z

Trist, E. L., & Bamforth, K. W. (1951). Some social and psychological consequences of the longwall method of coal-getting. *Human Relations*, *4*(1), 3–38. DOI: 10.1177/001872675100400101

Venkatesh, V., Thong, J. Y. L., & Xu, X. (2016). Unified theory of acceptance and use of technology: A synthesis and the road ahead. *Journal of the Association for Information Systems*, *17*(5), 328–376. https://aisel.aisnet.org/jais/vol17/iss5/1. DOI: 10.17705/1jais.00428

Wirtz, B. W., Weyerer, J. C., & Geyer, C. (2019). Artificial intelligence and the public sector Applications and challenges. *International Journal of Public Administration*, *42*(7), 596–615. DOI: 10.1080/01900692.2018.1498103

KEY TERMS AND DEFINITIONS

Agile Governance: Agile governance encompasses lightweight yet robust mechanisms for oversight, compliance, accountability, and risk management that align Agile autonomy with organizational, regulatory, and ethical requirements.

Agile Tooling Ecosystems: Agile tooling ecosystems comprise interconnected software platforms that support Agile and DevOps activities, including backlog management, continuous integration, forecasting, risk monitoring, and value tracking across multi-team and enterprise-scale environments.

AI-Augmented Agile: AI-Augmented Agile refers to the integration of artificial intelligence techniques such as machine learning, natural language processing, and predictive analytics into Agile practices to enhance planning, prioritization, estimation, and decision-making while retaining human oversight and iterative delivery principles.

Digital Delivery Metrics: Digital delivery metrics are quantitative and qualitative indicators such as flow efficiency, cycle time, predictability, and value realization used to assess performance and outcomes in Agile and DevOps delivery systems.

Ethical AI in Project Management: Ethical AI in project management involves the responsible design and use of AI systems that respect fairness, accountability, transparency, data privacy, and human agency throughout the project lifecycle.

Explainable AI (XAI): Explainable AI refers to methods and systems that make AI model behavior transparent and interpretable to stakeholders, enabling trust, accountability, and informed decision-making in high-impact environments.

MLOps and LLMOps: MLOps and LLMOps denote operational practices for deploying, monitoring, governing, and continuously improving machine learning and large language models in production systems, ensuring reliability, reproducibility, and compliance.

Reference Architectures: Reference architectures are standardized, reusable architectural models that define core components, integration patterns, governance layers, and data flows, serving as blueprints for designing scalable and interoperable AI-enabled delivery environments.

Chapter 11
Intelligent Facilitation: Exploring AI's Role in Agile Leadership

Otmane Azeroual
http://orcid.org/0000-0002-5225-389X
University of Hagen, Germany

ABSTRACT

Agile frameworks such as Scrum depend on the human-centered roles of Product Owner (PO) and Scrum Master (SM), who balance strategic prioritization, team facilitation, and stakeholder alignment. As artificial intelligence (AI) advances, these roles increasingly gain support from intelligent systems capable of analyzing complex data, generating insights, and automating routine tasks. This chapter examines how AI can augment PO and SM responsibilities, focusing on applications such as backlog analysis, predictive risk assessment, meeting facilitation, and team sentiment monitoring. At the same time, it highlights challenges related to transparency, bias, and the preservation of accountability in agile environments. By exploring human-AI collaboration dynamics and emerging hybrid role profiles, the chapter offers guidance for practitioners and researchers seeking to integrate AI responsibly while maintaining the essential human dimensions of agile leadership.

INTRODUCTION

In the rapidly evolving landscape of software development, the emergence of artificial intelligence (AI) is changing not only how teams build products, but also how they organize themselves (Deshmukh et al., 2023). Agile methodologies such as Scrum rely on deeply human roles — the Product Owner (PO), who crafts the product vision, prioritizes features, and negotiates stakeholder demands; and the

DOI: 10.4018/979-8-3373-6851-1.ch011

Scrum Master (SM), who coaches teams, moderates processes, and helps remove impediments (Moldovan & Georgousis, 2024). These roles have always required a strong mix of leadership, empathy, strategic thinking, and interpersonal skills. As AI systems become more powerful, able to analyze large datasets, generate natural language, and even mimic decision-support, a pressing question arises: can AI support or potentially replace Product Owners (POs) and Scrum Masters (SMs) — and what would that mean for agile teams?

This chapter explores this question in depth. It seeks to understand not just the technical possibilities, but also the organizational, social, and ethical implications of integrating AI into core agile roles. By weaving together theoretical foundations, empirical research, and practical examples, the chapter aims to present a balanced view of how AI might transform these crucial agile functions — and where its limitations lie.

Agile frameworks like Scrum are underpinned by a clear role structure. The PO is accountable for maximizing the value of the product: defining what the team should build, maintaining and prioritizing the product backlog, and serving as a bridge between stakeholders and the development team. According to Atlassian, the PO must balance customer needs and business value, translating them into backlog items and ordering them to deliver maximum impact (Nath et al., 2024). Meanwhile, the SM ensures that the Scrum process is followed, supports the team in self-organization, resolves impediments, and fosters continuous improvement (see Fig. 1). These responsibilities reflect a blend of vision, process stewardship, and servant leadership — tasks deeply rooted in human judgment and social interaction.

Figure 1. Agile Role Structure and Responsibilities.

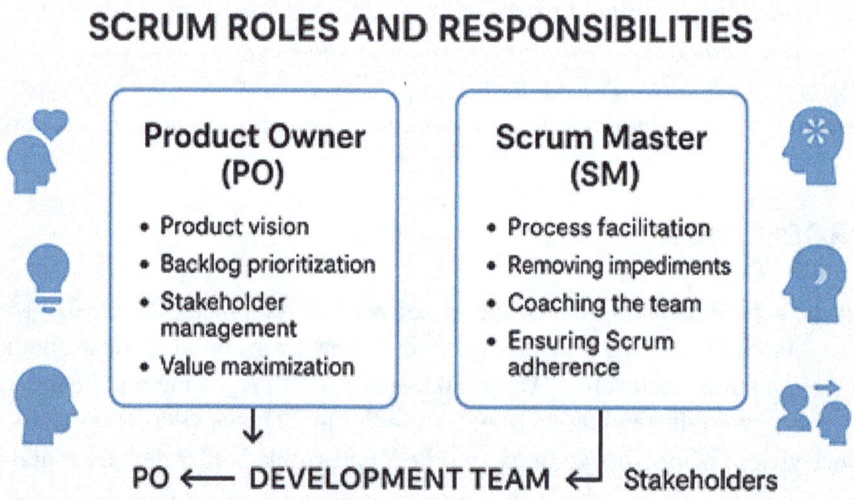

Moreover, Scrum explicitly separates these roles: the PO focuses on the "what" and "why" of the product, while the SM focuses on "how" the team works together, encouraging collaboration and adherence to Scrum values (Patrucco, Canterino & Minelgaite, 2022). This separation helps avoid conflicts of interest and ensures clarity in decision-making. Many agile experts warn against combining the two roles, as they require distinct mindsets and skills (Hofert, 2022; Neumann et al., 2024). Without this distinction, the balance between team process and product value can be lost, undermining the benefits of Scrum.

In parallel with the evolution of agile practices, AI has matured at a remarkable pace. Academically, early work already foresaw the integration of AI into project management. In their seminal paper "Towards effective AI-powered agile project management," Dam et al., 2019 propose a framework in which AI can support estimation, risk prediction, task automation, and recommendation, helping project teams to cope with uncertainty and complexity. More recently, research into "Multimodal Generative AI for Story Point Estimation" has shown how advanced models can combine text, categorical data, and even images to produce more accurate and context-aware estimations of story points — a fundamentally agile metric (Islam & Sandborn, 2025). Another promising development is the prototype RetroAI++, described by Spichkova et al. 2025, which uses AI to improve sprint planning and retrospective analysis by automating insights, recognizing patterns, and suggesting actionable improvements. Meanwhile, forward-looking conceptual work, such as that by Mahboob et al., 2024 in "Future of Artificial Intelligence in Agile Software Development," argues that generative AI and agent-based systems could support decision-making, strategy design, and risk assessment in agile teams — though also raising important concerns about explainability, trust, and responsibility.

These scholarly contributions sketch out a future in which AI does more than process data: it can become an active assistant in agile workflows. For the PO, AI might sift through customer feedback, analyze usage data, and propose backlog prioritization; for the SM, AI could monitor team dynamics, detect impediments by analyzing communication patterns, and even help facilitate meetings. But while these possibilities are seductive, they raise profound questions: Where are the boundaries of AI's competence? Can AI replicate the emotional intelligence, coaching, and human stewardship that define high-performing agile teams? And how do we govern AI's role so that decisions remain accountable, transparent, and aligned with human values?

Despite growing interest in AI-assisted agile work, academic understanding is still limited. The body of literature that directly examines how AI can or should interweave with the PO and SM roles remains sparse. Many studies focus on general project management support or on technical tasks (like estimation), but do not deeply engage with role-specific responsibilities such as stakeholder negotiation, conflict resolution, vision setting, coaching, or team culture. At the same time, real-world practices are already developing. Some organizations experiment with AI-powered tools for retrospective mining, backlog suggestions, or even automated facilitation. These hybrid practices suggest new role designs — but also raise risks around over-reliance, de-skilling, and accountability.

If AI becomes deeply embedded into these agile roles, we may see new hybrid profiles emerge: AI-augmented POs, "AI-assisted SMs," or even entirely new roles that combine human creativity with algorithmic insight. Such a transition, however, must be carefully managed. It requires not only technology, but also governance, education, and ethical consideration.

This chapter therefore aims to chart a path through this emergent terrain. It synthesizes theoretical literature, reviews practical innovations, and critically examines the limits and risks of integrating AI into PO and SM functions. Ultimately, it argues that while AI will not fully replace these human roles anytime soon, it has the potential to become a powerful co-pilot. By augmenting decision-making, automating routine tasks, and providing predictive insight, AI can free POs and SMs to focus on high-value, deeply human work — shaping vision, coaching teams, and maintaining the ethical and social fabric of agile development.

To provide a clear roadmap for the chapter, it is organized into several interconnected sections. The first section, Theoretical Foundations: Agile Roles and AI Augmentation, establishes a conceptual understanding of the responsibilities of POs and SMs, and examines how AI can potentially augment these functions without supplanting the human judgment central to agile practice. Building upon this, Practical Applications of AI for POs and SMs presents concrete use cases, detailing how AI tools are employed in backlog management, meeting facilitation, risk assessment, and knowledge management. The chapter then addresses Risks, Limitations, and Ethical Considerations, highlighting challenges such as algorithmic bias, data quality, privacy, and the maintenance of accountability in AI-augmented decision-making. Following this, Human-AI Interaction and Collaboration Dynamics explores the social, psychological, and organizational implications of integrating AI into team workflows, emphasizing trust, motivation, and adaptive leadership. The penultimate section, Future Perspectives and Role Evolution, provides a forward-looking analysis of emerging hybrid roles, new competencies required, and open research questions. Finally, the Conclusion synthesizes the insights, offers recommendations for research and practice, and reflects on the enduring role of humans in AI-supported agile teams.

This chapter is primarily intended for an interdisciplinary audience, including agile practitioners, software development managers, organizational leaders, and researchers in software engineering, project management, and human-computer interaction. By linking theoretical insights with practical applications and ethical considerations, the chapter provides actionable guidance for teams exploring AI integration while highlighting the implications for skill development, team collaboration, and organizational strategy.

The relevance of this chapter is underscored by several current pain points in agile practice. POs often face the challenge of managing increasingly complex backlogs while aligning competing stakeholder priorities under tight timelines. SMs contend with distributed teams, remote collaboration, and the need to detect early signals of disengagement or conflict. Both roles must navigate high uncertainty, rapid change, and intensive decision-making demands. AI offers tools to address these pain points: automated backlog analysis, predictive risk assessment, sentiment monitoring, and facilitation support can reduce cognitive load, enhance decision quality, and free human practitioners to focus on relational and strategic responsibilities. At the same time, the chapter critically examines the limits of AI, ensuring that human agency, ethical governance, and social cohesion are not compromised in pursuit of efficiency.

By combining a structured overview of AI capabilities with attention to ethical, social, and organizational dimensions, this chapter aims to provide both practical value and scholarly insight. It demonstrates how AI can serve as an augmentation rather than a replacement for the deeply human skills that define effective Product Ownership and Scrum Mastery, and positions readers to understand both the opportunities and challenges of this rapidly evolving landscape.

THEORETICAL FOUNDATIONS: AGILE ROLES AND AI AUGMENTATION

Agile frameworks such as Scrum are fundamentally grounded in clearly defined roles, among which the PO and SM play pivotal, yet distinct, parts. The PO is entrusted with maximizing the product's value by prioritizing the backlog, defining the product vision, and acting as a bridge between stakeholders and the development team (Podeswa, 2021). According to empirical and theoretical literature, this role requires not only business acumen, but also strong interpersonal and decision-making skills (Schmidt & Heidenreich, 2018). The PO must understand stakeholder needs, reconcile competing demands, and communicate effectively with the team — tasks that are deeply human and socially embedded (Pichler, 2020).

In contrast, the SM is dedicated to facilitating the Scrum process, removing impediments, coaching the team, and maintaining the integrity of the agile framework (Shastri, Hoda & Amor, 2021). Research on the SM's role highlights its inherently social nature: a study on distributed Scrum teams identifies six core activities of SMs, such as process anchoring, facilitating stand-ups, sprint planning, and coordinating across teams (Mojabi, 2024). These findings reflect that SMs act as servant-leaders whose influence is rooted in coaching, conflict resolution, and capacity building — not in command-and-control.

The conceptual and practical separation of these roles is crucial. The Scrum Primer warns that conflating PO and SM duties often leads to role confusion, micro-management, or even the collapse of Scrum's self-organizing ethos. Indeed, merging these roles subverts the balance between value-driven prioritization and team autonomy (Paterniti & Manzoni, 2018). Additionally, Scrum's philosophy deliberately avoids the classical project-manager archetype: rather than consolidating authority, it distributes responsibilities among PO, SM, and the development team (Patary, 2019). This separation is echoed in agile practice: for example, in many organizations, attempts to combine SM and PO result in conflict and inefficiency (Rigby, Elk & Berez, 2020).

As AI matures, it introduces a new dimension to this role architecture. AI techniques — especially large language models (LLMs), predictive analytics, and pattern recognition — now enable systems that can partly mimic or support tasks historically reserved for human POs and SMs (see Fig.2).

Figure 2. AI-Augmentation for Product Owner and Scrum Master Roles.

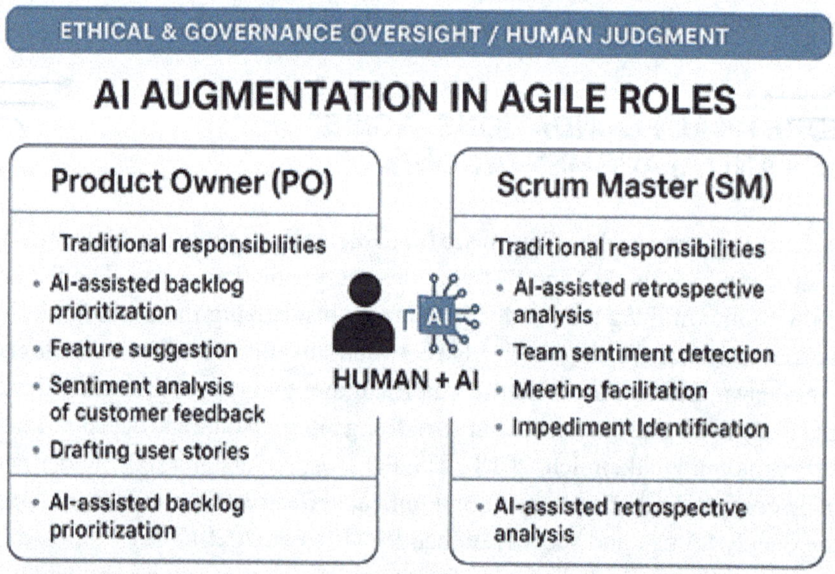

For the PO, AI augmentation can begin in the domain of backlog management and prioritization. AI tools can analyze large volumes of user feedback, sentiment data, usage metrics, and market signals to generate prioritized feature proposals or even draft user stories. For example, Scrum.org's blog on the "Augmented PO" describes how generative AI can craft user stories, suggest UI mockups, and integrate business value estimations in real time, thus accelerating the translation from vision to backlog (Sindiramutty et al., 2025). This amplification does not replace the PO's human judgment; rather, it supplies structured, data-based input that a PO can leverage to make more informed decisions.

From a theoretical standpoint, AI offers cognitive augmentation: by offloading analytical and repetitive tasks, POs can dedicate more of their capacity to strategic thinking, stakeholder engagement, and value negotiation. In this way, AI acts as a co-pilot rather than an autopilot. Such augmentation aligns with the evolving understanding of leadership as a collaborative process, where decision-makers interweave human insight with algorithmic support.

For the SM, AI presents a similarly compelling opportunity. Advanced research demonstrates prototypes where AI assists in critical Scrum ceremonies and process analysis. For instance, the "RetroAI++" project provides a prototype that uses AI for retrospective analysis, detecting patterns in team feedback, generating actionable insights, and suggesting improvements for future sprints (Spichkova et al., 2025). By automating parts of the retrospective, AI can help SMs identify recurring impediments or systemic issues more quickly, giving them more time to focus on coaching and team development.

Moreover, cognitive agents powered by LLMs have been proposed to assist in Agile project management broadly. Recent work explores how such agents might simulate or support roles in scaled agile environments, communicating with human team members, delegating tasks, and managing interdependencies (Cinkusz & Chudziak, 2025). These agents could potentially serve as digital proxies for SM tasks, particularly in analyzing language, tracking sentiment, generating meeting summaries, and alerting to risks — all while the human SM preserves responsibility for relational leadership and resolving nuances beyond AI's reach.

Research into human–AI collaboration in agile settings further underlines potential synergies. In one action-research study, custom LLM-based meeting assistants were embedded in Scrum rituals (e.g., daily stand-ups and backlog refinement). The authors found that these AI assistants could foster new team dynamics, help maintain meeting focus, and reduce administrative burden, but integration required careful calibration of trust, prompt design, and human oversight (Herda et al., 2025).

These theoretical foundations suggest a reimagining of agile roles: rather than replacing POs or SMs, AI may serve as augmentation, amplifying their capabilities while preserving core human functions. Such an arrangement raises important conceptual implications. First, it challenges traditional boundaries: if AI can help generate backlog items or propose priorities, what remains uniquely human in the PO role? Is it conflict resolution, vision-setting, and stakeholder diplomacy?

Similarly, if AI can perform retrospective sentiment analysis, what uniquely human contributions does the SM make? Perhaps it is in coaching, relational trust building, and facilitating sense-making in ambiguous situations.

Second, the integration of AI calls for a re-examination of authority and accountability in Agile teams. Who owns the AI's suggestions? Does the PO simply accept them, or must they justify deviations from them? How do teams ensure that AI-driven recommendations do not undermine the empirical, constructivist nature of Scrum? These questions bring forward governance concerns, such as transparency of AI models, traceability of decisions, and mechanisms for human override.

Third, the augmentation of PO and SM roles by AI introduces ethical and epistemic challenges. AI systems trained on historical project data may reflect biases or perpetuate suboptimal patterns embedded in past sprints. If POs rely on such systems uncritically, they risk amplifying flawed heuristics. If SMs use AI agents to detect team mood or sentiment, they must carefully manage privacy, consent, and psychological safety.

Furthermore, theoretical frameworks from leadership studies may need to evolve. The traditional view of the SM as a servant-leader assumes human empathy, moral agency, and reflexivity. When augmented by AI, the concept of leadership may shift: SMs may become meta-coaches who coach not only people but people working with AI, guiding interpretation of AI outputs, mediating between AI and humans, and ensuring that AI remains a servant, not a dominator.

Another theoretical consideration is the evolution of role hybridization. Rather than strict human-only PO or SM roles, we may see new configurations emerge: the AI-augmented PO, the AI-assisted SM, or even an AI–Human hybrid agent that co-manages certain administrative or analytical tasks. These hybrid roles suggest that the future of agile teams may be less about human-versus-AI and more about *collaboration architecture*: how to structure human-AI partnerships so that strengths are leveraged and responsibilities are appropriately distributed.

Finally, examining the theoretical foundations of these augmented roles points toward a broader research agenda. Scholars need to investigate empirically how these augmented roles affect team effectiveness, trust, psychological safety, and innovation. Specifically, questions include: How does reliance on AI affect a PO's sense of ownership? How do SMs mediate between AI suggestions and organic team conversations? What governance structures are needed to ensure responsible use of AI in agile contexts?

In sum, the theoretical foundation of Agile Roles and AI Augmentation suggests that AI has significant potential to enhance, but not fully replace, the roles of PO and SM. By automating analytical and repetitive tasks, AI frees these roles to concentrate on human-centered capabilities: coaching, leadership, negotiation, and strategic thinking. However, this new paradigm also demands fresh frameworks for authority, accountability, role definition and ethical oversight. As AI becomes more integrated in agile workflows, both practitioners and researchers will need to rethink what it means to lead, serve, and produce value in agile teams.

While theoretical foundations clarify the potential and limitations of AI in augmenting the responsibilities of POs and SMs, the question remains: how are these concepts instantiated in real-world practice? The next section examines concrete applications of AI within agile workflows, illustrating how theory translates into actionable tools and measurable outcomes.

PRACTICAL APPLICATIONS OF AI FOR POs AND SMs

The practical integration of AI into agile project management has transitioned from theoretical exploration to tangible, data-driven applications that enhance productivity, decision-making, and team coordination. AI's ability to process vast amounts of structured and unstructured data, detect patterns, and generate actionable recommendations allows both POs and SMs to operate more efficiently, particularly in complex, distributed, or stakeholder-intensive environments (Oloyede & Owen, 2025). Importantly, AI does not replace human judgment but serves as an augmentation mechanism that amplifies capabilities while preserving the relational, ethical, and strategic responsibilities of agile leadership.

For POs, AI is predominantly applied to backlog management, refinement, and prioritization. Natural language processing (NLP) and machine learning algorithms can analyze multiple input sources—including customer feedback, support tickets, usage analytics, and social media content—to identify recurring themes, emerging requirements, and sentiment trends (Owusu-Berko, 2025). These insights support evidence-based decision-making regarding feature implementation, sequencing, and release planning. AI-assisted modules within platforms such as Jira or Azure DevOps operationalize this capability, automating scoring of backlog items according to projected business value, effort estimates, and anticipated user impact.

Beyond backlog management, AI enhances market analysis and strategic roadmap planning. Predictive models aggregate competitive intelligence, historical product performance, and industry trends to generate scenario-based recommendations. These models allow POs to simulate alternative prioritization strategies, estimate potential delivery timelines, adoption rates, and financial outcomes, and align multiple interdependent teams in scaled agile frameworks (Dugbartey & Kehinde, 2025).

SMs also benefit from AI, particularly in team performance monitoring, facilitation, and risk identification. AI-driven analytics assess collaboration patterns, communication frequency, and sentiment indicators from project management tools or digital communication platforms, providing early warnings of disengagement, bottlenecks, or emerging conflicts (Spichkova et al., 2025). Tools like RetroAI++ utilize NLP to analyze retrospective data and identify recurring impediments, allowing SMs to focus on targeted interventions rather than routine monitoring. Automated transcription, summarization, and task-tracking further enhance the efficiency of sprint planning, daily stand-ups, and review meetings, particularly in distributed or asynchronous teams (Herda et al., 2025).

AI also supports risk assessment, predictive decision-making, and knowledge management. By analyzing historical sprint data, task dependencies, and resource allocations, AI can estimate the likelihood of delays, identify critical dependencies, and recommend mitigation strategies. Centralized, AI-powered knowledge repositories facilitate onboarding, document decision histories, and suggest best practices, ensuring continuity and adherence to organizational standards.

To summarize and make practical applications explicit, Table 1 presents key use cases of AI for both POs and SMs, the type of AI applied, and the expected benefits:

Table 1. AI Use Cases for POs and SMs in Agile Project Management.

Role	Use Case	AI Type / Technology	Practical Application	Expected Benefits
PO	Backlog prioritization	NLP, ML predictive models	Analyzes stakeholder feedback, usage analytics, and support tickets to score backlog items	Evidence-based prioritization, reduced cognitive load, improved alignment with business value
PO	Roadmap planning	Predictive analytics, scenario modeling	Simulates feature sequencing, forecasts adoption and delivery outcomes	Strategic decision support, better alignment across interdependent teams
PO	Customer sentiment analysis	NLP, sentiment analysis	Evaluates customer feedback, social media, and product reviews	Identification of emerging trends, improved user-centric decision-making
SM	Team performance monitoring	Data analytics, sentiment analysis	Analyzes communication frequency, collaboration patterns, and sentiment	Early detection of disengagement, conflicts, or workflow bottlenecks
SM	Retrospective analysis	NLP, pattern recognition	Identifies recurring impediments and improvement opportunities	Enhanced continuous improvement, focused interventions
SM	Meeting facilitation	Automated transcription, summarization, task tracking	Summarizes meetings, assigns action items, tracks progress	Reduced administrative overhead, improved meeting efficiency
Both	Risk assessment	Predictive modeling	Forecasts delivery delays, identifies dependencies, suggests mitigation strategies	Proactive risk management, optimized sprint planning
Both	Knowledge management	AI-powered repositories, recommendation systems	Stores project knowledge, recommends best practices and guidelines	Continuous learning, reduced information loss, faster onboarding

The deployment of AI, however, necessitates careful human oversight to mitigate risks such as automation bias, data quality issues, and misinterpretation of outputs (Holzinger, Zatloukal & Müller, 2025). Historical data may encode biases or sub-optimal practices, and sentiment or predictive analyses require contextual human judgment. Consequently, AI is most effective when implemented as a decision-support system, complementing human expertise rather than substituting for it.

Overall, evidence from industry implementations, pilot studies, and academic research illustrates that AI materially enhances operational efficiency for POs and SMs. By automating analytical and administrative tasks, providing predictive insights, and enabling proactive interventions, AI allows agile practitioners to concentrate on strategic, relational, and value-creation activities, thereby preserving the human-centric competencies critical to successful agile project management. The table of use cases highlights both the versatility of AI applications and the tangible benefits realized in modern agile environments.

Although AI demonstrates significant potential in backlog management, meeting facilitation, and risk assessment, practical deployment is not without challenges. The subsequent section explores the inherent risks, limitations, and ethical considerations that accompany AI integration, emphasizing the need for human oversight and governance.

RISKS, LIMITATIONS, AND ETHICAL CONSIDERATIONS OF AI IN AGILE ROLES

While AI offers significant augmentation opportunities for POs and SMs, its integration into agile project management introduces a spectrum of risks, limitations, and ethical challenges that warrant careful consideration. The primary concern revolves around the inherent limitations of AI in replicating human judgment, emotional intelligence, and ethical reasoning — competencies that are essential to both PO and SM responsibilities (Parikh, 2025; Naithani, Tiwari & Kumari, 2025). AI systems operate on historical data and algorithmic models, which can reflect biases, incomplete information, or misrepresentations of context, potentially leading to flawed recommendations if used without appropriate human oversight (Parikh, 2025).

For POs, reliance on AI for backlog prioritization or market analysis carries the risk of over-dependence on algorithmic outputs. Machine learning models are trained on past project data, which may encode historical inefficiencies, stakeholder biases, or patterns that are no longer relevant. If such recommendations are adopted uncritically, there is a danger of perpetuating systemic errors, overlooking innovative opportunities, or misaligning product development with evolving market demands (Balzano, 2025). Moreover, AI systems may inadequately capture qualitative aspects of stakeholder feedback, such as nuanced expectations, emotional undertones, or conflicting priorities, which are central to strategic decision-making and value maximization.

SMs face analogous limitations in their augmented roles. AI-driven analyses of team communication and sentiment can detect trends and anomalies, but they cannot fully comprehend complex interpersonal dynamics, subtle conflict signals, or cultural and contextual subtleties that influence team behavior (Spichkova et al., 2025). Misinterpretation of AI-generated insights could result in inappropriate interventions, undermining trust, psychological safety, and team cohesion. Furthermore, overreliance on automated facilitation or sentiment monitoring might diminish the SM's active engagement and observational judgment, which are critical for fostering self-organization and adaptive learning within agile teams.

Ethical considerations extend beyond technical limitations. Privacy and data protection are paramount when AI systems monitor team communication, analyze stakeholder inputs, or process sensitive organizational data. Without clear consent, transparency, and secure handling, the use of AI could violate ethical standards and regulatory requirements, including data protection laws such as GDPR (Herda et al., 2025). Additionally, algorithmic opacity — the "black box" problem — raises accountability concerns. Decisions or recommendations generated by AI may lack explainability, making it difficult for POs and SMs to justify actions to stakeholders, teams, or management. This creates potential liability and challenges the principle of responsible leadership.

Bias represents another critical ethical risk. AI models can inadvertently amplify existing biases embedded in historical project data, including gender, cultural, or hierarchical biases. For instance, task allocation suggestions may favor historically dominant team members, or sentiment analysis may misinterpret communication styles associated with minority groups. Without careful monitoring and mitigation strategies, AI-assisted decisions could reinforce inequities, reduce inclusivity, and compromise team morale (Parikh, 2025).

From an operational perspective, AI integration introduces systemic limitations. Effective use of AI requires high-quality, comprehensive data, as well as infrastructure capable of processing and analyzing it. Organizations lacking mature data collection practices or agile measurement frameworks may experience suboptimal outcomes or unreliable recommendations. Furthermore, AI systems require continuous training, validation, and adaptation to remain relevant in dynamic project environments, which imposes ongoing resource demands (Mahboob, et al., 2024).

Another limitation concerns the potential erosion of human skills. As AI assumes tasks such as backlog analysis, sentiment monitoring, or meeting summarization, there is a risk that POs and SMs may underutilize or lose critical judgment, facilitation, and decision-making capabilities over time. Maintaining a balance between automation and human engagement is essential to prevent skill atrophy and ensure that teams continue to rely on human-centered leadership when necessary.

Mitigating these risks requires a framework that combines technical, managerial, and ethical strategies. Human-in-the-loop approaches, in which AI provides recommendations but human practitioners retain ultimate authority, are critical for preserving accountability and ethical oversight. Governance protocols, including audit trails, transparency mechanisms, and performance validation, help ensure that AI outputs are interpretable, traceable, and aligned with organizational objectives. Training programs for POs and SMs that emphasize AI literacy, critical evaluation, and ethical decision-making are equally important to cultivate informed adoption and responsible usage (Rajnath & Kumar, 2025).

Finally, organizations must consider the cultural and social dimensions of AI integration. The acceptance of AI-augmented roles depends on trust between human practitioners, teams, and AI systems. Transparent communication about AI capabilities, limitations, and decision boundaries is essential to maintain team cohesion and psychological safety. Additionally, continuous feedback loops, iterative evaluation of AI performance, and collaborative adjustment of workflows ensure that AI serves as a supportive tool rather than a disruptive force.

Collectively, these considerations illustrate that while AI offers significant advantages in augmenting PO and SM functions, its deployment entails complex risks spanning technical, operational, ethical, and social domains. Addressing these challenges requires deliberate governance, human oversight, and ethical frameworks that preserve human judgment, accountability, and the relational dimensions of agile practice.

Beyond technical and ethical considerations, AI integration fundamentally alters team dynamics, communication, and trust relationships. The following section delves into these socio-technical interactions, examining how human-AI collaboration shapes motivation, engagement, and decision-making within agile teams.

HUMAN-AI INTERACTION AND COLLABORATION DYNAMICS

AI is increasingly embedded within agile workflows, fundamentally reshaping interactions among team members and between humans and digital agents. This shift has significant implications for communication, trust, and decision-making processes in PO and SM roles (Bonghez, 2025; Spichkova et al., 2025). Rather than functioning merely as a tool, AI can be conceptualized as a collaborative participant that both informs and is informed by human activity, creating a socio-technical system in which human judgment and machine analytics are interdependent.

One central aspect concerns the calibration of trust in AI outputs. Research on human-computer interaction emphasizes that reliance on AI is mediated by perceived reliability, transparency, and interpretability of recommendations (Chae & Yoon,

2025). In agile contexts, excessive dependence may lead to automation bias, where decisions are followed uncritically, while insufficient trust may result in underutilization of valuable insights. POs and SMs therefore must balance efficiency gains with critical evaluation, ensuring that AI contributions complement rather than override human expertise.

Interpretive challenges represent another important dimension. Agile methods rely heavily on tacit knowledge, informal cues, and context-sensitive reasoning (Yan et al., 2025). AI systems, including those utilizing natural language processing, cannot fully grasp nuanced social signals, such as team morale, subtle disagreements, or implicit expectations. Misinterpretation of AI-generated sentiment or analytics may result in inappropriate interventions if not carefully contextualized by human leaders. Consequently, the SM assumes a mediator role, translating machine insights into actionable strategies while preserving the team's social and emotional balance.

AI's presence also alters collaboration patterns within the team. Digital agents participating in meetings, backlog refinement, or progress monitoring may change communication hierarchies and workflow dynamics. Teams may direct questions or feedback toward AI systems, which can improve task efficiency but may also introduce social friction if the AI is perceived as evaluative or intrusive (Herda et al., 2025). Establishing clear interaction protocols and defining boundaries of AI involvement is essential to maintain human agency and team cohesion.

The influence on motivation and engagement is equally significant. By automating repetitive and analytical tasks, AI can free POs and SMs to focus on strategy, coaching, and decision-making, potentially enhancing job satisfaction and perceived value contribution. Conversely, over-automation may reduce perceived autonomy and self-determination, undermining intrinsic motivation and impairing team self-organization. Thus, careful design of AI-supported workflows is required to sustain meaningful human involvement.

Organizationally, AI facilitates iterative learning through continuous feedback loops. Insights generated by AI inform human decisions, and human corrections refine AI models, creating a co-adaptive system. However, this requires structured mechanisms for accountability, error correction, and conflict resolution between AI recommendations and human judgment. Without such mechanisms, there is a risk of reinforcing biases or propagating errors throughout the team.

Cultural and social variables further shape AI adoption. Distributed or multicultural teams exhibit varying degrees of acceptance, trust, and interaction norms with AI systems. Transparent communication regarding AI capabilities and limitations is critical to mitigate resistance and maintain equitable team dynamics (Joshi, 2025).

Finally, the introduction of AI in agile teams necessitates reconsideration of leadership and accountability. While AI may guide analytical decisions, ultimate responsibility rests with human POs and SMs. This hybrid leadership model requires advanced competencies in AI literacy, ethical judgment, and socio-technical reasoning to ensure that AI functions as an augmentative resource rather than a decision-maker (Çeri & Erhan, 2025).

Taken together, these factors indicate that the effectiveness of AI in agile environments depends not only on technological sophistication but also on the management of human-AI interaction, trust calibration, interpretive oversight, and organizational culture. When integrated thoughtfully, AI can enhance decision-making, reduce cognitive burden, and provide actionable insights, all while preserving the human-centered principles critical to agile project management.

Understanding current interaction patterns provides a foundation for anticipating future developments. Building on these insights, the next section offers a forward-looking perspective on the evolution of agile roles, the emergence of hybrid human-AI profiles, and the competencies required for effective collaboration in AI-augmented environments.

FUTURE PERSPECTIVES AND ROLE EVOLUTION

The ongoing integration of AI into agile project management not only transforms current workflows but also necessitates a forward-looking perspective on the evolution of PO and SM roles. Emerging technologies, increasing data availability, and advanced machine learning models are likely to produce a paradigm shift in which human responsibilities, competencies, and organizational structures are redefined. Understanding these future dynamics is essential for researchers, practitioners, and organizations seeking to anticipate the capabilities required for successful AI-augmented agile teams.

One of the most significant developments is the emergence of hybrid or AI-augmented roles. Rather than viewing AI as a mere tool, future frameworks may conceptualize it as an active collaborator that co-manages specific aspects of PO and SM responsibilities. For POs, AI-augmentation could extend beyond backlog analysis or feature prioritization to encompass predictive scenario modeling, automated stakeholder analysis, and continuous evaluation of product-market fit. In such a configuration, the PO functions as a strategic integrator, synthesizing AI-derived recommendations with human judgment, domain knowledge, and ethical considerations. Similarly, AI-assisted SMs may rely on intelligent agents for sentiment analysis, workload optimization, and retrospective pattern recognition, allowing the SM to focus on relational leadership, conflict mediation, and the cultivation of psychological safety. These hybrid roles exemplify a collaborative human-AI ecosystem in which decision-making responsibilities are shared, and human competencies are amplified rather than replaced (Dili & Ansong, 2025).

The shift toward AI-augmented roles implies substantial changes in required competencies and skill sets. Traditional PO and SM capabilities, such as stakeholder negotiation, facilitation, and domain expertise, will remain critical; however, new competencies will gain prominence. AI literacy, including the ability to interpret algorithmic outputs, assess data quality, and validate model predictions, will become essential. Moreover, ethical discernment will be increasingly important as POs and SMs navigate decisions influenced by AI recommendations, ensuring fairness, transparency, and accountability. Leadership skills may evolve to include digital mediation: understanding how AI influences team behavior, communication patterns, and autonomy, and designing workflows that optimize collaboration between humans and machines (Bock & von der Oelsnitz, 2025). Consequently, organizational training programs must adapt to equip agile practitioners with interdisciplinary skills that blend technical literacy, strategic decision-making, and socio-emotional intelligence.

Future role evolution may also involve structural transformations in team composition and responsibilities. Hybrid PO-AI or SM-AI systems may enable the delegation of routine analytical or monitoring tasks to digital agents, reducing the number of human hours required for administrative functions. This could allow agile teams to operate at larger scales or across more complex product portfolios without proportional increases in human resources. Additionally, AI may facilitate distributed and asynchronous collaboration, allowing for more flexible team configurations while maintaining cohesion and accountability. As these dynamics unfold, organizations will need to reconsider traditional definitions of team roles, reporting structures, and performance evaluation metrics, shifting from purely human-centered assessments to frameworks that account for AI-assisted contributions (Herda et al., 2025).

The evolution of AI-augmented roles also raises important research questions and knowledge gaps. First, the long-term impact on human judgment, expertise, and skill retention is not well understood. As AI assumes analytical and repetitive tasks, there is a risk that POs and SMs may become over-reliant on algorithmic recommendations, potentially diminishing critical thinking or relational capabilities. Empirical research is needed to assess how human decision-making evolves in hybrid settings, particularly regarding bias detection, ethical reasoning, and creativity. Second, the optimal balance between AI autonomy and human oversight remains an open question. Investigating frameworks for dynamic task allocation, human-in-the-loop processes, and trust calibration will be crucial to ensure both efficiency and accountability. Third, the psychological and social implications of AI integration require careful study, including effects on team motivation, cohesion, and cultural acceptance. Understanding these dynamics is essential to maintain effective collaboration and preserve the adaptive, self-organizing principles central to Scrum (Orozco, 2025).

From a methodological perspective, future research should explore longitudinal and cross-context studies. Observing AI-augmented agile teams over extended periods will illuminate how roles evolve, how skills are redistributed, and how AI influences organizational learning. Comparative analyses across industries and cultural contexts can reveal variations in adoption strategies, acceptance levels, and performance outcomes. Additionally, action-research approaches, in which researchers actively participate in AI-enhanced agile workflows, can provide rich qualitative insights into the negotiation of human-AI collaboration, decision-making practices, and ethical dilemmas.

Technological developments will continue to shape these role evolutions. Advances in natural language processing, predictive modeling, and reinforcement learning may allow AI systems to handle increasingly complex tasks, from forecasting market trends to mediating team conflicts. Future AI agents might not only provide recommendations but also simulate potential outcomes, assess ethical implications, and adapt dynamically to team feedback. These capabilities could redefine the boundaries of human responsibility, positioning POs and SMs as evaluators, orchestrators, and ethical stewards in a human-AI collaborative environment.

Finally, the broader organizational and societal implications must be considered. AI-augmented roles may influence workforce composition, skill requirements, and career trajectories. Organizations may need to implement governance mechanisms to ensure transparency, accountability, and equitable distribution of AI benefits. Regulatory frameworks and ethical guidelines will play an increasing role in shaping how AI is deployed in agile environments, ensuring that technological augmentation supports human-centered values rather than undermining autonomy or fairness.

Overall, the future perspective suggests that PO and SM roles will transition toward hybrid, AI-augmented configurations that blend human judgment with machine intelligence. Competencies will evolve to integrate technical literacy, ethical reasoning, and socio-emotional awareness, while team structures and workflows may adapt to accommodate AI-enabled scalability and distributed collaboration. These developments open new avenues for research, practical experimentation, and methodological innovation, emphasizing the need for interdisciplinary approaches that unite organizational science, computer science, ethics, and human factors. By anticipating these changes, practitioners and researchers can proactively shape the evolution of agile roles, ensuring that AI augmentation enhances value creation, preserves human agency, and strengthens team adaptability in increasingly complex and data-intensive project environments.

Insights from both current practice and future projections converge to highlight the strategic, ethical, and operational implications of AI in agile roles. The concluding section synthesizes these findings, providing recommendations for research and practice while reflecting on the enduring significance of human judgment in AI-supported agile teams.

CONCLUSION

The analysis of POs and SMs in the context of AI-augmented agile project management demonstrates the multifaceted impact of AI on contemporary and future workflows. Across theoretical frameworks, practical applications, human-AI interaction dynamics, and ethical considerations, AI emerges as a transformative tool capable of enhancing efficiency, decision-making, and value creation. At the same time, the integration of AI introduces significant complexities, requiring critical reflection on human agency, ethical responsibility, and skill evolution. This conclusion synthesizes the key insights from preceding sections, identifies recommendations for research and practice, and offers a reflective perspective on the evolving role of humans in AI-supported agile environments.

From a theoretical standpoint, AI augmentation challenges traditional conceptualizations of the PO and SM roles. POs have historically been responsible for value maximization, backlog prioritization, and stakeholder alignment, while SMs serve as facilitators, coaches, and guardians of the agile process (Dugbartey & Kehinde, 2025). The introduction of AI adds a layer of analytical and predictive capability that can assist in data-driven decision-making, scenario planning, and workflow optimization. Theoretical literature emphasizes that while AI can replicate certain cognitive and analytical functions, it cannot replace the relational, ethical, and judgment-driven aspects that define these roles. Consequently, AI functions most effectively as an augmentation tool rather than a substitute, enabling POs and SMs to focus on high-value tasks that require emotional intelligence, ethical discernment, and complex decision-making (Mishra & Mishra, 2025).

Practical applications of AI illustrate the tangible ways in which these augmentations manifest. For POs, AI enables automated backlog refinement, prioritization based on predictive analytics, and data-informed scenario modeling. These capabilities reduce cognitive load, accelerate decision cycles, and provide evidence-based guidance that can improve product-market alignment. For SMs, AI supports meeting facilitation, team sentiment analysis, and retrospective evaluation, offering early detection of bottlenecks, conflicts, or emerging risks (Herda et al., 2025). By automating repetitive or analytical tasks, AI frees human practitioners to concentrate on coaching, leadership, and relational facilitation, thus enhancing overall team performance.

Despite these opportunities, the integration of AI carries inherent risks and limitations. Bias in training data, algorithmic opacity, and privacy concerns can compromise decision-making or undermine ethical standards. Over-reliance on AI may reduce human judgment or skill retention, while misinterpretation of AI outputs can lead to inappropriate interventions or conflict within teams (Doh, 2025; Parikh, 2025). Furthermore, cultural and organizational factors influence the acceptance and effectiveness of AI augmentation, particularly in distributed or multicultural teams where communication norms and trust levels vary. Ethical frameworks, governance protocols, and human-in-the-loop mechanisms are therefore essential to ensure accountability, transparency, and responsible use of AI in agile settings.

The study of human-AI interaction and collaboration dynamics underscores the importance of trust calibration, interpretive oversight, and workflow design. AI does not operate in isolation; its outputs must be interpreted, validated, and integrated by human practitioners. POs and SMs must act as mediators between AI recommendations and team realities, translating analytical insights into actionable strategies that maintain psychological safety, autonomy, and motivation. This socio-technical perspective highlights that AI is not merely a technical artifact but a participant in collaborative processes, shaping communication, behavior, and decision-making in complex ways (Tsarouhas & Grigoriadis, 2025; Spichkova et al., 2025).

Looking toward the future, the evolution of agile roles suggests the emergence of hybrid human-AI configurations. POs and SMs will increasingly operate as strategic integrators and ethical stewards, synthesizing AI-derived recommendations with human judgment, relational skills, and domain expertise. These hybrid roles will require new competencies, including AI literacy, data interpretation, ethical reasoning, and socio-emotional intelligence. Organizations will need to redesign training programs, performance metrics, and governance structures to support these changes, ensuring that AI augmentation enhances value creation without compromising human agency or accountability (Khera, Sharma & Kumar, 2025).

From a research perspective, several priorities emerge. Longitudinal studies are necessary to examine how hybrid roles evolve over time, particularly regarding skill retention, decision-making quality, and team performance. Comparative studies across industries, cultural contexts, and organizational sizes can provide insights into best practices for AI integration and the contextual factors that influence success. Moreover, the development of standardized evaluation frameworks and metrics for assessing AI's impact on agile roles will support evidence-based decision-making and responsible technology adoption. Interdisciplinary research, bridging organizational science, human-computer interaction, ethics, and machine learning, will be critical to fully understand and guide the evolution of AI-augmented agile roles.

In practice, organizations should adopt a phased and deliberate approach to AI integration. Clear definitions of AI responsibilities, human oversight protocols, and ethical guidelines are essential. Training and support for POs and SMs should focus on interpretive judgment, ethical decision-making, and collaborative human-AI workflows. Additionally, continuous evaluation of AI performance and its impact on team dynamics, decision quality, and psychological safety will help ensure that augmentation delivers intended benefits while mitigating risks. Pilot implementations, iterative adjustments, and stakeholder engagement are recommended strategies to align AI capabilities with organizational goals and team needs.

Finally, reflection on the role of the human in AI-supported agile teams reveals that human judgment, relational expertise, and ethical reasoning remain irreplaceable. AI can enhance analytical capacity, reduce cognitive load, and provide predictive insights, yet it cannot replicate the socio-emotional intelligence, moral discernment, and adaptive decision-making that are central to effective Product Ownership and Scrum Mastery. The future of agile project management lies in a collaborative partnership between humans and AI, in which human practitioners retain ultimate responsibility, guide ethical and strategic decisions, and ensure that AI functions as a supportive, rather than directive, agent.

Taken together, these insights suggest that AI-augmented agile roles represent both an opportunity and a challenge. They offer the potential to improve efficiency, decision-making, and responsiveness to market and team dynamics, while simultaneously demanding careful attention to ethics, human skill development, and socio-technical integration. By embracing AI as a partner rather than a replacement, organizations can harness its capabilities to enhance agile practices, preserve human-centered leadership, and prepare for the evolving demands of complex, data-intensive project environments.

REFERENCES

Balzano, M. (2025). Post-error adjustments: Strategic agility and organizational zemblanity. *California Management Review, 67*(4), 121–153. DOI: 10.1177/00081256251332311

Bock, T., & von der Oelsnitz, D. (2025). Leadership-competences in the era of artificial intelligence–a structured review. *Strategy and Leadership, 53*(3), 235–255. DOI: 10.1108/SL-09-2024-0100

Bonghez, S. (2025). Scrum team tales: conquering challenges with scrum masters and product owners. In *Case Studies on Project Management in Practice* (pp. 99–105). Edward Elgar Publishing. DOI: 10.4337/9781035311279.00016

Çeri, Ş. Ö., & Erhan, T. (2025). A Conceptual Study on the Effects of Artificial Intelligence in Managerial Decision-Making. *European Journal of Digital Economy Research, 6*(1), 5–21.

Chae, H. S., & Yoon, C. (2025). Factors Affecting Human-Generated AI Collaboration: Trust and Perceived Usefulness as Mediators. *Information (Basel), 16*(10), 856. DOI: 10.3390/info16100856

Cinkusz, K., & Chudziak, J. (2025). Agile Software Management with Cognitive Multi-Agent Systems. In *17th International Conference on Agents and Artificial Intelligence.* SciTePress. DOI: 10.5220/0013153000003890

Dam, H. K., Tran, T., Grundy, J., Ghose, A., & Kamei, Y. (2019). Towards effective AI-powered agile project management. In *2019 IEEE/ACM 41st international conference on software engineering: new ideas and emerging results (ICSE-NIER)* (pp. 41-44). IEEE. DOI: 10.1109/ICSE-NIER.2019.00019

Deshmukh, A., Patil, D. S., Mohan, J. S., Balamurugan, G., & Tyagi, A. K. (2023). Transforming next generation-based artificial intelligence for software development: current status, issues, challenges, and future opportunities. In *Emerging Technologies and Digital Transformation in the Manufacturing Industry* (pp. 30–66). IGI global. DOI: 10.4018/978-1-6684-8088-5.ch003

Dili, G., & Ansong, E. D. (2025). Human–AI Collaboration: A Paradigm Shift in Decision-Making. In *The Power of Agentic AI: Redefining Human Life and Decision-Making: In Industry 6.0* (pp. 59–80). Springer Nature Switzerland. DOI: 10.1007/978-3-031-89424-4_5

Doh, W. (2025). *Systematically Predicting and Preventing Overreliance Through the Human-AI-System Concordance (HASC) Matrix and Cognitive Interventions* (Doctoral dissertation).

Dugbartey, A. N., & Kehinde, O. (2025). Optimizing project delivery through agile methodologies: Balancing speed, collaboration and stakeholder engagement. *World J. Adv. Res. Rev*, *25*(1), 1237–1257. DOI: 10.30574/wjarr.2025.25.1.0193

Herda, T., Pichler, V., Zhang, Z., Abrahamsson, P., & Hanssen, G. K. (2025). AI and Agile Software Development: From Frustration to Success XP2025 Workshop Summary. In *International Conference on Agile Software Development* (pp. 3-13). Cham: Springer Nature Switzerland.

Hofert, S. (2022). *The agile mindset: Developing employees, shaping the future of work*. Springer Nature. DOI: 10.1007/978-3-658-34910-3

Holzinger, A., Zatloukal, K., & Müller, H. (2025). Is human oversight to AI systems still possible? *New Biotechnology*, *85*, 59–62. DOI: 10.1016/j.nbt.2024.12.003 PMID: 39675423

Islam, M. R., & Sandborn, P. (2025). Multimodal Generative AI for Story Point Estimation in Software Development. *arXiv preprint arXiv:2505.16290*.

Joshi, S. (2025). The Role of AI in Enhancing Teamwork, Resilience and Decision-Making: Review of Recent Developments. *International Journal of Computer Applications*, *187*(8), 9–26. DOI: 10.5120/ijca2025925036

Khera, P., Sharma, M., & Kumar, A. (2025). Reforming Organization Development Through AI: Strategies for Improved Processes and Performance. In *Achieving Organizational Diversity, Equity, and Inclusion with AI* (pp. 315-336). IGI Global Scientific Publishing.

Mahboob, M., Ahmed, M. R. U., Zia, Z., Ali, M. S., & Ahmed, A. K. (2024). Future of artificial intelligence in agile software development. *arXiv preprint arXiv:2408.00703*.

Mishra, K., & Mishra, S. (2025). Artificial and Emotional Intelligence for Employee Engagement with E-Human Resource Management. *Intellectuals' Book Palace*.

Mojabi, O. (2024). Harmonizing Agile transformation: Navigating software startup success through a hybrid journey of Scrum, Kanban-a Case Study analysis.

Moldovan, A., & Georgousis, I. (2024). Navigating Scrum-The Impact of Agile Leadership and Coaching on IT Project Outcomes.

Naithani, K., Tiwari, S., & Kumari, S. (2025). *AI for Product Development*. Taylor & Francis Group. DOI: 10.1201/9781003536901

Nath, J., Kurni, M., & Choudhuri, S. S. (2024). *A Comprehensive Guide to Agile Transformation, Enterprise Innovation, and Productivity*. Cambridge Scholars Publishing.

Neumann, M., Kuchel, T., Diebold, P., & Schön, E. M. (2024). Agile culture clash: Unveiling challenges in cultivating an agile mindset in organizations. *arXiv preprint arXiv:2405.15066*.

Oloyede, J., & Owen, J. (2025). AI-Driven Knowledge Extraction: Managing Unstructured Data for Business Intelligence Author. *Available at SSRN* 5144223. DOI: 10.2139/ssrn.5144223

Orozco, E. (2025). *FAST: Fully aligned strategic teams*. Solo Unicorn Press.

Owusu-Berko, L. (2025). Harnessing big data, machine learning, and sentiment analysis to optimize customer engagement, loyalty, and market positioning. *Int. J. Comput. Appl. Technol. Res*, *14*, 1–16.

Parikh, N. A. (2025). Managing ai-first products: Roles, skills, challenges, and strategies of ai product managers. *IEEE Engineering Management Review*, *53*(5), 232–244. DOI: 10.1109/EMR.2025.3530942

Patary, C. L. (2019). *The Scrum Master Guidebook: A Reference For Obtaining Mastery*. Notion Press.

Paterniti, G. G., & Manzoni, L. (2018). Does scrum methodology impact team's subculture? A multiple case study exploration.

Patrucco, A. S., Canterino, F., & Minelgaite, I. (2022). How do scrum methodologies influence the team's cultural values? A multiple case study on agile teams in Nonsoftware industries. *IEEE Transactions on Engineering Management*, *69*(6), 3503–3513. DOI: 10.1109/TEM.2022.3146717

Pichler, R. (2020). *How to lead in product management: practices to align stakeholders, guide development teams, and create value together*. Pichler Consulting.

Podeswa, H. (2021). *The Agile Guide to Business Analysis and Planning: From Strategic Plan to Continuous Value Delivery*. Addison-Wesley Professional.

Rajnath, Y. K., & Kumar, V. (2025). Training and Skills Development for AI in Product Development. In *AI for Product Development* (pp. 123–145). CRC Press. DOI: 10.1201/9781003536901-7

Rigby, D., Elk, S., & Berez, S. (2020). *Doing agile right: Transformation without chaos*. Harvard Business Press.

Schmidt, J., & Heidenreich, S. (2018). The role of human capital for entrepreneurial decision-making-investigating experience, skills and knowledge as antecedents to effectuation and causation. *International Journal of Entrepreneurial Venturing*, *10*(3), 287–311. DOI: 10.1504/IJEV.2018.093226

Shastri, Y., Hoda, R., & Amor, R. (2021). Spearheading agile: The role of the scrum master in agile projects. *Empirical Software Engineering*, *26*(1), 3. DOI: 10.1007/s10664-020-09899-4

Sindiramutty, S. R., Prabagaran, K. R. V., Akbar, R., Hussain, M., & Malik, N. A. (2025). Generative AI for secure user interface (UI) design. In *Reshaping CyberSecurity With Generative AI Techniques* (pp. 333–394). IGI Global Scientific Publishing.

Spichkova, M., Iwan, K., Zwart, M., Lee, H., Yoon, Y., & Qin, X. (2025). Advanced approach for Agile/Scrum Process: RetroAI++. *arXiv preprint arXiv:2506.15172*.

Tsarouhas, P., & Grigoriadis, K. (2025). A socio-technical framework for AI trust in public administration. *Transforming Government: People, Process and Policy*, 1-22

Yan, L., Cheng, C., Zhang, Y., & Miao, Z. (2025). Large Language Models in International Business Research: Opportunities, Challenges, and Prospects. *MIR. Management International Review*, *65*(6), 1–29. DOI: 10.1007/s11575-025-00601-8

Chapter 12
Change Management and Upskilling for AI-Augmented Teams

Priyadarshani Singh
http://orcid.org/0000-0002-5474-1440
Noida International University, India

Syed Hassan Imam Gardezi
http://orcid.org/0009-0006-6171-1238
Union Investments LLC, UAE

P. Selvakumar
http://orcid.org/0000-0002-3650-4548
Department of Science and Humanities, Nehru Institute of Technology, Coimbatore, India

Ganesh Pathak
http://orcid.org/0000-0003-0427-2145
Sri Balaji University, Pune, India

Asita Ghewari
http://orcid.org/0000-0003-1686-1588
Dnyansagar Institute of Management and Research, Pune, India

Ashok Raut
http://orcid.org/0009-0006-2259-8607
Global Business School and Research Centre, Dr. D.Y. Patil Vidyapeeth, Pune, India

ABSTRACT

The integration of artificial intelligence (AI) into organizational environments is reshaping not only workflows and operational efficiency but also the very nature of team dynamics and change management. Traditionally, change management has revolved around structured strategies for transitioning people, processes, and technologies from one state to another while minimizing resistance and maximizing adoption. However, the introduction of AI introduces unique challenges and opportunities that extend beyond conventional frameworks, influencing how teams interact, collaborate, and adapt to constant transformation. AI is not merely another tool or incremental technological advancement; it represents a paradigm shift in how

DOI: 10.4018/979-8-3373-6851-1.ch012

decisions are made, tasks are executed, and roles are defined within organizations. This shift impacts interpersonal trust, communication, leadership styles, employee identity, and the overall resilience of teams navigating technological disruption.

THE IMPACT OF AI ON TEAM DYNAMICS AND CHANGE MANAGEMENT

The integration of artificial intelligence (AI) into organizational environments is reshaping not only workflows and operational efficiency but also the very nature of team dynamics and change management. Traditionally, change management has revolved around structured strategies for transitioning people, processes, and technologies from one state to another while minimizing resistance and maximizing adoption. However, the introduction of AI introduces unique challenges and opportunities that extend beyond conventional frameworks, influencing how teams interact, collaborate, and adapt to constant transformation. AI is not merely another tool or incremental technological advancement; it represents a paradigm shift in how decisions are made, tasks are executed, and roles are defined within organizations. This shift impacts interpersonal trust, communication, leadership styles, employee identity, and the overall resilience of teams navigating technological disruption. Understanding the nuanced impact of AI on team dynamics and change management is essential for organizations seeking sustainable digital transformation. One of the most profound ways AI influences team dynamics is through the redistribution of roles and responsibilities. Tasks that were once exclusively human-driven—such as data analysis, customer service interactions, or even elements of decision-making—are increasingly automated or augmented by AI systems. This reallocation of responsibilities can create both opportunities for efficiency and tension within teams. On the positive side, AI alleviates employees from repetitive, low-value tasks, enabling them to focus on higher-order responsibilities that require creativity, empathy, and strategic judgment.

AI also reshapes team communication and collaboration by acting as both a mediator and a participant in interactions. Collaborative AI platforms—ranging from intelligent project management systems to chatbots that streamline communication—can facilitate smoother workflows, automate meeting scheduling, analyze team performance, and even suggest strategies for conflict resolution. These capabilities have the potential to enhance team cohesion, reduce inefficiencies, and improve coordination across geographically distributed workforces. Yet, the integration of AI in collaborative settings also raises questions of authenticity and trust: how do team members perceive decisions or insights generated by AI? Will they treat AI-generated suggestions with equal legitimacy as those from human colleagues, or will skepticism undermine effectiveness? Change management must address these psychological aspects by fostering digital trust, ensuring transparency in AI decision-making processes, and promoting a balanced human–AI partnership that preserves the value of human intuition alongside computational precision. Another critical area where AI impacts team dynamics is in leadership and decision-making. AI's ability to process vast amounts of data and generate predictive insights challenges traditional hierarchies by providing team members with direct access to knowledge that was once the exclusive domain of managers or experts. This democratization of data can flatten organizational structures, fostering more inclusive decision-making where employees at different levels can contribute informed perspectives. However, it may also disrupt traditional authority, as leaders must adapt from being the primary sources of knowledge to becoming facilitators who interpret and contextualize AI-driven insights.

UNDERSTANDING THE NEED FOR UPSKILLING IN AI-AUGMENTED TEAMS

The accelerated integration of artificial intelligence (AI) into workplaces across industries has brought about a profound transformation in how teams' function, collaborate, and deliver value. (Barrett & Miller, 2024) AI-augmented teams—where human professionals work alongside intelligent systems—represent the future of organizational productivity, but they also introduce a fundamental challenge: the urgent need for upskilling. Upskilling, broadly defined as the process of equipping employees with new competencies and knowledge to meet evolving job requirements, has never been more critical than in the era of AI. Unlike previous waves of technological change, which often replaced physical tasks with machinery, AI impacts cognitive and decision-oriented tasks, compelling workers to adapt their skills, mindsets, and professional identities. Understanding the drivers, scope, and urgency of upskilling in AI-augmented teams is essential for organizations to thrive in the digital economy while ensuring employee engagement, resilience, and equity in the face of disruption. At the heart of this need lies the shifting nature of job roles in AI-augmented teams. Many tasks traditionally performed by humans—such as data collection, basic analysis, customer support interactions, or routine decision-making—are increasingly automated by AI systems. However, this does not eliminate the role of humans but instead redefines it, emphasizing higher-order skills such as critical thinking, creativity, empathy, and ethical judgment. (Barrett & Miller 2024) For instance, in healthcare, AI systems may perform preliminary diagnostic analysis, but it is the clinicians who interpret these insights in context, communicate them empathetically to patients, and make final treatment decisions.

The need for upskilling also arises from the complexity of working with AI tools themselves. Employees must not only understand how to operate AI systems but also develop the literacy to interpret AI outputs critically. (Charan J. K. et al. 2025) This includes acquiring foundational knowledge in data literacy, algorithmic logic, and bias detection, enabling workers to engage with AI-generated recommendations in an informed manner rather than passively accepting them. For example, a marketing professional using AI-powered analytics must understand how predictive models function, recognize potential biases in training data, and contextualize outputs for real-world campaign strategies. Without upskilling, teams risk overreliance on AI or misinterpretation of results, leading to errors, ethical dilemmas, and a loss of trust in both technology and leadership. (Charan J. K. et al. 2025) Thus, upskilling is not about transforming all employees into data scientists, but rather about ensuring that every professional possesses sufficient AI fluency to engage meaningfully with augmented systems. Beyond technical literacy, upskilling is critical for nurturing the soft skills that AI cannot replicate. AI excels at data processing and pattern recognition, but it lacks emotional intelligence, ethical reasoning, and the ability to navigate complex interpersonal dynamics. In AI-augmented teams, human strengths such as empathy, creativity, cultural sensitivity, and leadership become even more valuable. Upskilling programs must therefore balance technical training with the cultivation of soft skills, preparing employees to complement AI by excelling in areas where human judgment is irreplaceable.

STRATEGIES FOR EFFECTIVE CHANGE MANAGEMENT IN AI-DRIVEN ENVIRONMENTS: STRATEGIES

The integration of artificial intelligence (AI) into organizational operations represents one of the most significant transformations in modern business and societal ecosystems. Unlike previous technological shifts that primarily automated routine physical labor, AI directly affects cognitive processes, decision-making, and collaborative structures, redefining how organizations function at every level. (Goel A. et al. 2024) While AI offers unprecedented opportunities for efficiency, innovation, and growth, its implementation often triggers resistance, uncertainty, and cultural disruption within the workforce. These challenges highlight the necessity of effective change management strategies specifically tailored to AI-driven environments. Change management in this context involves not only the technical deployment of AI systems but also preparing people, processes, and organizational cultures to embrace new ways of working. Successful strategies require a combination of clear vision, strong leadership, employee engagement, continuous upskilling, ethical governance, and agile adaptation to ensure that AI adoption enhances organizational resilience and value creation rather than fueling anxiety or disengagement. The first critical strategy lies in establishing a clear vision and purpose for AI adoption. Many AI initiatives fail when employees perceive them as vague, threatening, or irrelevant to their daily work. Leaders must articulate a compelling narrative that positions AI as a tool for augmenting human capability rather than replacing it. (Goel A. et al. 2024).

A second core strategy is employee engagement and participation throughout the change process. Traditional top-down approaches to technology implementation often alienate workers, fostering resistance or passive compliance. (Gonzalez K. et al. 2024) In contrast, involving employees in the design, testing, and feedback loops of AI tools promotes a sense of ownership and empowerment. Participatory approaches allow workers to highlight practical challenges, suggest improvements, and align AI systems with the realities of day-to-day operations. For example, in healthcare settings, involving clinicians in the adoption of AI diagnostic tools ensures that the technology supports rather than disrupts clinical workflows. Similarly, in customer service, co-creating AI-driven chatbots with frontline staff improves usability and acceptance. By treating employees as partners in innovation rather than passive recipients of change, organizations foster a culture of collaboration and trust that is essential for successful AI adoption. Another vital strategy is comprehensive training and upskilling initiatives. AI-driven environments demand new skill sets that go beyond basic technical literacy. Employees must develop competencies in data interpretation, algorithmic awareness, critical thinking, and digital collaboration, while leaders must acquire the skills to manage AI-augmented teams effectively. (Gonzalez K. et al. 2024) Training programs should be continuous, personalized, and practical, offering employees the opportunity to experiment with AI tools in safe learning environments. Microlearning modules, mentoring systems, and cross-functional workshops can make upskilling more accessible and engaging.

OVERCOMING RESISTANCE TO AI ADOPTION IN TEAMS: OVERCOMING RESISTANCE

The integration of artificial intelligence (AI) into organizational settings has been transformative, but it has also encountered significant resistance from teams and individuals who feel threatened, uncertain, or overwhelmed by the pace of technological change. Resistance to AI adoption is not inherently negative; rather, it often signals deeper concerns about job security, autonomy, trust, and the perceived fairness of technological decision-making. (Goryunova & Yawson, 2025) Understanding and addressing these concerns is critical for ensuring that AI achieves its potential as a tool for augmenting human work rather than fueling disengagement and anxiety. Overcoming resistance requires a comprehensive set of strategies that blend communication, education, cultural transformation, and leadership practices, while also ensuring that employees feel supported, valued, and empowered throughout the adoption process. Successful management of resistance is less about suppressing opposition and more about transforming skepticism into active participation and ownership of AI-driven initiatives. A primary source of resistance stems from fear of job displacement. Many employees perceive AI as a replacement for human roles, particularly in sectors where automation has already reduced workforce numbers. This fear can manifest as reluctance to engage with AI tools, avoidance of training programs, or outright opposition to their use. To address this, organizations must proactively emphasize AI's role as a tool for augmentation rather than substitution. (Goryunova & Yawson, 2025) Clear communication about how AI will be used to reduce repetitive tasks, streamline operations, and free employees for more complex, creative, or people-oriented responsibilities can shift the narrative from one of replacement to one of empowerment.

Transparent communication plays a central role in overcoming resistance. Employees are more likely to oppose AI adoption when they lack information or suspect hidden agendas. Organizations should communicate openly about why AI is being adopted, what its limitations are, and how it will affect workflows and roles. (Guru Basava Aradhya S. et al. 2025) Avoiding vague promises and instead providing realistic expectations builds credibility and trust. Communication should not be one-way; employees need opportunities to ask questions, voice concerns, and receive meaningful responses. Town hall meetings, open forums, and internal communication channels can provide platforms for dialogue. Leaders who address skepticism directly and acknowledge potential challenges—such as the need for reskilling or workflow adjustments—are better positioned to build trust and reduce fear-driven resistance. Another crucial strategy is employee involvement in the AI implementation process. Resistance often arises when employees feel that decisions are imposed upon them without their input. By involving teams in pilot projects, feedback loops, and testing phases, organizations can increase ownership and reduce opposition. (Guru Basava Aradhya S. et al. 2025) Employees bring valuable domain expertise that can help tailor AI systems to the realities of daily operations, thereby ensuring that the technology complements rather than disrupts existing workflows. For example, in customer service, frontline employees can provide insights into how AI-driven chatbots should handle nuanced queries, making the tools more effective and user-friendly. Participation not only improves the quality of AI systems but also fosters a sense of empowerment, signaling to employees that their knowledge and contributions remain central to organizational success.

LEADING CHANGE IN AI-AUGMENTED TEAM ENVIRONMENTS: LEADING CHANGE

The advent of artificial intelligence (AI) is fundamentally transforming the way teams function, collaborate, and deliver value across industries. (Harmanpreet et al. 2025) As organizations adopt AI to optimize operations, enhance decision-making, and increase productivity, leaders face the critical task of guiding their teams through this complex transformation. Leading change in AI-augmented team environments requires more than simply introducing new technologies; it involves reshaping organizational culture, fostering trust, redefining roles, and ensuring employees embrace AI as a strategic partner rather than viewing it as a threat. Unlike traditional change management efforts that focus on incremental adjustments, AI-driven transformation demands a deeper shift in mindset, behavior, and skillsets. Leaders must navigate uncertainty, address resistance, and balance technological integration with human factors such as empathy, communication, and inclusion. Effective leadership in this context is not only about managing technology but also about creating an environment where humans and machines collaborate synergistically to drive innovation and sustainable success. One of the primary responsibilities of leaders in AI-augmented environments is establishing a clear vision and purpose for the transformation. (Harmanpreet et al. 2025) Teams are more likely to embrace AI when they understand how it aligns with broader organizational goals and their own professional growth. A compelling vision articulates how AI will enhance performance, improve outcomes, and create opportunities for innovation rather than merely focusing on efficiency gains or cost reduction. For example, in healthcare, leaders can emphasize how AI-driven predictive analytics improves patient care by identifying risks earlier, thereby empowering clinicians to provide more personalized treatment.

Another essential aspect of leading change is building trust and psychological safety. AI adoption can trigger fear and skepticism, particularly if employees worry about job displacement, loss of autonomy, or lack of control. Leaders must establish trust not only in themselves but also in the AI systems being implemented. Trust is built through transparency—communicating openly about AI's capabilities, limitations, and implications for work processes. (Huzooree G. et al. 2025) Leaders should address concerns directly, explaining how AI complements human judgment rather than replacing it. For instance, in financial services, employees are more likely to trust AI risk assessment tools if leaders explain that final decision-making still rests with human experts. Psychological safety further ensures that team members feel comfortable expressing concerns, asking questions, and experimenting with AI tools without fear of judgment or repercussions. (Huzooree G. et al. 2025) This environment fosters innovation by allowing employees to engage actively in the learning and adaptation process. Role modeling and leading by example are critical leadership practices in AI-augmented environments. Leaders who demonstrate curiosity, adaptability, and willingness to experiment with AI tools set a tone that encourages their teams to do the same. When leaders visibly adopt AI systems in their own workflows, it signals that the technology is valuable, practical, and worth engaging with.

IDENTIFYING SKILL GAPS IN AI-AUGMENTED TEAMS: IDENTIFYING GAPS

As artificial intelligence (AI) continues to permeate workplaces and reshape how organizations function, the ability of teams to adapt and thrive in AI-augmented environments depends largely on their skills and competencies. (Koparde S. A. et al. 2026) AI tools can automate repetitive tasks, process massive datasets, and provide advanced analytics, but their success relies on human collaborators who can effectively interpret, manage, and integrate these technologies into workflows. Identifying skill gaps in AI-augmented teams has thus emerged as a strategic priority for organizations across industries, as it determines not only the efficiency of AI adoption but also long-term competitiveness, innovation capacity, and workforce resilience. Skill gaps refer to the discrepancies between the skills employees currently possess and those required to operate effectively in AI-enhanced contexts. (Koparde S. A. et al. 2026) These gaps are often multidimensional, encompassing technical expertise, digital literacy, critical thinking, ethical reasoning, collaboration, and change adaptability. Addressing these gaps requires leaders to conduct comprehensive skill audits, anticipate future needs, and align training strategies with organizational goals, ensuring that employees are empowered rather than left behind in the digital transformation journey. One of the first steps in identifying skill gaps is recognizing that technical skills alone are insufficient for AI-augmented work environments. While proficiency in areas such as programming, data analysis, machine learning, and system integration is critical for certain roles, broader competencies such as problem-solving, adaptability, communication, and creativity are equally essential.

Skill gap identification in AI-augmented teams is best approached through structured skill assessments and workforce analytics. Organizations increasingly rely on tools such as digital competency frameworks, self-assessment surveys, and performance analytics to map current skills against future requirements. (Marion T. et al. 2025) These assessments can be role-specific or team-wide, capturing both technical proficiencies (e.g., knowledge of data visualization tools or cloud computing) and soft skills (e.g., collaboration across human-machine workflows). For example, in healthcare, an AI-augmented clinical team may need physicians to develop greater familiarity with diagnostic AI tools, while also requiring nurses to strengthen digital communication skills to interact effectively with AI-driven patient monitoring systems. Without systematic assessments, organizations risk underestimating the depth of gaps and misaligning training investments with actual workforce needs. A significant challenge in identifying skill gaps lies in the dynamic and evolving nature of AI technologies. Unlike traditional skill requirements that remain relatively stable, AI adoption often results in continuously shifting demands, as new tools, models, and applications emerge rapidly. This means that skill gap analysis cannot be treated as a one-time exercise but must be an ongoing process integrated into organizational strategy. (Marion T. et al. 2025) Leaders must anticipate not only current skill deficiencies but also emerging competencies that may be required in the near future. For example, as AI systems become increasingly explainable and regulated, employees may need skills in ethical AI usage, compliance management, and bias mitigation—skills that were not traditionally prioritized. Failure to forecast these evolving needs can leave organizations vulnerable to both technical inefficiencies and ethical risks.

DEVELOPING TRAINING PROGRAMS FOR AI UPSKILLING: TRAINING PROGRAMS

The rapid advancement of artificial intelligence (AI) technologies has made it imperative for organizations to develop well-structured training programs that equip employees with the necessary skills to thrive in AI-augmented work environments. (Martino D. et al. 2025) As AI becomes deeply embedded in decision-making, process automation, data analysis, and customer engagement, employees across all functions must learn not only how to use AI tools but also how to collaborate effectively with them. Developing training programs for AI upskilling is therefore a strategic priority that ensures workforce readiness, minimizes disruption during digital transformation, and fosters a culture of continuous learning. Unlike traditional training initiatives that focus narrowly on technical competencies, AI upskilling programs must adopt a holistic approach that combines technical skills, human-centric competencies, ethical awareness, and adaptive learning strategies. These programs must be tailored to the specific contexts of industries, job functions, and organizational cultures, while also being flexible enough to adapt to the rapid pace of technological change. In essence, training programs for AI upskilling are not just about teaching employees how to use new tools; they are about preparing the workforce for a future where human-machine collaboration becomes central to value creation. (Martino D. et al. 2025) The first step in developing effective AI upskilling programs is conducting a comprehensive skills assessment to identify the gaps between current workforce capabilities and the skills required for AI-augmented roles. These assessments can include surveys, digital competency frameworks, performance reviews, and data-driven workforce analytics. For instance, while data scientists may require deeper technical training in machine learning algorithms and natural language processing, frontline employees may need introductory training in AI-enabled platforms that support customer service or logistics.

Once skill gaps are identified, organizations must design tiered training pathways that cater to employees at different levels of expertise. For beginners, training may focus on digital literacy, foundational understanding of AI concepts, and practical applications in their daily roles. For intermediate learners, programs can delve into data handling, algorithmic thinking, and AI tool integration. (Mishra B. R. et al. 2025) Advanced learners, such as data scientists and AI specialists, may require specialized training in areas like deep learning, computer vision, reinforcement learning, and AI ethics. By creating these tiered pathways, organizations enable employees to learn at their own pace, progress incrementally, and build confidence as they advance. Moreover, tiered programs reduce the intimidation often associated with AI technologies, making them more accessible to non-technical employees. A critical component of AI upskilling programs is the integration of real-world applications and experiential learning. Theoretical knowledge alone is insufficient in preparing employees for the dynamic challenges of AI-augmented environments. Training programs should therefore include simulations, case studies, hackathons, and project-based learning opportunities where employees can apply AI concepts to solve real business problems. For example, a retail company might design a training module where employees use AI tools to analyze sales data and predict inventory needs, thereby understanding how AI enhances decision-making. Such experiential learning not only reinforces technical skills but also cultivates problem-solving abilities, creativity, and adaptability. (Mishra B. R. et al. 2025).

UPSKILLING STRATEGIES FOR AI-DRIVEN WORK ENVIRONMENTS: UPSKILLING STRATEGIES

The rise of artificial intelligence (AI) across industries has fundamentally reshaped the structure of work, necessitating a strategic approach to workforce development. As organizations integrate AI into core processes such as decision-making, customer engagement, operations, and data-driven forecasting, employees must be equipped with new competencies to remain effective and relevant. (Mollah M. A. et al. 2024) This transition requires not just the acquisition of technical skills but also the cultivation of adaptive, ethical, and collaborative abilities that support human-AI interaction. Upskilling strategies for AI-driven work environments therefore extend beyond traditional training, embracing holistic frameworks that combine continuous learning, practical application, interdisciplinary collaboration, and cultural transformation. Unlike one-time training sessions, effective upskilling strategies recognize AI as a constantly evolving ecosystem, demanding flexible and iterative approaches that evolve alongside technology. (Mollah M. A. et al. 2024) By embedding structured upskilling initiatives into organizational strategy, companies can enhance workforce agility, foster innovation, and maintain competitiveness in an era where human-machine synergy drives value creation. One of the cornerstone strategies for upskilling in AI-driven environments is conducting a comprehensive skill gap analysis to identify the mismatch between current workforce capabilities and the demands of AI-augmented roles.

Figure 1. Understanding Human-AI Augmentation in the Workplace

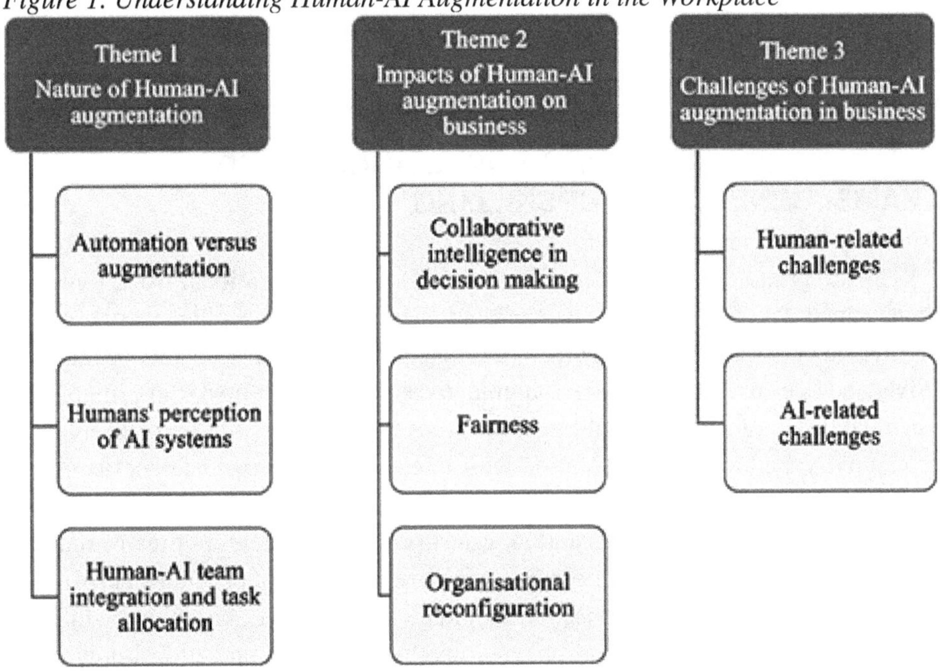

Based on the findings of such assessments, organizations can implement tiered learning pathways that accommodate varying levels of expertise across the workforce. Entry-level employees may benefit from introductory modules that focus on AI literacy, digital fluency, and practical applications of AI tools in daily tasks. (Nirupama E. et al. 2025) Mid-level employees, who often interact with AI-driven systems in managerial or operational contexts, can progress to more advanced modules that cover data handling, AI-enabled decision-making, and interdisciplinary problem-solving. For highly technical staff, such as data scientists and engineers, specialized pathways can include training in deep learning, reinforcement learning, natural language processing, and ethical AI design. Tiered learning pathways not only make training inclusive but also allow employees to progress at their own pace, reducing the intimidation often associated with complex technologies. This structured progression ensures that employees at all levels are prepared for meaningful participation in AI-driven work environments. (Nirupama E. et al. 2025) Another key strategy involves leveraging experiential and project-based learning to bridge the gap between theory and practice. Traditional lecture-based training is insufficient in preparing employees for the dynamic, real-world challenges posed by AI technologies. Instead, organizations can implement hands-on workshops, hackathons, case studies, and sandbox environments where employees experiment with AI tools in simulated or real scenarios. For instance, in a financial institution, employees could be tasked with building models to detect fraudulent transactions, gaining both technical and problem-solving skills.

BENEFITS OF UPSKILLING FOR AI-AUGMENTED TEAMS: BENEFITS OF UPSKILLING

The integration of artificial intelligence (AI) into organizational workflows has transformed not only the nature of work but also the dynamics of teamwork, creating hybrid ecosystems where human and machine capabilities operate in tandem. (Sivanand R. et al. 2025) In such AI-augmented environments, upskilling emerges as a critical driver of success, enabling employees to adapt to evolving roles, enhance productivity, and foster collaboration with intelligent systems. The benefits of upskilling extend far beyond individual learning, influencing organizational resilience, innovation, ethical governance, and long-term competitiveness. For teams that are increasingly reliant on AI technologies, structured upskilling programs ensure that members can interpret, supervise, and strategically leverage AI outputs while retaining the uniquely human qualities of empathy, creativity, and ethical judgment. Without targeted upskilling, the introduction of AI risks creating knowledge divides, resistance, and inefficiencies; with it, organizations can harness the synergy of human and machine intelligence to achieve greater effectiveness. One of the most immediate benefits of upskilling in AI-augmented teams is the enhancement of AI literacy and confidence among employees. Many workers initially perceive AI as a threat to job security or as an opaque "black box" whose decisions are difficult to understand. Through upskilling initiatives that teach the basics of AI functionality, data handling, and algorithmic logic, employees gain the knowledge needed to demystify AI technologies. (Sivanand R. et al. 2025) This literacy not only reduces fear but also equips team members to engage constructively with AI systems, ask critical questions, and identify potential errors or biases in automated outputs.

Another critical benefit lies in improving decision-making quality and speed. AI systems excel at processing vast volumes of data and identifying patterns that are invisible to humans, but it is upskilled employees who interpret these insights and apply them in context. When teams possess the knowledge to understand AI outputs, they can integrate them into their decision-making processes more effectively, balancing computational accuracy with human judgment. For instance, in healthcare settings, clinicians trained in AI-assisted diagnostic tools can combine data-driven recommendations with their expertise and patient knowledge, leading to faster and more accurate diagnoses. In business environments, managers who understand AI-generated forecasts can make quicker, evidence-based decisions that enhance agility. Thus, upskilling not only improves the quality of decisions but also accelerates response times in fast-paced markets, where speed is often a competitive differentiator. Upskilling also contributes significantly to increased innovation and creativity within AI-augmented teams. Far from replacing creativity, AI often serves as a catalyst for new ideas by handling repetitive tasks and offering novel insights derived from data. (Rahayu & Bablu, 2023) However, teams must be trained to recognize and exploit these opportunities. Through upskilling, employees learn to use AI tools as co-creators—whether by experimenting with generative AI for design, exploring predictive analytics for new market opportunities, or employing natural language processing to uncover emerging customer sentiments. This ability to leverage AI for creative problem-solving transforms teams into engines of innovation.

OUTCOMES OF EFFECTIVE CHANGE MANAGEMENT IN AI TEAMS

The rapid adoption of artificial intelligence (AI) within organizations has created unprecedented opportunities for innovation, efficiency, and strategic growth. However, the success of AI initiatives depends not only on the technical sophistication of the systems implemented but also on how well human teams adapt to this transformation. (Rahayu & Bablu, 2023) Effective change management in AI teams is therefore a decisive factor that determines whether organizations realize the full potential of AI or struggle with disruption, resistance, and underutilization. When change management processes are well designed and executed, the outcomes extend across multiple dimensions—ranging from enhanced adoption rates and workforce adaptability to improved collaboration, ethical governance, and long-term competitive advantage. These outcomes shape not only the immediate success of AI projects but also the resilience of organizations in an era of continuous technological evolution. One of the most significant outcomes of effective change management in AI teams is higher adoption and utilization of AI technologies. Research and practice consistently show that the introduction of advanced technologies often fails because employees resist change, either due to fear of job displacement, lack of clarity, or insufficient training. By implementing structured change management strategies—such as transparent communication, stakeholder engagement, and gradual rollouts—organizations create an environment where employees understand the value of AI, trust its outputs, and integrate it into their daily workflows.

Another critical outcome is the enhancement of workforce adaptability and resilience. Effective change management equips employees with not just the technical skills to use AI tools but also the mindset to embrace continuous transformation. In AI-driven environments, where algorithms, models, and platforms are constantly updated, adaptability becomes a core competency. (Raman M. S. et al. 2025) Change management interventions—such as training programs, upskilling initiatives, and coaching—foster a culture of learning where employees are comfortable navigating uncertainty and change. Over time, teams develop resilience, becoming capable of pivoting quickly in response to evolving technologies or market demands. This outcome is particularly valuable in industries like healthcare, finance, and manufacturing, where the rapid evolution of AI capabilities can disrupt traditional roles. Teams that are adaptable through effective change management are not merely surviving technological disruption but thriving within it. Effective change management also leads to greater alignment between human expertise and AI capabilities, creating synergistic workflows that enhance decision-making and performance. AI excels at data processing, predictive modeling, and automating repetitive tasks, but its full potential is only realized when human teams can interpret, contextualize, and apply its outputs. Change management helps clarify role definitions, ensuring that employees understand how their responsibilities evolve in collaboration with AI.

THE ROLE OF CONTINUOUS LEARNING IN AI-AUGMENTED TEAMS: ROLE OF CONTINUOUS LEARNING

In the evolving landscape of artificial intelligence (AI), where technologies continuously advance and reshape organizational practices, the role of continuous learning in AI-augmented teams has become indispensable. (Raman M. S. et al. 2025) Unlike traditional teams, which could rely on periodic training programs or static knowledge bases, AI-augmented teams operate in dynamic environments where algorithms, platforms, and data-driven processes evolve at a rapid pace. Continuous learning, defined as the ongoing acquisition of knowledge, skills, and competencies through formal and informal channels, enables teams to remain agile, relevant, and resilient amidst constant change. It is not a peripheral or supportive activity but a central pillar of AI integration that directly influences how teams adapt, innovate, and thrive in technologically driven workplaces. The necessity of continuous learning stems from three interlinked realities of AI environments: the accelerating pace of technological evolution, the need to align human expertise with machine intelligence, and the organizational imperative to maintain competitiveness and ethical responsibility in an AI-driven economy. One of the most critical roles of continuous learning in AI-augmented teams is ensuring adaptability in response to rapid technological advancements. AI systems are not static tools but dynamic platforms that evolve through new models, upgraded algorithms, and changing datasets. For instance, natural language processing models or predictive analytics frameworks may be updated regularly to improve accuracy, requiring teams to adjust their usage and interpretation strategies. Without continuous learning, employees' risk being left behind, unable to effectively harness the capabilities of evolving AI systems.

Another fundamental role of continuous learning is to strengthen human-AI collaboration by aligning human expertise with machine outputs. While AI excels in processing massive datasets, identifying patterns, and executing repetitive tasks, humans bring contextual judgment, ethical reasoning, and creative problem-solving to the partnership. Continuous learning helps employees understand the strengths and limitations of AI, enabling them to make informed decisions about when to rely on machine-generated insights and when to exercise human discretion. (Seufert & Spirgi, 2024) For example, in healthcare, continuous training ensures that medical professionals can interpret AI-generated diagnostic suggestions while applying clinical judgment to account for patient history or unique conditions. In finance, ongoing learning allows analysts to complement AI-driven predictive models with market insights and risk assessments. This alignment fosters trust in AI systems, minimizes errors arising from blind reliance, and enhances the overall effectiveness of AI-augmented decision-making. Continuous learning also plays a vital role in fostering innovation and creativity within AI teams. Far from being restricted to technical knowledge, continuous learning cultivates interdisciplinary skills and diverse perspectives that encourage employees to explore novel applications of AI. When teams are empowered to learn continuously, they develop the confidence and curiosity to experiment with AI tools, test hypotheses, and co-create solutions. This culture of learning-driven innovation allows organizations to unlock new opportunities for value creation, whether through improved product development, enhanced customer experiences, or reimagined business processes.

IMPLEMENTING AI-AUGMENTED CHANGE MANAGEMENT STRATEGIES: IMPLEMENTATION

The implementation of AI-augmented change management strategies represents a transformative step for organizations navigating the complexities of digital transformation, workforce evolution, and competitive market dynamics. Change management, traditionally rooted in structured methodologies such as Kotter's 8-step model or Lewin's three-stage approach, has historically relied on human-driven processes such as communication campaigns, training programs, and leadership alignment to facilitate organizational adaptation. However, in today's environment where artificial intelligence (AI) increasingly permeates business operations, conventional approaches to change management are no longer sufficient to address the speed, scale, and unpredictability of technological disruption. (Seufert & Spirgi, 2024) AI-augmented change management involves leveraging AI tools and data-driven insights to design, execute, and continuously refine change initiatives, creating an adaptive and intelligent framework that empowers organizations to manage transitions with greater precision, agility, and inclusivity. The successful implementation of such strategies requires a careful balance between technological capabilities and human-centered approaches, ensuring that AI strengthens rather than replaces the role of leaders and employees in the change journey. One of the primary dimensions of implementing AI-augmented change management is the integration of predictive analytics and data-driven insights into change processes. Traditionally, change managers relied on surveys, interviews, and manual performance metrics to assess readiness, resistance, and progress. While valuable, these methods often lacked real-time accuracy and suffered from biases or delays. AI-driven analytics allow organizations to process vast amounts of employee, operational, and market data to anticipate barriers to adoption, identify skill gaps, and detect early signs of resistance. For example, natural language processing (NLP) tools can analyze employee feedback from digital platforms, uncovering sentiments, concerns, and recurring themes that might otherwise remain hidden. Predictive models can forecast which departments or teams are most likely to struggle with AI adoption, enabling targeted interventions such as additional training, mentoring, or leadership engagement. This proactive, evidence-based approach transforms change management from reactive to anticipatory, ensuring that strategies are aligned with evolving organizational realities.

Implementing AI-augmented change management also involves the automation of repetitive change management tasks, thereby freeing leaders to focus on higher-value responsibilities such as vision-setting and culture-building. (Tangi L. et al. 2025) AI-powered chatbots and virtual assistants, for instance, can deliver consistent communication about change initiatives, answer frequently asked employee questions, and provide on-demand resources such as training materials, policies, or troubleshooting guidance. This automation reduces the cognitive load on change managers while enhancing employee experience by offering accessible, real-time support. Furthermore, AI-enabled platforms can monitor progress on change initiatives by tracking key performance indicators (KPIs) such as adoption rates, system usage, or productivity metrics, providing instant feedback loops for managers. By integrating these automated mechanisms, organizations not only reduce the administrative burden of managing change but also ensure that support is tailored, timely, and responsive to employee needs. Another critical aspect of implementation is the personalization of learning and development initiatives through AI-driven adaptive systems. Change management often requires employees to acquire new skills, adapt to new workflows, or reframe their roles within the organization. Traditional training programs, delivered uniformly, often fail to address the diverse learning styles, prior knowledge levels, and pace preferences of employees. AI-augmented learning platforms leverage machine learning algorithms to customize training experiences, providing personalized content, adaptive assessments, and real-time recommendations. For instance, an employee who demonstrates proficiency in certain AI tools may be directed toward advanced learning modules, while another struggling with foundational concepts receives additional support. This personalized approach accelerates skill development, boosts confidence, and reduces frustration, thereby smoothing the change process and increasing the likelihood of sustained adoption.

CONSIDERATIONS FOR UPSKILLING IN DIVERSE TEAM ENVIRONMENTS: CONSIDERATIONS

Upskilling in diverse team environments has emerged as a critical organizational priority in the context of rapid digital transformation, artificial intelligence (AI) integration, and evolving workforce dynamics. Diverse teams—comprising individuals from different cultural backgrounds, age groups, educational experiences, professional disciplines, and socio-economic contexts—bring unique perspectives that can enhance innovation, creativity, and problem-solving. (Tangi L. et al. 2025) However, this diversity also creates unique challenges in designing and implementing effective upskilling strategies, as learning needs, preferences, and access to resources can vary significantly across individuals. To ensure equitable and effective upskilling in such contexts, organizations must consider not only the technical aspects of training but also the social, cultural, psychological, and structural factors that shape how team members acquire, apply, and retain new skills. Effective upskilling in diverse team environments, therefore, requires a multidimensional strategy that prioritizes inclusivity, adaptability, equity, cultural sensitivity, and long-term capacity-building.

A key consideration is the recognition of diverse learning styles and preferences. Research in adult learning theory emphasizes that individuals absorb information differently—some thrive in visual or auditory formats, while others prefer hands-on, experiential approaches. In diverse teams, these preferences may be influenced by prior educational systems, cultural norms, or generational experiences. For example, younger employees who grew up in digital-first environments may prefer self-paced e-learning modules, while older employees may value instructor-led, collaborative sessions. Similarly, team members from cultures that emphasize collective learning may thrive in group-based training, while those from individualistic contexts may prefer independent study. Organizations must therefore provide multimodal training programs that integrate varied approaches—such as workshops, online platforms, peer learning groups, and simulation-based exercises—to ensure inclusivity and engagement across diverse learners.

Another central consideration is addressing language and communication barriers. In global organizations, diverse teams often consist of members with varying levels of fluency in the primary language of instruction, which can affect comprehension and participation. Upskilling programs that rely solely on technical jargon or culturally specific metaphors may inadvertently disadvantage certain employees. (Tenakwah E. S. et al. 2025) To mitigate this, training content should be designed with linguistic inclusivity in mind, using clear, accessible language and providing translation, subtitles, or multilingual support where necessary. AI-driven language tools, such as real-time translation platforms and adaptive glossaries, can play a role in overcoming communication gaps, ensuring that all team members have equal access to learning resources. Furthermore, incorporating cross-cultural communication training into upskilling initiatives helps build mutual understanding and empathy among diverse team members, enhancing collaboration beyond the training context. The equity of access to resources is another significant factor in upskilling diverse teams. Differences in access to technology, internet connectivity, or even physical spaces for learning can create disparities in participation. For instance, remote employees in regions with limited digital infrastructure may face barriers in accessing e-learning platforms or virtual simulations, while employees in headquarters may enjoy uninterrupted access. Organizations must proactively address these inequities by investing in inclusive technologies, offering offline learning options, and ensuring that resource allocation does not inadvertently favor certain groups over others. Equity also extends to providing opportunities for participation: women, minorities, or individuals from underrepresented backgrounds may face systemic barriers to engaging fully in training due to workload inequities, caregiving responsibilities, or unconscious biases. Designing flexible training schedules, offering micro-learning modules, and actively encouraging participation from marginalized groups ensures that upskilling initiatives reach all team members equitably.

MEASURING THE SUCCESS OF UPSKILLING INITIATIVES: MEASURING SUCCESS

As organizations across industries invest heavily in upskilling initiatives to address the challenges of digital transformation, artificial intelligence (AI) adoption, and rapidly evolving skill requirements, measuring the success of these initiatives has become a critical priority. Without robust measurement, even well-designed training programs risk being reduced to symbolic gestures rather than transformative drivers of workforce adaptability and organizational competitiveness. (Tenakwah E. S. et al. 2025) Success in upskilling cannot be assessed solely by participation rates or the number of training sessions conducted; instead, it requires a multidimensional evaluation framework that captures learning outcomes, behavioral changes, employee satisfaction, and long-term organizational impact. Moreover, measurement processes must account for diverse team environments, where cultural, generational, and contextual factors shape how skills are acquired, applied, and retained. A comprehensive approach to measuring success not only validates the value of investments in training but also provides actionable insights for improving program design, aligning with organizational strategy, and ensuring inclusivity. One of the foundational aspects of measuring upskilling success is assessing learning outcomes at the individual level. Traditional metrics such as pre- and post-training assessments, certification completion, or skill proficiency tests provide direct evidence of knowledge acquisition. These quantitative measures allow organizations to track improvements in employees' technical competencies or domain-specific expertise. However, measuring success should go beyond simple test scores, as real-world application of skills often requires contextual adaptation, critical thinking, and collaboration. For this reason, organizations are increasingly incorporating project-based evaluations, simulations, and scenario-based assessments to test not just whether employees can recall information but whether they can apply it effectively in complex work environments. In AI-augmented workplaces, for instance, success might be measured by an employee's ability to use AI tools ethically and effectively, interpret algorithmic outputs, and make informed decisions that balance automation with human judgment.

Another key dimension is evaluating behavioral and performance changes on the job. The true test of upskilling is whether newly acquired skills translate into improved work performance and contribute to organizational outcomes. (Warale P. N. et al. 2025) Organizations can measure this through performance metrics such as productivity improvements, error reduction, faster project completion times, or increased innovation in problem-solving. For example, in a healthcare setting, training clinicians in data analytics might be measured by improvements in diagnostic accuracy or patient outcomes, while in a retail context, employee training in digital platforms might be reflected in higher customer engagement or smoother omnichannel operations. Managers play a crucial role in this evaluation by observing behavioral changes, providing feedback, and assessing whether employees demonstrate confidence, adaptability, and collaboration after training. By combining quantitative performance data with qualitative insights from managers and peers, organizations can develop a holistic view of training effectiveness. Employee engagement and satisfaction form another critical measure of success. Upskilling initiatives are not just about technical competence but also about motivating employees, boosting morale, and fostering a sense of belonging in AI-augmented teams. Surveys, focus groups, and feedback tools can capture employees' perceptions of training relevance, accessibility, and value to their career development. High satisfaction levels indicate that training programs are well-aligned with employee expectations and learning styles, while low satisfaction can signal gaps in inclusivity, content design, or delivery methods. For diverse teams, satisfaction surveys must also consider whether training programs are culturally sensitive, accessible in multiple languages, and adaptable to different learning preferences. Engagement metrics, such as completion rates, voluntary participation in optional training modules, and employee advocacy for further learning opportunities, also provide valuable insights into the overall success of upskilling efforts.

EMERGING TRENDS IN AI-AUGMENTED TEAM MANAGEMENT: EMERGING TRENDS

The rapid integration of artificial intelligence (AI) into organizational workflows has not only transformed how work is performed but also redefined the very dynamics of team management. Traditional approaches to managing teams, which relied primarily on human intuition, leadership experience, and standardized organizational frameworks, are increasingly being supplemented and reshaped by AI-driven tools that enhance decision-making, communication, coordination, and employee engagement. (Warale P. N. et al. 2025) As AI becomes more deeply embedded in the fabric of organizational life, new trends are emerging that highlight both opportunities and challenges in managing AI-augmented teams. These trends reveal a shift from reactive management practices to proactive, predictive, and adaptive models of leadership where data, automation, and machine learning algorithms play a central role. Far from replacing human managers, AI is increasingly positioned as a co-pilot—an intelligent assistant that supports leaders in navigating the complexities of distributed workforces, evolving skill demands, and fast-changing market conditions. Understanding these emerging trends is critical for organizations seeking to remain competitive, agile, and inclusive in the era of

AI-augmented team management. One of the most prominent trends is the rise of AI-driven decision support systems for team management. Managers are increasingly using AI to analyze employee performance data, predict workload imbalances, and identify early indicators of burnout or disengagement. By processing vast amounts of information in real-time, AI enables leaders to make more informed, data-backed decisions rather than relying solely on intuition. For instance, workforce analytics platforms can assess productivity trends across remote and hybrid teams, identifying areas where additional support or redistribution of tasks is needed. Similarly, natural language processing (NLP)-based sentiment analysis tools are being used to gauge team morale by analyzing communication patterns across emails, chat platforms, and collaboration tools. These developments allow managers to take preemptive actions to maintain team cohesion, reduce attrition, and optimize resource allocation.

Another key trend is the emergence of hyper-personalized employee experiences facilitated by AI. Traditional one-size-fits-all management approaches are giving way to tailored strategies that adapt to the unique needs, preferences, and learning styles of individual team members. AI-powered platforms can recommend personalized learning and development opportunities, suggest task assignments aligned with employees' strengths, and even provide individualized wellness interventions. (Weiner S. P. et al. 2020) In AI-augmented team environments, this personalization extends to communication and collaboration, where AI systems help managers adapt their leadership style to suit diverse personalities and work preferences. For example, adaptive management platforms can identify whether an employee thrives under frequent feedback or prefers more autonomy, enabling managers to fine-tune their approach accordingly. This trend enhances inclusivity, engagement, and retention by ensuring that management practices respect individual differences while still promoting collective goals. A closely related development is the growing role of predictive and prescriptive analytics in workforce planning. Instead of relying on historical data alone, AI systems are being leveraged to anticipate future skill needs, identify potential gaps, and recommend targeted upskilling strategies. This capability is particularly critical in industries undergoing rapid technological disruption, where traditional workforce planning approaches often lag behind market realities. In AI-augmented team management, predictive analytics can help managers allocate resources more efficiently, anticipate project bottlenecks, and prepare teams for emerging challenges. For example, in a software development context, AI can predict which project modules are most likely to face delays based on historical data, enabling managers to proactively assign additional support. Over time, these predictive systems evolve into prescriptive tools that not only forecast challenges but also recommend optimal solutions, positioning managers as strategic enablers rather than reactive problem solvers.

THE FUTURE OF WORK: AI'S ROLE IN TEAM DYNAMICS: FUTURE OF WORK

The future of work is being shaped by the rapid advancement of artificial intelligence (AI), which is fundamentally altering not only the technical and operational aspects of organizations but also the social and relational fabric of teams. (Weiner S. P. et al. 2020) Team dynamics—the ways in which individuals interact, collaborate, resolve conflicts, and align around shared goals—are central to organizational success, and AI is poised to transform these dynamics in profound ways. As organizations integrate AI across industries and workflows, its role in shaping communication, decision-making, leadership, trust, and collaboration within teams becomes increasingly evident. Unlike earlier technological revolutions that focused largely on mechanizing tasks or digitizing processes, AI introduces cognitive capabilities such as natural language processing, pattern recognition, and predictive modeling, which bring machine intelligence into the social sphere of teamwork. (Shmueli G. et al. 2024) This development raises important questions: How will AI reshape traditional roles within teams? What new opportunities and challenges will arise in balancing human creativity, empathy, and judgment with machine-driven efficiency and accuracy? And, perhaps most importantly, what will team management and collaboration look like in an AI-augmented future of work? Addressing these questions requires a forward-looking perspective that examines the emerging shifts AI is introducing into team dynamics and considers strategies for leveraging these changes constructively. One of the most significant shifts in team dynamics is the integration of AI as a non-human "team member." Increasingly, AI systems are not just background tools but active participants in workflows, influencing how team members interact with one another and how decisions are made. For instance, AI-powered project management platforms allocate tasks, monitor progress, and provide real-time feedback, while conversational AI assistants participate in meetings by transcribing, summarizing, and even suggesting action points. These systems effectively occupy roles that once required human effort, thereby altering the balance of contributions within teams. This creates new dynamics where human members may focus more on higher-order problem-solving and creativity, while AI takes on repetitive or data-intensive tasks. However, this integration also challenges traditional notions of accountability and trust. Teams must learn to navigate questions such as: Should AI be treated as a collaborator or simply as a tool? How do teams reconcile disagreements between human intuition and AI recommendations? These issues will shape the cultural and ethical dimensions of team dynamics in the future of work.

Another emerging feature of AI's role in team dynamics is the transformation of communication patterns. Communication lies at the heart of effective teamwork, and AI is increasingly mediating how information flows between team members.

For example, AI-based communication tools can automatically translate languages in real-time, enabling seamless collaboration across global, multilingual teams. They can also summarize conversations, highlight unresolved issues, and ensure that no critical input is overlooked, thus making communication more inclusive and efficient. (Shmueli G. et al. 2024) Additionally, sentiment analysis tools can help managers identify underlying tensions or disengagement within teams by analyzing language use in emails, chat systems, or meeting transcripts. This evolution reduces the risks of miscommunication and allows for proactive interventions to maintain harmony and productivity. However, the reliance on AI-mediated communication also risks depersonalizing interactions if not managed thoughtfully. In the future of work, teams will need to balance the efficiency of AI-enhanced communication with the emotional nuances and empathy that only humans can provide. AI is also revolutionizing decision-making processes in team environments. Traditionally, teams relied on deliberation, brainstorming, and consensus-building to arrive at decisions, processes often constrained by limited data or subjective biases. AI introduces data-driven objectivity by analyzing vast datasets, identifying trends, and recommending evidence-based options. For example, in supply chain teams, AI can forecast demand fluctuations and suggest resource allocation strategies, thereby reducing uncertainty and disagreement among team members. In healthcare teams, AI can assist clinicians by offering diagnostic recommendations, which then inform collaborative treatment decisions. These shifts foster a new dynamic where AI serves as a "decision catalyst," expediting consensus and grounding discussions in empirical evidence. Yet, this also raises the challenge of algorithmic overreliance—where teams may defer too heavily to AI outputs at the expense of human judgment. The future of work will require cultivating a balanced dynamic where AI informs but does not dictate decisions, with human members exercising critical oversight to ensure ethical and context-sensitive outcomes.

CONCLUSION

The transformative potential of artificial intelligence (AI) in the workplace extends beyond automation and efficiency; it also encompasses the ability to enhance team performance while simultaneously creating opportunities for upskilling and professional growth. In today's rapidly evolving digital economy, organizations are under increasing pressure to remain competitive, agile, and innovative. Teams must not only deliver high performance but also continuously adapt to changing technologies, markets, and customer expectations. AI has emerged as both a performance enabler and a learning catalyst, helping organizations unlock new levels of productivity while empowering employees with the tools, insights, and resources they need to upgrade their skills. Harnessing AI for enhanced team performance and upskilling requires a holistic approach that considers technical, social, and cultural factors, ensuring that the integration of AI into workflows augments rather than displaces human potential. One of the primary ways AI enhances team performance is through intelligent automation and augmentation. Unlike traditional automation, which focuses on replacing repetitive, rule-based tasks, AI-driven augmentation allows teams to offload time-consuming activities such as data entry, reporting, or basic customer queries to AI systems, thereby freeing employees to focus on higher-value activities like problem-solving, strategic planning, and creative innovation. For example, in finance teams, AI tools can analyze large datasets to detect anomalies, forecast market trends, or provide real-time compliance checks, enabling professionals to make faster, more informed decisions. In healthcare, AI can assist medical teams by generating diagnostic insights or suggesting treatment options based on patient histories, allowing doctors and nurses to focus on personalized care. By reducing cognitive load and eliminating inefficiencies, AI not only increases team productivity but also creates opportunities for employees to deepen their expertise and expand their roles.

AI also plays a pivotal role in data-driven decision-making, which directly impacts team performance. Traditionally, teams have relied on intuition, experience, or limited data to make decisions, often leading to delays, biases, or inaccuracies. With AI's ability to analyze vast volumes of structured and unstructured data, teams can base decisions on evidence, predictive analytics, and scenario modeling. For instance, sales teams can leverage AI-driven customer relationship management (CRM) systems to identify leads with the highest conversion probability, while operations teams can optimize supply chains by predicting demand fluctuations and adjusting resource allocations in real time. This data-driven environment enhances team confidence, reduces conflicts rooted in subjective judgments, and fosters a culture of accountability and transparency. At the same time, engaging with AI-driven insights encourages employees to develop data literacy skills, a critical upskilling dimension in AI-augmented workplaces. In addition to performance optimization, AI contributes significantly to personalized learning and skill development, making upskilling a natural outcome of AI integration. AI-powered learning management systems (LMS) can assess individual team members' strengths, weaknesses, and learning preferences, and then design tailored training paths that maximize engagement and knowledge retention. For example, an AI platform might recommend technical modules such as coding, data analysis, or cybersecurity for one employee, while suggesting leadership, communication, or project management training for another. This personalization ensures that team members acquire skills most relevant to their roles and aspirations, fostering both immediate performance improvements and long-term career growth. Furthermore, AI can identify emerging skill gaps at the team or organizational level by analyzing work outputs, project outcomes, and industry trends, enabling proactive upskilling initiatives that future-proof the workforce against technological disruptions.

REFERENCES

Barrett, B., & Miller, C. (2024). Ensuring inclusive workplace training in an age of rapid technological advancement: an examination of the impact of artificial intelligence (ai) rollout. In *ICERI2024 Proceedings* (pp. 7796-7802).

Charan, J. K., Chandra, S., Vaissnave, V., Ragupathi, T., Satyanarayana, P., & Manjunath, T. C. (2025). Impact of Generative AI on Industries and Organizations. In Zhao, J., Kumar, V., Katina, P., & Richards, J. (Eds.), *Humans and Generative AI Tools for Collaborative Intelligence* (pp. 509–528). IGI Global Scientific Publishing. DOI: 10.4018/979-8-3693-8332-2.ch022

Goel, A., Dede, C., Garn, M., & Ou, C. (2024). AI-ALOE: AI for reskilling, upskilling, and workforce development. *AI Magazine*, *45*(1), 77–82. DOI: 10.1002/aaai.12157

Gonzalez, K., Kanitz, R., & Briker, R. (2024). "AI can't steal my soul": In the age of AI, the human touch is paramount for the craft of managing change. *The Journal of Applied Behavioral Science*, *60*(4), 589–602. DOI: 10.1177/00218863241279916

Goryunova, E., & Yawson, R. M. (2025). "Nested Complexity" Framework for Human-Centered AI-Augmented Leadership. *Journal of Leadership Studies*, *19*(2), e70016. DOI: 10.1002/jls.70016

Guru Basava Aradhya, S., Chithambar Gupta, V., Raman, M. S., Singh, J., Manjunath, T. C., & Sharma, M. (2025). Health Crises and Digitalization: Digital Health. In Yıldırım, D., Yıldırım, S., & Kandpal, V. (Eds.), *Sustainable Digitalization Strategies in Business and Healthcare* (pp. 171–198). IGI Global Scientific Publishing. DOI: 10.4018/979-8-3373-5087-5.ch007

Harmanpreet, C. S., Kalshetti, P., Satyanarayana, P., Sharma, M., & Manjunath, T. C. (2025). Digital Transformation in the Public Sector Entities. In A. Santos Ferreira & C. Lourenço dos Santos (Eds.), *Enhancing Public Sector Accountability and Services Through Digital Innovation* (pp. 353-380). IGI Global Scientific Publishing.

Huzooree, G., Subramanian, J., & Dewasiri, N. J. (2025). Reskilling for the AI Age: Project Management Approaches and Organisational Strategies for Workforce Readiness. In *Global Work Arrangements and Outsourcing in the Age of AI* (pp. 471-494). IGI Global Scientific Publishing.

Koparde, S. A., Selvakumar, P., Jha, R. P., Deepthi Reddy, K., Kuchipudi, J. D., Manjunath, T. C., & Sharma, M. (2026). Generative AI in Predicting and Preventing Foodborne Illnesses. In Madaan, G., Singh, A., Chahal, B., David, A., & Singh, G. (Eds.), *Generative AI in Food Systems: Predictive Demand, Smart Supply Chains, and Sustainable Service Futures* (pp. 205–232). IGI Global Scientific Publishing.

Marion, T., Yuan, C., & Moghaddam, M. (2025). Integrating AI into the Front End of New Product Development: A Case Comparison of Traditional and Augmented Processes. *Research Technology Management, 68*(2), 10–22. DOI: 10.1080/08956308.2024.2444142

Martino, D., Perlangeli, C., Grottoli, B., La Rosa, L., & Pacella, M. (2025). A Knowledge-Driven Framework for AI-Augmented Business Process Management Systems: Bridging Explainability and Agile Knowledge Sharing. *AI, 6*(6), 110. DOI: 10.3390/ai6060110

Mishra, B. R., Selvakumar, P., Kaur, R., Kalshetti, P., Mishra, K. K., Sharma, M., & Manjunath, T. C. (2025). Innovation and Digital Transformation in the Public Sector Entities. In Santos Ferreira, A., & Lourenço dos Santos, C. (Eds.), *Enhancing Public Sector Accountability and Services Through Digital Innovation* (pp. 409–436). IGI Global Scientific Publishing. DOI: 10.4018/979-8-3693-9251-5.ch013

Mollah, M. A., Rana, M., Amin, M. B., Sony, M. A. A. M., Rahaman, M. A., & Fenyves, V. (2024). Examining the role of AI-augmented HRM for sustainable performance: Key determinants for digital culture and organizational strategy. *Sustainability (Basel), 16*(24), 10843. DOI: 10.3390/su162410843

Nirupama, E., Seenivasan, S., Bhardwaj, K., Karunakaran, N. B., & Basava Aradhya, S. G., & Manjunath, T. C. (2025). Transforming Digital Supply Chains With Gamification and Metaverse Integration. In G. Malik, D. Singh, & R. Bansal (Eds.), *Addressing Practical Problems Through the Metaverse and Game-Inspired Mechanics* (pp. 123-152). IGI Global Scientific Publishing.

Rahayu, S., & Bablu, T. A. (2023). AI-Augmented Learning and Development Platforms: Transforming Employee Training and Skill Enhancement. *Journal of Computing Innovations and Applications, 1*(01), 19–38.

Raman, M. S., Koppa, K. B., Chithambar Gupta, V., Bhat, V. A., & Guru Basava Aradhya, S. (2025). Digital Transformation and Sustainability Artificial Intelligence and Sustainable Development. In Yıldırım, D., Yıldırım, S., & Kandpal, V. (Eds.), *Effects of Digitalization and Circular Economy on Sustainable Policy and Climate Change Prevention* (pp. 69–96). IGI Global Scientific Publishing. DOI: 10.4018/979-8-3693-9909-5.ch003

Seufert, S., & Spirgi, J. (2024). Navigating AI Transformation: Human Resource Development Strategies for Corporate Learning. *International Journal of Advanced Corporate Learning, 17*(4), 80–93. DOI: 10.3991/ijac.v17i4.47443

Shmueli, G., & Ray, S. (2024). Reimagining the Journal Editorial Process: An AI-Augmented Versus an AI-Driven Future. *Journal of the Association for Information Systems*, *25*(1), 10. DOI: 10.17705/1jais.00864

Sivanand, R., Selvakumar, P., & Sharma, N. (2025). Navneet Sharma, Nanotechnology Applications in Cancer Drug Delivery Systems: A Review. *Journal of Environmental Nanotechnology*, *14*(2), 458–470. DOI: 10.13074/jent.2025.06.2511221

Tangi, L., Müller, A. P. R., & Janssen, M. (2025). AI-augmented government transformation: Organisational transformation and the sociotechnical implications of artificial intelligence in public administrations. *Government Information Quarterly*, *42*(3), 102055. DOI: 10.1016/j.giq.2025.102055

Tenakwah, E. S., & Watson, C. (2025). Embracing the AI/automation age: Preparing your workforce for humans and machines working together. *Strategy and Leadership*, *53*(1), 32–48. DOI: 10.1108/SL-05-2024-0040

Warale, P. N., Limbore, N. V., Anute, N., Ahluwalia, G. K., & Raut, A. (2025). AI-Enhanced Customer Engagement and Experience: Chatbots, Virtual Assistants, and AI-Powered Customer Interactions. In Hussain, Z., Khan, A., Uzir, M., Sharipudin, M., & Shaheen, A. (Eds.), *Impacts of AI-Generated Content on Brand Reputation* (pp. 335–362). IGI Global Scientific Publishing. DOI: 10.4018/979-8-3373-4327-3.ch014

Weiner, S. P., & McMahon, M. (2020). Action taking augmented by artificial intelligence. *Employee surveys and sensing: Driving organizational culture and performance*, 338-354.

Chapter 13
Change Management and Skills Development in the Age of AI

Nesrine Barhoum
http://orcid.org/0009-0008-3542-9997
Faculty of Economics and Management, University of Sax, Tunisia

Sami Boudabbous
Faculty of Economics and Management, University of Sfax, Tunisia

ABSTRACT

Artificial intelligence (AI) is now emerging as a driver of organizational transformation, revolutionizing management models, work patterns, and human relationships within companies. While its potential for innovation, efficiency, and competitiveness is undeniable, its integration is prompting profound changes in skills and organizational structures. The success of this transition hinges on companies' ability to implement human-centered change management that reconciles technological progress with ethical considerations. This chapter explores the dynamics of organizational change in the AI era, drawing on both classic (Lewin, 1951; Kotter, 1996) and contemporary (Hiatt & Creasey, 2021; Barabel & Meier, 2023) models, while highlighting the new skills to be developed: digital literacy, critical thinking, creativity, emotional intelligence, and adaptability.

INTRODUCTION

Artificial intelligence (AI) is no longer a distant technological promise; it has become a powerful force that is already reshaping economies, organizations, and

DOI: 10.4018/979-8-3373-6851-1.ch013

everyday work. As part of a broader wave of digital innovation, AI is transforming value chains, employment patterns, and labor relations (Brynjolfsson & McAfee, 2021; Organisation for Economic Co-operation and Development [OECD], 2023). In line with Schumpeter's (1942) idea of creative destruction, this transformation brings both progress and disruption. While AI offers unprecedented opportunities to improve productivity and decision-making, it also generates deep human, managerial, and ethical challenges that organizations can no longer ignore.

The impact of AI goes far beyond technological change. It alters how organizations are structured, how decisions are made, and what it means to be competent at work (Borenstein & Howard, 2023). Traditional hierarchical models are increasingly questioned, and organizations are compelled to rethink how they manage change. In this context, change management can no longer be treated as a one-time response to innovation; it must be understood as a continuous process of learning, adjustment, and collective sense-making. In other words, the ability to manage change has become a strategic asset in itself.

Yet, the reality of digital transformation remains paradoxical. Despite massive investments in AI and digital tools, many organizations struggle to translate technology into real performance gains. McKinsey (2023) shows that nearly 70% of digital transformation initiatives fail, not because of technical shortcomings, but because of human and organizational barriers such as resistance to change, skills gaps, and the absence of a shared vision. This highlights a crucial point: technological success depends above all on people's ability and willingness to adopt and integrate new ways of working.

These difficulties are closely linked to the fears and uncertainties generated by AI. Many employees worry about being replaced by machines, losing control over their work, or seeing their skills become obsolete (International Labour Organization [ILO], 2023). At the same time, the growing role of data and automation makes work environments more complex, requiring employees to develop hybrid profiles that combine technical knowledge with cognitive and social capabilities (Barabel, 2023). In this context, training and skills development are no longer optional—they are essential conditions for organizational sustainability.

Change management theories offer useful lenses for understanding these dynamics. Lewin's (1951) model of unfreezing, change, and refreezing remains relevant for describing how organizations move away from old routines and stabilize new ones. Kotter's (1996) eight-step model further emphasizes the importance of leadership, urgency, and the consolidation of change. More recently, the ADKAR framework (Hiatt & Creasey, 2021) has highlighted the individual dimension of change, focusing on awareness, motivation, knowledge, and capability. However, in the age of AI, these models must be revisited to account for the ethical, cognitive, and technological complexity of contemporary transformations.

At the same time, AI is profoundly reshaping skill requirements. The World Economic Forum (2024) estimates that more than half of workers will need significant reskilling by 2027. Technical skills such as data analysis, programming, and the use of intelligent systems are becoming indispensable, but they are no longer sufficient. They must be complemented by human capabilities such as critical thinking, creativity, empathy, and emotional intelligence (Goleman, 2022). These skills enable individuals not only to work with AI, but also to question it, interpret it, and use it responsibly.

In this context, the role of managers becomes even more critical. They are expected to guide their teams through uncertainty, give meaning to change, and support learning and adaptation. As Amabile (2021) points out, organizations that innovate successfully are those in which leadership encourages experimentation, trust, and psychological safety. When AI disrupts established work practices, these human qualities of leadership become decisive.

Finally, no discussion of AI would be complete without addressing its ethical implications. Algorithmic bias, digital surveillance, and the massive use of personal data raise fundamental questions about fairness, transparency, and privacy (Floridi, 2021; Institute of Electrical and Electronics Engineers [IEEE], 2023). For organizations, this means that technological transformation must be accompanied by clear ethical governance in order to preserve trust and legitimacy.

Although a large body of research exists on AI, change management, skills, and ethics, these topics are too often treated separately. What is still missing is an integrated perspective that brings together technology, human capital, leadership, and ethical responsibility. This chapter seeks to fill that gap by adopting a human-centered approach to AI-driven organizational transformation.

Accordingly, the chapter is organized around five main themes: (1) change management in a context of technological disruption; (2) the identification of key skills required in the AI era; (3) innovative approaches to training and learning; (4) the role of leadership and managers in supporting change; and (5) the ethical challenges associated with the integration of AI. The overall objective is to show that the success of digital transformation depends less on technology itself than on organizations' ability to learn, adapt, and evolve in a way that is both inclusive and ethically responsible.

SECTION 1 – THE IMPORTANCE OF EFFECTIVE CHANGE MANAGEMENT

1.1. Change Management in the Era of Artificial Intelligence

The integration of artificial intelligence into organizations represents far more than a technological upgrade; it reshapes organizational structures, work processes, and social relations at work. As highlighted by Kotter (1996) and Hiatt and Creasey (2021), the outcome of such transformations depends less on the sophistication of the technology than on the way employees understand, interpret, and accept it. By automating tasks and redefining roles, AI often triggers emotional reactions such as anxiety, resistance, or disengagement, which can seriously undermine transformation efforts (Schein, 2017).

In this context, change management plays a central role in helping organizations navigate uncertainty and build trust. In environments where technological change evolves faster than human adaptation, the objective is no longer to impose new systems from the top down, but to involve employees in shaping the transformation. This perspective echoes Lewin's (1951) three-stage model—unfreezing, changing, and refreezing—but it also requires a significant reinterpretation. In the AI era, change cannot be stabilized once and for all; it must be continuously renewed through learning and experimentation (Burnes & Cooke, 2013). To achieve this, organizations need to develop dynamic capabilities that allow them to sense technological shifts, seize new opportunities, and integrate innovation into everyday practices (Teece, 2018).

1.2. Human and Organizational Challenges of Technological Change

The introduction of AI into the workplace gives rise to a set of interrelated human and organizational challenges. One of the most significant is resistance to change. Fear of automation and job displacement remains widespread, and many employees still perceive AI as a threat rather than as a support to their work (ILO, 2023). Such perceptions can generate withdrawal, lower engagement, and reduced productivity.

Another major barrier lies in the shortage of digital and analytical skills. Working effectively with AI requires the ability to understand data, interpret algorithmic outputs, and interact with automated systems—competencies that many employees have not yet fully developed (Brynjolfsson & McAfee, 2021). At the same time, AI disrupts organizational culture by challenging traditional hierarchies. Authority increasingly derives from the capacity to learn, adapt, and collaborate, rather than from formal position alone (Barabel & Meier, 2023).

Trust also becomes a critical issue. Concerns about algorithmic bias, data privacy, and digital surveillance can weaken the social contract between employees and organizations (Floridi, 2021). These concerns are not marginal: a Deloitte study (2023) reports that 64% of employees believe their organizations are not sufficiently prepared to manage the human consequences of automation. This underlines the urgent need for change management approaches that integrate communication, training, and ethical leadership.

1.3. Contemporary Models of Change Management

Several theoretical frameworks help to structure how organizations can manage AI-driven transformation. Kotter's (1996) eight-step model—ranging from creating a sense of urgency to anchoring change in organizational culture—remains a valuable guide, provided that it incorporates ethical and participatory dimensions. Similarly, the ADKAR model developed by Hiatt and Creasey (2021) highlights the individual trajectory of change by focusing on awareness, desire, knowledge, ability, and reinforcement. This model is particularly useful in understanding why AI initiatives succeed or fail at the employee level.

More recent approaches, such as Prosci's model (2024), place strong emphasis on co-creation and two-way communication. Evidence suggests that organizations that actively involve employees in the design and implementation of AI systems are significantly more likely to complete their digital transformations successfully. Agile and self-managed approaches to change, advocated by Appelo (2019) and Laloux (2016), further stress the importance of rapid experimentation and continuous adaptation in complex technological environments.

In practice, no single model is sufficient. Organizations benefit most from hybrid approaches that combine the structure and discipline of classical change frameworks with the flexibility and responsiveness of agile methods. This balance allows firms to provide direction while still encouraging innovation and employee participation.

1.4. Communication and Engagement as Drivers of Change

Clear and credible communication is one of the most powerful levers of successful change management. It must be ongoing, transparent, and sensitive to employees' concerns. McKinsey (2023) shows that digital transformation initiatives with strong communication strategies are about 40% more likely to succeed.

Effective communication rests on three complementary pillars. First, organizations must inform employees by explaining why AI is being introduced and how it supports the overall strategy. Second, they must involve them by creating spaces for dialogue and co-design. Third, they must inspire by showing how AI can improve daily work and create new opportunities. Storytelling, pilot projects, and internal success cases are particularly effective in making abstract technologies more concrete and meaningful (Barabel & Meier, 2023).

Leadership plays a decisive role in this process. Managers are expected to embody the vision of change, encourage open dialogue, and foster psychological safety within their teams (Edmondson, 2019). In AI-driven transformations, transformational leadership—based on trust, motivation, and shared purpose—proves far more effective than traditional command-and-control styles (Bass & Riggio, 2018).

1.5. Employee Training and Support

Training is a cornerstone of any AI-related change strategy. To be effective, it must go beyond technical instruction and include broader economic, social, and ethical dimensions of AI. When employees understand not only how AI works but also why it is used and what its implications are, their confidence and engagement increase.

Continuous learning initiatives are particularly important in this regard. LinkedIn Learning (2023) reports that employees are far more likely to remain committed to organizations that invest in their development. Tailored training programs, practical workshops, and simulations enable employees to experiment with AI tools in a safe environment and to recognize their value in everyday work.

Leading organizations such as Google, IBM, and Orange have adopted "learning by doing" approaches, allowing employees to interact with AI systems before large-scale deployment. This experiential learning process reduces uncertainty and helps transform fear into competence and curiosity (Kolb, 2015).

1.6. Measuring Impact and Ensuring Continuous Improvement For change management to be effective, it must be continuously assessed. Organizations need to define clear indicators to monitor technology adoption, employee engagement, and productivity outcomes. Tools such as HR dashboards, satisfaction surveys, and 360-degree feedback systems provide valuable insights that allow managers to adjust their strategies in real time (Deloitte, 2023). This emphasis on measurement and feedback reflects a broader culture of organizational learning, in which mistakes are viewed as opportunities for improvement rather than as failures (Argyris & Schön, 1996). Finally, AI-driven change must always be guided by ethical principles. As Floridi (2021) argues, technological progress is meaningful only if it remains aligned with human values, fairness, and social responsibility.

SECTION 2 – IDENTIFYING KEY SKILLS IN THE AGE OF ARTIFICIAL INTELLIGENCE

2.1. Artificial Intelligence and the Structural Reconfiguration of Work

Artificial intelligence represents a general-purpose technology that is reshaping the organization of production, coordination, and decision-making across sectors. Unlike earlier waves of automation, AI not only replaces routine manual and cognitive tasks but also augments analytical, predictive, and interpretative functions (Brynjolfsson & McAfee, 2021). This dual dynamic profoundly alters the architecture of work and the nature of professional competence. According to the World Economic Forum (2024), nearly half of current workforce skills will become obsolete or require substantial upgrading by 2027. However, this transformation should not be interpreted merely as a technical reskilling challenge. It reflects a deeper shift in the sources of value creation. As AI increasingly performs standardized processing and optimization, human labor is reallocated toward functions that involve judgment under uncertainty, social interaction, and ethical responsibility. This chapter builds on the OECD's (2023) concept of a "cognitive and emotional economy" and extends it by proposing that AI accelerates the transition from task-based to capability-based work. In such a regime, performance depends less on the execution of predefined procedures and more on the ability to navigate complexity, interpret algorithmic outputs, and coordinate across organizational and technological boundaries.

2.2. Technical and Digital Skills as Enabling Infrastructures

Technical competence constitutes the infrastructural layer of all other skills in AI-enabled organizations. Digital literacy, defined by the OECD (2022) as the capacity to access, evaluate, and apply digital technologies, is no longer a specialized competence but a general condition of employability. A central component of digital literacy is data literacy. As Cukier and Mayer-Schönberger (2021) argue, data functions as the primary factor of production in the digital economy. Employees must therefore be capable of interpreting data, assessing its quality, and translating quantitative information into actionable organizational knowledge. Without this capacity, AI systems remain opaque tools rather than instruments of augmented intelligence. Moreover, AI deployment requires familiarity with automation, predictive modeling, and cybersecurity. LinkedIn Learning (2023) identifies data analytics, AI system management, and process automation as the fastest-growing professional skills. However, this chapter argues that technical competence is inherently unstable: technologies evolve faster than formal training systems. Consequently, the most critical technical skill is not mastery of a particular tool, but the capacity for continuous technological learning (Barabel & Meier, 2023).

2.3. Cognitive Skills and the Limits of Algorithmic Rationality

While AI excels at optimization and pattern recognition, it remains limited in dealing with ambiguity, novelty, and conflicting objectives. These limitations explain why cognitive skills become increasingly valuable as AI diffuses throughout organizations. Critical thinking enables individuals to evaluate algorithmic recommendations, identify biases, and challenge erroneous or ethically problematic outputs (Kahneman, 2011). In a data-intensive environment, this skill protects organizations from automation bias and over-reliance on machine-generated insights. Creativity, in turn, allows humans to generate solutions that cannot be derived from historical data. As Amabile (2021) demonstrates, innovation depends on the interaction between knowledge, motivation, and an environment that tolerates experimentation. Florida (2020) further shows that creative occupations play a central role in regional and organizational competitiveness in digital economies. Complex problem-solving integrates analytical reasoning with contextual understanding and interdisciplinary knowledge. In AI-based organizations, effective problem-solving increasingly occurs within hybrid teams that combine technical, managerial, and domain-specific expertise (Nonaka & Takeuchi, 2019).

2.4. Emotional and Relational Skills as Organizational Stabilizers

The diffusion of AI intensifies emotional and relational demands at work. As tasks become more abstract and mediated by technology, employees face uncertainty about their roles, identity, and future prospects. Emotional intelligence, defined as the ability to recognize, regulate, and mobilize emotions (Goleman, 2022), therefore becomes a core organizational capability. Emotional skills contribute to organizational performance in three ways. First, they support collaboration between humans and AI systems by enabling employees to manage frustration, uncertainty, and cognitive overload. Second, they reinforce trust and cohesion in digitally mediated teams. Third, they underpin ethical judgment by grounding decisions in empathy and social awareness. Empirical evidence confirms their importance. Harvard Business Review (2023) reports that emotionally intelligent leaders achieve substantially higher levels of engagement and psychological safety, both of which are essential for learning and innovation in AI-driven environments.

2.5. Ethical Competence and the Governance of Algorithmic Power

As AI systems increasingly shape hiring, evaluation, and resource allocation, ethical competence becomes inseparable from professional competence. Ethical skills involve more than regulatory compliance; they require the capacity to anticipate social consequences, recognize moral dilemmas, and exercise responsibility in algorithmic decision-making (Floridi, 2021; IEEE, 2023).

PwC (2024) shows that while most executives consider AI ethics strategically important, few organizations provide systematic training in this area. This creates a structural risk: organizations may deploy powerful technologies without the human capacity to govern them responsibly. Ethical literacy—combining technological understanding with moral reasoning—must therefore be institutionalized as a core professional skill.

2.6. Metacognitive and Adaptive Skills in a Learning Economy

In volatile technological environments, no fixed set of skills remains sufficient for long. Adaptability and metacognition—the ability to reflect on and regulate one's own learning—become decisive sources of resilience (Knowles, 2020).

Metacognitive skills allow individuals to identify knowledge gaps, select appropriate learning strategies, and transfer competencies across contexts. At the organizational level, this translates into the concept of the learning organization, in which experimentation, feedback, and reflection are embedded in everyday work (Senge, 2019).

2.7. An Integrated Human–AI Skills Architecture

Based on the preceding analysis, this chapter proposes a multi-layered skills architecture that integrates technical, cognitive, emotional, and ethical-adaptive dimensions.

Table 1. Human–AI Skills Architecture

Layer	Core Skills	Strategic Function
Technical	Digital literacy, data analytics, AI tools	Enable effective human–machine interaction
Cognitive	Critical thinking, creativity, problem-solving	Provide judgment and innovation
Emotional	Empathy, collaboration, emotional intelligence	Stabilize social systems
Ethical–Adaptive	Accountability, transparency, continuous learning	Govern AI responsibly over time

This architecture conceptualizes skills as an interdependent system rather than a list of attributes. It supports the central argument of this chapter: the future of work in the age of AI will be shaped not by the power of machines, but by the capacity of humans to interpret, regulate, and ethically integrate intelligent technologies into organizational life.

SECTION 3: SKILLS DEVELOPMENT STRATEGIES

In a context marked by the rapid diffusion of artificial intelligence (AI), skills development has become a central strategic issue for organizations seeking to maintain their competitiveness, resilience, and capacity for innovation. Far from being limited to technical training, skills development now encompasses cognitive, behavioral, ethical, and collaborative dimensions. This section analyzes the main strategies that enable companies to structure sustainable and inclusive skills development systems, while fully integrating the opportunities offered by AI.

3.1. Continuing Education As A Strategic Lever For Competitiveness

Continuing education constitutes a fundamental pillar of organizational adaptation in the face of technological, economic, and social transformations driven by AI. Its primary objective is to continuously update employee skills, strengthen innovation capacity, and reduce resistance to change within organizations.

According to the World Economic Forum (2024), 85% of companies consider continuing education a decisive success factor for digital transformation. This observation reflects a paradigm shift: learning is no longer perceived as a one-time stage in a professional career, but rather as an ongoing process of reinvention.

Barabel and Meier (2023) emphasize that in an environment characterized by rapid skills obsolescence, employability depends on individuals' ability to learn continuously, while organizations benefit from a workforce capable of adapting and innovating. Continuing education therefore plays a dual role: it secures individual career paths and enhances overall organizational performance. Modern training systems are structured around four major principles, summarized in Table 3.1.

Table 2. Core principles of contemporary continuing education models

Principle	Description	Key Reference
Individualization	Tailoring learning content to individual needs, roles, and skill levels	Knowles (2020)
Hybridization	Combining face-to-face and online learning formats	Clark & Mayer (2023)
Interactivity	Encouraging active learning through simulations, case studies, and problem-solving	Experiential learning approaches
Continuous assessment	Ongoing measurement of learning outcomes to adjust training paths	McKinsey (2023)

Empirical evidence supports the strategic value of such investments. McKinsey (2023) shows that organizations allocating at least 1.5% of their payroll to digital training achieve productivity levels approximately 20% higher than the industry average.

Figure 1. Role of continuing education in organizational competitiveness

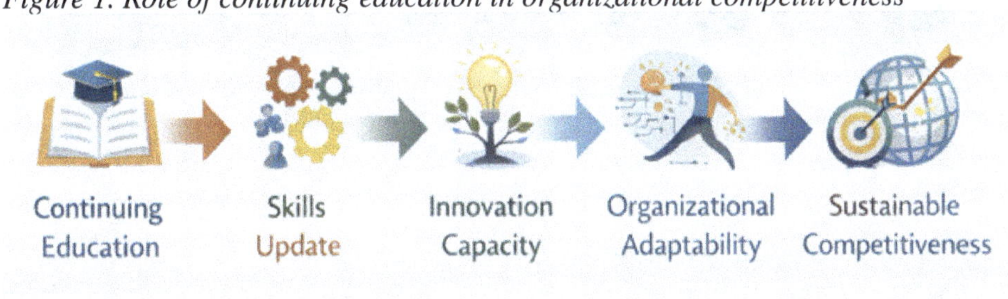

3.2. Personalized And Adaptive Learning

The development of AI-based learning technologies has profoundly transformed training systems by enabling personalized and adaptive learning experiences. These systems rely on algorithms capable of analyzing learners' performance, preferences, and skill gaps in order to propose customized learning paths (365Talents, 2024).

Adaptive learning significantly enhances knowledge retention and learner engagement. A Gartner study (2024) indicates that personalized training programs increase employee engagement by 40% and operational performance by 32%. One of the major advantages of AI-driven platforms lies in their ability to identify skill gaps in real time and redirect learners toward targeted modules.

Concrete examples illustrate this dynamic. IBM Skills Build offers a free global platform integrating AI, data analytics, and digital skills training, accessible to more than 2 million users worldwide. Similarly, Google Digital Garage provides free certification programs aimed at strengthening the digital capabilities of employees, entrepreneurs, and job seekers.

These initiatives reflect a broader trend toward the democratization of access to learning and the promotion of learner autonomy. They are fully aligned with the principles of andragogical pedagogy developed by Knowles (2020), which stress that adults learn more effectively when they:

- Are actively involved in the learning process;
- Understand the purpose and relevance of the content;
- Can immediately apply newly acquired knowledge.

Figure 2. Functioning of adaptive learning systems

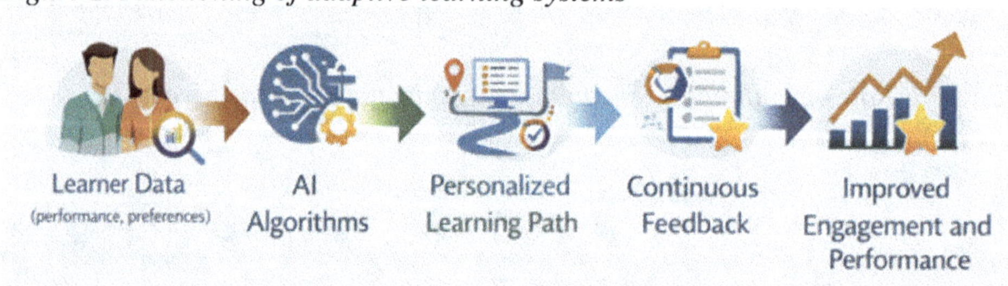

3.3. Mentoring And Coaching As Catalysts For Human Development

Mentoring and coaching represent complementary mechanisms for developing soft skills, managerial competencies, and emotional intelligence. In periods of technological uncertainty, these human-centered approaches play a crucial role in supporting employees.

According to Goleman (2022), mentoring provides emotional support, facilitates knowledge transfer, and strengthens cultural alignment within organizations. It contributes to confidence-building and resilience, particularly in contexts of rapid technological change. Effective mentoring programs are generally structured around three key dimensions, presented in Table 3.2.

Table 3. Dimensions of mentoring programs

Dimension	Objective
Transfer of experience	Sharing tacit knowledge and proven practices
Emotional support	Helping employees manage stress and uncertainty
Stimulation of innovation	Encouraging reflection on AI-driven opportunities

Deloitte (2023) reports that 68% of organizations implementing structured mentoring programs observe improvements in organizational climate and collective performance.

Coaching, by contrast, focuses more strongly on individual accountability and self-awareness. As highlighted by Whitmore (2019) and Baron & Morin (2020), managerial coaching enables employees to identify internal barriers, enhance decision-making autonomy, and align personal objectives with organizational goals.

Digital technologies further extend the reach of these practices. E-mentoring platforms, hybrid coaching sessions, and conversational AI tools improve accessibility and scalability. Solutions such as CoachHub and MentorcliQ already use algorithms to match mentors and mentees based on skills, values, and development needs.

3.4. Communities Of Practice And Collaborative Learning

Communities of practice, initially conceptualized by Wenger and Snyder (2021), are collective spaces where individuals share experiences, exchange knowledge, and co-create solutions. They play a crucial role in the informal diffusion of knowledge and the emergence of collective intelligence.

In the AI era, these communities are strengthened by digital collaboration tools such as Slack, Microsoft Teams, and Notion, as well as open innovation platforms. Learning thus becomes social, participatory, and continuous. The main benefits associated with communities of practice include:

- Higher employee engagement ;
- Reduced organizational silos ;
- Enhanced creativity and innovation ;
- Strengthened sense of belonging.

A notable example is Orange France's "Digital Academy," launched in 2021. This initiative brings together internal communities focused on AI, cybersecurity, and customer data, enabling employees to share projects, tutorials, and feedback, thereby fostering continuous collective learning.

Figure 3. Knowledge dynamics within communities of practice

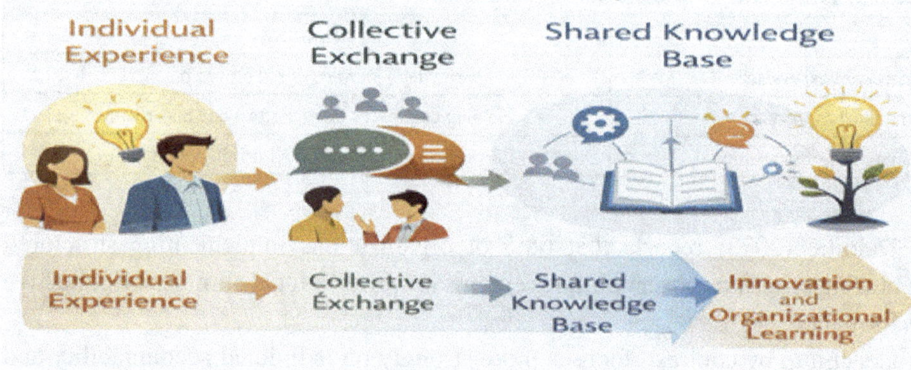

3.5. Self-Directed Learning And The Culture Of Lifelong Learning

The acceleration of skills obsolescence has made lifelong learning a strategic necessity. As Senge (2019) argues, learning organizations are those capable of transforming individual learning into collective value.

Self-directed learning relies primarily on intrinsic motivation, including curiosity and the desire for self-improvement. Online platforms such as Coursera, Udemy, and edX offer thousands of certified courses in fields ranging from programming to occupational psychology.

Progressive organizations integrate these platforms into their HR strategies, encouraging employees to allocate dedicated time to autonomous learning. AI further enhances these approaches by recommending personalized learning modules based on observed performance gaps or project requirements.

Microlearning, supported by AI-driven analytics, enables agile, flexible, and context-adapted training that aligns with modern work rhythms.

3.6. Skills Assessment And Recognition

Effective skills development strategies must be accompanied by transparent evaluation and recognition mechanisms. Increasingly, organizations rely on digital badges and internal certifications to formally acknowledge learning achievements (SHRM, 2023).

Assessment systems may be based on multiple tools:

- Individual performance indicators ;
- 360° feedback mechanisms ;
- Formative assessments embedded in learning modules;
- Data analytics generated by learning platforms.

Digital credentials enhance the visibility and portability of skills, facilitating both internal and external mobility. LinkedIn (2023) reports that profiles displaying verified certifications are 2.5 times more likely to lead to promotion or recruitment.

Table 4. Benefits of digital skill recognition systems

Stakeholder	Benefits
Employees	Motivation, career mobility, skill visibility
Organizations	Talent retention, objective evaluation, workforce planning

3.7. Integration Of Ethical And Inclusive Dimensions Into Training

Skills development in the AI era must integrate ethical and inclusive considerations. Digital transformation should be equitable, accessible, and respectful of cultural and social diversity. Training programs must avoid reinforcing pre-existing inequalities (Floridi, 2021; IEEE, 2023).

Inclusive training policies aim to ensure that women, senior workers, and low-skilled employees are not excluded from digital transformation. UNESCO (2024) emphasizes that equal access to digital training is a key driver of social cohesion and sustainable competitiveness.

Leading organizations such as Microsoft, Accenture, and BNP Paribas have introduced digital diversity charters that combine equal training access with awareness of algorithmic bias. These initiatives reinforce.

SECTION 4: THE ROLE OF MANAGERS IN CHANGE MANAGEMENT AND SKILLS DEVELOPMENT

The integration of artificial intelligence (AI) within organizations represents not only a technological shift, but also a profound human and managerial transformation. In this context, managers play a decisive role in aligning strategic objectives with employees' expectations, emotions, and skills. Far from being simple supervisors, managers become agents of meaning, facilitators of learning, and guarantors of ethical and sustainable change. This section analyzes the multiple dimensions of managerial action in change management and skills development, highlighting leadership styles, communication mechanisms, human support, and performance evaluation.

4.1. The Manager As A Catalyst For Change

The successful introduction of AI into organizations requires leadership capable of guiding teams through uncertainty and complexity. As emphasized by Kotter (1996) and Hiatt & Creasey (2021), the managerial role has evolved beyond task supervision toward inspiration, communication, and facilitation of change adoption. Empirical research confirms this evolution. For instance, a quantitative study conducted by Oreg, Vakola, and Armenakis (2011) on organizational change processes demonstrates that managerial support and leadership commitment significantly influence employees' readiness and acceptance of technological transformations. Similarly, a survey-based analysis by Al-Haddad and Kotnour (2015), based on data collected from multiple industries, shows that organizations where managers actively support change initiatives report higher success rates in digital transformation projects.

In the digital era, managers act as catalysts for transformation (Barabel & Meier, 2023). They must articulate a clear strategic vision while providing human-centered support. Bass and Riggio (2018) demonstrate that high-performing organizations are led by transformational leaders who foster emotional engagement through trust, recognition, and the communication of a shared vision. Supporting this theoretical perspective, an empirical study by Wang, Oh, Courtright, and Colbert (2011), based on a meta-analysis of 113 independent samples, reveals that transformational leadership has a strong positive effect on employee performance, job satisfaction, and organizational commitment, which are key determinants of successful technological change adoption.

A key condition for such leadership lies in the creation of psychological safety (Edmondson, 2019). By encouraging employees to express doubts, test new ideas, and learn from errors without fear of sanctions, managers stimulate creativity and innovation—critical capabilities in environments shaped by AI. Empirical evidence provided by Frazier, Fainshmidt, Klinger, Pezeshkan, and Vracheva (2017), through a meta-analysis covering over 136 independent samples, demonstrates that psychological safety significantly enhances knowledge sharing, learning behaviors, and innovative performance within organizations undergoing digital transformation. Likewise, Newman, Donohue, and Eva (2017) confirm through empirical investigation that psychologically safe environments improve employee engagement and adaptability, which are essential for AI-driven organizational change. In this sense, managerial action is no longer about "driving" change, but about co-constructing it with teams, integrating their feedback, aspirations, and concerns.

Figure 4. Manager as a catalyst for change

4.2. Communication As A Tool For Mobilization

Communication constitutes one of the most powerful levers of managerial influence in AI-driven transformations. A McKinsey study (2023) shows that transformation initiatives supported by clear, structured, and continuous communication enjoy a

40% higher success rate. Effective communication relies on three complementary pillars, summarized in Table 4.1.

Table 5. Pillars of effective managerial communication

Pillar	Description	Key Reference
Transparency	Explaining the rationale, objectives, and impacts of change	Kotter (2022)
Proximity	Maintaining frequent and direct interactions with teams	Barabel (2023)
Inspiring storytelling	Translating strategy into meaningful and motivating narratives	Denning (2011)

Through communication, managers act as facilitators of meaning, transforming technological challenges into professional and human opportunities. For instance, in a banking context, the deployment of AI tools can be framed as a way to reduce repetitive tasks and allow advisors to focus on high value-added customer relationships.

Communication should be dialogical rather than unidirectional. Active listening and feedback mechanisms allow managers to adjust the pace and modalities of change. This participatory logic aligns with agile management principles (Appelo, 2019), which emphasize flexibility, experimentation, and continuous improvement.

4.3. Human Support And Psychological Assistance

Digitalization and automation often generate emotional tensions, including fear of job loss, perceived skills obsolescence, and anxiety toward new technologies. Managers must therefore assume a supportive and coaching-oriented posture.

Emotional intelligence, as highlighted by Goleman (2022), is a cornerstone of modern leadership. It enables managers to recognize employees' emotions, respond empathetically, and foster intrinsic motivation. Such leadership strengthens trust and mitigates resistance to change.

Transformational coaching practices (Whitmore, 2019) are particularly effective in this context. They involve asking open-ended questions, recognizing progress, encouraging autonomy, and valuing effort. The manager thus shifts from the role of "expert" to that of learning facilitator.

Empirical evidence supports this approach. Deloitte (2023) reports that teams led by empathetic managers exhibit 25% higher productivity and 31% greater job satisfaction.

Figure 5. Human support during digital transformation

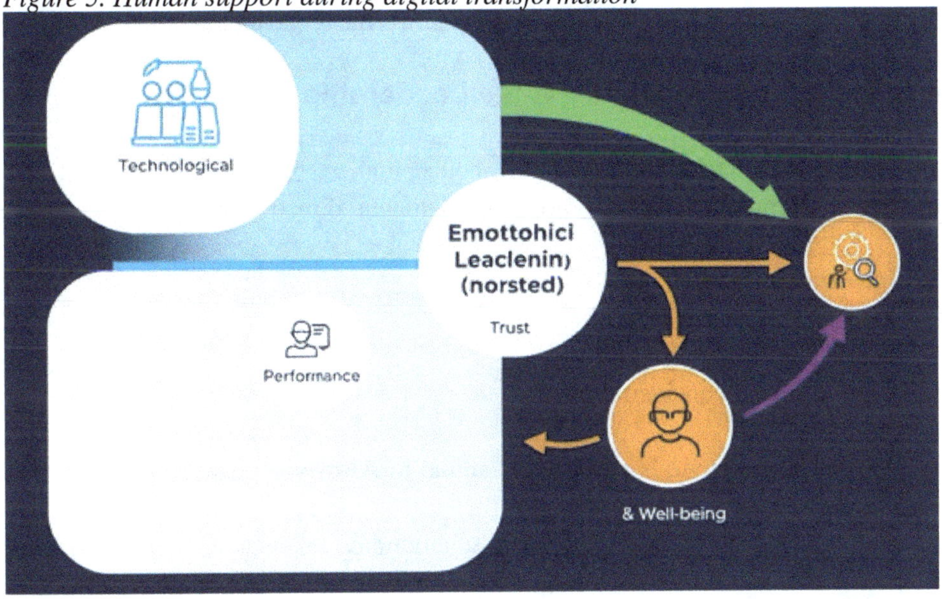

4.4. Identification And Development Of Skills

Managers play a central role in identifying, assessing, and developing employee skills. Their proximity to operational realities enables them to detect training needs, skills gaps, and emerging potential.

Workforce Planning and Skills Management (WPSM) approaches rely on close collaboration between managers, HR departments, and employees. Digital HR analytics tools now allow managers to monitor skills trajectories, anticipate future needs, and align training investments with strategic objectives (SHRM, 2023).

The ADKAR model (Hiatt & Creasey, 2021) provides a structured framework for individual skills development, presented in Table 4.2.

Table 6. ADKAR model for skills development

Stage	Objective
Awareness	Understanding the necessity of change
Desire	Building motivation to engage
Knowledge	Acquiring theoretical and technical knowledge
Ability	Applying skills in practice
Reinforcement	Sustaining and consolidating change

Managers orchestrate these stages through feedback, training opportunities, and recognition, creating a virtuous cycle of empowerment and engagement.

4.5. Transformational And Agile Leadership

Transformational leadership, initially conceptualized by Bass (1985) and refined by Bass & Riggio (2018), rests on four fundamental dimensions:

1. Idealized influence ;
2. Inspirational motivation ;
3. Intellectual stimulation ;
4. Individualized consideration.

This leadership style is particularly suited to AI-driven change, as it nurtures trust, innovation, and commitment.

In parallel, agile leadership (Rigby, Sutherland & Takeuchi, 2016) emphasizes adaptability, rapid decision-making, and continuous experimentation. In AI environments characterized by constant evolution, managers must prioritize learning over perfection.

Amabile (2021) demonstrates that managerial contexts fostering experimentation and tolerance for error significantly enhance creativity. Errors thus become learning opportunities rather than failures.

4.6. Managing Trust And Managerial Ethics

As AI increasingly supports organizational decision-making, trust becomes a critical managerial challenge. Employees must trust both leadership and the technologies deployed.

Managers are responsible for ensuring transparency regarding AI usage: explaining decision criteria, algorithmic limits, and ethical safeguards (Floridi, 2021; IEEE, 2023).

This responsibility aligns with ethical leadership theory (Brown & Treviño, 2006), which is grounded in integrity, fairness, and accountability. Managerial ethics can be structured around four pillars, summarized in Table 4.3.

Table 7. Pillars of ethical managerial leadership

Pillar	Description
Transparency	Clarity in AI-based decisions
Responsibility	Accountability for human impacts
Equity	Fair access to opportunities
Privacy	Protection of personal data

Organizations such as Microsoft and Accenture have established AI Ethics Boards in which managers actively participate to ensure alignment between innovation and organizational values.

4.7. Collective Learning and a Culture of Innovation

Beyond supervision, managers must cultivate collective learning ecosystems. Learning organizations, as described by Senge (2019), are characterized by shared reflection, knowledge exchange, and continuous improvement.

Managers act as conductors of collective intelligence by encouraging cross-functional collaboration, experimentation, and knowledge sharing. Tools such as lessons learned (REX), co-development workshops, and internal hackathons support this dynamic.

Companies such as Airbus, Capgemini, and Orange have institutionalized "learning labs," collaborative spaces dedicated to experimentation and innovation around AI.

4.8. Leadership Assessment and Performance Indicators

To ensure managerial effectiveness, organizations must evaluate leadership practices using both qualitative and quantitative indicators. Common metrics include:

- Employee engagement levels ;
- Job satisfaction rates ;
- Participation in training programs ;
- Productivity and innovation outputs.

360-degree feedback tools and employee experience surveys provide valuable insights. Deloitte (2023) reports that organizations institutionalizing leadership assessments achieve 35% higher employee retention.

Feedback thus becomes a developmental tool, enabling managers to align vision, behavior, and organizational culture.

4.9. The Manager as the Architect of Human Transformation

In the context of rapid digitalization and the widespread adoption of artificial intelligence, the role of the manager has undergone a profound transformation. Traditionally viewed as a coordinator of operational activities and organizational processes, the modern manager increasingly assumes the role of an architect of human transformation. This evolving role involves balancing technological efficiency with the preservation of human values, employee well-being, and organizational sustainability. As organizations integrate AI-driven technologies into their operations, managerial leadership becomes essential in ensuring that digital transformation processes remain socially responsible and strategically aligned with long-term organizational objectives.

Managers play a critical role in embedding technological change within the organizational culture. According to Kotter (2012), successful organizational transformation requires leadership that promotes employee engagement, communication, and shared vision. Managers facilitate this process by encouraging openness to innovation, reducing resistance to change, and promoting a culture that embraces continuous adaptation. In AI-driven environments, this cultural transformation becomes even more crucial, as employees must adapt to new work processes, decision-support systems, and digital collaboration tools. By promoting transparency and participatory leadership, managers contribute to the sustainable integration of technological innovation into daily organizational practices.

Furthermore, managerial leadership significantly influences the development of trust and organizational cohesion. Trust represents a fundamental element in digital transformation, particularly when employees interact with algorithmic decision-making systems. Mayer, Davis, and Schoorman (1995) emphasize that organizational trust depends on perceived competence, integrity, and benevolence of leadership. Managers who demonstrate ethical responsibility, transparency in technological adoption, and concern for employee well-being strengthen interpersonal relationships and organizational commitment. This trust is essential for facilitating collaboration between humans and intelligent technologies, as employees are more likely to accept AI-driven tools when they perceive managerial decisions as fair and accountable (Raisch & Krakowski, 2021).

In addition, managers play a strategic role in promoting creativity and continuous learning within AI-enabled organizations. Digital transformation requires employees to continuously update their skills, adapt to technological innovations, and develop interdisciplinary competencies. According to Senge (2006), learning organizations foster knowledge sharing, experimentation, and collaborative problem-solving. Managers encourage these dynamics by creating supportive environments where employees feel empowered to innovate and experiment with new technological solutions. Moreover, AI technologies themselves can enhance organizational learning by providing data-driven insights that support strategic decision-making and innovation processes (Brynjolfsson & McAfee, 2017).

Another crucial managerial responsibility concerns the ethical adoption of technological innovations. As AI systems increasingly influence decision-making processes, managers must ensure that these technologies are implemented in accordance with ethical principles such as fairness, transparency, and accountability. Floridi et al. (2018) highlight that responsible AI governance requires organizational leaders to establish ethical guidelines, risk assessment mechanisms, and stakeholder engagement processes. Managers serve as intermediaries between technological developers, employees, and external stakeholders, ensuring that AI deployment respects both regulatory frameworks and societal expectations.

Barabel (2023) emphasizes that digital transformation can only be sustainable if it is supported by humanistic leadership that prioritizes social progress and organizational well-being. In this perspective, managers are not replaced by artificial intelligence but rather become strategic facilitators who provide meaning, guide professional development, and humanize technological modernization. Their ability to integrate emotional intelligence, ethical judgment, and strategic vision enables organizations to navigate the complexities of digital transformation successfully.

Ultimately, the manager of the AI era must combine technological literacy with human-centered leadership. By balancing innovation with ethical responsibility, managers contribute to building resilient, inclusive, and sustainable organizations capable of adapting to the evolving demands of the digital economy. This transformation of managerial roles highlights the importance of leadership that places human values at the core of technological progress, ensuring that AI remains a tool that enhances, rather than replaces, human potential.

SECTION 5: ETHICS AND ORGANIZATIONAL RESPONSIBILITY IN THE AGE OF ARTIFICIAL INTELLIGENCE

5.1. The Moral Dimension of Technological Progress

Artificial intelligence (AI) represents one of the most profound technological transformations of the twenty-first century. Its rapid diffusion across strategic sectors such as healthcare, finance, education, industry, and public administration has deeply reshaped economic structures, production systems, and social interactions. AI enables improved productivity, enhanced decision-making accuracy, and new forms of innovation. However, alongside these benefits, the expansion of AI technologies raises significant ethical challenges, including digital surveillance, algorithmic discrimination, data manipulation, and the potential erosion of human decision-making autonomy. Empirical evidence supports these concerns. For example, a large-scale experimental study conducted by Buolamwini and Gebru (2018) demonstrates that facial recognition systems exhibit significantly higher error rates when identifying women and individuals with darker skin tones, highlighting the presence of algorithmic bias in widely used AI applications. Similarly, Raji et al. (2020), through an audit of commercial facial recognition technologies, reveal systematic disparities in algorithmic performance across demographic groups, confirming the existence of fairness risks in real-world AI deployment.

From a philosophical and normative perspective, Floridi (2021) argues that AI ethics should be understood as a reflection on how digital technologies reshape fundamental human values such as dignity, justice, freedom, and responsibility. AI should therefore not be perceived solely as an operational or productivity-enhancing tool. Instead, it contributes to the formation of a new socio-technical paradigm structured around massive data exploitation, automation, and predictive analytics. This transformation imposes new responsibilities on organizations, which must ensure that technological development respects fundamental human rights while contributing to social welfare and sustainable development. Empirical research reinforces this perspective. Brynjolfsson and Mitchell (2017), based on cross-sector analyses of AI implementation, show that while AI improves productivity and decision accuracy, organizations that neglect human-centered governance mechanisms experience greater resistance, ethical controversies, and reputational risks. Likewise, a survey conducted by the MIT Sloan Management Review in collaboration with the Boston Consulting Group (Ransbotham et al., 2020) indicates that companies integrating ethical governance frameworks into AI deployment report higher levels of employee trust, customer acceptance, and long-term performance sustainability.

The importance of this ethical responsibility is reinforced by international institutional frameworks. UNESCO's Ethical Framework for Artificial Intelligence (2023) identifies four essential guiding values: human dignity, justice, transparency, and sustainability. These principles highlight that the legitimacy of AI integration depends not only on technical efficiency but also on its capacity to promote fairness, protect individuals, and contribute to long-term societal well-being. Empirical evidence further confirms this relationship between ethical governance and organizational outcomes. For instance, a multi-country study conducted by Jobin, Ienca, and Vayena (2019), based on the analysis of 84 global AI ethics guidelines, demonstrates that organizations adopting structured ethical governance mechanisms tend to develop more transparent AI systems and face fewer regulatory and social acceptance challenges. Moreover, empirical findings by Cowls and Floridi (2018) indicate that companies implementing formal ethical AI frameworks are more likely to achieve stakeholder legitimacy and strengthen corporate social responsibility performance. Consequently, companies must embed ethical reflection into their governance structures and strategic decision-making processes.

5.2. Core Principles of Artificial Intelligence Ethics

In response to the growing societal influence of AI, several international institutions, including the European Union, the OECD, and the IEEE, have developed regulatory and ethical frameworks aimed at promoting responsible technological innovation. Despite institutional differences, these frameworks converge around six fundamental principles that structure ethical AI governance.

The first principle is transparency, which requires algorithms to be explainable, traceable, and auditable. Stakeholders must understand how automated decisions are generated, particularly when such decisions influence employment, credit access, healthcare treatment, or security measures. Transparency strengthens trust and allows for the identification of potential errors or biases.

The second principle concerns responsibility. Organizations must assume full legal and moral accountability for decisions produced by AI systems. The delegation of decision-making to automated systems does not remove corporate responsibility but instead reinforces the need for oversight and governance.

The third principle is fairness, which aims to ensure that AI systems are designed to prevent discrimination and systemic bias related to gender, ethnicity, age, or socio-economic background. Ethical AI must promote equal opportunity and social justice.

The fourth principle focuses on safety and reliability. AI systems must operate according to clearly defined objectives and must not generate unintended risks for individuals, organizations, or society.

The fifth principle concerns privacy protection. Personal data must be collected, stored, and processed in compliance with strict legal standards such as the General Data Protection Regulation (GDPR, 2018). Privacy protection is essential to maintaining public trust in digital technologies.

Finally, the sixth principle addresses sustainability and well-being. AI should contribute positively to economic and social development while minimizing environmental impacts and preserving the interests of future generations.

These principles are not purely theoretical constructs. They have been progressively incorporated into regulatory frameworks. The European Union's AI Act (2024), for example, represents the first legally binding international regulation classifying AI systems according to their level of societal risk and imposing strict compliance obligations on high-risk applications.

5.3. Algorithmic Bias and Organizational Fairness

Algorithmic bias represents one of the most critical ethical challenges associated with AI adoption. Biases occur when datasets, model architectures, or training processes reproduce or amplify existing social inequalities. Rather than eliminating discrimination, poorly governed AI systems may reinforce structural inequities.

A well-known example is Amazon's experimental recruitment algorithm, abandoned in 2018 after evidence revealed systematic discrimination against female candidates for technical roles. The algorithm reproduced historical gender imbalances embedded in training datasets, demonstrating the importance of ethical data governance.

O'Neil (2016) describes such systems as "weapons of mathematical destruction," emphasizing their opacity, scalability, and capacity to produce harmful decisions without accountability. To mitigate these risks, organizations must implement several preventive measures, including diversifying training datasets, conducting systematic bias testing across demographic groups, and performing regular algorithmic audits.

Many multinational companies, such as Google, IBM, and BNP Paribas, have established data ethics committees responsible for monitoring algorithmic neutrality, evaluating social impacts, and ensuring compliance with ethical standards. These committees contribute to strengthening organizational legitimacy and preventing reputational risks.

5.4. Data Protection and Confidentiality: GDPR Compliance

Data protection constitutes a cornerstone of digital ethics. The General Data Protection Regulation (GDPR), implemented by the European Union in 2018, imposes strict requirements on organizations processing personal data. These requirements include obtaining explicit user consent, limiting data collection to strictly necessary information, guaranteeing the right to erasure (the "right to be forgotten"), and ensuring cybersecurity protections. Empirical research confirms the transformative impact of GDPR on organizational practices. For instance, a large-scale empirical study conducted by Johnson, Shriver, and Goldberg (2020), based on web traffic and advertising market data, demonstrates that GDPR significantly reduced the availability of personal data for online advertising, forcing firms to redesign their data governance strategies. Similarly, Jia, Jin, and Wagman (2021), using cross-country firm-level data, show that GDPR compliance has increased data protection investments while simultaneously improving consumer trust and corporate reputation.

AI systems rely heavily on big data analytics, which increases both operational efficiency and exposure to privacy breaches. According to a PwC survey (2024), 63% of consumers express concern about how their personal data is used by AI applications. This growing mistrust highlights the importance of transparent data governance. Empirical evidence further supports this relationship between transparency and user acceptance. Martin and Murphy (2017), through survey-based research on consumer privacy perceptions, demonstrate that perceived transparency and responsible data handling significantly increase customer trust and willingness to share personal information. Likewise, a multi-industry empirical study by Aguirre, Mahr, Grewal, de Ruyter, and Wetzels (2015) reveals that while personalized AI-driven marketing improves service efficiency, excessive data collection without transparency generates consumer discomfort and reduces engagement levels.

To ensure compliance, companies must appoint Data Protection Officers (DPOs), implement data encryption technologies, establish formal data governance policies, and provide continuous employee training on data protection practices. Empirical studies confirm the effectiveness of these governance mechanisms. For example, a European firm-level study by Kuner, Bygrave, and Docksey (2020) shows that organizations with formal data protection governance structures and dedicated DPO roles demonstrate higher compliance levels and fewer data breach incidents. Similarly, research by Bada, Sasse, and Nurse (2019), based on cybersecurity training experiments, indicates that continuous employee awareness programs significantly reduce human-related security vulnerabilities, which remain one of the primary sources of data breaches.

Leading technology firms such as Microsoft and Salesforce have adopted the principle of "Privacy by Design," integrating data protection mechanisms from the earliest stages of system development. Empirical evidence provided by Cavoukian (2019) demonstrates that organizations implementing Privacy by Design frameworks achieve stronger regulatory compliance and improved stakeholder confidence. Furthermore, a comparative case study conducted by Gürses, Troncoso, and Diaz (2011) highlights that embedding privacy protections during system architecture development reduces long-term compliance costs and strengthens organizational resilience against cyber threats.

5.6. Automated Decision-Making and the Human-In-The-Loop Principle

A fundamental principle of AI ethics is the concept of "Human in the Loop" (HITL), which emphasizes maintaining human supervision over automated decision-making processes. According to Floridi (2021) and Caldara & Iacoviello (2022), AI systems should support rather than replace human judgment, particularly in sensitive sectors such as recruitment, credit evaluation, healthcare, public safety, and judicial systems.

Implementing the HITL principle requires ensuring the traceability of algorithmic decisions, enabling human intervention at all stages of decision-making, and developing mechanisms that explain algorithmic outputs in accessible terms. The OECD (2023) reinforces this principle by asserting that legal and moral responsibility remains with human decision-makers, even when AI tools assist decision processes.

5.7. Inclusion, Diversity, and Social Justice

AI ethics is closely linked to broader issues of social justice and inclusion. Automation may increase economic inequality if technological benefits are unevenly distributed. The World Economic Forum (2024) estimates that approximately 26% of existing jobs could disappear by 2030, particularly within low-skilled sectors. Empirical evidence supports these projections. For instance, Frey and Osborne (2017), using an econometric analysis of occupational data in the United States, estimate that nearly 47% of jobs are at high risk of automation, particularly routine and low-skilled occupations. Similarly, Acemoglu and Restrepo (2020), based on panel data from U.S. labor markets, demonstrate that the adoption of industrial robots has contributed to employment displacement and wage inequality in affected regions. Their findings highlight that technological diffusion, if not accompanied by adequate social policies and organizational support mechanisms, can reinforce labor market polarization.

Organizations therefore have a crucial role in promoting a just digital transition. This includes investing in reskilling and upskilling programs for employees affected by automation, promoting diversity within AI development teams, and integrating inclusion criteria into recruitment and training policies. Empirical research confirms the effectiveness of such initiatives. For example, a large-scale empirical study by Bughin, Hazan, Lund, Dahlström, Wiesinger, and Subramaniam (2018), based on surveys across multiple industries, shows that companies investing in workforce reskilling programs experience significantly higher productivity growth and employee retention during digital transformation. Likewise, Nedelkoska and Quintini (2018), using OECD labor market data, demonstrate that training and lifelong learning programs significantly reduce workers' vulnerability to automation and improve employment resilience.

Empirical research also demonstrates that diverse innovation teams are more effective in identifying ethical risks and designing inclusive technological solutions. A comprehensive quantitative study conducted by Hunt, Prince, Dixon-Fyle, and Yee (2018), based on data from over 1,000 companies across 12 countries, reveals that organizations with higher gender and ethnic diversity within leadership and innovation teams show significantly higher innovation performance and financial results. Similarly, Page (2007), through computational modeling and empirical analysis of group decision-making, demonstrates that cognitively diverse teams outperform homogeneous teams in solving complex problems, particularly in innovation and technological design contexts.

More recent empirical evidence reinforces these findings in the context of AI development. For instance, a multi-sector study conducted by Cowgill, Dell'Acqua, Deng, Hsu, Verma, and Chaintreau (2020) demonstrates that diverse development teams are more effective in detecting algorithmic bias and improving fairness in AI systems. Likewise, Leslie (2019), based on empirical case studies of AI governance frameworks, shows that inclusive design approaches significantly enhance ethical compliance and public trust in AI technologies. By incorporating diverse perspectives across gender, age, culture, and educational backgrounds, organizations improve both ethical decision-making and innovation performance.

5.8. Sustainability and Environmental Responsibility

Artificial intelligence (AI) ethics extend beyond human-centered considerations to encompass environmental sustainability and ecological responsibility. The rapid expansion of digital infrastructures, particularly data centers and advanced deep learning models, has significantly increased global energy consumption, thereby raising concerns about the environmental footprint of digital technologies. As AI systems require vast computational resources for training, storage, and deployment, their carbon emissions have become a critical issue in discussions surrounding sustainable technological development.

According to the International Energy Agency (IEA, 2023), training large-scale AI models can generate substantial greenhouse gas emissions, sometimes reaching up to 500 tonnes of CO_2. This level of emission highlights the urgent need to incorporate environmental sustainability into the design and implementation of AI systems. Similarly, Strubell, Ganesh, and McCallum (2019) demonstrate that natural language processing models require significant computational power, leading to high energy consumption and environmental costs. Their findings underline the necessity of evaluating AI models not only based on their performance but also on their energy efficiency.

In response to these challenges, the concept of Green AI has emerged as a strategic approach aimed at designing computational models that minimize energy consumption while maintaining acceptable levels of performance. Schwartz et al. (2020) emphasize that Green AI encourages researchers and developers to prioritize efficiency, transparency in reporting computational costs, and optimization of algorithms to reduce environmental impact. This approach promotes the development of sustainable technological innovation by balancing performance improvements with ecological responsibility.

At the international level, initiatives such as the United Nations' AI for Good program advocate for the use of AI technologies to support the achievement of Sustainable Development Goals (SDGs). AI applications in healthcare, precision agriculture, climate monitoring, and water resource management demonstrate the potential of technology to address global environmental and social challenges (Vinuesa et al., 2020). Consequently, corporate social responsibility (CSR) becomes inseparable from ethical AI governance, as organizations are increasingly expected to consider environmental externalities when adopting digital technologies (Porter & Kramer, 2011).

5.9. Ethics Training and Awareness for Employees

The successful implementation of ethical AI governance requires a sustainable organizational transformation that emphasizes continuous training and awareness programs for employees and managerial staff. Ethical awareness cannot be assumed to exist naturally within organizations; rather, it must be actively cultivated through structured educational initiatives. Stahl (2022) argues that organizations must integrate ethical considerations into professional development programs to ensure responsible technological decision-making. Similarly, Borenstein and Howard (2023) highlight that employees who receive ethics training are better equipped to identify algorithmic biases, data privacy risks, and governance challenges associated with AI deployment.

Leading organizations in digital transformation increasingly incorporate mandatory training modules covering topics such as algorithmic fairness, data protection regulations, ethical risk assessment, and responsible innovation practices. These training initiatives often rely on interactive methodologies, including simulation-based learning, case studies, and participatory workshops, which allow employees to engage directly with ethical dilemmas in real-world contexts (Mittelstadt, 2019).

Beyond regulatory compliance, ethical training contributes to fostering an organizational culture based on transparency, accountability, and shared responsibility. A strong ethical culture encourages employees to critically assess the social and technological consequences of their actions. According to Deloitte (2024), companies that implement structured digital ethics programs report significantly higher levels of employee engagement and trust, demonstrating that ethical awareness contributes positively to organizational performance and internal cohesion.

Furthermore, ethical education supports the development of interdisciplinary collaboration between engineers, data scientists, legal experts, and management teams. This collaborative approach strengthens governance frameworks and ensures that ethical considerations are embedded throughout the entire AI lifecycle, from development to implementation and evaluation (Jobin, Ienca, & Vayena, 2019).

5.10. Towards a Humanistic and Responsible Artificial Intelligence

The integration of ethics into AI governance represents not merely a regulatory obligation but a fundamental requirement for ensuring technological legitimacy, sustainability, and long-term organizational performance. Organizations cannot claim to achieve sustainable innovation without guaranteeing fairness, transparency, accountability, and inclusivity in their AI-driven processes.

Ethical governance of AI must adopt a transversal and multidisciplinary approach, ensuring that ethical principles are incorporated at all stages of the technological life-cycle, including system design, deployment, monitoring, and continuous evaluation. This governance framework should involve not only engineers and decision-makers but also end users, regulators, and civil society stakeholders, thereby promoting participatory and inclusive technological development.

Floridi et al. (2018) argue that the primary objective of AI ethics is not to moralize machines but to reinforce the ethical responsibility of institutions that design, deploy, and regulate technological systems. This perspective highlights the importance of institutional accountability in maintaining trust between organizations and society. Similarly, the OECD (2019) emphasizes that responsible AI governance contributes to building public confidence and ensuring that technological progress aligns with human values and societal well-being.

Ultimately, the organization of the future will be characterized not only by digital transformation but also by ethical maturity, social inclusiveness, and environmental sustainability. By placing responsibility at the core of innovation strategies, organizations can successfully reconcile technological advancement with humanistic values. Such a balanced approach represents an essential condition for maintaining social cohesion, organizational legitimacy, and sustainable economic development in an increasingly automated world.

6. CONCLUSION

Artificial intelligence (AI) is emerging as one of the most transformative forces shaping modern organizations. Its rapid development is redefining work structures, managerial practices, and governance models. AI represents not only a technological revolution but also a profound human and cultural transformation that requires organizations to rethink their operational frameworks, decision-making processes, and organizational values. The integration of intelligent technologies demands a fundamental reconfiguration of competencies, leadership styles, and institutional structures to ensure sustainable and responsible digital transformation.

In this context, change management appears as a central pillar of successful organizational transformation. Traditional approaches to change, which rely primarily on planning and hierarchical communication, are no longer sufficient in digital environments characterized by rapid innovation, uncertainty, and complexity. Modern change management must become interactive, participatory, and inclusive, encouraging employees to actively engage in transformation processes. Change should be viewed as a continuous learning journey rather than a temporary transition phase. Organizational agility increasingly depends on the capacity to learn, adapt, and innovate at a pace that matches technological evolution.

This chapter highlights the critical importance of human capital in the successful implementation of AI. The digital economy requires the development of hybrid competencies combining technical, cognitive, emotional, and ethical dimensions. Digital literacy and analytical thinking enable employees to interact effectively with intelligent technologies, while creativity and emotional intelligence support innovation, collaboration, and problem-solving. These complementary skills allow organizations to harness the potential of AI while preserving the unique contribution of human capabilities.

Consequently, organizations must adopt lifelong learning strategies that promote continuous professional development. Training programs, digital learning platforms, mentoring initiatives, and collaborative knowledge-sharing systems illustrate the transition toward a learning-oriented organizational culture. Investment in human capital development strengthens employee adaptability, stimulates innovation, and enhances organizational resilience. Continuous learning is therefore becoming a strategic necessity rather than a supplementary activity, enabling organizations to maintain competitiveness in rapidly evolving technological environments.

The managerial role plays a decisive part in facilitating this transformation. Managers act as catalysts of change by translating strategic vision into operational practices, fostering employee engagement, and supporting the psychological adaptation of teams. Leadership approaches based on trust, transparency, and empowerment are particularly effective in digital environments. By placing people at the center of transformation processes, managers help maintain a balance between technological performance and employee well-being. They also contribute to strengthening collaboration between humans and intelligent systems, ensuring that technological innovation enhances rather than disrupts organizational cohesion.

Despite the opportunities offered by AI, digital transformation also raises significant ethical and social challenges. The increasing automation of decision-making processes and the large-scale use of data introduce risks related to fairness, transparency, accountability, and privacy. Responsible governance requires organizations to establish regulatory compliance mechanisms, ethical oversight structures, and risk management frameworks to ensure that AI systems operate in accordance with societal expectations. Ethical training and awareness programs must become integral components of professional development, enabling employees and decision-makers to understand the broader implications of technological innovation.

Beyond regulatory requirements, ethical governance represents a strategic advantage that strengthens organizational legitimacy, stakeholder trust, and corporate reputation. Organizations that integrate ethical principles into their digital transformation strategies are more likely to build sustainable relationships with employees, customers, and society. Responsible AI fosters organizational transparency, enhances public confidence, and supports long-term sustainable performance.

This chapter also promotes the development of humanistic artificial intelligence, emphasizing the complementary relationship between human intelligence and technological innovation. The objective of digital transformation is not to replace human capabilities but to enhance them. AI technologies can support decision-making, improve efficiency, and stimulate creativity when they are designed to complement human expertise. Ensuring that AI remains aligned with human values requires strong governance frameworks, ethical accountability, and inclusive stakeholder participation.

Ultimately, the future of work depends on the ability of organizations to balance three fundamental and interconnected dimensions. Technology represents a powerful driver of efficiency, productivity, and innovation. Human capital remains the primary source of creativity, adaptability, and organizational meaning. Ethics serves as a guiding framework that ensures technological progress contributes to equitable and sustainable development.

By integrating these three pillars, organizations can transform artificial intelligence into a strategic opportunity rather than a disruptive threat. The company of the future will combine digital performance with social responsibility, promoting inclusive growth, knowledge development, and human dignity. Such an integrated approach represents a fundamental condition for achieving sustainable economic progress and strengthening social cohesion in an increasingly automated world.

REFERENCES

Acemoglu, D., & Restrepo, P. (2020). Robots and jobs: Evidence from US labor markets. *Journal of Political Economy, 128*(6), 2188–2244.

Aguirre, E., Mahr, D., Grewal, D., de Ruyter, K., & Wetzels, M. (2015). Unraveling the personalization paradox: The effect of information collection and trust-building strategies on online advertisement effectiveness. *Journal of Retailing, 91*(1), 34–49.

Al-Haddad, S., & Kotnour, T. (2015). Integrating the organizational change literature: A model for successful change. *Journal of Organizational Change Management, 28*(2), 234–262.

Amabile, T. (2021). *Creativity in Context: Update to the Social Psychology of Creativity*. Westview Press.

Appelo, J. (2019). *Managing for Happiness: Games, Tools, and Practices to Motivate Any Team*. Wiley.

Argyris, C., & Schön, D. (1996). *Organizational Learning II: Theory, Method, and Practice*. Addison Wesley.

Bada, M., Sasse, M. A., & Nurse, J. R. C. (2019). Cyber security awareness campaigns: Why do they fail to change behaviour? *International Conference on Cyber Security for Sustainable Society*, 118–131.

Barabel, M. (2023). Management and Digital Transformation: Humanistic Leadership in the AI Era.

Barabel, M., & Meier, O. (2023). *Management 4.0: Agility, Innovation and Digital Transformation*. Dunod.

Barabel, M., & Meier, O. (2023). *Management et transformation digitale*. Dunod.

Baron, L., & Morin, L. (2020). *Coaching and Transformational Leadership*. Presses de l'Université Laval.

Bass, B. M., & Riggio, R. E. (2018). *Transformational leadership* (3rd ed.). Routledge.

Bass, B. M., & Riggio, R. E. (2018). *Transformational Leadership* (3rd ed.). Psychology Press.

Borenstein, J., & Howard, A. (2023). *Trustworthy AI*. MIT Press.

Brown, M., & Treviño, L. (2006). Ethical leadership: A review and future directions. *The Leadership Quarterly, 17*(6), 595–616.

Brynjolfsson, E., & McAfee, A. (2017). *Machine, Platform, Crowd: Harnessing Our Digital Future*. Norton.

Brynjolfsson, E., & McAfee, A. (2021). *The Second Machine Age: Work, Progress, and Prosperity in a Time of Brilliant Technologies*. WW Norton.

Brynjolfsson, E., & Mitchell, T. (2017). What can machine learning do? Workforce implications. *Science, 358*(6370), 1530–1534. PMID: 29269459

Bughin, J., Hazan, E., Lund, S., Dahlström, P., Wiesinger, A., & Subramaniam, A. (2018). *Skill shift: Automation and the future of the workforce*. McKinsey Global Institute.

Buolamwini, J., & Gebru, T. (2018). Gender shades: Intersectional accuracy disparities in commercial gender classification. *Proceedings of Machine Learning Research, 81*, 1–15.

Burnes, B., & Cooke, B. (2013). Kurt Lewin and the Planned Approach to Change: A Re-appraisal. *Journal of Management Studies, 50*(6), 977–1002.

Caldara, D., & Iacoviello, M. (2022). Measuring Geopolitical Risk. *The American Economic Review, 112*(4), 1194–1225.

Cavoukian, A. (2019). Privacy by Design: The definitive workshop. *Identity in the Information Society, 12*(1), 3–18.

Clark, R. C., & Mayer, R. (2023). *E-Learning and the Science of Instruction*. Wiley.

Cowgill, B., Dell'Acqua, F., Deng, S., Hsu, D., Verma, N., & Chaintreau, A. (2020). Biased programmers? Or biased data? A field experiment in operationalizing AI ethics. Management Science Working Paper.

Cowls, J., & Floridi, L. (2018). Prolegomena to a white paper on an ethical framework for a good AI society. SSRN Electronic Journal.

Cukier, K., & Mayer-Schönberger, V. (2021). *Big Data: A Revolution That Will Transform How We Live, Work, and Think*. Eamon Dolan.

Deloitte. (2023). *Human Capital Trends Report*. Deloitte Insights.

Deloitte. (2024). *Ethical AI and Workforce Engagement*. Deloitte University Press.

Denning, S. (2011). *The Leader's Guide to Storytelling*. Jossey-Bass.

Edmondson, A. (2019). *The Fearless Organization: Creating Psychological Safety in the Workplace for Learning, Innovation, and Growth*. Wiley.

Edmondson, A. C. (2019). *The fearless organization: Creating psychological safety in the workplace for learning, innovation, and growth.* Wiley.

Florida, R. (2020). *The Rise of the Creative Class Revisited.* Basic Books.

Floridi, L. (2021). *The Ethics of Artificial Intelligence.* Oxford University Press.

Floridi, L. (2021). *The ethics of artificial intelligence: Principles, challenges, and opportunities.* Oxford University Press.

Floridi, L., Cowls, J., & Beltrametti, M.. (2018). AI4People—An ethical framework for a good AI society. *Minds and Machines, 28*(4), 689–707. PMID: 30930541

Frazier, M. L., Fainshmidt, S., Klinger, R. L., Pezeshkan, A., & Vracheva, V. (2017). Psychological safety: A meta-analytic review and extension. *Personnel Psychology, 70*(1), 113–165.

Frey, C. B., & Osborne, M. A. (2017). The future of employment: How susceptible are jobs to computerisation? *Technological Forecasting and Social Change, 114,* 254–280.

Gartner. (2024). Adaptive Learning in Corporate Environments. Gartner Research.

Goleman, D. (2022). *Emotional Intelligence: Why It Can Matter More Than IQ.* Bantam Books.

Gürses, S., Troncoso, C., & Diaz, C. (2011). *Engineering privacy by design.* Computers, Privacy & Data Protection Conference.

Hiatt, J., & Creasey, T. (2021). *ADKAR: A Model for Change in Business, Government, and Our Community.* Prosci Learning Center Publications.

Hiatt, J., & Creasey, T. (2021). *Change Management: The People Side of Change.* Prosci.

Hiatt, J., & Creasey, T. J. (2021). *Change management: The people side of change.* Prosci Research.

Hunt, V., Prince, S., Dixon-Fyle, S., & Yee, L. (2018). *Delivering through diversity.* McKinsey & Company.

IEEE. (2023). *Ethically Aligned Design: A Vision for Prioritizing Human Well-being with Autonomous and Intelligent Systems.* IEEE Global Initiative.

International Energy Agency (IEA). (2023). *Energy Efficiency and Digitalization Report.* IEA Publications.

International Labor Organization (ILO). (2023). The Future of Work in a Digital World.

Jia, J., Jin, G. Z., & Wagman, L. (2021). The short-run effects of GDPR on technology venture investment. *Marketing Science, 40*(4), 661–684.

Jobin, A., Ienca, M., & Vayena, E. (2019). The global landscape of AI ethics guidelines. *Nature Machine Intelligence, 1*(9), 389–399.

Johnson, G., Shriver, S., & Goldberg, S. (2020). Privacy and market concentration: Intended and unintended consequences of the GDPR. *Management Science, 66*(10), 5349–5371.

Knowles, M. (2020). *The Adult Learner: The Definitive Classic in Adult Education and Human Resource Development*. Routledge.

Kotter, J. (2012). *Leading Change*. Harvard Business Review Press.

Kotter, J. (2022). *Change: How Organizations Achieve Hard-to-Imagine Results in Uncertain and Volatile Times*. Wiley.

Kuner, C., Bygrave, L., & Docksey, C. (2020). *The EU General Data Protection Regulation (GDPR): A commentary*. Oxford University Press.

Leslie, D. (2019). *Understanding artificial intelligence ethics and safety: A guide for the responsible design and implementation of AI systems*. The Alan Turing Institute.

Lewin, K. (1951). *Field Theory in Social Science*. Harper & Row.

LinkedIn Learning. (2023). Global Workplace Learning Report.

Martin, K., & Murphy, P. (2017). The role of data privacy in marketing. *Journal of the Academy of Marketing Science, 45*(2), 135–155.

Mayer, R., Davis, J., & Schoorman, F. (1995). An integrative model of organizational trust. *Academy of Management Review, 20*(3), 709–734.

McKinsey & Company. (2023). The State of AI Transformation.

Nedelkoska, L., & Quintini, G. (2018). Automation, skills use and training. OECD Social, Employment and Migration Working Papers, No. 202.

Newman, A., Donohue, R., & Eva, N. (2017). Psychological safety: A systematic review of the literature. *Human Resource Management Review, 27*(3), 521–535.

Nonaka, I., & Takeuchi, H. (2019). *The Wise Company: How Companies Create Continuous Innovation*. Oxford University Press.

O'Neil, C. (2016). *Weapons of Math Destruction: How Big Data Increases Inequality and Threatens Democracy*. Crown.

Oreg, S., Vakola, M., & Armenakis, A. (2011). Change recipients' reactions to organizational change: A 60-year review of quantitative studies. *The Journal of Applied Behavioral Science*, *47*(4), 461–524.

Page, S. E. (2007). *The difference: How the power of diversity creates better groups, firms, schools, and societies*. Princeton University Press.

Porter, M., & Kramer, M. (2011). Creating shared value. *Harvard Business Review*, *89*(1–2), 62–77.

PwC. (2024). AI and Ethics in the Digital Economy. PwC Global Report.

PwC. (2024). *Global consumer insights survey on data trust and artificial intelligence*. PricewaterhouseCoopers.

Raisch, S., & Krakowski, S. (2021). Artificial intelligence and management: The automation–augmentation paradox. *Academy of Management Review*, *46*(1), 192–210.

Raji, I. D., Smart, A., White, R. N., Mitchell, M., Gebru, T., Hutchinson, B., Smith-Loud, J., Theron, D., & Barnes, P. (2020). Closing the AI accountability gap: Defining an end-to-end framework for internal algorithmic auditing. *Proceedings of the 2020 Conference on Fairness, Accountability, and Transparency*, 33–44.

Ransbotham, S., Kiron, D., Gerbert, P., & Reeves, M. (2020). Expanding AI's impact with organizational learning. *MIT Sloan Management Review*.

Rigby, D., Sutherland, J., & Takeuchi, H. (2016). Embracing Agile. *Harvard Business Review*, *94*(5), 40–50.

Schein, E. (2017). *Organizational Culture and Leadership*. Wiley.

Senge, P. (2006). *The Fifth Discipline: The Art and Practice of the Learning Organization*. Doubleday.

Senge, P. (2019). *The Fifth Discipline*. The Art & Practice of The Learning Organization.

Stahl, B. (2022). *Ethics of Emerging Technologies: The AI Context*. Routledge.

UNESCO. (2023). *Recommendation on the Ethics of Artificial Intelligence*. UNESCO Publishing.

UNESCO. (2024). Gender Equality and Digital Inclusion Report.

Wang, G., Oh, I. S., Courtright, S. H., & Colbert, A. E. (2011). Transformational leadership and performance across criteria and levels: A meta-analytic review. *Journal of Management*, *37*(2), 223–270.

World Economic Forum. (2024). The Future of Jobs Report. WEF Publications.

World Economic Forum. (2024). The future of jobs report. WEF.

Compilation of References

Abdelzaher, T., Diao, Y., Hellerstein, J. L., Lu, C., & Zhu, X. (2008). Introduction to control theory and its application to computing systems. In *Performance Modeling and Engineering* (pp. 185–215). Springer US. https://link.springer.com/chapter/10.1007/978-0-387-79361-0_7

Abras, J., Burnay, C., & Faulkner, S. (2025). Can Generative AI Mitigate Strategic Decision-Making Complexity? An Empirical Exploration of RAG-Augmented Decision-Support Systems. *Lecture Notes in Business Information Processing, 548 LNBIP*, 3–19. DOI: 10.1007/978-3-031-92471-2_1

Acemoglu, D., & Restrepo, P. (2020). Robots and jobs: Evidence from US labor markets. *Journal of Political Economy, 128*(6), 2188–2244.

Agarwal, R., Bacco, F., Camuffo, A., Coali, A., Gambardella, A., Msangi, H., Sonka, S., Temu, A., Waized, B., & Wormald, A. (2025). Does a theory-of-value add value? Evidence from a randomized control trial with Tanzanian entrepreneurs. *Organization Science*, *36*(2), 601–625. DOI: 10.1287/orsc.2023.17590

Agrawal, G. (2024). Accountability, trust, and transparency in AI systems from the perspective of public policy: Elevating ethical standards. In *AI healthcare applications and security, ethical, and legal considerations* (pp. 148–162). IGI Global. DOI: 10.4018/979-8-3693-7452-8.ch009

Aguirre, E., Mahr, D., Grewal, D., de Ruyter, K., & Wetzels, M. (2015). Unraveling the personalization paradox: The effect of information collection and trust-building strategies on online advertisement effectiveness. *Journal of Retailing*, *91*(1), 34–49.

Ahuchogu, M. C. (2025). Real-Time Image-Based Data Processing and its Applications in Managerial Decision-Making and Risk Analysis. *EKSPLORIUM-BULETIN PUSAT TEKNOLOGI BAHAN GALIAN NUKLIR*, *46*(1), 1552–1565.

Alam, M. A. U. (2020). AI-fairness towards activity recognition of older adults. *ACM International Conference Proceeding Series,* December 2020, 108–117. DOI: 10.1145/3448891.3448943

Alenezi, M., & Akour, M. (2025). AI-Driven Innovations in Software Engineering: A Review of Current Practices and Future Directions. In *Applied Sciences* (Vol. 15, Issue 3, p. 1344). DOI: 10.3390/app15031344

Al-Haddad, S., & Kotnour, T. (2015). Integrating the organizational change literature: A model for successful change. *Journal of Organizational Change Management, 28*(2), 234–262.

Almalki, S. S. (2025). AI-Driven Decision Support Systems in Agile Software Project Management: Enhancing Risk Mitigation and Resource Allocation. In *Systems* (Vol. 13, Issue 3, p. 208). DOI: 10.3390/systems13030208

Amabile, T. (2021). *Creativity in Context: Update to the Social Psychology of Creativity.* Westview Press.

Amershi, S., Weld, D. S., Vorvoreanu, M., Fourney, A., Nushi, B., Collisson, P., & Horvitz, E. (2019). Guidelines for human-AI interaction. *Proceedings of the 2019 CHI Conference on Human Factors in Computing Systems,* 1–13. DOI: 10.1145/3290605.3300233

Ameta, U., Patel, M., & Sharma, A. K. (2022). Scaled Agile Framework Implementation in Organizations', its Shortcomings and an AI Based Solution to Track Team's Performance. *2022 IEEE 3rd Global Conference for Advancement in Technology (GCAT),* 1–7. DOI: 10.1109/GCAT55367.2022.9971968

Ansari, W. (2023). The Ethical Implications of Artificial Intelligence on the Human Society. SSRN *Electronic Journal, 9*(6), 94–101. DOI: 10.2139/ssrn.4512301

Ansari, I., Barati, M., Sadeghi Moghadam, M. R., & Ghobakhloo, M. (2025). Empowering Industry 4.0: Systemizing readiness assessment and strategic roadmapping for digital transformation. *Journal of Manufacturing Technology Management, 36*(5), 937–960. DOI: 10.1108/JMTM-05-2024-0257

Anwar, N., Sekti, B. A., Widodo, A. M., Erzed, N., Gunawan, H., Tangkudung, R. R. S., Muchlis, M., & Budhisantosa, N. (2025). Emerging innovations in AI and green computing for cybersecurity. In *Sustainable Information Security in the Age of AI and Green Computing* (pp. 17–38). DOI: 10.4018/979-8-3693-8034-5.ch002

Anwar, R., & Bashir, M. B. (2023). A Systematic Literature Review of AI-Based Software Requirements Prioritization Techniques. *IEEE Access : Practical Innovations, Open Solutions, 11,* 143815–143860. DOI: 10.1109/ACCESS.2023.3343252

Appelo, J. (2019). *Managing for Happiness: Games, Tools, and Practices to Motivate Any Team.* Wiley.

Argyris, C., & Schön, D. (1996). *Organizational Learning II: Theory, Method, and Practice.* Addison Wesley.

Assres, G., Bhandari, G., Shalaginov, A., Gronli, T.-M., & Ghinea, G. (2025). State-of-the-Art and Challenges of Engineering ML- Enabled Software Systems in the Deep Learning Era. *ACM Computing Surveys, 57*(10), 1–35. Advance online publication. DOI: 10.1145/3731597

Azeroual, O. (2025a) Beyond Black Boxes: Adaptive XAI for Dynamic Data Pipelines. In *Proceedings of the 17th International Joint Conference on Knowledge Discovery, Knowledge Engineering and Knowledge Management* - (Volume 2), p.428-437. DOI: 10.5220/0013736100004000

Azeroual, O. (2025b). Streamlining Research Information Management with Large Language Models: Automation, Analysis, and User-Centric Solutions. in *Proceedings of the 10th International Conference on Big Data Analytics (ICBDA2025),* Nanyang Technological University, Singapore, pp. 281-287, IEEE. DOI: 10.1109/ICBDA65366.2025.11211236

Bada, M., Sasse, M. A., & Nurse, J. R. C. (2019). Cyber security awareness campaigns: Why do they fail to change behaviour? *International Conference on Cyber Security for Sustainable Society*, 118–131.

Baghalzadeh Shishehgarkhaneh, M., Keivani, A., Moehler, R. C., Jelodari, N., & Roshdi Laleh, S. (2022). Internet of Things (IoT), Building Information Modeling (BIM), and Digital Twin (DT) in construction industry: A review, bibliometric, and network analysis. *Buildings (Basel, Switzerland), 12*(10), 1503.

Bai, S., Fang, D., & Zhang, Q. (2019). Research and application of artificial intelligence technology in the field of risk perception. *Journal of Physics: Conference Series, 1302*(2), 022002. DOI: 10.1088/1742-6596/1302/2/022002

Baltà-Salvador, R., Brasó-Vives, E., & Peña, M. (2026). Evaluating AI-assisted creative ideation: A crossover study in higher education. *Thinking Skills and Creativity, 59*, 101958. Advance online publication. DOI: 10.1016/j.tsc.2025.101958

Balzano, M. (2025). Post-error adjustments: Strategic agility and organizational zemblanity. *California Management Review, 67*(4), 121–153. DOI: 10.1177/00081256251332311

Bandara, R. B. M. T., & Wickramarachchi, R. (2025). Developing an AI Readiness Model for Software Project Management: A Thematic Analysis. In *2025 5th International Conference on Advanced Research in Computing (ICARC)* (pp. 1-6). IEEE. DOI: 10.1109/ICARC64760.2025.10962923

Barabel, M. (2023). Management and Digital Transformation: Humanistic Leadership in the AI Era.

Barabel, M., & Meier, O. (2023). *Management 4.0: Agility, Innovation and Digital Transformation*. Dunod.

Barabel, M., & Meier, O. (2023). *Management et transformation digitale*. Dunod.

Barker, M., Chue Hong, N. P., Katz, D. S., Lamprecht, A. L., Martinez-Ortiz, C., Psomopoulos, F., Harrow, J., Castro, L. J., Gruenpeter, M., Martinez, P. A., & Honeyman, T. (2022). Introducing the FAIR Principles for research software. *Scientific Data*, *9*(1), 1–6. DOI: 10.1038/s41597-022-01710-x PMID: 36241754

Baron, L., & Morin, L. (2020). *Coaching and Transformational Leadership*. Presses de l'Université Laval.

Barrett, B., & Miller, C. (2024). Ensuring inclusive workplace training in an age of rapid technological advancement: an examination of the impact of artificial intelligence (ai) rollout. In *ICERI2024 Proceedings* (pp. 7796-7802).

Bass, B. M., & Riggio, R. E. (2018). *Transformational Leadership* (3rd ed.). Psychology Press.

Bass, B. M., & Riggio, R. E. (2018). *Transformational leadership* (3rd ed.). Routledge.

Baxter, G., & Sommerville, I. (2011). Socio-technical systems: From design methods to systems engineering. *Interacting with Computers*, *23*(1), 4–17. DOI: 10.1016/j.intcom.2010.07.003

Beck, K., Beedle, M., van Bennekum, A., Cockburn, A., Cunningham, W., Fowler, M., . . . Thomas, D. (2001). Manifesto for Agile Software Development. Agile Alliance. https://agilemanifesto.org/

Beck, K., Beedle, M., van Bennekum, A., Cockburn, A., Cunningham, W., Fowler, M., . . . Thomas, D. (2001). *Manifesto for Agile software development*. https://agilemanifesto.org

Behravan, M. (2025). Generative ai framework for 3d object generation in augmented reality. arXiv preprint arXiv:2502.15869.

Bello, O. A., Ogundipe, A., Mohammed, D., Adebola, F., & Alonge, O. A. (2023). AI-driven approaches for real-time fraud detection in US financial transactions: Challenges and opportunities. *European Journal of Computer Science and Information Technology*, *11*(6), 84–102.

Belton, V., & Stewart, T. J. (2002). *Multiple criteria decision analysis: An integrated approach*. Springer. https://link.springer.com/book/10.1007/978-1-4615-1495-4

Benbya, H., Nan, N., Tanriverdi, H., & Yoo, Y. (2020). Complexity and information systems research in the emerging digital world. *Management Information Systems Quarterly*, *44*(1), 1–17. DOI: 10.25300/MISQ/2020/13304

Bengio, Y., Hinton, G., Yao, A., Song, D., Abbeel, P., Darrell, T., Harari, Y. N., Zhang, Y.-Q., Xue, L., Shalev-Shwartz, S., Hadfield, G., Clune, J., Maharaj, T., Hutter, F., Baydin, A. G., McIlraith, S., Gao, Q., Acharya, A., Krueger, D., & Mindermann, S. (2024). Managing extreme AI risks amid rapid progress. *Science*, *384*(6698), 842–845. DOI: 10.1126/science.adn0117 PMID: 38768279

Bethune, K. G. (2025). *Nonlinear: Navigating Design with Curiosity and Conviction*. MIT Press. DOI: 10.7551/mitpress/14993.001.0001

Bhatt, J., Patel, B., Prajapati, A., & Vasa, J. (2026). Adopting Agile Methodologies for Digital Newsrooms: A Case Study of BBC News. *Lecture Notes in Networks and Systems, 1457 LNNS*, 231–241. DOI: 10.1007/978-981-96-7496-1_18

Bock, T., & von der Oelsnitz, D. (2025). Leadership-competences in the era of artificial intelligence–a structured review. *Strategy and Leadership*, *53*(3), 235–255. DOI: 10.1108/SL-09-2024-0100

Bodendorf, F. (2025). A data-driven use case planning and assessment approach for AI portfolio management. *Electronic Markets*, *35*(1), 22. Advance online publication. DOI: 10.1007/s12525-025-00759-x

Bonghez, S. (2025). Scrum team tales: conquering challenges with scrum masters and product owners. In *Case Studies on Project Management in Practice* (pp. 99–105). Edward Elgar Publishing. DOI: 10.4337/9781035311279.00016

Borenstein, J., & Howard, A. (2023). *Trustworthy AI*. MIT Press.

Bose, M. (2025). Bias in AI: A societal threat: A look beyond the tech. In *Open AI and Computational Intelligence for Society 5.0* (pp. 197-224). IGI Global Scientific Publishing.

Bostrom, N., & Yudkowsky, E. (2014). The ethics of artificial intelligence. In K. Frankish & W. Ramsey (Eds.), The Cambridge Handbook of Artificial Intelligence (pp. 316–334). Cambridge University Press. DOI: 10.1017/CBO9781139046855.020

Bouzeria, Z., Asli, L., & Brahmi, B. (2026). Local search-based approach for cardinality constrained portfolio selection problem. *Expert Systems with Applications*, *296*, 128950. Advance online publication. DOI: 10.1016/j.eswa.2025.128950

Brandthav, T., & Elzaki Adam, S. (2025). Human-AI Symbiosis in Public Sector: Exploring Delegation and Constant Recalibration of Agency Through Generative AI.

Brown, M., & Treviño, L. (2006). Ethical leadership: A review and future directions. *The Leadership Quarterly*, *17*(6), 595–616.

Brunner, D., Legat, C., & Seebacher, U. (2024). Towards Next Generation Data-Driven Management: Leveraging Predictive Swarm Intelligence to Reason and Predict Market Dynamics. In Collective Intelligence (pp. 152-203). CRC Press.

Brynjolfsson, E., & McAfee, A. (2017). *Machine, Platform, Crowd: Harnessing Our Digital Future*. Norton.

Brynjolfsson, E., & McAfee, A. (2021). *The Second Machine Age: Work, Progress, and Prosperity in a Time of Brilliant Technologies*. WW Norton.

Brynjolfsson, E., & Mitchell, T. (2017). What can machine learning do? Workforce implications. *Science*, *358*(6370), 1530–1534. PMID: 29269459

Bughin, J., Hazan, E., Lund, S., Dahlström, P., Wiesinger, A., & Subramaniam, A. (2018). *Skill shift: Automation and the future of the workforce*. McKinsey Global Institute.

Buolamwini, J., & Gebru, T. (2018). Gender shades: Intersectional accuracy disparities in commercial gender classification. *Proceedings of Machine Learning Research*, *81*, 1–15.

Burnes, B., & Cooke, B. (2013). Kurt Lewin and the Planned Approach to Change: A Re-appraisal. *Journal of Management Studies*, *50*(6), 977–1002.

Busby, L. P., Courtier, J. L., & Glastonbury, C. M. (2018). Bias in radiology: The how and why of misses and misinterpretations. *Radiographics*, *38*(1), 236–247. DOI: 10.1148/rg.2018170107 PMID: 29194009

Caldara, D., & Iacoviello, M. (2022). Measuring Geopolitical Risk. *The American Economic Review*, *112*(4), 1194–1225.

Campos, L. N., Bryce-Alberti, M., Gerk, A., Hill, S. K., Calderon, C., Zaigham, M., del Valle, D. D., Mita, C., Juran, S., Ferreira, J. L., & Uribe-Leitz, T. (2024). Examining the surgical backlog due to COVID-19 in Latin America and the Caribbean: Insights from a scoping review. *Lancet Regional Health. Americas*, *40*, 100908. Advance online publication. DOI: 10.1016/j.lana.2024.100908 PMID: 39493415

Cao, Y., Chen, Y., Fan, X., Fu, H., & Xu, B. (2026). Advanced Design for High-Performance and AI Chips. *Nano-Micro Letters*, *18*(1), 13. Advance online publication. DOI: 10.1007/s40820-025-01850-w PMID: 40728678

Cavoukian, A. (2019). Privacy by Design: The definitive workshop. *Identity in the Information Society*, *12*(1), 3–18.

Çeri, Ş. Ö., & Erhan, T. (2025). A Conceptual Study on the Effects of Artificial Intelligence in Managerial Decision-Making. *European Journal of Digital Economy Research*, *6*(1), 5–21.

Cervini, P., Farri, E., & Rosani, G. (2023). Generative AI for strategy & innovation. Harvard Business Review Italia, 4.

Chae, H. S., & Yoon, C. (2025). Factors Affecting Human-Generated AI Collaboration: Trust and Perceived Usefulness as Mediators. *Information (Basel)*, *16*(10), 856. DOI: 10.3390/info16100856

Chakrabarti, M., Fabozzi, F. J., Narain, A., & Sood, A. (2025). Ethical AI in Asset Management: Frameworks for Transparency, Compliance, and Trust. *The Journal of Financial Data Science*, *7*(1), 18–35. DOI: 10.3905/jfds.2025.7.1.018

Charan, J. K., Chandra, S., Vaissnave, V., Ragupathi, T., Satyanarayana, P., & Manjunath, T. C. (2025). Impact of Generative AI on Industries and Organizations. In Zhao, J., Kumar, V., Katina, P., & Richards, J. (Eds.), *Humans and Generative AI Tools for Collaborative Intelligence* (pp. 509–528). IGI Global Scientific Publishing. DOI: 10.4018/979-8-3693-8332-2.ch022

Cheng, Q., Sahoo, D., Saha, A., Yang, W., Liu, C., Woo, G., . . . Hoi, S. C. (2023). AI for IT operations (AIOps) on Cloud Platforms: Reviews, Opportunities and Challenges. arXiv preprint arXiv:2304.04661.

Chinta, S. (2021). The impact of AI-powered automation on agile project management: Transforming traditional practices. [IRJET]. *International Research Journal of Engineering and Technology*, *8*(10), 2025–2036. DOI: 10.2139/ssrn.5034076

Chong, H.-Y., Yang, X., Goh, C. S., & Luo, Y. (2025). BIM and AI Integration for Dynamic Schedule Management: A Practical Framework and Case Study. In *Buildings* (Vol. 15, Issue 14, p. 2451). DOI: 10.3390/buildings15142451

Chou, J.-S., Lin, K.-C., & Pham, T.-B.-Q. (2025). AI-fused construction portfolio investment system with risk hedging using machine learning and long-short strategies. *Applied Soft Computing*, *183*, 113555. Advance online publication. DOI: 10.1016/j.asoc.2025.113555

Chou, J.-S., & Pham, T.-B.-Q. (2025). Leveraging ensemble learning-based stock preselection with multiobjective investment optimization for stepwise decision-supported portfolio management. *Journal of Big Data*, *12*(1), 196. Advance online publication. DOI: 10.1186/s40537-025-01202-w

Chowdhury, P., Mishra, S., Srivastava, S., Ghosh, R., Singh, D., Jena, J. J., & Darshana, S. (2024). Scalability and AI: An Insight on Software Project Management. *2024 6th International Conference on Computational Intelligence and Networks (CINE)*, 1–6. DOI: 10.1109/CINE63708.2024.10881438

Chui, M., Manyika, J., & Miremadi, M. (2016). Where machines could replace humans-and where they can't (yet). *The McKinsey Quarterly*, •••, 1–12.

Chukwunweike, J., & Aro, O. E. (2024). Implementing agile management practices in the era of digital transformation. *World Journal of Advanced Research and Reviews*, *24*(1), 2223–2242. DOI: 10.30574/wjarr.2024.24.1.3253

Chu, X., Zhang, B., & Xu, R. (2021). FairNAS: Rethinking Evaluation Fairness of Weight Sharing Neural Architecture Search. *Proceedings of the IEEE International Conference on Computer Vision*, 12219–12228. DOI: 10.1109/ICCV48922.2021.01202

Cinkusz, K., & Chudziak, J. (2025). Agile Software Management with Cognitive Multi-Agent Systems. In *17th International Conference on Agents and Artificial Intelligence*. SciTePress. DOI: 10.5220/0013153000003890

CIO – Wiki. IT Operations (Information Technology Operations). Retrieved 8 Jan 2026 from https://cio-wiki.org/wiki/IT_Operations_(Information_Technology_Operations)

Clark, R. C., & Mayer, R. (2023). *E-Learning and the Science of Instruction*. Wiley.

Coniglio, I. M., Cimino, A., & Corvello, V. (2026). Artificial Intelligence and the Future of Supply Chain Management. *Springer Proceedings in Complexity*, 43–52. DOI: 10.1007/978-3-031-78623-5_4

Cowgill, B., Dell'Acqua, F., Deng, S., Hsu, D., Verma, N., & Chaintreau, A. (2020). Biased programmers? Or biased data? A field experiment in operationalizing AI ethics. Management Science Working Paper.

Cowls, J., & Floridi, L. (2018). Prolegomena to a white paper on an ethical framework for a good AI society. SSRN Electronic Journal.

Cukier, K., & Mayer-Schönberger, V. (2021). *Big Data: A Revolution That Will Transform How We Live, Work, and Think*. Eamon Dolan.

Dam, H. K., Tran, T., Grundy, J., Ghose, A., & Kamei, Y. (2019, May). Towards effective AI-powered agile project management. In *2019 IEEE/ACM 41st international conference on software engineering: new ideas and emerging results (ICSE-NIER)* (pp. 41-44). IEEE. DOI: 10.1109/ICSE-NIER.2019.00019

Dameski, A. (2020). Foundations of an Ethical Framework for AI Entities: the Ethics of Systems. *Doctoral Dissertation, University of Luxembourg, Esch-Sur-Alzette, Luxembourg*. https://orbilu.uni.lu/handle/10993/45285

Dang, Y., Lin, Q., & Huang, P. (2019, May). Aiops: real-world challenges and research innovations. In 2019 IEEE/ACM 41st International Conference on Software Engineering: Companion Proceedings (ICSE-Companion) (pp. 4-5). IEEE. DOI: 10.1109/ICSE-Companion.2019.00023

Davenport, T. H., & Ronanki, R. (2018). Artificial intelligence for the real world. *Harvard Business Review*, *96*(1), 108–116.

Davis, F. D. (1989). Perceived usefulness, perceived ease of use, and user acceptance of information technology. *Management Information Systems Quarterly*, *13*(3), 319–340. https://www.jstor.org/stable/249008. DOI: 10.2307/249008

Davis, M. A., Wu, O., Ikuta, I., Jordan, J. E., Johnson, M. H., & Quigley, E. (2024). Understanding Bias in Artificial Intelligence: A Practice Perspective. *AJNR. American Journal of Neuroradiology*, *45*(4), 371–373. DOI: 10.3174/ajnr.A8070 PMID: 38123951

De Brito, M. M., & Evers, M. (2016). Multi-criteria decision-making for flood risk management: A survey of the current state of the art. *Natural Hazards and Earth System Sciences*, *16*(4), 1019–1033. DOI: 10.5194/nhess-16-1019-2016

De la Cruz Cabello, M., Sales, T. P., & Machado, M. R. (2025). AIOps for log anomaly detection in the era of LLMs: A systematic literature review. *Intelligent Systems with Applications*, *200608*. Advance online publication.

de Oliveira Garcia Coutinho, V., de Almeida Souza, M. R., & Freire, A. P. (2024). Application of human-centered design practices in the agile requirements engineering process: a case study in a public company. *ACM International Conference Proceeding Series*, 498–507. DOI: 10.1145/3701625.3701635 de Sousa Leite, G., Maciel, R. S. P., Vieira, R. E. P., Freire, S., Cerqueira, L., & Mendonça, M. (2024). Technical Debt Management in Agile Software Development: A Systematic Mapping Study. *ACM International Conference Proceeding Series*, 309–320. DOI: 10.1145/3701625.3701669

Deloitte. (2023). *Human Capital Trends Report*. Deloitte Insights.

Deloitte. (2024). *Ethical AI and Workforce Engagement*. Deloitte University Press.

Denning, S. (2011). *The Leader's Guide to Storytelling*. Jossey-Bass.

Derby, E., Larsen, D., & Horowitz, D. (2024). *Agile Retrospectives: A Practical Guide for Catalyzing Team Learning and Improvement*. The Pragmatic Programmers LLC.

Deshmukh, A., Patil, D. S., Mohan, J. S., Balamurugan, G., & Tyagi, A. K. (2023). Transforming next generation-based artificial intelligence for software development: current status, issues, challenges, and future opportunities. In *Emerging Technologies and Digital Transformation in the Manufacturing Industry* (pp. 30–66). IGI global. DOI: 10.4018/978-1-6684-8088-5.ch003

Deshpande, M. (2024). Leveraging AI and Machine Learning to Revolutionize IT Service Management. *Journal of Artificial Intelligence & Cloud Computing, 353*, 2-5. DOI: 10.47363/JAICC/2024(3)353

DevOps Research & Assessment (DORA). (2022). Accelerate: State of DevOps Report 2022. Google Cloud.

Diao, Y. (2007, July). Using control theory to improve productivity of service systems. In *IEEE International Conference on Services Computing (SCC 2007)* (pp. 435-442). IEEE. DOI: 10.1109/SCC.2007.78

Diaz-De-Arcaya, J., Torre-Bastida, A. I., Zárate, G., Miñón, R., & Almeida, A. (2023). A joint study of the challenges, opportunities, and roadmap of mlops and aiops: A systematic survey. *ACM Computing Surveys*, *56*(4), 1–30.

Dignum, V. (2019). *Responsible artificial intelligence: How to develop and use AI in a responsible way* (Vol. 2156). Springer.

Dili, G., & Ansong, E. D. (2025). Human–AI Collaboration: A Paradigm Shift in Decision-Making. In *The Power of Agentic AI: Redefining Human Life and Decision-Making: In Industry 6.0* (pp. 59–80). Springer Nature Switzerland. DOI: 10.1007/978-3-031-89424-4_5

Dingsøyr, T., Moe, N. B., Fægri, T. E., & Seim, E. A. (2018). Exploring software development at the very large-scale: A revelatory case study and research agenda for agile method adaptation. *Empirical Software Engineering*, *23*(1), 490–520. DOI: 10.1007/s10664-017-9524-2

Doh, W. (2025). *Systematically Predicting and Preventing Overreliance Through the Human-AI-System Concordance (HASC) Matrix and Cognitive Interventions* (Doctoral dissertation).

Doshi-Velez, F., & Kim, B. (2017). Towards a rigorous science of interpretable machine learning. *arXiv*. https://arxiv.org/abs/1702.08608

Drosos, I., Sarkar, A., & Toronto, N. (2025). " It makes you think": Provocations Help Restore Critical Thinking to AI-Assisted Knowledge Work. arXiv preprint arXiv:2501.17247.

Drukker, K., Chen, W., Gichoya, J., Gruszauskas, N., Kalpathy-Cramer, J., Koyejo, S., Myers, K., Sá, R. C., Sahiner, B., Whitney, H., Zhang, Z., & Giger, M. (2023). Toward fairness in artificial intelligence for medical image analysis: Identification and mitigation of potential biases in the roadmap from data collection to model deployment. *Journal of Medical Imaging (Bellingham, Wash.)*, *10*(06). Advance online publication. DOI: 10.1117/1.JMI.10.6.061104 PMID: 37125409

Dugbartey, A. N., & Kehinde, O. (2025). Optimizing project delivery through agile methodologies: Balancing speed, collaboration and stakeholder engagement. *World J. Adv. Res. Rev*, *25*(1), 1237–1257. DOI: 10.30574/wjarr.2025.25.1.0193

Durrani, U. K., Akpinar, M., Adak, M. F., Kabakus, A. T., Öztürk, M. M., & Saleh, M. (2024). A Decade of Progress: A Systematic Literature Review on the Integration of AI in Software Engineering Phases and Activities (2013-2023). *IEEE Access : Practical Innovations, Open Solutions*, *12*, 171185–171204. DOI: 10.1109/ACCESS.2024.3488904

Edmondson, A. (2019). *The Fearless Organization: Creating Psychological Safety in the Workplace for Learning, Innovation, and Growth.* Wilcy.

Edmondson, A. C. (2019). *The fearless organization: Creating psychological safety in the workplace for learning, innovation, and growth.* Wiley.

Ehtsham, M., Parisi, G., Pedone, F., Rossi, F., Zincani, M., Congiu, E., & Marchionni, C. (2025). AI-Powered Advanced Technologies for a Sustainable Built Environment: A Systematic Review on Emerging Challenges. In *Sustainability* (Vol. 17, Issue 17, p. 8005). DOI: 10.3390/su17178005

Ekambaram, A., Vågbø, P. C., & van der Leyen, B. S. (2022). The role of machine learning in managing uncertainty in projects–A view on early warning systems. In *European Conference on Management, Leadership & Governance* (pp. 536-XV). Academic Conferences International Limited. DOI: 10.34190/ecmlg.18.1.932

El Aouni, F., Moumane, K., Idri, A., Najib, M., & Jan, S. U. (2025). A systematic literature review on Agile, Cloud, and DevOps integration: Challenges, benefits. *Information and Software Technology, 177*, 107569.

Ellefsen, A. P. T., Oleśków-Szłapka, J., Pawłowski, G., & Toboła, A. (2019). Striving for excellence in AI implementation: AI maturity model framework and preliminary research results. *LogForum, 15*(3).

Elumalai, D. (2025). Leveraging AI and Machine Learning to Improve Agile Backlog Prioritization. *The American Journal of Engineering and Technology, 7*(05), 211–218. DOI: 10.37547/tajet/Volume07Issue05-21

Eyieyien, O. G., Idemudia, C., Paul, P. O., & Ijomah, T. I. (2024). Effective stakeholder and risk management strategies for large-scale international project success. *Int. J. Front. Sci. Technol. Res, 7*(1), 013-024.

Fathi, N. (2025). *The Role of AI in Enhancing Project Success Rate in Project Management* (Doctoral dissertation, Dublin, National College of Ireland).

Favari, E. (2023). *Project management: leading change in the age of complexity*. Springer Nature. DOI: 10.1007/978-3-031-25031-6

Felemban, H., Sohail, M., & Ruikar, K. (2024). Exploring the readiness of organisations to adopt artificial intelligence. *Buildings (Basel, Switzerland), 14*(8), 2460. DOI: 10.3390/buildings14082460

Filho, R. C. D., Silva, M. J., & Marinho, M. L. M. (2024). Low-Code Quality Metrics for Agile Software Development. *ACM International Conference Proceeding Series*, 417–425. DOI: 10.1145/3701625.3701626

Florida, R. (2020). *The Rise of the Creative Class Revisited*. Basic Books.

Floridi, L., & Cowls, J. (2022). A unified framework of five principles for AI in society. Machine learning and the city: Applications in architecture and urban design, 535-545. doi:DOI: 10.1162/99608f92.8cd550d1

Floridi, L. (2021). *The Ethics of Artificial Intelligence*. Oxford University Press.

Floridi, L. (2021). *The ethics of artificial intelligence: Principles, challenges, and opportunities*. Oxford University Press.

Floridi, L., Cowls, J., & Beltrametti, M.. (2018). AI4People—An ethical framework for a good AI society. *Minds and Machines*, *28*(4), 689–707. PMID: 30930541

Floridi, L., Cowls, J., Beltrametti, M., Chatila, R., Chazerand, P., Dignum, V., Luetge, C., Madelin, R., Pagallo, U., Rossi, F., Schafer, B., Valcke, P., & Vayena, E. (2018). AI4People An ethical framework for a good AI society. *Minds and Machines*, *28*(4), 689–707. DOI: 10.1007/s11023-018-9482-5 PMID: 30930541

Forsgren, N., Humble, J., & Kim, G. (2018). *Accelerate: The science of lean software and DevOps*. IT Revolution Press. https://itrevolution.com/book/accelerate/

Frazier, M. L., Fainshmidt, S., Klinger, R. L., Pezeshkan, A., & Vracheva, V. (2017). Psychological safety: A meta-analytic review and extension. *Personnel Psychology*, *70*(1), 113–165.

Freedman, E. B. (2023). "Not a Word Was Said Ever Again": Silence and Speech in Women's Oral History Accounts of Sexual Harassment. *The Oral History Review*, *50*(1), 4–22. DOI: 10.1080/00940798.2023.2182695

Frey, C. B., & Osborne, M. A. (2017). The future of employment: How susceptible are jobs to computerisation? *Technological Forecasting and Social Change*, *114*, 254–280.

Furberg, A., Azizi, S., Bieser, J., Bol, D., Coroamă, V., Eriksson, E., Fuso-Nerini, F., Golard, L., Höjer, M., Kamiya, G., Lundén, D., Lövehagen, N., Malmodin, J., Schien, D., & Finnveden, G. (2026). Guidelines for assessments of the global information and communication technology sector's direct energy use and climate impact: Key aspects and future scenarios. *Renewable & Sustainable Energy Reviews*, *226*, 116176. Advance online publication. DOI: 10.1016/j.rser.2025.116176

Gade, K., Geyik, S. C., Kenthapadi, K., Mithal, V., & Taly, A. (2020). Explainable AI in industry: Practical challenges and lessons learned. *Companion Proceedings of the Web Conference, January 2020*, 699–699. DOI: 10.1145/3351095.3375664

Gandomi, A., & Haider, M. (2015). Beyond the hype: Big data concepts, methods, and analytics. International Journal of Information Management, 35(2), 137–144. (Ransbotham, Kiron, & Prentice, 2021)

Gaona-Cuevas, M., Guerrero, V. B., & Vera-Rivera, F. H. (2024). The Smart Product Backlog: A Classification Model of User Stories. *IEEE Access : Practical Innovations, Open Solutions*, *12*, 150008–150019. DOI: 10.1109/ACCESS.2024.3478833

García Martínez, J. R. (2023). Letters of blood and fire: writing and accumulation in Latin America, from the chronicles of the Indies to the present (Doctoral dissertation, University of British Columbia).

Gartner – AIOps. (n.d.). *Information Technology Glossary*. Retrieved Jan 2, 2025, from https://www.gartner.com/en/information-technology/glossary/aiops-artificial-intelligence-operations

Gartner - Hype Cycle. (2020). *Hype Cycle for I and O Automation.* Available: https://automationedge.com/news/gartner-hyper-cycle-for-io-automation-2020-report-mentions-automationedge-as-a-key-vendor-for-intelligent-automation/#. Accessed 2 Mar 2026

Gartner. (2017). I*nnovation Insight for AIOps: Artificial Intelligence for IT Operations*. Gartner Research. Retrieved from https://www.gartner.com/en/research/methodologies/aiops-artificial-intelligence-for-it-operations

Gartner. (2024). Adaptive Learning in Corporate Environments. Gartner Research.

Geis, J. R., Brady, A., Wu, C. C., Spencer, J., Ranschaert, E., Jaremko, J. L., Langer, S. G., Kitts, A. B., Birch, J., Shields, W. F., van den Hoven van Genderen, R., Kotter, E., Gichoya, J. W., Cook, T. S., Morgan, M. B., Tang, A., Safdar, N. M., & Kohli, M. (2019). Ethics of artificial intelligence in radiology: Summary of the joint European and North American multisociety statement. *Insights Into Imaging*, *10*(1), 101. Advance online publication. DOI: 10.1186/s13244-019-0785-8 PMID: 31571015

George, A. S. (2024). The symbiotic relationship between visionary and pragmatic leadership in propelling organizational success. *Partners Universal International Innovation Journal*, *2*(3), 57–79.

Ghiglino, P., Harshe, M., Doran, H. D., & Tordoya Taquichiri, C. R. (2026). High-Performance AI Inference for Agile Deployment on Space-Qualified Processors: A Performance Benchmarking Study. *Lecture Notes in Computer Science, 15955 LNCS*, 267–280. DOI: 10.1007/978-3-032-02018-5_20

Gichoya, J. W., Banerjee, I., Bhimireddy, A. R., Burns, J. L., Celi, L. A., Chen, L. C., Correa, R., Dullerud, N., Ghassemi, M., Huang, S. C., Kuo, P. C., Lungren, M. P., Palmer, L. J., Price, B. J., Purkayastha, S., Pyrros, A. T., Oakden-Rayner, L., Okechukwu, C., Seyyed-Kalantari, L., & Zhang, H. (2022). AI recognition of patient race in medical imaging: A modelling study. *The Lancet. Digital Health*, *4*(6), e406–e414. DOI: 10.1016/S2589-7500(22)00063-2 PMID: 35568690

Gichoya, J. W., Thomas, K., Celi, L. A., Safdar, N., Banerjee, I., Banja, J. D., Seyyed-Kalantari, L., Trivedi, H., & Purkayastha, S. (2023). AI IN IMAGING AND THERAPY: INNOVATIONS, ETHICS, AND IMPACT: REVIEW ARTICLE AI pitfalls and what not to do: mitigating bias in AI. *The British Journal of Radiology*, *96*(1150), 20230023. Advance online publication. DOI: 10.1259/bjr.20230023 PMID: 37698583

Gil, Y., & Varshney, K. R. (2019). Towards accountable AI: Hybrid human–machine analyses for responsible decision-making. AI Magazine, 40(4), 56–70.

Gilbert, T. K., & Mintz, Y. (2019). Epistemic therapy for bias in automated decision-making. *AIES 2019 - Proceedings of the 2019 AAAI/ACM Conference on AI, Ethics, and Society, March*, 61–67. DOI: 10.1145/3306618.3314294

Giudici, P., Centurelli, M., & Turchetta, S. (2024). Artificial Intelligence risk measurement. *Expert Systems with Applications*, *235*, 121220. DOI: 10.1016/j.eswa.2023.121220

Goel, A., Dede, C., Garn, M., & Ou, C. (2024). AI-ALOE: AI for reskilling, upskilling, and workforce development. *AI Magazine*, *45*(1), 77–82. DOI: 10.1002/aaai.12157

Gohring, N. (2024, Jan). *Cost May Be a Bigger Issue for AIOps than Observability*. Retrieved 14 Jan 2024 from https://www.idc.com/getdoc.jsp?containerId=US51608423#:~:text=The%20median%20annual%20spend%20by,observability%20tools%20is%20%241.4%20million

Goleman, D. (2022). *Emotional Intelligence: Why It Can Matter More Than IQ*. Bantam Books.

Gonzalez, K., Kanitz, R., & Briker, R. (2024). "AI can't steal my soul": In the age of AI, the human touch is paramount for the craft of managing change. *The Journal of Applied Behavioral Science*, *60*(4), 589–602. DOI: 10.1177/00218863241279916

González, P., González, V., Molenaar, K., & Orozco, F. (2014). Analysis of causes of delay and time performance in construction projects. *Journal of Construction Engineering and Management*, *140*(1), 04013027. DOI: 10.1061/(ASCE)CO.1943-7862.0000721

González-Sendino, R., Serrano, E., Bajo, J., & Novais, P. (2024). A Review of Bias and Fairness in Artificial Intelligence. *International Journal of Interactive Multimedia and Artificial Intelligence*, *9*(1), 5–17. DOI: 10.9781/ijimai.2023.11.001

Goryunova, E., & Yawson, R. M. (2025). "Nested Complexity" Framework for Human-Centered AI-Augmented Leadership. *Journal of Leadership Studies*, *19*(2), e70016. DOI: 10.1002/jls.70016

Gozman, D., Liebenau, J., & Mangan, M. (2018). The innovation mechanisms of fintech start-ups: Insights from SWIFT's innotribe competition. *Journal of Management Information Systems*, *35*(1), 145–179. DOI: 10.1080/07421222.2018.1440768

Grigoliene, R., Kiyak, D., Olsauskas, V., & Juknyte-Petreikiene, I. (2025). Public Governance of Sustainable Development Implementation: A Case Study of Coastal Municipalities in Lithuania. *Sustainability (Basel), 17*(18), 8170. Advance online publication. DOI: 10.3390/su17188170

Grimm, P. W., Grossman, M. R., & Cormack, G. V. (2021). Artificial intelligence as evidence. *Nw. J. Tech. & Intell. Prop., 19*, 9.

Gül, C., & Özder, A. (2025). The Effects of Hotel Managers' Perceptions about Refugees on Their Operational Decisions in Istanbul: A Research in the Framework of Affect Heuristic Theory. *Electronic Turkish Studies, 20*, 747–767.

Gürses, S., Troncoso, C., & Diaz, C. (2011). *Engineering privacy by design*. Computers, Privacy & Data Protection Conference.

Guru Basava Aradhya, S., Chithambar Gupta, V., Raman, M. S., Singh, J., Manjunath, T. C., & Sharma, M. (2025). Health Crises and Digitalization: Digital Health. In Yıldırım, D., Yıldırım, S., & Kandpal, V. (Eds.), *Sustainable Digitalization Strategies in Business and Healthcare* (pp. 171–198). IGI Global Scientific Publishing. DOI: 10.4018/979-8-3373-5087-5.ch007

Habbal, A., Ali, M. K., & Abuzaraida, M. A. (2024). Artificial Intelligence Trust, Risk and Security Management (AI TRiSM): Frameworks, applications, challenges and future research directions. *Expert Systems with Applications, 240*(November 2023). DOI: 10.1016/j.eswa.2023.122442

Haidabrus, B., Grabis, J., Druzhinin, E., & Kolesnikova, K. (2026). Implementing Lean-Agile Principles in Data Programme. *Lecture Notes in Mechanical Engineering*, 149–158. DOI: 10.1007/978-3-032-07144-6_13

Halperin, B., & Mazlish, J. Z. (2025). Overreaction and forecast horizon: longer-term expectations overreact more, shorter-term expectations drive fluctuations.

Hanna, M. G., Pantanowitz, L., Jackson, B., Palmer, O., Visweswaran, S., Pantanowitz, J., Deebajah, M., & Rashidi, H. H. (2025a). Ethical and Bias Considerations in Artificial Intelligence/Machine Learning. *Modern Pathology, 38*(3), 100686. DOI: 10.1016/j.modpat.2024.100686 PMID: 39694331

Harmanpreet, C. S., Kalshetti, P., Satyanarayana, P., Sharma, M., & Manjunath, T. C. (2025). Digital Transformation in the Public Sector Entities. In A. Santos Ferreira & C. Lourenço dos Santos (Eds.), *Enhancing Public Sector Accountability and Services Through Digital Innovation* (pp. 353-380). IGI Global Scientific Publishing.

Harris, C. (2020). Mitigating Cognitive Biases in Machine Learning Algorithms for Decision Making. *The Web Conference 2020 - Companion of the World Wide Web Conference, WWW 2020, 2020*(April 2020), 775–781. DOI: 10.1145/3366424.3383562

Hartley, J. (2007). Cognitive bias mitigation and transparency in decision-making. Public Administration Review, 67(6), 1045–1056.

Hassan, M., Aziz, L. A.-R., & Andriansyah, Y. (2023). The Role Artificial Intelligence in Modern Banking: An Exploration of AI-Driven Approaches for Enhanced Fraud Prevention, Risk Management, and Regulatory Compliance. *Reviews of Contemporary Business Analytics*, *6*(1), 110–132. https://researchberg.com/index.php/rcba/article/view/153

Herda, T., Pichler, V., Zhang, Z., Abrahamsson, P., & Hanssen, G. K. (2025). AI and Agile Software Development: From Frustration to Success XP2025 Workshop Summary. In *International Conference on Agile Software Development* (pp. 3-13). Cham: Springer Nature Switzerland.

HERMES Foundation. (2022). [– Method overview. https://www.hermes.admin.ch/en/project-management/method-overview.html]. *Hermes*, *5*, •••.

Hiatt, J., & Creasey, T. (2021). *ADKAR: A Model for Change in Business, Government, and Our Community*. Prosci Learning Center Publications.

Hiatt, J., & Creasey, T. (2021). *Change Management: The People Side of Change*. Prosci.

Hiatt, J., & Creasey, T. J. (2021). *Change management: The people side of change*. Prosci Research.

Hidalgo, E. S. (2019). Adapting the scrum framework for agile project management in science: Case study of a distributed research initiative. *Heliyon*, *5*(3), e01447. DOI: 10.1016/j.heliyon.2019.e01447 PMID: 30976706

Highsmith, J. (2009). *Agile project management: Creating innovative products* (2nd ed.). Addison-Wesley Professional.

Highsmith, J. (2009). *Agile project management: creating innovative products*. Pearson education.

Hofert, S. (2022). *The agile mindset: Developing employees, shaping the future of work*. Springer Nature. DOI: 10.1007/978-3-658-34910-3

Hofmann, P., Jöhnk, J., Protschky, D., & Urbach, N. (2020, March). Developing Purposeful AI Use Cases-A Structured Method and Its Application in Project Management. In *Wirtschaftsinformatik (zentrale tracks)* (pp. 33-49). DOI: 10.30844/wi_2020_a3-hofmann

Hokmabadi, H., Rezvani, S. M. H. S., Hokmabadi, H., & de Almeida, N. M. (2025). Business Resilience Through AI-Agent Automation for SMEs and Startups: A Review on Agile Marketing and CRM. In *Information* (Vol. 16, Issue 11, p. 1000). DOI: 10.3390/info16111000

Holloway, S. (2025). Navigating Supply Chain Disruptions with Technology-Driven Agility and Coordination. Available at *SSRN* 5136960. DOI: 10.2139/ssrn.5136960

Holzinger, A., Zatloukal, K., & Müller, H. (2025). Is human oversight to AI systems still possible? *New Biotechnology*, *85*, 59–62. DOI: 10.1016/j.nbt.2024.12.003 PMID: 39675423

Hort, M., Chen, Z., Zhang, J. M., Harman, M., & Sarro, F. (2024). Bias Mitigation for Machine Learning Classifiers: A Comprehensive Survey. *ACM Journal on Responsible Computing*, *1*(2), 1–52. DOI: 10.1145/3631326

Howells, J. R. (1995). Going global: The use of ICT networks in research and development. *Research Policy*, *24*(2), 169–184. DOI: 10.1016/0048-7333(93)00760-Q

Hoxhaj, O., Halilaj, B., & Harizi, A. (2023). ETHICAL IMPLICATIONS AND HUMAN RIGHTS VIOLATIONS IN THE AGE OF ARTIFICIAL INTELLIGENCE. *Balkan Social Science Review*, *22*(22), 153–171. DOI: 10.46763/BSSR232222153h

Hua, Y. (2021). A systems approach to effective aiops implementation (Doctoral dissertation, Massachusetts Institute of Technology). hdl.handle.net/1721.1/139422

Humble, J., & Farley, D. (2010). *Continuous delivery: Reliable software releases through build, test, and deployment automation.* Addison-Wesley Professional.

Hunt, V., Prince, S., Dixon-Fyle, S., & Yee, L. (2018). *Delivering through diversity.* McKinsey & Company.

Hussain, K. (2024). Revolutionizing healthcare: The impact of artificial intelligence on patient care, diagnosis, and treatment.

Huzooree, G., Subramanian, J., & Dewasiri, N. J. (2025). Reskilling for the AI Age: Project Management Approaches and Organisational Strategies for Workforce Readiness. In *Global Work Arrangements and Outsourcing in the Age of AI* (pp. 471-494). IGI Global Scientific Publishing.

Ibidunmoye, O., Hernández-Rodriguez, F., & Elmroth, E. (2015). Performance anomaly detection and bottleneck identification. *ACM Computing Surveys*, *48*(1), 1–35. DOI: 10.1145/2791120

IBM - AIOps. (n.d.). *What is AIOps?* Retrieved 20 Dec 2025 from https://www.ibm.com/think/topics/aiops

IBM – ITOps. (n.d.). *What is IT operations (ITOps)?* Retrieved 8 Jan 2026 from https://www.ibm.com/think/topics/it-operations

IEEE. (2023). *Ethically Aligned Design: A Vision for Prioritizing Human Well-being with Autonomous and Intelligent Systems*. IEEE Global Initiative.

Ilieva, G., Yankova, T., Staribratov, P., Ruseva, G., & Iliev, Y. (2025). Industrial Digitalization: Systematic Literature Review and Bibliometric Analysis. In *Information* (Vol. 16, Issue 12, p. 1080). DOI: 10.3390/info16121080

Intel – IT Transformation. (n.d.). *What Is IT Transformation? Overview and Strategy – Intel*. Retrieved 10 Jan 2025, from https://www.intel.com/content/www/us/en/business/resources/it-transformation.html#:~:text=IT%20transformation%20is%20the%20strategic,respond%20quickly%20to%20ecosystem%20changes

Intelligence, M. (n.d.). *IT Operations Management (ITOM) Market Size & Share Analysis - Growth Trends & Forecast* (2025 - 2030). https://www.mordorintelligence.com/industry-reports/it-operations-management-market#:~:text=The%20IT%20Operations%20Management%20Market,integration%20of%20AI%20and%20automation

International Energy Agency (IEA). (2023). *Energy Efficiency and Digitalization Report*. IEA Publications.

International Labor Organization (ILO). (2023). The Future of Work in a Digital World.

Iorliam, A. (2023). A Novel Additive Internet of Things (IoT) Features and Convolutional Neural Network for Classification and Source Identification of IoT Devices. *Sakarya University Journal of Computer and Information Sciences*, *6*(3), 218–225. DOI: 10.35377/saucis...1354791

Islam, M. R., & Sandborn, P. (2025). Multimodal Generative AI for Story Point Estimation in Software Development. *arXiv preprint arXiv:2505.16290.*

ISO/IEC. (2011). *ISO/IEC/IEEE 42010: Systems and software engineering Architecture description*. International Organization for Standardization. https://www.iso.org/standard/50508.html

ISO/IEC. (2021). ISO/IEC 23894:2021 Artificial Intelligence — Risk Management. International Organization for Standardization.

ISO/IEC. (2023). ISO/IEC 42001: Artificial Intelligence Management System Standard. International Organization for Standardization.

Ispas, L., Mironeasa, C., Severin, T.-L., Cerlincă, D.-A., & Mironeasa, S. (2025). Artificial Intelligence Applications in Risk Management Within Integrated Management Systems: A Review. In *Systems* (Vol. 13, Issue 11, p. 967). DOI: 10.3390/systems13110967

Jacobsen, A., de Miranda Azevedo, R., Juty, N., Batista, D., Coles, S., Cornet, R., & Schultes, E. (2020). FAIR principles: Interpretations and implementation considerations. *Data Intelligence*, *2*(1-2), 10–29. DOI: 10.1162/dint

Jedličková, A. (2024). Ethical considerations in Risk management of autonomous and intelligent systems. [in Central Europe]. *Ethics and Bioethics*, *14*(1–2), 80–95. DOI: 10.2478/ebce-2024-0007

Jia, J., Jin, G. Z., & Wagman, L. (2021). The short-run effects of GDPR on technology venture investment. *Marketing Science*, *40*(4), 661–684.

Ji, Z., Lee, N., Frieske, R., Yu, T., Su, D., Xu, Y., Ishii, E., Bang, Y. J., Madotto, A., & Fung, P. (2023). Survey of Hallucination in Natural Language Generation. *ACM Computing Surveys*, *55*(12), 1–38. Advance online publication. DOI: 10.1145/3571730

Jobin, A., Ienca, M., & Vayena, E. (2019). The global landscape of AI ethics guidelines. *Nature Machine Intelligence*, *1*(9), 389–399.

Johnson, G., Shriver, S., & Goldberg, S. (2020). Privacy and market concentration: Intended and unintended consequences of the GDPR. *Management Science*, *66*(10), 5349–5371.

Joshi, S. (2025). The Role of AI in Enhancing Teamwork, Resilience and Decision-Making: Review of Recent Developments. *International Journal of Computer Applications*, *187*(8), 9–26. DOI: 10.5120/ijca2025925036

Junqué de Fortuny, E., Martens, D., & Provost, F. (2013). Predictive modeling with big data: Is bigger really better? *Big Data*, *1*(4), 215–226. DOI: 10.1089/big.2013.0037 PMID: 27447254

Kalluri, R. (September 2025). Socio-Technical System Challenges in The Era of Artificial Intelligence: A Comprehensive Analysis. *International Journal of Business & Management Studies*, *6*(9). 75-91. DOI: 10.56734/ijbms.v6n9a8

Kaminski, M. E. (2023). Regulating the Risks of Ai. *SSRN, 103*(5), 1347–1411. DOI: 10.2139/ssrn.4195066

Karaboga, M., Matzner, T., Obersteller, H., & Ochs, C. (2017). Is There a Right to Offline Alternatives in a Digital World? In *Data Protection and Privacy:(In) visibilities and Infrastructures* (pp. 31–57). Springer. DOI: 10.1007/978-3-319-50796-5_2

Karamthulla, M. J., Malaiyappan, J. N. A., Muthusubramanian, M., & Tillu, R. (2024). From theory to practice: Implementing AI technologies in project management. *International Journal for Multidisciplinary Research, 6*(2), 1–11.

Kayabay, K., Kılınç, A., Gökalp, M. O., Gökalp, E., & Daim, T. U. (2024). Technology Roadmapping: Data Science Roadmapping of Networked Organizations' Strategic Planning for Artificial Intelligence. In *Future-Oriented Technology Assessment: A Manager's Guide with Case Applications* (pp. 273–300). DOI: 10.1002/9781119909880.ch10

Kelleher, J. D., & Tierney, B. (2018). *Data science.* MIT press.

Kerzner, H. (2025). *Project management: a systems approach to planning, scheduling, and controlling.* John Wiley & Sons.

Khan, A., & Jilani, A. A. A. (2025). From Algorithms to Intelligence: The Historical Perspective of AI in Software Development. In Generative AI in Software Engineering (pp. 1-56). IGI Global Scientific Publishing.

Khan, M. F. I. (2024). Predictive Analytics And Machine Learning For Real-Time Detection Of Software Defects.

Khan, F. S., Mazhar, S. S., Mazhar, K. A., AlSaleh, D., & Mazhar, A. (2025). Model-agnostic explainable artificial intelligence methods in finance: A systematic review, recent developments, limitations, challenges and future directions. *Artificial Intelligence Review, 58*(8). Advance online publication. DOI: 10.1007/s10462-025-11215-9

Khera, P., Sharma, M., & Kumar, A. (2025). Reforming Organization Development Through AI: Strategies for Improved Processes and Performance. In *Achieving Organizational Diversity, Equity, and Inclusion with AI* (pp. 315-336). IGI Global Scientific Publishing.

Kim, G., Humble, J., Debois, P., & Willis, J. (2016). *The DevOps handbook.* IT Revolution Press. https://itrevolution.com/book/the-devops-handbook/

Kim, G., Humble, J., Debois, P., Willis, J., & Forsgren, N. (2021). *The DevOps handbook: How to create world-class agility, reliability, & security in technology organizations*. It Revolution. IT Revolution Press., DOI: 10.5555/3044729

Kim, J., Park, G., Woo, M., & Geum, Y. (2025). How Big Data Has Changed Technology Roadmapping: A Review on Data-Driven Roadmapping. *IEEE Access : Practical Innovations, Open Solutions*, *13*, 8297–8309. DOI: 10.1109/ACCESS.2025.3526173

Kim, Y., Park, K., Kim, Y., Yang, W., Han, D., & Kim, W. S. (2020). The Impact of Visual Art and High Affective Arousal on Heuristic Decision-Making in Consumers. *Frontiers in Psychology*, *11*(November), 1–16. DOI: 10.3389/fpsyg.2020.565829 PMID: 33324278

Knowles, M. (2020). *The Adult Learner: The Definitive Classic in Adult Education and Human Resource Development*. Routledge.

Koçak, B. (2022). Key concepts, common pitfalls, and best practices in artificial intelligence and machine learning: Focus on radiomics. *Diagnostic and Interventional Radiology*, *28*(5), 450–462. DOI: 10.5152/dir.2022.211297 PMID: 36218149

Kolt, N., Shur-Ofry, M., & Cohen, R. (2025). Lessons from complex systems science for AI governance. *Patterns*, *6*(8), 2025, 101341, ISSN 2666-3899,

Kontogiannis, K., Grigoriou, M., Brealey, C., & Giammaria, A. (2021, November). Compliance by design: software analytics and aiops. In *Proceedings of the 31st Annual International Conference on Computer Science and Software Engineering* (pp. 294-295). https://dl.acm.org/doi/abs/10.5555/3507788.3507847

Koparde, S. A., Selvakumar, P., Jha, R. P., Deepthi Reddy, K., Kuchipudi, J. D., Manjunath, T. C., & Sharma, M. (2026). Generative AI in Predicting and Preventing Foodborne Illnesses. In Madaan, G., Singh, A., Chahal, B., David, A., & Singh, G. (Eds.), *Generative AI in Food Systems: Predictive Demand, Smart Supply Chains, and Sustainable Service Futures* (pp. 205–232). IGI Global Scientific Publishing.

Košinár, M. A., Štolfa, S., Lašinská, M., Štolfa, J., & Spanyik, M. (2026). Catalogue of Pathological Patterns of Self-managed Teams in Scrum. *Communications in Computer and Information Science, 2658 CCIS*, 197–211. DOI: 10.1007/978-3-032-04291-0_14

Kotter, J. (2012). *Leading Change*. Harvard Business Review Press.

Kotter, J. (2022). *Change: How Organizations Achieve Hard-to-Imagine Results in Uncertain and Volatile Times*. Wiley.

Kreuzberger, D., Kühl, N., & Hirschl, S. (2023). Machine learning operations (MLOps): Overview, definition, and architecture. *ACM Computing Surveys*, *55*(8), 1–37. https://dblp.dagstuhl.de/rec/journals/access/KreuzbergerKH23.html

Kumar, R., & Sharma, V. (2023). The AI revolution: Financial services in the age of intelligent machines. In *Leveraging AI and Emotional Intelligence in Contemporary Business Organizations* (pp. 287–305). DOI: 10.4018/979-8-3693-1902-4.ch017

Kumar, S. (2023). Data silos a roadblock for AIOps. *International Journal for Research Trends and Innovation. 9*(1). ISSN: 2456-3315. 33-39. arXiv preprint DOI: 10.5281/zenodo.10471800

Kumari, M., Yamang, C., & Saxena, R. S. D. A. (2023). Artificial Intelligence in Project Management: Opportunities, Challenges, and Future Prospects. *Artificial Intelligence*, *16*(4).

Kuner, C., Bygrave, L., & Docksey, C. (2020). *The EU General Data Protection Regulation (GDPR): A commentary*. Oxford University Press.

Larrazabal, A. J., Nieto, N., Peterson, V., Milone, D. H., & Ferrante, E. (2020). Gender imbalance in medical imaging datasets produces biased classifiers for computer-aided diagnosis. *Proceedings of the National Academy of Sciences of the United States of America*, *117*(23), 12592–12594. DOI: 10.1073/pnas.1919012117 PMID: 32457147

Lavin, A., & Ahmad, S. (2015). Evaluating real-time anomaly detection algorithms--the Numenta anomaly benchmark. 2015 IEEE 14th international conference on machine learning and applications (ICMLA)

LeCun, Y., Bengio, Y., & Hinton, G. (2015). Deep learning. nature, 521(7553), 436-444.

Lee, T., Puyol-Antón, E., Ruijsink, B., Shi, M., & King, A. P. (2026). Does a Rising Tide Lift All Boats? Bias Mitigation for AI-Based CMR Segmentation. *Lecture Notes in Computer Science, 15976 LNCS*, 84–93. DOI: 10.1007/978-3-032-05870-6_9

Lee, W.-J. (2024). SERVICE FAILURE BY HUMAN, SERVICE RECOVERY BY AI CHATBOT: THE IMPACT OF JUSTICE, AI EFFICACY ON RECOVERY EFFORT. *Virtual Economics*, *7*(4), 48–63. DOI: 10.34021/ve.2024.07.04(3)

Leslie, D. (2019). *Understanding artificial intelligence ethics and safety: A guide for the responsible design and implementation of AI systems*. The Alan Turing Institute.

Lewin, K. (1951). *Field Theory in Social Science*. Harper & Row.

Li, H., Yazdi, M., Nedjati, A., Moradi, R., Adumene, S., Dao, U., Moradi, A., Haghighi, A., Obeng, F. E., & Huang, C.-G. (2024). Harnessing AI for project risk management: a paradigm shift. In *Progressive decision-making tools and applications in project and operation management: Approaches, case studies, multi-criteria decision-making, multi-objective decision-making, decision under uncertainty* (pp. 253–272). Springer. DOI: 10.1007/978-3-031-51719-8_16

Li, J., Shen, Y., Zhou, W., & Chen, H. (2026). SearchExpert: A GenAI-driven framework for reasoning-intensive multimedia information fusion through fine-tuning and reinforcement learning. *Information Fusion, 126*, 103665. Advance online publication. DOI: 10.1016/j.inffus.2025.103665

LinkedIn Learning. (2023). Global Workplace Learning Report.

Linke, K. (2019). Traditional and agile management approaches. In *12th ILERA European Congress,* Düsseldorf, Deutschland.

Linkinen, T. (2024). *Generative artificial intelligences: Challenges and benefits for game development* Master's thesis, Tampere University].

Liontou, A. K., Zisimopoulos, S., & Dermitzakis, A. (2024). Leveraging Web Scraping and API Integration for Efficient Medical Device Data Management. *Global Clinical Engineering Journal, 6*(Special Issue 6), 51–56. DOI: 10.31354/globalce.v6iSI6.252

Liu, G., Tan, Q., Kou, H., Zhang, L., Wang, J., Lv, W., Dong, H., & Xiong, J. (2018). A flexible temperature sensor based on reduced graphene oxide for robot skin used in internet of things. *Sensors (Basel), 18*(5), 1400. DOI: 10.3390/s18051400 PMID: 29724037

Lizzio, A. (2025). From Artificial to Humane Intelligence (HI)–The Necessary Evolution of Ethical Diversity in AI.

Mahboob, M., Ahmed, M. R. U., Zia, Z., Ali, M. S., & Ahmed, A. K. (2024). Future of artificial intelligence in agile software development. *arXiv preprint arXiv:2408.00703.*

Maier-Hein, L., Reinke, A., Godau, P., Tizabi, M. D., Buettner, F., Christodoulou, E., Glocker, B., Isensee, F., Kleesiek, J., Kozubek, M., Reyes, M., Riegler, M. A., Wiesenfarth, M., Kavur, A. E., Sudre, C. H., Baumgartner, M., Eisenmann, M., Heckmann-Nötzel, D., Rädsch, T., & Jäger, P. F. (2024). Metrics reloaded: Recommendations for image analysis validation. *Nature Methods, 21*(2), 195–212. DOI: 10.1038/s41592-023-02151-z PMID: 38347141

Malhotra, R., & Meena, S. (2024). Empirical validation of machine learning techniques for heterogeneous cross-project change prediction and within-project change prediction. *Journal of Computational Science*, *76*, 102230. DOI: 10.1016/j.jocs.2024.102230

Marçal, D., Metrôlho, J., & Ribeiro, F. (2025). Integrating Sentiment Analysis into Agile Feedback Loops for Continuous Improvement. In *Applied Sciences* (Vol. 15, Issue 22, p. 12329). DOI: 10.3390/app152212329

Marchenko, V. (2025). Digital Freight Command. Available at *SSRN* 5527858.

Marion, T., Yuan, C., & Moghaddam, M. (2025). Integrating AI into the Front End of New Product Development: A Case Comparison of Traditional and Augmented Processes. *Research Technology Management*, *68*(2), 10–22. DOI: 10.1080/08956308.2024.2444142

Marr, B. (2019). *Artificial intelligence in practice: how 50 successful companies used AI and machine learning to solve problems*. John Wiley & Sons.

Martin, K., & Murphy, P. (2017). The role of data privacy in marketing. *Journal of the Academy of Marketing Science*, *45*(2), 135–155.

Martino, D., Perlangeli, C., Grottoli, B., La Rosa, L., & Pacella, M. (2025). A Knowledge-Driven Framework for AI-Augmented Business Process Management Systems: Bridging Explainability and Agile Knowledge Sharing. In *AI* (Vol. 6, Issue 6, p. 110). DOI: 10.3390/ai6060110

Martin, R., Hughes, D. J., Epitropaki, O., & Thomas, G. (2021). In pursuit of causality in leadership training research: A review and pragmatic recommendations. *The Leadership Quarterly*, *32*(5), 101375. DOI: 10.1016/j.leaqua.2019.101375

Maya, G. (2021 Jun 28). *Lists 26 ITIL Processes & 4 ITIL Functions*. Retrieved Jan 5, 2005, from https://www.itsm-docs.com/en-in/blogs/itil-concepts/itsm-processes-functions#:~:text=The%20function%20is%20a%20team,Technical%20Management%2C%20and%20Operations%20Management

Mayer, R., Davis, J., & Schoorman, F. (1995). An integrative model of organizational trust. *Academy of Management Review*, *20*(3), 709–734.

McAfee, A., & Brynjolfsson, E. (2017). *Machine, platform, crowd: Harnessing our digital future*. WW Norton & Company.

McKinsey & Company. (2023). The State of AI Transformation.

Mehrabi, N., Morstatter, F., Saxena, N., Lerman, K., & Galstyan, A. (2022). A Survey on Bias and Fairness in Machine Learning. *ACM Computing Surveys, 54*(6), 1–35. Advance online publication. DOI: 10.1145/3457607

Memarian, B., & Doleck, T. (2023). Fairness, Accountability, Transparency, and Ethics (FATE) in Artificial Intelligence (AI) and higher education: A systematic review. *Computers and Education: Artificial Intelligence, 5*(May), 100152. DOI: 10.1016/j.caeai.2023.100152

Menezes, R., Marinho, M., & Sampaio, S. (2024). Metrics for Large-Scale Agile Development: A Survey of the Brazilian Software Industry. *ACM International Conference Proceeding Series*, 210–219. DOI: 10.1145/3701625.3701660

Mergel, I., Gong, Y., & Bertot, J. C. (2018). Agile government: Systematic literature review and future research. *Government Information Quarterly, 35*(2), 291–298. DOI: 10.1016/j.giq.2018.04.003

Merkle, C. (2022). The Affect Heuristic and Financial Expectations: Risk, Return, and ESG. SSRN *Electronic Journal, July*. DOI: 10.2139/ssrn.4157854

Meyer, S., Newsome, D., Fuller, T., Newsome, K., & Ghezzi, P. M. (2021). Agility: What it is, how to measure it, and how to use it. *Behavior Analysis in Practice, 14*(3), 598–607. DOI: 10.1007/s40617-020-00465-4 PMID: 34631367

Miceli, M., Posada, J., & Yang, T. (2022). Studying up machine learning data: Why talk about bias when we mean power? Proceedings of the ACM on Human-Computer Interaction, 6(GROUP), 1-14.

Min, A. (2023). Artifical Intelligence and Bias: Challenges, Implications, and Remedies. *Journal of Social Research, 2*(11), 3808–3817. DOI: 10.55324/josr.v2i11.1477

Mishra, K., & Mishra, S. (2025). Artificial and Emotional Intelligence for Employee Engagement with E-Human Resource Management. *Intellectuals' Book Palace.*

Mishra, B. R., Selvakumar, P., Kaur, R., Kalshetti, P., Mishra, K. K., Sharma, M., & Manjunath, T. C. (2025). Innovation and Digital Transformation in the Public Sector Entities. In Santos Ferreira, A., & Lourenço dos Santos, C. (Eds.), *Enhancing Public Sector Accountability and Services Through Digital Innovation* (pp. 409–436). IGI Global Scientific Publishing. DOI: 10.4018/979-8-3693-9251-5.ch013

Misslisch, J., Bauer, T., Eibl, F., Neumann, M., Spanke, J., Schön, E.-M., & Przybyłek, A. (2026). Unlocking the OKR Framework: Insights into Benefits and Barriers for an Effective Implementation in Practice. *Lecture Notes in Computer Science, 16082 LNCS*, 90–107. DOI: 10.1007/978-3-032-04200-2_7

Mitchell, V. L. (2006). Knowledge integration and information technology project performance. *Management Information Systems Quarterly*, *30*(4), 919–939. DOI: 10.2307/25148759

Mohamed Noor, A. F., Moghavvemi, S., & Tajudeen, F. P. (2025). Identifying key factors of cybersecurity readiness in organizations: Insights from Malaysian critical infrastructure. *Computers & Security*, *159*, 104674. Advance online publication. DOI: 10.1016/j.cose.2025.104674

Mohammad, A., & Chirchir, B. (2024). Challenges of Integrating Artificial Intelligence in Software Project Planning: A Systematic Literature Review. In *Digital* (Vol. 4, Issue 3, pp. 555–571). DOI: 10.3390/digital4030028

Mohammadi, E., Thelwall, M., Cai, Y., Collier, T., Tahamtan, I., & Eftekhar, A. (2026). Is generative AI reshaping academic practices worldwide? A survey of adoption, benefits, and concerns. *Information Processing & Management*, *63*(1), 104350. Advance online publication. DOI: 10.1016/j.ipm.2025.104350

Mojabi, O. (2024). Harmonizing Agile transformation: Navigating software startup success through a hybrid journey of Scrum, Kanban-a Case Study analysis.

Moldovan, A., & Georgousis, I. (2024). Navigating Scrum-The Impact of Agile Leadership and Coaching on IT Project Outcomes.

Mollah, M. A., Rana, M., Amin, M. B., Sony, M. A. A. M., Rahaman, M. A., & Fenyves, V. (2024). Examining the role of AI-augmented HRM for sustainable performance: Key determinants for digital culture and organizational strategy. *Sustainability (Basel)*, *16*(24), 10843. DOI: 10.3390/su162410843

Mons, B., Neylon, C., Velterop, J., Dumontier, M., Da Silva Santos, L. O. B., & Wilkinson, M. D. (2017). Cloudy, increasingly FAIR; revisiting the FAIR Data guiding principles for the European Open Science Cloud. *Information Services & Use*, *37*(1), 49–56. DOI: 10.3233/ISU-170824

Morello, L. T., & Chick, J. C. (2025). Human-AI Symbiotic Theory (HAIST): Development, Multi-Framework Assessment, and AI-Assisted Validation in Academic Research. *Informatics (MDPI)*, *12*(3), 85. Advance online publication. DOI: 10.3390/informatics12030085

Morris, P. (2013). Reconstructing project management reprised: A knowledge perspective. *Project Management Journal*, *44*(5), 6–23. DOI: 10.1002/pmj.21369

Mullapudi, A. (2025). Predictive Paradigms and Strategic Insights for Enhancing AnalyticsDriven Project Management.

Munoko, I., & Miklos, H. L. B. (2025). The Ethical Implications of Using Artificial Intelligence in Auditing. *Journal of Business Ethics, 167*(2), 209–234. DOI: 10.1007/s10551-019-04407-1

Nabeel, M. Z. (2024). AI-enhanced project management systems for optimizing resource allocation and risk mitigation: Leveraging big data analysis to predict project outcomes and improve decision-making processes in complex projects. *Asian Journal of Multidisciplinary Research & Review, 5*(5), 53–65. DOI: 10.55662/AJMRR.2024.5502

Nabot, A., Alnaimat, F., Jebreen, I., Al-Qerem, A., & Ali, A. M. (2025). AI for Software Project Management: Predicting Delivery Times & Resource Allocation. *2025 12th International Conference on Information Technology (ICIT)*, 277–284. DOI: 10.1109/ICIT64950.2025.11049089

Naithani, K., Tiwari, S., & Kumari, S. (2025). *AI for Product Development.* Taylor & Francis Group. DOI: 10.1201/9781003536901

Nath, J., Kurni, M., & Choudhuri, S. S. (2024). *A Comprehensive Guide to Agile Transformation, Enterprise Innovation, and Productivity.* Cambridge Scholars Publishing.

Nedelkoska, L., & Quintini, G. (2018). Automation, skills use and training. OECD Social, Employment and Migration Working Papers, No. 202.

Nenni, M. E., De Felice, F., De Luca, C., & Forcina, A. (2025). How artificial intelligence will transform project management in the age of digitization: A systematic literature review. *Management Review Quarterly, 75*(2), 1669–1716. DOI: 10.1007/s11301-024-00418-z

Nesanır, M. O., Zenezini, G., Senvar, O., & Ottaviani, F. M. (2026). A Literature Review on the Integration of System Dynamics and Machine Learning/Artificial Intelligence in Addressing Environmental Matters. *IFIP Advances in Information and Communication Technology, 764 IFIPAI*, 370–384. DOI: 10.1007/978-3-032-03515-8_26

Neumann, M., Kuchel, T., Diebold, P., & Schön, E. M. (2024). Agile culture clash: Unveiling challenges in cultivating an agile mindset in organizations. *arXiv preprint arXiv:2405.15066.*

Newman, A., Donohue, R., & Eva, N. (2017). Psychological safety: A systematic review of the literature. *Human Resource Management Review, 27*(3), 521–535.

Nirupama, E., Seenivasan, S., Bhardwaj, K., Karunakaran, N. B., & Basava Aradhya, S. G., & Manjunath, T. C. (2025). Transforming Digital Supply Chains With Gamification and Metaverse Integration. In G. Malik, D. Singh, & R. Bansal (Eds.), *Addressing Practical Problems Through the Metaverse and Game-Inspired Mechanics* (pp. 123-152). IGI Global Scientific Publishing.

Nonaka, I., & Takeuchi, H. (2019). *The Wise Company: How Companies Create Continuous Innovation*. Oxford University Press.

Notaro, P., Cardoso, J., & Gerndt, M. (2021). A Survey of AIOps Methods for Failure Management. *ACM Trans. Intell. Syst. Technol. 12*, 6, Article 81 (December 2021), 45 pages. DOI: 10.1145/3483424

Ntoutsi, E., Fafalios, P., Gadiraju, U., Iosifidis, V., Nejdl, W., Vidal, M. E., Ruggieri, S., Turini, F., Papadopoulos, S., Krasanakis, E., Kompatsiaris, I., Kinder-Kurlanda, K., Wagner, C., Karimi, F., Fernandez, M., Alani, H., Berendt, B., Kruegel, T., Heinze, C., & Staab, S. (2020). Bias in data-driven artificial intelligence systems—An introductory survey. *Wiley Interdisciplinary Reviews. Data Mining and Knowledge Discovery*, *10*(3), 1–14. DOI: 10.1002/widm.1356

O'Neil, C. (2016). *Weapons of Math Destruction: How Big Data Increases Inequality and Threatens Democracy*. Crown.

Oloyede, J., & Owen, J. (2025). AI-Driven Knowledge Extraction: Managing Unstructured Data for Business Intelligence Author. *Available at SSRN* 5144223. DOI: 10.2139/ssrn.5144223

Oreg, S., Vakola, M., & Armenakis, A. (2011). Change recipients' reactions to organizational change: A 60-year review of quantitative studies. *The Journal of Applied Behavioral Science*, *47*(4), 461–524.

Organisation for Economic Co-operation and Development. (2019). *OECD principles on artificial intelligence*. https://www.oecd.org/going-digital/ai/principles/

Orozco, E. (2025). *FAST: Fully aligned strategic teams*. Solo Unicorn Press.

Owusu-Berko, L. (2025). Harnessing big data, machine learning, and sentiment analysis to optimize customer engagement, loyalty, and market positioning. *Int. J. Comput. Appl. Technol. Res*, *14*, 1–16.

Page, S. E. (2007). *The difference: How the power of diversity creates better groups, firms, schools, and societies*. Princeton University Press.

Pahune, S., & Akhtar, Z. (2025). Transitioning from MLOps to LLMOps: Navigating the unique challenges of large language models. *Information (Basel)*, *16*(2), 87. DOI: 10.3390/info16020087

Palani, H. K., Shelke, R., & Pagi, S. AIOps with Multi Cloud (June 8, 2023). Available at *SSRN*: https://ssrn.com/abstract=4473251 or , from https://papers.ssrn.com/sol3/papers.cfm?abstract_id=4473251DOI: 10.2139/ssrn.4473251

Pandey, B. K. (2023). AI-Based Automation Frameworks for IT Operations in a Digitally Transformed Environment. Distributed Learning and Broad Applications in Scientific Research, Annual, 9. https://ssrn.com/abstract=5101691

Pan, Y., & Zhang, L. (2021). A BIM-data mining integrated digital twin framework for advanced project management. *Automation in Construction*, *124*, 103564. DOI: 10.1016/j.autcon.2021.103564

Paramesha, M., Rane, N., & Rane, J. (2024). Big data analytics, artificial intelligence, machine learning, internet of things, and blockchain for enhanced business intelligence. *Artificial Intelligence, Machine Learning, Internet of Things, and Blockchain for Enhanced Business Intelligence (June 6, 2024).*

Parikh, N. A. (2025). Managing ai-first products: Roles, skills, challenges, and strategies of ai product managers. *IEEE Engineering Management Review*, *53*(5), 232–244. DOI: 10.1109/EMR.2025.3530942

Park, P. S., Goldstein, S., O'Gara, A., Chen, M., & Hendrycks, D. (2024). AI deception: A survey of examples, risks, and potential solutions. *Patterns (New York, N.Y.)*, *5*(5), 100988. DOI: 10.1016/j.patter.2024.100988 PMID: 38800366

Patary, C. L. (2019). *The Scrum Master Guidebook: A Reference For Obtaining Mastery*. Notion Press.

Patel, A., Laudya, R., Ragothaman, H., & Pandey, P. (2025). Applying Artificial Intelligence to DevOps: A Study on AI-Driven Anomaly Detection and Predictive Maintenance in Cloud Environments. *2025 1st International Conference on Secure IoT, Assured and Trusted Computing (SATC)*, 1–8. DOI: 10.1109/SATC65530.2025.11137316

Patel, D. K., Doshi, D. R., & Rawal, A. R. (2025). From Heuristics to AI: A Deep Dive into Software Project Resource Allocation. *2025 International Conference on Artificial Intelligence and Machine Vision (AIMV)*, 1–6. DOI: 10.1109/AIMV66517.2025.11203447

Paterniti, G. G., & Manzoni, L. (2018). Does scrum methodology impact team's subculture? A multiple case study exploration.

Patrucco, A. S., Canterino, F., & Minelgaite, I. (2022). How do scrum methodologies influence the team's cultural values? A multiple case study on agile teams in Nonsoftware industries. *IEEE Transactions on Engineering Management, 69*(6), 3503–3513. DOI: 10.1109/TEM.2022.3146717

Pawar, S., & Dhumal, V. (2024). The role of technology in transforming leadership management practices. *Multidisciplinary Reviews, 7*(4), 2024066–2024066. DOI: 10.31893/multirev.2024066

Pedreschi, D., Giannotti, F., Guidotti, R., Monreale, A., Ruggieri, S., & Turini, F. (2019). Meaningful explanations of black box AI decision systems. *Proceedings of the AAAI conference on artificial intelligence* DOI: 10.1609/aaai.v33i01.33019780

Pektaş, Ş. T. (2026). An Inquiry on the Usability of Generative AI in Design Education. *Lecture Notes in Computer Science, 15914 LNCS*, 393–402. DOI: 10.1007/978-3-031-98197-5_42

Pérez-Castillo, Y. J., Orantes-Jiménez, S. D., & Letelier-Torres, P. O. (2024). A systematic literature review on machine learning applications for agile project management. *Ingeniería, Investigación y Tecnología, 25*(3), 1–11. DOI: 10.22201/fi.25940732e.2024.25.3.017

Peurala, N. (2025). Preserving creative performance through AI integration–A qualitative study on how to lead AI integration in creative agencies.

Pichler, R. (2020). *How to lead in product management: practices to align stakeholders, guide development teams, and create value together*. Pichler Consulting.

Pillai, V. (2022). *Anomaly Detection for Innovators: Transforming Data into Breakthroughs*. Libertatem Media Private Limited.

Pineda, V. G., Valencia-Arias, A., Giraldo, F. E. L., & Zapata-Ochoa, E. A. (2026). Integrating artificial intelligence and quantum computing: A systematic literature review of features and applications. *International Journal of Cognitive Computing in Engineering, 7*, 26–39. DOI: 10.1016/j.ijcce.2025.08.002

Ping, D. (2024). *The Machine Learning Solutions Architect Handbook: Practical strategies and best practices on the ML lifecycle, system design, MLOps, and generative AI*. Packt Publishing Ltd.

Plante, M. (2025). A new symbiotic, holistic and gradualist model proposal for the concept of "living organism". *Theory in Biosciences, 144*(1), 45–65. DOI: 10.1007/s12064-024-00429-0 PMID: 39636364

Podeswa, H. (2021). *The Agile Guide to Business Analysis and Planning: From Strategic Plan to Continuous Value Delivery*. Addison-Wesley Professional.

Porter, M., & Kramer, M. (2011). Creating shared value. *Harvard Business Review, 89*(1–2), 62–77.

Portman, D. G. (2020). *Are you an elite DevOps performer? Find out with the four keys project.*

Potts, W. C., & Carver, C. (2024, May). Best practices implementing aiops in large organizations. In *2024 International Conference on Smart Applications, Communications and Networking (SmartNets)* (pp. 1-5). IEEE. DOI: 10.1109/SmartNets61466.2024.10577643

Prasad, P., & Rich, C. (2018). *Market guide for AIOps platforms*. Retrieved March, 12(2020), 2-9. https://cloudaims.co.in/wp-content/uploads/2021/02/Market-Guide-for-AIOps-Platforms-Gartner-Reprint-1.pdf. Gartner ID: G00340492

Project Management Institute. (2021). *Pulse of the Profession 2021: The Future of Work*. PMI.

Psyché, V., Tremblay, D. G., Miladi, F., & Yagoubi, A. (2023). A competency framework for training of AI projects managers in the digital and AI Era. *Open Journal of Social Sciences, 11*(5), 537–560. DOI: 10.4236/jss.2023.115032

Puplampu, R. (2024). *What Everyone Should Know About the Rise of AI: AI Transparency, Privacy, and Ethics Best Practices*. Puplampu Books.

PwC. (2024). AI and Ethics in the Digital Economy. PwC Global Report.

PwC. (2024). *Global consumer insights survey on data trust and artificial intelligence*. PricewaterhouseCoopers.

Quaquebeke, N. V., & Gerpott, F. H. (2023). The now, new, and next of digital leadership: How Artificial Intelligence (AI) will take over and change leadership as we know it. *Journal of Leadership & Organizational Studies, 30*(3), 265–275. DOI: 10.1177/15480518231181731

Radwan, A. M., Abdel-Fattah, M. A., & Mohamed, W. (2025). Smart Agile Prioritization and Clustering: An AI-Driven Approach for Requirements Prioritization. *IEEE Access : Practical Innovations, Open Solutions, 13*, 127335–127350. DOI: 10.1109/ACCESS.2025.3589959

Rahayu, S., & Bablu, T. A. (2023). AI-Augmented Learning and Development Platforms: Transforming Employee Training and Skill Enhancement. *Journal of Computing Innovations and Applications, 1*(01), 19–38.

Rahmadi, D., & Anjani, K. T. (2024). A COMPREHENSIVE REVIEW OF BIAS IN AI ALGORITHMS. *Nusantara Hasana Journal, 1*(7), 132–137.

Rai, A., Constantinides, P., & Sarker, S. (2020). Next-generation digital platforms: Toward human–AI hybrids. *Management Information Systems Quarterly, 44*(3), iii–ix. https://aisel.aisnet.org/misq/vol43/iss1/2/. DOI: 10.25300/MISQ/2020/441E0

Raikov, A. N., & Pirani, M. (2022). Human-machine duality: What's next in cognitive aspects of artificial intelligence? *IEEE Access : Practical Innovations, Open Solutions, 10*, 56296–56315. DOI: 10.1109/ACCESS.2022.3177657

Raisch, S., & Krakowski, S. (2021). Artificial intelligence and management: The automation–augmentation paradox. *Academy of Management Review, 46*(1), 192–210.

Raji, I. D., Smart, A., White, R. N., Mitchell, M., Gebru, T., Hutchinson, B., & Barnes, P. (2020). Closing the AI accountability gap. *Proceedings of the 2020 Conference on Fairness, Accountability, and Transparency*, 33–44. DOI: 10.1145/3351095.3372873

Raji, I. D., Smart, A., White, R. N., Mitchell, M., Gebru, T., Hutchinson, B., Smith-Loud, J., Theron, D., & Barnes, P. (2020). Closing the AI accountability gap: Defining an end-to-end framework for internal algorithmic auditing. *Proceedings of the 2020 Conference on Fairness, Accountability, and Transparency*, 33–44.

Raj, M., & Seamans, R. (2019). Artificial intelligence, labor, productivity, and the need for firm-level data. In *The economics of artificial intelligence: An agenda* (pp. 553–565). University of Chicago Press.

Rakova, B., Yang, J., Cramer, H., & Chowdhury, R. (2021). Where responsible AI meets reality: Practitioner perspectives on enablers for shifting organizational practices. *Proceedings of the ACM on Human-Computer Interaction*, 5(CSCW1), 1-23.DOI: 10.1145/3449081

Raman, M. S., Koppa, K. B., Chithambar Gupta, V., Bhat, V. A., & Guru Basava Aradhya, S. (2025). Digital Transformation and Sustainability Artificial Intelligence and Sustainable Development. In Yıldırım, D., Yıldırım, S., & Kandpal, V. (Eds.), *Effects of Digitalization and Circular Economy on Sustainable Policy and Climate Change Prevention* (pp. 69–96). IGI Global Scientific Publishing. DOI: 10.4018/979-8-3693-9909-5.ch003

Ranjeeth, S. (2026). An Organisational Culture Framework to Guide the Transition to an Agile Software Development Methodology. *Communications in Computer and Information Science, 2583 CCIS*, 112–128. DOI: 10.1007/978-3-031-96262-2_9

Ransbotham, S., Kiron, D., Candelon, F., Khodabandeh, S., & Chu, M. (2022). Achieving individual—and organizational—value with AI. *MIT Sloan Management Review*.

Ransbotham, S., Kiron, D., Gerbert, P., & Reeves, M. (2020). Expanding AI's impact with organizational learning. *MIT Sloan Management Review*.

Rauscher, K. (2024). *Successful Strategies Government Executive Stakeholders Use to Mitigate Higher Project Costs and User Adoption Failure Rates* (Doctoral dissertation, Walden University).

Reddy, S., Allan, S., Coghlan, S., & Cooper, P. (2020). A governance model for the application of AI in health care. *Journal of the American Medical Informatics Association : JAMIA, 27*(3), 491–497. DOI: 10.1093/jamia/ocz192 PMID: 31682262

Reger, E. A., & Rozell, E. J. (2023). The master of accountancy:understanding factors influencing intentions and behaviors toward accounting graduate education. In *Journal of Theoretical Accounting Research* (Vol. 19, Issue 1).

Remil, Y., Bendimerad, A., Mathonat, R., & Kaytoue, M. (2024). Aiops solutions for incident management: Technical guidelines and a comprehensive literature review. arXiv preprint /arXiv.2404.01363DOI: 10.48550

Reznikov, R. (2025). Enhancing Project Management Success through Artificial Intelligence. *International Journal of Multidisciplinary Research and Growth Evaluation, 6*(1), 1036–1046. DOI: 10.54660/.IJMRGE.2025.6.1.1036-1046

Riedinger, C., Netscher, M., Zimmermann, S., & Huber, M. (2026). Implementing Business-IT Integration in Digital Enterprises Using Organizational Capabilities. *Lecture Notes in Business Information Processing, 555 LNBIP*, 58–78. DOI: 10.1007/978-3-031-93580-0_3

Rigby, D. K., Sutherland, J., & Noble, A. (2018). Agile at scale. *Harvard Business Review, 96*(3), 88–96.

Rigby, D., Elk, S., & Berez, S. (2020). *Doing agile right: Transformation without chaos*. Harvard Business Press.

Rigby, D., Sutherland, J., & Takeuchi, H. (2016). Embracing Agile. *Harvard Business Review, 94*(5), 40–50.

Rodrigues, P. G., Bárrios, M. J., & Mendes, M. S. G. (2025). Waiting for Specialists: A Multi-Priority and Multi-Speciality Analysis. *The International Journal of Health Planning and Management, 40*(6), 1248–1278. DOI: 10.1002/hpm.70007 PMID: 40650993

Romao, L., Villamizar, H., Oliveira, R., Alonso, S., & Kalinowski, M. (2026). Agile Management for Machine Learning: A Systematic Mapping Study. *Lecture Notes in Computer Science, 16082 LNCS*, 350–360. DOI: 10.1007/978-3-032-04200-2_24

Rouzrokh, P., Khosravi, B., Faghani, S., Moassefi, M., Garcia, D. V. V., Singh, Y., Zhang, K., Conte, G. M., & Erickson, B. J. (2022). Mitigating Bias in Radiology Machine Learning: 1. Data Handling. *Radiology. Artificial Intelligence*, *4*(5), e210290. Advance online publication. DOI: 10.1148/ryai.210290 PMID: 36204544

Russell, S., Norvig, P., & Intelligence, A. (1995). A modern approach. Artificial Intelligence. Prentice-Hall. *Egnlewood Cliffs*, *25*(27), 79–80.

Saaty, T. L. (2008). Decision making with the analytic hierarchy process. *International Journal of Services Sciences*, *1*(1), 83–98. DOI: 10.1504/IJSSCI.2008.017590

Salimimoghadam, S., Ghanbaripour, A. N., Tumpa, R. J., Kamel Rahimi, A., Golmoradi, M., Rashidian, S., & Skitmore, M. (2025). The Rise of Artificial Intelligence in Project Management: A Systematic Literature Review of Current Opportunities, Enablers, and Barriers. *Buildings (Basel, Switzerland)*, *15*(7), 1130. DOI: 10.3390/buildings15071130

Samhan, A. AlHajHassan, S., Dabaa't, S. A., & Elrashidi, A. (2024). A Review of AI-Assisted Impact Analysis for Software Requirements Change: Challenges and Future Directions. *2024 25th International Arab Conference on Information Technology (ACIT)*, 1–13. DOI: 10.1109/ACIT62805.2024.10877072

Sami, M. A., Rehman, A., Ahmad, Z., & Bano, N. (2025). *Explainable AIOps: A Deep Survey on Trust worthy and Transparent AI in Cloud-Scale DevOps Automation. Spectrum of Engineering Sciences.*

Samuel, S., Meilani, Y. F. C. P., Wanasida, A. S., & Napitupulu, P. E. (2025). *Human Capital in The AI Era*. Penerbit NEM.

Sandén, T. (2024). U*nveiling Anomaly Detection: Navigating Cultural Shifts and Model Dynamics in AIOps Implementations.* https://www.diva-portal.org/smash/get/diva2:1878820/FULLTEXT01.pdf

Sanusi, B. O. (2024). The role of data-driven decision-making in reducing project delays and cost overruns in civil engineering projects. *SAMRIDDHI: A Journal of Physical Sciences. Engineering and Technology*, *16*(04), 182–192.

Sarker, I. H. (2021). Machine learning: Algorithms, real-world applications and research directions. *SN Computer Science*, *2*(3), 1–21.

Sarma, A. D. N. (2021). A generic architecture for alert notification and monitoring system based on event processing framework. *International Journal of Business Performance Management*, *22*(4), 426–442. DOI: 10.1504/IJBPM.2021.118612

Sartori, L., & Theodorou, A. (2022). A sociotechnical perspective for the future of AI: Narratives, inequalities, and human control. *Ethics and Information Technology*, *24*(1), 4. DOI: 10.1007/s10676-022-09624-3

Sarwar, H., & Rahman, M. (2024). A Systematic Short Review of Machine Learning and Artificial Intelligence Integration in Current Project Management Techniques. *2024 IEEE 4th International Conference on Software Engineering and Artificial Intelligence (SEAI)*, 262–270. DOI: 10.1109/SEAI62072.2024.10674089

Savaş, S. (2025). Artificial intelligence in construction project management: Trends, challenges and future directions. *Journal of Design for Resilience in Architecture and Planning*, *6*(2), 221–238. DOI: 10.47818/DRArch.2025.v6i2165

Schär, B., Jüngling, S., & Thönssen, B. (2015). Towards an agile requirements engineering process combining HERMES 5 and SCRUM. In *2015 International Conference on Enterprise Systems (ES)* (pp. 98-109). IEEE. DOI: 10.1109/ES.2015.17

Schein, E. (2017). *Organizational Culture and Leadership*. Wiley.

Schmidt, J., & Heidenreich, S. (2018). The role of human capital for entrepreneurial decision-making-investigating experience, skills and knowledge as antecedents to effectuation and causation. *International Journal of Entrepreneurial Venturing*, *10*(3), 287–311. DOI: 10.1504/IJEV.2018.093226

Schwaber, K., & Sutherland, J. (2020). The scrum guide. *Scrum Alliance*, *21*(19), 1.

Sciences, N. A. o., Medicine, Engineering, D. o., Sciences, P., Science, C., Board, T., Alert, C. o. t. F. o. E., Systems, W., & Directions, R. (2018). Emergency alert and warning systems: Current knowledge and future research directions.

Sculley, D., Holt, G., Golovin, D., Davydov, E., Phillips, T., Ebner, D., . . . Dennison, D. (2015). Hidden technical debt in machine learning systems. *Advances in Neural Information Processing Systems*, 28, 2503–2511. https://proceedings.neurips.cc/paper_files/paper/2015/file/86df7dcfd896fcaf2674f757a2463eba-Paper.pdf

Seffe, N. S., Odzaly, E. E., & Samah, K. A. F. A. (2024). Data-driven Strategies for Enhanced Risk Management Performance in Software Development Perspective: an Agile Implementation. *2024 IEEE 22nd Student Conference on Research and Development (SCOReD)*, 122–127. DOI: 10.1109/SCOReD64708.2024.10872763

Sekar, A. (2025). AIOps: Transforming Management of Large-Scale Distributed Systems. *European Journal of Computer Science and Information Technology, 13*(5), 1–17.

Sekti, B. A. (2025a). Machine learning and artificial intelligence (AI) in manufacturing. In *Integrating Digital Innovation and Integrated Frameworks in Manufacturing* (pp. 255–292). DOI: 10.4018/979-8-3373-1082-4.ch011

Sekti, B. A. (2025b). Machine Learning vs. AI: Key Concepts. In *Implementing Enterprise Cybersecurity With AI* (pp. 1–27). DOI: 10.4018/979-8-3373-2252-0.ch001

Sekti, B. A., Laksono, M. N. G., Laksono, M. I. A., Widodo, A. M., Anwar, N., & Tiaraputri, Z. A. (2025). Principles of green computing in information security. In *Sustainable Information Security in the Age of AI and Green Computing* (pp. 1–16). DOI: 10.4018/979-8-3693-8034-5.ch001

Semenov, S., Tsukur, V., Molokanova, V., Muchacki, M., Litawa, G., Mozhaiev, M., & Petrovska, I. (2025). Mathematical Model of the Software Development Process with Hybrid Management Elements. In *Applied Sciences* (Vol. 15, Issue 21, p. 11667). DOI: 10.3390/app152111667

Senge, P. (2006). *The Fifth Discipline: The Art and Practice of the Learning Organization*. Doubleday.

Senge, P. (2019). *The Fifth Discipline*. The Art & Practice of The Learning Organization.

Seufert, S., & Spirgi, J. (2024). Navigating AI Transformation: Human Resource Development Strategies for Corporate Learning. *International Journal of Advanced Corporate Learning, 17*(4), 80–93. DOI: 10.3991/ijac.v17i4.47443

Sharma, K., Kumar, P., & Özen, E. (2024). Ethical Considerations in Data Analytics: Challenges, Principles, and Best Practices. In *Data Alchemy in the Insurance Industry: The Transformative Power of Big Data Analytics* (pp. 41-48). Emerald Publishing Limited.

Sharma, S., & Arjunan, T. (2023). Natural language processing for detecting anomalies and intrusions in unstructured cybersecurity data. *International Journal of Information and Cybersecurity, 7*(12), 1–24.

Shastri, Y., Hoda, R., & Amor, R. (2021). Spearheading agile: The role of the scrum master in agile projects. *Empirical Software Engineering, 26*(1), 3. DOI: 10.1007/s10664-020-09899-4

She, Y., & Yin, B. (2026). Enabling Authenticated Query Services on Multi-dimensional Data in Collaborative Blockchain. *Lecture Notes of the Institute for Computer Sciences, Social-Informatics and Telecommunications Engineering, LNICST, 625 LNICST*, 3–22. DOI: 10.1007/978-3-031-93254-0_1

Shen, S., Zhang, J., Huang, D., & Xiao, J. (2020, August). Evolving from traditional systems to AIOps: design, implementation and measurements. In *2020 IEEE International Conference on Advances in Electrical Engineering and Computer Applications (AEECA)* (pp. 276-280). IEEE. DOI: 10.1109/AEECA49918.2020.9213650

Shevchenko, I., Liubokhynets, L., Zvarych, I., Brodovska, O., & Bril, M. (2023). ANTIFRAGILE IN THE GLOBAL ECONOMY AS AN INDICATOR OF ECONOMIC DEVELOPMENT. *Financial and Credit Activity: Problems of Theory and Practice*, *6*(53), 274–286. DOI: 10.55643/fcaptp.6.53.2023.4203

Shmueli, G., & Ray, S. (2024). Reimagining the Journal Editorial Process: An AI-Augmented Versus an AI-Driven Future. *Journal of the Association for Information Systems*, *25*(1), 10. DOI: 10.17705/1jais.00864

Silva, R., & Santos, G. (2023). Surveying the Academic Literature on the Use of OKR (Objective and Key Results). *ACM International Conference Proceeding Series*, 427–434. DOI: 10.1145/3592813.3592934

Sindiramutty, S. R., Prabagaran, K. R. V., Akbar, R., Hussain, M., & Malik, N. A. (2025). Generative AI for secure user interface (UI) design. In *Reshaping CyberSecurity With Generative AI Techniques* (pp. 333–394). IGI Global Scientific Publishing.

Singh, A., Sethu, S. G., & Chaudhary, R. (2024). Artificial Intelligence in Storytelling: A Critical Analysis of Narrative Authenticity, Cultural Impact, and the Future of Creative Industries. Library of Progress-Library Science, Information Technology & Computer, 44(3).

Singh, M. (2025). Enhancing site reliability engineering through AIOps: A framework for next-generation IT operations. *Asian Journal of Research in Computer Science*, *18*(4), 10–9734. https://journalajrcos.com/index.php/AJRCOS/article/view/619. DOI: 10.9734/ajrcos/2025/v18i4619

Sivanand, R., Selvakumar, P., & Sharma, N. (2025). Navneet Sharma, Nanotechnology Applications in Cancer Drug Delivery Systems: A Review. *Journal of Environmental Nanotechnology*, *14*(2), 458–470. DOI: 10.13074/jent.2025.06.2511221

Slimi, Z., & Carballido, B. V. (2023). Navigating the Ethical Challenges of Artificial Intelligence in Higher Education: An Analysis of Seven Global AI Ethics Policies. *TEM Journal*, *12*(2), 590–602. https://doi.org/DOI: 10.18421/TEM122-02

Sokol, K., Santos-Rodriguez, R., & Flach, P. (2022). Fat Forensics: A Python toolbox for algorithmic fairness, accountability and transparency. *Software Impacts*, *14*, 100406. DOI: 10.1016/j.simpa.2022.100406

Spichkova, M., Iwan, K., Zwart, M., Lee, H., Yoon, Y., & Qin, X. (2025). Advanced approach for Agile/Scrum Process: RetroAI++. *arXiv preprint arXiv:2506.15172.*

Sreerangapuri, A. (2021). IT Service Management Transformation: Implementing AIOps for Proactive Service Delivery. *NeuroQuantology: An Interdisciplinary Journal of Neuroscience and Quantum Physics*, *19*(10). Advance online publication. DOI: 10.48047/nq.2021.19.10.NQ21220

Stahl, B. (2022). *Ethics of Emerging Technologies: The AI Context*. Routledge.

Steimers, A., & Schneider, M. (2022). Sources of Risk of AI Systems. *International Journal of Environmental Research and Public Health*, *19*(6), 3641. Advance online publication. DOI: 10.3390/ijerph19063641 PMID: 35329328

Sun, L., Chan, A., Chang, Y. S., & Dow, S. P. (2024, March). ReviewFlow: Intelligent scaffolding to support academic peer reviewing. In *Proceedings of the 29th International Conference on Intelligent User Interfaces* (pp. 120-137). DOI: 10.1145/3640543.3645159

Sutherland, J., & Schwaber, K. (2013). The scrum guide. *The definitive guide to scrum: The rules of the game. Scrum. org, 268*, 19.

Tangi, L., Müller, A. P. R., & Janssen, M. (2025). AI-augmented government transformation: Organisational transformation and the sociotechnical implications of artificial intelligence in public administrations. *Government Information Quarterly*, *42*(3), 102055. DOI: 10.1016/j.giq.2025.102055

Tansurat, P., & Gerdsri, N. (2024). Responsive Scenario-based Roadmapping: Applying System Dynamics to Enhance Scenario-based Roadmapping. *PICMET 2024 - 2024 Portland International Conference on Management of Engineering and Technology: Technology Management in the Artificial Intelligence Era, Proceedings.* DOI: 10.23919/PICMET64035.2024.10653350

Tarafdar, M., Cooper, C. L., & Stich, J. F. (2019). The technostress trifecta Techno eustress, techno distress and design. *Information Systems Journal*, *29*(1), 6–42. DOI: 10.1111/isj.12169

Tasneem, N., Zulzalil, H. B., & Hassan, S. (2025). Enhancing Agile Software Development: A Systematic Literature Review of Requirement Prioritization and Reprioritization Techniques. *IEEE Access : Practical Innovations, Open Solutions*, *13*, 32993–33034. DOI: 10.1109/ACCESS.2025.3539357

Teece, D. J., Pisano, G., & Shuen, A. (1997). Dynamic capabilities and strategic management. *Strategic Management Journal*, 18(7), 509–533. : AID-SMJ882>3.0. CO;2-Z

Teece, D. J. (2018). Business models and dynamic capabilities. *Long Range Planning*, *51*(1), 40–49. DOI: 10.1016/j.lrp.2017.06.007

Teichmann, F. (2026). Cybersecurity risks in mining's operational technology: Implications of OT vulnerabilities and EU NIS2 compliance. *The Extractive Industries and Society*, *25*, 101774. Advance online publication. DOI: 10.1016/j.exis.2025.101774

Tejani, A. S., Ng, Y. S., Xi, Y., & Rayan, J. C. (2024). Understanding and Mitigating Bias in Imaging Artificial Intelligence. *Radiographics*, *44*(5), e230067. Advance online publication. DOI: 10.1148/rg.230067 PMID: 38635456

Telkamp, J. B., & Anderson, M. H. (2022). The Implications of Diverse Human Moral Foundations for Assessing the Ethicality of Artificial Intelligence. *Journal of Business Ethics*, *178*(4), 961–976. DOI: 10.1007/s10551-022-05057-6

Tenakwah, E. S., & Watson, C. (2025). Embracing the AI/automation age: Preparing your workforce for humans and machines working together. *Strategy and Leadership*, *53*(1), 32–48. DOI: 10.1108/SL-05-2024-0040

Tong, B. G., Liang, Z., He, X., Yang, F., Yang, L., & Gao, L. (2025). AI-driven dynamic psychological measurement: Correcting university student mental health scales using daily behavioral and cognitive data. *Frontiers in Digital Health*, *7*, 1615250. Advance online publication. DOI: 10.3389/fdgth.2025.1615250 PMID: 41395629

Trist, E. L., & Bamforth, K. W. (1951). Some social and psychological consequences of the longwall method of coal-getting. *Human Relations*, *4*(1), 3–38. DOI: 10.1177/001872675100400101

Truss, A. (2024). Agile development processes in IT support work.

Tsarouhas, P., & Grigoriadis, K. (2025). A socio-technical framework for AI trust in public administration. *Transforming Government: People, Process and Policy*, 1-22

Tupsakhare, P. (2022). Enhancing Agile Methodologies with AI: Driving Efficiency and Innovation. *European Journal of Advances in Engineering and Technology*, *9*(10), 66–71.

UNESCO. (2023). *Recommendation on the Ethics of Artificial Intelligence*. UNESCO Publishing.

UNESCO. (2024). Gender Equality and Digital Inclusion Report.

Uys, G., Meyer, A., & Niemann, W. (2019). Taxonomies of trust in supply chain risk management in the South African third party logistics industry. *Acta Commercii, 19*(1). Advance online publication. DOI: 10.4102/ac.v19i1.792

Van Der Aalst, W. (2016). Data science in action. In *Process mining: Data science in action* (pp. 3–23). Springer Berlin Heidelberg.

Van Veenstra, A. F., Klievink, B., & Janssen, M. (2018). Governance of AI: Balancing benefits and risks. Government Information Quarterly, 35(4), 611–619.

Velikov, V., & Ivanova, G. (2025). Intelligent Software Project Management: A Novel Approach to Risk Analysis and Resource Allocation. *2025 International Conference on Computer Systems and Technologies (CompSysTech)*, 1–8. DOI: 10.1109/CompSysTech65493.2025.11136946

Venkatesh, V., Thong, J. Y. L., & Xu, X. (2016). Unified theory of acceptance and use of technology: A synthesis and the road ahead. *Journal of the Association for Information Systems, 17*(5), 328–376. https://aisel.aisnet.org/jais/vol17/iss5/1. DOI: 10.17705/1jais.00428

Vitui, A., & Chen, T. (2025). Empowering AIOps: Leveraging Large Language Models for IT Operations Management. In *Companion Proceedings of the 33rd ACM Symposium on the Foundations of Software Engineering* (FSE '25), June 23–27, 2025, Trondheim, Norway. ACM, New York, NY, USA ArXiv, abs/2501.12461. DOI: 10.48550/arXiv.2501.12461

Vos, P., & Van der Voordt, T. (2002). Tomorrow's offices through today's eyes: Effects of innovation in the working environment. *Journal of Corporate Real Estate, 4*(1), 4865. DOI: 10.1108/14630010210811778

Voutama, A. V. (2025). Generative Artificial Intelligence in Agile Product Management: Optimizing Task Coordination and Team Efficiency in Software Development. *The Indonesian Journal of Computer Science, 14*(3).

Wach, K., Duong, C. D., Ejdys, J., Kazlauskaitė, R., Korzynski, P., Mazurek, G., Paliszkiewicz, J., & Ziemba, E. (2023). The dark side of generative artificial intelligence: A critical analysis of controversies and risks of ChatGPT. *Entrepreneurial Business and Economics Review, 11*(2), 7–30. DOI: 10.15678/EBER.2023.110201

Wamba, S. F., Akter, S., Edwards, A., Chopin, G., & Gnanzou, D. (2015). How 'big data'can make big impact: Findings from a systematic review and a longitudinal case study. *International Journal of Production Economics, 165*, 234–246.

Wang, G., Oh, I. S., Courtright, S. H., & Colbert, A. E. (2011). Transformational leadership and performance across criteria and levels: A meta-analytic review. *Journal of Management*, *37*(2), 223–270.

Wang, S., Liu, W., Wu, J., Cao, L., Meng, Q., & Kennedy, P. J. (2016). Training deep neural networks on imbalanced data sets. *Proceedings of the International Joint Conference on Neural Networks, 2016-Octob*, 4368–4374. DOI: 10.1109/IJCNN.2016.7727770

Warale, P. N., Limbore, N. V., Anute, N., Ahluwalia, G. K., & Raut, A. (2025). AI-Enhanced Customer Engagement and Experience: Chatbots, Virtual Assistants, and AI-Powered Customer Interactions. In Hussain, Z., Khan, A., Uzir, M., Sharipudin, M., & Shaheen, A. (Eds.), *Impacts of AI-Generated Content on Brand Reputation* (pp. 335–362). IGI Global Scientific Publishing. DOI: 10.4018/979-8-3373-4327-3.ch014

Wasserkrug, S., Boussioux, L., & Sun, W. (2024). Combining large language models and or/ms to make smarter decisions. In *Tutorials in Operations Research: Smarter Decisions for a Better World* (pp. 1–49). INFORMS. DOI: 10.1287/educ.2024.0275

Weiner, S. P., & McMahon, M. (2020). Action taking augmented by artificial intelligence. *Employee surveys and sensing: Driving organizational culture and performance*, 338-354.

Wezel, A., Gemmill Herren, B., Kerr, R. B., Barrios, E., Luiz, A., Gonçalves, R., & Sinclair, F. (2019). Agroecological principles and elements and their implications for transitioning to sustainable food systems. A review. *Agronomy for Sustainable Development*. Advance online publication. DOI: 10.1007/s13593-020-00646-z

White, G. R. T., Samuel, A., Jones, P., Madhavan, N., Afolayan, A., Abdullah, A., & Kaushik, T. (2024). Mapping the ethic-theoretical foundations of artificial intelligence research. *Thunderbird International Business Review*, *66*(2), 171–183. DOI: 10.1002/tie.22368

Wilkinson, M. D., Dumontier, M., Aalbersberg, I., Appleton, G., Axton, M., Baak, A., Blomberg, N., Boiten, J.-W., da Silva Santos, L. B., Bourne, P. E., Bouwman, J., Brookes, A. J., Clark, T., Crosas, M., Dillo, I., Dumon, O., Edmunds, S., Evelo, C. T., Finkers, R., & Mons, B. (2016). Comment: The FAIR Guiding Principles for scientific data management and stewardship. *Scientific Data*, *3*(1), 1–9. DOI: 10.1038/sdata.2016.18 PMID: 26978244

Williams, J. L. (2007). *Information theoretic sensor management*. Massachusetts Institute of Technology.

Wilson, C., Ghosh, A., Jiang, S., Mislove, A., Baker, L., Szary, J., Trindel, K., & Polli, F. (2021). Building and auditing fair algorithms: A case study in candidate screening. *FAccT 2021 - Proceedings of the 2021 ACM Conference on Fairness, Accountability, and Transparency, March*, 666–677. DOI: 10.1145/3442188.3445928

Wilson, R., & Tyson, J. (2025). *Age of Invisible Machines: A Guide to Orchestrating AI Agents and Making Organizations More Self-Driving, Revised and Updated.* John Wiley & Sons.

Wirtz, B. W., Weyerer, J. C., & Geyer, C. (2019). Artificial intelligence and the public sector Applications and challenges. *International Journal of Public Administration, 42*(7), 596–615. DOI: 10.1080/01900692.2018.1498103

Witten, I. H., Frank, E., Hall, M. A., Pal, C. J., & Data, M. (2005, June). Practical machine learning tools and techniques. In Data mining (Vol. 2, No. 4, pp. 403-413). Amsterdam, The Netherlands: Elsevier.

World Economic Forum. (2024). The Future of Jobs Report. WEF Publications.

World Economic Forum. (2024). The future of jobs report. WEF.

Wu, Y., Sicard, B., & Gadsden, S. A. (2024). A review of physics-informed machine learning methods with applications to condition monitoring and anomaly detection. *arXiv preprint arXiv:2401.11860.*

Xiao, L., Madanian, S., Li, W., & Xiao, Y. (2023). Enhancing resource allocation in IT projects: the potentials of deep learning-based recommendation systems and data-driven approaches. In *Australasian Conference on Data Science and Machine Learning* (pp. 226-238). Singapore: Springer Nature Singapore.

Xu, R. (2026). Optimizing ML classifiers for superior intrusion detection in resource-constrained smart homes. *International Journal of Cognitive Computing in Engineering, 7*, 58–73. DOI: 10.1016/j.ijcce.2025.08.003

Yang, J., Qi, X., & Yu, G. (2005). Disruption management in production planning. [NRL]. *Naval Research Logistics, 52*(5), 420–442. DOI: 10.1002/nav.20087

Yan, L., Cheng, C., Zhang, Y., & Miao, Z. (2025). Large Language Models in International Business Research: Opportunities, Challenges, and Prospects. *MIR. Management International Review, 65*(6), 1–29. DOI: 10.1007/s11575-025-00601-8

Yarram, S., & Bittla, S. R. (2023). Predictive Test Automation: Shaping the Future of Quality Engineering in Enterprise Platforms. Available at *SSRN* 5132329.

Yigitcanlar, T., Desouza, K. C., Butler, L., & Roozkhosh, F. (2020). Contributions and risks of artificial intelligence (AI) in building smarter cities: Insights from a systematic review of the literature. *Energies, 13*(6), 1473. Advance online publication. DOI: 10.3390/en13061473

Yilmaz, K., & Deniz, K. Z. (2024). Natural Language Processing and Machine Learning Applications For Assessment and Evaluation in Education: Opportunities and New Approaches. *Egitimde ve Psikolojide Ölçme ve Degerlendirme Dergisi, 15*(4), 421–445. DOI: 10.21031/epod.1551568

Yu, A. C., Mohajer, B., & Eng, J. (2022). External Validation of Deep Learning Algorithms for Radiologic Diagnosis: A Systematic Review. *Radiology. Artificial Intelligence*, *4*(3), 1–9. DOI: 10.1148/ryai.210064 PMID: 35652114

Zadeh, E. K., Khoulenjani, A. B., & Safaei, M. (2024). Integrating AI for agile Project Management: Innovations, challenges, and benefits. [IJIECM]. *International Journal of Industrial Engineering and Construction Management*, *1*(2), 1–10. https://www.ijiecm.com/index.php/ijiecm/article/view/1#

Zaripour, M. (2024). *Boost Your Team's Speed: Quick and Easy Ways to Get Things Done Faster*. Mohammad Zaripour.

Zhang, C., & Zhao, P. (2021). Federated learning for edge computing: Challenges and opportunities. IEEE Network, 35(1), 12–18.

Zhang, W., Bifet, A., Zhang, X., Weiss, J. C., & Nejdl, W. (2021). FARF: A Fair and Adaptive Random Forests Classifier. *Lecture Notes in Computer Science (Including Subseries Lecture Notes in Artificial Intelligence and Lecture Notes in Bioinformatics), 12713 LNAI*, 245–256. DOI: 10.1007/978-3-030-75765-6_20

Zhang, J., & Bareinboim, E. (2018). Fairness in decision-making the causal explanation formula. *32nd AAAI Conference on Artificial Intelligence, AAAI 2018*, 2037–2045. DOI: 10.1609/aaai.v32i1.11564

Zhang, J., Qi, Y., Xu, H., Chang, M., & Yang, L. (2025). Promoting the Sustainable Development of Organizations: Technological Capability, Environmental Uncertainty, and Enterprise Exploratory Innovation. *Sustainability (Basel)*, *17*(14), 6251. Advance online publication. DOI: 10.3390/su17146251

Zhang, L., Jia, T., Jia, M., Wu, Y., Liu, A., Yang, Y., & Li, Y. (2025). A survey of aiops in the era of large language models. ACM Computing Surveys, 58(2), 1-35. .

Zhang, Y., & Ramesh, A. (2020). Learning fairness-aware relational structures. *Frontiers in Artificial Intelligence and Applications*, *325*, 2543–2550. DOI: 10.3233/FAIA200389

Ziolkowski, P. (2023). Computational complexity and its influence on predictive capabilities of machine learning models for concrete mix design. *Materials (Basel), 16*(17), 5956. DOI: 10.3390/ma16175956

Zmuda, A., & Kuklis, R. (2004). *Transforming schools: Creating a culture of continuous improvement*. ASCD.

Zysman, J., & Nitzberg, M. (2020). Governing AI: Understanding the Limits, Possibility, and Risks of AI in an Era of Intelligent Tools and Systems. SSRN *Electronic Journal, c*. DOI: 10.2139/ssrn.3681088

About the Contributors

Otmane Azeroual is a world-renowned senior researcher, lecturer, and thought leader in digital transformation, artificial intelligence, and advanced data-driven research infrastructures. His groundbreaking interdisciplinary work at the nexus of computer science, higher education research, innovation management, and industry has set new standards in how data and AI reshape science and society. His research on the design, deployment, and critical evaluation of Current Research Information Systems (CRIS) — combined with cutting-edge AI-powered analytics — is internationally acclaimed and among the most cited in the field. Dr. Azeroual's pioneering contributions drive the evolution of intelligent data ecosystems that empower Open Science, elevate transparency, and revolutionize strategic decision-making in science policy worldwide. Holding a Ph.D. in Engineering Informatics and a robust foundation in business information systems and software engineering, he has authored numerous high-impact publications in top-tier journals and has been a sought-after keynote and plenary speaker at prestigious global conferences. His expertise is recognized by editorial boards and scientific committees internationally, where he shapes the future agenda of research data science. Bridging academia and private industry, Dr. Azeroual uniquely fuses rigorous theoretical insight with practical innovation. His leadership in both sectors fuels transformative digital strategies and sustainable technological solutions. As an inspiring educator, he equips emerging researchers and professionals with cutting-edge knowledge in AI, data science, research analytics, and project management — preparing them to excel in complex, dynamic environments. Passionate about harnessing AI for evidence-based governance, Dr. Azeroual actively collaborates across disciplines to build resilient, transparent, and data-driven research infrastructures that set global benchmarks. His visionary work not only advances scientific understanding but also catalyzes paradigm shifts that benefit institutions, governments, and society at large.

***

Bhavanam Amarnath Reddy is working as an Assistant Professor, Department of Finance & Marketing, Vignana Jyothi Institute Of Management (VJIM) A Premium Business School, Hyderabad, Telangana, India. In his 16 years of teaching and research experience, he has served in an array of designations as Assistant Professor, Associate Professor and HOD of MBA Department, Head, Entrepreneurship Development Cell, President to Institution Innovation Council (IIC) and National Institutional Startup Policy (NISP) under MHRD Innovation Cell, also Mentor to various innovations under Innovation Cell, MHRD Has authored 6 Text Books, published 31 patents, 82 National & International Paper Publications, presented papers in 34 International Conferences, Participated in more than 62 FDPs, 91 Webinars, Workshops, Refresher courses and has 24 Coursera Certifications, Won 6 International Awards, life time member in 6 International associations. Reviewer&Editor for 12 International Journals Has presented many Guest lectures and was Resource person for Workshops & Refresher Courses in several Universities, Engineering Colleges and Business Schools on a variety of topics.

Rahul Bharadwaj is an Assistant Professor at the School of Hospitality and Tourism, Galgotias University. He earned his Ph.D. from Banaras Hindu University and is dedicated to advancing research and education in hospitality and tourism management.

Neha Dubey, with 8 years of academic and research experience… On her credit there are more then 40 research articles which is from ugc care list, Scopus indexed and WOS. She is NAAC coordinator at faculty level and also INTERNATIONAL STUDENT FACULTY ADVISOR, MEMBER OF VIGILANCE COMMITTEE At faculty level, Member of Student Service Center at university level, BOARD MEMBER at faculty level, Member of Anti Raging committee at faculty level. Attended short term training program, refresher course, Nep 2020, research methodology course, all sponsored by MMTTC. Guided more 40 master degree student for dissertation. There are three PhD scholar under my supervision.

Syed Hassan Imam Gardezi serves as the Executive Director and Board Member at Union Investments LLC, based in Ras Al Khaimah, United Arab Emirates. With a strategic leadership role in the organization, Dr. Gardezi brings extensive experience in corporate governance, investment planning, and executive management. His contributions to Union Investments LLC reflect a strong commitment to driving business growth, fostering innovation, and ensuring sustainable development. Through his role on the board, he plays a key part in shaping the company's strategic direction and long-term vision.

Asita Ghewari is an accomplished academic and researcher currently serving as an Associate Professor at Dnyansagar Institute of Management & Research, Pune. With a strong background in management education and research, she has contributed significantly to the academic community through her teaching, mentoring, and scholarly work. Dr. Ghewari is known for her expertise in contemporary management practices, her commitment to fostering innovation in business education, and her active involvement in conferences, workshops, and research publications. Dedicated to shaping future leaders, she emphasizes practical learning, ethical values, and strategic thinking in her academic approach. Through her years of experience, Dr. Ghewari has established herself as a respected educator and thought leader in the field of management studies.

Alphonsa Diana Haokip is an Assistant Professor in the Department of Education at Don Bosco College (Autonomous), Maram.

|Abishek J - Contributing Author|I am Abishek J, pursuing my Bachelor of Engineering in Computer Science and Engineering at Dr. G. U. Pope College of Engineering, Tamil Nadu, India. My areas of interest include Artificial Intelligence, Machine Learning, and Human–AI Collaboration. I am passionate about learning, research, and exploring innovative ideas in the field of computer science.

Inayatul Janah is affiliated with Universitas Esa Unggul, where she focuses on strategic management and organizational transformation in the context of emerging technologies. Her professional interests include the integration of artificial intelligence into strategic decision-making processes, agile portfolio management, and adaptive organizational governance. With a strong analytical and conceptual background, she explores how intelligent systems can enhance strategic agility, improve decision coherence, and foster sustainable business innovation. In her recent works, she emphasizes the intersection of human judgment and machine intelligence in shaping the future of strategic leadership. Inayatul Janah's research contributions reflect a forward-thinking perspective on how AI-driven strategy can empower organizations to remain competitive, resilient, and ethically grounded in dynamic business environments.

Shruti Jose is a Research Enthusiast and an Assistant Professor in the Department of Professional Studies under the School of Commerce, Finance and Accountancy at CHRIST (Deemed to be) University, Bangalore (India). Her research interests lie in banking, finance, technology adoption, consumer behaviour, payments, eCommerce, artificial intelligence, and innovation research.

Daniel Raj K. holds a Master of Engineering in Computer Science and Engineering from Dr. G.U. Pope College of Engineering and a Bachelor of Technology in Information Technology from Kings Engineering College with a CGPA of 8.1. His research interests include Artificial Intelligence, Machine Learning, Deep Learning, and Neuromorphic Computing. Beyond academia, he has served as a System Administrator, Teaching Assistant, and Media Archiver at St. Joseph's College of Engineering, Chennai. Known among peers as Jojo, he is also a violinist and a YouTuber sharing educational and inspirational insights. Passionate about teaching and mentorship, he aspires to pursue a Ph.D. and contribute to shaping the next generation of engineers and researchers.

P. Selvakumar is currently an Associate Professor in the Department of Science and Humanities at Nehru Institute of Technology, Coimbatore, Tamil Nadu, India. Prior to joining Nehru Institute of Technology, he held positions as an Assistant Professor in the Department of Science and Humanities various engineering colleges in Coimbatore, Tamil Nadu, India, spanning from 2011 to 2023. Dr.P. Selvakumar's academic and research interests lie primarily in the field of phytochemistry. He has made significant contributions to his field, with an impressive record that includes 30 journal publications, 12 patents, and 20 conference papers. Additionally, he has organized 5 seminars and conferences, further demonstrating his commitment to academic and scientific exchange. Throughout his career, Dr. P.Selvakumar has been recognized for his dedication and excellence in teaching, having been honored with several awards, including the Best Teacher Awards. He holds a prominent position in the academic community, contributing actively to research.

Shagufta Parween, Head & Assistant Professor, Department of English, Chaitanya Bharathi Institute of Technology, Hyderabad, has more than 16 years of experience in teaching and research. She holds a Gold Medal in M.A. English and has won 4 Awards. She has done her PhD in Indian English Novels. She is the author of many research papers published in reputed international journals. Dr. Parween is also a member of ELTAI, IATEFL WMS and ICPSCE.She has significantly contributed to the academic community as a reviewer of journal articles and provided best practices in English Language and Literature, Business Communication, Technical Writing Skills, Gender Sensitization, Soft Skills and Employability Skills at the undergraduate and post-graduate levels. In addition. She has organized International conference, conducted a workshop and FDP, and has also presented her research in many prestigious International conferences.

Ganesh Pathak is an Associate Professor at Sri Balaji University, Pune (SBUP). With extensive academic and professional experience, Dr. Pathak is dedicated to excellence in teaching, research, and mentorship. His academic interests span across management studies, organizational behavior, and leadership development. At SBUP, he plays a key role in guiding students toward academic success and practical industry readiness, contributing significantly to the university's vision of nurturing future leaders.

U. D. Prasan, B.Tech, M.Tech, Ph.D., is a distinguished Professor in the Department of Computer Science and Engineering at Aditya Institute of Technology and Management (AITAM), Tekkali, Srikakulam District, Andhra Pradesh. He has been an integral part of AITAM since 2007, shaping generations of engineers through his inspiring teaching and research mentorship. With over 24 years of academic experience, Dr. Prasan's contributions reflect a deep commitment to advancing education and technology. He obtained his Ph.D. in Computer Science and Engineering in May 2016, with specialization in Sensor Networks. His scholarly work includes numerous publications in reputed international journals and presentations at national and international conferences. He also holds patents and serves as a reviewer for several international journals and conferences. The author of five books on emerging technologies, Dr. Prasan's research interests encompass Sensor Networks, Computer Networks, Data Mining, Image Processing, Artificial Intelligence, and Machine Learning.

Sindy Rahmahsari is an undergraduate student in Informatics Engineering with research interests in Artificial Intelligence, Machine Learning, and data-driven technologies for sustainable industrial transformation.

Ashok Raut is a dedicated academic professional currently serving as an Assistant Professor at Dr. D. Y. Patil Vidyapeeth's Global Business School and Research Centre, Pune. With a strong foundation in management education, he brings a blend of academic excellence and practical insights to his teaching. Mr. Raut is passionate about nurturing students' managerial and analytical skills, preparing them to meet the dynamic challenges of the business world. His areas of interest include contemporary management practices, business strategy, and organizational development. Known for his engaging teaching style and commitment to academic excellence, Mr. Raut actively contributes to research, seminars, and academic initiatives that promote holistic learning. Through his dedication and professional approach, he continues to make a significant impact in the field of management education.

V. Muthu Ruben is a distinguished Associate Professor at the School of Law, Christ University, situated in Bengaluru, Karnataka, India. Driven by an extensive scholarly foundation and a steadfast dedication to legal education, Dr.

Ruben makes substantial contributions to both the academic community and the domain of law. His proficiency transcends numerous spheres within the realm of law, and he significantly influences the educational journeys of students enrolled at Christ University. Motivated by an ardent interest in legal research, he actively participates in scholarly endeavors, thereby making significant contributions to the ongoing legal dialogue. In addition to his scholarly responsibilities, Dr. V. Muthu Ruben is renowned for his commitment to cultivating an atmosphere that encourages intellectual engagement. His mentorship and counsel motivate pupils to explore into the complexities of the law, fostering the development of critical thinking skills and a profound comprehension of legal principles. In his role as an Associate Professor, Dr. Ruben provides the School of Law with an abundance of expertise, experience, and a forward-thinking perspective, thereby enhancing the institution's dedication to providing superior legal education.

Himanshu Sanghavi Assistant Professor C Z Patel College of Business and Management, The Charutar Vidya Mandal (CVM) University. Vallabh Vidyanagar. Gujarat. himanshu.sanghavi@cvmu.edu.in Cell No: 98253 11588 Dr. Himanshu Sanghavi, a scholarly academic background, has 19 years of teaching experience to his credit. Dr. Sanghavi has participated and presented research papers in various workshops and seminars of National and International level. His area of interest is General Management, Human Resource Management, Organizational Behavior, Entrepreneurship, etc.

Binastya Anggara Sekti has been a lecturer at the Faculty of Computer Science, Esa Unggul University, Jakarta, since 2016. He is actively involved in the Artificial Intelligence and Information Security Study Group. He holds a Bachelor's degree in Informatics Engineering from the Bandung Institute of Technology and a Master's degree in Information Systems Management from Trisakti University, Jakarta. Prior to entering academia, he accumulated over 25 years of professional experience as an IT practitioner in various companies across Jakarta. His work focused on developing data centers for internet service providers and delivering IT solutions for the manufacturing and oil & gas sectors. His research interests include artificial intelligence, cybersecurity, and the development of IT infrastructure.

Priyadarshani Singh is a distinguished academician, entrepreneur, and thought leader with a multidisciplinary academic background including a Ph.D. in Management, MBA, M.Com, M.Sc., and LLB. A qualified professional in Management, she brings over 17 years of diverse experience spanning higher education, corporate leadership, and entrepreneurial ventures. Currently an Associate Professor at Noida International University, she has previously contributed her academic expertise at renowned institutions such as Lovely Professional University, IILM Lucknow, and the University of Allahabad. In addition, she has worked with the All India Management Association (AIMA) local chapter and has played pivotal roles in various faculty development and academic initiatives. Her research contributions include papers published in renowned journals, with interests in AI-enabled HR analytics, sustainable HRM, and digital learning systems. She holds two Indian patents focused on AI in HR optimization and adaptive learning in classrooms. As an editor of the International Journal of Research in Business Studies, she is actively involved in promoting quality academic discourse. Dr. Singh has presented her work at prestigious platforms including IIM Bangalore, Cambridge University, and international conferences across Dubai and Malaysia. She has authored several books ranging from research compendiums to exam preparation and personal development, and has successfully organized multiple international conferences on business and innovation.

Ranjit Singha is a Doctorate Research Fellow at Christ (Deemed to be University) and holds a prestigious membership in the American Psychological Association (APA). With a strong background in Research and Development, he has significantly contributed to various fields such as Mindfulness, Addiction Psychology, Women Empowerment, UN Sustainable Development Goals, and Data Science. With over 15 years of experience in Administration, Teaching, and Research, both in Industry and Higher Education Institutions (HEI), Mr Ranjit has established himself as a seasoned professional. Mr Ranjit is dedicated to research and teaching endeavours, primarily focusing on mindfulness and compassion-based interventions. His work in these areas aims to promote well-being and foster positive change in individuals and communities.

Surjit Singha is a passionate academician and researcher with over 16+ years of professional experience spanning administration, teaching, and research. Currently serving as a faculty member at Kristu Jayanti (Deemed to be University), Dr. Singha is deeply committed to fostering academic growth and guiding students in their research pursuits. His multidisciplinary interests include the UN Sustainable Development Goals, Organizational Climate, Workforce Diversity, Organizational Culture, Human Resource Management (HRM), Marketing, Finance, International Business, Global Business, Artificial Intelligence, K12 & Higher Education, Gender, and Cultural Studies. An accomplished author and editor, Dr. Singha contributes to renowned global publications and journals and holds prominent editorial roles, including being on the Editorial Review Board of the Information Resources Management Journal (SCOPUS & WoS). With an impressive academic portfolio, Dr. Singha has published over 160+ articles, book chapters, and textbooks, including

100+ SCOPUS-indexed publications. He also holds 2+ US Copyrights and one Patent, demonstrating his dedication to innovation and originality. Additionally, he has successfully completed two fully funded minor research projects from Kristu Jayanti (Deemed to be University). As a research mentor, Dr. Singha has guided numerous students and young scholars toward academic excellence. His academic qualifications include a PhD, M.Phil, and MBA (Distinction) from Christ University, M.Com, BBM from Kristu Jayanti College (Bangalore University), and PGDHE (Higher Education) from IGNOU (Central University). He is also a UGC-NET (Commerce) qualifier and serves as an Examiner for International Baccalaureate (IB).

Varadharajan Bhoopathy is a Professor at Sree Rama Engineering College. He holds a Ph.D. in Information and Communication Engineering from Anna University and has over 16 years of academic experience. Specializing in wireless sensor networks and IoT, he has published numerous research papers and holds several international patents. Dr. Bhoopathy is a recipient of prestigious awards for his contributions to education and research. His commitment to academia continues to drive innovation and excellence in the field of computer science.

Index

A

Agile Delivery Forecasting 111, 113, 116, 118, 134, 138, 145, 146, 152
agile frameworks 1, 28, 75, 248, 255, 258, 261, 300, 337, 338, 341, 345
Agile Governance 159, 265, 267, 335
Agile Management 73, 87, 95, 103, 109, 148, 157, 158, 159, 255, 295, 296, 406
Agile Project Management 28, 30, 37, 40, 51, 57, 58, 59, 66, 67, 69, 70, 73, 74, 76, 80, 188, 255, 260, 263, 266, 268, 296, 297, 299, 302, 303, 306, 307, 310, 311, 312, 313, 314, 321, 322, 332, 334, 339, 343, 345, 346, 347, 351, 354, 356, 357
Agile Tooling Ecosystems 335
AI-Augmented Agile 299, 300, 301, 302, 305, 306, 307, 309, 311, 315, 316, 318, 319, 320, 321, 322, 325, 329, 330, 331, 332, 336, 351, 353, 354, 355, 356
AI-Augmented Strategic Loop 83, 88, 97, 100, 105
AI governance 65, 78, 173, 174, 175, 176, 177, 178, 180, 181, 182, 183, 184, 185, 186, 254, 262, 264, 265, 302, 324, 329, 331, 411, 413, 417, 418, 419
AIOps 27, 28, 29, 30, 32, 33, 40, 41, 42, 44, 45, 46, 47, 48, 49, 50, 51, 52, 53, 54, 55, 56, 57, 58, 59, 60, 61, 62, 63, 64, 65, 66, 67, 68, 69, 70, 71, 72, 73, 74, 75, 76, 77, 78, 79, 80
Anomaly Detection 4, 45, 48, 51, 52, 61, 69, 74, 76, 79, 131, 139, 148, 154, 168, 179, 217, 219, 220, 224, 225, 226, 230, 238, 242, 243, 244, 286
Artificial Intelligence (AI) 1, 2, 16, 23, 24, 27, 29, 40, 41, 44, 45, 56, 67, 76, 77, 78, 80, 83, 85, 86, 87, 89, 90, 92, 94, 95, 97, 98, 99, 100, 101, 105, 106, 108, 109, 110, 113, 119, 130, 145, 154, 155, 157, 158, 159, 175, 178, 179, 183, 187, 188, 192, 193, 194, 195, 196, 197, 198, 199, 207, 209, 210, 211, 212, 213, 214, 215, 218, 219, 221, 223, 225, 232, 233, 240, 242, 243, 244, 245, 246, 248, 252, 255, 258, 259, 263, 266, 268, 270, 272, 273, 275, 295, 296, 297, 298, 300, 302, 304, 306, 308, 313, 324, 331, 334, 335, 336, 337, 339, 357, 358, 361, 362, 363, 364, 365, 367, 368, 369, 370, 372, 373, 374, 376, 377, 379, 380, 382, 383, 386, 387, 388, 389, 392, 395, 398, 404, 410, 411, 412, 413, 417, 419, 421, 424, 425, 426
Artificial Intelligence Systems (AIS) 94, 98, 195, 196, 197, 213

C

Change Management 36, 64, 65, 67, 133, 141, 143, 145, 150, 172, 277, 278, 280, 328, 361, 362, 363, 364, 367, 373, 374, 376, 377, 389, 390, 391, 392, 393, 394, 404, 420, 422, 424
Change Management and Upskilling for AI-Augmented Teams 361

D

Decision Intelligence 186
Decision Support Systems 96, 99, 153, 169, 171, 248, 381
Deep Learning (DL) 71, 91, 92, 121, 163, 188, 208, 214, 230, 231, 235, 237, 256, 257, 270, 298, 370, 372, 417
DevOps 30, 33, 42, 48, 57, 58, 66, 68, 70, 75, 77, 78, 79, 81, 134, 137, 142, 154, 162, 171, 173, 177, 183, 187, 255, 260, 264, 267, 300, 302, 303, 304, 305, 307, 309, 315, 317, 327, 328, 329, 331, 333, 334, 335, 336, 345
Digital Delivery Metrics 336
Digital Project Coaching 275, 281, 282, 283, 286
Digital Transformation 27, 40, 44, 59, 84, 98, 108, 277, 295, 357, 362, 368, 369, 376, 377, 379, 386, 387, 390, 391, 393, 398, 403, 404, 405, 410, 411,

416, 418, 419, 420, 421, 422
Dynamic Resource Allocation 88

E

Early Warning Systems 217, 219, 227, 229, 295
Effort Estimation 255
Ethical AI in Project Management 336
Ethical Implications 175, 195, 205, 209, 211, 213, 287, 288, 291, 322, 325, 338, 353, 391
Explainable AI (XAI) 55, 56, 64, 90, 94, 101, 103, 105, 106, 170, 174, 182, 186, 210, 232, 236, 237, 257, 261, 265, 289, 306, 307, 336

F

Flow Metrics 6, 111, 113, 117, 118, 119, 124, 125, 134, 139, 152

H

HERMES 275, 276, 277, 278, 279, 280, 281, 282, 283, 284, 285, 286, 287, 288, 289, 290, 291, 292, 295, 297
Human-AI Collaboration 97, 100, 173, 176, 245, 248, 254, 265, 275, 287, 289, 290, 291, 337, 349, 353, 375
human-in-the-loop 5, 47, 49, 65, 111, 113, 114, 118, 130, 131, 135, 140, 141, 143, 145, 146, 151, 157, 159, 162, 168, 170, 172, 178, 179, 181, 182, 183, 186, 262, 302, 306, 309, 313, 314, 315, 317, 320, 322, 325, 329, 331, 349, 352, 355, 415
Human-in-the-Loop Governance 111, 113, 114, 118, 130, 131, 135, 140, 141, 143, 145, 179, 322

I

IT Operations 27, 28, 29, 30, 31, 32, 33, 34, 35, 36, 37, 38, 39, 40, 41, 42, 43, 44, 45, 46, 48, 49, 50, 51, 53, 54, 56, 57, 59, 60, 61, 62, 66, 67, 70, 71, 72, 73, 74, 75, 76, 77, 78, 79, 80, 81
ITOps 27, 28, 30, 31, 32, 33, 34, 35, 37, 40, 41, 45, 46, 48, 51, 58, 59, 60, 62, 68, 71, 73, 74, 77, 81

L

Lessons Learned Analysis 275, 281, 283, 286
LLMOps 24, 30, 33, 75, 81, 300, 302, 307, 313, 315, 323, 327, 330, 331, 336

M

Machine Learning (ML) 2, 23, 24, 27, 29, 42, 44, 45, 46, 47, 48, 49, 50, 51, 52, 54, 56, 58, 64, 66, 67, 68, 69, 70, 71, 76, 80, 81, 85, 87, 89, 91, 95, 98, 100, 103, 106, 108, 109, 111, 113, 118, 119, 123, 135, 136, 138, 144, 147, 148, 151, 155, 163, 171, 177, 187, 188, 189, 208, 211, 212, 213, 218, 219, 220, 221, 224, 225, 230, 232, 234, 238, 240, 243, 244, 245, 247, 248, 251, 252, 253, 255, 264, 268, 272, 273, 275, 276, 279, 281, 283, 286, 287, 295, 296, 297, 298, 301, 304, 308, 311, 313, 314, 333, 334, 335, 336, 345, 347, 351, 355, 359, 368, 370, 380, 423
MLOps 5, 10, 24, 30, 33, 41, 55, 75, 77, 81, 103, 105, 119, 138, 140, 300, 302, 307, 313, 315, 323, 327, 330, 331, 334, 336
Monte Carlo Simulation 111, 113, 116, 118, 119, 126, 127, 141, 142, 147, 149

N

National Institute of Standards and Technology (NIST) 194
Natural Language Processing (NLP) 2, 85, 91, 92, 94, 98, 106, 166, 198, 245, 247, 248, 251, 252, 256, 268, 273, 275, 276, 278, 282, 292, 293, 298, 301, 304, 308, 313, 336, 345, 350, 353, 370, 372, 373, 375, 376, 381, 382, 417

O

OKR Alignment 83, 84, 86, 90, 94, 96, 101, 105
Organizational Agility 51, 142, 159, 302, 307, 308, 311, 313, 314, 420

P

Predictive Analytics 2, 13, 14, 15, 16, 17, 23, 41, 42, 58, 61, 67, 68, 98, 100, 119, 120, 162, 168, 169, 171, 178, 179, 180, 183, 184, 186, 187, 219, 221, 238, 245, 261, 268, 275, 276, 278, 286, 292, 293, 300, 311, 314, 317, 325, 336, 342, 346, 354, 367, 373, 375, 376, 381, 384, 412
Probabilistic Models 111, 113, 116, 118, 119, 124, 130, 152
Product Owner 8, 9, 169, 248, 250, 251, 253, 256, 260, 337
Project Management 1, 2, 3, 8, 12, 13, 16, 17, 19, 20, 21, 22, 23, 27, 28, 30, 32, 33, 37, 40, 51, 57, 58, 59, 66, 67, 69, 70, 73, 74, 76, 80, 99, 153, 154, 155, 171, 177, 188, 217, 218, 221, 222, 229, 230, 232, 234, 236, 237, 238, 239, 240, 241, 243, 244, 246, 255, 260, 263, 266, 268, 275, 276, 277, 278, 279, 280, 281, 283, 284, 286, 287, 288, 289, 290, 291, 292, 293, 294, 295, 296, 297, 299, 300, 301, 302, 303, 306, 307, 308, 309, 310, 311, 312, 313, 314, 320, 321, 322, 326, 329, 331, 332, 334, 336, 339, 340, 343, 345, 346, 347, 351, 354, 356, 357, 362, 382, 384, 386

R

Reference Architectures 299, 300, 301, 302, 305, 306, 307, 308, 309, 315, 316, 317, 318, 319, 320, 322, 323, 324, 326, 327, 331, 332, 336
Risk Management 62, 70, 86, 88, 104, 125, 127, 152, 154, 155, 168, 171, 172, 174, 177, 178, 179, 180, 181, 188, 191, 192, 194, 195, 203, 208, 209, 211, 214, 218, 220, 221, 222, 223, 224, 225, 234, 235, 236, 238, 241, 242, 243, 275, 276, 278, 283, 286, 293, 296, 301, 335, 346, 421
risk sensing 157, 166, 186, 217, 220, 224, 225, 313, 320
Roadmapping 83, 85, 86, 91, 92, 106, 108, 109, 110, 157, 163, 179
Role of ITOps 37

S

Scrum 9, 75, 169, 188, 248, 250, 251, 254, 255, 259, 265, 268, 271, 275, 276, 277, 278, 279, 280, 281, 282, 283, 284, 285, 286, 287, 289, 292, 296, 297, 298, 337, 338, 339, 341, 342, 343, 344, 352, 356, 357, 358, 359, 360
Scrum Master 248, 250, 251, 286, 337, 338, 359, 360
Skills Development 359, 389, 390, 398, 402, 403, 404, 407
Strategic Portfolio Management 83, 86, 89, 90, 91, 105, 291

www.ingramcontent.com/pod-product-compliance
Lightning Source LLC
LaVergne TN
LVHW062334300926
849161LV00007B/1688
9798337368511